Risk Assessment and Management

ADVANCES IN RISK ANALYSIS

This series is edited by the Society for Risk Analysis.

A Continuation Order Plan is available for this series. A continuation order will bring delivery of each new volume immediately upon publication. Volumes are billed only upon actual shipment. For further information please contact the publisher.

Risk Assessment and Management

Edited by
Lester B. Lave
Carnegie-Mellon University
Pittsburgh, Pennsylvania

PLENUM PRESS • NEW YORK AND LONDON

Library of Congress Cataloging in Publication Data

Risk assessment and management / edited by Lester B. Lave.
    p.   cm.—(Advances in risk analysis; v. 5)
    "Proceedings of the annual meeting of the Society for Risk Analysis, held
November 1985, in Washington, D.C."—T.p. verso.
    Includes bibliographical references and index.
    ISBN 0-306-42683-8
    1. Risk management—Congresses. 2. Risk—Congresses. I. Lave, Lester B. II. Socie-
ty for Risk Analysis. III. Series.
    HD61.R5684   1987
    658—dc19   87-21288
                                                                          CIP

Proceedings of the annual meeting of the Society for Risk Assessment,
held November 1985, in Washington, D.C.

© 1987 Plenum Press, New York
A Division of Plenum Publishing Corporation
233 Spring Street, New York, N.Y. 10013

Printed in the United States of America

PREFACE

This is a collection of papers presented at the 1985 annual meeting of the Society for Risk Analysis. As always seems to occur at these meetings, the discussion was lively, the sessions were filled, and people complained about not being able to hear all the papers they wanted to because of concurrent sessions. If ever someone is in charge of a meeting, I wish them the good luck to have it be one for the Society for Risk Analysis.

While I was responsible for the meeting, it could not have taken place without the efforts of the general chairman, Alan Moshissi. The program committee was chaired by Janice Longstreth, and included Lee Abramson and Vincent Covello. Together we assembled disparate papers into reasonably coherent sessions, prodded authors into getting us manuscripts on time, and dealt with all the last minute changes that are required for a major meeting.

The Washington chapter of the Society for Risk Analysis hosted the meeting. Dr. Longstreth was president of the chapter during this fateful year and deserves a great deal of thanks for her organizational skills and efforts. Rick Cothern, Jerry Chandler, Kathleen Knox, Sue Perlin, and Paul Price played major roles in organizing the meeting and making it run smoothly. Special thanks go to Richard J. Burk, Jr., Executive Secretary of the Society, and his staff for handling the logistics.

The greatest debt is to the members of the Society for Risk Analysis who made this such a stimulating meeting, and to the authors of these papers. The intent was stimulation, keeping the intellectual pot boiling. I think that intent has been amply realized.

Lester B. Lave
Carnegie-Mellon University

CONTENTS

RISK ANALYSIS: ESTIMATING SAFETY RISKS

BLACK HATS, ECONOMISTS AND SOCIETAL RISK ASSESSMENT

Marina v.N. Whitman

General Motors Corporation

Appearing before this organization reminds me of three pieces of immortal advice from Winston Churchill: "never try to walk up a wall that's leaning toward you...never try to kiss a person that's leaning away from you...and never speak to a group that knows more about a subject than you do."

I've done very well with the first two precepts, but I may be in danger of violating the third one today. As I discuss public policy. economics, and risk analysis, I'll try not to stray too far into your territory, if I can help it.

I would like to begin, though, by congratulating this organization on the remarkable impact it's recently had on regulation and policy-setting. All of you deserve tremendous credit for your ground-breaking and immensely important work.

"IMMORAL" ECONOMISTS?

Since at least the time of Malthus, economics has been called the "dismal science" and economists have been roundly condemned for having a callous attitudes toward issues that affect public health and safety.

Our attempts to quantify some of the benefits and costs associated with public health and safety initiatives have been criticized as tasteless at best and downright immoral at worst. We are told that it is wrong to place a monetary value--or in fact any finite value--on human life and health. It even seems to some that the mere linking of the words "acceptable risk" is a contradiction, like "criminal justice" or "jumbo shrimp"--an oxymoron that violates Judeo-Christian moral precepts, which hold human life to be absolutely sacred.

I admit that we economists can get carried away with number-crunching..that we sometimes ignore-at our peril-the qualitative, human aspects associated with health and safety issues. So it's little wonder that in the public eye, we're so often the ones in the black hats.

That reminds me of the popular distinction between a dead dog on a highway and a dead economist: there are skid marks in front of a dog! I trust that everyone here brakes for economists.

LIMITS OF ECONOMIC ANALYSIS

To be sure, there are significant limitations to the use of economics in risk analysis. The reasons for these limitations will no doubt sound familiar-because they arise from the very nature of risk analysis itself.

To begin with, the very idea of assigning a finite value to human life, health and safety is something that we quite naturally find abhorrent.

Also, most problems, of course, simply have no "correct"-that is, totally risk-free-solution. Our everyday activities involve accepting risks-my flight to National Airport as opposed to Dulles indicated a willingness to accept increased risk for the reduction in travel time. And on a societal scale, what's good for one group is not necessarily optimal for another.

Another reason for the imprecision is that it's so dauntingly difficult to quantify long-range adverse health effects.

Also, some occupations are inherently riskier than others-and, as you will know, there are libraries full of literature on occupational wage premiums.

Some societies are willing to accept more risk than others (the affluence of the society is a factor here, and I'll return to it a bit later on).

DECIDING WHAT TO FEAR

Finally, risks are selected and prioritized in different ways by different societies. You'll remember that in their book Risk and Culture, Mary Douglas and Aaron Wildavsky argue that
> "[in selecting and prioritizing perceived threats, there] is not
> much difference between modern times and ages past. They
> politicized nature by inventing mysterious connections between
> moral transgressions and natural disasters, as well as by their
> selection among dangers. We moderns can do a lot of politicizing
> merely by our selection of dangers" [p. 30].

The authors cite the example of the Lele tribe of Zaire. These people are more afraid of three things than anything else: bronchitis, barrenness, and being struck by lightning. Of course, they are subject to the full gamut of tropical diseases. But they fear lightning, bronchitis, and barrenness more. And "they attribute these troubles to specific types of immorality in which the victim would generally be seen as innocent and some powerful leader or village elder would be blamed" (Ibid, p. 7].

The point is that what we regard as risky has to do with more than verifiable threats to health and safety. It is strongly related to our concept of nature and to our view of moral and immoral conduct.

A classic example is the modern belief that all pollution is caused by human beings. This attitude sees nature as somehow pristine and harmless, if only it were left alone, whereas in fact, many harmful substances occur naturally and were around long before there were corporations and industries.

Despite all of these concerns,-and this is a big "despite," but one that I hope to justify-I believe that economic considerations are relevant to public health and safety policy, and I'll explain why I think so. Then I'll give you some ways in which I think that the tools of the economists and risk analysts can contribute analyses that will benefit policymakers in this difficult area.

THE TRANSFER OF RISK

There are two broad reasons why sound public health and safety policy ignore economic considerations at their peril.

First, when we mandate what we think are risk reductions, we sometimes do little more than transfer risks from one segment of the population to another or from one economic activity to another.

Your past President, Chris Whipple, made this observation in a recent piece in Regulation magazine ("Redistributing Risk," Regulation, May/June, 1985, pp. 37-44.)

He cites a study by the International Atomic Energy Agency and the International Institute for Applied Systems Analysis. The authors found that "beyond a certain point the occupational and public risk of producing safety equipment becomes higher than the reduction achieved in an existing risk. They found that, based on data for West Germany, one so-called "equivalent" death or 6000 equivalent lost man-days are caused during the construction and installation of safety equipment costing about $33 million. "Thus," they concluded, "expenditures on safety at marginal costs of risk reduction higher than $33 million per equivalent life saved would actually lead to an increase in risk."

ACCEPTING RISKS VS. DENYING BENEFITS

Another case of "transferred risk" involves the problem of Type I/Type II errors. Some new products are valuable for their contribution to life and health. Yet they also entail risks of their own. But to ban or restrict them out of fear of the increased risks may actually be counterproductive, since by doing so, we keep some people from enjoying their benefits.

Consider our nation's experience with drug regulations and product liability lawsuits on children's vaccines.

As Whipple observes, "[manufacturers are becoming unwilling, for reasons of liability and licensing cost, to produce vaccines and other drugs that entail a small probability of adverse side effects-for example, pertussis [whopping cough] vaccine."

Under such circumstances, according to Edmund Kitch, University of Virginia Professor of Law, the "principal competitive" issue for such firms has become "not the quality of their product, research and development, or [even] marketing," but rather how to "price the risk of liability." In just a few years' time, for example, the wholesale price of DPT vaccine has risen 28 times ("Vaccines and Product Liability; A Case of Contagious Litigation," Regulation [May/June], p. 17).

A number of studies have shown how the ponderous regulations of the FDA have substantially delayed the introduction of new life-saving drugs into the United States.

Alvin Weinberg, writing in Issues in Science and Technology (Fall '85), calls the Delaney clause "the worst example of how a disregard of an intrinsic limit of science can lead to bad policy...". He says that the clause "is of no help in resolving such issues as the relative risks [from] carcinogenic compounds that can be formed in the body from nitrites [versus the risks of] digestive diseases caused by meat untreated with nitrites."

POVERTY IS UNHEALTHY-AND UNSAFE

Let me turn now to the other major reason why economic considerations are relevant to public health and safety policy: there's a direct relationship between economic growth, on the one hand, and health and safety, on the other.

A number of studies have shown a positive relationship between economic growth and trends in health and safety. Samuel Preston, for example, has estimated that for the period between 1938 and 1963, rising per capita income accounted for about 16% of the world's increase in longevity [cited by Whipple, p. 42].

And as for regulation, economists have estimated that during the 1970s, in the nation's manufacturing sector, federal health and safety rules were responsible for between 8% and 39% of the slowdown in the growth of productivity.

Thus, if we retard economic growth through unwise or excessive regulation, we may actually hold down the overall level of health and safety. Poverty is both unhealthy and unsafe!

Economic growth not only facilitates improvements in health and safety; it also increases the demand for them. For example, what a wealthy society finds morally unacceptable a poor society may find economically essential. I recall a trip to a Chinese steel mill a few years ago-a mill that was actually a showcase for foreign tourists. Buckets of molten steel were being carried around by workers wearing open-toed rubber sandals.

TRADE-OFFS AND RELATIVE RISK

This situation presents a very difficult moral problem: should there by different standards for different parts of the world? Should an accident of birth determine the appropriate level of risk? We are morally repelled by such disparities. Yet economic conditions will inevitably be reflected in each society's standard. Is it appropriate for us to force our more stringent standards on others and make them poorer and quite possibly less safe and healthy? I don't think so.

Even within the same society, there can be trade-offs between safety and other goals. As Lester Lave observes, there are very real trade-offs between auto safety and fuel economy objectives: it is a law of physics that-other things being equal-small, light, more fuel-efficient vehicles provide less protection in a collision than large, heavy ones.

And so, as circular as it may seem, we need to increase productivity and economic growth if we are to sustain aggregate reductions in risk. And if our efforts to reduce risk are excessive or inefficient, we will only keep productivity from increasing, and we will limit our ability to reduce risk. That's why those efforts which achieve few benefits and are not cost-effective may actually reduce health and safety in the aggregate.

RESULTS, NOT WISHES

Given, then, that economic considerations bear heavily on public health and safety decisions, what specifically do economists and risk analysts have to offer?

First, we are trained to evaluate alternatives, not on the basis of wishful thinking, but in terms of expected results. That's an important difference in the arena of policymaking: private individuals and even public officials may be judged by their intentions-but when it comes to policies themselves, it's the results that matter.

Closely related is the fact that we try to anticipate those results within a general, comprehensive framework. And we do that by taking account, to the extent we can, not only of the immediate and direct effects, but also of the chain of indirect effects associated with a particular course of action.

In light of my earlier comments, that sort of broad perspective is critical. Without it, how could we tell whether some proposed policy would actually reduce risks or merely redistribute them to other segments of the population who are less well represented in government? Or how could we predict whether, because of its potentially adverse economic effects, such a policy might actually reduce overall health and safety?

Let me outline briefly the kind of framework I'm talking about.

TO REGULATE OR NOT TO REGULATE?

We begin with a complete assessment of the risks associated with a particular issue: we try to define the relevant ones, to explain how they are generated, and to determine whether they are de minimis.

Second, we try to assess whether a regulatory approach is appropriate. What is there, for example, about ordinary market forces that might make government intervention in a specific area necessary-or, in economist's terms, are there significant market imperfections?

Take pollution control as an example. Although reasonable people may disagree as to specific cases, the concept of government intervention is readily justified, since the market might not effectively take into account the so-called "externalities"-in this case, the effects of pollution on third parties.

There's also the effect of third parties on pollution: why should I buy an anti-pollution device for my car, if I can't be sure that practically everybody else will do the same? This is the economist's classic problem of the "commons," or public goods.

Another example: Auto safety regulations are based partly on the underlying premise that the costs of accidents are shared by society in the form of social insurance programs (again, an externalities argument) and partly on the premise that individuals cannot correctly evaluate the low probabilities of catastrophic events-or the safety attributes of a particular car. Here again, inadequate information can lead to a failure of the market, in and of itself, to deliver the optimal level of safety.

True, it takes a lot of dispassionate analysis to evaluate whether such considerations are important enough to justify preempting the consumer's choice in any particular case. Nonetheless, it is clear that auto safety regulation must be a fundamental concern of public policy.

CHOOSING THE MECHANISM

Third, once we have decided to regulate, economics can help in determining the best mechanism for achieving the stated policy objectives.

In the case of auto safety, for example, should we try to modify the driver's behavior? Or the roadway? Or the vehicle itself?

Over the years, emphasis has shifted. Until 1966, safety efforts focused on modifying the roadway and the driver's behavior. But since the passage of the Highway Safety Act, the premise of auto safety regulation has been that vehicle modifications should be the primary means of reducing auto accidents and injuries. And during the last few years, relatively more attention has been paid to modifying the driver's behavior and the roadway.

Of course, it may be hard to judge the overall impact of what we do in any one of these areas, because our various regulatory efforts may interact, sometimes in unpredictable ways. Peltzman, for instance, argues that drivers adjust their risk-taking so as to offset the greater safety of their regulated vehicles.

There's a lot of controversy about the significance of this effect. But again, it's largely an economic issue: in Peltzman's model the key variables include the cost of accidents, which shows up in such before-the-fact elements as experience-rated insurance premiums. Peltzman suggests that anything that increases these costs will encourage drivers to be more careful.

ASSESSING COST-EFFECTIVENESS: THE AUTO SAFETY DEBATE

Fourth, after we settle on what is to be regulated and to what extent, we ask how to achieve the desired result in a cost-effective way.

In our industry, this point is powerfully made by our current public-policy debate over the various forms of protection for the occupants of a vehicle. Is it better to focus on supporting manual safety belts by getting mandatory use laws passed? Or are such efforts merely red herrings that distract from a drive toward mandated passive-restraint systems, such as air bags?

If we ask which alternative achieves maximum benefits for society's limited resources, the answer seems fairly obvious.

If drivers and passengers do in fact buckle up, then the existing belt systems are not only far less expensive than the passive systems, but they can also afford far greater protection to users of current and past auto models. That's because they are already in place in virtually all 130,000,000 cars on the road. We don't have to wait the twelve years or more that it would take to put a passive restraint system in every vehicle.

ACTIVE VS. PASSIVE SYSTEMS

I should also add that the passive systems do not represent a significant improvement over the manual ones. According to a study by the Department of Transportation, a manual seat belt is as effective as an automatic belt in reducing injuries and deaths. The same study concludes that the manual belt is more effective than an air bag by itself. And the overall level of protection offered by an air bag plus a lap belt is roughly comparable to that of a lap-shoulder belt alone.

To be sure, we don't yet know how effective the safety belt laws will be. However, we don't know how effectively the air bags or passive belts would function either, because we don't know how many people will disconnect the automatic belt, or fail to wear a manual belt in a vehicle that has an air bag.

We know that passive belts, to be fully effective, would have to be covered by mandatory-use laws. And we know that the cost of the air bags is substantial. Finally, the air bags are not substitutes for the safety belts. To be fully effective, the two must be used together.

Eventually, we may dramatically reduce the cost and perhaps improve the effectiveness of air bags-or achieve some other technological breakthrough that makes safety belts unnecessary.

But in the meantime, there are other areas of research as well that can significantly improve the passive safety features of our vehicles. GM research scientists are creating what we call "built-in safety." To do so, they study, among other things, the energy-absorbing properties of the car body, with special attention to the steering column and other points most likely to be struck by the occupants if there's a collision.

So, before we conclude that air bags or passive belts are the way to go, we must consider their incremental cost and effectiveness, as compared to what can be achieved with built-in safety.

In short, mandatory belt use laws seem a sensible way of proceeding, given the present state of knowledge and technology, and the characteristics of the vehicles that are currently in use.

In this regard, I am heartened by the initial results from New York's mandatory-use law: for the first five months after the law went into effect, safety belt use rose from 16 percent to 57 percent. It's too early to tell how far fatalities will fall. But the early results are encouraging. And there's every reason to expect that we can achieve the same kind of reductions that we've already seen in other countries with similar laws.

BELT-USE LAWS AS A TEST CASE

The seat belt laws will provide an excellent set of data for testing the risk compensation hypothesis and real world effectiveness. The results should point the way for future auto safety efforts; they should help us decide whether we should concentrate on the vehicle, on the driver's behavior, or the roadway-or on some combination of the three.

In other words, if it's proven that safety-belt laws are indeed effective over a sustained period of time, then we should be encouraged to try other strategies to modify drivers' behavior-such as redoubling our efforts to enforce speed limits or drunk-driving laws more strictly.

7

Of course, some might argue that such laws are inconsistent with the economist's approach-that the effects on third parties are minimal. However, anyone who thinks this way is ignoring the social costs generated by drivers who do not wear the belts and who are injured in collisions. Besides, society has already made the decision to regulate; the only question is how to ensure that our health and safety resources are used as effectively as possible.

NO GUARANTEES

Finally, appropriate economic and risk analyses can help force policy-makers to consider the broadest possible effects of any specific policy.

As I said, a truly well constructed regulation must consider the nature and extent of any risk transfers that it may cause.

Such a global assessment must also consider the impact on productivity-upon our ability to generate future economic growth and achieve risk reductions in the aggregate.

After all, in the real world there is no guarantee that a particular regulatory approach will achieve its objectives-or even that it will do more good than harm.

A MORAL IMPERATIVE

I really think, then, that economists are justified in trading in their black hats for white ones. When we talk about "productivity" and "efficiency," it's too often assumed that we're exchanging lives for dollars. But where the efficient approach can be shown to save lives as well as dollars-where inefficiency actually shortens lives rather than extending them-the economist's search for a cost-effective solution becomes a moral imperative as well.

INTRASPECIES EXTRAPOLATION: EFFORTS AT ENHANCING DOSE-RESPONSE

RELATIONSHIPS

Janice Longstreth

ICF - Clement, Inc.

INTRODUCTION

I think that it is safe to say that the process of assessing the
human health risk posed by exposure to toxic chemicals is far more often
based on animal toxicity data than on human data. That being the case,
those who perform such risk assessments (myself included) are often faced
with the need to extrapolate from animal data to estimates of human
risk. This requirement for intraspecies extrapolation has been around a
long time and is the practical basis for toxicology; unfortunately, it is
fraught with uncertainty because of the large number of assumptions
normally required due most frequently to insufficient information.

There are no perfect animal models for a human response to a toxic
chemical. Indeed even humans are not perfect models for other humans
(with the possible exception of one identical twin for another). Thus,
in order to extrapolate from animals to humans, we are forced to make many
adjustments -- leaps of faith, if you will -- in any attempt to estimate
human risk on the basis of animal information. Figure 1 shows a
simplified overview of the process of making estimates of human cancer
risk using data from an animal bioassay. It is simplified in that the
process diagramed is one in which the route, duration, and pattern of
administration is the same for both humans and animals -- an optimal
situation, rarely encountered.

I have divided the extrapolation into two parts: Part I - the high-
to-low dose extrapolation, generally involves the use of a statistical
model which fits the experimental data points in the observable range and
is then used to predict the risks associated with very low doses or the
doses associated with very low risks. A number of models exist for this
extrapolation. The most common ones in current use assume a linear non-
threshold response. For cancer risk assessment this high to low dose
extrapolation is generally performed using as input doses the intake or
exposure dose of the test animal; this is plotted against the incidence of
a given tumor. Most often, the doses are expressed in mg/kg-day and are
determined using information on the food or water intake or estimated for
inhalation exposures by assuming the appropriate respiratory minute
volume. Under these conditions, this process (when used with a linear
non-threshold model) requires three important assumptions:

A. That absorption at the high dose is equivalent to absorption at
the low dose,

B. That metabolism (or degradation) at the high dose is equivalent to
    metabolism at the low dose, and

C. That cancer incidence is linearly related to dose and that this
    relationship has no threshold.

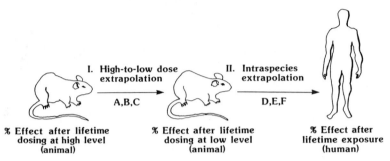

Figure 1. Extrapolations in human health risk assessment

Thus, the high-to-low dose extrapolation has under these (the typical)
conditions at least three large areas of uncertainty: absorption,
metabolism and mechanism of carcinogenesis.

    Extrapolation II, the intraspecies extrapolation, generally takes the
predictions of the model in the low dose range and converts them to human
equivalents. This is most commonly done on the basis of surface area,
i.e., mg/m^2, (although there are those who feel that mg/kg doses are
equivalent among species). The human doses (which are generally
expressed in mg/kg-day) then have to be equated to concentrations in food
and water. For carcinogenic risk assessment, this extrapolation is based
on three additional critical assumptions:

D. That the route of metabolism is the same in both species.

E. That an animal lifespan (2-3 years) is equivalent to a human
    lifespan (70 years).

F. That the response of a genetically homogeneous animal population
    is relevant to that of a genetically heterogeneous human
    population.

These six assumptions underlie most human health risk assessments. Some
of them can be addressed through the collection of adequate ancillary
data, but others, notably the lifespan = lifespan, the heterogeneity vs.
homogeneity and the linear non-threshold dose response for carcinogenesis
are still at the point of being debated philosophically -- without much
hope of arriving at scientific data to prove or disprove them.

    With this background I would now like to turn to the real point of
this paper -- one risk analyst's attempt to assemble and use additional
ancillary data in order to deal with some small part of the uncertainty in
this process. This uncertainty is derived from relying on exposure doses
as the input into the dose-response relationship used in human health risk
assessments. This paper deals with two risk assessments in which an
effort was made to go beyond the exposure dose available from the
literature to develop effective doses -- those that make it to the target
site -- or barring that -- are absorbed into the bloodstream.

BROMOETHYLENE

The first risk assessment was on the compound bromoethylene. Bromoethylene is mono bromo-substituted, two carbon alkene, which at ambient temperature and pressure is a colorless gas. An inhalation bioassay (Ter Haar 1979) performed in Sprague-Dawley rats resulted in a dose-related increase in angiosarcomas in both males and females. Exposure concentrations and their associated tumor incidences are given in Figure 2. In the absence of additional information, in order to have doses to associate with these incidences, these concentrations would have been converted to mg/kg-day doses using a standard respiratory minute volume of 0.2 liter for rats (Leong et al. 1964) and information on the body weights. The resulting doses are presented in the Table 1.

However, in this instance there was additional information about the uptake of bromoethylene. Pharmacokinetic studies in rats by several authors indicate that the uptake of bromoethylene is a dose-dependent but saturable process (Filser and Bolt 1979, Andersen et al. 1980). When described by Michaelis-Menten kinetics, the uptake of bromoethylene in rats was found by Andersen et al. (1980) to have a K_m of 18.4 ppm (80.59 ug/l) and a V_{max} of 2.1 mg/kg/hr. As detailed by Gehring et al. (1978) and Anderson et al. (1980), these pharmacokinetic parameters are useful because they can be used to estimate the amount (v) of bromoethylene metabolized or taken into the bloodstream after exposure to a given concentration, according to the formula:

$$v = \frac{V_{max} \cdot S}{K_m + S} \qquad (1)$$

where

$$
\begin{aligned}
v &= \text{amount metabolized or taken in (mg/kg/hr)} \\
V_{max} &= \text{maximum velocity of metabolism or intake (mg/kg/hr)} \\
K_m &= \text{Michaelis-Menten constant (ug/l)} \\
S &= \text{concentration of the compound (ug/l).}
\end{aligned}
$$

These estimates of v are the intake doses received by the animal, and they can then be indexed to incidence information so that a more accurate assessment of dose-response relationships is possible. The resulting doses are presented in the next table (Table 2) in contrast to those developed in the more conventional fashion. Also given are the percent of the respiratory doses calculated in Table 1. This comparison indicates that saturation is probably occurring at the higher exposive concentrations and thus that the dose actually delivered to the blood stream would be over estimated by the standard method.

Having indexed the rat toxicity information to an intake dose, however, our next need was to extrapolate this dose-response relationship to humans. Thus, we needed a way to estimate the amount of bromoethylene to enter the human blood stream following inhalation exposure. Ideally, this should have been based on a knowledge of the human V_{max} and K_m for uptake of bromoethylene. Unfortunately, such information was not available. (It rarely is.)

What was available, however, was the information that for a compound whose metabolism or uptake is perfusion limited, the rate of metabolism or uptake, u_T, can be approximated by the equation (Andersen 1980, 1981):

$$u_T = \frac{V_A (N - N_{eff}) C_{inh}}{N} \qquad (2)$$

where

u_T = rate of uptake (mg/kg/hr)
V_A = alveolar ventilation rate (1/kg/hr)
N = thermodynamic blood:gas partition coefficient
N_{eff} = steady-state blood:gas concentration ratio
C_{inh} = inhaled concentration (mg/l).

The human dose is calculated by multiplying u_T by the length of exposure (in hours).

Table 1. Estimated doses based on rodent respiratory parameters

Exposure Concentration a/ (μg/l)	42.7	229	1110
Estimated Respiratory Dose b/ (mg/kg-d)	7.5	40.65	197.06

a/ Nominal concentrations administered under regimen detailed in Figure 2.

b/ Estimated with a rat respiratory minute volume of 0.2 liter.

Structure:

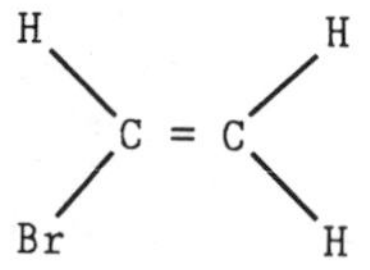

Effect: Dose-related increase in angiosarcomas in Sprague Dawley rats following inhalation exposure 6 hr/day, 5 day/week for 24 months

Exposure Concentrations mg/m³	42.7	229	1110
Incidence (%)	8.89	46	65

Figure 2. Risk assessment for bromoethylene

Table 2. Estimated doses based on Michaelis-Menten kinetics

Exposure Concentration (µg/1)	42.7	229'	1110
Estimated Michaelis-Menten Dose (mg/kg-d)	4.36	9.32	11.74
Percent of Respiratory Dose	58	22	5

Andersen (1980) defines N_{eff} as,

$$N_{eff} = N/(1 + Cl_t \times N) \tag{3}$$

where Cl_t is the fraction of cardiac output cleared of toxicant by metabolism. Andersen (1980) considers bromoethylene to be a compound whose metabolism is perfusion limited. Furthermore, he indicates that for a chemical such as bromoethylene, which because of the high affinity of its metabolism should be completely cleared from the hepatic blood by one pass through the liver, the Cl_t will be about 0.3 (Andersen 1980).

Although a value for N, the true blood:gas partition coefficient, of bromoethylene was not found in the literature, Andersen et al. (1980) calculated a number of mixed partition coefficients ("S"); for bromoethylene, "S" = 3. These authors suggest that while "S" is generally larger than the reported literature values of N, the choice of which to use is arbitrary; that is, "S" can replace N in these calculations. Thus the steady-state blood: gas concentration ratio (N_{eff}) for bromoethylene can be calculated as follows:

$$N_{eff} = 3/[1 + (0.3)(3)] = 1.58$$

The alveolar ventilation rate (V_A) can be defined as follows (Menzel and McClellan 1980, ICRP 1975):

$$V_A = (TV - VD) \times f = (TV \times f) - (VD \times f) \tag{4}$$

where

V_A	=	alveolar ventilation rate
TV	=	tidal volume
VD	=	dead space

f   = frequency (breaths/min).

Further (ICRP 1975),

$$TV \times f = \text{minute volume (MV)} \tag{5}$$

Substituting (Eq. 5) into (Eq. 4), the alveolar ventilation rate can be calculated:

$$V_A = MV - (VD \times f) \tag{6}$$

For a 70-kg human, under conditions of light activity, $f = 16$, $VD = 160$ ml/breath, and $MV = 20$ 1/min (ICRP 1975).
    Thus, during light activity, such as during a workday, the V_A of a 70-kg human can be calculated as,

$$V_A = [20 \text{ 1/min} - (160 \text{ ml/breath} \times 16 \text{ breaths/min})] - 70 \text{ kg}$$
$$= 0.25 \text{ 1/kg-min} = 15 \text{ 1/kg-hr}$$

From the foregoing derivation, it follows that the amount of material taken up (u_T) by a 70-kg human exposed to bromoethylene in the workplace can be estimated as follows:

$$u_T = (15 \text{ 1/kg-hr}) \times (3 - 1.58) \times C_{inh} - 3$$
$$= 7.1 \text{ 1/kg-hr} \times C_{inh}$$

which allows one to calculate the does received at a given concentration thereby allowing the assessment of risk.

ALPHA CHLOROTOLUENE

    The second risk assessment that I wish to discuss was one for the compound alpha-chlorotoluene (ACT). alpha-Chlorotoluene is a side chain chlorinated aromatic which is a colorless to light yellow liquid at normal temperatures. Also known as benzyl chloride, ACT was used in the production of benzyl alcohol in which it may remain as a contaminant at levels as high as 1000 ppm. Benzyl alcohol was often a component of shampoos and other toiletries. Thus this risk assessment was concerned with estimating the dose received dermally by consumers using contaminated shampoos.

    The dose received from the dermal application of a compound can be estimated by the use of the following formula (Shell Development Company 1980):

$$d = J_s \bullet t \bullet A \tag{7}$$

where

d = dose
J_s = the absorption flux of the compound
t = the duration of use
A = the surface area of application

Determining the J_s of ACT, however, requires the use of a number of assumptions which have been underlined in the following discussion in order to emphasize the contribution they make to the development of an uptake dose.

The rate limiting step of the absorption of a compound through the skin is generally considered to be diffusion through the stratum corneum (SC) (Scheuplein 1965). Under steady state conditions, this rate or flux, J_s, varies inversely with the thickness (δ) and is directly proportional to the solute concentration difference (ΔC) across the SC according to the following expression (Scheuplein 1965):

$$J_s = \frac{K_M D}{\delta} \Delta C \qquad (8)$$

where

J_s = the amount of solute that penetrates a unit of SC per unit time
K_m = the partition coefficient of solute between SC and water
D = diffusion coefficient of solute in SC (cm^2/sec)
ΔC = the concentration difference of solute across SC (mg/cm^3)
δ = thickness of SC in cm.

Substituting equation 8 into equation 7, it is possible to derive a dose in terms of the partition coefficient and diffusion coefficient of the solute in SC:

$$d = \frac{K_M D}{\delta} \Delta C \cdot t \cdot A \qquad (9)$$

where,

d = the daily dermal absorption of the solute in mg/day
K_m = the partition coefficient of solute between SC and water
D = the diffusion coefficient of solute in SC (cm^2/sec)
ΔC = the concentration difference of solute against SC (mg/cm^3)
δ = thickness of SC.

If it is assumed that the diffusion process is very slow and that once the solute crosses the SC it is rapidly removed by the capillary circulation, then the amount of solute retained inside the SC will be much less than that remaining on the SC surface, i.e., $\Delta C \simeq C$ where C is the initial concentration of solute applied to the SC. With this assumption Equation 9 now can be written as follows:

$$d = \frac{K_M D}{\delta} C \cdot t \cdot A. \qquad (10)$$

15

Roberts et al. (1977) have shown that for a number of phenolic compounds and aromatic alcohols, the partition coefficient, K_M, of a compound can be derived from its octanol/water partition coefficient (log P) using the following equation

$$\log K_M = 0.57 \log P - 0.1 \tag{11}$$

where

K_M = partition coefficient of solute in SC
$\log P$ = octanol/water partition coefficient

Although the authors point out that this relationship may not hold true for solutes that are more polar than those examined, it seemed reasonable to assume that this relationship will hold true for ACT which should be less polar than the chlorophenols that were examined. Given that the log P for ACT = 2.30, equation 11 can be used to calculate the K_M of ACT as follows:

$$\log K_M = (0.57 \times 2.30) = 0.1 = 1.211$$
$$K_M = 16.26.$$

The diffusion coefficient (D) for ACT in SC depends on the thickness (δ) of the SC and the thermodynamic and chemical properties of ACT. Although no D value for ACT in SC was found in the available literature, based on theoretical considerations[1] it seemed reasonable to assume that the value Scheuplein and Blank determined for non-polar alcohols (5×10^{-10} cm^2/sec for an SC of thickness (δ) equal to 40 u.) probably can be used. Substituting 5×10^{-10} cm^2/sec for D, 40 u (4×10^{-3} cm) for δ and 16.26 for K_M into equation 10, equation 12 can then be derived:

$$u - \frac{16.26 \bullet (5 \times 10^{-10} cm^2/sec)}{4 \times 10^{-3} \ cm} \bullet C \bullet t \bullet A \tag{12}$$

$$d = (2.03 \times 10^{-6} \ cm/sec) \bullet C \bullet t \bullet A$$

With equation 12 it was then now possible to estimate doses received under various exposure scenarios. As a worst case scenario assume the following:

(1) that a class of individuals exists that uses a shampoo containing the highest concentration of benzyl alcohol (25%)

---

[1]Scheuplein and Blank (1971) indicate that more bulky, non-polar molecules (e.g., ACT) will probably have lower diffusion coefficients (10^{-11}, 10^{-12} cm^2/sec) thus the value they determined for the non-polar alcohols probably represents an upper limit on the D for ACT.

(2) that the benzyl alcohol used in that shampoo contains 1,000 ppm (0.1%) ACT

(3) that the shampoo is used daily

(4) that this is diluted 1:5 for use (Shell Development Company 1980)

(5) that the duration of exposure is 0.08 hour (Shell Development Company 1980)

(6) that the major body areas exposed are the scalp and palms and that these comprise a surface area of approximately 1,600 cm^2.

Based on assumptions 1 and 2, the postulated shampoo contains 250 ppm ACT. Diluted 1:5 for use the concentration applied to the skin is 50 ppm (5×10^{-5} g/cc). The dose received by individuals using this shampoo is calculated as follows:

$$d = 2.03 \times 10^{-6} \text{ cm/sec} \bullet 5 \times 10^{-5} \text{ g/cm}^3 \bullet \text{hr} \bullet 3600 \text{ sec/hr} \bullet 1,600 \text{ cm}^2$$

$$d = 4.68 \times 10^{-5} \text{ g}$$

Under this scenario a 70 kg human would receive 6.69×10^{-1} ug/kg/day (4.68×10^{-5} g $\bullet$ 10^6 ug/g $\div$ 70 kg).

Information in the voluntary registry of cosmetic products indicates that only 1.08% of the shampoos used should contain benzyl alcohol. If these data are representative and, if the above scenario was expanded to all individuals that wash their hair daily, then the average daily dose of this population would be 7.22×10^{-3} ug/kg/day (6.69×10^{-1} ug/kg/day $\bullet$ 0.0108). Expand the scenario to apply to those individuals that on the average washed their hair once a week, and the average daily dose becomes 1.03×10^{-3} ug/kg/day.

It should also be noted that the initial scenario may not be the extreme worst case. Shampoos generally contain surfactants and surfactants can cause damage to the stratum corneum (Scheuplein and Blank 1971). This in turn would enhance the uptake of ACT. Furthermore, although the scenario has been limited to shampoo, the use of other cosmetics may also increase the dose. Dosimetry for such usage is very hard to estimate, however.

This presentation has outlined two attempts to develop better dose response relationships: the first, on bromoethylene, used available pharmacokinetic data from animals and physiologically based information from humans to develop a method to estimate human exposure concentrations comparable on a blood-intake level to those which in rats were associated with increased risk of tumors. The second, on alpha-chlorotoluene, made use of a variety of physico-chemical parameters and relationships to estimate the dose of a compound delivered across the stratum corneum to the blood supply. Of the two, I put more faith in the first for the second required a large number of assumptions. Both exercises were very educational in that the detailed review of uptake mechanisms required in order to derive them clearly highlighted the kind of data required in order to develop better dose estimates and subsequent work has just as clearly indicated how rarely such data are available.

REFERENCES

Anderson ME. 1980. Saturable metabolism and its relationship to toxicity. Wright-Patterson AFB, OH: Air Force Aerospace Medical Research Laboratory, AFAMRL-TR-80-18.

Andersen ME. 1981. A physiologically-based toxicokinetic description of the metabolism of inhaled gases and vapors: analysis at steady-state. Wright-Patterson AFB, OH: Air Force Aerospace Medical Research Laboratory, AFAMRL-TR-81-8.

Andersen ME, Gargas ML, Jones RA, Jenkins LJ. 1980. Determination of the kinetic constants for metabolism of inhaled toxicants in vivo using gas uptake measurements. Toxicol. Appl. Pharmacol. 54:100-116.

Anderson MW, Hoel DG, Kaplan NL. 1980. A general scheme for the incorporation of pharmacokinetics in low-dose risk estimation for chemical carcinogenesis: example - vinyl chloride. Toxicol. Appl. Pharmacol. 55:154-161.

Gehring PJ, Watanabe PG, Park CN. 1978. Resolution of dose-response toxicity data for chemicals requiring metabolic activation: example - vinyl chloride. Toxicol. Appl. Pharmacol. 44:581-591.

ICRP (International Commission on Radiological Protection). 1975. Physiological data for reference man. In: Report of the task group on reference man, no. 23. New York: Pergamon Press, pp. 335-365.

Leong KJ, Dowd GF, MacFarland HN. 1964. A new technique for tidal volume measurement in unanaesthetized small animals. Can. J. Physiol. Pharmacol. 42:189-198.

Menzel DB, McClellan RO. 1980. Toxic responses of the respiratory system. In: Doull J. Klaassen CD, Amdur MO, eds. Casarett and Doull's toxicology. The basic science of poisons, 2nd edition. New York: Macmillan Publishing Co., Inc., pp. 246-274.

Roberts MS, Anderson RA, Moore DE, Swarbrick J. 1977. The distribution of non-electrolytes between human stratum corneum and water. Aust. J. Pharm. ci. 6(3):77-82.

Scheuplein RJ. 1965. Mechanism of percutaneous adsorption I. Routes of penetration and the influence of solubility. J. Invest. Dermatol. 45(5)334-346.

Scheuplein RJ, Blank IH. 1971. Permeability of the skin. Physiol. Rev. 51(4):702-747.

Shell Development Company. 1980. Product literature. 1,4-dioxane in alcohol ethoxysulfate products. Houston: Shell Development Company. Ter Haar G, Ethyl Corporation, Baton Rouge, LA 70801. April 16, 1979b. Submission to Docket Officer, OSHA on the histopathology of vinyl bromide.

A RETROSPECTIVE LOOK AT THE CARCINOGENIC POTENCY OF VINYL CHLORIDE

John T. Barr

Air Products and Chemicals, Inc.
Allentown, PA 18105

ABSTRACT

Failure to find any cases of vinyl chloride-induced cancer outside the heavily exposed reactor cleaner group calls into question the human relevance of predictive methods for carcinogenic potency. Potency estimates by six conventional routes are reviewed with special attention to the implication of each route for vinyl chloride. New metabolic and mechanistic data are used to suggest a basis for the failure of "classical" risk assessment methods to provide accurate predictions for humans in this instance.

KEY WORDS: Angiosarcoma, Carcinogenicity, Epidemiology, Latency, Potency, Risk Assessment, Vinyl Chloride

The practice of estimating the quantitative risk to humans from exposure to carcinogens has expanded widely in the last ten years. In many cases the thrust has come from the need or the desire to evaluate long lists of chemicals for regulatory decision making. There has been a concomitant increase in the effort to standardize the procedure in order to save time, and to provide means of obtaining estimates in the absence of a complete data base, as is often the case.

This situation has led to the widespread use of the deceptively simple expression. Risk = Potency times Exposure. There often are problems in estimating exposures of the past, but frequently they can be estimated with about as great precision as potency can be estimated. Current exposures can be determined accurately, and acceptable future exposures could be determined if only the potency was known. Thus, the value of potency, although equal in weight to exposure in determining the risk, usually is the primary subject of investigation.

Some regulatory agencies have practiced projection of carcinogenic risks for exposure to substances whose carcinogenicity has not been determined. This "what if" type of approach would have some utility if the finding of an impossible rate of mortality by such a calculation would result in the withdrawal of the estimate or assist in concluding that the substance is not a carcinogen. Unfortunately, that has not occurred regularly, and such potency estimates acquire a life of their own, living on in agency control requirements and in the popular press long after any scientific support for such action has vanished.

It is reasonable to expect that the subject of a potency estimation should have at least some some epidemiological or experimental support for being a suspect carcinogen. The substance to be discussed today is unquestionably a human and animal carcinogen, and there is an enormous amount of data available on its properties. Vinyl chloride is a classical procarcinogen which is metabolized by Cytochrome P-450, primarily in the liver, to some as yet unidentified carcinogenic metabolite. It thus is a suitable paradigm for exploring the six most frequently used methods for estimating the potency of carcinogens.

Epidemiology

The great amount of public interest in and the high commercial value of vinyl chloride and its polymers has led to development of substantial epidemiological data on both occupational and ambient exposures. Occupational deaths have occurred in every PVC-producing country in the free world with an adequate latency period (Purchase, et al, 1985). The only tumor excess found consistently in these workers is angiosarcoma of the liver (ASL). We can therefore make a rough potency calculation using occupational data from the United States, and conventional assumptions (Barr, 1982).

About 25,000 workers were exposed to vinyl chloride in VC and PVC plants by the early 1970's. At least 10% were very heavily exposed, to an average of 1,000 ppm or more in their work. Of these, some 35 have died, and it has been estimated by some authorities (Purchase, et al., 1985) that an additional 30 or so may eventually develop the disease. The average latency period has been 25 years. Thus,

$$\frac{65}{2,500} = P \frac{1,000 \times 25}{70}, \text{ and}$$

$$P = 7.3 \times 10^{-5} \text{ ppm}^{-1}, \text{ or } 10^{-4}.$$

If, as we hope, the number 65 is too large, this estimate is too high. And if, as many with personal experience in the industry feel, the 10% fraction of highly exposed persons is too low, the potency value also is overstated. Also, if the 1,000 ppm value is too low, as many also feel, the value is reduced further. A total effect of up to nearly two orders of magnitude would result from the use of different, but equally defensible numbers. For example, if

$$\frac{50}{25000} = P \frac{5000 \times 25}{70}, \text{ then } P = 2 \times 10^{-6}$$

The most likely value probably lies somewhere between these two estimates.

Another factor often overlooked is that any exposures that are experienced after the irreversible initiation of a tumor (by an initiator) or after the first irreversible promotion of the tumor (by a promoter) are irrelevant. That fact has important implications for most risk estimates as they are currently being conducted. Total lifetime dose is a cornerstone of the EPA methodology (Anderson, 1983), but is is obvious upon reflection that it is an incorrect basis for potency estimation. Thus, the figure 25 in the above expression is too large, and therefore the actual potency is greater than the value shown by a factor of about 5 or 10. However, all potency calculations are also in error, so the relative potency ratings are not affected as much.

If the first potency value calculated by this method is accepted as stated, a person exposed at work to 1 ppm of VC for 25 years would have about a 1 in 10,000 chance of ASL over a lifetime. That would seem on its face to be a reasonably sound estimate, because it is based on epidemiology. It appears to be confirmed roughly by a study of 15,000 PVC fabrication workers, who were exposed to 10-20 ppm in their work until 10 years ago, which failed to find any cases in 1976, and none have been reported since then. About 1 or 2 cases would have been predicted from the above estimates.

The EPA estimated that about 4.6 million persons lived within 5 miles of VC/PVC plants in 1975, and were being exposed to an average of 17 ppb, and among whom the EPA estimated 20 cases per year of cancer (Kusmack and McGaughy, 1975).

Some of these persons have (or could have) lived there for fifty years by now; many of them could have been there for over 30 years, well over the needed latency period. Yet, not one person has been found to have developed ASL as the result of such exposure. Based on well over 200 million person years of exposure, the potency thus can be shown to be less than 10^{-7}. How much less is only speculation because negative epidemiology can only set an upper limit.

The potency value derived from the general population and that from the occupational studies do not agree by 1-3 orders of magnitude. Therefore, one must conclude that either one of the potency values is in error, or the potency of vinyl chloride varies with level of exposure, as does that of some other substances (Lijinsky and Reuber, 1984). We should not lose sight of the fact that a potency is calculated from only one data point on the dose response curve, and there is no compelling reason why it should be constant over the entire dose range (ECETOC, 1982). In either chloride is found to be a relatively weak carcinogen.

Animal Bioassays

Results from animal lifetime bioassays are the best source of data if epidemiological studies are not adequate, and thus are the data used in most instances. Several hundred such studies, of varying degrees of reliability are now available (Gold, et al., 1984). The conventional agency method of calculating potency from a bioassay is to determine the slope of the line from the origin (based on a no threshold policy) to the upper 95% limit of the lowest observed effect for the most sensitive species. Various groups have published potency estimates based on the dose required to produce 10% mortality (EPA, 1985) or 50% mortality (Peto, et al., 1984), as well as using just the slope to compute a potency index (Anderson, 1983). The results can show wide variation among the various studies on a single substance, with the 50% value varying over 3 orders of magnitude in some cases (Gold, et al., 1984). Even within one series of studies, widely varying dose response curves can be found (Barr, 1982).

Projections from such data invariably yield mortality estimates far higher than actually seen. The National Cancer Advisory Board found the estimate for vinyl chloride from the rat data was 500 times higher than that expected for humans (NCAB, 1979). Gehring, et al. (1978) and Anderson, et al. (1980), found that unless comparative pharmacokinetics are applied, the animal data cannot be predictive of human results. This problem of trying to determine the proper interspecies extrapolation factor is, of course, the single largest difficulty in the use of animal data. No generic solution has been found, and only a case-by-case analysis can produce appropriate results.

An interesting point is that each of the major animal studies on vinyl chloride that have been reported in detail found a no-effect level for each of the different organs that are attacked (Matoni, et al. 1981) and a no-observed-effect level below which no visible health effects at all were seen.

At the lowest levels, the only biological response was an increase in liver nodules or foci, and there were no overt effect on mortality or lifespan. These results are due to saturable metabolic and detoxification pathways, which allow a spillover of vinyl chloride or its metabolites to other, more distant organs at high doses, but appears to be able to confine the damage to a nonfatal response in the liver at low doses (Barr, 1985). Such effects as these show that caution is needed in the rote application of animal data to humans, and require careful analysis of the data. Even rats and mice correlate very poorly with one another, and therefore should not be always expected to be adequate surrogates for humans (DiCarlo and Fung, 1984).

Animal Skin Painting

Of all the methods being discussed, this has perhaps the least applicability to vinyl chloride because of its physical state. Vinyl chloride can be absorbed through the skin, but at a much lower rate than by inhalation. Thus, skin data could not be relevant to the expected exposure rates.

Further, skin painting studies are most effective in the study of promoters, and there is no question that VC is a complete carcinogen. A small fraction of recognized animal carcinogen do produce tumors at remote organs when applied to rodent skin, but many do not, and so the method has limited potential at best for potency measurements of other than local promoters (Tobin, et al., 1982).

In-vitro Tests

For many years, no reliable test procedure was available for showing the clastogenic properties of vinyl chloride, and it is, in fact, negative in the true mutagenic tests, i.e., those which test for heritable defects, such as the dominant lethal test. It is positive, however, in some of the Ames and other similar short-term tests which are taken by some as indicators of carcinogenicity, but which often are labeled improperly as tests for mutagenicity. It is necessary to take proper steps to overcome the gaseous nature and poor water solubility of the substance in order to obtain these results, however.

Perhaps because of this mechanical problem, no potency estimates have been made for vinyl chloride based on short-term results. The usual procedure when such data are reported is to state the minimum concentration or quantity of a test substance which yields positive results under standard conditions, but this concept of no-effect levels can lead to serious conflicts when utilized in conjunction with a potency estimate derived from a no-threshold extrapolation of bioassay data. Obviously, the two estimates are not comparable, and should not be used in conjuction with each other, although some regulatory agencies have attempted to do so.

Therefore, the available short-term data for vinyl chloride, while acting as an after-the-fact confirmation of its carcinogenicity, are not helpful in understanding its potency.

Acute Toxicity

There is a recognized relationship between the carcinogenicity and the chronic toxicity of some classes of substances, and it is recognized

22

that many of these substances do not induce cancer until other chronic health effects have occurred. There often also is a relationship between acute and chronic health effects, in that chronic effects sometimes are an extension of the acute effects, and utilize some of the same mechanistic pathways. Richard Wilson and coworkers at Harvard have investigated (Zeise, et al., 1984) the possibility of a relationship between carcinogenic potency and acute toxicity, and have examined the relationship:

$$\beta = D/(LD_{50})^C + k,$$

where β is the potency, C and D are empirically-derived constants, k contains an expression of the variance of the estimate, and LD_{50} is the 50% acute lethal dose.

They then estimated that, based on an inhalation LD_{50} of 26 g/kg for vinyl chloride in the rat, workers exposed to 5,000 ppm of VC for 15 years would have a lifetime risk of between 1 and 10%. As was shown earlier, this is about 3 or 4 orders of magnitude too high.

They also estimated that, based on an oral rat LD_{50} of 30 g/kg for sucrose, and an average intake of 1.7 g/kg day by humans, there should be between 200,000 and 2,000,000 deaths per year from cancer because of that sucrose intake. Similarly, table salt would be predicted to add 300,000 to 1,000,000 more deaths. It does not appear, therefore, that a useful estimate of human carcinogenic potency can be obtained by a direct extrapolation of oral rodent LD_{50} data without other facts being considered.

Structure-Activity Relationships

It is rare to read a report on the chronic hazards of an unsaturated substance without finding a statement that the "similarity" of the substance to vinyl chloride was one basis for suspicion of its carcinogenicity. Without vinyl chloride the ethylenic products would enjoy a much better reputation. However, among the unsaturated aliphatic compounds, there is no other similar substance which has been shown unquestionably to be a human carcinogen, or for which even the animal data are unequivocal. Therefore, possession of a carbon-to-carbon double bond is not a credible indication of carcinogenicity, and neither in the C-H bond, of course. This leaves only the Cℓ bond as a possible signal. Certainly, adding more chlorine does nothing to increase the potency significantly (EPA, 1985). Table 1 contains potency data calculated by EPA by two of its current procedures for a series of suspect carcinogens and a comparison with the IARC classification of those substances. Thus, we find nothing in QSAR to help us understand the potency of vinyl chloride. This table does illustrate perhaps the most valuable use for potency estimates, the comparison of closely-related substances.

SUMMARY

Of the six methods now being used for potency estimation, we find that four of them, QSAR, acute toxicity, short-term tests, and skin painting, are of no significant value in evaluating the strength of this recognized human carcinogen. Although the reasons for this vary from case to case, it suggests that caution should be used when attempting to apply such data to less well characterized substances.

Animal bioassays offer confirmatory evidence, but present both

TABLE 1

Potency Values for Several Substances
as Calculated by Two Current EPA Methods,
and Comparison with the IARC Classification

	$\log_{10}$[a] Potency Index	Potency[b] Factor I/ED_{10}	IARC[c] Class
Vinyl Chloride	0	0.16	1
Vinylidene Chloride	1	4.60	3
Trichloroethylene	0	0.18	3
Tetrachloroethylene	1	0.18	3
Acrylonitrile	1	0.06	2A
Styrene	--	--	3

Source:

(a) EPA (1985 b)

(b) EPA (1985)

(c) (1982)

qualitative and quantitative differences from humans, in the target organs and in the potency. Animal data can be understood better in light of the human data now available, but the animal data have been of only limited value in explaining the human results.

We cannot explain fully the human data. Thee appear to be too few (zero, actually) cases in the general public based on those which would be predicted from the occupational results. It is not easy to understand why only about 1% of the highly exposed workers have developed ASL. It is apparent that we do not understand yet the mechanism of the disease or its actual eitiology.

What do we know? Vinyl chloride is a weak human carcinogen. If it had been more potent, it certainly would have been recognized as such much sooner. It is qualitatively and quantitatively different from structurally similar substances. We have very encouraging indications from epidemiology that low-level exposures to the public cause no ill effect.

We have a strong reaffirmation of the value of epidemiology data, where available, and also of the fact that animal data must be interpreted only after careful application of appropriate adjustment factors.

Potency estimates can play a very useful part in both risk estimation and risk management. We must be careful in our application of these estimates not to destroy their credibility by carelessness in our calculations or use.

REFERENCES

Anderson, C. (1983), "Quantitative Approaches in Use to Assess Cancer Risk," Risk Anal., 3 277.

Anderson, M. W., Hoel, D. G., and Kaplan, N. L. (1980), "A General Scheme for the Incorporation of Pharmacokinetics in Low Dose Risk Estimation for a Chemical Carcinogenesis. Example--Vinyl Chloride," Toxicol. Appl. Pharmacol., 55 154.

Barr, J. T. (1982), "Risk Assessment for Vinyl Chloride in Perspective," Paper 82-9.2 at the 75th Annual Meeting of the Air Pollution Control Association, New Orleans, LA, June 20-25.

Barr, J. T. (1985), "The Calculation and Use of Carcinogenic Potency--A Review," Reg. Toxicol. Pharmacol., in press.

DiCarlo, F. J. and Fung, V. A. (1984), "Summary of Carcinogenicity Data Generated by the National Cancer Institute /National Toxicology Program," Drug Metabol. Rev., 15 1251.

Environmental Protection Agency (1985), "Methodology for Ranking the Degree of Hazard Associated with Exposure to Carcinogens and Other Toxic Chemicals," EPA/600/D-85-/040, PB85-167906.

Environmental Protection Agency (1985 b), "Mutagenicity and Carcinogenicity Assessment of 1,3-Butadiene," EPA/600/8-85-004A, February.

European Chemical Industry Ecology and Toxicology Centre (1982), Monograph No. 3, Risk Assessment of Occupational Chemical Carcinogens, January, Brussels.

Gehring, P. J., Watanabe, P. G., and Park, C. N. (1978), "Resolution of Dose-Response Toxicity Data for Chemicals Requiring Metabolic Activation. Example--Vinyl Chloride," Tox. Appl. Pharmacol., 44 581.

Gold. L. S., Sawyer, C. B., Magaw, R., Backman, G. M. deVeciana, M., Levinson, R., Hooper, N. K., Havender, W. R., Bernstein, L., Peto, R., Pike, M. C., and Ames, B. N. (1984), "A Carcinogenic Potency Database of the Standardized Results of Animal Bioassays," Environ. Health Perspect., 58 9.

International Agency for Research on Cancer (1982), "Annual Report 1982," World Health Organization, Lyon, France.

Kusmack, A. M. and McGaughy, R. E. (1975), "Quantitative Risk Assessment for Community Exposure to Vinyl Chloride," U.S. EPA, Washington, DC, Dec. 5.

Lijinsky, W. and Reuber, M. D. (1984), "Carcinogenesis in Rats by NDMA and Other Nitrosos at Low Doses," Can. Let., 22 83.

Maltoni, C., et al. (1981), "Carcinogenicity Bioassays of Vinyl Chloride Monomer," Environ. Health Perspect., 41 3.

National Cancer Advisory Board Subcommittee on Environmental Carcinogenesis (1979), "The Relationship of Bioassay Data for Chemicals to the Assessment of the Risk of Carcinogens for Humans Under Conditions of Low Exposure," January.

Peto, R., Pike, M. C., Bernstein, L., Gold, L. S., and Ames, B. N. (1984), "The TD_{50}: A proposed General Convention for the Numerical Description of the Carcinogenic Potency of Chemicals in Chronic-Exposure Animal Experiments," Environ. Health Perspect., 58 1.

Purchase, I. F. H., Stafford, J., and Paddle, G. M. (1985), "Vinyl Chloride, A Cancer Case Study," in Toxicological Risk Assessment, Vol. II, Ch. 8, D. B. Clayson, D. Krewski, and I. Munro, eds., CRC Press, Boca Raton, FL.

Tobin, P. W., Kornhauser, A., and Scheuplein, R. J. (1982), An Evaluation of Skin Painting Studies as Determinants of Tumorigenesis Potential Following Skin Contact with Carcinogens," Reg. Tox. Pharm., 4 187.

Zeise, L., Wilson, R., and Crouch, E. (1984), "Use of Acute Toxicity to Estimate Carcinogenic Risk," Risk Analysis, 4 187.

ANALYSIS OF HEALTH EFFECTS CAUSED BY MULTIPLE INSULTS

Fritz A. Seiler

Lovelace Inhalation Toxicology Research Institute
Albuquerque NM 87185

ABSTRACT

A method is presented for the analysis of the risk of health effects caused by a combination of insults. The approach is entirely phenomenological and has no built-in restrictions. Also, interactions between the effects of various toxicants are treated in a general manner. The only restrictions arise from the finite set of functions relating exposure parameters and the risk of health effects. As an example, the incidences of oral and esophageal cancer in man are analyzed as a function of alcohol and tobacco consumption. The properties of the solutions obtained are discussed, together with conclusions about the processes involved in the etiology of these cancers.

KEY WORDS: Multiple Insults, Synergism, Antagonism, Data Analysis.

INTRODUCTION

In the environment, no toxicant can act on an organism all by itself, there is always a mixture of many agents acting in combination. In order to study the health effects of multiple insults, the investigation of exposures to only one and two toxicants provides the basic information needed for a theoretical approach. At present, experiments involving two toxicants are being planned with increasing frequency both in chemical and in radiological toxicology, because the presence of other toxic agents can enhance or diminish the effects of a toxicant and yield results which are significantly different from those expected for an additivity of damages.

Most of the data available involve the exposure to a dose of either toxic agent alone, followed by an exposure to the combination of the doses. A simple comparison then shows whether the effects are at, above or below additivity (Reif, 1984). However, a measurement at a single dose combination does not allow a detailed study of the interaction between the effects of the two toxicants. For such an analysis, more elaborate data sets are needed. At present, sufficiently large sets are available only from epidemiological studies (Tuyns et al., 1977; Walter, 1980; Whittemore and McMillan, 1983) but corresponding experiments both in vitro and in vivo are being planned by many experimenters.

In the absence of sufficient experimental data, a multitude of mathematical forms can be constructed for the interaction of two toxicants. It is, therefore, important to approach the analysis without preconceived notions as to the nature of the interaction and to rely on a phenomenological approach to reach conclusions which are, as far as

27

possible, subject only to the requirements of the data set. In addition, the first priority is to find the dominant ones among the many contributions possible, neglecting for the time being those of lesser importance.

It is the purpose of this study, to introduce a formalism which is completely phenomenological and has as few built-in restrictions as possible, and to use it in the analysis of epidemiological data to demonstrate the viability of the method.

SYNERGISMS, COERGISMS AND ANTAGONISMS

Combination of Risks

Risk are probabilities and the risks due to a combination of insults must, therefore, combine probabilities appropriately. Thus, the risk of a health effect due either to agent 1 or agent 2 is given by the sum of the two probabilities minus their overlap. The overlap is zero if and only if the effects caused by the two toxicants are mutually exclusive; it is equal to their product if the two probabilities are independent of each other; otherwise more complex forms apply. If more than two causes with probabilities r_i, are possible, the general expression for the combined risk of toxicants with independent actions is given by

$$r_{ind} = 1 - \prod_{i=1}^{n} (1 - r_i).$$ (1)

Experimentally, it is often found, however, that the actions of several toxicants are not independent of each other, but that there are interactions between the effects of different insults. In that case, a risk higher or lower than r_{ind} is found. An experimental value R for the combined risk which is characterized by

$$R = r_{ind}, \text{ is said to indicate } \begin{matrix} > & \text{Synergism} \\ & \text{Coergism}, \\ < & \text{Antagonism} \end{matrix}$$ (2)

respectively. For small risks, that is, for $r_i \ll 1$, the higher order products of the risks r_i are much smaller still, and the criterion for independent action on the right-hand side reduces approximately to the sum of the risks. This sum of risks is often - but incorrectly - used as a general criterion for the existence of synergisms or antagonisms. It is for this reason that the condition for equality in relation (2) is not labeled with the generally inappropriate term 'additivity', but with the broader term 'coergism'.

Combined Risks in the Presence of Interactions

If interactions are possible, the difference in inequality (2) can be assigned to interaction terms of second or higher order which describe the interaction between the effects of two or more toxic agents, respectively. The most general expression for the total risk of a mixture of n toxicants is thus

$$R = 1 - \prod_{i=1}^{n} (1 - r_i) + \sum_{i=1}^{n} \sum_{j=i+1}^{n} r_{ij} +$$

$$+ \sum_{i=1}^{n} \sum_{j=i+1}^{n} \sum_{k=j+1}^{n} r_{ijk} + \cdots$$ (3)

The second term on the right-hand side is the source of the overlap terms of up to nth order between the risks r_i, if they are assumed to be independent. The third and fourth terms describe the interaction between the effects of two and three toxicants, respectively. This basic structure of eq. (3) is determined by the requirement that it must reduce to the marginal risk r_i if all exposures but the one to agent i are set equal to zero. Similarly, the interaction terms $r_{ij...k}$ must be zero if any of the exposures to agents i, j,...,k is zero.

For further discussions, it will become necessary to assume explicit cause-effect relationships for the marginal risks r_i. These may assume a variety of mathematical forms, but it will be assumed here that

    a)   the relevant exposure quantity is the accumulated dose D_i of the toxicant, and that

    b)   the dose-effect relationship is given by a power function of the dose D_i, that is, by

$$r_i = a_i D_i^{m_i} . \qquad (4)$$

Whereas these assumptions will influence the detailed form of the results given here, the methods employed are general and can be used to analyze data involving dose-effect relationships which have several terms or which involve exposure quantities other than dose.

In view of the basic requirements for the interaction term $r_{12...m}$ between m toxicants, its most simple possible form is the product of all doses D_i. The next higher level of complexity is a product of powers n_j of the doses D_j.

$$r_{12...m} = a_{12....m} \prod_{j=1}^{m} (D_j)^{n_j} , \qquad (5)$$

where the parameter $a_{12...m}$ is determined from experimental data. This form is appropriate for simultaneous exposures and, under certain conditions, for some consecutive exposures. If the interaction depends in any way on the sequence of some of the exposures, then a mathematical form has to be chosen which is asymmetric in the relevant doses.

Explicit Formula for Two Agents and Background

For two agents and a health effect with a background risk r_0, the most general form for the combined risk is

$$R = r_0 + r_1 + r_2 + r_{12} - \{ Q \}, \qquad (6)$$

where the overlap Q for independent action is defined by

$$Q = r_0 r_1 + r_0 r_2 + r_1 r_2 - r_0 r_1 r_2. \qquad (7)$$

Here, the marginal risks and the interaction term are potentially of the same order, whereas the overlap terms in Q are at least quadratic in the marginal risks r_i. Thus, for small values of the risks, the overlap Q can often be neglected.

In terms of the exposure parameters, the combined risk R is then given by

$$R = a_0 + a_1 D_1^m + a_2 D_2^n + a_{12} D_1^p D_2^q , \qquad (8)$$

The representation of the risks in which eqs. (6) and (8) are given is called the absolute risk model. It assumes that the marginal risks r_0, r_1, r_2 and the interaction term r_{12} all have different dependences on age, sex, and some lifestyle parameters. Its 4 parameters a_i and a_{ij} are the absolute risk coefficients, to be determined from experimental data.

If it is assumed that all dependences except those on exposure are the same, the background risk r_o can be factored out, resulting in the relative risk model, which thus assumes that the combined risk is proportional to the background risk

$$R = r_o[1 + f_1 + f_2 + f_{12} - \{ Q' \}], \tag{9}$$

where

$$Q' = r_o[f_1 + f_2 + f_1 f_2 - r_o f_1 f_2]. \tag{10}$$

Here, the symbols f_i and f_{ij} denote the fractional excess risks for the two agents and their interaction, respectively, and Q' is the relative overlap for independent action of the toxicants. The quantity in square brackets is called the relative risk and is independent of age, sex and some lifestyle parameters.

In the low-dose region, if the relative overlap Q' is very small and can be neglected, the combined risk in terms of the doses D_i is

$$R = a_o[1 + b_1 D_1^{m} + b_2 D_2^{n} + b_{12} D_1^{p} D_2^{q}], \tag{11}$$

with the relative risk coefficients b_1 and b_{1j}. Thus, if the relative risk R/a_o is fitted to an experimental data set, 3 parameters have to be determined.

ANALYSIS OF EPIDEMIOLOGICAL DATA

Analytical Approach

The characteristics of some biological processes which lead to the endpoint under consideration manifest themselves not only in the dose-effect relations of the marginal risks, but are particularly evident in the algebraic form of the interaction terms. The main purpose of the analysis is, therefore, an attempt to extract the mathematical essence of the information contained in the data set.

Geometrically speaking, the fitting of a data set by eqs. (8) or (11) is equivalent to fitting a risk surface to the data points in the 3-dimensional space defined by the two dose axes D_1 and D_2 and the risk axis R (For an aid to visualization, see Fig. 3). The approach used here is to determine the surface with the most simple algebraic structure which gives an acceptable fit to the data. Thus, the first trial functions are planes, then surfaces are used which are curved in one or more dimensions.

Algebraically speaking, this means that at first all linear and quadratic forms of both doses are tested in all combinations. There are 44 such trial functions, characterized by their exponents in eq. (11) which are combined in the symbol (mn pq). In addition, the interference term is given a special form, found already in previous evaluations of synergisms (Reif, 1984; Whittemore and McMillan, 1983). This results in a separable form of eq. (11), that is, in a product of factors each related to only one toxicant

$$R = a_o[1 + b_1 D_1^{m}][1 + b_2 D_2^{n}]. \tag{12}$$

For linear and quadratic forms of the marginal risks, there are 4 such functions. Separable functions will be denoted by the symbol (mn*mn), whereas the absence of a marginal risk or of an interference term is characterized by (m0 pq) and (mn 00), respectively.

Analysis of Two Data Sets

There are two data sets that relate the incidence of cancer of the upper gastro-intestinal tract to the consumption of alcohol and tobacco. The first is a study of Tuyns et al. (1977) of esophageal cancer in the province Ille-et-Villaine of France; the second an investigation of the incidence of oral cancer in the United States (Walter, 1980). A full discussion of the details of both data sets and of their analyses are given elsewhere (Seiler, 1985), only results and conclusions will be summarized here.

The 48 trial functions were tested not only for the quality of their fit to the data but also for the stability of these fits for moderate changes in the doses. Both the fitted surfaces and the values of the parameters fitted proved to be surprisingly stable, although the sum of weighted least-squares per data point sometimes changed considerably. The best fits were determined on the basis of goodness of fit and the requirement that the coefficients obtained be clearly nonzero.

Four trial functions consistently yielded the best fits, and two of these also fulfilled the criteria for nonzero coefficients. They are the functions characterized by (22 00) and (12*12). The first assumes independent action of the toxicants and quadratic marginal risks; the second assumes a synergistic, but separable risk function and relative risks linear in tobacco and quadratic in alcohol consumption. It should be noted that whereas most of the 48 trial functions have 3 free parameters, the best fits were obtained by two more restrictive functions with only 2 parameters (Figs. 1 and 2).

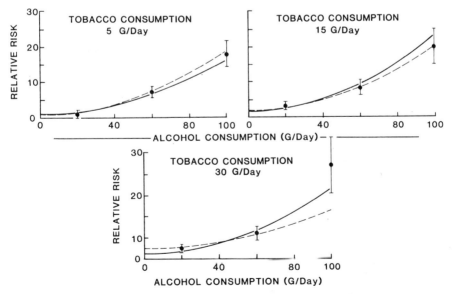

Fig. 1. Relative risk of esophageal cancer as a function of alcohol and tobacco consumption. The data points are those of Tuyns et al. (1977) and the solid and dashed lines are fits for the trial functions (12*12) and (22 00), respectively.

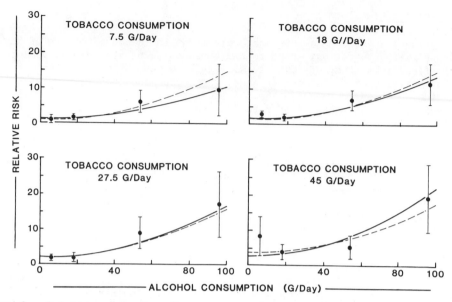

Fig. 2. Relative risk of oral cancer as a function of alcohol and tobacco consumption. The data points are those of Walter (1980) and the solid and dashed lines are fits for the functions (12*12) and (22 00), respectively.

For both oral and esophageal cancer, the best trial functions were the same, and even more important, the relative risk coefficients were the same, resulting in the same risk surface (Fig. 3). This implies that cancer of the oral cavity and the esophagus due to the consumption of alcohol and tobacco have a similar, if not the same etiology. Also, it allows to combine both organs into one critical organ for these toxicants.

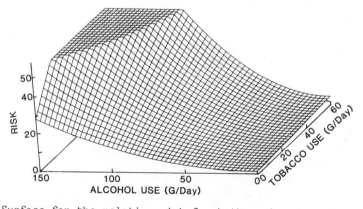

Fig. 3. Surface for the relative risk for both oral and esophageal cancer as a function of alcohol and tobacco consumption. In order to show the curvature of the surface it has been cut off at a relative risk of 50.

Mathematically, there are no valid reasons to prefer one of the two best solutions over the other. Biologically, however, there are reasons for a preference. In the complex multi-stage evolution from a normal cell to a cancerous cell, there are likely to be several steps where interaction can occur and result in a nonzero interaction term. On the other hand, the existence of two totally independent multi-stage pathways leading to the same cancer, one induced by alcohol and the other by tobacco seems considerably less plausible. For this biological reason, the solution (22 00) is considered the less likely one.

The separable structure of the more likely solution (12*12) requires that the synergistic interaction is of a kind which allows the risk enhancement due to one toxicant to be totally independent of the enhancement due to the other agent. Thus, although there is a dependence in a statistical sense, there must be independence in the mechanism of the interaction. This requirement restricts the type of processes that mechanistic models may use to describe the pathogenesis of oral and esophageal cancer by alcohol and tobacco.

Finally, the separability of the most probable solution and the equality of the risk surfaces for both cancers can lead to the formulation of some hypotheses with regard to the histologogy of the cancers or particular processes in their etiology. These hypotheses could then be verified in future experiments.

DISCUSSION

The purpose of this study was to introduce a formalism for the analysis of data from experimental studies involving a combination of insults. The method involves a minimum of a priori assumptions and attempts to distill the mathematical essence of the way in which biochemical processes influence the dependence of health effects on exposure.

The implementation of this method which is discussed here in detail uses an approach common in other fields by assuming that, until more is known about the processes studied, only the dominant contributions are of interest and that only the simplest solutions which are compatible with the data should be determined. More complex approaches to eqs. (3) to (5) can be devised easily, once additional knowledge on the health effects is available.

The application of this methodology to two totally independent sets of epidemiological data on cancers with different locations in the upper gastro-intestinal tract leads to several important results, demonstrating the capability to determine the numerical values of risk coefficients, and to discriminate between different algebraic structures of the interaction term. From these results, inferences can drawn and hypotheses formulated, which lead to new, clearly defined experimental questions.

ACKNOWLEDGMENTS

The author would like to express his gratitude to several members of the staff at the ITRI for helpful discussions and reviews of the manuscript. This research was performed under U.S. Department of Energy Contract Number DE-AC04-76EV01013.

REFERENCES

Reif, A.E., Synergism in Carcinogenesis, JNCI, 73, 25-39, 1984.

Seiler, F.A., Oral and Esophageal Cancer and the Consumption of Alcohol and Tobacco, Inhalation Toxicology Research Institute, Annual Report 1983-1984, LMF-113, p. 327-331, 1984, available from National Technical Information Service, Springfield, VA, 22161; and to be published.

Tuyns, A.J., G. Peuquignot, and D.M. Jensen, Le Cancer de l'Oesophage en Ille-et-Villaine en Function des Niveaux de Consummation d'Alcool et de Tabac: Des Risques qui se Multiplient, Bulletin du Cancer, 64, 45-60, 1977.

Walter, S.D., Prevention of Multifactorial Disease, Am. J. Epidemiol., 112, 409-416, 1980.

Whittemore, A.S., and A. McMillan, Lung Cancer Mortality Among U.S. Uranium Miners: A Reappraisal, JNCI, 71, 489-499, 1983.

MANAGING ECONOMIC RISKS DUE TO ELECTRICAL EQUIPMENT CONTAINING PCBS:

ANALYTICAL TOOLS TO SUPPORT UTILITY DECISIONS

Deborah A. L. Amaral, Dean W. Boyd, David Cohan,
Michael S. Hohnson and Donald S. Wilson

Decision Focus Incorporated

ABSTRACT

For industries that make use of hazardous materials, the direct economic consequences of alternative courses of action are often the most important factors in decisions about how to manage risks, but may be difficult to predict. The analysis of alternatives can be very complex, and uncertainty about actual and perceived risks may impede company efforts to manage risks.   A mathematical model designed to assist electric utility personnel in the financial analysis of management options for PCB-containing equipment has been developed and implemented as an interactive software tool. Based on the methods of decision analysis and utility finance, this specific application allows the user to represent uncertainty about possible PCB incidents (fires or spills), including frequency of occurrence, incident severity, and the costs of cleanup, plant shutdown, and legal liabilities. Predictions of total life-cycle equipment and incident costs can be compared for utility ratepayers and shareholders in order to facilitate risk management decisions. While the approach is general enough to be useful for many types of hazardous materials,   this paper presents a PCB transformer risk management case study using this tool.

KEY WORDS: Risk management, Risk analysis, PCB, Software, Utility,
           Decision, Model, Transformer

The PCB Economic Risk Management Model (ASK) and the Contaminated Oil Economic Risk Management Model (COIL) are decision support tools designed to help utility personnel manage equipment containing or contaminated with PCBs. Based on the methodology of decision analysis, the models provide techniques for comparing alternative strategies in terms of equipment costs and the costs of potential incidents such as fires and spills.

INTRODUCTION

Electric utilities typically have a variety of equipment containing or contaminated with PCBs. Accidents or failures involving such equipment may lead to very large economic costs for the utility. These costs can include cleanup of the facility and the surrounding area, repair or replacement of utility and third-party equipment, and possible legal liabilities. The possibility of incurring such losses may exist even when

35

the PCB contamination is very low. The need to weigh these highly
uncertain but potentially large losses against the costs of various
management alternatives prompted the development of the two decision
support tools discussed in this paper. The development of ASK was
motivated by the need to manage askarel transformers and PCB capacitors in
the face of the potential for large financial impacts due to incidents
such as fires. COIL was developed to help utilities choose management
alternatives for potentially contaminated mineral oil equipment. Both
tools focus on economic risks, which include direct equipment and cleanup
costs, and costs that may be incurred due to real or perceived health or
environmental effects from releases of PCBs.

Management Alternatives

Utilities have a variety of options available to manage equipment
containing PCBs, including replacing existing equipment with one or more
alternative types of equipment, isolating the equipment or installing
electrical protection devices to reduce risks, retrofilling to reduce PCB
levels, or retaining the existing equipment as is. Replacement may
involve significant costs for a new unit and for installation, but may
improve the operating efficiency and will eliminate the possibility of a
PCB incident. Incidents involving substitute equipment may occur with
greater frequency and with greater risk of conventional damage, but
probably will not lead to the larger costs sometimes associated with PCB
incidents.

There is often considerable uncertainty regarding the degree of PCB
contamination of mineral oil transformers. Testing the equipment can help
guide the choice of a management strategy and may help a utility avoid the
costs associated with an incident involving PCBs. If the likelihood of
severe contamination is low and incidents are rare, however, the cost of
testing may exceed the value of the information gained.

Balancing Equipment Costs Against Economic Risks

Choosing the best management strategy requires careful weighing of
uncertain losses against known cost and performance considerations. Is an
investment in risk reduction measures or new equipment merited to remove
the possibility of a potentially very expensive but relatively unlikely
incident? Management questions such as these are challenging due to the
large uncertainties in the likelihood, severity, and cost of incidents, as
well as the complexity of the cost, performance, and financial
considerations.

For example, consider the case of a utility that has a number of
askarel transformers in its generating stations. There is a small chance
that a fault in one of the transformers could lead to a major fire, one in
which PCBs and combustion by-products would be distributed widely through
the plant in the form of smoke and soot. How large would the probability
of a major fire need to be, and how great would the likely costs of an
incident need to be, before the company should decide to remove its
askarel transformers and replace them with non-PCB equipment? The cost of
installing new equipment is relatively easy to determine, but the
potential incident costs are not. Utility personnel may find it difficult
to estimate the costs since incidents are unlikely and the costs could be
quite large. The challenges posed by decisions such as this have
motivated the development of the risk management models and decision
support tools described in this paper.

ASK AND COIL: AIDS TO DECISION MAKING

ASK and COIL are designed to help utility personnel make the
difficult management decisions regarding PCB and contaminated mineral oil
equipment. Both ASK and COIL incorporate equipment cost and performance
calculations, a financial model to account for costs to ratepayers and
shareholders, and explicit representation of uncertainties in the
occurrence, severity, and cost of incidents. These features are combined
in interactive software packages that implement the risk management
models. The software implementations have been designed to facilitate and
guide analyses performed by relatively inexperienced computer users, yet
remain convenient and efficient for experienced users. They provide
complete capabilities for the user to enter, display, edit, save, and
retrieve data, to run the models, and to display and save both summary and
detailed results.

Decision Trees

The management decisions and key uncertainties are represented in ASK
and COIL using decision trees. The tree for ASK, shown in Figure 1, can
be used to calculate expected costs and the range of uncertainty over a
large number of scenarios. The tree in this figure is a shorthand
representation of the complete tree, in which specific decision
alternatives and uncertain events are defined, and each node is connected
to every branch of the previous node. The decision tree for COIL is
similar, but includes explicit representation of the sample/no sample
choice prior to the equipment management alternative.

If each of five uncertainty nodes shown in the ASK decision tree had
three possible outcomes, there would be a total of 243 scenarios,
represented as distinct paths through the tree. The likelihood, or
probability, of each scenario is simply the product of each likelihood
associated with the branches along its path through the tree.

Models

For each scenario defined by the tree, the calculations in ASK and
COIL are carried out using the models shown in Figure 2. The equipment
model calculates all costs associated with existing and replacement
equipment. It can take into account different operating and maintenance
costs and efficiencies for different types of equipment. The incident
occurrence model calculates the likelihood, potential timing, and likely
severity of an incident using values for the uncertain parameters, such as

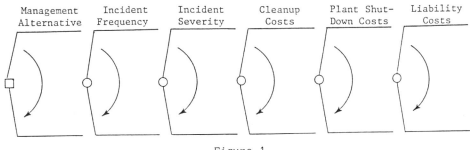

Figure 1

Key Uncertainties Are Represented as a Decision Tree in ASK

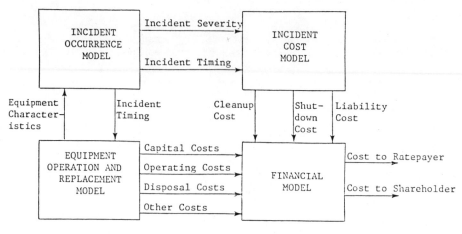

Figure 2

A Set of Models Are Used to Calculate Costs in ASK and COIL

the rate of occurrence of incidents, from the decision tree.

The incident cost model calculates all costs of an incident, given that one occurs. Cost elements can include equipment replacement costs, cleanup and repair costs, costs of legal liabilities, and costs due to the shutdown of a generating plant during the cleanup and repair period. The frequency and cost probabilities and estimates will depend on the specific scenario or path through the tree. The model incorporates utility cost-of-service calculations, distinguishes between capitalized and expensed costs, and calculates costs to both ratepayers and shareholders.

AN EXAMPLE USING ASK

As an example of a PCB equipment management decision problem, consider the question of whether an askarel transformer in a generating station should be replaced with a mineral oil transformer. Suppose the total capital cost of replacement is $75,000 for a 1000 KVA mineral oil transformer. Assume that the existing askarel would be replaced in about 14 years if no incident occurs, and the useful life of the slightly more efficient new transformer would be about 30 years. Also, assume that ratepayers will pay all of the costs associated with new equipment, but shareholders will pay a portion of the costs of an incident involving PCBs.

Utility personnel are typically uncertain about how likely an incident might be and what one would cost. Most utilities have not had major fires involving their askarel equipment, and thus have no historical data to draw upon to estimate fire frequencies or potential PCB fire costs. Using the decision tree structure in ASK, the uncertainty can be represented as two or more possible scenarios and industry data and subjective judgment can be used to assign likelihoods to each representative scenario [1,2]. Figure 3 shows the decision tree for this example and contains estimates for the uncertain parameters. For example, it has been assumed that the frequency of fires ranges from once every 1000 to 10,000 transformer-years and that fires in mineral oil equipment

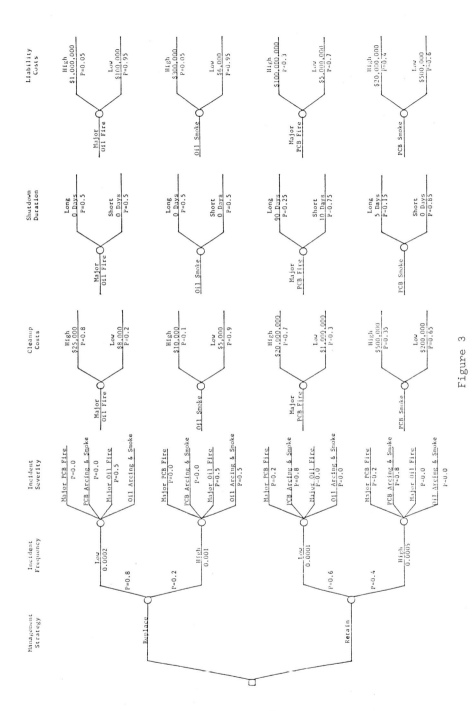

Figure 3

Decision Tree for ASK Example

39

are twice as likely as fires in askarels, but less expensive to clean up.

Rolling back this decision tree using ASK, it becomes apparent that the total expected life cycle cost of replacing the equipment is only slightly less than the expected cost of doing nothing and risking a fire. Figure 4 summarizes the expected equipment and incident costs by category. The nonincident costs are significantly higher when the equipment is replaced, but they are more than offset by the lower incident costs when no PCBs are present. Also, the decision tree generates a cumulative distribution that can be used to compare the range of possible costs for the management alternatives. Using the cumulative distribution, we find that for this example there is approximately a one in one thousand chance that the cost of choosing to replace the transformer will be $250,000 or more, which may be compared to the same chance that the cost of doing nothing will be $11 million or more. A utility may be unwilling to accept the chance of the higher cost.

What if fires in mineral oil transformers are ten times more likely than in askarels, rather than twice as likely? Figure 5 shows that changing this assumption about mineral oil fire frequency increases the cost of the option of replacing the askarel, but would probably not lead one to switch the choice of options, since the total expected cost of replacement is still lower. When should the decision change? Figure 6 shows the results of a sensitivity analysis performed using ASK. Assumptions about askarel incident frequency are compared with assumptions about the liability costs of major PCB incidents, and the curve indicates the points where the decision switches. For a wide range of expected liability costs, the frequency of incidents need not be very high before replacement becomes the preferred option. This figure demonstrates the advantages offered by a tool that can be used to quickly analyze the implications of differing judgments about the uncertain factors in this decision problem.

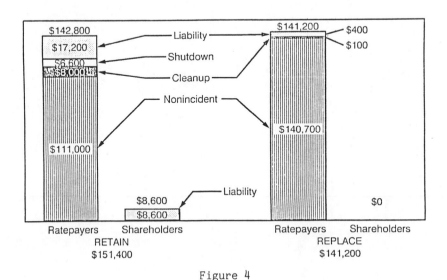

Figure 4

Present Value of Expected Equipment and Incident Costs

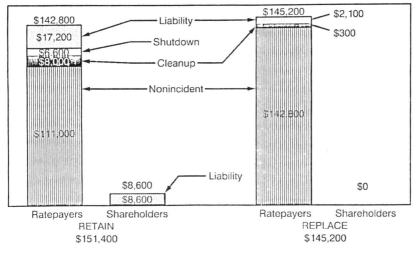

Figure 5

Expected Costs When Mineral Oil Fires are 10 Times as Likely

AN EXAMPLE USING COIL

COIL provides the same capabilities for analysis as ASK, but adds the ability to examine the value of testing, since the PCB content of a potentially contaminated transformer may be uncertain. Consider a 1000 KVA mineral oil transformer that might contain PCBs. Should it be retrofilled with clean insulating fluid to remove the risk of PCB spread in a spill incident? Retrofilling will not change the likelihood of a spill, but could substantially reduce the costs to the utility should an incident occur.

Assume that there is an 80 percent chance that the transformer contains less than 50 ppm PCB, a 15 percent chance of moderate contamination in the 50-500 ppm range, and a five percent chance that it contains 500 ppm or more. Retrofilling costs $5,000 and testing for PCB level costs $400. Assume that cleanup and liability costs will depend on the severity of an incident, which in turn will depend on the extent of PCB contamination in the transformer. Suppose that cleanup costs may range from $3,000 to $25,000 for an oil spill, and from $50,000 to $400,000 for a PCB spill. Assume that no liability costs are incurred in an oil spill, but that liabilities may range from $200,000 to $50,000,000 when PCBs are spilled.

Table 1 presents the a summary of the COIL results from an analysis of this example. The value of sampling is found to exceed the cost of sampling for PCBs, and the contamination level where action should be taken to reduce risks is identified as above 50 ppm PCB. In general, testing is worthwhile if it can change the choice of equipment management options. For this example, there is a significant chance that the transformer will contain less than 50 ppm, and testing has the potential to save the utility from the cost of retrofilling such a unit.

41

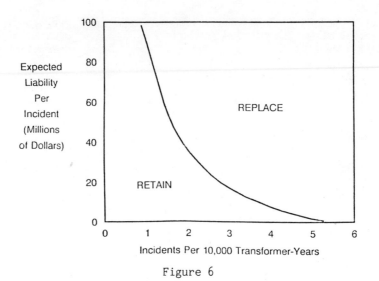

Figure 6

When the Decision Should Change

Table 1

Summary of Results in Coil Example

Sampling Alternative	Expected Cost
* SAMPLE	92,987
DON'T	93,769

The Value of Sampling Is: 1182

The Cost Of Sampling Is: 400

Contamination Level	Response Alternative	Expected Cost
Less than 50ppm	* NO ACTION	91881
	RETROFILL	93359
50 to 500 ppm	NO ACTION	99154
	* RETROFILL	94761
More than 500ppm	NO ACTION	108801
	* RETROFILL	97364
Uncertain	NO ACTION	93818
	* RETROFILL	93769

SUMMARY

ASK and COIL are decision support tools that allow utility personnel to evaluate PCB equipment management options for a wide range of situations. Comprehensive analyses can be carried out quickly and efficiently, comparing different management options in terms of direct costs and costs due to incidents. Uncertainties in incident occurrence, severity, and cost may be accounted for explicitly, and a wide variety of "what if?" questions can be answered rapidly.

In addition to serving as a useful analytical aid, ASK and COIL can help utility personnel communicate with top management, regulators, and public groups about the complex nature of PCB and contaminated mineral oil problems, as well as provide key insights from the analyses. The tables produced by ASK and COIL show both the assumptions and the results clearly. The implications of alternative viewpoints and opinions can be tested and displayed quickly and easily, thus facilitating discussion and consensus building on difficult PCB management issues.

REFERENCES

1. Resource Planning Corporation, "Report of the Study of Risks Posed by Askarel Transformer Fires," for the Edison Electric Institute and the Utilties Solid Waste Activities Group, June 1984.
2. Decision Focus Incorporated, "Economic Risk Management Models for Electrical Equipment Containing PCBs: A Guide to the ASK and COIL Decision Support Models," Draft Final Report to the Elecric Power Research Institute, RP 2595, July 1985.

ESTIMATING RISKS OF KNOWN AND UNKNOWN CARCINOGENS

Richard Wilson

Energy and Environmental Policy Center
and Department of Physics
Harvard University

ABSTRACT

Risk assessment is well accepted for those carcinogens for which there is human epidemiology. When there is only an animal bioassay, or only toxicity data, the calculated risk is very uncertain. Many people reject the idea of calculating risks and suggest that only a priority order is possible. But a risk still exists, however uncertain its calculation. A priority order based on uncertainty of information is different from one based on risk; yet it is the latter that is needed to improve public health.

KEY WORDS: Magnitude of risk, Priority, Non-carcinogen, Comparison, and Interspecies.

INTRODUCTION

This talk follows the two excellent talks by Dr. Elizabeth Anderson and by Dr. Roy Albert. They have been estimating risks for many years in the Carcinogen Assessment Group (CAG) of the Environmental Protection Agency (EPA). Their primary purpose is to address those toxic chemicals of concern to the Agency, with a view to deciding upon possible regulation. They make assumptions, some of them arbitrary, but assumptions that are deemed necessary to get the job done. I and my colleagues, particularly Dr. E.A.C. Crouch and Dr. L. Zeise, have been estimating risks with a particular aim of studying the assumptions, and with an effort to be logically complete. To the extent that our numbers agree with those of CAG, we help to give a logical underpinning; to the extent they disagree, we suggest that the disagreement be examined so that perspective can be gained. In addition we believe that deciding upon possible regulation is only one of the uses of risk assessment, and probably the least important use. We argue that public health can often be improved by steps that do not involve regulation, and that finding ways to continuously improve public health is a more important use.

In performing a risk assessment for a toxic chemical, we all will agree upon the first rule: use human data whenever it is available. The proper study of man is man. The human data is rare, and very precious. The exposures were high because of ignorance, accident, or stupidity, and we hope not to repeat such high exposures for any toxic chemical. Table I gives a partial list of some of the chemicals for which adequate human data are available.

Table I

Chemical	Reason
Cigarette Smoke	Stupidity
β napthylamine	Occupation
Benzidine	Occupation
Arsenic inhalation	Occupation
ingestion	Impure water
Benzene	Occupation
Aflatoxin B1	Food
Radiation	Mistakes

There are often more human data than generally realized. There may be, either implicitly or explicitly, negative epidemiological data which are adequate to give an upper limit to the possible risk. For example there is no firm evidence that those who work near refineries develop cancer. An upper limit can be placed upon the number of workers who might develop cancer as a result of the exposure. This upper limit is of the order of magnitude of the natural incidence. Those who inhale gasoline at gas stations probably have a lower exposure, and presumably have a correspondingly smaller risk.

The two key assumptions made in using human epidemiology are:
1) The exposure in the situation being assessed is similar in type to the exposure in the epidemiological study, and

2) If the magnitude of the exposure differs, a dose response relationship must be assumed.

Acute and Chronic Effects

In both the two preciding talks, emphasis has been placed upon cancer risks. Yet these are not the only possible adverse health effects that can occur. What risks are being ignored? Can we justify the idea that cancer risks are the most important? In discussing these questions it is useful to distinguish acute problems and chronic problems. A large, single, exposure to a chemical can poison an animal or a person. the effect is usually observed very quickly. These are acute, or prompt, toxic effects. They have been observed for centuries and man has learned to keep away from these poisons. To describe the ability of a chemical to cause adverse health effects toxicologists have defined several quantities. The LD50 - the least dose at which 50% or more of the animals die; the No Observable Effect Level or NOEL is the largest dose at which no effect is observed in a group of animals of reasonable size - typically 10 - 50. The LD50 is, according to this view, a short term dose, and a dose well below the LD50 can be repeated after a delay of a day or two without untoward effects. but this is certainly too simple. For example, in the animal bioassys for dioxin, the LD50 varied roughly as $1/\sqrt{t}$ where t is the number of daily repeated exposures. This is illustrated in figure 1. Toxicologists believe that these acute effects follow a sharp, threshold type of dose - response curve as illustrated in figure 2. Then provided that a single exposure is well below the LD50, or below the NOEL, the risk is believed to be zero or close to zero. To extrapolate between animal and man safety factors are used. For example if the dose is a 10 times below the NOEL when data is derived from human exposure, or 100 times if it is derived from animal exposure, the exposure is considered to be safe. A century of experience has shown the usefulness of this concept.

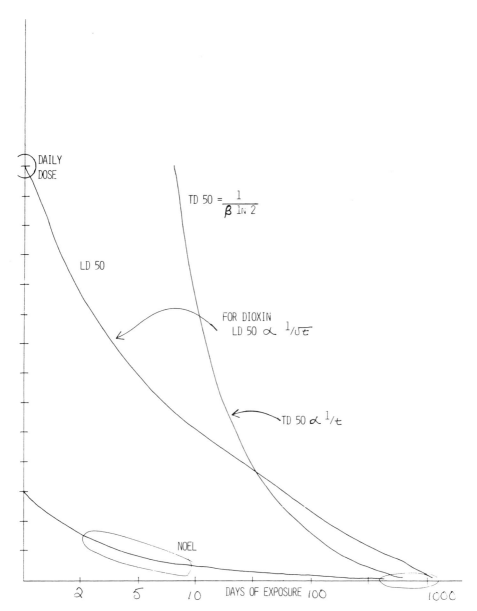

Figure 1. A schematic plot showing dangerous acute toxic doses (LD50) and Chronic doses such as the carcinogenic dose (TD50).

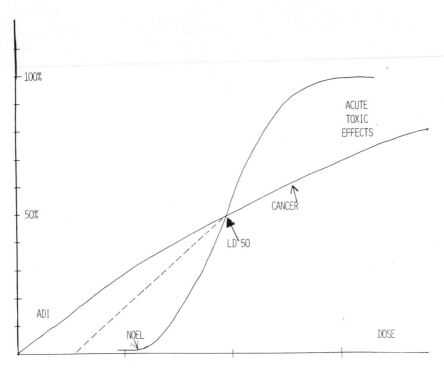

Figure 2. Typical dose response relationships for acute and chronic effects.

There are other chronic effects that appear with continuous exposure, of which cancer is a good example. To the extent that it is the cumulative dose that determines the cancer risk, the risk varies with average daily exposure as 1/t as shown in figure 1. Cancer incidence is expected to follow a dose response curve which is much less sharp than the acute toxic dose, and the effect might be proportional to dose, as shown in figure 2. Cancer is expected to proceed by damage to the DNA in a cell, and to the extent that such damage can also cause hear disease and other problems, a cancer risk assessment can be thought of as a surrogate for these other risks. The total risk is probably a small multiple of the cancer risk - as it is for cigarette smoking.

Certainty or Magnitude?

I now make a second rule about risk assessments. It is important to distinguish between the strength of evidence or certainty of the information and the magnitude of a risk. All too often, someone wants to set a priority order for risk-reduction on the basis of certainty of information (Squires, 1981). I submit that this procedure is not the best procedure to protect public health and illustrate this point by an example.

Vinyl chloride certainly has caused angiosarcoma in people. The epidemiology is unequivocal. Angiosarcoma is a rare tumor. Only 30 cases were observed in New York State in a 25 year period, and when one is seen attribution to a cause is often easy. In the epidemiological studies, the Risk Ratio was 400. Yet vinyl chloride has only caused 100 or so angiosarcomas, world wide, over 30 years. New that exposures are reduced over a hundredfold, the risk is surely minute.

Saccharin causes in cancer in rats. It may cause cancer in people, and there is certainly a chance and therefore a risk that it does. Yet, the FDA calculates that 500 cancers per year could be caused by saccharin consumption and this is over 1,000 times the number of cancers that could be caused by vinyl chloride. The risk of saccharin ingestion is clearly begger than the risk of vinyl chloride exposure, but the certainty is less. By avoiding vinyl chloride exposure we would not even reduce one cancer a year, but by avoiding saccharin consumption we expect to reduce 500 cancers a year, although the number might be more and might be less. If we want to reduce risk, and by doing so to improve public health, we must often take action on chemicals where the data are uncertain.

This distinction is hard to get across. Yet if we only address the issues of public health about which we are certain, we miss most of the opportunities to reduce risk. We did not demand pure water in the last century, because we had firm epidemiology to tell us that this disease or that disease was definitely caused by a particular microbe in the water; it was done on sound general principles with uncertain data.

An example may be in order. A committee of the Commonwealth of Massachusetts is recommending a policy for considering toxic air pollutants. This committee must include both the assessment step and the management step in its' recommendations. In their present draft, they reject making a priority order soley on the basis of the numerical value of risk, but combine this with the weight of evidence in a multiplicative scoring system. Maybe, given all the constraints and influences on a risk manager, this will be the list he should have, or will wish to have, to aid in his decision making. But an assessor, would in my view be delinquent if he did not also produce an ordered list of risks for comparison, with appropriate statements of uncertainty, based upon the strength of evidence. Unfortunately, in the present draft of the Massachusetts policy the roles of the assessor and of the manager are hopelessly confused.

Criticisms of Risk Assessments

It is important to note that although risk assessment using human epidemiology is generally accepted, risk assessment using other data, such as animal bioassys, is still widely criticized. for example, Richard Peto, in a keynote address at a meeting similar to this one, (Peto 1985) urges caution in using the assessments for any regulatory purpose. He argues that all that can be properly done is to take some index of nastiness of the chemical, multiply it by the exposure, and create a priority order for action. I do not completely accept his criticism, because if the carcinogenic potency in a bioassay is taken as an index of nastiness, the product of the exposure and the index, is just the risk magnitude we all talk about. In creating a priority order Peto also notes that it is distracting and seems absurd to reduce the exposure to a man made chemical much below that found to occur naturally - a point also made by Bruce Ames (1984).

I believe that the crucial issue is the creation of a priority order. Other critics of risk assessment have also accepted that the usual risk assessment procedure is probably adequate for a priority order (Ahmed 1984, Foy 1983). I therefore emphasize those uses of risk assessment that depend primarily upon this order. However, some aspects of the present EPA system for risk assessment and for presentation of risk assessments, are deficient in this they do not create a priority order, and make it hard for others to create one.

In few, or perhaps none, of the EPA assessments is a risk comparison made at the end. Therefore it is not possible to set a priority order without looking at all the CAG reports at the same time. Yet, so far as one can tell from outside, only one assessment is presented to the EPA administrator when he makes a decision, and therefore the risk assessors are withholding information that many people believe is useful or even crucial. The assessments might be more acceptable to Peto if there is a comparison of risk.

Another bad example is the risk assessment for dioxin made by the Center for Disease Control (CDC). Dioxin and aflatoxin B1 are both nasty chemicals. Both are acutely very toxic. Both give cancer in rodents, with a carcinogenic potency that is about equal. If animal data is used to calculate risk, the calculated risks will be similar. When it comes to the strength of evidence, or certainty of information, aflatoxin B1 is worse. It has been shown to cause cancer in people. In my view, a comparison of the risk of aflatoxin ingestion to the risk of dioxin ingestion, can be very instructive; yet CDC declined to make it, thereby reducing the information content of their assessment. CDC <u>did</u> go beyond risk assessment to a statement about risk management; by saying that one part in a billion of dioxin in soil is a cause for concern. This statement was not justified, and in my view cannot be justified without a risk comparison.

When I make such a comparison I find that FDA only regulates aflatoxin B1 in peanut butter when the concentration exceeds 20ppb. Yet CDC are worried about 1 ppb of dioxin in soil. When one do the CDC risk assessors eat?

Of course I am not suggesting that dioxin and aflatoxin should be regulated in the same way; I am merely suggesting that such risk comparisons provide important information which a risk manager must have, and to the extent that the risk manager decides to regulate dioxin more strongly, he should make it clear that it is not because of the risk. One possible reason might be that aflatoxin is not heavily regulated is that it is a natural carcinogen, whereas dioxin is manmade - an argument illustrated by the New Yorker cartoon of Figure 3.

"Non-carcinogens"

The EPA is inconsistent and stresses the strength of evidence over the risk magnitude, when they fail to calculate, and present for comparison, the risk of a chemical for which the animal bioassay is not statistically significant. They declare the chemical to be a "non-carcinogen" which I maintain is a legal but not a scientific declaration. In other cases EPA makes a big issue of calculating a conservative upper limit to the risk. Even if there is no statistical significance, an upper 95th percentile can be calculated. In a number of papers, (Zeise et. al. 1983,1984,1985a, 1985b) we have shown how to use other information about a chemical when an animal bioassay is absent. In particular we have suggested using the acute toxic LD50 to give a crude estimate. This is based on our noticing that there is an approximate correlation between carcinogenic potency β and acute toxicity LD50. Such a correlation is shown in figure 4. I note that Peto (1979) suggested the use of several possible indices of nastiness of a chemical in deciding which chemicals are of concern to be sure that no particularly dangerous chemical has been missed. One of his suggested indices was acute toxicity.

"It's going to be great! All natural ingredients."

Figure 3. An illustration from the New Yorker showing the willingness to accept natural chemicals - even if dangerous.

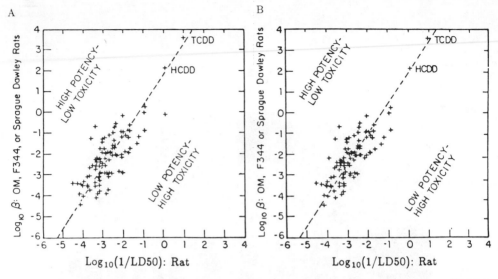

Figure 4. A plot of carcinogenic potency β versus acute toxicity. Figure 4A shows all data; in figure 4B data are censored if there is reason to doubt the LD50 value.

There are three reasons that the consideration of these "noncarcinogens" is important. The first is logical completeness. The second, is that they are important for comparison purposes. Crouch and Wilson (1981) show that the upper limit of carcinogenic potency of common salt is large enough that if this is put into the formula for carcinogenic risk, the calculated risk is 1000 times the risk level at which FDA regulate. In a forthcoming paper, Clayson and Krewski (1986) derive a similar result for distilled water. This suggests to me, that the level of risk EPA and FDA take as "acceptable" and above which they often regulate may be too low. Still a third reason is that this can give use preliminary estimates of risk for planning purposes. This is, in my view, a far more important use of risk assessment than the use to suggest, or justify, regulation which is a prime use of EPA and FDA assessments.

Uncertainty

The whole issue here should be coupled with a discussion of uncertainty (Wilson Crouch and Zeise (1985). The very word risk implies uncertainty -- there is a risk that I will die of cancer. If I get cancer the risk suddenly rises to 50% or more; and when the cancer is diagnosed as fatal, the risk becomes a certainty. The number or magnitude of the risk is an expression of our knowledge: knowledge that can change with time. Likewise, when there is uncertainty about whether, or not a chemical causes an adverse health effect there is a risk that is does.

I illustrate this by considering the risk of a new, untested, chemical. An ardent environmentalist might say it is unity because we do not know that it is not; an insensitive industrialist might say that it is zero, because it hasn't been tested. A risk assessor uses whatever information he has at his disposal to find a number somewhere in between and to state whatever error is appropriate. In the cases of the declared noncarcinogens, the EPA imply that the risk is well defined and zero, whereas it is badly determined and finite.

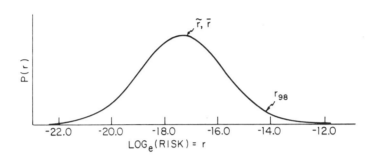

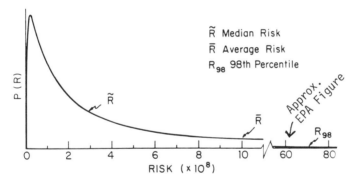

Figure 5. A typical risk distribution showing the moment of the distribution typically calculated by EPA.

In our work, we try to find a number for the risk magnitude, with its' error or uncertainty, for exposure to any chemical of concern. We try to state not merely one number but a risk distribution. The biggest uncertainty we find is that of the comparison of carcinogenic potency in animal and man - which can vary over a factor of 10 in either direction. (Crouch and Wilson 1979, 1985a, 1985b) A typical risk distribution is shown in figure 5. Although both EPA and FDA take the comparison of animal and human potencies to be a fixed number without uncertainty, which is formally incorrect, they take a sufficiently conservative number that their value lies close to our upper 95th percentile. To this extent, therefore, we confirm, or underpin their procedure, but only for those chemicals for which they calculate a risk and not for the chemicals they ignore.

A Priority List

I return to my defense of risk assessment, and of my insistence that risk comparison is needed. Firstly I show by figure 6 that comparing risks is a common activity, approved by the Charles Schulz cartoon, Peanuts. Secondly I show in Table II a priority list for a selected group of chemicals. This is not a priority based upon risk alone, but upon the product of risk and persons exposed in the USA giving an annual cancer incidence from the selected causes.

The first column is a priority list of the sort that I believe Peto would approve. I believe that it is a better priority list when the numbers in the second column are attached. Even though the numbers at the bottom portion of the list are uncertain by at least a factor of 10, the very smallness of the values at the bottom makes this uncertainty relatively unimportant. The first entry is by direct human epidemiology -- at high doses. The second is from a mixture of epidemiology and historical experience. The third entry is by human epidemiology in uranium mines and by comparing exposures of radon gas in homes to those in mines. The fourth is also from epidemiology. The others are calculated from animal bioassays.

We all know about cigarettes -- though many of us go in smoking. But how many of you are aware than radon gas in houses is calculated to cause enough lung cancers to make it number three on the list? If you did not know before, this list has given you some useful information. This then brings me to the last item in this talk; the use of risk assessment for planning purposes in various ways. Radon gas is not the only important indoor air pollutant. In table III I present risks calculated for 45 organic air pollutants measured in 4 Dutch houses. (Tancrede, Zeise, Crouch and Wilson (1985) At the bottom I put the risk from the U.S. average radon gas exposure of 1.5pCi/1. There are several conclusions one might draw.

1) Each of the chemicals pose a risk greater than 10^{-6} per life - a value often used as an acceptability criterion by FDA and EPA. These risks therefore should not be ignored.

2) For some of these chemicals, the upper 98th percentile of the risk might be reduced if better data are available. A good animal bioassay may reduce the uncertainty, and this is underway for limonene.

Figure 6. A PEANUTS cartoon illustrates the general acceptance of the procedure of comparing risks.

Table II
Deaths in U.S. from selected cases (approximate)

	Deaths/yr	Source
Cigarette smoking (including heart attacks)	400,000	Surgeon General
Alcohol (including alcohol -caused accidents)	50,000	Crouch Wilson
Radon gas in houses	20,000	
Asbestos from exposures of 1940-50	10,000	J. Peto
Aflatoxin in corn, nuts, milk	5,000	FDA
Saccharin	500	FDA
Hair dyes	<1/10	FDA
Vinyl Chloride in plastic bottles	<1/10	FDA

Table III
The 98th Percentile <u>Annual</u> Risk For Indoor Air in Four Dutch
Houses (x 1,000,000)

No.	Chemical	House A	House B	House C	House D
1	n-hexane	0.04	0.80	0.09	1.58
2	n-heptane	0.19	0.23	0.45	2.25
3	n-octane	0.17	0.09	0.25	0.37
4	n-nonane	1.66	0.62	1.88	1.23
5	n-decane	5.46	1.60	3.47	1.86
6	n-undecane	12.59	0.68	1.00	0.47
7	n-dodecane	12.43	0.11	0.16	0.11
8	n-tridecane	8.06	0.01	0.06	0.08
9	n-tetradecane	0.91	0.21	0.08	0.15
10	n-pentadecane	0.22	0.14	0.07	0.18
11	n-hexadecane	0.02	0.01	0.00	0.06
12	3-methylpentane	0.01	0.06	0.02	0.18
13	2-methylhexane	0.40	0.67	0.33	6.78
14	3-methylhexane	0.31	0.53	0.27	4.95
15	cyclohexane	0.04	0.53	0.03	1.10
16	methylcyclohexane	0.02	0.02	0.01	0.15
17	dimethylcyclopentane 1	0.03	0.03	0.03	0.20
18	dimethylcyclopentane 2	0.03	0.03	0.03	0.36
19	dimethylcyclopentane 3	0.06	0.06	0.03	0.52
20	limonene	12.79	13.00	12.60	23.65
21	benzene	1.11	1.76	1.84	2.05
22	toluene	8.23	11.60	7.51	51.46
23	xylenes	2.96	2.23	3.21	2.93
24	ethylbenzene	0.22	0.35	0.34	0.41
25	n-propylbenzene	0.10	0.07	0.29	0.13
26	isopropylbenzene	0.16	0.14	0.24	0.24
27	o-methylethylbenzene	2.04	0.61	3.07	2.27
28	m-methylethylbenzene	2.88	1.29	4.25	2.45
29	p-methylethylbenzene	0.98	0.31	0.88	0.71
30	1,2,3-trimethylbenzene	3.29	1.88	7.29	3.07
31	1,2,4-trimethylbenzene	4.18	1.84	4.44	2.42
32	1,3,5-trimethylbenzene	1.24	0.60	1.38	0.64
33	n-butylbenzene	1.19	0.31	1.24	0.59
34	p-methylisopylbenzene	3.47	18.25	2.93	1.90
35	napthalene	1.23	0.53	0.56	0.40
36	1-methylnapthalene	0.14	0.07	0.07	0.07
37	tetrachloromethane	8.53	196.00	8.53	15.95
38	trichloroethene	1.83	1.75	1.04	18.09
39	tetrachloroethene	11.92	11.37	7.65	126.50
40	chlorobenzene	0.23	0.23	0.23	0.23
41	m-dichlorobenzene	1.41	1.41	1.41	1.41
42	p-dichlorobenzene	-----	-----	-----	-----
43	1,2,3-trichlorobenzene	7.28	7.28	7.28	7.28
44	1,2,4-trichlorobenzene	2.28	2.28	2.28	2.28
45	1,3,5-trichlorobenzene	7.28	7.28	7.28	7.28

RADON GAS
1.5 pc/l   100   100   100   100

Asbestos
Formaldehyde

<u>NOTE THAT</u> IN <u>ALL</u> CASES R > 10^{-6}/LIFETIME

3) These risks are inversely proportional to the air ventilation rate. Since 1973, the need to conserve fuel has led to a reduction of the ventilation rate of US houses by 30%. Even the increase of risk associated with this conservation measure exceeds the reduction of risk from EPA actions to date, suggesting that future energy conservation measures by coupled with active measures to reduce sources of pollution, or public health will be reduced.

4) For those chemicals which appear to pose the highest risks, it seems appropriate to make more detailed exposure measurements.

5) An individual may choose to change his lifestyle, or avoid certain products, to avoid exposure to those chemicals with the highest risks.

6) A builder or architect may use such a list in his selection of building materials for building new, or repairing old, houses.

I remind the risk managers, who are often ourselves as members of the general public, that by evaluating a risk, we can often see how to take steps to reduce it, and although the risk of radon gas exposure is a natural and not a man made risk, it can be avoided just as we can avoid being trapped by earthquakes and floods.

Such reductions of risk is what risk analysis, and it's subset, risk assessment, is all about.

REFERENCES

Ahmed A.K. (1984) Testimony to U.S. congress on the "Risk Bill." also private communication.
Ames, Bruce (1984), "Dietary Carcinogens and Anti-Carcinogens," Science, 221:1256 (see also subsequent correspondence, Science, 224:668 and 757 (1984).
Clayson, D.B. and D. Krewski (1985) Draft: the Concept of negativity in experimental carcinogenesis, Health Production Branch, Health and Welfare Canada, Ottawa, Ontario.
Crouch, E.A.C. and Richard Wilson (1979), "Interspecies Comparisons of Carcinogenic Potency," Jrnl. Tox. Environ. Hlth. 5:1095.
Crouch E.A.C. and Richard Wilson, (1981), "The regulation of carcinogens," Risk Analysis, 1, 47.
Crouch, E.A.C. and Richard Wilson, (1985a), "Problems in Interspecies Comparison," in: "Mechanism of DNA Damage and Repair," Conference at National Bureau of Standards, June.
Crouch, E.A.C. and Richard Wilson, (1985b), "Problems in Interspecies Comparison," Toxicology Forum, July, 1985.
Foy, D., (1983), Comments at Risk Management Seminar, Harvard University.
Peto, R., (1979), Detection of Risk of Cancer to Man, Prox. Rep. Soc. Land. (Bio.), 205, 111-120. Peto, Richard, (1985), "Epidemiological Reservation about Risk Assessment," in: Assessment of Risk from Low Level Exposure to Radiation and Chemicals, Ed. Woodhead et al. Plemum, NY and London.
Squires, (1981), Ranking of Animal Carcinogens, a proposed regulatory approach, Science, 214, 877-880.
Tancrede M., L. Zeise, Richard Wilson, and E.A.C. Crouch, (1986), "Risks posed by indoor air pollution by Organic compounds," Preprint to be published.
Wilson, Richard, E.A.C. Crouch and L. Zeise, (1985), "Uncertainty in Risk Assessment," Banbury Report, 19, 133.

Zeise, L., E.A.C. Crouch and Richard Wilson, (1983), "The risks of Drinking Water," Water Resources Research, 19, 1359.

Zeise, L., E.A.C. Crouch and Richard Wilson, (1984), "The use of acute toxicity to estimate carcinogenic risk," Risk Analysis, 4, 187.

Zeise, L., E.A.C. Crouch and Richard Wilson, (1985a), "A possible relation between toxicity and carcinogenicity?" J. Am. Coll. Tox., in press.

Zeise, L., E.A.C. Crouch and Richard Wilson, (1985b), "Reply to comments: On the relationship to toxicity and carcinogenicity," Risk Analysis, in press.

THE CLEANUP OF CHEMICAL WASTE SITES -

A RATIONAL APPROACH

Charles A. Staples and Richard A. Kimerle

Monsanto Co., St. Louis, Missouri

ABSTRACT

A conceptual hazard assessment design is presented here for addressing waste site cleanup. Three main steps to be carried out in an evaluation of any potential waste site include, identification of potential chemical exposure, assessment of that exposure in relation to established `safe' concentrations, and control measures to remediate the exposure. Hazard assessment techniques are used to establish the appropriate `how clean is clean enough' endpoints based on calculated margins of safety (MS), where MS = toxicologically safe concentration/exposure concentration. A successful remedial action endpoint is achieved when the targeted exposure reduction action results in a margin of safety that is greater than 1.0 (MS > 1.0) including the uncertainty of the estimate. This assessment program is carried out in a cost effective step by step tiered approach to guide selection of a remediation endpoint.

INTRODUCTION

There are estimated to be well over 20,000 solid and contained liquid waste sites (both legal and illegal) in the U.S. (1-3). Many of the sites have been abandoned and are perceived as or are known to be sources of chemical contamination. Costs for cleanup of these sites has been estimated at up to $10-20 billion. The 1984 RCRA amendments (4) are forcing review of current waste disposal practices and are geared towards prevention and reduction of future problems from hazardous waste facilities. The 1980 `Superfund' Law is aimed at cleaning up those past sites which are or may threaten human health and the environment. Technically sound, cost effective approaches are needed to determine `how clean is clean' for remedial or corrective action under both programs. A hazard assessment based approach is presented here to utilize rational decision making in addressing the cleanup of any contaminated site. The hazard assessment approach suggested here addressed the critical issue of how extensive the remedial practices must be to protect the ecosystem and humans from exposure to toxic chemicals (5).

How Clean Is Clean?

A key factor in any remedial action program must be the establishment of a justifiable endpoint which is established by answering `how clean is clean?'. This endpoint is a reduction in the concentration of the chemical(s) to a point where no adverse impact is expected to man or the environment now or in the future. The factors that affect the establishment of the target performance standard include subsurface or surface hydrology, chemical fate and transport properties and toxicological characteristics.

The answer to, `how clean is clean?' is indeed complex. All aspects of a problem resolution scheme must take part (Figure 1). The potential problem must be identified in terms of what compound(s) or groups of compounds are present. The levels of these compounds must be quantified. This is to be followed by a comprehensive assessment. The assessment addresses both chemical exposure and chemical effects in a rational manner. Both short and long term exposures and effects are addressed. This assessment process allows the thorough understanding of the implications of the exposure. The general formula for addressing both exposure and effects together also considers uncertainty of exposure calculations (equation 1).

$$\text{Margin of Safety (MS)} = \frac{\text{Safe Concentration}}{(\text{Exposure Conc.})(\text{Uncertainty})} \tag{1}$$

We will assume that a safe concentration can be established for a particular exposure scenario. A margin of safety, then, is a function of the measured exposure concentration and the uncertainty or variability that exists in the exposure determination. The exposure concentration is unacceptably high when the MS is less than 1.0 (6). An exposure concentration is desired that causes the MS to exceed 1.0. Assessment, then is the coupling of chemical exposure concentrations (whether measured or predicted) with the toxicologically safe concentrations that is appropriate for the exposure scenario (figure 2). This type of assessment guides the choice and development of control actions and provides an iterative review of post-remedial action results. The site is `clean' when these processes are complete and margin of safeties are scientifically judged to be adequate.

Decision-making Steps for Cleanup at Waste Sites

Cleanup of any waste site may be carried out in a stepwise fashion as described in Figure 3 and Table 1. The steps required include both decision points and more complex activity steps. Moving through the described decision-making process represented in the simple flowchart results in a rational stepwise approach to correctly ascertaining the necessary extent of remediation of an identified waste site problem.

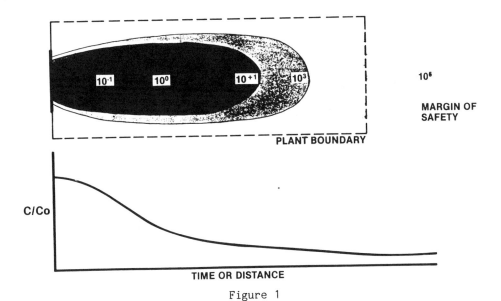

Figure 1

Predicted Concentrations and Margins of Safety

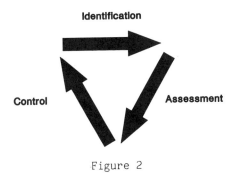

Figure 2

The Cycle of Problem Solving

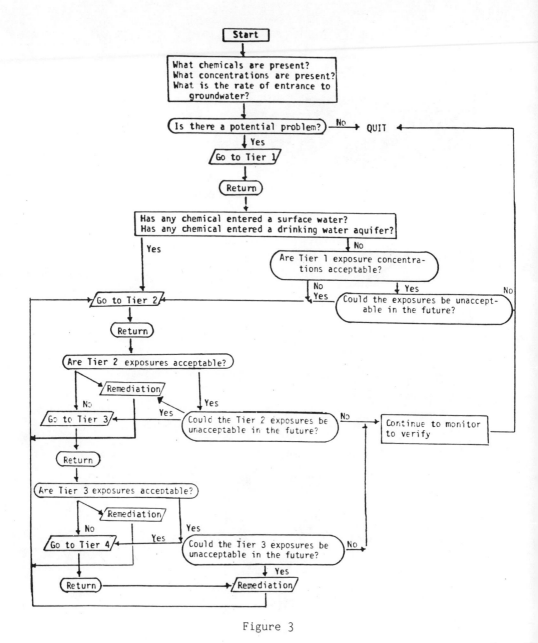

Figure 3

Decision Pathway for Evaluation of Potential Waste Site Problems

Table 1

Summary of Risk Results and Research Recommendations from a Hypothetical
Million BPD Oil Shale Fuel Cycle

Tier	Data Requirements	Cost	Uncertainty of Exposure Calc.	Required Exposure: Conc.=$\frac{Safe\ Conc.}{(MS)(Uncertainty)}$
I	• Monitoring onsite • General site geology & characteristics • ADI's and/or Screening Toxicology Tests • Simple one dimensional modeling	$	LARGE $(10^0\text{-}10^5)$	10^{-5}
II	• Monitoring (con't) • Leachate rate or source loading rate • Hydrologic characteristics • 2 dimensional solute transport in groundwater or surface waters • ADI's	$$	MEDIUM $(10^0\text{-}10^3)$	10^{-3}
III	• Offsite (if needed) hydrologic data • Offsite monitoring (if needed) • 2-3 dimensional solute transport modeling • Sorption, biodegradation, hydrolysis rates • Toxicity data for complex mixtures • ADI's	$$$	SMALL $(10^0\text{-}10^1)$	10^{-1}
IV	• Complete field chemical analyses (spatial & temporal) • ADI's for all constituents	$$ to $$$$	ONE (10^0)	10^{-0}

* $MS = \dfrac{Safe}{Exposure}$,MS ≥ 1.0 is required so rearranging allows calculation of maximum allowable exposure:

Exposure = Safe/(MS)(Uncertainty)

Four main assumptions are considered here. First, the existence of
contamination substantial enough to be of potential concern has been
established. Second, the source is considered sufficiently large such
that the problem will not rapidly correct itself. Third, an acceptable
safe concentration has been or can be established for the chemicals of
concern. Fourth, when safe concentration is used a margin of safety (MS)
in excess of 1.0 is an appropriate `clean' target. The concept of a safe
level is used by EPA and others in an attempt to establish safe chemical
concentrations for the protection of human life and the environment (7).
The use of the term safe concentration in this paper directly assumes that
an acceptable or safe concentration can be correctly established. The
exact technical procedures for establishment of safe or acceptable levels
of exposure are not an issue here.

Beginning with Figure 3, the first steps for the site evaluation include ascertaining the scope of the problem. The main emphases are 'what chemicals are found where and in what concentrations?' This is followed by determination of approximate rates of continued chemical input from the source. Rapid or catastrophic release of chemicals to groundwater would call for a different response than a slow leaching of a source. The leaching could, for example, be defined by the Toxicity Characteristic Leaching Procedure (TCLP) being developed by EPA. These data provide definition of the contaminants at the waste site. Then, the following question is asked: Does this preliminary data suggest any potential problems? If not, one ends the investigation. If potential problems are indicated, a Tier 1 assessment (Table 1) is carried out to estimate the existing exposure concentrations.

Tier 1 Assessment

Tier 1 assessments include continued monitoring of chemicals at the site as well as conducting a hydrogeologic evaluation of the site. Identified compounds would have a 'safe' concentration determined. The safe concentration must be selected with regard to the existing and future exposure scenarios.

Determining the correct exposure scenario is critical. Chronic toxicity requires chronic exposure. Carcinogenicity requires lifetime (70 years) exposures. Long term exposures must be considered possible if the source is very large and is essentially considered infinite. However, if a contaminated aquifer is not a drinking water aquifer (it may be saline, for example), application of a carcinogenic endpoint may be inappropriate. Discharge of the chemical into a surface water body from such a saline aquifer would then alter the useful endpoint to perhaps a site specific water quality criteria. It is therefore possible to require different endpoints for the different aspects of the exposure scenario. Initial analytical data plus site hydrogeologic characteristics can then be coupled with simple one dimensional modeling to yield short and long term chemical exposure estimates. Necessary exposures (that result in MS > 1.0) can then be calculated based on the safe concentration, required margin of safety and the related uncertainty (eq. 1). At this point, return to the flow chart (Figure 3).

More specific data concerning leaching rates, transport times (which take into account appropriate chemical for the processes) and exposure estimations with lower uncertainty would be required if the chemical(s) have entered either a drinking water aquifer or surface water body from subsurface flow. No further testing would be required if drinking water supplied were not in the chemical flow path and Tier 1 exposures were acceptable. If the exposures are unacceptable than Tier 2 assessment is required.

Tier 2 Assessment

Tier 2 assessments focus on improvement of understanding of existing and future chemical exposure, fate and transport. Existing chemical exposure is further evaluated by additional chemical measurements made both spatially and temporally. These measurements may require more monitoring wells and an expanded site based on the results of Tier 1 assessments. Additionally, a leachate rate (from TCLP) should be generated if deemed necessary and not already accomplished. Additional hydrogeologic parameters required for exposure analysis that may not be known or are needed for 1 dimensional solute transport modeling, should be generated. Properly calibrated 2 dimensional models can generate exposure concentrations with less uncertainty than 1 dimensional models. A lesser gap between exposure concentrations and uncertainty factors is allowed with the Tier 2 efforts, while still achieving a MS > 1.0.

Upon return to Figure 3, judgment of Tier 2 exposure predictions are made. Acceptable MS's (MS > 1.0), coupled with continued monitoring for verification purposes allow the site investigation to move to completion. Unacceptable MS's require moving to Tier 3 or carrying out remediation.

Tier 3 Assessment

Tier 3 assessments may require offsite (i.e. expanded beyond original natural site boundaries) hydrogeologic data to be determined. Many solute transport models carry assumptions of homogeneity and isotropy. These assumptions are often valid for short distances or areas but usually become unsupportable with greater distances from a source. Variability over a site of transmissivities, conductivities and dispersivities can lead to unacceptable uncertainty factors. Therefore, improvement of future chemical exposures may require more extensive and costly data. Existing analytical data may not fully describe chemical transported beyond initial discovery (Tier 1 and 2) efforts. This may be especially important if deeper aquifers are potentially impacted.

These more extensive data collection efforts are coupled with estimated or measured chemical equilibrium and decay processes for key individual compounds. These loss (sink) mechanisms become increasingly important as greater exposure prediction accuracy is required. In place of toxicological data that may not be available, `safe' toxicologic endpoints may have to be established for the complex mixtures of compounds that may exist (8-10). These tests may include acute tests (plant root elongation, algal assays, Ceriodaphnia mortality) or chronic tests (earthworm growth or Ceriodaphnia reproduction that are currently being evaluated by EPA). New exposure concentrations can be determined for each set of new data, modeling predictions and their uncertainty factors. More comprehensive data sets obtained under Tier 3 guidelines (chemical and hydrogeologic data) should reduce uncertainty related to predicted exposure concentrations from that of Tiers 1 and 2. The allowed exposure concentration to achieve MS > 1.0 would be greater by an equivalent margin.

Tier 4 Assessment

Complete field chemical analyses would be required (spatially and temporally) throughout the entire site if Tier 3 exposure values are considered inadequate to guide remedial actions. Many more monitoring points (than with Tier 1 to 3) would be needed to analytically describe a chemical waste site fully 3 dimensionally. Costs could become prohibitive relative to possible remedial practices.

Decision points for remedial action can occur at any of the return points in Figure 3 from Table 1. A remediation is selected that will obtain a particular tier's required exposure concentration yielding MS > 1.0. If the remediation is judged to be excessive in either cost or scope then the next tier assessment is conducted. Determination of the necessity, extent and specifics of remediation at any site must be carried out using these assessment procedures. Data requirements may include chemical specific parameters such as soil partitioning, degradation rates, aqueous solubility and aquifer characteristics such as permeabilities, gradients, densities, direction of flows and storage. Needed toxicological data, if absent, may include aquatic acute and chronic tests and mammalian chronic studies. Obtaining these data may become expensive should the scale of the site be large. However, control of chemical

exposure without sufficient assessment could result in gross over-
expenditures far in excess of assessment costs.

Identifying appropriate remedial actions to address the various
affected regions is the next step to carry out. Possible remedial actions
of groundwater contamination are many in number. Various categories range
from simple water withdrawal to walls or trenches to divert groundwater
flow to complete removal of contaminated aquifer material. The specific
actions taken must reflect both the desired goal of reducing chemical
exposure as well as being cost effective. Following choice of remedial
actions, mathematical modeling should again be used to estimate the new or
altered chemical concentrations. Plotting the new exposure isopleths gives
guidance as to the ultimate success of the remediation.

Hypothetical Use of the Waste Site Decision Tree

Examination of a hypothetical case study illustrates the principles
behind the approach. The demonstration involves a leachate moving from a
waste site through soil to groundwater, then to a stream. The chemical of
concern is tetrachloroethylene, a slightly soluble solvent (Table 2).
Chemical concentrations were measured in surface soils, a groundwater and
surface waters. Concentration isopleths were drawn. Long term
tetrachloroethylene fate predictions through mathematical modeling were
used to evaluate the steps that follow.

Choice of toxicological endpoints requires examination of the
exposure scenario. The aquifer is not considered to be a potential
drinking water source (salinity > 4%) nor used to feed stock animals. The
groundwater discharges into a stream. Fish may be consumed from the
stream. The safe concentration utilized here will be the aquatic life
criteria (1500 ug/L).

Calculated uncertainty can then be overlain on the exposure
concentration isopleths (Figure 2). Now the identified chemical exposures
can be adequately understood through this assessment. Clearly, all of the
chemical levels present are not unsafe (based on exposures). The extent
to which the site must be remediated can now be clearly identified.
Exposures considered unacceptable would trigger either further work (e.g.
advanced tiers) to better establish chemical concentrations or remedial
action.

Remedial activities are called for by the decision tree analysis when
exposure concentrations are deemed unacceptable. Possible remedial
actions include: (1) doing nothing, (2) using a combination of best
engineering practices or (3) digging it up. Chemical fate modeling is
used to evaluate the results of the various remedial actions. The overall
effect of doing nothing may cause exposures to get worse (i.e. MS's
smaller) as the concentrations increase through time. The combination of
engineering practices reduces chemical levels. Evacuation and removal from
the site of all contaminated material does improve the margin of
safeties. However, consideration of another factor, cost, reveals the
drawbacks of the `dig-it-up' approach to cleanup. Excavation of even a
small (1 acre) site 30-40 feet deep (to bottom aquifer) generates over
80,000 tons of aquifer material. A 200 acre site with a contaminated
aquifer 100 feet deep would generate 40,000,000 tons of aquifer
material. Even a combination of source excavation and removal coupled
with complete aquifer withdrawal and treatment would be unduly costly for
such a large site. Clearly, rational remedial actions or control measures
must be dictated by all facets of the identification and assessment
processes.

SUMMARY

Cleanup of contaminated waste sites is possible in a manner that is
scientifically adequate, technologically feasible and cost effective.
Remedial activities must be guided by a complete comprehension of the
identified problems through assessment. Failure to do so can be costly.
Efficient use of existing resources can yield the best results not only
for a particular site but also for effectively addressing the nation's
overall toxic wastes problems.

The general approach to the addressing of waste site cleanup is not
new. The principles elucidated here have been used to address work place
chemical exposure limits, set permitted effluent discharge limits and
guide industrial waste treatment plant designs. The approach outlined
here should not be considered as an `out' or as a means to avoid
acceptance of responsibility by affected parties. Rather, use of the
methods presented here can successfully guide the cleanup of contaminated
waste sites in the most rational and feasible manner.

REFERENCES

Adrian, G.W., 1981, Development of a National Groundwater Strategy. In:
    Proceedings AWWA Seminar entitled, `Organic Chemical Contaminants in
    Groundwater: Transport and Removal'. AWWA (American Water Works
    Association) Denver, CO.
Cairns, J., Jr., K.L. Dickson and A.W. Maki, 1978. Estimating the Hazard
    of Chemical Substances to Aquatic Life. ASTM STP 657. American
    Society for Testing and Materials, Philadelphia, PA.
Callahan, C.A. 1984, Earthworms as Ecotoxicological Assessment Tools, U.S.
    environmental Protection Agency Report No. EPA-600/D-84-272.
Frost, E.G., 1982. Risk Assessment Under the Revised National Contingency
    Plan to Superfund. In: Risk Assessment of Hazardous Waste Sites,
    Edited by F.A. Long and G.E. Schweitzer, ACS No. 204, American
    Chemical Society, Washington,D.C.
Gilford, J.H. 1985, Environmental Effects Assessment of New Chemicals
    under the Toxic Substances Control Act. Presented at 1985 Summer
    National Meeting, American Institute of Chemical Engineers, Seattle,
    WA.
Houk, V.N., 1982, Determining the Impact on Human Health Attributable to
    Hazardous Waste Sites. In: Risk Assessment of Hazardous Waste Sites,
    Edited by F.A. Long and G.E. Schweitzer, ACS No. 204, American
    Chemical Society, Washington, D.C.
PL-98616, 1984, Hazardous and Solid Wastes Amendments of 1984.
Stephan, C.E., D.A. Mount, D.J. Hausen, J.H. Gentile, G.A. Chapman and
    W.A. Brungs, 1983. Draft U.S. Environmental Protection Agency
    Document.
Thomas, J.M., 1984, Characterization of Chemical Waste and its Extent
    Using Bioassays. Report to U.S. Environmental Protection Agency.
    Contract D.E.-AC06-76RLO 1830, Pacific Northwest Laboratory, Richland,
    WA
Thomas, J.M. and J.F. Cline, 1985. Modification of the Neubauer Technique
    to Assess Toxicity of Hazardous Chemicals in Soils. Environmental
    Toxicology and Chemistry, 4:201:207.

IDENTIFICATION OF KEY RISKS UNDER DIFFERENT MEASURES

FOR A FUTURE OIL SHALE INDUSTRY

Lawrence B. Gratt

IWG Corp.

Risk management can be enhanced for a future oil shale industry by identification of the key health and environmental risks. Different risk measures and associated uncertainties can be used to establish research requirements. The risk measures analyzed were cases (occurrences of accidents or disease), premature fatalities, and life-loss expectancy. The analysis for the occupational risks in the oil shale fuel cycle resulted in silicosis from the dust environment as the worker disease of primary concern, following by other forms of pneumoconiosis, chronic bronchitis, chronic airway obstruction, internal cancer, and skin cancers, respectively. Design of mine environments at 1 mg/m^3 dust as opposed to current nuisance dust level of 5 mg/m^3 results in a balancing of the accident, cancer, and dust-induced disease risks. Comparison of safety, dust-induced disease and cancer for the workforce show safety of prime concern for cases while dust-induced diseases dominant for fatalities and life-loss expectancy. Cancer has a low priority except for the high uncertainty range estimates for life-loss expectancy. The public sector cancer risk estimates are very small although other public and environmental risks issues require further analysis.

KEYWORDS: Oil Shale, Occupational Disease Risk, Occupational Safety Risk, Risk Measurement Comparison

INTRODUCTION

The results of the 1984 oil shale risk analysis for the fuel cycle (extraction through delivery of the products) representing a steady-state, one million barrels-per-day (BPD) oil shale industry in the United States in the year 2010 are summarized using graphics to show different risk measures. The 1984 analysis (1) complements and updates the results of both the 1981 (2) and 1982 (3) oil shale risk analyses, concentrating on the recommendations of the National Academy of Sciences' review (4). The methodology to establish and prioritize key research is a useful process to aid in risk management.

OIL SHALE AND SHALE OIL

A future oil shale processing industry will not be developed until the proper economic conditions prevail. The industry will be a massive solids handling industry generating large amounts of hazardous materials. Oil shale is a sedimentary rock that produces a petroleum-like liquid through destructive distillation (pyrolysis). Oil shale deposits in

the United States represent an immense fossil fuel resource. The world's
premier oil shale deposit is found in the Green River geologic formation
in Colorado, Utah, and Wyoming, representing proven reserves of over one-
trillion barrels. Shale oil is produced from the oil shale mined from
these deposits by a process called retorting. This process involves
crushing oil shale into small pieces and heating for extended periods.
There are many different shale retorting technologies and each attempts to
produce oil and other marketable products in an efficient and economical
manner. The retorting process scheduled to be the first modern
commercial-sized production at Union Oil's Parachute Creek site uses
oxygen free retort gases heated to 540° C recycled through the shale to
supply the needed heat.

OIL SHALE RISKS AND UNCERTAINTIES

Methodology

The purpose of the oil shale risk analysis was to identify those
aspects of the oil shale industry which could impact human health and the
environment, and which need further investigation, analysis, or
research. The risk results were estimated for annual premature deaths
from occupational accidents, occupational disease, and public disease.
Other measures of the estimated risk include the number of cases, the
life-loss expectancy, and the life-loss expectancy per man. A methodology
was developed for this analysis which allows tracking of component
uncertainties into the uncertainty of the risk estimate, including the
objective and subjective contributions. The analysis used available
information about surrogate industries. The information itself, as well
as the process of extrapolation from surrogate industries, contains a
number of assumptions and uncertainties. The effect of these assumptions
and uncertainties was estimated by assigning an uncertainty range of the
risk estimate. This uncertainty range was based on both objective and
subjective considerations. In essence, a narrow uncertainty range denotes
more confidence about the health risk estimate and wide uncertainty range
denotes less confidence. Apart from this subjective indication of
confidence, the range does not have any precise statistical meaning. Thus,
relatively high risk estimate with a wide range indicates a relatively
significant risk, which requires further analysis or research to reduce
the uncertainty in the estimate. While these types of estimates are
useful in identifying needed information and research, they are
inappropriate for other uses, especially regulatory purposes.

The research recommendations for reducing the uncertainties of the
risk estimates are presented in Table 1. Research needs based on lack of
information to estimate a risk are summarized elsewhere (1).

Occupational Risks

The risk analysis considered two dust exposure scenarios for the
occupational workforce: Scenario A representing exposures about the
nuisance dust limit of 5 mg/m^3 dust and Scenario B representing exposures
about the free-silica limit of 100 ug/m^3 for an assumed 10% silica content
of dust (corresponding to 1 mg/m^3 dust).

A graphical depiction of the analysis results are shown in Figures 1
through 3. Figure 1 presents the results for the occupational accidents
and disease discussed above. The area of the circles is proportional to
the magnitude of the risk estimate. The solid circle represents the "best
estimate" of the risk. The dash-lined circle represents the lower
uncertainty and the dash-dot-dash lined circle the upper uncertainty. The
intent of these figures is to depict how the uncertainties change for

72

component risk areas. The corresponding risk areas (accidents, cancers, and dust-induced diseases) are denoted by the designated shading for the upper uncertainty and nominal estimates only. Both Table 1 and Figure 1 show that accidents dominate the aggregated total cases of disease and injury (although it is not informative to compare a minor industrial accident to a disabling lung disease). The uncertainty analysis for occupational disease risk shows that dust-induced disease (for both exposure scenarios) has the largest potential for reducing the uncertainty range through research. The dust-induced diseases analyzed were pneumoconiosis, silicosis, chronic bronchitis, and chronic airway obstruction (5).

Figure 2 summarizes the annual fatalities and again shows that dust-induced disease has the largest potential for uncertainty range reductions derived from research. For Scenario A, dust-disease fatalities are the dominant risk, representing 86% of the total premature fatalities and 89% for the upper uncertainty estimate. For Scenario B, the corresponding values are 47% and 59%, respectively, indicating a lesser importance of the dust at the lower scenario level and increased potential for research uncertainty reduction through cancer research.

Another risk measure shown in Figure 3, the annual life-loss expectancy in total years, indicates that the accidents dominate the total occupational risk estimate at 61%, but falls to 30% in the upper uncertainty estimate, again indicating the high potential for uncertainty reduction in the Scenario A dust-induced disease risks. For Scenario B, the accidents dominate all risks and offer the most potential for risk uncertainty reduction, followed by cancers and dust-induced disease.

Table 1. Summary of risk results and research recommendations from a hypothetical million BPD oil shale fuel cycle

Health or Environmental Effects	Exposure	Risk Per Year (Uncertainty Range) Cases	Deaths	Research Recommendations
WORKERS (Population at Risk: 41,000 persons)				
Injury	Accident with days lost	2400 (1700-3700)	13	Underground mining and crushing safety improvements; Improved workforce estimates; New Process (retorting) safety; Use of large equipment safety; Life-long expectancies for disabling injuries.
Injury	Accident with days lost	1500 (1200-2200)	NA	
Cancers	Hydrocarbons, Radiation, As	26 (0-300)	4 (0-49)	Occupational hydrocarbon exposure characterization Latency of carcinogenic effects; Comparative toxicology; Industrial hygiene characterization; Improved refinery worker cancer studies.
Silicosis	Dust*	232 (0-1070)	76 (0-387)	Dust exposure to silica; Improved silica exposure control; Characterization of exposure; Combined effects with diesel exhausts.
Pneumoconiosis	Dust*	100 (33-310)	17 (9-98)	Fundamental research on pneumoconiosis regarding causations; Relative fibrogenicity; Mine dust control; Characterization of exposure; Industrial hygiene.
Chronic Bronchitis	Dust*	41 (13-130)	15 (4-51)	Mine dust control; Characterization of dust exposure; Comparative toxicology; Industrial hygiene characterization.
Airway Obstruction	Dust*	10 (3-36)	5 (1-17)	Mine dust control; Characterization of dust; Comparative toxicology; Industrial hygiene characterization
High Frequency Hearing Loss	Noise	3 (0-8)	NA	Occupational noise level measurements

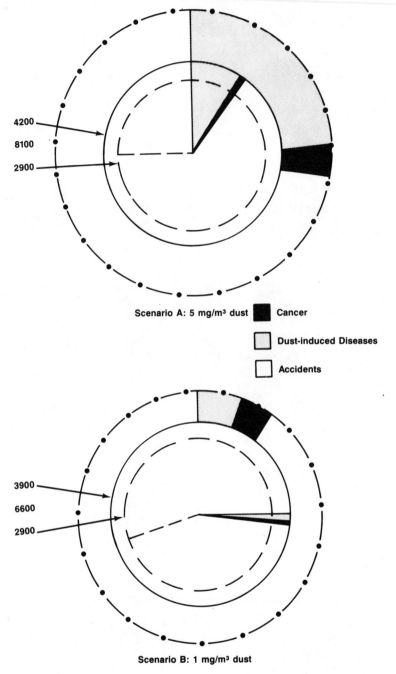

Scenario A: 5 mg/m³ dust

4200
8100
2900

■ Cancer

▨ Dust-induced Diseases

□ Accidents

3900
6600
2900

Scenario B: 1 mg/m³ dust

Figure 1.   Annual occupational cases of injury and disease for a one
million barrels-per-day oil shale industry

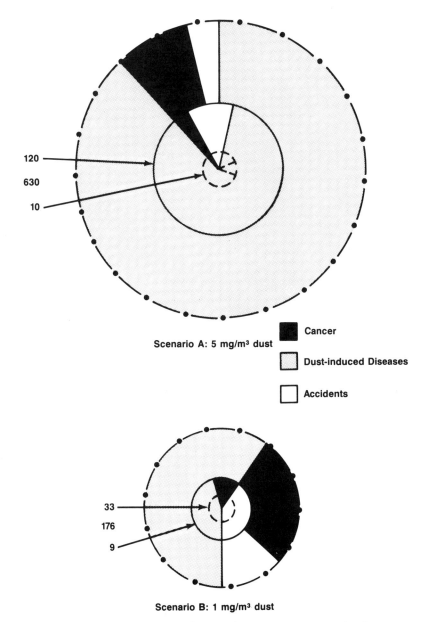

Scenario A: 5 mg/m³ dust

120
630
10

Cancer

Dust-induced Diseases

Accidents

33
176
9

Scenario B: 1 mg/m³ dust

Figure 2.   Annual occupational fatalities for a one million barrels-
per-day oil shale industry

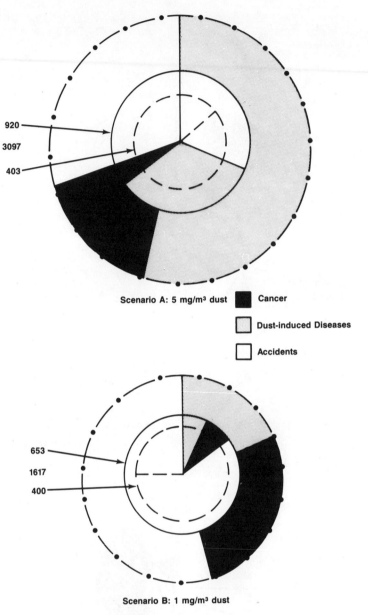

Scenario A: 5 mg/m³ dust

■ Cancer

▦ Dust-induced Diseases

□ Accidents

Scenario B: 1 mg/m³ dust

Figure 3. Annual occupational life-loss expectancy for a one million barrels-per-day oil shale industry

Life-loss expectancy per man estimates were used to establish high risk occupational groups in the oil shale fuel cycle workforce. Silicosis in mining and crushing is the key occupational concern followed by lung cancer and brain cancer from hydrocarbon exposure for this risk measure.

The risk results indicate that from safety considerations the workers in the extraction phase of the oil shale industry, mining and crushing, are at a higher risk than those in the other portions of the fuel cycle (6). When large relative uncertainties are considered, safety in the transportation and retorting/upgrade populations become of concern.

The retorting/upgrading upper uncertainty estimates are large due to the lack of relevant historical safety statistics for large-scale retorting. The oil shale industry will be a massive solids handling industry. There is no applicable surrogate for the large vessel heating of solids that occurs during retorting. Applicable data should be compiled during the commercial demonstration phase to allow these uncertainties to be reduced. The overall safety results indicate that research to improve underground mining safety is desirable. The safety aspects of the use of large equipment in the underground oil shale mines will be important to the developing oil shale industry. It is also important for oil shale mine accidents to be monitored as the industry grows because the use of coal mine data cannot accurately predict the potential oil shale accident rates.

One research area to fill a data need for occupational health and safety is the Life-Loss-Expectancy (LLE) due to non-fatal accidents. This would allow a better comparison of disease-induced LLE with the LLE from accidents. An epidemiologic study of mortality of persons with various disabilities could provide useful data.

Risks of non-neoplastic lung diseases for future U.S. oil shale worker dust exposures were estimated between 56 and 390 cases annually. In the absence of an active industry, health effects rates from surrogate industries were utilized. The risk of chronic bronchitis, chronic airway obstruction, and pneumoconiosis was quantified from British coal worker data (5). The risk of occupational silicosis in oil shale miners was estimated using worker studies from Peruvian metal mines, Vermont granite sheds, West Virginia potteries, and Utah non-ferrous metal mines. Ten percent free silica composition of the dust in the respirable range from oil shale mining and crushing was assumed (with a $\pm 5\%$ uncertainty range). Silicosis was the dominant pulmonary health effect, but at the Scenario A dust level, pneumoconiosis, chronic bronchitis, and chronic airway obstruction are also important risks. Designing oil shale facilities to meet the nuisance dust threshold limit value may not provide adequate protection to the future workers involved in oil shale extraction and processing.

An estimate of 26 cases of occupational cancer risks due to hydrocarbon exposure during retorting, upgrading, and refining was derived using epidemiological studies in a surrogate industry. The oil refining industry was selected as a surrogate, with an attempt to adjust the refining cancer incidence using oil shale toxicologic and exposure data. Risk estimates were derived for those cancers which may be excessive in refinery workers, namely lung, stomach, kidney, brain, and skin cancer (7,8). The magnitude of health risks for these diseases was very small, with the estimated 15,000 exposed workers suffering 4 excess internal cancers per year and 21 excess skin cancers per year. The cancer risks from the radiation dose from inhalation of radon and thoron daughters in addition to inhalation of arsenic dust by the miners and crushers was also calculated. The total occupational cancer disease is expected to produce less than 5 deaths per year.

Other occupational diseases were considered, including: hearing loss (with an excess prevalence of 8.2% for mines); dermatitis (prevalence based on hygiene practices); vibration disease (prevalence based on preventive practices); and adverse reproductive outcomes (an important future consideration for the industry).

In spite of considerable uncertainty, hydrocarbon-induced cancers are overshadowed by dust-related respiratory disease occupational health risks in the oil shale industry (6).

Public Risks

In the public sector, the fine particulate surrogate health-damage function replaced the sulfur surrogate function used in previous analyses (9). The resulting risks in the public sector were lower than previous estimates. To reduce the fine particulate health damage function uncertainty, an improved exposure index in the epidemiological study of health effects of air pollution is needed. This would couple the spatial and temporal activities of people to establish the person-exposure distributions for indoor vs. outdoors and occupational vs. public. Apportionment of the aerosol components to the health effects should also provide a means for reducing the uncertainty. Also, time series data for other parts of the United States would be beneficial for reduction of the standard errors of the damage function.

The long range transport of oil shale pollution across the entire U.S. resulted in a risk estimate of about half of the regional risk. The uncertainty of this estimate was much greater than the regional uncertainty. The source of the additional uncertainty is the exposure modeling, with the wet and dry deposition uncertainty terms dominating other modeling term uncertainties.

The public cancer risk estimates are very small, which limits the importance of any associated research recommendations. Nonetheless, the major component uncertainty is in the health dose-response functions which could be reduced by re-assessment with better epidemiologic studies of carcinogenic risk. Better extrapolation methods from high to low doses may also reduce uncertainty.

Other public health issues continue to be sources of uncertainty. The channelling of air pollution in valleys and canyons could raise pollutant concentrations above the disease thresholds during upset operating conditions or very unusual meteorological conditions. New pollutants not yet recognized as an oil shale concern could be identified. Region-specific factors could affect the dose-response relationship of know pollutants which were found to be of little consequence in this analysis. The additional quarter-million people associated with the growth of the oil shale industry, would have a significant impact on the pollution levels of the region, almost as much as the industry itself. The impact of these pollutants should be considered in further analyses.

Environmental Risks

The need to process 1 to 3 tons of shale per barrel of oil results in a major solid waste disposal problem. Retorted shale is by far the most substantial solid waste produced by a surface retort. Results of the analysis of potential impacts on the semi-arid, high altitude ecosystem yielded minimal risks from air pollutants and land disturbances, but of potential concern for aquatic systems under extreme conditions (10).

Aqueous wastes from oil shale processing originate from direct and indirect sources. Direct sources are waste waters generated from unit operations and processes. Indirect sources include: leachate from retorted shale disposal areas; run-off and erosion resulting from construction and site use activities; and run-off from mining and transport activities. Approximately 45 to 50 percent of the water required for an oil shale plant is expected to be used for moisturizing of

retorted shale. Much of this water requirement will be supplied by
minewater and process wastewaters. Because of the large quantities of
water utilized and the exposure of retorted shale to rain and snowfall, a
source of indirect water pollution may occur via leaching or run-off from
retorted shale piles. Leaching experiments in the laboratory and with
small field studies indicate that inorganic salts (eg. sodium, magnesium,
chlorides, fluorides, and sulfates), small quantities of organic
substances, and/or trace elements may be leached from both raw-shale
storage piles and spent-shale disposal piles.

The impact of an oil shale industry on the water resources of the
Western United States involves several controversial issues. Release of
oil shale process waters, by intention or accident, may expose local area
residents of toxic pollutants in drinking water. However, there is major
uncertainty regarding the probability of such occurrences, the reliability
of a "zero-discharge" system, and the attenuation of released pollutants
in surface waters. Leaching of solid wastes is a potential environmental
problem which may extend several centuries after final abandonment of an
industry. Percolating water from rainfall and snowmelt through spent
shale piles and abandoned in-situ retorts may dissolve a portion of the
spent shale matrix. This polluted water could migrate a surface waters
and ultimately to drinking water. Also, the issue of water availability
is a perennial controversy due to the large amount of water needed by the
industry and the limited amount of water available on the western slope.

The analysis indicated that significant water shortages begin to
appear somewhere between 2000 to 2040 depending on the assumptions made
about growth of non-oil shale uses. This does not imply that oil shale
could not be developed; water rights can be brought and sold. However, it
does mean that the economics of water rights purchase may affect oil shale
development.

Research recommendations based on the water quality and solid
leachates analyses include the following: a description of water
management within an oil shale facility including probabilities of leaks,
overflows, and accidents; characterization of leachate attenuation in
groundwater; and data for waterborne organics release rates and
transformation in the environment.

Risk Analysis Methodologies

Further research into risk analysis methodologies and implementations
are also recommended. The dust-induced risk analysis should be extended
to all types of underground mining and compared to historical
statistics. The LLE for disabling accidents would allow a better
comparison of occupational accidents and diseases. Finally, the results
of this analysis should be tested in research planning, generation of
useful results, and risk management processes. The potential utility of
the current risk analysis for research planning (11) would be increased by
updating with the results of current oil shale health effects research on
the defunct Scottish industry (12) and measurements from commercial-scale
U.S. oil shale facilities.

SUMMARY

The management of the health and environmental risks of a future
oil shale industry will require a proper scientific basis for their
quantification and, if necessary, mitigation. Research is needed for
providing the scientific basis for this decision making process. The
current risk analysis presents a methodology and the initial estimates for

health and environmental risks of a steady-state million BPD oil shale industry. The effort was based on existing and novel approaches. The estimated uncertainty factors associated with the key risks can be used to assess and prioritize research needs to reduce the important uncertainties. The use of the analysis for aid in research management is a dynamic and interactive process. As new information becomes available, the risk analysis can be iterated and updated as part of the research prioritization process to focus on critical risk management issues.

ACKNOWLEDGMENTS

This analysis was performed under sponsorship of the U.S. Department of Energy (DOE) Contract DE-AC02-82ER60087, Dr. Paul Cho, Project Officer, and Lawrence Livermore National Laboratory (LLNL), Subcontract 4554105, Dr. David Layton, Project Officer, by IWG Corp. and the University of Colorado. Mr. Bruce Perry, Dr. David Savitz, Dr. William Marine, and Dr. Willard Chappell all provided significant contributions to the reported effort.

REFERENCES

1. Gratt, L.B., B.W. Perry, W.M. Marine, D.A. Savitz, and W.R. Chappell, "Health and Environmental Effects Document for Oil Shale - 1982," IWG-FR-085-01, IWG Corp., San Diego, California, 1984.
2. Gratt, L.B., W.R. Chappell, B.W. Perry, J.L. Feerer, K.J. Berger, J.A. Lanning, R.A. Molano, and F.X. Siroky, "Health and Environmental Effects Document for Oil Shale - 1981," IWG-FR-082-01, IWG Corp., San Diego, California, 1981.
3. Gratt, L.B., W.R. Chappell, B.W. Perry, W.M. Marine, D.A. Savitz, and J.L. Feerer, "Health and Environmental Effects Document for Oil Shale - 1982," IWG-FR-003-01, IWG Corp., San Diego, California, 1982.
4. National Research Council, "A Review of the 1982 Department of Energy Health and Environmental Effects Assessments on Coal Liquefaction and Oil Shale Technologies," Committee on Health and Ecological Effects of Synfuels Industries, National Academy Press, Washington, D.C., 1983.
5. Marine, W.M., D.A. Savitz, L.B. Gratt, and B.W. Perry, "Risk of dust-induced lung disease in oil shale workers." In: Gary, J.H., ed., Seventeenth Oil Shale Symposium Proceedings, pp. 414-425, Colorado School of Mines Press, Golden, Colorado, 1984.
6. Gratt, L.B., B.W. Perry, W.M. Marine, and D.A. Savitz, "High Risk Groups in an Oil Shale Workforce," In: Gary, J.H., ed., Seventeenth Oil Shale Symposium Proceedings, pp. 403-413, Colorado School of Mines Press, Golden, Colorado, 1984.
7. Savitz, D.A., W.M. Marine, L.B. Gratt, and B.W. Perry, "Hydrocarbon-induced Cancer Risks in Oil Shale Processing," In: Gary, J.H., ed., Seventeenth Oil Shale Symposium Proceeding, pp. 426-432, Colorado School of Mines Press, Golden, Colorado, 1984.
8. Cho, P.C., L.B. Gratt, "Oil Shale Processing Occupational Cancer Risks from Polynuclear Aromatic Hydrocarbons," Presented at the International Chemical Congress to the Pacific Basing Society in Honolulu, Hawaii, December 1984.
9. Perry, B.W. and L.B. Gratt, "Public Health Risks from an Oil Shale Industry," In: Gary, J. H., ed., Seventeenth Oil Shale Symposium Proceedings, pp. 391-402, Colorado School of Mines Press, Golden, Colorado, 1984.

10. Gratt, L.B., "Risk Analysis of Hazardous Materials in Oil Shale," Journal of Hazardous Materials, 10, pp. 317-350, Elsevier Science Publishers, the Netherlands, 1985.

11. Cho, P.C., "Oil Shale Health and Environmental Effects Research Projects and Risk Analysis Requirements," In: Seventeenth Oil Shale Symposium Proceedings, Gary, J.H., ed., pp. 384-390, Colorado School of Mines Press, Golden, Colorado, 1984.

12. Seaton, A., "Studies of The Scottish Oil Shale Industry," Final Report to the U.S. Department of Energy on Research Project No. DE-AC02-82ER60036, Institute of Occupational Medicine, Edinburgh, Scotland, May 1985.

RISK ASSESSMENT OF DELIBERATE RELEASE OF GENETICALLY-ENGINEERED

MICROORGANISMS

Vlasta Molak and Jerry Stara

Environmental Protection Agency
Environmental Criteria and Assessment Office
Cincinnati, Ohio

ABSTRACT

Hazard identification and evaluation of dose response and exposure, the standard approach to risk assessment, take on a new meaning when one evaluates the risks associated with deliberate release of genetically-engineered microorganisms (GEMs). Hazard identification of GEMs may be quite complex since one must consider not only their potential toxic effects on humans and animals, but also disruptions that the introduction of novel GEMs may cause in the ecological equilibrium. Initially, these changes might not be as obvious as direct toxic effects. Unlike with chemicals, for which the risk assessment scheme was initially developed, exposure to GEMs does not necessarily decrease with time due to dilution and degradation. This paper will describe conceptual models of risk assessment applicable to deliberate release of GEMs.

KEY WORDS: Risk assessment, genetic engineering, microorganisms, deliberate release

INTRODUCTION

New genetically-engineered microorganisms (GEMs) promise a great benefit to humanity, yet their use may pose a risk to public health or cause ecological damage. Thus, the potential adverse effects need to be reviewed and evaluated.

Application of genetic engineering results in three categories of products:

(1) Macroscopic plants and animals with altered genes, presumably improved from the original species; for example, more pest- and drought resistant plants, "super" cows, and "super" sheep.

(2) Products made by GEMs, such as insulin, growth hormone, interferon, various polypeptides, and vitamins.

(3) A GEM is itself a product designed to perform a specific task, and may be deliberately released into the environment for the following purposes:

(a) Pollution control, such as oil-digesting bacteria; xenobiotics-digesting bacteria, yeasts and fungi.

(b)   Pest control; e.g., <u>Pseudomonas fluorescens</u> with inserted genes from <u>Bacillus thuringiensis</u>.

(c) Other uses, such as frost prevention by ice (-) strain of <u>Pseudomonas syringae</u>, nitrogen fixing bacteria, metal and oil recovery bacteria.

The data needed to evaluate risks posed by the use of products of genetic engineering are quite different for each category. This paper will focus primarily on category 3 because of its potential for the most immediate impact (products are already waiting for field testing), and potentially widespread use in various environments. Since the purpose of these GEMs is to perform their function in the natural environment such as soil, sewage, plant leaves, and water, a parent organism is generally selected that can survive well in these media. This is in clear distinction to microorganisms in category 2, which were specifically selected to be less able than the wild type to survive outside the container.

In order to place potential risks posed by a deliberate release of GEMs in the proper perspective, one must first address the misconception that naturally occurring products are safe, and that man-made products are inherently hazardous and unsafe. An example of a dangerous natural product is aflatoxin a potent hepatotoxin and liver carcinogen. Aflatoxin is a by product of the metabolism of the mold <u>Aspergillus Plauus</u> which grows on grains and peanuts. It is, therefore, a natural, but potentially very hazardous contaminant of grain products and peanut butter. Another example of naturally occuring hazardous entities is the numerous types of microorganisms causing infectious diseases, which certainly present a human health hazard. Just as naturally occurring microorganisms are not necessarily safe, GEMs created using recombinant DNA techniques are not necessarily more dangerous.

Another important fact to consider in risk assessment of a deliberate release of GEMs is that the degree of change in a genome of an organism does not necessarily correlate with physiological properties that this change in genome confers (Sharples, 1983). Slight differences in the genome can be associated with large differences in the organism's properties. For example, chestnut-blight fungus (<u>Endothia parasitica</u>) in Asia co-exists with Asian chestnut and causes no harm. When Asian chestnut-blight fungus was imported into the United States, however, it destroyed American chestnut trees, although it is not very different from the fungus that normally lives on American chestnuts and causes no harm.

Therefore, in the risk assessment of a deliberate release of GEMs one should not differentiate between naturally-occurring microorganisms and genetically-engineered microorganisms, and one should not assess risks based on the degree of human intervention used in the modification of the microorganism. Whenever the release of a <u>large number</u> of microorganisms into the environment (both natural and GEMs) is contemplated, the risks should be determined based on a specific organism. A case-by-case approach has to be applied because causal relationships between genome structure and functional properties are unknown at the present time. Knowing the DNA sequence of a gene does not provide information on how this gene will function in a particular cell. Therefore, risk assessment should be based on functional properties of the microorganism, and should be performed for each microorganism that is going to be released in large quantities into the environment.

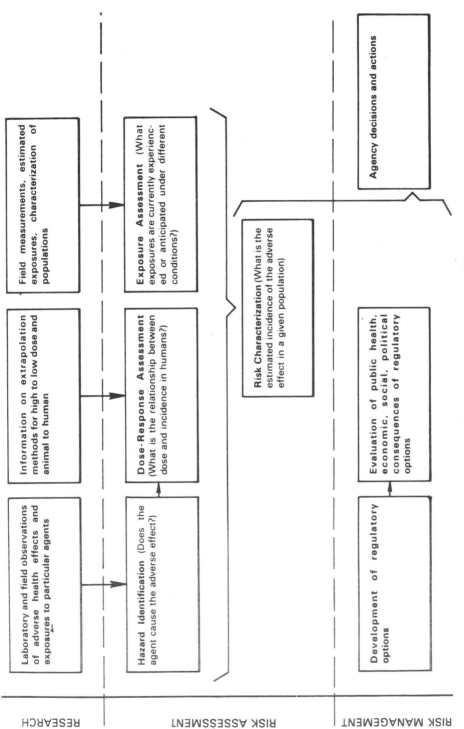

Figure 1. Elements of risk assessment and risk management

Hazard Identification

Figure 1 describes the risk assessment scheme for chemicals. In this scheme the main components of the assessment are hazard identification, dose-response determination and exposure assessment, leading to the risk characterization (Ruckelshaus, 1984; 1985). On the basis of risk characterization for a particular chemical, one can then perform qualitative or quantitative risk assessment. Can one use a similar scheme for microorganisms that are going to be released deliberately into the environment? In the case of chemicals, hazard identification is based on observed endpoints (presumably undesirable acute and chronic toxic effects or cancer); with microorganisms, the endpoints are not that clear. In general, microorganisms can be divided into two categories with respect to hazard identification, pathogens and non-pathogens.

In the case of pathogens, a scheme for hazard identification can be constructed somewhat similar to the scheme for chemicals. Minimal infectious dose (ID50), analogous to LD50 for chemicals, is the number of microorganisms that would cause infection (by ingestion, inhalation or dermal exposure) in 50% of the tested population. The ingestion ID50 is between 10^2 and 10^8 for most pathogenic bacteria; 1-10 for virusus and 1-100 for parasites (Battelle, 1985; Ward and Akin, 1984). Risk characterization of naturally-occurring pathogens can be performed similarly to risk characterization of chemicals by measuring the exposure levels (intake through food, air or water), and calculating the likelihood of infection.

Recently, an attempt has been made to perform a risk assessment for pathogens that may contaminate various environmental media as the result of sludge disposal (Battelle, 1985). The environmental fate and transport of various pathogens naturally found in sludge are being determined and combined with known infectivity dose response values. Various options of sludge disposal are considered (land application, distribution and marketing, landfill, ocean dumping), and an attempt is made to assess the risk of pathogens causing diseases resulting from each sludge disposal option. Such methodology could be applied for risk assessment of GEMs with known ID50. The transport and fate models have to be developed for each specific microorganism and the environment into wnich this microorganism is released.

Most of the newly constructed GEMs, however, are probably not pathogenic in human, animals, or plants. Therefore, for most GEMs an ID50 does not exist, nor does one know which endpoints to observe or even to expect. Since these GEMs must survive in the environment in order to perform their task, the question to ask in the case of a deliberate release of GEMs into the environmental media is not if they will survive (Alexander, 1985), but how long will these microorganisms survive in each particular environment, and what effects on the environment will they have during their survival. Obviously, the survival of each specific microorganism will depend on its interactions with the environment into which it is released.

Exposure

Figure 2 shows some of the environmental media into which GEMs could possibly be released. Microorganisms that might serve as pesticides, will be released into soil or onto plant surfaces. Microorganisms for pollution control will be released into sewage and water (Johnson and Robinson, 1984) or contaminated soil (Ghosal et al. 1985). Microorganisms used for oil recovery or metal recovery will be released into ore fields or oil drills (Moses and Springham, 1982; Curtis, 1983). In addition, certain GEMs are planned to be released on plant surfaces to prevent frost (Lindow, 1983).

All the cited environmental media into which microorganisms might be released are already occupied by their natural biota. For example, to a depth of 15 centimeters in moderate temperatures, a hectare of average soil contains about 2×10^{18} bacteria, which weigh 2.6 metric tons. This soil also contains 8×10^{16} fungi weighing approximately 2 metric tons; 6×10^{17} actinomycetes, 7×10^{16} protozoa; and 3×10^{14} algae (Foth, 1984). In total, each hectare of soil into which GEMs would be released already contains about five tons of naturally occuring microorganisms. The interaction of microorganisms already present in the soil with the newly-introduced agents will determine their survivability and growth. It is possible that it would be safe to release a certain limited number of microorganisms, but unsafe to release a larger number (critical mass). Release of a critical mass of microorganisms into a specific environment could enable the introduced microorganisms to replace the natural populations. Therefore, quantitative relations between introduced and endogenous microorganism populations should be taken into account because ecological effects might depend, to a great extent, on the number of microorganisms that are introduced into a unit space.

Risk Characterization

From the above discussion it is clear that numerous factors must be considered before release of a large number of microorganisms into any environmental media can be contemplated (Figure 3). Such factors include the physiological properties of GEMs (nutritional requirements, growth, and metabolism); the quantity of GEMs released into a particular environment; and detailed characteristics of the environmental media. This includes physical characteristics such as soil porosity, structure of the soil particles, and water content; chemical characteristics, such as presence of mineral and organic materials; and biological characteristics which depend on the species already occupying each medium. Environmental interaction will be determined by a combination of these three factors. For example, survival and transport of GEMs will be determined by characteristics of GEMs and their interaction with physical and chemical factors in the environment. Intra- and interspecies gene transfer will depend on interaction of GEMs with biological factors. The interaction of GEMs with other species would again depend on biological characteristics of the particular environment. Potential exposure of humans, animals and plants would be also determined by these three factors.

1. soil

2. sewage

3. water

4. plant surfaces

5. ore fields

6. oil drills

Figure 2. Environments for deliberate release of GEMs

1. GEMs characteristics (nutritional requirements, growth, Survival)

2. Quantity of GEMs released into particular environmental unit

3. Characteristics of the environment:

    a. Physical

    b. Chemical

    c. Biological species occupying same space

4. Environmental interaction

    a. Survival and transport of GEMs

    b. Intra and interspecies gene transfer

    c. Interaction of GEMs with other species

5. Possible exposures of human, animals and plants

Figure 3. Points to consider

Examples of GEMs for Deliberate Release

Examples of GEMS intended for deliberate release are listed in
Figure 4. Pseudomonas fluorescens is a bacterium that normally lives on
roots of various plants (including corn). This species has been
genetically altered by the introduction of a gene from Bacillus
thuringiensis, which renders Pseudomonas fluorescens poisonous to soil
parasites such as cutworms. Bacillus thuringiensis itself is used as a
natural microbial pesticide against mosquito larvae, by spraying it over
ponds which are breeding grounds for mosquitoes (Luthy et al., 1982).
Therefore, plants that contain genetically-engineered Pseudomonas
fluorescens on their roots are resistant to attacks from cutworms because
their roots are poisonous to cutworms. In this example, the environment
for a deliberate release is soil, and one must determine the fate and
transport of this GEM in soil as well as its interaction with the soil's
natural biota. Moreover, the toxic effects of this GEM on other species
which might be exposed to soil should be established. If genetically-
engineered Pseudomonas fluorescens has a prolonged survival time in soil,
one would also need to consider its environmental fate and transport.
Existing models for pathogen transport in soil may be useful to follow the
environmental fate and transport of this GEM (BDM, 1980).

1. **Pseudomonas fluorescens with inserted gene from**

   Bacillus thuringiensis

2. **Pseudomonas syringae (ice (-) strain)**

3. **Pollution control microorganisms**

Figure 4. Examples of GEMs intended for deliberate release

The second example is genetically-engineered Pseudomonas syringae,
which has been obtained from the wild type by deleting the ice nucleation
gene. This change lowers the temperature at which this organism serves as
an ice nucleation center. The bacteria that normally live on plant leaves
are the sources of ice nucleation; therefore, the temperature at which
these bacteria freeze determines the temperature at which leaves freeze
(Lindow, 1983). In order to assess the risk of a deliberate release of
Pseudomonas syringae, its survival on plant leaves should be considered,
as well as its fate and transport in the environment where it is
applied. Also, the possible pathogenic properties of this genetically-
engineered species should be determined.

A third example of a possible deliberate release is pollution-control
microorganisms. Many processes in decontamination of toxic wastes might
involve the use of biological agents (Johnston and Robinson, 1984).
Microorganisms are already used in sludge treatment and in wastewater
treatment plants (Powledge, 1983). Presumably, with the help of genetic
engineering, one can construct microorganisms that would have specific
properties for desired pollution control. Such microorganisms will be

then released at various contamination sites, which might vary from sewage and sludge environment to water and contaminated soil (Chakrabarty, 1985). Again, to assess the risk posed by this type of a deliberate release, first it must be established whether these microorganisms are pathogens and what effect they have on the environment into which they are released.

CONCLUSION

What can be done with the information on microorganisms intended for deliberate release? The final goal should be to develop models for deliberate release of microorganisms that will accurately predict the fate and transport of these microorganisms and their public health and ecological effects. Ideally, a mathematical model that <u>adequately</u> describe <u>all</u> the environmental factors involved would be developed. The final output of the series of equations would describe the state of the system (environment) into which the new variable (GEM) is to be introduced. For example, given the number of GEMs introduced into a particular volume of soil, sludge, water or surface of plants, one should be able to predict the subsequent density of these GEMs at any chosen time and space. Provided that one knows the initial values (distribution and density of GEMs), and all relevant parameters for the model, this goal is achievable. The major difficulty lies in finding which equations <u>adequately</u> describe processes in nature (survival, competition, growth, transport, gene transfer), and in testing experimentally the relevant parameters in these equations. Because of the diversity of GEMs and the diversity of environments into which they will be released, it appears impossible to construct a generic model that would cover all possible instances of a deliberate release of GEMs. For example, mathematical equations describing the density of GEMs in aquatic environment will undoubtedly be different from the equations applicable to GEMs released into soil or onto plant leaves.

Since GEMs are not basically different from natural microorganisms (except for some special functions), models describing the fate and transport of natural microorganisms could be applied to a deliberate release of GEMs. However, only a few such models exist at present. Most of the models are   designed for very specific purposes that do not take into account all the factors described in Figure 3. Therefore, new and more realistic models, requiring a great deal of interdisciplinary knowledge will have to be developed. These models should be designed taking into consideration knowledge from various disciplines such as ecology, microbiology, biochemistry, molecular genetics, soil science, agriculture and toxicology. Finally, the models should be tested in simulated real-life situations of deliberate release of microorganisms.

REFERENCES

Alexander, M., 1985. "Ecological Consequences: Reducing Uncertainties." Issues in Science and Technology 1 (3): 57-68, 1985.
Battelle, Inc. 1985. Pathogen Risk Assessment Feasibility Study. Contract No. 68-01-6986, U.S. EPA, 1985.
BDM Corporation, 1980. Sewage Sludge Pathogen Transport Model Project. The BDM Cooperation, Albuquerque, NM, Contract No. IAG-78-D-X0116, U.S. EPA, Request No. 224.

Chakrabarty, A.M. 1985. Genetically-manipulated Microorganisms and Their Products in the Oil Service Industries. Trends in Biotech. 3(2): 32-38. Curtin, M.E. 1983. Microbial Mining and Metal Recovery: Corporations Take the Long and Cautious Path, Biotechnology 1: 229-230.

Foth, H.D. 1984. Fundamentals of Soil Science, John Wiley and Sons, New York, 1984.

Ghosal, D., You, I.S., Chatterjee, D.K., Chakrabarty, A.M. 1985. Microbial Degradation of Halogenated Compounds. Science 228: 135-142.

Johnston, J.B., and S.G. Robinson, 1984. Genetic engineering and the development of new pollution control technologies. EPA-600/2-84-037, January 1984.

Lindow, S.E., 1983. The Role of Bacterial Ice Nucleation in Frost Injury to Plants. Ann. Rev. Phytol. 21: 363-384.

Lythy, P., Cordiev, J.L., Fisher, H.M. 1982. Bacillus thuringiensis as a bacterial insecticide: Basic considerations and application in microbial and viral pesticides, Ed. E. Kurstak, p. 35-74.

Moses, V. and D.G. Springham, Ed. 1982. Bacteria and the Enhancement of Oil Recovery, Elsevier Science Publishers, NY

Powledge, T.M. 1983. Prospects for pollution control with microbes. Biotechnology 1: 743-755.

Ruckelshaus, W.D. 1984. Risk Assessment and Management: Framework for Decision Making, U.S. EPA 600/9-85-002. December 1984.

Ruckelshaus, W.D. 1985. Risk, Science and Democracy. Issues in Science and Technology 1 (3): 19-38, 1985.

Sharples, F.E. 1983. Spread of organisms with novel genotypes: thoughts from an ecological perspective. Recombinant DNA Technical Bull 6: 43-56.

ASSESSING THE RISKS ASSOCIATED WITH BIOTECHNOLOGY: THE REGULATORY PROBLEM

Janis C. Kurtz

Dynamic Corporation
11140 Rockville Pike
Rockville, MD 20852

ABSTRACT

In examining the regulatory problem posed by biotechnology, three areas must be considered: 1) the potential benefits to mankind, 2) the generation of profits to industry, and 3) the mitigation of risk presented to human health and the environment. Environmental risk assessments involving exposure and effects assessments must consider the potential for establishment in the environment, the potential for altering ecosystem processes and the potential for unexpected events as they relate to biotechnology applications. Predictive and analytical tools must be developed and used by regulators to ensure that the rewards of genetic engineering to both mankind and industry are realized with minimal consequence.

KEY WORDS: Biotechnology, Regulation, Genetic Engineering, Risk, Risk Assessment, Environmental Release, Microcosm, Differential Light Scattering.

ASSESSING THE RISKS ASSOCIATED WITH BIOTECHNOLOGY: THE REGULATORY PROBLEM

Biotechnology presents us with the possibility for solutions to many of mankind's problems and presents industry with unique opportunities for new markets, yet is perceived to present novel risks also - defining a regulatory problem. My objective is to further explore this problem, examining the sources of risk and the techniques that can help to predict and mitigate it.

The genetic engineering of microorganisms involves the introduction of new genetic sequences into existing microorganisms to enhance their capabilities to perform a function. One method of engineering is DNA recombination. Figure 1 presents a simplistic representation of DNA recombination. A selected characteristic present in the donor DNA molecule is removed using restriction enzymes and inserted or recombined into plasmid DNA. The recombinant DNA is then cloned into a bacterial host where the desired function can be expressed. The application of genetic engineering technology by recombinant DNA and other methods has come to be known as biotechnology (OTA, 1981).

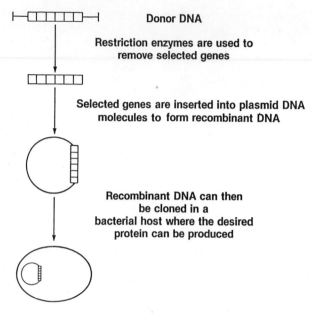

Donor DNA

Restriction enzymes are used to
remove selected genes

Selected genes are inserted into plasmid DNA
molecules to form recombinant DNA

Recombinant DNA can then
be cloned in a
bacterial host where the desired
protein can be produced

Figure 1

Recombinant DNA

The technique of recombining genes from
one species with genes from another

Biotechnology's potential impact for the benefit of mankind is
enormous. The treatment of human, animal, and plant diseases may be
revolutionized. Commercial applications will enhance the chemical,
energy, mining, electronic, textile, and waste treatment industries.
Business and market analysts predict that biotechnology may benefit 70% of
current US industries, due to the wide variety of potential applications.

Although tremendous potential exists, profits have not been realized
to any significant degree, nor have products been marketed to benefit
consumers. Notable exceptions are interferon, insulin, and human growth
hormone, which are produced by genetically engineered organisms in
fermentation cultures. These products have been approved for use by the
Food and Drug Administration (FDA). Reasons for the delay in bringing
other genetically engineered products to the market are related to the
risks posed by the products of biotechnology.

These three possibilities 1) the benefits to mankind, 2) the
profitability to industry and 3) the risk posed, combine to describe a
regulatory problem. How can we guarantee that the inherent benefits and
profitability will be captured while avoiding the potential risks to
health and the biosphere?

This is not a new problem, but is one that has been faced by the
chemical industry and the nuclear energy industry. A tool that was
developed to assist in defining the unknown risks posed by these
technologies is risk assessment. Biotechnology has an advantage in that
this tool has already been developed; however, it must be modified to
allow application to new types of risk.

Risk assessment methods can assist the regulatory community in solving this problem. Regulation should be designed to mitigate risk, and is often based on risk management endpoints. But before risk can be mitigated or endpoints can be determined, the risk must be defined.

Risk questions can be divided into three areas:

1) Potential for establishment in the environment. Engineered organisms may have the ability to find a suitable niche once they are released, and may reproduce, disperse, and evolve in new environments. They may also interact with native species creating new community structures and predator-prey relationships.

2) Potential for altering ecosystem processes. Releases and establishment of novel organisms could cause changes in decomposition pathways, primary production, oxygen consumption, and/or nitrogen fixation. Climatic and geologic processes could also be affected as pointed out in Eugene Odum's recent letter to Science. Normal, wild type ice-nucleating bacteria cause frost to form on potato crops as the temperature drops. Recently it has been suggested that these normal bacteria decompose contributing their lipoprotein coats to detritus, which is blown about into the atmosphere. Here the coat fragments serve as nuclei for raindrop formation. The use of ice minus strains, strains deficient for the character that causes frost formation, might reduce frost damage to potato crops. However, the establishment of ice minus strains in the environment might ultimately result in the reduction of total rainfall amounts, since nuclei for raindrop formation would not be contributed. The reduction in overall rainfall would be worse for crops than frost damage (Odum, 1985).

3) Potential for unexpected events. Novel genes and genetic changes cannot be specifically controlled or predicted, nor can the stability of genetic changes within an organism be assured. Conjugation and plasmid transfer can take place between organisms that are not generically related. Figure 2 shows some of the pathways of possible genetic exchange that have been demonstrated under laboratory conditions. Exchange is possible between many microorganisms, although spontaneous transfers in nature have not been investigated to any degree. Another point for consideration is that this gene transfer may result in transfer of genetic change from one ecosystem to another, such as from aquatic to terrestrial communities. Instability of genetic change could result in the loss of desired traits, as well as the creation of undesirable traits such as virulence or pathogenicity.

Most researchers are convinced that the chance for untoward events is very small. Surveys of science, environmental, and religious policy leaders demonstrate perceptions that the benefits of biotechnology far outweigh the risks (C & E News, 1985). Most agree that biotechnology risk factors can be classified as low probability/high consequence, and that environmental endpoints must be considered in addition to human health endpoints.

Environmental risk assessment will be more important to the regulation of biotechnology products than they have been with any other technology. These assessments must reflect the complex interaction of wide spectrum of animals, plants, and microorganisms with inanimate processes such as nutrient cycling and material balances.

Environmental risk assessments for deliberately released, genetically engineered products will involve the familiar components of exposure

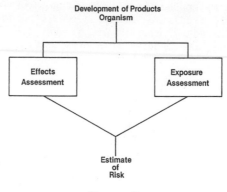

Figure 2

Environmental Risk Assessment

assessment and effects assessment, which will be combined to yield an estimate of risk (See Figure 3). Exposure assessments will rely on models of release, dispersal and persistence to estimate the probability that organisms and ecosystem processes will be exposed. Effects assessment will be used to define the magnitude and likelihood of response of organisms and ecosystem processes produced by the estimated range of exposure.

Two factors compromise our ability to conduct environmental risk assessments for the products of biotechnology: a lack of predictive tools and a lack of appropriate analysis techniques.

With regard to predictive tools; tools must be developed to allow simulation of environmental conditions. Simulated, contained conditions are needed so that we can gather data from which to make predictions.

Microcosms are laboratory systems that allow for this simulation. A variety of designs are possible, ranging from flasks containing soils and microbial communities to larger systems containing vertebrates and higher plants. They have advantages (safety, cost and time effectiveness, and simplification of complex interactions) and disadvantages (may be unrepresentative of natural conditions in surface-to-volume ratio, oversimplification, and elimination of immigration and emigration for population studies). Microcosms seem the obvious tools to utilize, yet development and standardization are needed to make them a viable regulatory tool (Pritchard, 1982).

Appropriate analysis tools are also needed. They must allow for the detection and identification of genetically engineered organisms, and their unique genetic sequences. Biotechnology products must be identifiable by their functional character before they are released into the environment. Detection and quantification will be important after release in microcosms for testing and in the environment for monitoring sites of release.

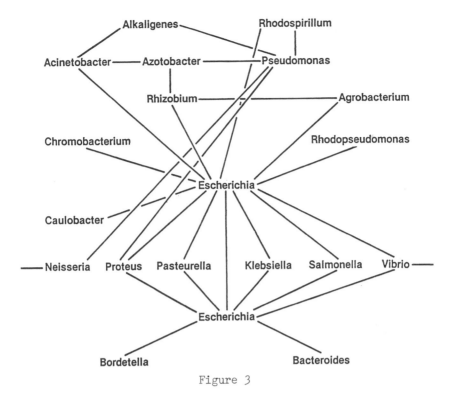

Figure 3

Pathways of possible genetic exchange
(after Reaaney et al.; 1982)

Possible methods include the addition or insertion of unique genetic
sequences, such as antibiotic resistance markers, as identifiers.
However, these sequences may be transferred from species to species with
or without the traits being monitored. Spontaneous mutation may also
alter both the marker and the useful trait.

Another analysis technique is under investigation. This technique
utilizes a battery of 19 recombinant DNA mutants of Bacillus subtilis.
The isogenic Bacillus mutants differ only by defects in DNA repair which
involve specific recombination, excision or polymerase activity. A laser
beam is used to produce unique differential light scattering patterns
based on bacterial count, morphology and size, and will monitor changes
produced by exposure of the test organisms to various physiological
conditions. Distinctive signatures or fingerprints are generated by input
of the laser readout data directly into a computer system to produce a
visual image. We hypothesize that this system will allow identification
of newly introduced novel genetic sequences, thereby allowing us to
develop an assay designed to detect and monitor genetically engineered
organisms and the products produced by biotechnology (Felkner, 1983).

Further research and development in these areas, and in microbial
ecology as a science, will allow us to better predict the ecosystem
consequences posed by the release of engineered organisms. This
predictive ability will allow the regulatory community to define endpoints

that can be used as indicators of safety for the management of biotechnology products.

A clear framework must be devised to ensure that a balance is achieved between risk and reward or cost and benefit. As biotechnology leaves the developmental stage and moves into the applied, industrial arena, the framework of regulations designed to control medical, agricultural, and industrial products will be applied.

This application must be tempered by risk management decisions that rely on environmentally based assessments. These assessments should examine the potential of genetically engineered organisms to become established in the environment, to alter ecosystem processes, and to cause unexpected events. Both predictive and analytical tools will be needed to ensure that the rewards of genetic engineering to both mankind and industry are achieved with minimal consequence.

REFERENCES

Anon. Biotechnology gets good marks in survey. Chemical and Engineering News (C & E News) 63(34): 16, August 26, 1985.
Felkner, IC. Rapid Detection of Genotoxic Chemicals in the Environment; IN: Proceedings of the ASCE Specialty Conference on Environmental Engineering, p.204, 1983.
Odum, Eugene P. Biotechnology and the biosphere (letter). Science 229:1338, September 27, 1985.
Office of Technology Assessment (OTA). Impact of Applied Genetics: Micro-Organisms, Plants, and Animals, p.5, April, 1981.
Pritchard, P.H. Model Ecosystems; IN: Conway, Richard A (Editor) Environmental Risk Analysis for Chemicals. Van Nostrand Reinhold Co., New York, 1982.
Reanney, DC et al. Genetic interactions among microbial communities; IN: Bull, A.T. and Slater J.H. (Editor), Microbial Interactions and Communities. Academic Press: London, 1982.

METHODOLOGICAL APPROACH TO THE STUDY OF RISK POLICY DECISION-MAKING:

THE CASE OF DELIBERATE RELEASE OF GENETICALLY ENGINEERED ORGANISMS

Smita K. Siddhanti,

University of Pittsburgh

ABSTRACT

Policy making for regulating genetically engineered organisms is fraught with uncertainty and incomplete information. Risk assessment studies useful for policy decision-making require the knowledge of multiple perspectives on the nature of risk and influence of variation in perspectives on the judgements for policy decisions. The proposed methodological approach combines Repertory grid and Social judgement analysis to examine variation in problem formulation and perspectives, and influence of this variation in decision-making in deliberate release of genetically engineered organisms.

KEY WORDS: Multiple perspectives; Problem structure; Judgment; Decision-making Criteria; Repertory grid; and, Social judgement analysis.

INTRODUCTION

Along with the present and potential benefits due to advancement of science and technology, the past decade has seen a rise in concern for unanticipated consequences and potential risk to health, safety and environment in the formation of public policy related to technological development. Policy making in these areas is fraught with uncertainty of impacts of technological application and the probable or unknown risks associated with it.

Policy decision making in the advances of biotechnology, which is the focus of this research, also faces the problem of uncertainty of impacts and potential risks. While the potential benefits of genetic engineering are widely acknowledged, legitimate concerns about its safety have also been raised as additional products of biotechnology move from contained research laboratories into full contact with the public and the environment through commercial testing and application. The great promise that genetic engineering holds also raises anxieties about the effects of reshaping nature to fit our needs, goals and aspirations. The importance of a sound decision-making system has been emphasized in most public hearings, as seen in the opening statement of the presiding chairman, John Dingell,

"It is essential to create a trustworthy system for avoiding problems associated with biotechnology. Government has the responsibility to protect the public health and environment - - - -- Beyond the

99

immediate harm of any mistake, we are sure to lose some of the public confidence in science, in industry, and in government. If a frightening accident were to occur in the face of faulty predictions, there could be a very strong public reaction against further development or use of this technology" (Hearing Report, Dec. 1984: 2).

New technology creates many risks but determining which risks are socially acceptable is an important national issue. The question arises how should group decision processes operate to minimize social costs and maximize social benefits. Social costs include intangibles, and the question immediately evident is what costs are included and how are they weighted. Decisions are not made by institutions, the decision process involves people. The government typically works through agencies and committees, where a few people really decide what happens. To improve the quality of decision-making, it is imperative to explore the subject of individual decision-making in relation to risk assessment and risk management of new technology.

In recent years, empirical and theoretical research on the psychology of decision-making under risk and uncertainty has produced a body of knowledge that should be of value to those who seek to understand and improve societal decisions (Slovic, Fischhoff and Lichstenstein, 1983; 1984). These efforts are grounded in cognitive psychology, psychometrics, and decision theory. The basic assumption is that those who promote and regulate low-probability-high-risk technologies need to understand the ways in which people (including themselves and the decision-makers) think about risk, the outcome of technology that people deem to be important, and the values that they attach to these outcomes. Without such understanding, well intended policies may be ineffective and even counterproductive.

This paper summarizes a research approach to make the decision making process more explicit and help improve policy-making in this new area. The study will elicit the criteria for the decisions in the field of deliberate release of genetically engineered organisms into the environment. The specific aim is to understand how 'actively involved' stakeholders/policy-makers perceive risk and how their variation of perspective on risk affect their judgements influencing policy decisions. The importance of problem structuring in the policy process is studied and how the alternative formulations of the problem affect the solution space. Not only will the study describe the variations in criteria relating to deliberate release, but will also examine the explanatory value of several variables on the judgement of the decision-makers. The purpose here is to be able to explain the variance in judgement with such cognitive variables as relative weights, functional relations between criteria and judgements, organizing principle, self-consistency of judgements, and other socio-demographic variables as organizational affiliations and disciplinary orientation. Ultimately the goal of this study is to increase understanding of how decisions are made under uncertainty and potential risk.

Nature of the Debate and Policy Decision-Making in Deliberate Release

The possibility of creating a genetically engineered organism derives fro advances in the means of synthesizing, analyzing, transposing and transporting deoxyribonucleic acid (DNA) in and between organisms. Recent research accomplishments in the genetic modification of microorganisms, plants and animals appear to have wide potential applications in both agriculture and industry. Potential new products include plants with greater disease resistance; bacteria that enhance the nitrogen fixing capability of plants; microbes that detoxify hazardous wastes, cleanup oil spills, or facilitate the recovery of minerals from the ground; and many, many others (Office of Technology Assessment Report, 1984).

Products are making their way toward the marketplace at a rapidly increasing rate and have to go through some sort of regulation whether these products are new or better drugs, pesticides or corn plants. As the research and development of these products has gotten to the point of field testing in the past year, more private commercial ventures are coming to the Recombinant DNA Advisory Committee (RAC) of the National Institutes of Health. Until now most federal government overseeing of genetic engineering has been done by RAC, due to the belief that the main regulatory agencies - notably the EPA, the FDA and the USDA - do not yet have developed sufficient expertise to evaluate proposals for genetically engineered products.

Since 1983 a number of public hearings and conferences have been held where issues of costs and benefits of deliberate release have been raised. Issues are raised that bioengineered products can exhibit acute toxicity, carcigenocity or other harmful environmental and health effects. The long term fate of the engineered organisms in the environment may differ from that of the inanimate pollutants because the unique risks they pose by being alive. "In fact uncertainty about the risks of releasing genetically engineered material into the environment is the salient feature of the problem" (McChesney and Adler, 1983).

The 'genetic engineers' claim they know enough about their creations to guarantee their safety. But there is a wide array of critics at this point, ranging from those who merely want to ensure safe practices of biotechnology commercialization, to those like Jeremy Rifkin who argue against genetic engineering on a wholesale basis. With regard to field testing of genetically engineered organisms, Rifkin raises a number of points ranging from specific safety concerns to the ethics of modes of production.

If Rifkin can be considered to constitute one side of this debate and rDNA researchers the other, a not-very-well-defined group of biologists tends to fall in the middle. Although disassociating themselves for Rifkin's position, they do not feel completely comfortable with the answers provided by researchers eager to field test genetically engineered organisms. Some scientist, backed by a number of environmental and 'public interest' groups, contend that the safety of such deliberate release projects is anything but clear (Wines, 1983).

At present the federal agencies are assessing the need for regulation. The regulators are grappling with the questions about the nature and magnitude of risks of deliberate release, and whether the existing statutes and laws are sufficient to protect the environment from the new technology. There are questions about agency expertise and jurisdiction besides the fact that none of the statutes are broad enough to address the risks from all types of living organisms that are likely to be bioengineered. Neither the NIH guidelines, the only existing regulatory system, nor NEPA apply to private organizations. At the center of these efforts is a working group formed under the White House Cabinet Council on Natural Resources and the Environment, specifically to address the jurisdictional and regulatory problems of biotechnology.

The results of the interagency Working Group to date are reflected in the publication of notice for proposal of a coordinated framework for regulation of biotechnology which includes: (1) Regulatory matrix: a concise index of the current regulatory requirements that might be applicable to biotechnology; (2) Policy Statements: a compilation of

proposed statements of policy that describe how the US Department of
Agriculture, the Environmental Protection Agency, and the Food and Drug
Administration intend to apply to their existing regulatory authorities to
biotechnology products; (3) A Scientific Advisory Mechanism: a
coordinated structure of scientific review to promote consistent risk
assessment within statutory confines (Office of Science & Technology
Policy, 1984). The interagency proposal for coordinated framework for
regulation has been criticized for its defects, some of which include
"lack of coordinated view on whether biotechnology poses any unique or
novel risks," and, "lack of assurance for requirement of consistent data
for open and balanced review of deliberate release" (Ahmed, K.R., et al.,
1985).

The Research Problem of the Present Study

In the area of advances in biotechnology the current pursuit of the
federal government is to provide a clear understanding of how this new
industry will be regulated, and how the regulatory agencies will approach
this evolving technology.

Regardless of the criteria used to determine whether a product is
within the responsibility of a given agency, all the agencies will
approach the review of biotechnology products and processes in a similar
way. They will conduct their assessments on a case-by-case basis,
employing internal staff, consultants and expert advisory committees.
Each agency and the Cabinet Council Working Group are all in the process
of developing appropriate scientific evaluation methods and administrative
procedures for genetically engineered products. The focus of this
research concerns itself with the individual judgements which will impact
the policy decisions when the regulators and scientists in various
agencies have to make decisions on a case-by-case basis. Ultimately the
decisions have to be made by individuals with varying perspectives,
disciplinary backgrounds and organizational affiliations.

The Problem Statement

How do the relevant stakeholders/decision-makers, in regulating the
deliberate release of genetically engineered organisms into the
environment, vary in their perspective of the problem and in their
criteria for decisions, and how does this variation affect the policy
decisions in this area?

The research questions are as follows:

a. How do the relevant stakeholders formulate the problem of 'deliberate
release' and what are the alternative problem formulations?

b. How do the relevant stakeholders/decision-makers differ in their
criteria of a) assessing the risks posed by the release, b) evaluating the
proposal of release?

c. How does this variation in criteria and individual judgement affect
the decisions in this area?

Methodological Approach

The exploratory nature of this research proposes a methodological
beginning for involving multiple stakeholders in policy decision-making
for technological development by studying their frames of reference and
cognitive parameters relevant to the particular technological
application. The methodological approach can be divided into three phases
which are more or less linearly driven. The theoretical basis, instrument

102

and data analysis for the three phases can be summarized as follows.

Phase I - Identification of problem structure and variables that influence the decisions

The purpose of this phase is to examine the alternative formulations of the problem structured by various decisionmakers. The central thesis is that the structure of the problem determines the prescription of the policy solution. For instance variation in the basic assumption whether deliberate release poses regulatory issues - whether of environmental safety, human health, adequacy of information, risk assessment or other things - are in any way unique or novel, would lead to different decisions for regulation.

This is the descriptive phase where the instrument is an in-depth interview or open-ended questionnaire asking to state the problem as seen by the respondent and the concerns that should be addressed in making decisions in this area. These concerns could be referred to as 'perceived risks' by the various stakeholders 'actively involved' in the policy process for deliberate release.

Phase II - Evaluation of 'Perceived risk' by individual criteria

This step is designed to elicit the universe of criteria by which the 'perceived risk' of deliberate risk can be evaluated. The instrument used here will be the "Repertory grid technique', which is a semi-structured interview procedure in which the respondents classify and evaluate 'perceived risks', obtained from phase I, according to their unique personal criteria. Repertory grid is a testing procedure based on a highly developed and formal theoretical framework called personal construct theory (Kelly, 1955), which implies that an individual's response to a situation is directly dependent upon her/his current repertoire of personal constructs or their frame of reference (Dunn, W.N. and Dukes, M.J., 1982).

The Repertory grid will not only permit an efficient generation of individual 'criteria' for 'perceived risks' and their relations, it will also yield data that could be translated into a graphic representation of problem spaces of individuals and into distance-cluster analysis that would group individuals by similarities and differences of problem spaces. The inter-criteria correlation and distance cluster analysis of individual and comparative grid data would enable determination of importance of criteria, importance of 'perceived risks' and critical criteria for each 'perceived risk' (Dunn, W.N. et al. 1983).

Phase III - Specification of importance of key criteria in making decisions

The stages of decision-making call for judgements for risk assessment and risk management. Here the judgements must be used to: a. select the data to be considered in forming a judgement; decide how the criteria should be weighted; b. determine the functional relations between criteria and risk; c. decide how much material should be aggregated or organized into a judgement. Social Judgement Analysis is a methodology, developed from empirical research on human judgement and decision-making, which has been successfully used to achieve greater awareness of the four parameters of the judgement process (Hammond, K.R. and Wascoe, N.E., 1980).

This phase is designed to study how the decision-makers vary in their use of criteria to make judgements about deliberate release cases. The technique used here is Social judgement analysis in which a structured interview is conducted by presenting the respondents with a number of hypothetical scenarios to make judgements. The hypothetical scenarios of judgemental tasks varying in critical criteria measurements will be designed, and the respondents are asked to make the judgements on a scale.

The technique of Social judgement analysis stems from the Social Judgement Theory, according to which the integration of information to form a judgement includes: a. placing a particular degree of importance on each piece of information - referred to as Weight; b. developing a specific functional relationship between each piece of information and final judgement - referred to as function form; and, c. using a particular method for integrating all dimensions of the problem - referred to as the organizing principle (Hammond et al., 1975).

Social judgement theory posits that experts disagree, at least in part, because of the importance that each assigns to the available information and due to the various manners in which each functionally related the data to the final judgement. If experts are asked to make repeated judgements about appropriate task under a variety of well specified conditions, the entire covert cognitive process of each expert judgement policy can be mathematically modelled by the multiple regression equation

$$Y' = b \, X + C$$

where Y' is the predicted judgement, b is the weight and functional direction of each dimension, x is the datum for each dimension, and C is a constant value. The equation can be expanded to include quadratic and non-metric relations. This analysis, that is regressing the expert's judgement (as the criterion variable) on the critical condition (as predictor variable), is referred to as Social Judgement analysis. The algebraic description of an expert's judgement policy can be converted to a pictorial representation by means of interactive computer graphics (Cook, R.L., 1980).

Statistical analyses of the judgements made by the respondents and display of results of these analyses in a graphical form requires the use of computer program called 'POLICY'. The program computes and displays results indicating the

1) weight or relative importance placed on each factor by the decision-maker. These weights are the estimates of the tradeoffs being used by the decision-maker in assessing risk or evaluating release.

2) Predictability of the decision-makers' judgement is also computed by the program.

3) Functional relation between each of the criteria and the judgement are shown in the form of a plot. Similar plots can be used to show the relationship between two sets of judgement, and statistical analysis of these judgements can be performed. Policy descriptions of several decision makers can be compared and groups of similar policies can be identified using cluster analysis.

Significance of the Research Approach

It is to be anticipated that the technology with such novelty, broad application and social significance generates, along with opportunities, attendant problems and uncertainties which the society must address. Thus we find ourselves at crossroads with respect to the difficult question of safety of this rapidly expanding industry. Policy decisions in this area will have long range impacts on our society and environment. Any effort to make the decision process more explicit and improve policy making in this area is very timely and useful. This research intends to be a step in that direction.

Theoretically this approach adds to the literature on risk analysis and decision making under risk and uncertainty, which are crucial areas of study for managing risks in this growing technological age. Examination of the process by which individuals make judgements regarding risk and, ultimately, through societal and political processes to societal decisions about risk acceptability, has been recommended by researchers in the area of risk analysis.

"The study of the degree of similarity between individual perceptions of risk and the levels of risk and uncertainty suggested by scientific research is important, since differences between the two types of estimates may illuminate the basis for social disagreements about risk acceptability and appropriate courses of action (Covello, V.T. et al., 1982)."

This research will contribute to methodological improvements to study policy decision making under uncertainty and incomplete information. The knowledge of multiple perspectives on problem of deliberate release, the establishment of importance of criteria and its influence on judgements, should be an important finding for designing tools of risk assessment useful in policy making. The results of this approach should also provide some insights for designing decision-making system for policy in this area. On the basis of the findings, further research projects can be designed where the interactive phase of Social Judgement analysis can be applied to achieve consensus on policy decisions, by knowing the probable cause of variation in views among various stakeholders/decision-makers.

REFERENCES

Ahmed, K.A., R.E. Ayers, J. Thonton and L. Kenworthy (1985), Natural Resources Defense Council Inc.'s Comments on Proposal for a Coordinated Framework for Regulation of Biotechnology. Natural Resources Defense Council, New York, N.Y.

Cook, R.L. (1980), Brunswick Lens Model and the Development of Interactive Judgement Analysis," in K. R. Hammond and N.E. Wascoe (eds.) New Directions for Methodology of Social and Behavioral Science, San Francisco, CA: Jossey-Bass, Inc.

Covello, Vincent, Menkes, J. and Nehnevajsa, J. (1982), Risk Analysis, Philosophy, and Social and Behavioral Sciences: Reflections on the Scope of Risk Analysis Research, Risk Analysis, Vol. 2, No. 2.

Dunn, William D. and M.J. Dukes (1982), Multiattribute Procedures for Studying Adoption Decision Making, Working Paper of Program for the Study of Knowledge Use, University of Pittsburgh, KU-201.

Dunn, William D., K.P. Kearns, Cahill, A.G., Applications of the Policy Grid to Work-Related Frames of References, Working Paper of Program for the Study of Knowledge Use, University of Pittsburgh, KU-203.

Hammond, Kenneth R., T.R. Stewart, B. Brehmer and D. Steinmann (1975) Social Judgement Theory, in M.F. Kaplan and S. Schwartz (eds.) Human Judgement and Decision Processes: Formal and Mathematical Approaches, New York: Academic Press.

Hammond, Kenneth R. and N.E. Wascoe (1980), New Directions for Methodology of Social and Behavioral Sciences: Realizations of Brunswick's Representative Design, San Francisco: Jossey-Bass.

Hearing Report (1984), _Biotechnology Regulation,_ Hearing before the
    subcommittee on Oversight of the committee on environment and public
    works, United States Senate, Ninety-Eighth Congress, Washington D.C.:
    U.S. Govt. Printing Office.
Kelly, G.A. (1955), _The Psychology of Personal Constructs,_ 2 Vol., New
    York: W.W. Norton.
McChesney, Frances L. and Reid Adler (1983), Biotechnology Released From
    the Lab: The Environmental Regulatory Framework, _Environmental Law_
    Reporter, November.
Office of Science and Technology Policy (1984), Proposal For a Coordinated
    Framework for Regulation of Biotechnology, _Federal Register_, December
    31st.
Office of Technology Assessment (1984), _Commercial Biotechnology An_
    International Analysis, Washington, D.C.: U.S. Government Printing
    Office.
Slovic, Paul, B. Fischhoff and S. Lichstenstein (1984), Regulation of
    Risk: A Psychological Perspective, in Noll (Ed.) _Social Science and_
    Regulatory Policy, Berkeley, CA: University of California Press.
Wines, M. (1983), Genetic Engineering - Who will Regulate the Rapidly
    Growing Private Sector, _National Journal_, October 15.

HOW REAL IS THE RISK FROM TECHNOLOGICALLY ENHANCED

NATURAL RADIATION

Alica Bauman and Djurdja Hovat

Institute for Medical Research and Occupational Health
41000 Zagreb, Yugoslavia

Investigations of technologically enhanced natural radiation have
been worldwide. In most cases the degree of risk was low when large
populations were exposed. The public interest in the issue has arisen due
to involuntary exposure to carcinogenic agents.

Two specific industries, a coal fired power plant and a larger
fertilizer industry have been investigated as a source of natural
radiation with possible synergistic effects from chemical contaminants.

During the investigations indications of the existence of threshold
levels were obtained. In this case a de minimis level could be based on
the observability of health effects.

KEY WORDS: Technologically enhanced natural radioactivity, chemical
contaminants, synergistic effects, risk, environmental
monitoring, mutagenic monitoring, de minimis approach

INTRODUCTION

During the last decade much has been written about the risk to which
the environment, the society and the individual are exposed. Since the
second half of the sixties and above all during the seventies one assisted
to a real proliferation of cost benefit studies concerning the impact on
the environment and the society, originating from different sources of
energy production (Cirillo et al. 1984). The problems of diversification
of primary sources and major sensibility of our culture lead to elements
which have influenced the actual tendency to treat the problem of energy
not in an isolated manner but to include it in a context which is
environmental, social and institutional.

A great influence favouring the production of cost benefit studies,
had the approbation of the USA National Environmental Policy Act" of
1969. This Act gave rise to many environmental impact statements which
were first oriented toward the evaluation of large power production with
special emphasis on the health of the exposed workers.

Human health was and is the preferential reference point of the
technological risk assessment studies. The initial goal was at first to
help the decision making authorities to quantify the complex reality to
easily comparable order. Often the impressions which were obtained
lead the authorities in several directions (80-EHD-48 Canada,

1980), part of which were leading nowhere or crippling further technological progress.

One of the topics which fit into the above mentioned problems is the awareness of technologically enhanced natural radiation (IAEA Safety Ser. No. 9, 1982). Starting two decades ago it has become a favourite topic of research and its impact on the environment and the population has been investigated in many countries. Many of the results raised the question if a thorough investigation was worthwhile at all, or only part of queer deviations from the mainstream of established thought.

In many cases the degree of risk was low, not only for a large population but also what in this case must misleadingly be called "critical population". One such low risk from technologically enhanced natural radiation is the emission from coal fired power plants using coal for combustion with an average content of uranium and thorium (Jacobi et al. 1981). Wrong publicity made possible a wide field of action and even manipulation of public opinion.

In such cases the impact on the environment was usually assessed on the basis of calculated models instead of experimental data from field measurements (Jacobi, 1981). The reason is, that offsite an average coal fired power plant (CFPP) the difficulties in differentiating between the real background and an increase in background level due to normal daily fluctuations of natural radiation are enormous. Even when studies are extended over a longer period the results are inconclusive.

DESIGN OF THE STUDY

In the present study industries producing hardly detectable levels of technologically enhanced natural radiation were avoided by mere chance. The authors followed a different approach investigating a CFPP using anthracite coal for combustion with a very high sulphur content, approximately 10%, where during the seventies the coal with an average of 50 ppm uranium with descendants in secular equilibrium (Bauman et al. 1981, 1982) was mined. Since 1980 the amount of uranium has fallen to 25 ppm, but with wide fluctuations depending on the coal bed in exploitation in the mine. The CFPP uses no system for desulphurization, not even scrubbers, only electrofilters with an efficiency of 99.5% (Bauman et al., 1981). The impact on the environment from the CFPP emission has been extensively monitored to a distance of 15 km continuously and intermittently for several years. The pathways for the chemical and radiological contamination has been defined. Heavy metals, pyrenes with special emphasis on bezo(a)pyrene (BaP) have also been determined (Bauman et al. 1983).

Owing to the concentration of radionuclides during the process of coal combustion, the level of radioactive contamination can be compared to that of surface low-grade uranium mining, with the difference that the secular equilibrium of uranium descendants is here disrupted. Fly ash from anthracite coal usually has a higher concentration factor for ^{210}Pb and ^{210}Po between 5 and 20, exceeding for ^{210}Pb even 100, lower for ^{226}Ra - 1,6 and other radionuclides - ^{222}Rn of the uranium decay series (Bauman et al. 1982). This results in an increased contamination of occupationally exposed workers in the CFPP and in places in the environment where the impact from the CFPP and felt due to meteorological fluctuations (Horvat et al. 1980).

An apparently similar situation exists in the observed fertilizer industry using phosphates from North Africa for the production of phosphate containing agricultural chemicals. This is another industry where, depending on the source of phosphate minerals the same level of radiation exposure is expected as in the CFPP. The source of additional chemical contamination is different. In the CFPP heavy metals, sulphur dioxide and pyrene are prevalent. In the fertilizer industry the dust from rock phosphates, sulphur dioxide, phosphoric acid, fluoride and sulphuric acid and the stored up final products are the main sources of chemical contamination.

Parallelly with the CFPP a study has also been performed in a big fertilizer plant. Necessary changes in environmental monitoring and plant control appropriate to differences in chemical technology have been introduced and the control continuous now for the fifth year onsite and two years offsite, to a distance of 5 km, in the centre of a town with 15.000 inhabitants.

The impact on the environment differs significantly. The immission from the CFPP exceeds the regulatory limits for total alpha activity and in some cases for ^{226}Ra, as well, both in air at a distance of 4 km in the prevalent wind direction. The increases of radioactive contamination from the fertilizer plant are higher by a factor of 100-250 above the average background levels for alpha activity and single radionuclides of uranium and descendants in air but still inside regulatory limits. A network of thermoluminescent dosimeters (TLD); (CaF_2:Mn) was placed inside the CFPP and the fertilizer plant and offsite in concentric circles to a distance of 8 km and 4 km. A network for intermittent or continuous sample collection has been established in both industries. The control of radioactive contamination due to the CFPP includes air, fall-out meat, milk and vegatation. Offsite the fertilizer plant the control is limited to air, ground water and drinking water. Industrial water and waste deposits are included in the control of both plants.

EXPERIMENTAL

On the basis of the monitoring results offsite, WL and ^{222}Rn measurements, an additional type of health control above the usual medical control was introduced in the two investigated industries. The check up of occupationally exposed workers consisted in radiotoxicological urine analysis and mutagenic analysis. The results were compared to a control group.

In the CFPP urine analysis was limited to ^{210}Pb since uranium and ^{210}Po gave negligible or borderline results. In the fertilizer plant for the time being ^{210}Pb only was analysed.

The mutagenic analysis consisted in the beginning only of the analysis of chromosome aberrations, while later on sister chromatid exchange (SCE) was also included.

The first radiotoxicological results confirmed the hypothesis that even at the level of stochastic effects some internal contamination in occupationally exposed workers existed and through mutagenic analysis, that some changes of the gene pool took place (Horvat et al. 1980; Bauman et al. 1985).

On the basis of initial results a systematic screening for possibly contaminated workers was initiated which was easy in the CFPP since the total number of workers never exceeded 200. In the fertilizer plant a representative test group had to be chosen from 4.000 workers. It was possible to choose a representative group in both plants due to systematic measurements of gamma exposure rate around work places and WL measurements performed during different time intervals. All the workers in the group answered a questionnaire in which data on demography, health, family and work histories were included. Additional screening was aimed at selecting workers who had not been exposed to X-rays or irradiation for diagnostic or therapeutic purposes one year before the start of the investigations. Smoking and drinking habits were also checked. All the members of the test group spent part or the whole of their work history in the investigated industries. In both industries some of the workers came from coal mines.

The control group which was included in the study answered the same questionnaire and all members were chosen on the same basis, but were not exposed to natural radiation and chemical contaminants.

Onsite measurements of natural radioactivity showed in both plants that the workers were continuously exposed to radioactive dust. In the CFPP the concentration of ^{210}Pb in air was higher than that of uranium, while in the fertilizer plant uranium was in radioactive equilibrium with descendants most of the time. On this basis it was expected that internal contamination of occupationally exposed workers came from inhalation in the CFPP mainly from ^{210}Pb which was confirmed by urine analysis. In the fertilizer plant, where only ^{210}Pb was determined in urine, there still exists the possibility that part of the internal contamination was due to uranium as the source. The biological consequences of the prolonged exposure to chemical and radiochemical contamination were evaluated by analysis of structural chromosome aberrations and SCE in samples of peripheral blood taken from the workers examined.

In the CFPP 74 people were studied in all. The group comprised smokers and non-smokers. Forty per cent of the workers had an increased ^{201}Pb level in urine. The workers had parallel typical chromosome aberrations and SCE. A better correlation was found between SCE and ^{210}Pb than between ^{210}Pb and chromosome aberrations but all data confirmed the existence of some internal contamination with unpredictable future effects.

As the basic level of ^{210}Pb in urine the average level obtained from the control group 38.5 mBQ/24 h was deducted from all results. The average value found in workers from the CFPP was 120 and the highest 790 mBq/24 h. it seems that synergistic effects with chemical contaminants have a significant influence on ^{210}Pb retention.

In the fertilizer industry 100 workers were examined. The internal contamination with ^{210}Pb was lower than in the CFPP, being 70 mBq/24 h with the highest value of 334 mBq/24 which is less than half of that in the CFPP. Fewer SCE and fewer chromosome aberrations were detected. No correlation was found between heavy drinking-smoking and internal contamination, the habits which were also controlled.

A higher incidence of cancer and higher morbidity were registered in the population around the CFPP, but systematic investigations outside the group, for instance the analysis of fertility changes in the regional population or teratogenic changes to name a few, will start now.

DISCUSSION

The presented studies in two industries contaminated with radioactive materials are typical cases of the effects of technologically enhanced natural radiation as are defined in paragraph 706 introduced for the first time in the Safety Series No 9 published by the IAEA, 1982.

The problem of environmental contamination which cannot be neglected in addition to onsite contamination and the exposure of the workers which are in this paper continuously named "occupationally exposed people" must be regulated. Should all these workers fall into the category of "occupationally exposed people" with all the financial consequences, or should they be treated as a critical group allowing 1/10 of the annual dose limit of 50 mSv? Not to mention the population which feels the impact of the immissions. At present the decision maker is not willing to get tangled in a problem where the solution is still shrouded in mist. If these people in the fertilizer plant and around the CFPP, remain under the term "population", they will be treated by the Yugoslav Code of Federal Regulation" under the dose of 1.70 mSv/year, the limit for the population. At present no authorized limits are defined. A new Yugoslav "Code of Federal Regulations" will be passed based on the ALARA principle (as low as reasonably achieveable) at the beginning of next year. The dose limit for the population will be lowered to 0.5 mSv, thus placing the examined workers automatically into the category of the critical population. Even part of the population around the CFPP will fall into the category "Population at risk".

CONCLUSION

The two specific cases in this paper, the CFPP and the fertilizer industry offer the right circumstances for "de minimis" limitations. The exposure to technologically enhanced radiation is at least three times the background level, which furnishes the means for a clear basis for selecting cut off values.
1. The risk at present is small compared to other risks which are encountered in daily life but continuous and additive.

One of the most difficult circumstances to evaluate the total risk is the potential synergistic interaction between radioactivity and chemical contaminations.
2. The occupationally exposed workers are exposed to many small insults. The total risk is at present wrongly below regulatory concern despite the fact that the effective dose equivalent which the workers receive is higher than for the population at large. They should be treated at least as the critical population, some of them should be even included in the group of occupationally exposed people.
3. In the case of the CFPP the cumulative population risk should not be easily dismissed.
4. At the present stage of technology and the existing situation in both industries it is impossible to further reduce the risk by introducing counter measures.

Since we have embarked on this venture trying to find initially if internal contamination can be detected at the stochastic level, we believe in arriving at a feasible methodology for developing at least a "de minimis" regulatory concern criteria. Our only fear is that our results could be misused by the manipulation of public opinion, thus hindering any technical and scientific progress in these industries.

REFERENCES

1. Cirillo M. C. Ricci P.P. 1984. L'analisi e la valutazione dei rischi technologici, ENEA-RT/STUDI/84/7.

2. Assessing the Risk of Nuclear Energy, 80-EHD-48. Canada.

3. International Atomic Energy Agency. 1982. Basic Safety Standards for Radiation Protection. Ed. Safety Series No 9, IAEA, Vienna.

4. Jacobi W. 1981. Umweltradioaktivitat und Strahlenexposition durch radioactive Emission aus Kohlektraftwerken; GSF-Bericht S-760, Neuherberg.

5. Jacobi W., Paretzke H., Ehling U. 1981. Strahlenexposition und Strahlenrisiko der Bevölkerung. GSF--Bericht S-710, Februar.

6. Bauman Alica, Horvat Djurdja. 1981. The Impact of Natural Radioactivity from a Coal-Fired Power Plant, The Science of the Total Environment, 17, 75.

7. Bauman Alica, Horvat Djurdja, Kovac Jadranka, Lokobauer Nena. 1982. Technologically Enhanced Natural Radioactivity in a Coal Fired Power Plant. In: "Natural Radiation Environment", Editors; K.G. Vohra, K.C. Pillai, U.C. Mishra, S. Sadasivan, Wiley Eastern Limited, Bombay, p. 401.

8. Bauman Alica. 1983. Exposure to Radiation and Chemical Mutagenic Agents at a Coal Fired Power Station, Final Report IAEA Research contract No 2346, Working Paper for the Final Research Co-ordinated Meeting on Comparative Biological Hazards from Low-level Radiation and Major Chemical Pollutants, Bombay, 30. XI - 3. XII.1983.

9. Bauman Alica, Horvat Djurdja, Kovac Jadranka, Marović Gordana. 1982. Risk from Exposure to Radiation and Chemical Agents at a Coal Fired Power Plant. SFRP Annual Congress, X Regional Congress of IRPA, Avignon, p. 473.

10. Bauman Alica, Horvat Djurdja. 1982. Exposure to Radiation and Chemical Mutagenic Agents at a Coal Fired Power Station, SRP Proceed. III Int. Symp. Inverness, Vol. 1, p. 331.

11. Horvat Djurdja, Bauman Alica and Racić Jadranka. 1980. chromosomal Aberrations in Persons Exposed to Low Doses of Ionizing Radiation, Mutation Research, 74, p. 194.

12. Horvat Djurdja, Bauman Alica and Racic Jadranka. 1980. Genetic Effect of Low Doses of Radiation in Occupationally Exposed Workers in Coal Mines and in Coal Fired Plants, Radiation and Environmental Biophysics, 18 p. 91.

13. Bauman Alica, Horvat Djurdja, Kovac Jadranka. 1985. Assessment of Radioactive Contamination in Man from Technologically Enhanced Natural Radioactivity. Proceedings of an International Symposium. Assessment of Radioactive Contamination in Man. Paris, 19-23. November 1984, IAEA, Vienna, p. 555.

SAFETY MANAGEMENT OF LARGE OPERATIONS

Edwin L. Zebroski

EPRI, Palo Alto, CA

ABSTRACT

The discipline of risk management for large scale operations involves a variety of activities, skills, and judgments, in addition to risk assessment. The essential activities in effective risk management include: the continuous monitoring and evaluation of known and potential hazards; decision-making on protective actions or remedies together with marshaling the resources required; managing and tracking of the effectiveness of implementation with feedback to the decisions taken. The general elements of successful risk management activities are described and are subject to explicit functional descriptions and organizational procedures. However, the implicit issues of risk management pose many subtle issues involving the integration of: value systems; safety criteria; real world limitations on timely access to human and material resources; and the ability to achieve timely closure on making decisions and implementing them. Practices in several industries are compared; aerospace, dams, chemicals, EPA on carcinogens, nuclear safety.

KEY WORDS: Risk Management Process; Safety Criteria; Industry Practices; Large Scale Operations; Integration; Implicit Criteria

Scope of Safety Management

Safety management of large operations involves a considerable range of managerial and analytic activities in addition to the fundamentals of risk assessment. The safety manager function ideally must evaluate and integrate a spectrum of hazards ranging from those with high or medium frequency of occurrence to hazards with low frequencies, as well as hypothetical hazards for which there may be no experience, but which, at low probabilities may involve high levels of personnel and financial consequences. The relative weighting of resources allocated to high, medium and low frequency-of-occurrence hazards give rise to a fundamental dilemma in that societal and human values are involved. There is a further complex of financial, insurance, and litigation considerations that overlay the conventional ("expected-value") results of risk assessments.

Another spectrum of analysis and decision-making involves judgments on the adequacy of resources and talents available or accessible, and the effectiveness of the management and monitoring skills and disciplines required to achieve the timely and effective application of such resources. Especially intangible and subjective judgments are involved in determining the timeliness of the evaluations - decisions - and implementation cycle involved in large-scale risk management actions. The criteria for the sufficiency and timeliness of such activities are commonly implicit and ambiguous, and even when they are explicit, often subject to a considerable range of interpretation. The historical defense of "Acts of God" for low-probability, high- consequence accidents is becoming increasingly untenable in most industries, and even in governmental, medical, and educational activities. The broad function of responsible risk management involves, above all, the continuing integration of a set of balanced judgments in these somewhat incommensurable factors, together with a sensitivity to continuing changes in both the exposure estimates, and in the judgmental criteria involved.

Safety management using systematic probabilistic risk assessment has been widely used in aerospace, defense and nuclear industries, and is coming into use in several other areas, including chemical industry, bio-medical industry, and also for the safety of dams, buildings and other structures in respect to earthquake hazards.

Basic Elements of Successful Risk Management for Large Operations

It is possible to describe a near-optimum risk management process in general terms by examining industries or activities that have been highly successful relative to the average performance. It is possible to get a further check on those elements that are necessary as well as sufficient by examining the nature of the deficiencies present when unsatisfactory performance occurs. A third checkpoint can be derived from the recognition that the health and survival of an operation is strong motivation for a balanced allocation of efforts and resources to cover the spectrum of exposures mentioned. Several different formulations are possible, for convenience we can divide the essential risk management activities under five general headings;

- O MONITORING
- O EVALUATION
- O DECISIONS
- O IMPLEMENTATION
- O INTEGRATION

Each of these activities will be discussed in turn.

Monitoring Function

Monitoring is the function that provides for continuing awareness and perception of relevant hazard exposures. Such exposures are inherently subject to virtually continuous change, since they can be influenced by planned or inadvertent changes in the activities undertaken, in the processes or procedures used, in the materials handled, in public or worker proximity to hazard sources, and most fundamentally by changes in the personnel involved in operating, supervising, and managing large scale activities. The inherent abundance of factors leading to change require that monitoring must be a continuous and timely activity involving senior management personnel as well as health and safety professionals. For most industries, there are at least three sources of information that need to be monitored, including: local experience (for a given plant or operation); general experience (of similar plants or operations elsewhere); results of analysis, local and generic.

Local experience is relatively easy to monitor provided only that a systematic and reliable reporting system is established and maintained, and that the managerial and supervisory chain take pains to insure that obstacles to full, frank, and timely reporting are minimized. For either highly structured or informal reporting systems, an essential attribute of success is to provide motivations for the full, frank and timely flow of information that are strong enough, and renewed often enough, to offset the normal tendencies to misperceive or to conceal errors or deteriorating conditions.

The monitoring of local and general experience is essential for adequate risk management, but it cannot provide adequate assurance in respect to low-probability, high-consequence hazards, since only a partial sample of the spectrum of such hazards is ever available from experience. As with experience, analysis of the specific local operation is essential, but it should be supplemented with analysis from similar operations elsewhere. Local experience and analysis often tends to minimize attention to low-probability, high-consequence risk exposures.

EVALUATION

An essential managerial requirement is to assure the timeliness of the receipt and study of information from the three sources discussed above, and the discipline to assure that the significance of incoming information is perceived and communicated in a timely way. This might be called "consequentiality" of the monitoring personnel and operating organization in maintaining a high level of discipline in respect to comprehensive gathering of the relevant information and rigorousness of coverage and timeliness in understanding the data and messages received.

An important though somewhat intangible function in monitoring is the level of sensitivity, insight, and responsiveness of the personnel responsible for preliminary judgments of the significance of local or general experience. Ideally, a decision to move to the next stage-in-depth evaluation - does not depend exclusively on the occurrence of a damaging or injurious event or observation. Many significant or damaging events are seen, in retrospect, as having had precursor events or situations that, while not damaging of themselves, could have triggered the perception that a damaging event was likely. For example, nearly any system or mechanical device has a nominal level of reliability and maintenance or inspection requirements. Record keeping and analysis of trends in reliability or maintenance requirements can provide clues that additional circumstances contributing to failure rates or modes are present, or are developing.

In some industries, industry-wide data bases on reliability behavior of systems and components are gathered and disseminated. Any significant departure from the general reliability expectations, can provide an indication that some unusual factors leading to increased exposure are present.

The establishment and continued systematic support of structured information flow for the receipt and processing of both local and general monitoring information is one of the key requirements for adequate risk management.

Deterministic analysis has commonly been applied whenever an actual failure, or observation of an incipient failure has occurred. Deterministic analysis can range in breadth of coverage. A simple check to verify the presumed controlling factors in the failure or malfunction is sometimes adequate. When this gives ambiguous results, more general failure modes and effects analysis is required. This can be supplemented by a probabilistic analysis of the particular system. Deterministic analysis is also essential to confirm that the design and operating margins are adequate for whatever remedy is selected.

The Use of Probabilistic Analysis in Evaluation

Probabilistic risk analysis is an increasingly powerful and widely used tool for safety and reliability evaluations of various kinds. The term probabilistic risk assessment (PRA) is generally used for a systematic and comprehensive risk assessment of an entire operation. All of the conceivable modes of failure and malfunction are modeled and documented, and numerical estimates of probabilities are developed. Where such a risk assessment has been performed and documented, (and maintained in an updated state) it provides a powerful and convenient logic tool for the evaluation of the importance of a known or supposed failure. It is a basic logic tool for testing the probable adequacy of a proposed remedy. In many practical situations, a simpler and more accessible use of some of the related disciplines can be more practical without the requirement of a comprehensive PRA.

The classical tools of reliability analysis involve developing or finding the data on the expected rates of failure or malfunction. This leads to the concept of reliability centered maintenance (RCM). The frequencies of surveillance, inspection, or testing and the rework or replacement schedules, are adjusted to provide acceptably low rates of failure or malfunction in service. This approach involves the continuing monitoring of inspection and maintenance results.

Sequence Risk Analysis

Intermediate between reliability analysis and a full PRA is sequence risk analysis (SRA). This involves considering the various event chains that can lead to a particular malfunction or failure, typically at a system or subsystem level. It provides a systematic way of examining the various operations, malfunctions, or environmental conditions that can contribute to a particular undesired consequence. This can also provide an objective method for evaluation of alternate remedial measures. Remedies can be tested against the various event sequences, including changes in duty cycles, in environmental conditions of exposure, or in the functioning or introduction of redundancies, backup devices, or means for sensing preconditions that may contribute to malfunctions. The use of probability numbers in an SRA provides a convenient way to display the relative contributions of different factors that can contribute to malfunctions. Used in this fashion, sequence risk analysis (SRA) can be regarded as a subset of a PRA.

The basic output of the analysis and evaluation function is to provide physically correct insights into the principal contributing factors to an undesired type (or rate) of failure. Such evaluation may logically continue to provide a recommended preferred remedy and options together with their cost and schedule estimates.

Decision-Making

Depending upon the size of the risk exposure involved, and the resource requirements of the remedies, decision-making often occurs at different organizational levels. Typically the people charged with safety review and management have only limited authority for the allocation of personnel and resources. They provide recommendations to levels of management with resource authority. Risk exposures can be perceived narrowly; for example as primarily occupational health or safety, or primarily risk to capital equipment or structures, or to the general public in the vicinity of a particular operation, or litigation exposure. Some kinds of malfunctions, even if not damaging to the public or the environment, may nevertheless be perceived by the public as "near-misses" or threats, with consequences on public acceptance and market success. Ideally, the decision-making process should involve people at the organizational levels qualified to consider all of these dimensions of risk exposures and to reach balanced-best-interest decisions.

Given that a risk exposure is newly perceived, or an increase in a previously recognized risk exposure is in evidence, a wide range of issues must be digested and evaluated by the decision-maker. Perhaps the most basic is whether or not an in-depth study or remedial action is required, and if so, on what schedule. This is almost always a difficult decision since the criteria of "how is safe is safe enough? - or soon enough?" are rarely explicit, and }are ultimately subjective. Judgments made are often difficult to rationalize and justify. Nevertheless, such judgments must be faced and the historical record expresses the working of the implicit criteria.

There is evident a range of one to two orders of magnitude in the relative effectiveness of risk management of specific hazards by different organizations. For example, Figure 1 exhibits the distribution of the frequency of activation of safety functions in a population of operating nuclear units. The median value in the indicated time interval was four events. However, about one-fifth of the group had zero or one such event, while another one-fifth of the group had 15 or more such events - (ranging to 40 events or more for four percent of the group.) There are closely similar plant and equipment designs at both ends and middle of the distribution. The integration of safety management activities is not the only factor reflected in this distribution - but it is an important, and usually the dominant factor.

Challenges to safety systems do not necessarily constitute evidence of undue risk, but frequent activations are undesirable because they usually result in some hours or days of plant outage, and indicate at least momentary increase in the contingent probability of some more undesirable or damaging events. Similar distributions are found for various other indicators of performance in many different populations of plants or other large operations.

The next consideration is to reach a judgment on the adequacy of the data, analysis and evaluation leading to whatever remedies are recommended. This may require probing questions to neutralize some of the perception and decision biases that are commonly present in organizations. The deterministic analyst tends to believe in the precision of his results - but may overlook other comparably important scenarios - or important indirect costs. The probabilistic analyst may believe in the comprehensiveness of his event trees and probability numbers but may have oversimplified physical models, and often tends to overestimate low probability and hypothetical scenarios. Both deterministic and probabilistic analysts - when asked to provide uncertainty analysis - often find such a wide range of uncertainties that the recommendations made and the decisions implied become clouded. Operating and construction people tend to discount medium and low probability hazards, and also to discount as inapplicable actual experience in similar facilities elsewhere. People with backgrounds primarily in government and academia tend to focus on worst-case scenarios, and tend to discount the effectiveness of remedies or backup systems. The risk manager must evaluate the sources of each of the judgments, calculations, and recommendations. When a recommendation hinges on a particular calculation, a separate qualified review should be obtained - of the basic assumptions and inputs - as well as of the arithmetic.

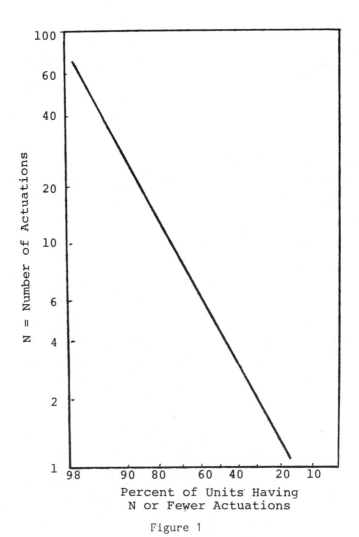

Figure 1

Number of Actuations of
Engineered Safety Functions in Nuclear Power Reactors
(U.S., First Half of 1984)

Allocation of Resources: Talents, Skills, and Materials

Taking an action on almost any recommendation involves diverting resources from other activities (if it can be managed within budget.) Some important issues arise that involve changes in overall budget levels if they are to be accomplished. Persuasive justification of needed corrective actions is a key function of risk management.

Once the hurdle of resource levels is surmounted, there is still a question of the adequacy of available local talents and skills, and the quality, reliability, and costs of whatever imported skills are used. An underlying factor is a judgment of the timing of implementation of a remedy. This is related to the practical working criteria of "how safe is safe enough? - and soon enough?". Conventional judgment at the level of operating supervision and management is pressed to give priority to those activities that are essential to maintain the scheduled and budgeted operation. Items that present a clear and present danger to the safety of continued operation obviously need to take precedence, provided the level of the exposure meets some rational criterion. Items of medium to low probability of occurrence can generally be tolerated as deficiencies for successively longer times.

Intuitive or qualitative judgments should be, and often are, in accord with a version of the Pareto principle on the most efficient use of resources. (C. Starr, 1985) That is to say, remedial measures are undertaken to an extent and with timing such that the expected value (measured by probability and consequences) is reduced to the same order of magnitude as other elements of the entire spectrum of risks. The force of the Pareto principle for intelligent risk management can be seen by an insurance analogy. If the insurance expenditure aimed at mitigating the impacts of one lower-level risk is excessive, then other, higher level, risks become relatively under-insured. Overall risk exposure can be reduced by transferring some of the resources from the lower level risk to the higher level risk. It can be argued that many of the observed deficiencies in risk management, and defects in regulation aimed at limiting risk, occur through neglect of this principle - through too narrow a scope of assigned or perceived responsibility, or too narrow choice of the possible options. The narrow view of options also can result in risk transfer - and overall risk increase - when the safety-motivated action reduces one apparent risk, but neglects the resulting likely increases in alternate risks. Another analogy is useful here. For example, for hazards that produce medium- or high- frequencies of accidents, the expenditures required per life saved or injury averted can often be reliably estimated. It is common to find disparities of factors of ten or more - between different types of hazards - in the historical record of expenditures actually made per life saved or injury averted. Clearly the total number of lives lost and injuries experienced would be reduced if some of the resources with high expenditures per life saved were transferred to the issues that have lower expenditures per life saved. The practical difficulty on a national scale is that the resources that protect one sector often come from different sources or are controlled by different political constituencies. A reduction in an area with an overexpenditure does not necessarily result in an increase in the availability of resources to areas with underexpenditures. This is a national tragedy of inadequate risk management. However, for a risk manager with the success and continued health of a given operation - and organization - as his responsibility, the balancing of resources in proportion to the size of the risk involved, viewed as broadly as possible, is essential to attain the best overall safety for the resources available.

Given that a decision to implement remedies is reached, resources allocated or appropriated, and the responsibilities for the execution of implementation are assigned and schedules projected, there is a further essential function of risk management. Namely; tracking of the implementation in sufficient detail to insure that the expected functional results are achieved and maintained.

Implementation of Safety-Improving Remedies

In some cases implementation is relatively simple and its achievement is objectively determinable by simple inspection. In other cases, implementation may involve the coordinated effort of several departments and many individuals with all the ramifications that are involved in achieving effective project management. If the issue involved has substantial safety impact, it is important that all of the participants understand the functional objectives, as well as the separate tasks and parts requirements. Organizations that have been exceptionally successful in achieving high levels of occupational safety have emphasized the participation of all levels of personnel - from the top to the bottom - in the functional objectives required to produce a safe operation. This helps to minimize the situation in which seemingly minor changes in interpretation of task requirements or specifications, or substitution of a seemingly equivalent component or material or procedure, can degrade the overall result. The attainment of the intended results by informed participation of all or most of the people involved is generally more successful, and often much less costly, than achieving the same result primarily through audit, surveillance, and rework after deficiencies are found or experienced.

Some Examples From Industries; Aerospace

The attainment of adequate levels of reliability and safety in the early years of the aerospace program was in substantial doubt after a high proportion of launch or mission failures. The remedies arose from a combination of classical reliability engineering, intensive component and system testing (including environmental conditions), and judicious use of redundancy and backup components and systems. Particularly with the advent of manned space missions, the reliability objectives for complex systems reached unprecedented levels. A common truism in the early days of this program was that any one of 10,000 components could cause failure of the mission. Even with 99.99 percent reliability of the individual components, there would be a substantial chance of failure. The systematic use of event tree methodology provided a powerful logic tool for guiding component, subsystem, and system testing - and also as a framework to incorporate the continuing lessons from failure and malfunction analysis. This insures that successive generations of designers, fabricators and operators can build on the cumulative experience of the industry and can avoid the need to relearn costly lessons. The observation of periodic repetition of similar errors in design, construction or operation are common in most industries where a systematic and readily accessible system for codification of prior experience is not available. The use of industrial, state or federal codes and standards is a partial response to this need, but it is not always sufficient when the nature of the application or environment, or elements involved are appreciably different from the historical experience.

Safety of Dams and Waterways

The Bureau of Reclamation and the Corps of Engineers have responsibility for large federal water projects. They also provide guidelines for non-federal dams and waterways and share some degree of statutory responsibility with individual states for this area. Although dam failures are relatively rare, historical data is now available for dozens of failures in tens of thousands of dams. Typical causes of dam failures have included over-topping by floods (or upstream avalanche), undermining by geological faults or inadequately sealed substrata, or structural failures from inadequate construction practices, inadequate compacting and sealing of earth-filled dams, and structural failures induced by severe earthquakes. According to the Bureau of Reclamation, a considerable number of smaller dams and several of the large ones have known deficiencies in respect to one or more known hazards. The cost of remedial measures to bring just the federally owned dams up to modern standards is upwards of several hundred million dollars more than the funding available.

The interim measures include increased frequency of periodic inspections, and in some cases sophisticated instrumentation to provide early indications of abnormal conditions, and increased attention to planning for warning and evacuation of downstream areas at risk. There is also increasing intensity of study of hydrology and geology conditions that might contribute to undermining or structural failures. Probabilistic techniques have been used for estimating flood over-topping of dams for many decades. However, more sophisticated probabilistic methods are being brought into use.

A five-step probabilistic procedure is used involving the following elements: (1) An inundation map for alternate loading scenarios; (2) estimates of potential forewarning available; (3) estimates of population at risk and effectiveness of evacuation warnings; (4) site-specific adjustment for degree of success of evacuation; (5) the probable lives saved for a given remedy versus no action.

Chemical Industry

The chemical industry has given primary attention - until recently - to occupational health and safety. Performance is measured in terms of lost work day accidents, with statistics ranging over nearly two orders of magnitude in workdays lost per million manhours worked. The DuPont Chemical Company has long been a leader in performance in this area with the results that its workers are seventy times safer than average for manufacturing industry, and more than forty times safer than the average for people away from work. In recent years, and especially since the dramatic accidents in Bhopal, India, and Soveso, Italy, attention has shifted to low-probability, high-consequence accidents involving the inadvertent release of toxic or carcinogenic chemicals. Also, much greater attention is now paid to the effects of chronic low-level exposures to chemicals. Work place standards set in recent years are commonly an order or magnitude lower than many historical exposure levels.

Probabilistic assessment methods are coming into greater use in the chemical industry and also in the Environmental Protection Agency. The occurrence of long delayed health effects - as for example from asbestos fibers - now poses an additional dimension for balancing efforts in risk management between known and experienced occupational hazards, and low-probability, high-consequence potential exposures to nearby public, and low-level chronic exposure effects.

Environmental Protection Agency

The EPA is representative of the risk management problems of a number of industries where exposure to both natural and manmade chemicals or materials can result in adverse effects on health and longevity. An important guiding principle has been the Delaney Amendment that stipulates that if a substance is carcinogenic at any dose level, then it must be banned, presumably even if the actual exposure levels are many orders of magnitude lower than those which show measurable effects in animal tests. However, rigid application of such a rule quickly faces an absurdity, namely that the natural constituents of most common foodstuffs and most of the essential trace elements are known to be either carcinogens or promoters of carcinogens (or mutagens or teratogens). (Ames, 1983) For a time, this dilemma was sidestepped by grandfathering "old" materials and natural products and concentrating on new chemicals and pharmaceutical products. This led to curious anomalies such as the banning of cyclamate but the retraction of several attempted bans on saccharin (with substantial technical doubts whether either of them is truly a carcinogen.) Different test animals are known to vary in their response to chemicals often by a factor of 1,000 or more with respect to toxicity levels, and with respect to carcinogenicity. Thus it becomes a truism that almost any substance - including ordinary untainted food products, can be found to be carcinogenic (or mutagenic or teratogenic) if fed at sufficiently high levels to a sufficient variety of test animals. Furthermore, the correspondence between animal sensitivities and human responses is extremely uncertain, and has been established to reasonable scientific standards for only a handful of substances. Because of the wide range of inter-species responses already known, it seems likely that when more complete understanding is developed by the techniques of molecular biology, the correspondence between a "worst case" animal test and human response will be rare indeed. A further anomaly with respect to the concept of the Delaney Amendment arises from the increasingly reliable observation that small doses of substances that are toxic or carcinogenic at high dose levels often have measurable beneficial effects at trace dose levels. For example, longevity and fertility of rodents is found to improve with low level exposures to several different toxic substances and also low levels of ionizing radiation. Another area of difficulty in the Delaney concept arises from the observation that some substances which are known carcinogens nevertheless reduce the overall morbidity (increase longevity) of a large sample of test animals. The effect seems to be that the carcinogen increases the incidence of a particular type of cancer or target organ effect, but at the same time reduces the incidence of other cancers sometimes enough to give significantly improved survival relative to controls. (Haseman, 1983) Finally, an additional incentive for reform derives from the increasing perception in both the technical community and in the public that with virtually no substance disprovable as a suspected carcinogen, the choice of things to be banned become subject to manipulation or misguided fear-mongering.

In addition to direct exposures in the work place and in the home, exposures to potentially damaging substances occur via atmospheric air pollution or via pollution of water supplies - either river or groundwater. The Clean Air Act (and Clean Water Act) involves language such as "an ample margin of safety" in respect to the need for control measures for hazardous pollutants. In recent years EPA has moved from the absolutes of zero risk, implied by the Delaney Amendment, or "ample margin of safety" in the Clean Air and Clean Water Acts, to a risk assessment and cost-benefit assessment basis for much of the regulatory decision-making and priority setting. This transition has not come easily since there is a substantial constituency for an absolutist treatment of safety questions, however impractical and unobtainable it may be. However, ecological and esthetic goals remain highly subjective. Nevertheless the pattern of regulatory decisions and recommendations for legislation based on the best available understanding of risks, benefits, and costs is beginning to attain considerable level of acceptance (W. D. Ruckelshaus, 1985).

Nuclear Power Safety Management

Perhaps because of its development as an outgrowth of the technology that led to nuclear bombs, civilian nuclear energy from its inception has involved extensive concern and consideration for "worst credible" accidents. In contrast society has lived for most of a century with large stores of substances that if released by accident could cause hundreds or thousands of immediate fatalities (for example, liquid natural gas, liquid hydrocyanic acid, methylisocyanate, liquid chlorine, etc.). Accidents involving dozens to hundreds of fatalities have occurred periodically with each of these substances and most dramatically the event at Bhopal with a death toll exceeding 2,000 people.

Society also has lived for much of the last century with large stocks of substances that if released can cause latent or long-delayed health effects including cancer (for example, PCBs, asbestos, and a fair number of the 403 toxic chemicals identified recently by the EPA, are stored in the millions of pounds in or near populated areas.) However, prior to the accident at Bhopal, only for the civilian nuclear industry was there continued systematic and open consideration of worst-case and hypothetical accidents that could lead to the spread of toxic agents. These include analysis of the potential for both near-term fatalities, and long-term latent health effects. The first large scale reactor built in a civilian context (as distinct from the military production reactors) was built with a large steel containment sphere to insure that even with inadvertent failures of several of the multiple barriers designed to contain radioactive fuel, radioactivity would still be retained safely.* In addition, current practice is to provide multiple "engineered safety systems" by design so that even if the normal heat removal systems all fail, several layers of backup systems can still be brought into operation. Similarly, redundant systems, with backups, are provided to shut off the nuclear reaction to limit the residual heat to the afterheat only without additional heat from fission.

Initially nuclear power plants were designed to the criterion that no single functional failure (component subsystem or system) would lead to the release of radioactivity. The principal objective of safety design was to insure the ability to cope with a major Loss Of Coolant Accident (LOCA) resulting from a postulated guillotine break of a large diameter pipe in the circulating water system. In the early 1970s a regulatory decision was reached that Emergency Core Cooling Systems (ECCS) should be installed in all reactors, and that these were to be entirely independent of the normal heat removal systems and their backup systems. The extended debate over the ECCS (nearly 30,000 pages of testimony) contributed to a decision to attempt a comprehensive risk assessment of nuclear systems using probabilistic risk analysis. The Reactor Safety Study - (Rasmussen, 1975), provided the first reasonably comprehensive documentation of all of the then conceivable scenarios that might eventually lead to severe damage of the reactor core and potential eventual release of radiation to the environment. One of the important results of the reactor safety study was that relatively small loss of coolant accidents (small break LOCA or stuck open relief valves) made a substantially larger contribution to the overall risk estimate than the more traditional large break LOCA. However, the full significance of this result was not generally perceived until after the accident at Three Mile Island Unit 2 that involved a stuck open relief valve, (together with delayed actions by the operators in turning

---

*Located at West Milton, New York, 1954

on the available backup water supplies, due in part to ambiguous
indications of relief valve closure and of water levels in the system.)

With the mandating of ECCS systems, the style of regulation in the
United States became increasingly voluminous and prescriptive. There were
frequent warnings that simply complying with regulations was not
sufficient to insure safety, and that some of the prescriptive
requirements had counterproductive aspects that could offset the nominal
improvements sought.

After the Three Mile Island accident, the process of licensing
reactors came to a halt for two years and a large number of additional,
generally prescriptive, requirements were drawn up under the heading of
the "TMI Action Plan". (NRC Staff, 1980). The cost of the delays and
backfits involved were estimated as more than $35 billion as of 1981 and
have increased substantially since then (perhaps doubling again if delays,
cancellations, and replacement power costs are included with backfit
costs.)

It became evident both to many of the regulatory people and to
industry people that a more systematic means was needed for the evaluation
of the need for changes and the balancing of potential counterproductive
or risk transfer effects of proposed changes. A sharp increase in the use
of probabilistic risk analysis to evaluate specific backfit issues has
often been useful to resolve such issues rationally. It appears to be
increasingly successful for generic issues that involve systematic review
by the Nuclear Regulatory Commission Headquarters staff. Most concerns
arising from malfunctions or events during plant operation are regarded as
having generic elements and are subject to such systematic reviews.

On the other hand, construction deficiencies, whether real or
suspected, whether physical or documentary, are regarded as plant-
specific, and the need for or timeliness of corrective action is often
treated as an absolute without regard to the safety significance of the
known or presumed deficiency. This has led to extensive delays and in
several cases cancellations of essentially completed plants despite a
reasonably strong presumption that the actual quality levels involved - if
given a valid probabilistic evaluation of safety significance, were at
least as good as most of the plants now operating in the U.S. and
worldwide. This has been a financial disaster, not only for the owning
utilities, but in a real sense for the regions involved and for the entire
national economy. For the nuclear units completed prior to 1979, total
generating costs were substantially lower than the alternative bulk
supplies (with the possible exception of old hydro capacity, but including
most future hydro capacity). There was further leverage from the rapid
displacement of use of highest-cost fuels (oil and gas), the use of which
for the production of electricity has declined sharply as nuclear capacity
has grown. About two-thirds of the nuclear units completed after 1980
will continue to be competitive or lower in cost than equivalent new coal-
fired generation. For another one-third, the generating cost, at least
initially, will be somewhat higher than for new coal-fired capacity.
However, even most of these plants are economically viable in the long run
since uranium fuel costs are stable at 30 to 40% of coal fuel costs for
the foreseeable future, whereas coal generation costs will continue to
increase as the environmental requirements on mining, transportation, and
control of combustion emissions and solid wastes, take greater effect.
Nuclear plant capital costs are largely written off in the first decade of
operation so that even plants with long delays and excessively high
initial capital costs are useful on a life- cycle basis. The problem of
"rate-shock" remains for any new capacity - coal as well as nuclear,

because of higher capital costs, and higher interest rates, relative to old capacity. Furthermore, the social contract implied for a regulated industry has, in effect, been broken. For the plants that have been built with attractive costs and which provide low cost power generation for utility systems, only normal returns on investment are permitted - even where such units represent a bonanza in low-cost energy relative to other contemporaneous sources available. However, projects that are delayed, experience high costs, or are not completed, are now commonly largely excluded from the allowable base for return on investment. With this "heads I win, tails you lose" arrangement, further investment in plants not already in the pipeline is effectively precluded, regardless of long term need or potential economic merit. Nevertheless, the effective operation of existing capacity (at present 91 units in operation - 26 more licensed for construction - and so far generating over 15 percent of all U.S. electricity) represents an enormous investment in dollars, human effort, materials and technology. Capacity factors of similar plants, in a more hospitable regulatory and legal environment in Europe and Japan, commonly attain operating factors of 80 percent or better while average factors range near 60 percent in the United States. The increased use of probabilistic risk assessment and a cost/safety benefit rationale that the NRC is beginning to practice is a very important and hopeful prospect for the future. It can contribute to producing additional energy equivalent of 30,000 megawatts of capacity - without any additional plant construction - from the existing plant investment, simply from the rationalizing of timely and effective risk management decisions.

French Program - Safety Management

An important example of this prospect is available in the French nuclear program. There is a near absence of prescriptive regulation. There are only several dozen pages of general functional requirements by law. Both operating and construction deficiencies or perceived hazards are evaluated by experienced teams of people involving designers, constructors, operators and risk analysts. Four levels of priority judgments are made. However unlike the U.S. situation, only the first level (the "zero level") covers items that are mandated to be on critical path to completion of construction, fuel loading, or startup and operation of a power plant. The other three levels reflect judgments of the relative importance, cost and time required to implement remedies that have been decided. These three levels carry no deadlines, but indicate a relative rate of effort or allocation of resources towards completion. (Bacher et al, 1985) There is a stipulation that the engineering, testing, checkout, incorporation into training and procedures, etc., be matured and tested before entering any changes into widespread routine use. With 40 reactors in operation and 23 under construction, there have been less than half a dozen "zero level" critical path remedies mandated since 1982. (This would contrast with hundreds or perhaps thousands of such items mandated by the NRC for plants currently under construction in the U.S.) Interestingly enough, the French program appears to have applied a major fraction of the improvements and backfits considered in the U.S. TMI action plan, often at a faster pace than in the U.S., and with virtually no impact on construction and operation schedules, and with costs that continue comparable to costs experienced in the U.S. in the 1970s.

CONCLUSION

The integration of risk management decision-making, is basically an unavoidable responsibility for the operator, but often influenced or dominated by the regulator. It appears to have reasonable prospects of finding common ground through well-disciplined risk analysis. The resulting social benefits can be considerable - substantially better safety results for the resources expended, and hopefully, less frequent occurrence of safety-motivated actions that sometimes result in risk transfer without significant overall reductions in risk experience.

REFERENCES

B. N. Ames, Science, 221, 1256 (1983)
P. Bacher, J. Kus, and D. Vignon, This volume (1986).
J. K. Haseman, Fund. and Applied Toxicology 3, 1-2 (1983)
Nuclear Regulatory Commission, Staff Study, NUREG-0660 (1980).
Rasmusssen, N., The Reactor Safety Study, WASH-1400, MIT and NRC, (1975).
Ruckelshaus, W.D., Issues in Science & Technology 1, No. 3, 1985.
C. Starr, Risk Analysis in the Private Sector, C. Whipple and V. Covello,
    Editors, Plenum Pub. Co., N.Y. (1985).

THE USE OF OPERATING EXPERIENCE TO REDUCE RISK

P. Bacher, J. P. Kus, and D. Vignon

Electricité de France

ABSTRACT

The French nuclear program is based on a high level of
standardization. However, operating experience of the first units,
information on operating experience from foreign units, technical
developments and new requirements from the safety authorities have led to
some modifications from the initial design of the plants.

A major problem is to maintain standardization of all the units when
at the same time modifications are implemented on units, some of which are
under construction and others in operation. Another problem is to assure
that an improvement on one point will not prove harmful on another. An
organization and procedures have been set up by Electricité de France to
collect operating experience data, analyze them, and decide where and when
to apply eventual remedies to different units of a given series and to
different series (900MW, 1300MW ...). These decisions take into account
risk analysis, and the state of construction, start-up, or operation.

A system of determining priorities has been used, and examples of
criteria and priority items are given.

KEY WORDS: Nuclear Plant Safety; Standardization; Risk Management;
           Operating Experience Feedback; Electricité de France

INTRODUCTION: THE REASONS FOR A NUCLEAR OPERATING EXPERIENCE FEEDBACK

In 1985, nearly 60% of the French electricity shall have been
generated by PWR system nuclear plants, equipped with nuclear steam supply
systems provided by FRAMATOME. This percentage will exceed 75% of 1990.
Owing to a thorough standardization policy, only two types of nuclear
steam power supply systems have been retained: in 1990, on the power grid,
there will be 34 units provided with similar 3 loop power steam supply
systems (900 MW units) which represent a total of 32000 MW and 18 units
equipped with similar 4 loop power steam supply systems (1300 MW units)
which represent a total of 23000 MW.

For EDF, the only owner and operator of a family of power plants that
are not diversified, the specific structure of its generating system has a
double effect, as far as concerns hazards:
- as a power supplier, not only must EDF consider the hazards
  represented by nuclear plants for people or for the environment:
  these hazards are analyzed by nuclear safety specialists as part of
  the design basis accidents studies, but it must also ensure the
  reliability and continuity of the power supply. This means getting

secured against the accidents that are the most likely to happen, constituting no radiological risk for the environment but which might entail unavailabilities of a generic kind. The identified risk is not only the risk for the environment, it is also the more subtle and more difficult situation stemming from repetitive technical incidents, affecting facilities directly or the acceptance of nuclear plants by the public opinion.

- on the other hand, even though it goes along with a certain vulnerability of the power generation system, the high degree of standardization can also be used to reduce hazards. In particular, it justifies a specific effort to ripe benefit from the operating experience by giving a special value to the precursor event analysis: an incident with a recurrence probability of 0.1 per year statistically occurs about 3 times a year out of a number of 30 similar units. Should it imply an unavailability - even a short one - or should it be a precursor of incidents having effects on safety, then efforts that are justified by the number of units must be made to reduce this frequency. The same incident could pass relatively unnoticed in non-standard plants.

With such a background, where the risks EDF is faced with are not only these of major accidents, no clear risk management system has been implemented yet: moreover, there is no certainty as to whether it is possible to present this problem in a totally rational manner that would permit solving it in a clear way.

However, in addition to the traditional methods of reducing risks (the good old safety analysis method; the design, construction and operation quality, the probabilistic studies, the personnel training and so on..) EDF undertakes a systematic analysis of the nuclear operating experience feedback, with the aim of taking the best advantage of the precursor incident analysis. In this respect, there is a double objective:

- to reduce the frequency of incidents likely to entail power generation unavailabilities, even though they have no effect on safety.
- to reduce the frequency of major incidents that are likely to have some effects on safety. Such are the design principles of the nuclear steam power supplies based on defense-in-depth and the presence of barriers that major accidents can only result form a simultaneous combination of independent and individually more frequent incidents.

As far as concerns nuclear safety which is the major concern of this presentation, the operating experience feedback aims at the following targets:

- Identifying the precursor events in order to define and implement the necessary corrective measures before the accidents occur.
- taking advantage of the standardization of PWR nuclear units.
- checking that changes -when changes are required- have no harmful side-effects before implementing them on all the units.
- taking full advantage of the data derived from the actual plant operation, in order, if necessary, to homogenize their safety level, especially on new standardized plant series.

1 - THE OPERATING EXPERIENCE FEEDBACK ORGANIZATION

In EDF, the operating experience feedback process is governed by the following guidelines:

- to gather systematically as much data as possible and to disseminate it widely both inside and outside EDF.
- to involve, as much as possible, designers, operators, manufacturers and safety authorities in their analysis.

-   to draw lessons from the experience so that units planned and under construction as well as operating units will benefit.

1.1 - The data gathering

The collected data refer to all abnormal events observed during units tests and operation. They can sometimes result from special audits requested by engineering and design departments. These data are gathered not only in the EDF units but can also originate from foreign power plants (through the Institute of Nuclear Power Operation, or through the UNIPEDE "USERS" system for instance).

The data supports used are mainly:
-   periodical reports issued by plants (daily, weekly, monthly or yearly reports).
-   incident reports, including the event description, the preliminary analysis and the considered provisional actions.
-   reports of audits considered as necessary to gather data on critical subjects (scrams, waste processing...).

The events thus gathered are stored with their main characteristics in a national computerized file called "The Event File." ALL EDF engineering and design departments and nuclear plants are connected to this computerized network as well as the safety authorities, and manufacturers such as FRAMATOME. Today, the event file updating is centralized, but plants will soon be able by themselves to enter events in the computer as soon as they occur.

1.2 - Data analysis and sorting out

All these data must be analyzed and sorted out in order to separate what is important and related to design from what is casual. Taking account of the units standardization, we also pay great attention to the events' generic aspect.

The available data and a first locally achieved analysis allow the operations or engineering and design departments to carry out their analysis, involving the manufacturers if necessary.

These analyses are submitted to specialized committees made up of the various EDF departments representatives (designers and operators). Any subject that seems to be important enough to justify a revision of the basic engineering documents will be submitted to analysis and further studies.

It should be noted that this main stage is achieved according to expert opinion. Then a follow-up report referring to the event is established. It gathers the first recommendations: its content is introduced in the second part of the national computerized file, the "Event File." This follow-up report will be used as a reference for all associated studies and application decisions. Besides, all references of the various documents concerned shall be stored in it.

1.3 - The change definition, study and decision

Taking account of the standardization of units, the study of all changes, other than minor changes, is generally achieved at the national level by the initial designer who defines the corrective measures to be taken as well as their mode of application. On the one hand, this is the guarantee of a better quality of change studies but on the other hand, it

could go along with a certain heaviness in the process. This is the reason why design changes studies are assigned a degree of urgency, which permits defining priority levels and to focus all means on what is considered - in accordance with the Safety Authorities - as important and urgent:
- Level 0:
  A study having priority, started at once, and carried out with all means that can be made available.
- Level 1:
  A study having priority, achieved with all normal available means.
- Level 2 and 3:
  A study normally achieved as part of short
  or
  medium-range programs.

  This priority concept is also found at the level of a dual plant modifications. Studies are carried out in two steps:
- In the first one, the design change principles and guidelines are defined.

  Once made, this proposal is submitted to the approval of the responsible persons who take into account the cost and duration of works in relation to the current state of each unit, the considered impact of the event if it recurs, and the expected benefit of the corrective measures.
- The second one takes place after the decision is made, and concerns the detailed design.

  The first step systematically includes a check to determine whether an incident having occurred in a certain kind of unit (900 MW for instance) is likely to happen in another type of unit (1300 MW). Documents of a generic type (specifications and technical sheets) are systematically updated.

1.4 - Achievement

  As far as concerns starting or operating units, the changes are implemented according to a program determined by EDF, with concurrence by the Safety Authorities. As regards units under construction or in startup, lists of the changes achieved or to be achieved are submitted to the approval of the Safety Authorities. This is done in each of the main steps requiring a preliminary agreement of these authorities.

  The last data stored in the computerized follow-up report is the implementation program (estimated and achieved).

1.5 - Taking the human factors into consideration

  According to present results, 60% of significant incidents are due to human failures. Thus, it is of the utmost necessity to take this phenomenon into account, and in this field, the following actions are taken:
- The design improvements, and we find here the above-mentioned process.
- The improvement of operation procedures.
- The integration of the EDF departments that are in charge of the personnel training in the operating experience feedback process.
- The distribution among the plant's personnel of a periodical report describing in a clear way the main incidents.
- The creation of an "incident library" that can be accessed from all the computer-assisted training units set up near control rooms.

1.6 - The manufacturers information and participation

Such an organization, which is so useful to gather the experience of a designer/operator such as EDF must also involve manufacturers in order to allow them to improve the design and manufacture of their equipments. This does not concern only future facilities but also the present units in which the required design changes will be made.

On the basis of the above-mentioned organization, manufacturers are informed and take part as follows:
- The accessibility to some events of the "Event File," selected according to the specific supply scope of the manufacturer (this is mainly the case of FRAMATOME),
- Periodical technical meetings allowing the exchange of detailed data on selected topics such as nuclear auxiliary systems and equipments, reactor coolant system components, fuel handling and storage system,
- Manufacturers are requested to achieve the analyses and studies that refer to the equipments or systems they supply. If necessary, they are also asked to carry out the design change: this is of the utmost importance to maintain the basic principles of the initial design.

1.7 - Relations with the Safety Authorities

As EDF is the unique counterpart of the French Safety Authorities, the implementation of close relations based on a wide ranging and real-time information flow and a strict control was facilitated.

The Safety Authorities defined criteria regarding the significant incidents that must be immediately reported by the operator and followed by the issuing of a detailed report on the incident within two months.

Concurrently, the Safety Authorities have access to the national "Event File" and thus are informed in real-time (within three days approximately nowadays) of all events regarding the equipments concerned by the operating technical specifications, and of the decision made by EDF.

Thus, concurrently with EDF, they can undertake the analysis allowing to compare the different points of view in specialized meetings. Besides, a systematic review is achieved twice or three times a year within the "Reactor Permanent Group" (the ACRS equivalent) on the "operating experience feedback" subject.

2 - EXAMPLES OF OPERATING EXPERIENCE FEEDBACK IN FRANCE

2.1 - Incidents on the reactors building air locks

A) Description

There were six incidents of this type which occurred on 900 MW units between August 1982 and September 1984. These incidents can be classified into two groups:
- The possibility of a common mode failure - due to a faulty design - entailing the loss of air supply of the inflatable seals of two airlock doors,
- The poor information and late reactions of operators in the case of deteriorated conditions of the air locks air supply (following periodic testing,...).

These incidents had no effect (negligible radiological effects, low

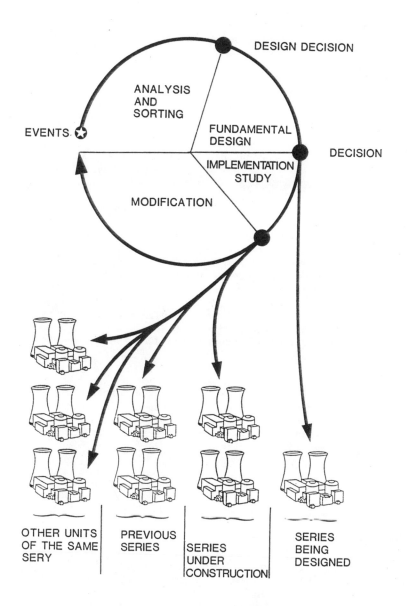

DESIGN DECISION

ANALYSIS
AND
SORTING

EVENTS

FUNDAMENTAL
DESIGN

DECISION

IMPLEMENTATION
STUDY

MODIFICATION

OTHER UNITS
OF THE SAME
SERY

PREVIOUS
SERIES

SERIES
UNDER
CONSTRUCTION

SERIES
BEING
DESIGNED

132

duration of the integrity loss) but they are precursors of the loss of a major safety function (the containment barrier integrity) and were reported as being significant to the Safety Authorities.

B) The causes analysis

In October 1982, the EDF operating experience feedback committee in charge of the operating incidents analysis decided the priority level 0 study of causes and lessons to be drawn. A follow-up report was established especially to allow the Safety Authorities to get informed of the development of this matter. The main causes appeared to be:
- the rupture of a plastic plug of a pressure reducing valve common to the two air lock doors,
- the presence of only one alarm signaling "air lock defect" which did not facilitate the operators diagnosis,
- the complexity of the air supply system of the door seals.

C) Lessons drawn - decisions

In order to bring the 900 MW units third barrier back to a suitable safety level, the following corrective actions were decided:
- the use of a stronger improved plug on pressure reducing valves,
- the doubling of the air supply system of an air lock doors seals with the addition of a device allowing the automatic isolation of the failing system,
- the addition on each air lock of a backup compressor,
- the setting of a specific "air lock untight" alarm.
The first modifications were implemented in November 1983, and are completed today in accordance with the Safety Authorities as units are shutdown.
Thus, following several incidents, the first of which occurred in August 1982, all identified causes of significant incidents were removed from 900 MW units air locks, while their safety level was improved. At the design stage, the 1300 MW units were provided with full sealing joints and so are not concerned with this matter.

2.2 - The break of the control valve stem on the steam inlet to an Auxiliary

Steam Generator   Feedwater System turbine

A) The event description

In July 1983, a break of the control valve stem occurred while an auxiliary feedwater turbine-driven pump of the first PALUEL unit was tested for the second time.

B) The causes analysis

After expert evaluation, it appeared that this break resulted from an excess of vibrations due to a faulty design of the valve-stem assembly and its guide. Because of its precursor feature, the incident was reported as being significant to the Safety Authorities. The EDF operating experience feedback committee in charge of the analysis of events occurring at the starting stage decided to achieve a priority "level 1" study of a design change. A follow-up report was established to inform the Safety Authorities of the development of the matter.

C) Lessons drawn - decisions

In 1985, i.e. one year after the first incident occurred, a solution

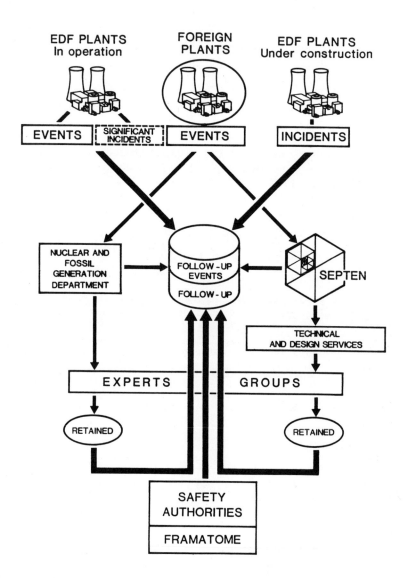

consisting in a forged monobloc valve-stem assembly with double guides was put into operation after qualification on test bench. It could then be implemented in all the 1300 MW units (as a modification on the first units and at the manufacture stage on the turbine driven pumps that had not been delivered yet).

Concurrently, taking into account the other precursor incidents that occurred in DAMPIERRE 2 in October 1983 and in KOEBERG, as well as the similarity between the 900 MW plant series turbine driven pumps and those of the 1300 MW plant series, it was decided to manufacture a prototype valve, to quality it on a 900 MW unit and then to generalize its use on 900 MW plant series. Modifications on the first 900 MW units were achieved in the summer 1985, and the others will take place as units are shutdown according to a schedule predefined with manufacturers.

2.3 - The cavitation of a containment spray system pump during transition from direct containment spraying to recirculation

A) The event description

In GRAVELINES-1 in January 1981 and in CRUAS-1 in August 1982, while tests were achieved at full rate, during transition from direct spraying to recirculation from the reactor building sump, the pump cavitated which entailed a flowrate loss in spray rings for dozens of seconds.

B) The causes analysis

Following the CRUAS incident which brought out the generic and precursor feature of the GRAVELINES incident:
- The incident was reported as significant to the Safety Authorities,
- In April 1983, a study of causes and lessons to be drawn was requested with a priority level 2 by the EDF operating experience feedback committee in charge of the analysis of events occurring at the startup stage.

A follow-up report was established and the analysis achieved showed that, taking into account the pipes geometry, an inclusion of air could be formed between valves and pumps on lines originating from sumps, the venting operation being critical during the system refilling.

C) Lessons drawn - decisions

A vent pipe and a valve were added on pipes, downstream from each check valve, in order to facilitate the venting operation, both on 900 MW and 1300 MW plant series.

The 900 MW plant series modifications were started in September 1983 and nowadays they are completed as units are shutdown. The design change is integrated as early as the new units are first achieved.

CONCLUSION

EDF evolved no particular risk management method in its nuclear program implementation. However, in addition to the usual actions taken to reduce risks, EDF has implemented a system allowing to take full advantage of the operating experience feedback. This system is based on the following principles:
- the systematic gathering and analysis of incidents,
- the strong involvement of the expert evaluation achieved by operators, designers (the EDF design and construction department) and

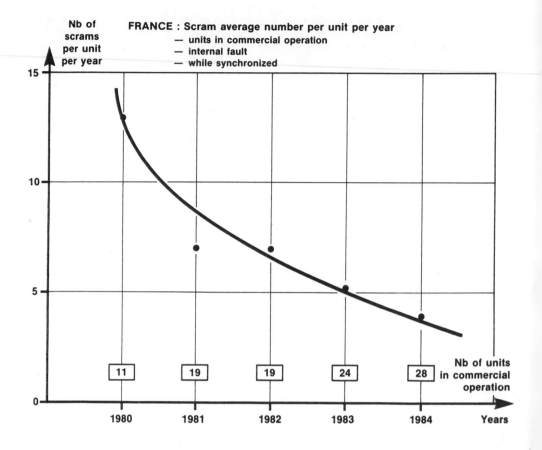

Nb of scrams per unit per year

FRANCE : Scram average number per unit per year
— units in commercial operation
— internal fault
— while synchronized

Nb of units in commercial operation

| 11 | 19 | 19 | 24 | 28 |

1980   1981   1982   1983   1984   Years

manufacturers when deciding which actions shall follow the analyses.
- The EDF motivation to run this system which allows steady improvements in operating availability,
- the continuous information of the Safety Authorities and the achievement by these very authorities of a strict and systematic control of the process performance.

This system has permitted the attainment of very good results in the availability factors, which exceeded 83% in 1984, (using U.S. definitions.) This percentage is also being maintained near this level for 1985.

It should be also noted the very significant reduction of the average number of scrams per unit per year during the last years. At present there are less than four scrams per unit per year and we hope to reach about two scrams per unit per year by the end of 1986.

A VIEW ON CONSISTENCY

OF NRC RISK POLICY

Robert M. Bernero

Director, Division of Systems Integration
Office of Nuclear Reactor Regulation

ABSTRACT

The occurrence of the Three Mile Island (TMI) accident greatly
accelerated the older, more conservative practice of imposing new safety
requirements to such a massive rate of change in safety requirements that
the safety of plant operations was threatened by the frantic pace of
keeping up with constantly changing requirements. The TMI accident also
accelerated development and use of probabilistic risk analysis (PRA), a
comprehensive, more balanced basis for evaluating safety requirements.
Four initiatives at the Nuclear Regulatory commission (NRC) define a
consistent risk policy for the NRC. They are the development of a safety
goal, the backfit policy, the Indian Point risk decision, and the Severe
Accident Policy Statement.

KEY WORDS: Risk, Risk Assessment, Safety, Safety Goal, Severe Accident,
NRC, Regulation, Backfit, Indian point

Ever since the beginning of nuclear power it has been recognized that
the central element of public risk is the severe accident, the accident in
which the reactor core is severely damaged or melted. This concern is the
origin of many of the fundamental safety requirements for nuclear power
plants, defense-in-depth, multiple barriers around the fuel, a substantial
containment structure, redundant systems for core cooling, etc. The
conception and application of safety requirements in the first two decades
of power plant development was without the benefit of a comprehensive
method of risk analysis which could be used to weigh the relative value of
specific requirements. Nevertheless, the conservatism born of the
underlying concern for public safety led to the imposition of many safety
requirements resulting in a relatively high degree of safety with, if
anything, a substantial number of superfluous requirements. The
occurrence of the Three Mile Island (TMI) accident greatly accelerated the
older, more conservative practice of imposing new safety requirements
leading beyond superfluous requirements to such a massive rate of change
in safety requirements that the safety of plant operations was threatened
by the frantic pace of keeping up with constantly changing requirements
(NRC-75).

A comprehensive, more balanced basis for evaluating safety
requirements, probabilistic risk analysis (PRA), came on the scene with

the Reactor Safety Study (NRC-81) just a few years before the TMI accident. It is ironic that the TMI accident also accelerated the development of risk analysis techniques. Thus, in the early 1980s we found the safety regulation of nuclear power in the U.S. greatly in need of a new discipline, at the same time that the means for that discipline fell to hand. I would like to offer my personal observations on four initiatives at the Nuclear Regulatory Commission (NRC) in these last few years which appear to be independent but which, I believe, constitute a coherent set defining a consistent risk policy for the NRC. These initiatives are the development of a safety goal, the backfit policy, the Indian Point risk decision, and the Severe Accident Policy Statement.

These closely related NRC actions will chart the general regulatory course for years to come. These four constitute a logical set, that should be mutually consistent in philosophy and approach even though the realities of administrative practice make it virtually impossible to deal with them together in a single combined action. Difficulties that may be apparent in one or the other, may be better understood in the broader context of the four actions. The development of the safety goal is the articulation of the clearly established principle that there is a level of sufficient safety for nuclear reactors where society's resources are better spent if they are left to other purposes. Certainly there are legitimate questions regarding just where that level of sufficient safety lies, and whether it is possible or useful to measure safety with available risk analysis techniques. Nevertheless, it is acceptable in principle that a threshold of concern does exist and the NRC, the responsible regulatory authority can seek to define it, or ways to determine whether a safety issue crosses it. For some years now the NRC has explored alternative formulations of safety goals and evaluation criteria. We are now just completing a two-year evaluation of a specific safety goal formulation (NRC-84) armed with a wealth of experience in the forms and methods of analysis that are needed to examine the potential utility of such a goal.

The essential basis of the safety goal under evaluation is that the risk of nuclear power plant operation should have a negligible effect on the risk of any person living near such a plant. As a measure of negligibility, the NRC is considering a risk increment of only 0.1%. This is certainly not a threshold of tolerance but rather a description of a clearly acceptable or timely negligible increment of risk for those closest to a plant. Taking such a strict standard as a goal comes somewhat easily because early conservative approaches to nuclear reactor safety achieved such a low level of risk. Taking such a strict standard also affords great advantage since it carries within it substantial margin for error. Undue risk to a member of the public is certainly not found at 0.1%, or at 1%, or at 10%, or perhaps even at 100%, although I certainly don't propose to argue that a factor of two change in background risk is acceptable for a regulatory goal. The point is that the goal, at 0.1%, holds orders of magnitude of margin against undue risk.

The NRC has not chosen a safety goal yet, nor even chosen to implement one. However, we must recognize now a formidable record that indicates that there is a general compatibility between most formulations of nuclear plant safety goals and most available quantitative estimates of risk or safety. In other words, it appears that our present estimates of risk all seem to indicate that the present generation of light water reactors are safe enough - if it is useful to consider a PRA-type formulation of safety goals and PRAs to compare to them.

I mentioned earlier that by the early 1980s it appeared that the poorly disciplined imposition of new requirements, or backfits, to existing plants actually threatened overall safety. The NRC has adopted a backfit policy and rule (NRC-85A) to bring discipline to this process. The NRC backfit policy does not rely slavishly on PRA or cost-benefit analysis derived from PRA. Rather, it calls for testing each proposed requirement in a systematic way including, where possible, good cost-benefit analysis. The essential questions are whether the total effects of the proposed change are a genuine and substantial improvement of plant safety, and whether the amount of safety improvement justifies the cost of that improvement. The backfit policy then is a corollary of the safety goal philosophy. Just as we can define an acceptable level of safety and use it as a threshold of consideration we can use methods and criteria to determine whether a safety issue crosses that threshold and warrants change.

The safety goal and backfit policy are initiatives dealing more with criteria for judging acceptable safety than with safety decisions themselves. The other tow initiatives reflect much more the actual safety decisions. The first of these two is the Indian Point risk decision (NRC-85B). From the time the Indian Point plants were first proposed there was intense interest in their degree of safety because of the proximity of the many people in New York City and its suburbs.

It is not surprising then that a petition was made after TMI accident to shut down these reactors because of the high population around them. After that petition the owners of those plants and the NRC engaged in an exhaustive risk analysis, which culminated in an NRC hearing and Commission decision passing judgment on the acceptability of the risk at those plants (NRC-85B).

The Indian Point risk decision was a test in a single preeminent case of the safety goal and backfit principles. Are the two large reactors, at that most populous of U.S. reactor sites, safe enough and, if not, what should be done about it? The decision in response to these questions was made after the most extensive risk analysis ever made of a nuclear power station. The finding was that after certain relatively modest changes were made to correct unique vulnerabilities in these plants, they are safe enough for continued operation. They were not found to be safe enough because they were exceptionally different and better than a typical light water reactor; they are safe enough because they are typical light water reactors which have been thoroughly screened for outliers, for significant unique vulnerabilities. The level of safety of a typical light water reactor can be safe enough, even on the most populous site. But this conclusion or any other conclusion on reactor safety does not lead us to dismantle our regulatory program, rather we are maintaining a vigorous program of surveillance and evaluation of experience to foresee causes of accidents and thereby prevent them. And from this experience alone even, we see the value of a systematic search for outliers in any plant.

And now there is the severe accident policy statement (NRC-85C). It enjoys the foundation of the arguments contained within it, the additional support of more detailed analysis in its companion document NUREG-1070 (NRC-85D). The massive support of the many other related works of this agency and others in this field (NRC-85E), and a logical consistency with the other three related actions of the Commission described above. In simple terms this policy statement says that, under certain conditions of assurance, light water reactors of current design are safe enough. For future plants the policy statement lays out those conditions of assurance. Those conditions for future plant licensing include the thorough satisfaction of the relevant current safety requirements, and the systematic use of risk analysis from the outset to test the resistance of the plant design and to discover its vulnerabilities. A new plant produced by this process is not expected to be greatly different from the latest reactor plant designs. Rather, I expect it to be a refinement of current designs, providing a much greater assurance of low risk rather than a dramatically lower estimated level of risk.

For existing plants the policy statement refers to the already well-developed interaction with the Industry Degraded Core Group (IDCOR) to develop and implement those conditions of assurance and the methods of their application which are appropriate and consistent with our safety goal and backfit philosophy and which presumably will be technically consistent with the Indian Point risk decision. The IDCOR activity is discussed in this same session by Dr. M. H. Fontana's paper.

NRC can stand with pride on its record of many years of pioneering work in quantitative risk analysis which I believe raises it to preeminent status in that field among regulatory agencies. The NRC has, in fact, now gone well along toward the development of two different safety evaluation processes which together provide great assurance of no undue risk to the health and safety of the public. The primary method is the classical or deterministic method of regulation which is standard practice for regulatory agencies. The supplementary independent method is PRA-based, used to illuminate alternatives in the classical method or to test the value of decisions made by it. The four initiatives I have discussed in this paper come together as a consistent building on this combination of methods. I believe they are activities which retain the good features of the conventional safety review process, which use PRA carefully and to good advantage, and which will lead to consistent policies and decisions in nuclear power plant safety requirements.

REFERENCES

(1) (NRC-75) WASH-1400 (NUREG-75/014) Reactor Safety Study, An Assessment of Accident Risks in U.S. Commercial Nuclear Power Plants, USNRC, October 1975.
(2) (NRC-81) NUREG-0839, A Survey by Senior NRC Management to Obtain Viewpoint on the Safety Impact of Regulatory Activities from Representative Utilities Operating and Constructing Nuclear Power Plants, USNRC, August, 1981.
(3) (NRC-84) NUREG-1050, Probabilistic Risk Assessment (PRA) Reference Document, USNRC, September, 1984.
(4) (NRC-85A) U.S. Nuclear Regulatory Commission CLI85-06, May 7, 1985.
(5) (NRC-85B) NUREG-1128, Trial Evaluation in Comparison with the 1983 Safety Goals, USNRC, June, 1985.
(6) (NRC-85C) NUREG-1070, NRC Policy on Future Reactor Designs, USNRC, July, 1985.
(7) (NRC-85D) U.S. Federal Register 50FR32138, August 8, 1985.
(8) (NRC-85E) U.S. Federal Register 50FR38097, September 20, 1985.

APPLICATION OF INTEGRATED RISK ANALYSIS AT EPA

Daniel Beardsley

Regulatory Integration Division
U.S. Environmental Protection Agency
Washington, D.C. 20460

ABSTRACT

The Environmental Protection Agency was created fifteen years ago as an umbrella organization for a large number of individual statues and programs distributed throughout the federal Executive Branch. This led to an often fragmented approach to environmental protection: pollution was removed from the air and water and put -- where? On the ground, or back into the air or water.

This presentation will focus on an alternative methodology for analyzing environmental problems -- one which attempts to define the range of exposures to substances across media that occur in any given community, to assess the relative significance of each, and then to develop cost-effective control strategies for reducing the environmental risk. This new "integrated" methodology takes into account residual risks from potential control strategies, thus allowing the decision-maker to minimize pollution transfer. The approach contains the potential for far better overall management of environmental problems. its principal limit is lack of scientific knowledge regarding pollutant effects.

KEY WORDS: Environmental Pollution; Control Strategies; Risk Management
              Exposure Assessment.

In a narrow sense, risk analysis is an array of technical tools and administration procedures EPA uses to support writing regulations and making policy decisions. But in EPA, it has come to represent a whole philosophy about what should be the fundamental premises upon which environmental protection decisions are made.

Let me briefly clarify some terms. By risk assessment I mean the scientifically based process of establishing the physical facts about risk -- defining probable effects, weighing evidence, discovering who might be exposed, and calculating estimates of possible harm. Risk management is the realm of policy, in which, taking into account economic and other considerations, we decide what action, if any, to take about a particular risk. Integration is an overarching process of setting priorities for pollution control actions given limited resources.

EPA has always been a risk management organization. It is only recently that we have taken care of assess explicitly the factors which support our decisions. This is happening because our agenda is quite

different from what it was in the early days. We now need to take some of
the priority setting responsibilities that Congress used to shoulder.
Examining why this is true brings us quickly into the domain of risk
assessment, risk management, and integration.

Ever since EPA was created, Congress has been the risk manager. Out
of the morass of issues under discussion in the 1960s, the Congress wisely
focused the new Agency's actions on controlling the grossest forms of
pollution first. EPA staff developed engineering solutions to obvious
pollution programs. In this initial phase we wrote basic regulations like
New Source Performance Standards for electric utilities, started up the
SIP planning process, and set the municipal construction grants program in
motion. Our emphasis was on swift, enforceable controls to protect public
health and the environment by getting large tonnages of "conventional"
pollutants out of the air and water. The results have been impressive.
By the mid-nineteen seventies, you could see the streetlamps in Pittsburgh
and fish in at least some of the rivers in Connecticut.

The Agency obviously must continue this work as the statutes require.
but we are now being asked to turn our attention to the much more subtle
and difficult problem of controlling toxic chemicals. By the end of the
last decade, advances in measurement technology revealed that air and
water that seemed pure ten years ago were, in the actuality, contaminated
with toxic chemicals. Often the degree of this contamination is
exceedingly small, but it is nevertheless significant because many of the
substances turn out to becarcinogens. Our dramatic early victories
against obvious environmental targets have given way to a campaign of
attrition against literally thousands of potential enemies.

In this hall of mirrors, risk analysis is the tool we hope to rely on
to distinguish real villains from phantoms, and to focus our limited
resources where they will do the most good.

Without risk analysis, where are we? The traditional engineering
approach, aimed at the conventional pollutants like sulfur dioxide and
particulates, was based on a clear consensus about what sources needed
control. We don't have that consensus today because toxic chemical risks
are so highly uncertain, so diffused throughout the environment, and ties
to so many different and unfamiliar sources. Scrubbers and catalytic
converters and activated sludge plants are expensive mechanical attachments
for controlling pollution from obvious sources like power plants, cars and
sewers. With toxics there is usually no appropriate way to employ this
hardware-oriented add-on approach on the scale that has been so successful
up to now.

It's hard to escape a military analogy here. EPA programs to control
conventional pollutants have been like a conventional military campaign,
fought with heavy machines against visible and empaced pollution
sources. Toxic chemical management is much more like a guerilla war, with
many of the same tactical and psychological problems that make guerilla
fighting the nightmare that it is. The targets are small and elusive, and
none of the traditional weapons seems to work very well. The population
is not only terrified about its own safety -- it's also deeply divided
over the means and ends of public policy being carried out in its own
name. To fight this campaign successfully we desperately need to build up
consensus, in all sectors, about what we are trying to do, and how we plan
to do it.

Inescapably, EPA must participate more in the priority setting
process that Congress has traditionally reserved for itself. Congress
sets the general guidelines, but the Agency must share in making many of

the tough decisions on what to control and in what order. In addition, these decisions have to be made on top of a whole history of other decisions, often made on the basis of different types of evidence. We now often find, for instance, the past actions have simply moved pollution from one part of the environment to another, sometimes with little or no measurable gain in health or environmental protection.

Cross-media pollution, as these inadvertant shifts are called, is an orphan that we have only recently, and begrudgingly, begun to acknowledge as largely our own creation. We shouldn't have been surprised that the massive effort to install sewage treatment would burden the country with a mammoth sludge disposal problem. But we were. We shouldn't have been surprised about the millions of tons of ash and scrubber sludge that our air pollution program produces. but we were. The reason was that our decentralized structure had set up bureaucratic incentives to virtually ignore these side effects when we wrote the regulations.

As the Agency's agenda moves towards control of toxics, it's especially important to find ways to bridge the distance between the different program fiefdoms. Many toxic chemicals are inherently mobile among media, so cross-media problems will probably be more of a problem in the future than they have been in the past. So long as the water program focused on BOD, there was no reason for the air program to take notice. but once it becomes apparent that volatile organic solvents tend to migrate to air -- even though they are originally discharged as water pollutants -- the air program has to pay attention.

The shift to a toxics-dominated regulatory agenda has raised other issues besides intermedia transfer. One glaring problem was that the different programs often worked from different data when dealing with the same chemical. One might be treating a chemical as a potent carcinogen when another was not. And there was the gobal question of setting overall priorities. How could we be sure that we were addressing the worst risks first? Setting toxic control priorities is difficult enough within a single program, but we have six major programs operating simultaneously on six essentially unrelated agendas. Can they ever by integrated?

Such questions were worrying people around the Agency when Bill Ruckelshaus took office in 1982. Ruckelshaus was the one who started the push to implement risk analysis systematically across the whole Agency, and during his tenure he occasioned a number of reforms.

One was the development of official guidelines for five major areas of risk assessment: cancer, reproductive risk mutagenicity, complex chemical mixtures, and exposure assessment. These go a long way toward improving the consistency of regulatory judgments from one program to the next.

In additions, EPA has set up a "Forum" on risk assessment that includes some of our most senior scientists. It meets regularly to discuss risk assessments in progress, areas where new guidance is needed, and developments in toxicology and other risk assessment disciplines.

But the scientific progress of assessing risk is only half the issue. Assessments have to be translated into decisions through the regulatory process. This is the domain of "risk management." While our different statutes do not allow us to achieve the same degree of quantitative consistency that we hope for from risk assessment, we have gone a long way to better document the values we bring to regulatory decisions, and make intelligent comparisons of what we are doing from decision to decision.

This brings us to the topic of how, and to what degree, we can integrate various program policies into some more coherent whole.

As you know, EPA has no umbrella statute that sets its primary agenda as the Occupational Safety and Health Act does for OSHA, but it wasn't until the dimensions of toxic chemical problem were known, and until major cross-media transfers began to show up, that we really had to face the basic inefficiencies of running a large regulatory agency with six major enabling statutes.

We decided to use risk analysis -- rather than more predictable bureaucratic approaches like reorganization -- as the integrating theme because risk reduction, either to human or ecological health, is the best working approximation we have to describe EPA's general mission. Within limits, we believe it can be a common denominator for measuring many different actions, a sort of Rosetta Stone for opening up communication among the separate programs.

To test this proposition we launched several integrated cost-effectiveness studies on existing and prospective controls on the most important industry sectors EPA regulates. The goal was to determine how close the agency had come, in the past, to an optimum pattern of risk control. Were we getting the most risk reduction available, per control dollar? Were we embarked on a course that would reduce risk efficiently in the future, given the choices still open? The analysis developed an integrated cost-effectiveness model that included, for typical industrial plants, information of all discharges to all media, the processes that emitted them, and the costs and removal efficiencies of all categories of possible emission control. It used dispersion models to estimate health and environmental effects of each industry's releases under all contingencies, then calculated total health risks to surrounding populations using available dose-response information. This data was used to determine which set of controls constitutes the most cost-effective set of regulations to apply.

Our first review was of the iron and steel industry. That analysis showed that we had not been particularly efficient, from a multi-media perspective, in developing regulations in the past. More important, perhaps, was that few of the regulations under consideration at the time of the study lay on the cost-effectiveness curve for reducing additional risk. Only two pending actions appeared cost-effective, in terms of human health protection, for regulating facilities in all regions of the country.

We are now using the exact same kind of analysis on some of the broad policy problems currently facing the Agency. For instance, we are developing an integrated strategy to address municipal sludge disposal -- the biggest example I know of an inadvertant cross-media pollutant shift. Our current will work creates a single integrated strategy encompassing land application, ocean dumping, incineration, and all other methods of sludge disposal.

But the place where I believe integrated risk analysis will lead to particularly significant long-term changes is in the way the Agency does business with its regional offices, and in our relationship with state and local governments. You can see this already in the Administrator's new air toxics strategy, which emphasizes local solutions. The trend is also clear in the RCRA, underground tank, ground-water and Superfund programs, all of which are beginning to demand accurate appraisals of risk on a geographic-specific basis.

Controlling toxic chemical risk on a local basis makes sense for several reasons. The most compelling is that even where all national standards are being met, risks might still be unreasonably high. There may be an usually high water table, bad meteorlogical conditions, or some other combinations of local factors that needs special attention. Looking at it the other way, it makes no sense to write a national regulation to solve a unique local problem. Finally, by closely analyzing what is going on locally in terms of toxic chemical exposure, we may reveal problems that escaped general notice at the national level.

Where chemical risks are concerned, local variations in conditions tend to be extremely important, and the best way to control toxics may well be through a cost-effective package of State, local and Federal controls.

For these reasons we have, over the last few years, been involved in pilot projects in several metropolitan areas -- Philadelphia, Baltimore, and the Silicon Valley -- to set up local programs to deal with toxic risks on a geographic basis. The projects are established as cooperative ventures. EPA supplies money and technical assistance, the local governments provide data and staff assistance, review the results of the analysis, and guide the scope and direction of the study.

So much for the sermon on integrated risk analysis and management. Now is the time for confession. Risk theory is analytically so seductive that it may be tempting us to ignore or downplay the significance of areas of environmental policy that cannot be reduced to numbers and equations. We have to remember at all times that risk analysis is simply a tool that can be used well or badly, and that it has important practical limitations.

Point one, risk management is a very data-hungry enterprise, and data is expensive. Good rat bioassay studies take two years to do, cost about $100,000, and you need at least two to draw any decent conclusions. Even if money were no object, there aren't many laboratories available, and there are tens of thousands of chemicals in line for evaluation.

Point two, we don't really understand the mechanisms of cancer, and are really still just speculating about the effects of chemicals at the very low levels at which we observe them in the environment. The next Nobel prize could conceivably invalidate half the regulations on our books -- or demonstrate convincingly that we should have twice as many.

Point three, nobody, except the helpless rate in the laboratory is exposed to just one chemical at a time. The rest of us are living in a dilute soup of hundreds of chemicals contaminating us from every conceivable direction. Somewhere along the line, all the one-in-a-million risks we worry about when we regulate benzene, or some other chemical, pile up to make the one-in-three chance we each have to getting cancer in our lifetime. Does this incremental, chemical-by-chemical, approach to regulation really make much sense?

Point four, cancer isn't the only risk we should care about, but it happens to be the easiest one to analyze. Is our regulatory program biased toward cancer risk simply because the risk equations are linear? Even though we have come up with risk assessment guidelines for mutagens, teratogens, and other effects, we really still know very little about environmental exposures and behavior health effects, and subtract ten years of lack of research.

Point five. Politics. I include this in the list of practical problems because it is one. Risk assessment is a creature that only a mother could love. Nobody on the outside has much use for it. One side thinks it's just an excuse for inaction, the other thinks any mention of cancer will start a firestorm of public alarm and heedless regulation.

Beyond these practical problems lie even deeper ones having to do with mission of environmental policy itself. Properly done, risk assessment unravels many problems quite nicely, laying out each thread to be measured and counted. We have fastened onto an intellectually elegant tool that works very well to rationalize one aspect of the Agency's mission -- the protection of human health. To do this it assumes that each chemical acts independently, and that each increment of control will provide an increment of benefit. While these are only assumptions, they are plausible ones and probably quite appropriate for developing cancer policy. But what happened to the old ecological adage that everything is connected to everything else? The assumptions of risk assessment are quite inappropriate for dealing with the environment as a whole -- with acid rain, with protection of sensitive areas like estuaries and wetlands, or with global issues like the greenhouse effect.

The important thing to remember is that risk assessment is an artifact for helping make necessary judgments in the face of considerable uncertainty. We are definitely riding the pendulum swing toward making more and more policy through risk analysis, but the approach is by no means a panacea. Over the past couple of years of EPA has invested a lot of intellectual capital designing and installing risk analysis procedures for our regulatory programs, but we now have created a predisposition to downplay problems that don't fit neatly into the new orthodoxy. Risk assessment, by itself, can't set broad policy directions.

What does all this mean for the future? While it is not clear how any individual action will be changed, we can at least conclude the following:

First, we are looking toward more efficient and centralized management of the policy and regulatory development process. Among other things, this will mean more attention on intermedia pollution transfer and a better regulatory decision process. This includes economic as well as risk data.

Second, we expect that environmental protection decision-making will be shifted increasingly to the regional, state and local levels, in response to out understanding of what will be the nature of toxics pollution problems in the future.

Last, I hope we see a resurgence of interest in long-term ecological issues, and a genuine attempt to find effective analytical tools for considering them in the balance along with human health risk.

DEVELOPMENT AND APPLICATION OF RISK ANALYSIS

IN DUKE POWER

Warren H. Owen

Executive Vice President
Engineering, Construction, and Production
Duke Power Company
Charlotte, North Carolina

ABSTRACT

Duke Power Company managers have available to them today a set of
analytical tools to provide risk evaluations for input into the decision-
making process. This paper describes the development of risk analysis
techniques within Duke Power Company and the growing application of these
techniques in our work.

Duke's initial involvement with risk analysis techniques began in
1973 with the formation of a small probabilistic reliability group in the
Design Engineering Department. The Reactor Safety Study (WASH 1400) and
the Three Mile Island accident accelerated interest in larger scale
applications for our nuclear plants. As a result, the Oconee
Probabilistic Risk Assessment, co-sponsored by Duke and the Nuclear Safety
Analysis Center, was undertaken. Shortly thereafter, dedicated groups
were established to develop and apply risk analyses in the design and
operation of our nuclear stations. A Probabilistic Risk Assessment (PRA)
for the McGuire Nuclear Station was completed in 1984, and a PRA on the
Catawba Nuclear Station is in progress.

Duke's PRA studies have been used to evaluate nuclear station
operational, design, and regulatory issues. Similar techniques are also
being applied beyond the nuclear area into such varied problems as
availability improvement, spare parts procurement, plant life extension
studies, and computer system contingency planning. Other areas of
potential application of risk analysis techniques are under study.
Duke's activities in risk analysis have not been developed as a
centralized risk management program. Senior management's approach has
been to monitor the application of risk analysis and to encourage managers
at all levels to use the results as inputs in decision-making.

KEY WORDS: Probabilistic Risk Assessment (PRA), Risk, Reactor Safety, and
Risk Management.

INTRODUCTION AND BACKGROUND

Duke Power Company managers have available to them today a set of analytical tools for use in decision making. These analytical tools facilitate the consideration of risk at all levels of decision making within Duke. Presently, both deterministic and probabilistic analytical capabilities exist within Duke's organization. Although each technique has its own strengths and weaknesses, each also provides a unique perspective for the decision maker. For example, deterministic analyses focus on the consequences of an event and probabilistic analyses focus on the likelihood of an event. The relationships between these analyses produce an assessment of risk. When combined with sound engineering judgment, these techniques provide valuable and complementary tools for prudent management.

"Risk Management", although only recently viewed as a unique subject, is a function that has always been performed by competent managers. Risk aversion and risk acceptance are factors to some degree in almost all decisions within large, technologically advanced organizations. Without question, the consideration of risk has always been present in the nuclear industry.

Historically, the nuclear industry has primarily addressed risk through the application of the "defense-in-depth" philosophy. This philosophy has resulted in the creation of functional barriers through the use of redundant and diverse plant features to provide protection for the public. The major managerial consideration is this philosophy is to determine the prudent number and types of functional barriers required to assure adequate protection of the public health and safety. These determinations have relied heavily upon engineering judgment and deterministic analyses. Little information regarding the likelihood of various accident conditions was initially available. As the sophistication of nuclear designs and the complexity of nuclear regulation increased, this lack of knowledge on event frequency, and scenario definition, was compensated for by increasing the degree of conservatisms in deterministic analyses and by expanding the use of "what if" engineering. Unfortunately, the proliferation of "what if" questions and the increasingly conservative analyses they spawned began yielding information that, in many cases, was focused on pursuing absolute protection rather than adequate protection. Consequently, the conservatisms were forgotten and the analyses considered as realistic. The inevitable result was the pervasive use of "what if" scenarios as a surrogate for risk in the selection of design bases.

The initiation of the Reactor Safety Study, WASH-1400, brought the powerful tools of probabilistic analysis into play within the nuclear industry. Probabilistic Risk Assessment (PRA) has now become relatively common in nuclear applications in an attempt to answer the questions of scenario definition and likelihood. PRA is moving toward maturity as a tool for engineering applications. Although questions remain on uncertainties in both data an methodologies, probabilistic calculations do provide information on event frequency. Therefore, probabilistic techniques provide the decision maker with a new a unique perspective not previously available. This additional perspective adds to and complements the knowledge obtained from engineering judgment and deterministic analyses to provide the decision maker with an enhanced understanding.

This paper summarizes the development and application of

probabilistic analysis capabilities within Duke.

DEVELOPMENT OF PROBABILISTIC CAPABILITIES

Duke began to incorporate probabilistic analysis capabilities into its engineering activities approximately ten years ago. At this time, a small reliability analysis group was formed within the Electrical Division of the Design Engineering Department. Although initially concerned with the reliability of electrical power systems, this group's scope eventually broadened to include equipment procurement evaluations and data analyses. The success of these initial efforts, combined with the demonstrated value of the technology provided by the Reactor Safety Study (WASH-1400), resulted in a formal internal assessment of probabilistic analyses for both reliability and safety applications with Duke. It was during this time frame that the Three Mile Island (TMI) accident occurred.

During the five years following the TMI accident, Duke placed heavy emphasis on the application of probabilistic techniques to safety analyses. There were many reasons for this emphasis. However, two of the more important reasons were: 1) the growing awareness of the need for studies that would provide additional insights into the design and operation, as well as training for operators of nuclear power plants, and 2) the recognition that PRA methods were going to play an important role in the regulation of the nuclear power industry.

Duke's first major undertaking was a joint project with the Nuclear Safety Analysis Center (NSAC) to perform a PRA on the Oconee Nuclear Station.[1,2] This project was an industry effort to provide other utilities, as well as Duke, with "hands on" experience with PRA and a tutorial document for other plant assessments. Eleven utility engineers, five from Duke, participated on the project team. Engineers from three leading PRA consulting firms provided technical expertise and NSAC provided project management. The Oconee PRA provided valuable insights into the design and operation of Oconee. These insights ultimately led to several Duke-initiated plant modifications. However, just as important, it provided "hands on" training in the use of state-of-the art PRA methods and valuable lessons in how to manage a PRA.[3]

Duke's participants on the Oconee PRA project team formed the core of the project team that conducted a PRA on the McGuire Nuclear Station.[4] Unlike the Oconee PRA, the McGuire PRA was a Duke-initiated effort, with Duke providing project management and a majority of the project's engineering labor. The project emphasized use of Duke personnel with solid design and operation experience. Contractors provided specialized technical expertise and guidance, as well as a portion of the engineering labor for the systems analysis segments of the study. The philosophy of the project was to develop a "production" PRA, i.e., the analysis was to use existing risk assessment methodologies and develop new ones only when deemed absolutely necessary. Additionally, the project's focus was to develop an engineering tool for future use.

Utilizing the experience gained and lessons learned from the Oconee PRA,[5] the McGuire PRA was successfully completed within the project's schedule and budget. Just as important, the McGuire PRA also provided Duke with additional "hands-on" training in probabilistic analysis techniques. In addition, the McGuire PRA provided a test case for a PRA review methodology developed under the auspices of NSAC.[6]

At present, Duke's probabilistic analysis efforts are centered in a group of approximately 20 engineers and technicians located within the Mechanical/Nuclear Division of the Design Engineering Department. The major ongoing activity at this time is a PRA of the Catawba Nuclear Station. Duke is providing project management and essentially all engineering labor for this study. In addition, the application of probabilistic analysis techniques, gained through Duke's PRA experience, is being aggressively pursued in many areas of power plant design and operation, e.g., maintenance practices and design modifications.

APPLICATION OF PROBABILISTIC CAPABILITIES

The most obvious application of probabilistic methods within Duke has been the use of PRAs to: 1) identify risk-important characteristics of nuclear plant design and operation, and 2) feed risk-related information into the design process. This assures that risk impact is a consideration in the design of plant modifications. For example, the turbine building flooding analysis in the Oconee PRA prompted an evaluation of several modifications to reduce the risk from internal floods. The obvious modification to implement was an automatic system for isolating condenser cooling water (CCW) flow. However, subsequent PRA analyses demonstrated that the proposed automatic isolation system would actually increase risk.[7] This was due to the fact that the CCW system supplies water to several important cooling water systems. As a result, other more appropriate modifications were designed and implemented to provide a substantial reduction in plant risk. Perhaps more importantly, though, the use of PRA analyses prevented the inadvertent creation of a larger problem.

An equally important application of PRAs has been in improving operating procedures and training. For example, the McGuire PRA identified a loss of nuclear service water scenario as an area where existing procedures were inadequate. In follow-up evaluations with design and operations personnel, it was found that a less prominent cooling water system could supplement nuclear service water in emergency conditions. Thus, not only was the need for an improved procedure identified, but valuable insights were gained on the beneficial interconnections possible between cooling water systems.[8] In addition, PRA results identify key operator actions, thus providing important focal points for training programs.

Probabilistic techniques must be fully integrated into the day-to-day design and operation activities in order to fully achieve successful and cost effective long term utilization. In striving for this goal, longer term PRA applications within Duke include the use of PRAs to evaluate design modifications and in addressing regulatory issues. Duke has recently implemented a program to evaluate the impact of proposed design modifications on a plant's risk profile. This program provides a risk-impact review on each proposed design modification. Based on the results of this review, more detailed analyses are performed as appropriate. The usefulness of such a program is demonstrated by a proposed modification to McGuire's Nuclear Service Water System. Although the original intent of the proposed modification was to reduce maintenance costs, the risk impact evaluation indicated that the dollar-equivalent of the resulting increase in risk was far greater than the anticipated savings. The modification was not implemented. Regulatory applications also include risk impact evaluations as well as technical specification evaluations. An example of the former is an evaluation of the NRC-mandated reactor vessel level monitoring system. Using the Oconee PRA, the monitoring system was shown not to be cost-effective. However, Duke was still required to install the system. Regarding technical specifications, Duke has been testing an EPRI-sponsored computer code, SOCRATES, for use in developing risk-based technical specifications. Duke is very optimistic about the use of PRAs in developing technical specifications and is continuing its investigations in this area.

As mentioned earlier, Duke is aggressively investigating the application of probabilistic techniques, learned primarily through PRA, into many areas of plant design and operation. Specific examples are reliability-centered maintenance (RCM), system reliability studies, and plant life extension studies. RCM is a procedure developed by the aircraft industry for establishing preventive maintenance (PM) programs.[9] The objective is to focus PM activities on areas that are important to plant reliability. Duke is currently testing this procedure on a system at McGuire with the intent of significantly improving the cost effectiveness of preventative maintenance. System reliability studies serve many purposes. However, the continuing focus is cost effectiveness. For example, the desirability and location of spare main step-up transformers are being evaluated. These analyses will provide a primary basis for Duke's decision.

Another application of system reliability studies is plant life extension evaluations. Duke is in the process of upgrading its older fossil units to increase their operating life. However, because of the many proposed modifications that evolve from these studies, it is difficult to select and then prioritize those modifications to be implemented. Probabilistic techniques will be tested as a means of guiding the selection and prioritization process.

It should be mentioned that uncertainties are associated with all applications of probabilistic techniques. However, these uncertainties are not unique to probabilistic analyses. All analyses, whether probabilistic or the traditional deterministic, contain uncertainties. In fact, many probabilistic analyses go to great lengths to identify and quantify uncertainties. The use of sensitivity studies also greatly enhances an analyst's understanding of the potential impacts of the identified uncertainties. Therefore, the quantitative estimation of uncertainty, combined with sensitivity studies, enhances the decisionmaker's understanding of his alternatives.

CONCLUSIONS

Duke has found probabilistic analysis techniques to be a valuable tool for use in decision making. Continued emphasis on the involvement of Duke's engineering and operations staff in the development of these tools is an important factor contributing to the success Duke has experienced with probabilistic techniques. Duke has found that the techniques, combined with deterministic analyses, provide the decision maker with a broader perspective of an issue. Probabilistic analyses have on occasions identified subtle problem areas not readily apparent in deterministic analyses. It is recognized that there are uncertainties associated with probabilistic analyses, that in some cases are rather large. These uncertainties, however, simply tend to reinforce the fact that even with a multitude of analyses present, judgment is an important factor in decision making.

Organizationally, Duke's activities have not been developed as a centralized risk management program. The approach has been to encourage and monitor the application of risk analysis at all levels of decision making. The result is improved decision making at the lowest practical level of the organization and a more cost-effective allocation of resources.

REFERENCES

1. Oconee Probabilistic Risk Assessment Project Plan, Nuclear Safety Analysis Center, NSAC-7, November, 1980.
2. A Probabilistic Risk Assessment of Oconee Unit 3, Nuclear Safety Analysis Center, NSAC-60, June, 1984.
3. Lewis, S. R., Managing PRA Projects: Some Lessons from the Oconee PRA, Paper presented at the Executive Conference on Methods for Probabilistic Risk Assessment, Arlington, Virginia, April, 1982.
4. McGuire Nuclear Station Unit 1 Probabilistic Risk Assessment, Duke Power Company, April, 1984.
5. Sugnet, W. R. and Lewis, S. R., Oconee Probabilistic Risk Assessment: Methodology, Applications, and Experience, Paper presented at the International ANS/ENS Topical Meeting on Probabilistic Risk Assessment, Port Chester, New York, September, 1981.
6. An Intensive Peer Review for Probabilistic Risk Assessment, Nuclear Safety Analysis Center, NSAC-67, March, 1984.
7. Daniels, T. A. and Canady, K. S., "A Nuclear Utility's View on the Use of Probabilistic Risk Assessment," Risk Analysis, Volume 4, Number 4, 1984.
8. Dougherty, E. M., Dolan, B. J., and Hudson, F. G., Plant Modification: Applying Human Reliability Analysis to the Risk Assessment of McGuire Nuclear Station, Paper presented at IEEE Topical Meeting on Human Factors and Power Plants, Monterey, California, June, 1985.
9. "Equipment Reliability Sets Maintenance Needs," Electrical World, August, 1985

THE PROCESS HAZARDS MANAGEMENT PROGRAM AT DUPONT

John G. Page

Director, Safety and Occupational Health
E. I. du Pont de Nemours and Company

ABSTRACT

Continual change is constant in risk management in large company that manufactures and handles hazardous materials. Unless one considers all factors in the real world of plant management, risk analysis may fail to take into account the risk of someone -- an employee, a contractor, a supplier -- making a change. Risk analysis accuracy is limited by the risk of the unknown -- those things that we haven't anticipated or given thought to. It is the challenge of the manager to manage change to reduce risk. In Du Pont operations, the process hazards management program includes: training to prevent unwanted change; process hazards reviews to detect change from original design; operating and emergency procedures and preventative maintenance to prevent change; audits and critical equipment inspections to detect change; and incident investigations to identify causes of change. Du Pont's 10 principles of safety will be presented and discussed.

KEY WORDS: Risk Management; Hazardous Materials; Process Changes; Principles of Safety

In learned forums of this type, there's always a risk of misjudging the quality of a message by measuring its quantity. That risk of miscalculation is greater, I'm sure, on the part of the speaker than on the part of the audience.

The urge to quantify has always been strong, as many of you know, across the river in official Washington. And I understand from a recent squib in the New York Times that the following list of calculations is informally circulating in government circles:

- The Lord's Prayer is stated in just 56 words.
- The 23rd Psalm consumes 118 words.
- Lincoln's Gettysburg Address -- 226.
- The Ten Commandments -- 297.
- And the U.S. Department of Agriculture's order on the price of cabbage -- 15,629 words:

I promise you that my talk today will be shorter than the USDA price order for cabbage, and at least as interesting.

The topic of today's presentations -- practical risk management of large operations in aerospace, chemicals, dams and nuclear power -- is probably more timely today than when-the program was first put together. It is a topic, also, much on the mind of the general public and the subject of widespread news coverage of tragic air crashes and toxic chemical releases.

One new columnist has speculated that perhaps this highly publicized rash of tragedies points to an inability on the part of industry to manage safety in today's high technology society.

Nonsense. I'm here today to refute any notion that safety and technology are not compatible. In fact, as we know, new technology is in many cases enabling us to improve the margin of safety for our employees and for citizens living in the vicinity of our operations.

A more likely explanation, I submit, is that in most of these incidents something changed. And so safety management, to a large extent, is managing change. I want to leave you with just two thoughts today: the importance of change and the importance of management commitment in managing that change.

Before I elaborate, let me give you a little background on our safety culture in Du Pont.

We've been managing safety for nearly two hundred years and everything has changed except basic human nature of our employees. I'll return to that later.

Safety and safety management have been at the bedrock of Du Pont's operations since the company's founding in 1802. Our first business was the manufacture of black powder. In that business, safety was not an afterthought; it was a matter of economic and, more importantly, personal survival, and safety was integrated directly into the production process.

Du Pont's safety performance, by any measure, is considered very good. Since the early 1900's, our lost workday injury rate has been steadily improving. During the last five years, we experienced 171 lost workday injuries. If we had been typically of all industry, we would have had more than 12,000 injuries. Another way to look at that record is that the average Du Pont worker is 73 times safer than the average American at work and 43 times safer than the average American away from work.

In addition to the incentive of sparing employees from the pain and suffering of injury, we estimate that our safety performance saves the company about $150 million annually.

An absolutely crucial element in influencing employees in any direction, I believe is the degree to which the culture of the organization supports that direction. Fortunately, our founder, E. I. du Pont, established that strong safety tradition from the very beginning.

Closely related to the organization culture is the importance of clear, consistent and well understood policy. In Du Pont, our policy is that we will not produce any product unless it can be "made, used, handled and disposed of safely." This is not just the policy we follow; it is the philosophy which we live every day.

Over the years, we have established certain principles on which our safety records is based. These also help define the all-important culture.

We believe all injuries and occupational illnesses can be prevented. I get asked frequently, do you really mean that? Of course I do. You may develop interim objectives, but the clearly stated goal must be zero. Anything short of that suggests that there is an acceptable level of injuries. The}second key in that belief is prevention, to take action to prevent injury and not just react to it after it occurs.

You may notice that I will use the word management several times. That's because we believe safety is a line management responsibility. By that I mean that the safety and health of all employees is the responsibility of every member of management from the chairman of the board to middle management, and to those who directly supervise or manage work groups in plants and offices around the world. Within Du Pont, I as the safety director am not responsible for injuries. Line management is.

To understand management's role in protecting the health and safety of employees at Du Pont, it is necessary to know a little history. The man I referred to earlier, E. I. du Pont, really believed in management's accountability and he called management to task in his earliest rules and regulations. For example, he prohibited employees from entering a new or rebuilt powder mill before he or his general manager went in first to operate the equipment to assess the risk. Now that's putting a lot of faith in your risk assessment! Remember, this was at the beginning of the previous century. Further, he chose to be close to his workers and he lived on site beside the mills in order to be part of the daily operations. Now that demonstrates management commitment, especially in the explosives business where, if you didn't make it right, you didn't make it long.

In our company, the chief executive officer also is the chief safety and health officer. He and the other senior executives spend a substantial amount of time on safety matters. In fact, the agenda for all meetings of the executive Committee and the vice presidents of all industrial and staff departments leads off with safety.

So the essence of an effective safety and health program is the complete exercise of management responsibility, with each level accountable to the level above and responsible for the level below.

In Du Pont we use the term "safety" frequently as a generic term to include the acute incidents traditionally called safety and the chronic incidents related to occupational health. In other words, we spell safety with a big "S" and it includes risk across a broad spectrum, beginning with our employees who are immediately at risk because they are on the front line of risk. Of equal concern is the general citizenry and particularly those people living in close proximity of our facilities, followed by concerns over protection of property and particularly the property of others. Ultimately there is the risk, if something goes wrong, of civil and/or criminal penalties, the possibility of future restrictive regulations, and harm to the company's reputation.

Essentially, we look at risk management as primarily the management of change. Almost always, when something goes wrong, the event followed a change of some kind. That change may even have been made to reduce the risk. Yet we sometimes overlooked the fact that it may be safer to leave a situation alone than to change it. Asbestos is an example that comes to

mind. Used extensively for decades as an effective fire proofing
material, asbestos in many installations poses essentially no risk if left
in place but can unleash a high risk when being removed.

There are several different kinds of change, in fact, that we have to
manage for safety:

• Planned changes such as new processes or process improvements
• Societal-imposed changes resulting from new regulations, laws,
court rulings, population shifts or attitude modifications reflecting
heightened public expectations.
• "Natural" changes including wear on equipment, fatigue, corrosion,
sludge buildup or deterioration.
• Human change such as discontent, forgetfulness, complacency,
inattentiveness, aging work force, new work force or substance abuse.

Risk analysis, after all, is limited by the risk of the unknown --
those things we had not anticipated. I am reminded of a situation at one
of our plants a number of years ago. After a series of leaks and
resultant small fires that posed the potential for a large fire some day,
we conducted a detailed risk analysis. As a result of that analysis, we
changed all the gaskets in a series of valves on a production line and the
myriad of little leaks went away. Later, however, the problem returned to
the original proportions. When we investigated, expecting perhaps to find
that our analysis may have been wrong, we discovered instead the
unanticipated. A purchasing agent had gone back to the old gaskets on the
basis of price.

Another time, after a lengthy fault tree was done, we experienced a
50-ton release of a highly toxic material. Two employees were killed and
several others injured. The accident was caused by bolt failures in a
valve. A contractor had replaced the bolts with the wrong type and they
stress corroded. Had we taken the risk into account in our fault tree? I
think the answer is apparent.

It's axiomatic in the business of safety that everything changes.
It's the job of the manager to manage that change, whether the change was
made to improve efficiency or safety or costs, because change is the
biggest factor in risk.

This leads me into a description of our process hazards management
program, the principal framework for managing athe risks of change in
chemical process operations:

• Training is paramount to prevent unwanted change. Safety awareness
is not naturally built into human nature. Du Pont may know how to do a
lot of exotic high tech things, such as exploring molecular chemistry to
understand the structure and processes of life, but we can't change basic
human nature by studying DNA molecules. So we must train and retrain for
safety. We transfer to the operator, the maintenance technician and the
supervisor the information and skills needed to operate and maintain the
process as intended by the designer. The goal is not to prevent change
but to force a critical examination of changes before they occur.

• Process hazards reviews, which in our language are formal risk
analyses, are not only intended to design a safe process in the first
place but are also done periodically to detect change from the original
design and assumptions. Even in the most well-established processes,
changes occur and not all of them are recognized at the time they occur.

A major purpose of the process hazards review is to identify these changes and assess their impact on and interaction with the whole.

• Operating and emergency procedures state what we expect of our employees under normal operating conditions as well as in emergencies. If we can't put them all in writing, it's probably because we haven't thought it through and don't have all the answers.

• Preventive maintenance programs, to prevent changes and possible system failures due to wear and tear, must be comprehensive enough to assure that the plant is always operating within design limits.

• Change of design procedures, intended to control change, can be critically important. Any change represents a new design and requires the same degree of scrutiny as the original design.

• Audits to detect change tell us how well we're doing. There are many kinds of audits; each must have a clear purpose and be designed to achieve that purpose. As the saying goes, "You can expect only what you inspect."

• Critical equipment inspections, like audits, are designed to detect change. We inspect a lot of things but it's important to give priority to those components critical to process safety.

• Emergency preparedness is a contingency plan for what to do when all else fails -- and history tells us that it will occasionally. A lack of such planning amounts to a denial of the potential for the worst case scenario.

• Incident investigation following an unanticipated event offers new information on change phenomena as well as an opportunity to test the integrity of the process hazard management system. For maximum benefit, the investigation must be probing, uninhibited and directed at finding the cause rather than a scapegoat.

• Safety during process phaseout, sale or transfer is one of the toughest challenges. Profitability may have eroded, maintenance budgets cut and key people transferred to more robust business, all forms of change. In this situation, attention to process safety must be even greater.

One final thought. I am often asked, in order to manage change or any part of a safety program, what are the three most important elements of an effective safety program. My answer: number one is management commitment, number two is management commitment, and number three is management commitment. And I could go on and on. Now there are other important elements, many of which I have described briefly here today, but management commitment is paramount and that commitment must start at the top.

RISK MANAGEMENT APPLICATIONS TO DAM SAFETY

ACTIVITIES WITHIN THE BUREAU OF RECLAMATION

Neil F. Parrett

U.S. Bureau of Reclamation

ABSTRACT

Historical practice of dam designers has been to provide for failure loading events from static loads, earthquakes and floods. The general practices differed somewhat for large and small dams and Federally and privately designed dams. Some ways individual existing dams now determined to be deficient for some loading conditions may be managed is discussed. The dam failures occurring in the 1970's, technology advances, and organizational activities have defined the national scope of deficient dams and brought national attention to the problem.

The Bureau of Reclamation now uses a Risk Management philosophy to establish the priorities for inspections and follow-up, engineering evaluations and assessments on 275 major dams. The paper discusses the process and the numerous elements being evaluated by the Bureau when assessing existing dams to recommended a level of structural and/or nonstructural modification.

KEY WORDS: Dam Safety; Structural Risk; Flood Risks; Dam Failures; Risk Management.

The USBR (United States Bureau of Reclamation) has been using risk analysis techniques in assessments for management decisions. Before presenting USBR practice and experience, it is appropriate to share some data on scope and history of dams and dam failures. The total number of dams in the U.S., with a height over 15 meters, exceeds 6,000. A review of the nations over 9,000 high hazard dams determined approximately 3,000 to be potentially unsafe. Many of these were unsafe only for extremely large and remotely occurring flood events. High hazard is determined by the location of the dam upstream from inhabited areas and not by the condition of the dam. Historic causes of dam failures are shown in the following table.

Table No. 1

HISTORICAL DAM FAILURE DATA

1. Dam Failure Data - U.S. Earth and Rockfill Dams > 50-Foot High

Failure Mode	Annual Failure Rate/Dam Year Of Operation
Piping	0.00006
Overtopping	0.00004
Slope Stability	0.00001
Piping (Outlet Works)	0.000006
Foundation and Other Causes	0.00005

2. U.S. Earthfill Dams Built Before 1930, 50 to 100 Feet High

Failure Mode	Annual Failure Rate/Dam Year of Operation		E	W
	Eastern U.S.	Western U.S.		
Piping	0.00032	0.00123	3	10
Overtopping	0.00042	0.00038	4	3
Slope Stability	0.00021	0.00024	2	2
Spillway	0.00010	0.00000	1	0
Foundation	0	0	0	0

Notes: 75 percent of all failures, except overtopping, occur in first 10 years of operation.

50 percent of all failures, except overtopping, occur in first filling

Specific dam failure data based on about 18,000 dam years of operation: 10,000 Eastern United States
                   8,000 Western United States

Table No. 2

NUMBER OF FAILURES vs. AGE OF FAILURE

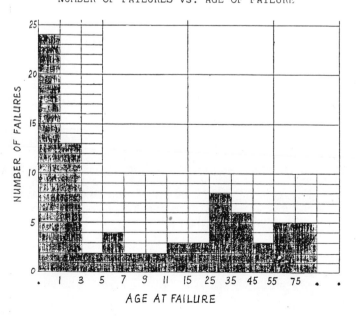

Table No. 1 demonstrates when dam failures occur with relation to the age of the dam.

Historically, the Bureau designed dams for structural stability under the most extreme loads believed probable. Recent improvements in data bases and procedures are predicting larger probable maximum loads resulting from floods or earthquakes. As the Bureau reviewed many existing dams for safety from a program perspective with constrained resources in people and money, and in terms of the need to find the dam most likely to fail before it failed, they chose to employ risk analysis evaluations. The following table illustrates some constraints and realities necessary to start up the Bureau's Safety of Dams Program:

Table No. 3

DAM SAFETY PROGRAM REALITIES

- Resources in people and dollars available were defined

- Records on past inspections of dams were not consistent in inspector experience, observation or evaluation as to criticality

- Historic data available on design, construction, and operations were not consistent for all dams

- Design loading data as to floods and earthquakes were not current with the state-of-the-art

- Engineering analyses on seepage and structural stability were not current with the state-of-the-art

- Authorities and budgets required to exercise program actions were not defined or restricted

Within the Bureau, the initial efforts were to establish a legislative base of authority and budget for a Safety of Dams Program. In addition, at the same time the agency was establishing inspection standards and training so that our onsite examinations of dams would have consistency.

The first applications of risk philosophy for dams was simple and logical. The agency assessed and rated damage potential, brought together factual data about each dam's size and location and graded each dam against a pre-established criteria. The same activity occurred for the condition information known about each dam. When a lack of knowledge existed that could not be supplied by the dam tender, a rank somewhat overly influenced by the hazard rating was assigned to the dam. This assured that lack of knowledge raised the attention level but did not move a dam into equality with a dam in a higher risk hazard category.

All USBR dams received in the order of the numerical rank assigned to them a review of the available historic information an appraisal level evaluation for PMF (probably maximum flood) and MCE (Maximum Credible Earthquake), and an onsite examination by a team which included a trained

Table No. 4

HAZARD RATING CRITERIA

Item	Low	Moderate	High	Extreme
DAMAGE POTENTIAL				
Capacity (acre-ft)	0-999 (0)	1,000-49,999 (3)	50,000-49,999 (6)	500,000- (9)
Hydraulic height (ft)	0-39 (0)	40-99 (3)	100-299 (6)	300- (9)
Hazard potential	(0)	(4)	(8)	
Hydrologic adequacy	Yes (0)	-	-	No (9)
Seismic zone	0-1 (0)	2 (3)	3 (6)	4 (9)
CONDITION				
Age (years) (0) (3)	Under 5 (4)	5-24 (9)	25-49	50
General condition	Excellent (0)	Good (3*)	Fair (6)	Poor (9)
Seepage problems	None (0)	Slight* (3)	Moderate (6)	High (9)
Structural behavior measurements current and within acceptable range	Yes (0)		Partial (6)	No (9)

*Assumed if not given

Note: Number in parenthesis is the weighting factor.

dam safety evaluation civil engineer, a geologist, and a mechanical
engineer. Also one individual was assigned to review all examination
reports and interview team inspectors as required for the second round of
numerical ranking against the same preestablished criteria.

The revised numerical ranking was used as the order for state-of-the-art
analyses for determining which dams required modification for safety of
dam decisions.

The analysis phase began before the inspection phase ended. A top-50 list
was maintained for the dams requiring analyses. While current inspection
findings could influence the order of dams to be analyzed, the agency did
not allow current inspection findings to influence the list to the extent
that any analysis begun was terminated because of priority. Several
analyses were stalled while needed data were obtained, but an attempt was
made to close all initial assessments with a decisions on each
recommendation on each dam.

Table No. 5 shows number of recommendations from examinations by subject
area and the number that had been analyzed by the end of 1984.

Table No. 5

DISTRIBUTION OF SEED RECOMMENDATIONS BY TOPIC

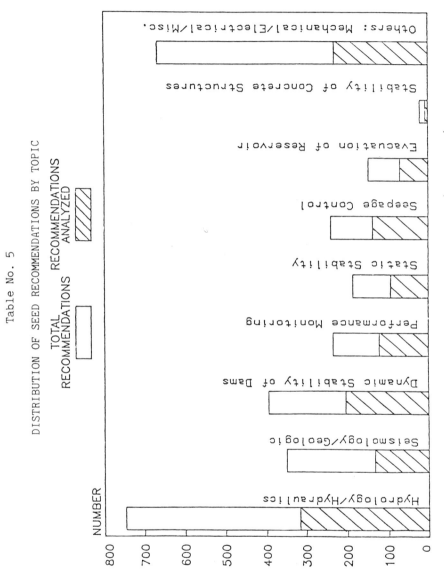

Recommendations Total = 2984 — (362 dams)
Recommendations Analyzed = 1291 — (140 dams)

Table No. 6

OVERALL SAFETY OF DAMS CLASSIFICATION

Overall safety of dams classification. - One of the following classifications is assigned to a dam following on onsite examination and subsequent analyses using available data and state-of-the art knowledge:

SATISFACTORY. - No existing or potential dam safety deficiencies are recognized. Safe performance is expected under all anticipated loading conditions, including such events as the MCE and the PMF.

FAIR. - No existing dam safety deficiencies are recognized for normal loading conditions. Infrequent hydrologic and/or seismic events would probably result in a dam safety deficiency.

CONDITIONALLY POOR. - A potential dam safety deficiency is recognized for unusual loading conditions that may realistically occur during the expected life of the structure. CONDITIONALLY POOR may also be used when uncertainties exist as to critical analysis parameters that identify a potential dam safety deficiency; further investigations and studies are necessary.

POOR. - A potential dam safety deficiency is clearly recognized for normal loading conditions. Immediate actions to resolve the deficiency are recommended; reservior restrictions may be necessary until problem resolution.

UNSATISFACTORY. - A dam safety deficiency exists for normal loading conditions. Immediate remedial action is required for problem resolution.

These terms, in lower case letters, are also used in a general sense throughout the SEED Report to describe various existing conditions but do not denote a classification of the dam.

Following the analyses, another ranking (this time a verbal one) was assigned to each dam.

- The condition of the dam is satisfactory and only continued surveillance is required.
- The condition is not in compliance with state-of-the-art practice but is not determined to be a safety of dam issue.
- A potential safety of dam condition exists.
- A decision cannot be made until the following data and/or analyses are accomplished.

To date, 140 SEED (Safety Evaluation of Existing Dams) analyses have been completed, and 20 dams have been identified for CAS (Corrective Action Studies) and probable Safety of Dams Modifications. If earlier rankings were anywhere near accurate, even in a relative sense, we should not generate many, if any, additional dams for CAS. We have completed, or have under construction, safety of dams modifications of 11 dams. Currently in final design for SOD (Safety of Dams) Modifications are 6 dams.

The way the Bureau applied risk analysis techniques for prioritizing dams for inspection and analyses is probably not controversial.

The Bureau also uses risk analysis as a method of assessing selected elements believed important to a decision on the modification of a dam that the agency needs to make. The risk analysis hopefully influences, but it does not make the decision. The decision is consciously made by the actions or unconsciously made by the inactions of people. Like other technical analyses tools, if accurate data and objectivity are not employed in a risk assessment, the results will be misleading. The benefits from risk assessments are:

- To increase comprehension as to interrelations of factors impacting on decisions
- To array information in a manner that will provide a good overall understanding of the problem
- To provide a concise presentation on comparative benefits of alternative actions
- To document the basis of decision

The following focuses on how the Bureau has employed risk-based or probability analysis in their decision process to 1) select a level of modification for an existing dam, and 2) select an alternative design that provides that level of protection.

The goals in the Bureau's modification of existing dams activities are to reduce risk for potential loss of life and reduce adverse effects of loss of reservoir. An example of a decision sequence is shown in table 7.

The application of Risk Analysis philosophies has been in the areas of hazard assessment, impacts of alternative actions and comparisons of hazard, impacts and other identified factors for a risk management decision. In a hazard assessment, separate relationships are prepared to illustrate the potential loss of life and property damage versus flood discharge.

Table No. 7

DECISION QUESTIONS FOR SAFETY OF DAMS MODIFICATION

A.	Will the dam fail if the leading event selected for safe design occurs:	No	Stop modification decision process, continue periodic assessment of dam for adequate performance.
		Yes	Describe modes of potential failure and continue to step B.
B.	Is failure possible from events likely to occur during normal anticipated operation?	No	Continue to step C.
		Yes	Define interim actions required and define priority to continued work. Continue to step C.
C.	Will the physical conse- quences of downstream flooding be worse because of dam failure?	No	This question needs to be addressed to interim level events if the answer to the maximum magnitude event is No. If No to all level of an event, stop modification decision process.
		Yes	Continue to step D.
D.	Are human lives likely to be lost as a result of dam failure?	No	Define most cost-effective level of protection and least cost modification alternative for that level of protection. consider use of a probability-based analysis. Stop modification decision analysis process.
		Yes	Continue to step E.
E.	Is level of protection required to minimize loss of lives the maximum magnitude event?	No	Determine if higher level of protection alternative is more cost-effective. Consider use of probability-based analysis. Continue to step F.
		Yes	Design least cost modification alternative for the maximum magnitude event. Stop modification decision analysis process.
F.	Is most cost-effective level of protection above level of pro- section required to minimize loss of lives?	No	Design least cost modification alternative for level of protection required to minimize loss of lives. Stop modification decision analysis process.
		Yes	Design at higher level of protection the least cost modification alternative. Stop modification decision analysis process.

Table No. 8

TYPICAL RESULTS FROM A HAZARD ASSESSMENT

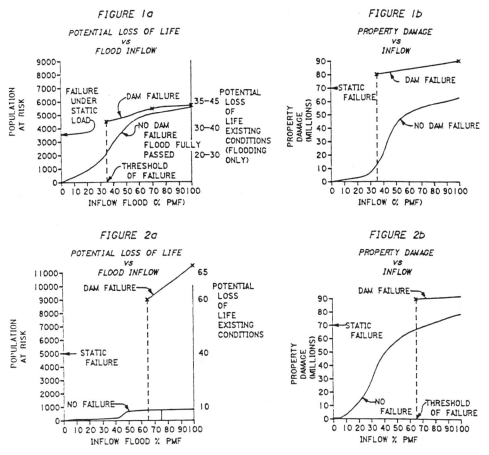

Note:

1. The incremental effects for dam failure due to static or earthquake loading are indicated at 0 discharge.

2. The relations between population at risk and estimated loss of life for the examples are purely a conjecture for this display and should not be considered an average or typical relationship.

Figure 1 illustrates a hypothetical case indicating a small incremental difference in population at risk and estimated loss of life for inflow flood levels above about 60 percent of the maximum discharge and significant incremental property damages for all flood levels with a failure of dam potential. A case can be established for a Safety of Dams modification above 60 percent of PMF (Probable Maximum Flood) being determined solely upon economic analyses. Figure 2 illustrates a case where the incremental estimated loss of life is significant for all flood levels up to the PMF. For some dam sites, the nature of the incremental hazard posed by potential dam failure can be discerned readily with a rather cursory assessment of the damages and population exposure. Other dam sites require expensive detailed assessments. Attention must be given to inundation mapping, location of affected population, method of flood wave detection, warning dissemination, route and time for escape, and other site-related factors.

Categories and examples of application of risk analyses between alternatives and various givens are illustrated in Table No. 9.

Case C may lead to selection of other than the least total cost alternative if a higher level of protection is mandated.

Table No. 9

EXAMPLES OF RISK ANALYSIS APPLICATIONS

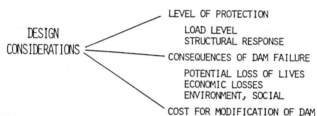

DESIGN CONSIDERATIONS
- LEVEL OF PROTECTION
  - LOAD LEVEL
  - STRUCTURAL RESPONSE
- CONSEQUENCES OF DAM FAILURE
  - POTENTIAL LOSS OF LIVES
  - ECONOMIC LOSSES
  - ENVIRONMENT, SOCIAL
- COST FOR MODIFICATION OF DAM

APPLICATION CATEGORY / DESIGN FACTOR	LEVEL OF PROTECTION	CONSEQUENCES FROM DAM FAILURE	COST FOR MODIFICATION OF DAM
A	FIXED	FIXED	VARIABLE FOR ALTERNATIVE SELECTED
B	FIXED	VARIABLE FOR ALTERNATIVE SELECTED	VARIABLE FOR ALTERNATIVE SELECTED
C	VARIABLE FOR ALTERNATIVE SELECTED	VARIABLE FOR ALTERNATIVE SELECTED	VARIABLE FOR ALTERNATIVE SELECTED

CASE A - PROBABILITY BASED ANALYSIS USUALLY NOT NECESSARY WHEN SELECTING A MODIFICATION ALTERNATIVE.

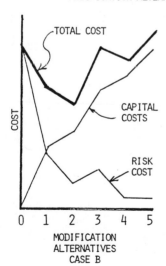

CASE B

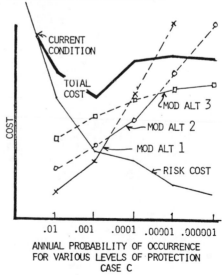

ANNUAL PROBABILITY OF OCCURRENCE FOR VARIOUS LEVELS OF PROTECTION

CASE C

CASE NO. 1 DAM
(Figures 1,2,3, & 4)

The following figures summarize, for Case No. 1 Dam, a hazard assessment
conducted for a series of dams upstream from a major population center.
An additional analysis, not illustrated, was a comparison of alternative
actions for management of a PMF through the system which selected the
storage of the PMF at the upstream dam as much less expensive than
modifying all spillways to pass the PMF through the series of dams.   The
hazard assessment includes the following steps:

1.   Flood routings to determine impact on dam as a function of flood
     level and establish outflow with no dam failure.
2.   Identify failure modes and failure threshold for each.
3.   Route flood with dam failure to obtain outflow.
4.   Determine consequences as a function of flow.
5.   Make hazard evaluation based on incremental consequences.

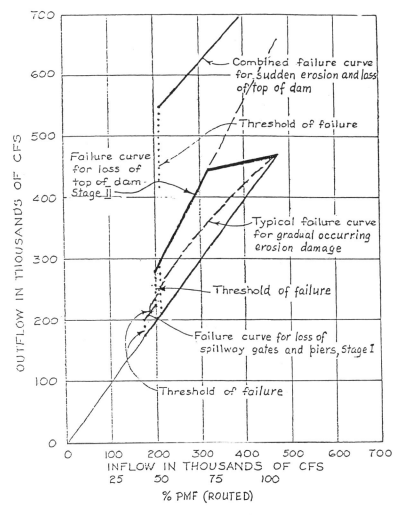

CASE #1, FIGURE #1

PMF - Probable Maximum Flood
CFS - Cubic Feet per Second

169

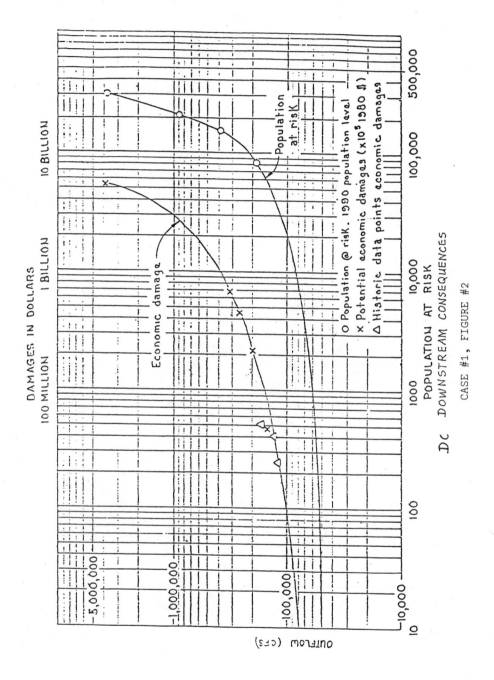

CASE #1, FIGURE #2

170

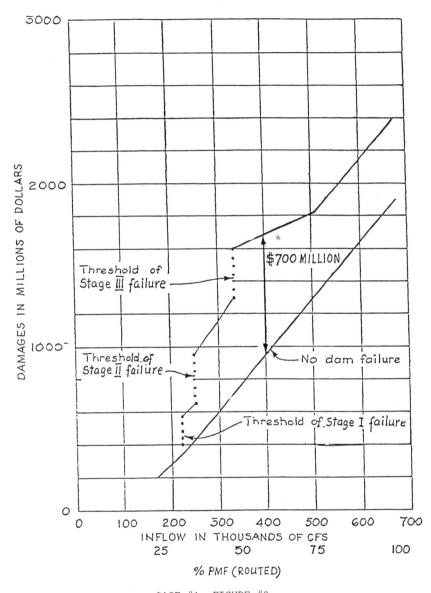

CASE #1, FIGURE #3

Incremental Economic Loss Due to Potential Dam Failure

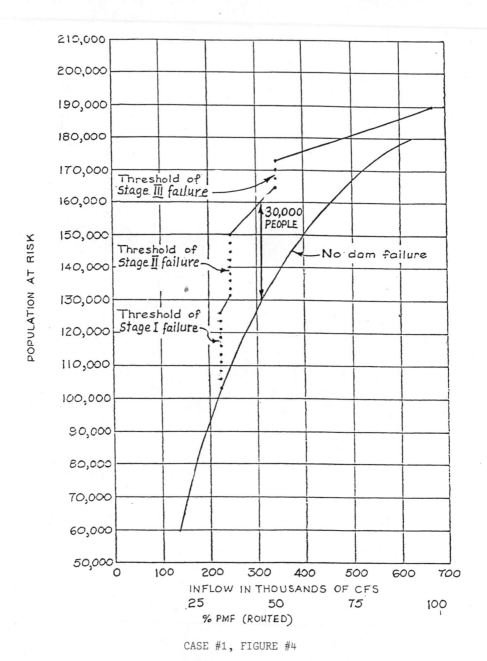

CASE #1, FIGURE #4

Incremental Population at Risk Due to Potential Dam Failure

CASE NO. 2 DAM
(Fig. 1,2 & 3)

The second case shows a risk-cost analysis, in which the apparent level of
modification would be to recommend balancing protection for remote events
to that which could be expected from extreme operational requirements, and
also the dependence of such a logic upon the frequency of reoccurrence
selected for large volume, remotely occurring floods.

Irrigation Project
Earth dam 40 feet height
Gated spillway 22,5000 ft^3/s capacity
Small reservoir outflow = Inflow
PMF (probable maximum flood) (revised) 84,000 ft^3/s
Condition of structures excellent
Existing single spillway may clog due to debris at about 10,000 ft^3/s flow

ALTERNATIVES   COSTS

1. Add second spillway of 20,000 ft^3/s and Roller $2.8 million
    Compacted Concrete to crest and downstream
    slope of embankment.
2. Add spillway of 40,000 ft^3/s and rise dam $4.8 million
    (no overtopping)
3. Add spillway of 60,000 ft^3/s $6.0 million
4. Add spillway of 84,000 ft^3/ $7.1 million
5. Establish and maintain downstream alert   ?
6. No action   Reputation

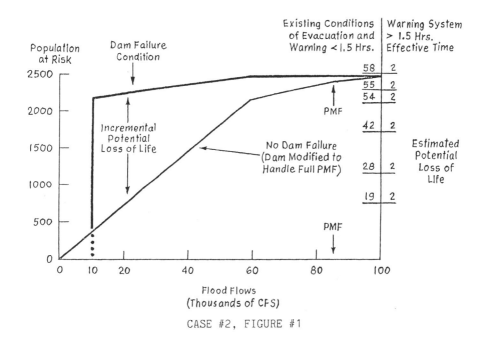

CASE #2, FIGURE #1

173

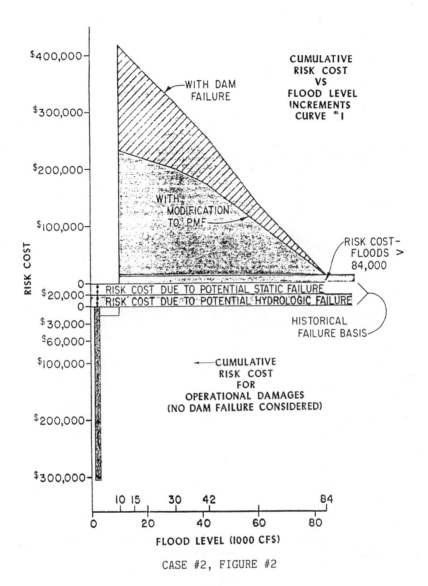

CUMULATIVE
RISK COST
VS
FLOOD LEVEL
INCREMENTS
CURVE #1

WITH DAM
FAILURE

WITH
MODIFICATION
TO PMF

RISK COST—
FLOODS >
84,000

RISK COST DUE TO POTENTIAL STATIC FAILURE

RISK COST DUE TO POTENTIAL HYDROLOGIC FAILURE

HISTORICAL
FAILURE BASIS

← CUMULATIVE
RISK COST
FOR
OPERATIONAL DAMAGES
(NO DAM FAILURE CONSIDERED)

RISK COST

$400,000

$300,000

$200,000

$100,000

0

$20,000
0

$30,000
$60,000

$100,000

$200,000

$300,000

10 15   30   42   84

0   20   40   60   80

FLOOD LEVEL (1000 CFS)

CASE #2, FIGURE #2

174

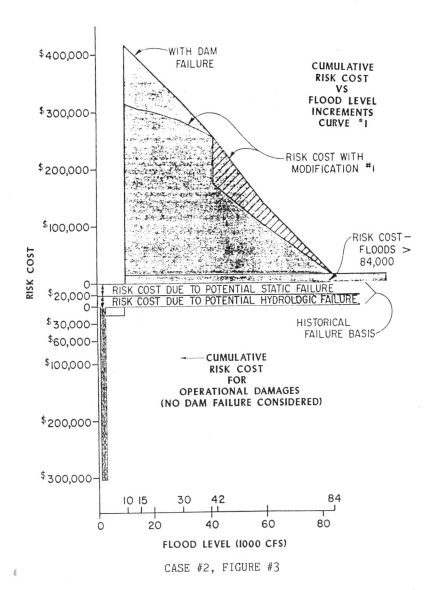

CASE #2, FIGURE #3

175

CASE NO. 3 DAM

The third case displays some data considered pertinent to selecting
between alternative actions for managing a large flood up to PMF magnitude
at a single project.

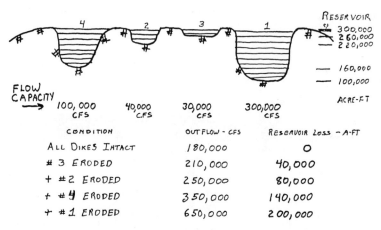

CONDITION	OUTFLOW - CFS	RESERVOIR LOSS — A-FT
ALL DIKES INTACT	180,000	O
# 3 ERODED	210,000	40,000
+ #2 ERODED	250,000	80,000
+ #4 ERODED	350,000	140,000
+ #1 ERODED	650,000	200,000

CASE #3, FIGURE #1

Controlled Dike Failure

ALTERNATIVES

1. No action
2. Remove Dam and Dikes
3. Direct all flows down north fork of the Red River
4. Divert flows partially or fully by spillways into Tepee Creek or
   unnamed creek.
5. Controlled dike failure
6. Non-structural actions
   * Flood detection
   * Warning systems
   * Operational control improvement

The recommended decision was a combination of alternative actions five and
six.

To summarize, the Bureau has used risk analyses in decision making on safety of dam modifications to assess:

- incremental consequences (human lives and property damage) with and without dam failure
- determination of likelihood of failure for a particular loading level (flood, earthquake)
- comparing consequences, benefits, and costs between an array of alternative actions
- comparing qualitative factors between alternative actions (social, environmental, political, likelihood of success)
- comparing qualitative factors between alternative actions (social, environmental, political, likelihood of success)

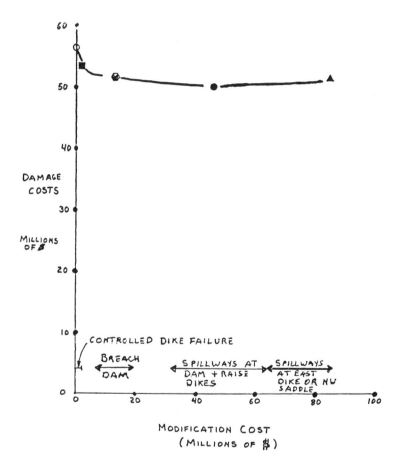

CASE #3, FIGURE #2

Effect of Actions on Damages at PMF Flow

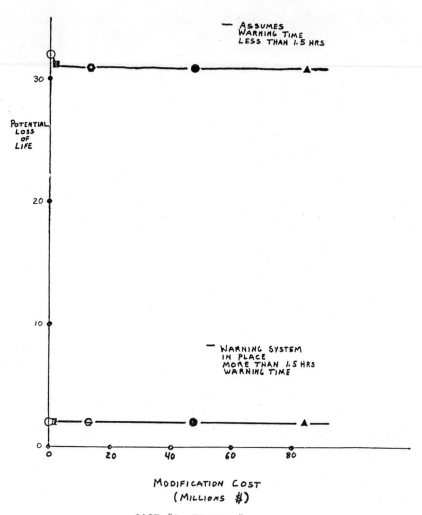

CASE #3, FIGURE #3

Effect of Actions on Potential Loss of Life at PMF Level

RISK MANAGEMENT OF COMPLEX, TECHNOLOGY-BASED SYSTEMS:

OBSERVATIONS ON SIMILARITIES AND DIFFERENCES

Rodney Lay and Gabor Strasser

The MITRE Corporation

ABSTRACT

There are great variations among the specific aspects of safety assurance for nuclear power plants, aircraft and space vehicles, large public projects, and industrial processes. Yet, each case is characterized by complexity, high technology content, concomitant hazards and risks, and public concern. The question that this paper addresses is: In light of the above, are there some significant, generic similarities in safety assurance, such that one system could benefit from the experience of others? Through informal discussions and review of such systems with representatives of the vendors, users, and regulators, the authors have highlighted similarities and differences in the various approaches to safety assurance.

Some preliminary findings show that there is much in risk management that could provide helpful insights among industries; both technical merit/validity and public acceptance are necessary but, by themselves, insufficient conditions for assuring acceptable levels of safety; it is becoming increasingly difficult to meet this dual requirement for large technology-based systems due to concurrent technical, operations, institutional, and political uncertainties and complexities; and it is not constructive to resolve issues of safety assurance primarily through adversarial processes. An adequate understanding of what goes into safety assurance should be fostered among all concerned parties. In this manner, decisions could be based on what is possible and acceptable, as opposed to what is desirable and legally mandated--but perhaps not feasible.

KEY WORDS: Comparative Risk, Risk Criteria, Safety Assurance, Risk Management, Safety Requirements.

INTRODUCTION

Our lifestyle today is based on a myriad of complex, large technology-based systems. Our remarkable--relative to the "good old days" (Bettmann 1974)--quality of life, to which technology has contributed so much, is marred by nagging doubts as to just how safe we are. As a result, we have evolved a variety of ways to cope with the apparent risks to our health and safety.

Engineering has provided many partial solutions to the dangers these technologies are seen to pose. To enforce the use of these solutions, our government acts on our behalf through a system of laws, licenses, permits, and guidelines and numerous regulatory agencies have been formed and charged with the task of ensuring our health and safety. This is frequently a thankless, frustrating, and at times even confusing challenge, particularly when it involves the analysis of rare events and has to deal with probabilities of occurrence which are themselves uncertain (Weinberg, 1985).

A relatively slow and often trial-and-error, evolutionary approach has worked for several of the technologies. A good example is the aviation industry, which has evolved into perhaps the most credible of the complex, technology-based systems insofar as safety issues are concerned. In the view of many, the aviation industry enjoys this position today in major part because of its slow, self-correcting growth; redundancy; and iterative development. The industry has applied sophisticated (and often not so sophisticated, but nevertheless highly relevant) testing practices which have iterated extensively between theory and practice.

Other technologies, due to the fault of no one individual or organization, simply have not grown in a similar way. Their progress is often stymied due to the risks to health and safety as perceived by the general public. In the final analysis it does not matter whether the perception is biased or even perhaps wrong. What counts is what is perceived; that is what the public acts upon. Many have cited the nuclear power industry in the United States as having fallen into this category.

A recent workshop held by the MITRE Corporation showed that there are many safety assurance issues common to both existing and emerging technologies. Systems that were discussed included nuclear power plants; aircraft and space vehicles; large public projects such as water works and dams; and hazardous, complex industrial processes. While the specifics differ, many interesting generic similarities were noted.

This paper suggest that a wide range of different technologies share significant aspects of risk management. By identifying and understanding these generic similarities we might better diagnose what has.gone wrong in specific situations, and improve our approach to assuring acceptable levels of safety in future systems.

An appropriate, applicable, and relevant generic framework would be a valuable basis for examining current practices. Either explicitly or implicitly, this framework starts with a philosophy of safety assurance (e.g., containment, fail-safe, safe-life, etc..). This is the subjective basis for all that must follow. The implementation of the system is highly objective (you cannot philosophize about rivet spacing, metal gages or safety factors; you apply them as they are prescribed in highly quantitative fashions). To link these two (philosophy and implementation) we need criteria to bridge the gap between the subjective philosophy and the objective implementation in some ingenious and pragmatic fashion.

In summary, we believe that there are generic issues involving risk in three major categories: (1) issues involving the nature of risk, (2) issues involving how risk is perceived by the public, and (3) issues surrounding the means we use to cope with the risk. Each of these is discussed further. The focus of this paper throughout is that there are important generic similarities within risk management across the board that could be beneficially exploited.

WHAT IS RISK?

A considerable segment of the public assumes a right to absolute safety from the actions taken by society at large. Many feel that absolute personal safety is an attainable, realistic, legislated public right. Regardless of the desirability of this condition, it is not feasible; complex and lengthy dialogues on the issues of public safety are based often on irreconcilable premises. At the limit, and we are more often than not trying to manage risk at the limit, "...one can argue that an accident whose occurrence requires an exceedingly unlikely sequence of untoward events may also be regarded as an act of God." (Weinberg, 1985)..that is, beyond secular safety assurance.

As has been pointed out a number of times, safety is a condition characterized by an absence of an imminent perceived threat to life and limb. The concept of safety is individual and judgmental. It cannot be measured by direct parameters. Furthermore, absolute safety does not exist. To be alive is to be, in fact unsafe---merely the degree is a variable.

Risk, on the other hand, is a measurably quantity. Expressions of risk are commonly a compound measure of the probability of a harmful occurrence and its severity. Management of risk can impact on the magnitude of the hazard, per se, and on the probability of its occurrence as well as on the mitigation of the severity of the results. Generic issues arising from the nature of risk include the following:

Magnitude of the Risk

Risk can be measured as the probability of an occurrence times the damage it can create (hazard). This provides a theoretical basis for comparing the impact of widely differing technologies. However, public attitudes are influenced by past history, familiarity, the media and lobbyists. These often override even the most sophisticated risk analyses. Perceptions, past experiences, and comparative assessments with more familiar situations carry much more weight with the public than risk measurements expressed in terms of the difference between 10^{-6} and 10^{-9} This use of math notation may even add to the level of apprehension.

Magnitude of the Hazard

If the potential harm from a technology is perceived by society as being "too great", the public shies away from concurring regardless of how low the concomitant probability of occurrence may be. This is a matter of personal feelings and subjective judgment and may only be remotely influenced by a scientific approach. A nuclear power plant core melt-down, an LNG super tanker exploding in New York Harbor, water supplies poisoned by industrial wastes, these are unfathomable dread possibilities. Reducing the likely probabilities of occurrence does not calm the anxiety.

Limiting the perceived hazard by breaking up the activity into smaller actions may help. For example, offloading a large LNG ship at sea onto six smaller ones, and allowing only one at a time in to New York Harbor. Even without the probability of an explosion having altered, the public may be more accepting of the implications for "only" part of New Jersey and the Battery, as opposed to the World Trade Center with lower Manhattan thrown in. Facts and values are always intermingled over a rare event (Whittemore 1983).

Many believe that the Monitored Retrievable Storage (MRS) system for nuclear waste has a good chance for public acceptance. This is not so much due to the public's knowledge of geological formations, radiation characteristics, and the waste material's half-life, nor is it due to the public's confidence in the government system that would be responsible for its management. Rather, it is due to the fact that the public understands monitoring, that is, watching what is happening to the stored material. Monitoring is believable and simple. Although simplification is a suspect panacea, "The desire for simplicity can be seen when people attempt to divide the participants in risk disputes into good guys and bad guys," (Fischhoff, 1985). In addition, the public believes that if they were to find out that something had gone wrong with the MRS they could got to it, and once they get to it, the technology required to "recontain it" is proven and represents no mystery. Note that a "structural" disaggregation of a hazard can take the form of a reduction in perceived exposure or a perceived improvement in procedure. To make it palatable to the public to have LNG ships in New York harbor requires the disaggregation of the cargo mass to which the public would be exposed at any given time. In the case of waste disposal, the "structural" disaggregation of the unacceptable hazard concerns the procedural aspects -- being on top of the situation and knowing what can and should be done in most of the likely future situations.

Uncertainties in Estimating Risk

Quantitative assessment of risk is frequently unreliable. Both the likelihood of an occurrence and the magnitude of damage it could cause may be impossible to determine with any acceptable accuracy. Scientific knowledge of health and safety impacts contains many gaps, making it difficult to set appropriate legislative standards.

For example, human health impacts are usually determined by extrapolating from animal data, but different species of animals may react very differently to various toxins. Estimates of potential cancer cases from saccharin, for example have ranged from 0.0001 to 5,200 cases per million exposed (Douglas, 1985). A new science, pharmacokinetics, attempts to quantify these differences, enabling scientists to better predict human response to toxic chemicals.

Risk assessment has to deal with many different kinds of uncertainties at all levels, many of which are subjective and governed by public perception based on myriad inputs and influences. Uncertainties keep compounding more on the subjective than on the objective level and officials responsible for assuring acceptable levels of safety for the public often turn to risk assessors and "managers" for "hard data." No wonder many feel that risk assessment is becoming one of the riskiest businesses in our society today. Learning how to worry together as a species may well be our next essential evolutionary turning point (Shodell, 1985).

Cost of Reducing Risk

Health and safety risks from technology can usually only be reduced at a cost. A recent calculation puts the cost of hazard-management in the United States at 3-5 percent of the GNP, excluding damages to people, material and the environment, (Tuller & Kates, 1985). Society must choose how best to spend its resources, although it appears repugnant to set a price on human life. Even if such choices are not made explicitly, because of the actions that government must take, implicit decisions will take place, whether or not anyone is aware of them. According to OMB's assistant director for public affairs, Edwin Dale, "...common sense tells you there is a limit on how much you can spend. If it costs 100 million dollars for a pollution control regulation to save one life, then to save 10,000 lives it would cost one third of the gross national product" (USNWR, 1985).

One approach to this problem has been developed by Kip Viscusi of the University of Chicago. Viscusi uses the extra income workers demand to take a more dangerous job to develop a measure of appropriate costs for pollution abatement. EPA has used this theory to establish limits for pollutants at a number of industrial facilities. For example, the agency "...set limits on radar exposure at uranium mines but not at enrichment plants, because the number of people and the risks were lower at the plants" (USNWR, 1985).

The cost of reducing a risk may also involve creating another risk: removing air pollutants from power plants emissions entails the creation of a solid waste, which must be disposed of in a land fill which, in turn, can contaminate water supplies. The hazards of each type of pollutant and the cost of their management must be compared and evaluated.

PUBLIC PERCEPTION OF RISK

The public's perception of risk is a somewhat elusive and often more subjective than objective phenomenon. For a large complex system to come into being, the public through its elected representatives and/or the courts, must accept (or rather not reject) the source of the perceived risk. This is not to say whether any system, so accepted or rejected, is deserving or undeserving. Nor is it to imply that those accepted will be the deserving ones, and the rejected ones, flawed. Hazardous technologies are in daily use when the "right" conditions are met; that is, when a level of safety deserving of public acceptance exists and is not in doubt. Both conditions are necessary; Each is essential, but insufficient on its own.

When a new system is being considered, several questions must be asked: (1) Can the new system be made safe from a theoretical point-of-view? If not, the system is already in trouble. (2) With the funds that are available, could a level of safety that the public would likely find acceptable be assured? If not, again, the system will probably be rejected. (3) Are there adequate plans to talk with the public, e.g., honest, justifiable public relations programs scheduled throughout the evolution of the system? If not, public rejection is invited.

In summary, the public simply cannot be neglected at any phase, and from the time the system is conceived to the time when the system would come on line, public acceptance must continuously be considered a critical design parameter. Factors involved include:

Newness of the Technology

The introduction of any new public system with inherent risk will cause public concern. As a rule, the public will prefer to avoid it. The technology may not be alarming in and of itself, so much as its newness. For example: existing dams cause less alarm than plans for new ones even though relative safety would favor the latter. Often it would appear that an existing unknown is acceptable because history and the regulators provide the confidence. This can and does work well until an unpredictable event, such as tampering (Tylenol), disrupts public confidence.

Evolution of the Technology

Public acceptance of technologies with slow, visible, evolutionary growth--such as the aviation industry--seems broader and more robust than for industries with a rapid growth pattern--nuclear power plants. Context is also important. The unpalatable weapons' heritage of nuclear power contrasts starkly with the pioneering, horizon-expanding image surrounding flight.

Perhaps there is much to learn from the history of evolutionary processes that have worked. the experience accumulated by the FAA and its predecessors for over half a century in assuring "airworthiness" of aircraft may be of particular value. Within this history, theory, design, experimentation, testing, operational experience and rigid maintenance schedules and practices have all played a part. As a result, complex operational systems have evolved that have often represented the leading edge of the scientific/technological state-of-the-art. There are other examples, such as the chemical industry with its highly complex plants, which may also provide valuable insights.

Voluntary vs. Involuntary Risk

Voluntary risks are those risks the individual chooses to accept: Involuntary risks are those imposed by society upon the individual. There is a great difference between the two insofar as attitude and tolerance toward them are concerned. Regardless of why, this fact must be recognized.

When one goes sky diving, or skiing, or mountain climbing, these are clearly individual choices and the risks associated with them must be assumed voluntary. On the other hand, the air pollutants from electric power generators or the general risks that a pedestrian is subjected to by city traffic are clear examples of involuntary risks to which society exposes individuals.

On the other hand, the difference between some of the voluntary and involuntary risks are becoming fuzzy. For example: Is driving of a car in congested city traffic really voluntary, if there is no other way to get to our jobs, and thus make a living? In the middle of the city we do not have much choice but to drink city water (irrespective of what the municipality does or does not put into it) even though bottled water is available in most supermarkets. Even here, for the skeptic, the question may arise: who fills the bottles and with what? Depending on the severity of the potential hazard most of the risks that we are dealing with fall into the range of 10^{-6} to 10^{-12}. Of late, more and more of the involuntary and voluntary ranges overlap. Besides, we do not believe that the variations in the negative exponents meant much in the past or won many arguments with the great majority of the public for their attitudes are governed by many other considerations.

Management of Risk

Chauncey Starr supports this last assertion in that he maintains that "public acceptance of any risk is more dependent on public confidence in risk management than on the quantitative estimates of risk consequences, probabilities and magnitudes." That is, to obtain and maintain public confidence, large systems need to show effective human intervention when necessary in addition to effective technical solutions (Starr, 1985).

Our multi-technology workshop discussions reinforced the notion that there has to be an appropriate technical solution <u>and</u> the public has to develop confidence as a foundation for acceptance. Both are necessary, but on there own each is insufficient.

We will never be able to come to grips with the risk aspects of our modern, technological society until we recognize that this is not a "zero-sum-game." Some people are more risk averse than others, while still others may be exceptionally risk tolerant, especially for a price. Sociologist tell us that we are all different with different values and needs. Depending where we, personally, are on the spectrum, the risks taken by some seem unacceptable while yet other behavior appears ultra-conservative. For example the traveling salesman who logs 150,000 airmiles per year whose wife will not accompany him on a flight from Los Angeles to San Francisco: Who is to say who is "right"? It is not a useful question at best. Rather, what is significant is that such nontechnology-specific differences in response do exist. The important issue is how can these differences be accommodated (managed at an acceptable cost)? Or, can we usefully apply what we learn from one system to another, because there are generic similarities among the various systems with which we must deal?

COPING WITH RISK

The business of "safety assurance" in general consists of three main elements: philosophy, criteria, and implementation. These elements are interdependent.

There must be some clearly articulated, philosophical basis for assuring system safety. Such philosophical bases, by their very nature, are more subjective than objective. On the other hand, the implementation (the specific design, operation, and maintenance practices) by their nature are pragmatic and highly objective. The criteria provide the essential link.

Philosophy

A philosophy must not only be appropriate and acceptable, but also implementable. But to be implementable which is obviously essential, the appropriateness and acceptability of a philosophy must sometimes be compromised. If the compromised version is inadequate, no amount of subsequent fine tuning and adjusting will make up for such a fundamental flaw. The only choice is to rethink the philosophy. For example, total containment of chemical processes is not feasible, and a philosophy based on such an assumption would be flawed from the start.

Different philosophical bases have evolved for various technical systems. If the philosophy of the safety assurance of nuclear power plants were to be characterized by one word, "containment" might serve best. In the case of aircraft, "fail-safe," "safe-life," and hybrids between the two would do the same. For civil engineering-type public works projects, the concept of exceedance frequencies (50-year or 100-year) or Standard Project Flood for flood control works and the Probable Maximum Flood for dams would convey the philosophical bases.

The level of integration is also an important philosophical aspect. Again, the aviation and nuclear industries provide contrasting examples.

The FAA always concentrates on the total system--with great emphasis on interactions and interfaces--and on the overall functioning of the system as a whole. The NRC has focused on independent subsystems identified as "safety related" with limited emphasis on their interface and integration in an engineering sense. Recently, the NRC has accelerated programs addressing systems interactions and the problems associated with the system as a whole.

Criteria

Criteria refer to the legislative and engineering design safety standards devised for technological systems. The criteria must be implementable through a practical design.

If the equipment is built to the design with appropriate quality assurance, the safety goals that originated in the safety philosophy will be, and will be seen to be, embodied in the plant. Note the philosophy cannot lead directly to safe design decisions, rather, it is the engineering criteria that must be developed as a practical link between the safety goals and the functioning plants. It is the criteria that will provide the basis on which to make the desired safe design decisions.

Implicit in the criteria is the concern for "responsibilities": who will ultimately be responsible for developing safety standards and controls. The aviation and nuclear industries again present an interesting contrast. Both the NRC and the FAA are greatly involved in all phases: design, manufacture, test, operation, and maintenance. However, their respective approaches are significantly different. The FAA, in cooperation with industry and airline representatives, approves specific procedures: The NRC request information from manufacturers and operators but makes final judgments and issues guidance, etc. based on its own evaluations.

Implementation

Implementation is the bringing of the system into being. Of course, the implementation phase does not end with the design, manufacture, testing, and delivery of the hardware. It continues under such headings as maintenance, operations, backfits, and any and all other actions that may have an impact on the hazards and their frequencies, that is, on the inherent safety of the system. The elements of implementation must include: what must happen? Who is responsible? What are the interfaces and where do the responsibilities lie to assure the interface problems will not compromise safety?

In the implementation phase, the man-machine interface issue has received much attention. Just as important is the proper distribution of roles between man and machine. Some systems (e.g., at NASA) are evolving greater reliance on "computer-controlled" safety when too many things that are too complicated are happening too fast for the operator to cope with in a timely fashion. Such system decisions invite a revisiting of the philosophy... an important concept in itself... but too demanding to be tackled in this short paper.

CONCLUSION

Society is hooked on technology but anxious about this dependence. "The capability and competence of the hazard-management system that has evolved in recent years is substantially limited" (Kates, 1985). Amongst the confusion and concern we are looking for order to replace the randomness and assurance to replace the insecurity.

Historically, each technological system evolved separately along with specific safety controls. There seem to be elements of risk management which are common to a wide range of technological systems, and the very commonality of some of the issues suggest the possibility of some generic overview of safety. Such an overview could be used in many ways: It could guide future safety assurance programs, it could lead to the recognition of holes in existing programs that need fixing, and perhaps even show some promising directions, and it could be used to review existing systems that work to see what improvements may still be possible and appropriate.

We will conclude with a "first cut" checklist as to what some such generic overview might address or include. We do not intend to imply that such a generic overview was accomplished at MITRE's workshop, merely to draw attention to the likely existence of such an overview and its utility, should it be properly developed by appropriate experts.

We are sure that his audience could add many items to this list. Then the questions are: Should some such list be completed? If so, how and by whom? And, finally, how could it be best used?

Generic Dimensions of Safety Assurance and Risk Management (A preliminary list)

1. Each successful safety assurance program has a Philosophy, Criteria and an Implementation associated with it, irrespective of whether these are explicitly recognized.

2. Safety assurance spans the spectrum from concept through design, manufacture/construction, testing, design verification, operation, maintenance, backfits and decommissioning, as well as their interfaces. Safety assurance can be compromised at any of these phases or their interfaces.

3. Overall system safety is the ultimate objective. A set of "safe" subsystems does not, as a rule, add up to overall system safety. Integration is an essential part of safety assurance and risk management.

4. Public acceptance of a system is an essential part of the success of the system. Public acceptance must be considered as one of the design variables and parameters. It does not come "cheap." It cannot be managed, as if by superposition, after the system has come into being. It must be addressed as an integral part throughout the development.

5. The public is concerned with hazard, equally if not more so, than with risk. This fact must be recognized and dealt with. Managing (reducing) risk, when the public concern is hazard, does not solve the problem. What was called in this paper "structural disaggregation of hazard" seems to have promise.

6. Past history, particularly of reliable human intervention when necessary, and comparative assessments, mean more to the public than 10^{-6} or even 10^{-20}. The public is more comfortable with existing systems (even of greater hazard) than with a new system (of provable lesser hazard).

7. There is a broad spectrum of public attitude towards safety and acceptance or aversion to risk. This variation should be fully explored as future systems are designed, for appropriate

compensations and other innovative means that may enhance safety assurance and acceptance.

8.   Public confidence and acceptance of large systems with inherent risks is difficult to gain. Objective arguments (versus subjective arguments) do not always carry the day with the public. Probably the only thing that is more difficult, is to regain confidence once it is lost.

9.   The success of a system is greatly dependent on the nature of the relationships among the advocates of the system, the public at large, and the regulators. When these relationships are "positive," the system "moves along," e.g., commercial aviation. When the relationship degenerates into an adversary situation, and lawyers enter the picture, it becomes virtually impossible to bring even an economically viable and technically feasible system on line. This is where the nuclear power industry seems to be heading in the United States, though not, it would appear, in France.

10.   As an extreme example of risk management, sometimes a system should be redesigned or even abandoned. This can occur when (a) a system's safety aspects become too controversial, (b) when the assurance of safety is unusually dependent on compound probabilities, some of which may be more subjective than objective, (c) when the opposing and supporting groups coalesce into highly vocal, more subjective than objective, lobbying groups, (d) when these groups each get competent legal representatives, (e) where there is sufficient money to be "awarded," once the "case" is settled. In general, the voices of experience argue for "back to the drawing board" before either lawyers enter the scene or there are monies that could be awarded.

11.   Even though the voluntary and involuntary risk domains tend to overlap, they are still different in many instances and respects. Such differences must be recognized and appropriately factored into the assurance of safety and the reduction of risk.

12.   ...

REFERENCES

Bettmann, O. L. 1974. The Good Old Days--They Were Terrible. New York: Random House Inc.
Doan, M. 1985. "What a Life is Worth: U.S. Seeks a Price." USNWR. September 16.
Douglas, J. 1985. "Measuring and Managing Environmental Risk." EPRI. July/August.
Fischhoff, B. 1985. "Managing Risk Perceptions," Issues in Science and Technology. II:1.
Kates, R. W. 1985. "Success, Strain and Surprises," Issues in Science and Technology. II:1.
Starr C. 1985. "Risk Management, Assessment and Acceptability." Risk Analysis. 5:2.
Shodell, M. 1985. "Risky Business," Science 85.
Tuller J. 1985. "Economic Costs and Losses," in Perilous Progress: Managing the Hazards of Technology. Referenced by R. W. Kates.
Weinberg, A. M. 1985. "Science and Its Limits: The Regulator's Dilemma," Issues in Science and Technology. II:1.
Whittemore, A. 1983. "Facts and Values in Risk Analysis for Environmental Toxicants," Risk Analysis 3. Referenced by Weinberg.

RISK-BASED MONITORING OF INDUSTRIAL SYSTEMS

M.E. Paté-Cornell and H.L. Lee

Department of Industrial Engineering
and Engineering Management
Stanford University

ABSTRACT

In this paper we studied different maintenance policies for the
control of production systems that are subject to deterioration over
time. Two types of basic maintenance policies are considered: scheduled
preventive maintenance and maintenance on demand. For both approaches the
policies could be further classified, based on the mode of observation:
the process itself for the outputs of the process. The performances of
these four policies are analyzed, and the long-run disutilities related to
them are derived. Numerical examples showed that by monitoring the
process using the appropriate optimal maintenance policy, significant
savings could result.

KEY WORDS: Maintenance, Inspection, Production, Probability, Markov Chain,
           Warning Signals

1. INTRODUCTION

Risk-based inspection and maintenance methods allow one to integrate,
in the choice of a particular risk management strategy, the probability of
errors and the costs of failures or defects. Industrial systems include
manufacturing systems, which are the focus of this paper, as well as
technical systems, such as aircrafts for which the maintenance of the
engines or control equipment are important safety issues. The basic
choice is to inspect and maintain on schedule or on demand; in the first
case one must choose a frequency and level of intervention, in the second
case one must determine what constitutes a "demand" and what response is
adequate.

Maintenance on demand is based on the observation of signals
revealing problems with the machines (equipment, set of machines, or
mechanical component of a production process). These signals come either
from the machines themselves or from the inspection of outputs and/or
customer reports. These signals, however, are imperfect. They may reveal
only a minor problem when a major one exists (Type I error: missing or
underestimating the system's problems), or suggest a problem more serious
than the one that actually exists (Type II error: false alert or
overestimation of system's problems).

Maintenance on schedule includes standard preventive maintenance
procedures at regular intervals as well as the inspection of the output on
schedule. Each inspection provides information about the state of the

machine when it produced the observed output. This information is imperfect and subject to the Type I and Type II errors described above.

The problem can, therefore, be considered as a particular application of a general theory of warning systems (Pate-Cornell, 1983) and studied by a Bayesian probabilistic method as a decision problem under uncertainty.

For each of the four policies, we study first the optimal frequency for maintenance or inspection on schedule, and the optimal responses to different signals suggesting problems at different levels of severity for maintenance on demand. Second, we find the optimal policy among the four poliaies considered. It is assumed here, however, that complete breakdowns and failures are immediately attended to and reparied within the following time unit. Repair may or may not be perfect, but restores the system to an operational state. Finally, we test the sensitivity of the decision to the risk attitude of the decision maker. The detail of the computations and the complete set of references can be found in the original paper (Paté-Cornell, Lee, and Tagaras, 1984).

2. PROBABILISTIC MODELLING

We first consider a "Policy 0" in which no maintenance is performed. There is only the response to failure, in which case the machine is restored to an operational state. This minimal policy is the limiting case of a policy of maintenance on schedule when the interval becomes infinite, or maintenance on demand when signals of problems are systematically ignored.

At any given point in time, the machine is assumed to be in one of four states: fine condition (state 1), a minor problem exists (state 2), a major problem exists (state 3), or the machine has broken down (state 4). The deterioration occurs following a Markov model characterized by the transition probabilities between two given states during any unit of time (See Figure 1).

2.1. Policy 1: Maintenance On Schedule

At regulate intervals, a maintenance operation is performed. We assume that it may not be perfect. The following time axis illustrates the process under this policy, assuming that failure occurs in the second period:

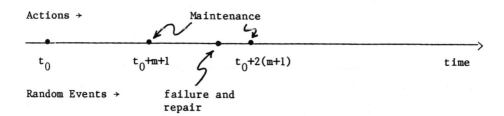

In what follows, E• denotes an expected value and $\bar{u}(\bullet)$ a disutility function associated with costs. The internal decision variable here is m, which is the number of time units between two scheduled maintenance procedures.

The state variables and parameters are:

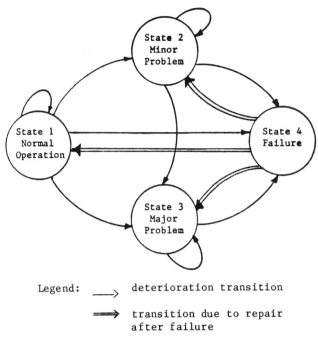

Legend: ⟶   deterioration transition

             ⟹   transition due to repair
                     after failure

Figure 1

Transition Diagram For The System's Deterioration

P   Transition probability matrix of the state of the system.

p_{ij}:   Generic element of matrix P.

$p_{ij}^{(t)}$:   Generic element of matrix P^t.

Q: Transition probability matrix characterizing the upgrading of the system by maintenance.

Π^*:   Vector with elements π_i's characterizing the limiting probability distribution of the state of the system after each maintenance.

C_M: Cost of a maintenance.

C_j: Costs per time unit of defective products (such as rework, scrap, loss of goodwill, etc.) associated with state j of the machine. For simplicity of notation, C_1 is kept equal to zero. C_4 includes also the cost of failure, and costs of repair.

Assuming that maintenance is scheduled every m+1 time units, then the steady state probabilities of the system after each maintenance can be obtained by solving the linear system of equations:

$$\Pi^* = \Pi^* \, P^m Q$$

The expected disutility of the costs per time unit associated with maintenance on schedule at interval m is the sum of regular maintenance costs, expected failure costs, and expected costs of defective products associated with minor or major problems of the machine:

$$\overline{Eu}_m = \frac{1}{m+1} \sum_{i=1}^{4} \pi_i^* \left[\sum_{t=1}^{m} \sum_{k=1}^{4} p_{ik}^{(t)} \overline{u}(c_k) \right] + \overline{u}(c_M)$$

2.2. Policy 2: Inspection Of Output On Schedule

In this case, the output product is inspected at regular intervals of m time units. There is a time lag of L time units, however, between the time when the machine becomes defective and the time when the defective product can be observed. We assume that $L \leq m$.

The following time axis illustrates the process described above, assuming that the first inspection occurs at time t_0.

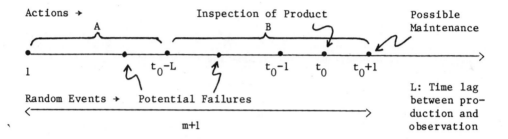

The internal decision variables are: the time interval m+1 between two scheduled inspections, and whether or not to respond to signals suggesting that the machine may be in state 2 (minor problem) or state 3 (major problem).

The state variables and parameters are:

q'_{ij}: Element of transition matrix characterizing the upgrading of the system after minor maintenance.

q''_{ij}: Element of transition matrix characterizing the upgrading of the system after major maintenance.

$P'^{(k)}_{ij}$: Probability that the machine is in state j at time t_0, given that it was in state i at time t_0-k and that there was no failure in the interim.

$r^{(k)}_{i4}$: Probability of first passage at state 4 (failure) after k time units, starting from state i.

s_{ij}: Probability that the machine is in state j at time t_0+1 given that it was in state i at time t_0-L. .

s'_{ij}: Probability that the machine is in state j at time t_0+1 given that it was in state i at time t_0-k and that there was no failure between time t_0-L and time t_0.

S: Transition probability matrix characterized by elements s_{ij}, denoting the evolution of the system between time t_0-L and t_0+1.

Z: Transition probability matrix characterizing the evolution of the system during each cycle (i.e., from a scheduled inspection to the next one).

$p(S_j|i)$: Probability of observing signal j, given that the machine is in state i (i = 1, 2, or 3; j = 2, 3).

$p(\overline{S}|i)$: Probability of observing no signal, given that the machine is in state i (i = 1, 2, or 3).

C_{IN}: Cost of one inspection of the output product.

$c_A^n(i)$: Costs at time n in phase A of cycle (from n = 1 to n = t_0-L), given that phase A begins in state i.

$c_B^n(i)$: Costs at time n in phase B of cycle (from n = t_0-L+1 to n = t_0+1), given that phase B begins in state i.

If the decision is to proceed to the level of maintenance suggested by the signals, then:

$$s'_{ij} = p(S_2|i) \sum_{k=1}^{3} p_{ik}^{(L)} q'_{kj} + p(S_3|i) \sum_{k=1}^{3} p_{ik}^{(L)} q''_{kj} + p(\overline{S}|i) \sum_{k=1}^{3} p_{ik}^{(L)} P_{kj}$$

The probability of first passage to state 4 (failure) after t time units starting at state i is:

$$f_{i4}^{(t)} = \begin{cases} \sum_{j=1}^{3} p_{ij}^{(t-1)} P_{j4} & \text{for } t > 1 \\ p_{i4} & \text{for } t = 1 \end{cases}$$

If a failure has occurred between t_0-L and t_0, then clearly the signal observed at time t_0 should be ignored. Hence, the matrix S has the following generic element:

$$s_{ij} = \begin{cases} \sum_{t=1}^{L} f_{i4}^{(t)} P_{4j}^{(L+1-t)} + \left[1 - \sum_{t=1}^{L} f_{i4}^{(t)} \right] s'_{ij} & \text{for } i \neq 4 \\ p_{4j}^{(L+1)} & \text{for } i = 4 \end{cases}$$

The inspection cycle can be divided into two phases: phase A in which the machine evolves following, at each time unit, the Markov process defined by matrix P, and phase B in which the machine evolves from time t_0-L+1 to time t_0+1 following the transitions defined by matrix S.

The evolution of the system from the beginning of the cycle (time 1) to the beginning of the next cycle is defined by matrix Z, where:

$$Z = P^{m-L}S$$

The expected disutility of the costs associated to inspection and maintenance during one time unit is equal to:

$$\overline{Eu}_m = \frac{1}{m+1} \sum_{i=1}^{4} z_i^* \left[\overline{u}(C_{IN}) + \sum_{n=1}^{m-L} \overline{Eu}(c_A^n(i)) + \sum_{n=m-L+1}^{m+1} \overline{Eu}(c_B^n(i)) \right]$$

The exact derivation of $\overline{Eu}(c_A^n(i))$ and $\overline{Eu}(c_B^n(i))$ are based on a probabilistic analysis of all possible events in phases A and B and can be found in the original paper (Paté-Cornell, Lee, and Tagaras, 1984) for details. The above model can be easily modified to include the case of responding to signal 3 only.

2.3. Policy 3: Maintenance On Demand Based On Monitoring Of Machines

The machine itself occasionally shows signs of problems, for example, unusual noises. Two levels of signals are considered here: signals noted S_2' that suggest minor problems, and signals noted S_3' that suggest major problems. Both types of signals are imperfect and subject to Type I or Type II errors. If one notes $\bar{S}'$, the non-occurrence of signals 2 and 3, the set of all scenarios that may occur is obtained by exhaustive combinations of a state (1, 2, or 3) and a signal ($\bar{S}'$, S_2', or S_3'). Because one directly observes the machine, there is no time lag between the appearance of problem and the observation of signals.

When a signal is observed, one can either respond to it or ignore it. There are, as in Policy 2, two types of maintenance operations: one in response to signal 2 (minor maintenance), and one in response to signal 3 (major maintenance).

The following time axis illustrates the process described above:

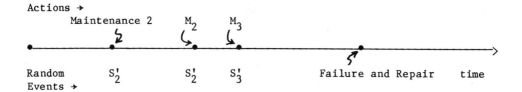

The internal decisions to be made are whether or not to respond to signal 2 by a low level maintenance, and whether or not to respond to signal 3 by a high level maintenance. The transition probability matrix characterizing the process of Policy 3 has generic elements denoted by t_{ij}, and steady state probabilities t_i^*.

Suppose that one responds to signal 2 by low level maintenance and to signal 3 by high level maintenance. The transition probability from state i to state j in one time unit is thus:

$$t_{ij} = \begin{cases} q_{ij}' \, p(S_2'|i) + q_{ij}'' \, p(S_3'|i) + p_{ij} \, p(\bar{S}'|i) & \text{for } i = 1,2,3 \\ p_{4j} & \text{for } i = 4 \end{cases}$$

The expected disutility per time unit of the costs associated with Policy 3 and response to all signals is then:

$$\overline{Eu} = \sum_{i=1}^{3} t_i^* [p(S_2'|i)\bar{u}(C_{M2}) + p(S_3'|i)\bar{u}(C_{M3}) + \sum_{j=1}^{4} p_{ij} p(\bar{S}'|i)\bar{u}(C_j)] + t_4^* \bar{u}(C_4)$$

One can define in a similar way the transitional probabilities and expected disutilities for the following cases: (1) one ignores signal 2 and responds only to signal 3; or (2) one ignores signal 3 but responds to signal 2 (which may be justified if maintenance 3 is very expensive and inefficient in preventing failure); or (3) one ignores all signals and waits for the failure to occur and be repaired.

2.4. Policy 4: Maintenance On Demand Based On Inspection Of Output

In this policy, no particular monitoring mechanism is used. The

product is routinely inspected and signals on the quality of the product
may indicate potential problems of the machine at the time when the output
was produced. There is a delay L' between the occurrence of problems and
their potential observation. Signals are meaningless if they characterize
a state anterior to a failure and repair, and, therefore, they are ignored
if failure has occurred within the L' previous time periods.

The following time axis illustrates the process just described:

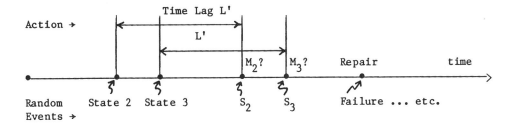

The internal decision to be made is whether or not to respond to
signal 2 and signal 3.

I: supra state, $(i^{(0)}, i^{(1)}, \ldots, i^{(L')})$,
        where $i^{(t)}$ corresponds to the state t time units before the
        current time unit.

R: Transitional probability among supra states.

r_i^*: steady state probability of the chain I.

Suppose that one responds by corresponding maintenance to signal 2
and signal 3, provided that no failure has occurred in the L' previous
time units. The generic element of R is thus zero unless the initial
state I and the subsequent state J have in common the first L' elements of
I and the last L' elements of J. The exact derivation of R is given in
Paté-Cornell, Lee, and Tagaras, 1984.

The steady state probabilities are computed by solving the linear
system $r^* = r^*R$. The corresponding steady state probabilities of the
simple states i, (i = 1, 2, 3, and 4) can be obtained by summing the r^*'s
for all supra states beginning, for example, with state i.

The expected disutility of the costs per time unit is given by:

$$\overline{Eu} = \sum_{\substack{I \text{ s.t. } \ni k \\ \text{with } i^{(k)} = 4}} r^*\left(i^{(0)}, i^{(1)}, \ldots, i^{(L')}\right) \overline{u}(C_{i^{(0)}})$$

$$+ \sum_{\substack{I \text{ s.t. } \ni k \\ \text{with } i^{(k)} = 4}} r^* \, p\left(S_2 | i^{(L')}\right) \overline{u}(C_{M2}) + p\left(S_3 | i^{(L')}\right) \overline{u}(C_{M3}) + p\left(\overline{S} | i^{(L')}\right) \overline{u}(C_{i^{(0)}})$$

The expected disutilities for the following cases: (1) one ignores
signal 2 and responds to signal 3; or (2) becomes equivalent to Policy 0
in which the system is not maintained and only failures are repaired, can
be similarly defined.

3. ILLUSTRATIVE EXAMPLE

An illustration of the method was developed and the data that were used are shown in Table 1. Four cases were considered: a stable system that deteriorates slowly and whose manager is risk indifferent as far as the costs involved are concerned; a stable system but a risk-averse decision maker; a sensitive system that deteriorates faster and the decision maker is risk indifferent; and a sensitive system with a risk-averse decision maker. For each case, each policy is evaluated and a first optimization is made internally: for Policy 1 and Policy 2 we determine the optimal time interval between two operations of maintenance or inspection corresponding to the minimum expected disutility of the costs involved; for Policy 3 and Policy 4 we identify the optimum strategy major problems) or response to signal 3 only (indicator of a major problem). The different policies are then compared to find the overall optimal strategy. Table 2 shows the results of all four models for both systems and both decision makers.

The first observation is that in all cases (except in the "sensitive-indifferent" case) any policy of one of the types considered here is better than doing nothing (Policy 0). The maximum potential benefit of a warning system in terms of decrease of the disutility function is in the order of 50% to 60%. Whereas the benefit is less important for the "sensitive-indifferent" case (9% improvement only is less important for the "sensitive-indifferent" case (9% improvement only from Policy 0 to optimal Policy 1), it is maximal for the "stable-risk averse" case (56%).

The optimal maintenance interval for Policy 1 varies, as one would expect: it decreases as the decision maker becomes more risk averse, and for a given risk attitude, as the system becomes more sensitive.
The same observation holds for Policy 2.

For Policy 3 and Policy 4, response to both signals is preferable in all four cases to response to signal 3 only. However, whereas Policy 3 is the best strategy (response to signals from the machine) in the case of the stable system, response to all signals is too costly in the case of the sensitive system. because it occurs too frequently. This is so because there is a continuous disruption of the process and overreaction as the steady state probability of being in state 2 or 3 exceeds, in our illustrative example, the probability of being in state 1 or 4.

Policy 4, which can be attractive if the time lag between production and observation is short ($L'=1$), becomes less attractive when this time lag increases ($L'=2$) and the detection delay is too long. The same is true for Policy 2. Overall, Policy 1 performs very well in all the cases considered. This confirms the importance of scheduled preventive maintenance often discussed in the literature.

4. CONCLUSION

This paper presents models to analyze different strategies of maintenance and inspection. These concepts apply to production processes in which a product as well as machines can be observed (all four policies are then relevant), such as the production of fabric yardage or the manufacturing of electronic components. With minor adaptations, the domain of application can be extended to equipment and structures for which there is no output to observe but whose monitoring and maintenance can be planned on schedule or on demand (Policy 1 and Policy 3), such as helicopters or dams. Mixed policies (e.g., monitoring of both the machine

Table 1

Illustrative Data:
Modelling The Deterioration And The Maintenance Decision
Of A Production System

TRANSITION PROBABILITY MATRICES							
STABLE SYSTEM				SENSITIVE SYSTEM			
P 0.85	0.10	0.05	0.00	0.45	0.35	0.15	0.05
0.00	0.80	0.175	0.025	0.00	0.60	0.30	0.10
0.00	0.00	0.85	0.15	0.00	0.00	0.75	0.25
0.95	0.05	0.00	0.00	0.85	0.10	0.05	0.00
D 0.95	0.04	0.01	0.00	0.85	0.10	0.05	0.00
0.90	0.08	0.02	0.00	0.85	0.10	0.05	0.00
0.85	0.10	0.05	0.00	0.85	0.10	0.05	0.00
0.95	0.05	0.00	0.00	0.85	0.10	0.05	0.00
D' 0.95	0.04	0.01	0.00	0.85	0.10	0.05	0.00
0.90	0.08	0.02	0.00	0.85	0.10	0.05	0.00
0.85	0.10	0.05	0.00	0.85	0.10	0.05	0.00
0.95	0.05	0.00	0.00	0.85	0.10	0.05	0.00
D" 0.99	0.01	0.00	0.00	0.90	0.07	0.03	0.00
0.95	0.04	0.01	0.00	0.90	0.07	0.03	0.00
0.90	0.07	0.03	0.00	0.90	0.07	0.03	0.00
0.90	0.06	0.04	0.00	0.90	0.07	0.03	0.00

PROBABILITY OF SIGNAL 2, SIGNAL 3, AND NO SIGNAL CONDITIONAL ON EACH STATE

$p(S_2|1) = 0.08$ $p(S_2|2) = 0.80$ $p(S_2|3) = 0.10$

$p(S_3|1) = 0.02$ $p(S_3|2) = 0.05$ $p(S_3|3) = 0.87$

$p(\bar{S}|1) = 0.90$ $p(\bar{S}|2) = 0.15$ $p(\bar{S}|3) = 0.03$

DISUTILITY OF THE COSTS FOR BOTH DECISION MAKERS

	$\bar{u}(M)$	$\bar{u}(C_1)$	$\bar{u}(C_2)$	$\bar{u}(C_3)$	$\bar{u}(C_4)$	$\bar{u}(C_{IN})$	$\bar{u}(C_{M2})$	$\bar{u}(C_{M3})$
Risk Indifferent	30	0	10	20	85	10	30	50
Risk Averse	42	0	12	23	400	12	42	100

Table 2

Optimal Policy And Expected Disutility of Costs
Sensitivity Of Results To System's Robustness And To
Risk Attitude of Decision Maker

	RISK INDIFFERENT		RISK AVERSE	
	POLICY	ū(OPTIMAL)	POLICY	ū(OPTIMAL)
STABLE SYSTEM	**3 (both)**	**9.56**	**3 (both)**	**15.19**
	1 (m*=5)	11.18	1 (m*=3)	18.51
	4 (L'=1,both)	11.33	2 (L=1,m*=2)	19.64
	2 (L=1,m*=4)	11.96	4 (L'=1,both)	19.93
	2 (L=2,m*=5)	12.48	2 (L=2,m*=2)	22.26
	4 (L'=2,both)	13.27	4 (L'=2,both)	24.04
	0	14.31	0	34.50
	Range: 9.56 to 14.31 Benefit (0 vs. optimum): 33%		Range: 15.19 to 34.50 Benefit (0 vs. optimum): 56%	
	POLICY	ū(OPTIMAL)	POLICY	ū(OPTIMAL)
SENSITIVE SYSTEM	**1 (m*=2)**	**20.55**	**1 (m*=1)**	**38.39**
	2 (L=1,m*=3)	21.33	2 (L=1,m*=1)	39.20
	4 (L'=1,both)	21.66	4 (L'=1,both)	47.76
	2 (L=2,m*=4)	21.80	2 (L=2,m*=2)	50.46
	0	22.51	4 (L'=2,both)	52.48
	4 (L'=2,both)	23.10	3 (both)	53.45
	3 (both)	23.42	0	67.99
	Range: 20.55 to 23.42 Benefit (0 vs. optimum): 9%		Range: 38.39 to 67.99 Benefit (0 vs. optimum): 44%	

Legend:
Policy 1: maintenance of machine on schedule
Policy 2: inspection of product on schedule
Policy 3: maintenance of machine on demand (signal observation)
Policy 4: delayed inspection of product
Policy 0: repair of machine after failure
m*:   optimal interval
L,L':   time lag for delayed inspection of product for Policy 2 and 4 respectively
"both":   response to both signals of minor or major problem and corresponding maintenance
ū: expected disutility of costs

Policies are ranked from most attractive (bold) to least attractive. Benefits are measured as percentage reduction of expected disutility.

and the product) have not been considered here but could constitute a
topic for future research.

REFERENCES

Paté-Cornell, M. E. <u>Probabilistic Assessment of Warning Systems: Signals
    and Response</u>. Center for Economic Policy Research, Paper No. 13,
    Stanford University, Stanford, California, 1984.
Paté-Cornell, M. E., H. L. Lee, and G. Tagaras. "Inspection and
    Maintenance of Production Systems: Method, Illustrations, and
    Computer Codes." Technical Report No. TR84-10, Stanford University,
    1984.

"LIVING PRA" CONCEPT FOR RISK MANAGEMENT OF NUCLEAR AND CHEMICAL

PROCESSING PLANTS

Selim Sancaktar

Westinghouse Electric Corporation

ABSTRACT

The "Living PRA" is based on placing a PRA plant model on an
interactive personal computer such as an IBM-XT. This model consists of
fault tree analyses for plant systems, event tree analyses for abnormal
events and site specific consequence analysis for public and/or financial
risks, for a given nuclear or chemical process plant. A living PRA allows
updates and sensitivity analyses by the plant owner throughout the
lifetime of a plant. Thus it enhances the risk management of the plant
both in personnel and public safety and also in economic risk tm the plant
owner. In addition, it can be used to track and improve the plant
availability and system reliabilities.

The above concept is well established for the Nuclear Power Plant
evaluation. It has also been used for the evaluation of process
facilities. Presently both the tools and the experience exists to set up
useful and viable living PRA models for nuclear and chemical processing
plants to enhance risk management by the plant owners through the in-house
use of micro computer based models.

KEY WORDS: PRA, Fault Trees, Event Trees, IBM-PC, Hazard Analysis.

INTRODUCTION

The "Living PRA" is based on placing a PRA plant model on an
interactive computer. It allows qualitative or quantitative
identification and ranking of single or multiple failures that would lead
to hazard states on or around the plant site. The model consists of fault
tree analyses for plant systems, event tree analyses for abnormal events
and site specific consequence analysis for public and/or financial risks,
for a given nuclear or chemical process plant. The plant owner can
perform updates and sensitivity analysis by using the}living PRA model
throughout the lifetime of a plant. Thus the model enhances the risk
management of the plant both in personnel and public safety and also in
economic risk to the plant owner. In addition, it can be used to track
and improve plant availability and system reliabilities.

The living PRA can be used to provide input in the following areas:

1. Evaluate catastrophic risks and plant response to abnormal
    events.

2. Seek insights into plant operations to maximize plant availability.
3. Enable both plant operations and plant engineering to gain a better understanding of system reliability, interactions and safety.
4. Respond to licensing issues.

Some references regarding the subjects summarized in this paper are provided at the end of the paper.

Model Description

The living PRA model can be implemented on an IBM Personal Computer. The following parts of the model are placed in the computer.

1. A Master Data Bank of Reliability/Availability Input

   This data bank includes component failure data, test and maintenance frequencies and times, operator action data, scheduled and unscheduled plant shutdowns (initiating event frequencies), system unavailabilities (event tree nodal probabilities), and site specific consequence analysis data.

2. System Fault Trees

   The system fault trees model random, common cause, operator, and test and maintenance-related failures or unavailabilities.

3. Event Trees

   The event trees model system responses and operator actions in postulated event sequences leading to plant unavailability or safety concerns.

4. Analysis and Data Processing Codes

   Existing computer codes are used to quantify fault trees and event trees and to generate output tables, graphs, and histograms.

5. Site Specific Consequence Model

   This model contains the various consequence categories of interest for a given plant.

Computer Codes and Files

A code library is developed on an IBM-XT (or IBM-AT) computer to construct a Living PRA for a plant. This library contains the following codes and data banks:

GRAFTER : Code for drawing, storing, and printing of fault trees.

SIMON : Code for management of fault tree master data bank.

SIMON.DAT : Fault tree master data bank containing random component failures; human errors; test and maintenance unavailability; common cause failures, etc.

WESCUT   : Code for quantification of system unavailability and
             identification of single and multiple failures.

COMP   : Code for importance ranking of failures.

SUPER   : Code for even tree drawing, quantification of accident
             scenario probabilities, and for printing of event trees.

SUPER.DAT : Event tree master data bank containing system failure
             probabilities; operator action failure probabilities and
             other phenomenological occurrence probabilities.

ADAM   : Code for identification of dominant accident sequences
             and ranking of system failures.

BORIS   : Code for calculation of the site specific plant risk and
             its dominant contributors.

BORIS.DAT : Plant analysis and site specific consequence data bank.

RIVET   : Code for uncertainty analysis through discrete
             probability distributions.

WTHERP   : Code for human error calculations.

WTHERP.DAT : Human error master data bank.

CONCLUSION

     Recently, event trees and fault trees from two major PRAs were placed
in a computerized format. The BYRON PRA study and the Living PRA and
Economic Risk examples for Indian Point Unit-3 enabled analysts to gain
experience and insight into the problems of plant operation. Presently,
the ZION Probabilistic Safety Study is being cast into a living PRA format
on an IBM-AT computer.

     The above concept is well established for the Nuclear Power Plant
evaluation. It has been also used for the evaluation of chemical
processing facilities. In these studies, systems modeling was carried out
by using the GRAFTER system for automated fault tree construction. These
hazard analyses were performed qualitatively to identify multiple failures
that lead to hazard states. Also an event tree code system (named SUPER)
is available on a micro computer to model multi-branched system states
(containing up to 8 branches per event tree node) and to identify dominant
accident sequences.

     Presently both the tools and the experience exist to set up useful
and viable living PRA models for nuclear and chemical processing plants to
enhance risk management by the plant owners through the in-house use of
micro computer based models.

REFERENCES:

"Financial Risk Assessment at the Plant Design Stage", S. Sancaktar,
    Plant/operations Progress, Vol 2, No. 3, July 1983.
"An Illustration of Matrix Formulation for a Probabilistic Risk Assessment
    Study", S. Sancaktar, RISK ANALYSIS, 1982 pp. 132.
Byron Generating Station Limiting Conditions for Operation Relaxation
    Program, WCAP 10526, April, 1984.

Living PRA and Financial Risk Assessment: Examples for Indian Point Unit-3, S. Sancaktar, T.L. Morrison, unpublished report, December 1983.

Hazard Evaluation of an Oil Recovery and Processing Facility, WCAP 10548, May 1984, (Westinghouse report to a customer).

Hazard Evaluation of an Oil Refining Facility, WCAP 10626, Sept. 1984. (Westinghouse report to a customer).

"Automated Fault Tree Analysis: The GRAFTER System", S. Sancaktar, D.R. Sharp. International ANS/ENS Topical Meeting on Probabilistic Safety Methods and Applications, San Francisco, Feb. 1985, (paper 116).

"Multi-branch Event Tree Analysis", S. Sancaktar, D.R. Sharp, IAEA Seminar on Implications of Probabilistic Risk Assessment, Blackpool, United Kingdom, March 1985.

THE IDCOR PROGRAM--SEVERE ACCIDENT ISSUES, INDIVIDUAL

PLANT EXAMINATIONS AND SOURCE TERM DEVELOPMENTS

Anthony R. Buhl, James C. Carter, Mario H. Fontana,
Robert E. Henry* and Harold A. Mitchell

Energex Associates, Inc., Oak Ridge, Tennessee 37820
*Fauske Associates, Inc., Burr Ridge, Illinois 60521

ABSTRACT

    The Industry Degraded Core Rulemaking (IDCOR) Program has established
a technical foundation for resolving the severe accident issues associated
with the operation of light water reactor (LWR) nuclear power plants. The
technical program began in early 1981 and was completed by 1984. IDCOR
cam to three primary technical conclusions and one major policy
conclusion.

- First, the probabilities of severe nuclear accidents occurring
  are extremely low.
- Second, the fission product source terms--quantities and types of
  radioactive material released in the event of severe accidents--
  are likely to be much less than had been calculated in previous
  studies.
- Third, the risks and consequences to the public of severe nuclear
  accidents are significantly below those predicted by previous
  studies and are much smaller than the risk levels incorporated in
  the NRC interim safety goals.
- From a policy standpoint, IDCOR concluded that major design or
  operational changes in reactors are not warranted.

The IDCOR program was extended through 1985 with the following new
directions:

- To maintain an industry presence with the NRC to close open
  technical issues and assure appropriate industry input into the
  NRC decision processes.
- To deomonstrate generic applicability of IDCOR results and
  support the development of an integrated approach for individual
  plant examinations.
- To use IDCOR results and other information to improve the source
  terms used in regulatory nuclear plants and to improve emergency
  planning.

this presentation provides the status of the IDCOR efforts on all three
fronts.

KEY WORDS: Industry Degraded Core Rulemaking Program, severe accidents, individual plant examinations, source terms, policy making

The Response to TMI

The accident at Three Mile Island (TMI) on March 28, 1979, prompted new initiatives for nuclear safety. The TMI degraded core reached conditions far more severe than those in a design basis accident. Several public inquiries questioned the existing regulatory process for licensing nuclear power plants.

As a result of the degraded core accident at TMI and subsequent re-evaluation of regulatory processes, the NRC initiated, on October 2, 1980, a "long-term rulemaking to consider to what extent, if any, nuclear power plants should be designed to deal effectively with degraded core and core melt accidents" (NRC, October 2, 1980). The NRC's rulemaking proposed to address the objectives and content of a degraded core-related regulation, the related design and operational improvements under consideration, their effects on other safety considerations, and the cost and benefits of design and operational improvements.

Recently, the NRC issued a Severe Accident Policy Statement (NRC, August 8, 1985) which withdrew the October 2, 1980, Advance Notice of Rulemaking and replaced it with a severe accident decision process on specific standard plant designs and with individual examinations for existing plants.

IDCOR: An Integrated Industry Evaluation

In late 1980 and early 1981, the nuclear industry organized an independent evaluation of the technical issues related to potential severe accidents in nuclear power plants with LWRs. The IDCOR technical program began in March 1981, under the direction of a Policy Group chaired by John Selby, Chairman of Consumers Power Company. A 12-member Steering Group chaired by Cordell Reed, Vice President of Commonwealth Edison Company, administers the Policy Group's direction and acts as the executive committee for IDCOR. The IDCOR Program Manager, originally Technology for Energy Corporation, then ENERGEX, and now IT provides the day-to-day program management.

The history, organization, technical program structure, and technical results of IDCOR are well documented (Fontan, November 1981; Buhl, October 20, 1982; Buhl, September 18-21, 1983; Fontana, August 28 - September 1, 1983; Sears, July 15-19, 1984; Fontana, September 11, 1984; Buhl, March 10-13, 1985; and Buhl, May 19-22, 1985.) Background material from the IDCOR program will not be repeated here except as needed to set the stage for describing IDCOR's present activities.

IDCOR developed a long list of severe accident issues and reviewed these with the NCR, Advisory Committee on Reactor Safeguards (ACRS), and many other interested organizations, both foreign and domestic.

This paper will address the following topics:

- IDCOR Contributions to Severe Accident Technology

- IDCOR Program for 1985

- NRC Interaction Process

- Major Technical Issues and Prescription for Resolution

- Individual Plant Evaluation Methodology

- Source Term Program

IDCOR CONTRIBUTIONS TO SEVERE ACCIDENT TECHNOLOGY

The original IDCOR mission was to gather and critically review existing technical work related to the severe accident issues and to perform the additional technical work required to develop a comprehensive and thorough understanding of these issues. IDCOR also served as the industry spokesman with the NRC on these matters.

IDCOR selected four reference plants, which are representative of the reactor and containment designs in the United States, for the most extensive technical evaluation of power plant response to severe accidents ever performed. The four plants selected for detailed analysis were: (a) Zion (Westinghouse pressurized water reactor (PWR) with a large dry containment system); (b) Sequoyah (Westinghouse PWR with ice condenser containment); (c) Peach Bottom (General Electric boiling water reactor (BWR) with Mark I pressure suppression containment); and (d) Grand Gulf (General Electric BWR with Mark III pressure suppression containment).

Accident progressions from initiation to core melt and containment failure were analyzed and quantified by IDCOR. In order to perform these analyzses, IDCOR developed a new suite of physical and chemical models, data, and computer codes based on analytical and experimental data from government and industrial research programs in several countries.

Application of this new understanding of key phenomena and new analytical techniques has yielded major new conclusions on the changes of occurrence and on the consequences of severe accidents (Fontana, November 1984). The key findings are:

- The release of fission products is greatly influences by the containment features and plant systems found in existing light water reactors (e.g., primary systems, containment volumes, suppression pools, and ice beds).

- The accident sequences which dominate the risk from severe accidents can be represented by a few categories of functional failures (e.g., pipe breaks with loss of emergency cooling, blackout, and transients with failure of decay heat removal).

- The frequency of these accidents is extremely low and only a small fraction of these lead to significant environmental releases.

- Debris from severely damaged cores can be cooled for an indefinitely long time, given water, power, and ways to remove the residual heat generated by core debris materials. The containment can hold in radioactivity for an indefinite period under these conditions.

- Previous risk studies, notably the 1975 NRC Reactor Safety Study, identified three mechanisms by which containments could fail early in an accident sequence: steam explosions, high pressures produced by rapid steam generation, and hydrogen combustion. Those postulated failures were the result of the overly conservative calculations and assumptions used in previous studies.

The IDCOR studies show that steam explosions and rapid steam generation are not likely to be the cause of early containment failure. Hydrogen detonation cannot occur in prototypical reactor accident conditions and hydrogen combustion would not cause failure of large, dry containments. Small containments have hydrogen control measures, such as inerted containment or igniters, that would be effective if needed.

• If containment should fail, failure would occur many hours after the start of the accident. Because of these long times before containment failure, there would be enough time to reduce the risk to the public by at least two methods: reactor operator intervention to correct the error or condition, and if that was not completely successful, emergency response measures away from the reactor. These long times also allow for reduction in the radioactive fission products that could be released by natural processes such as settling to the floors of the containment building.

There is one exception to this general rule. One BWR accident sequence is calculated to have a short time before containment fails. However, the amount of radioactive fission products that would be released to the environment would be small because of the filtering action of the suppression pool which is part of that design and existing emergency procedures.

• If a containment should reach failure pressure or temperature, it would be expected to fail by creating a small leak which would preclude further pressure increase and subsequent large size failure. In addition, IDCOR has shown that resuspension of previously settled fission products would not occur even during rapid depressurization caused by large size containment failure.

• Although it is possible that containment could be bypassed by simple events that have nothing to do with accident sequences, such as leaving a door or vent open by mistake, the likelihood of these conditions, given frequent inspection, is small. Even if the containment was to be partially circumvented by this or similar events, IDCOR calculated that the added risk to the public would be small.

• Fission product release to the environment, even if containment should fail, would be much less than estimated in past studies. Most accident sequences lead to volatile releases of one percent or less. A few exceptional accident sequences, as described above, lead to volatile releases of 10 percent or less. This is due to a number of factors. Some of them increase the estimated release while others decrease it.

Taken together, these factors decrease the effect on the public. The major reasons are: (a) more realistic analysis of core damage processes; (b) improved understanding of pressure and temperature loads on containment: (c) better understanding of the chemical and physical forms of fission products which have lower vapor pressures and less mobility than the forms assumed in prior analyses; and (d) more realistic analyses of the transport of these fission products from the fuel, through the primary coolant system, and in the containment system.

• The so-called "China Syndrome", where a mass of molten core debris penetrates the bottom of the reactor and the containment basemat, has been evaluated. If containment should fail by this mode, it would usually be much later than a failure due to high pressures. In any case, if this event were to occur, its added risk to the public, compared with other accident sequences, would be small.

Most of the discussion so far has dealt with events that are not caused by humans, at least directly. Humans can both start accident sequences by errors or halt them by taking corrective action. Whether corrective action can be counted on will depend, to a large extent, on how fast the accident sequence proceeds.

IDCOR found that most potentially severe accidents progress slowly, and that there are ample opportunities for human intervention to halt and reverse events. The industry has emergency procedure guidelines which direct the operator to act in accordance with a limited set of observed symptoms, without requiring diagnosis of a large mass of information. These guidelines correctly assist the operator and allow him multiple opportunities to prevent and terminate severe accidents.

The IDCOR analyses of the reference plants showed that those risks are generally less than those presented in previous studies. For example, in contrast to prior evaluations, the IDCOR calculations of consequences of severe accidents show that no early fatalities would result.

However, some risk is calculated as latent fatalities over a 30-year period. The risks calculated by IDCOR are less than those in previous studies, and much smaller than those set forth in NRC's interim safety goals.

Figure 1 illustrates the range of risks for the four reference plants calculated by IDCOR and contrasts these with pre-IDCOR values, the NRC interim safety goal, and normal cancer fatalities expected for the population over a thirty-year period.

IDCOR came to three primary technical conclusions and one overall policy conclusion.

• First, the probabilities of severe nuclear accidents occurring are extremely low and only a small fraction of those sequences result in significant releases.

The risk of latent cancer fatalities from operating the IDCOR reference nuclear plants is 1,000 times lower than the interim NRC safety goal. The risk from potential severe accidents at these plants is only one millionth of the normally occurring cancer fatalities for the population living within 50 miles of the plants.

• Second, the fission product source terms--quantities and types of radioactive material released in the event of severe accidents--are much less than were calculated in previous studies.

• Third, the risks and consequences to the public of severe nuclear accidents are significantly below those predicted by previous studies and are much smaller than the risk levels incorporated in the NRC interim safety goals.

• From a policy standpoint, IDCOR concluded that major design or operational changes in reactors are not warranted.

THE IDCOR PROGRAM FOR 1985

Based on the findings of NRC and IDCOR, the Commission has agreed with IDCOR's overall conclusion that major backfits to plants are not needed for severe accidents (Nuclear Regulatory Commission, August 8, 1985). The Commission and staff now believe that only confirmatory research and individual plant evaluations are needed to resolve the long-

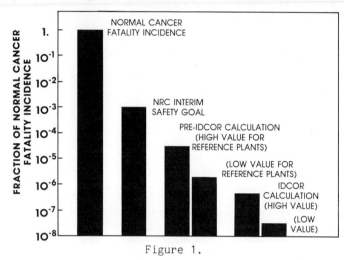

Figure 1.

Risk of Latent Cancer Fatalities From IDCOR Reference Plants

The risk of latent cancer fatalities from operating the IDCOR reference nuclear plants is 1,000 times lower than the interim NRC safety goal. The risk from potential severe accidents at these plants is only one millionth of the normally occurring cancer fatalities for the population living within 50 miles of the plants.

standing severe accident issues for existing plants.

The industry has maintained an IDCOR presence for several reasons. First, all technical issues have not been resolved. Second, IDCOR is developing the methodology needed to perform the individual plant evaluations now being required by the NRC. Third, the industry can take advantage of the reduced source terms from IDCOR to obtain relief in emergency preparedness and perhaps in other areas as well.

IDCOR has pursued three basic objectives in 1985:

1) Resolving the remaining technical issues with NRC.

2) Developing and obtaining NRC and industry acceptance of an individual plant analysis methodology for demonstration of generic applicability of the positive IDCOR severe accident conclusions.

3) Developing the technical basis for changes in regulatory requirements for emergency planning through utilization of new source term information.

Technical Resolution of Open Issues

IDCOR has assessed the original set of technical issues and identified a few key issues that needed to be addressed in 1985. IDCOR initiated specific tasks to develop additional technical information on these issues. Resolution is progressing through meetings with NRC senior management and technical exchange meetings with NRC staff. The technical exchange meetings are better defining the issues and working toward agreement on an acceptable basis for resolution. Senior management meetings between IDCOR and the NRC are guiding this process.

Individual Plant Methodology for Generic Applicability and Individual Plant Evaluations

IDCOR is developing a methodology for demonstrating whether individual plants are comparable with IDCOR reference plants with respect to severe accident issues. The methodology will be structured to identify unusual system designs or operational situations. The methodology will address accident prevention, containment response, and accident management. The activities leading to acceptance of the methodology include the following:

- Evaluating potential approaches and selecting an acceptable methodology.

- Reviewing the approach with NRC management and obtaining concurrence

- Applying the methodology for the IDCOR reference plants.

- Verifying the methodology as necessary and applying it to three additional plants.

- Developing positions on methodology use and interpretation.

- Presenting results to IDCOR groups.

- Presenting final results to the NRC.

- Preparing an implementation report.

- Briefing utilities on methodology application to individual plants.

Source Term Reduction and Emergency Planning

The 1985 IDCOR effort is focused on the technical work necessary to provide a basis for reducing source terms and to support emergency planning relief. IDCOR established a technical foundation for source terms which is an excellent starting point for pursuing source term reduction. Additionally, in 1985, IDCOR is pursuing resolution of a few remaining issues that can affect the source term. Once the technical bases are established, IDCOR will interact with the NRC to establish the requirements for emergency planning relief which will focus initially on graded response and increased public notification times.

Existing IDCOR results and other available and ongoing work will be integrated with the additional work tasks defined below to establish technically sound source terms. These tasks are scheduled for presentation of IDCOR positions to the NRC staff and the ACRS in late 1985 or early 1986.

The source term program logic includes:

- Documenting the present IDCOR source terms and determining emergency planning relief attainable at present.

- Recommending improvements in source term models, incorporating them into MAAP, and performing analyses of selected sequences.

- Determining further source term reductions required to justify relief in emergency planning.

- Evaluating technical uncertainties and aspects of plant design and operation which affect source terms for IDCOR plants.

- Determining practical improvements which could reduce source terms and documenting the technical basis for source terms.

NCR INTERACTION PROCESS

IDCOR was chartered by the industry to develop the technical basis for resolving the severe accident issues and to be the industry's spokeman with the NRC on these matters. IDCOR and the NRC have met many times to review IDCOR planning, progress, and results. From late 1983 through 1984, IDCOR provided documented technical results of all its work to the NRC. IDCOR and the NRC conducted five multi-day technical exchange meetings to review these IDCOR results. Following this intensive interaction process, early in 1985 the NRC defined 18 remaining open issues. Most of these are either resolved or near resolution. Five or six will likely extend beyond 1985.

The NRC has been conducting a major severe accident research program in parallel with IDCOR. Their program is similar to IDCOR in philosophy and content but is on an extended schedule. The NCR program is funded at a level about 10 to 20 times the IDCOR effort. Many of the major results of the NRC program will be forthcoming in the next few months. IDCOR expects to participate in extensive reviews of the NRC reference plant results, of NUREG-0956 on source term technology, and of other important research products.

The NRC and IDCOR developed precise definitions of the remaining technical issues and identifies the necessary technical work required to address these issues. Further meetings were proposed by the NRC to arrive at a closer technical understanding before developing final technical positions. Also, the NRC requested meetings to present their reference plant results.

IDCOR has the technical work under way to achieve resolution of these remaining open technical issues. The major differences and resolution needs are discussed in the next section. IDCOR expects to obtain documented agreement from the NRC management on the resolution of all issues.

MAJOR TECHNICAL ISSUES AND PRESCRIPTION FOR RESOLUTION

The many severe accident technical issues originally perceived to be important have been reduced to a tractable few. The IDCOR '85 technical task was directed toward identifying the important remaining issues and an appropriate path to resolution. That work has been completed.

Many issues were resolved in 1984, including containment failure due to in-vessel steam explosion, rate and magnitude of fission product release from fuel in-vessel, resuspension of desposited fission products, and selection of importantly types of sequences. The effort in 1985 has resulted in additional information which should address concerns raised by the NRC in other areas, including treatment of the interaction of tellurium and zirconium, importance of natural circulation in high pressure sequences, fission product and aerosol deposition in reactor coolant systems and containments, direct containment heating, and revaporization of fission products. Essentially no additional effort was required in several additional areas including modeling of emergency response, aerosol production from control materials, revaporization of fission products, and behavior in secondary containments.

In general, progress has been made in providing a technical basis for the few remaining areas of disagreement with the NRC. The more important remaining issues which may extend into 1986 are:

- Hydrogen production (Issue 5)

- Ex-vessel release of fission products (Issue 9)

- Coolability of debris on concrete in the presence of water (Issue 10)

- Hydrogen combustion in ice condenser containments (Issue 17)

- Direct containment heating (Issue 8)

- Containment performance (Issue 15)

The NRC analyses of core relocation and hydrogen production lead to early containment failure in ice condenser transients and in large LOCA sequences in Mark I BWR containments. IDCOR efforts have been directed toward comparison of models with integral experiments and TMI-2 experiences, to the degree possible, and further effort may be necessary. The behavior of core debris interaction with concrete and the related release of fission products is complicated by the dearth of information on chemical forms of low volatile fission products and adequate experimental data under appropriate conditions. This area will probably require additional effort as experimental data becomes available. These areas are treated in detail in the IDCOR analyses and are expected to be the focus of important discussions with the NRC.

GENERIC APPLICABILITY AND INDIVIDUAL PLANT EVALUATIONS

IDCOR analyzed the potential for, and consequences of, severe accidents for the reference plants, Grand Gulf, Peach Bottom, Sequoyah, and Zion. These analyses demonstrated that the probabilities for severe accidents were low and that the releases of fission products to the environment were well below those considered in the Reactor Safety Study (WASH-1400). The IDCOR '85 Program is directed at developing a methodology to determine if these results are generally applicable through individual plant analyses.

IPE methodology concentrates on two major aspects of the accident evaluation: (1) the core damage prevention capability and (2) environmental releases given a severe accident. In this regard, the analysis focuses on the controlling areas for each, such that major outliers in either area can be detected. For this to be executed in a timely manner, the methodology must be an approximate representation of both a Level 1 probabilistic risk assessment. (PRA and a containment response analysis for the dominant sequences as would be performed in a Level 2 PRA.) However, since the specific task of the analysis is to identify major outliers, concentrating on the controlling systems and/or physical processes for the different designs is a sufficient approach.

The IDCOR approach is divided into the two main areas and further subdivided into areas associated with BWR designs and PWR systems. The systems analysis for both designs concentrate on the front line core protection systems and their major support systems such as electrical power and service water. The basis for the structure of the BWR and PWR systems analysis is the extensive work performed on PRAs for both types of designs. Both methods concentrate on system level fault trees and the dependencies between the front line systems and the major support systems as well as the dependencies between support systems. The net result of performing these analyses is an approximate assessment of the core damage frequency which identifies those systems, operator actions, design dependent configurations, etc., which control the order of magnitude of the probability for a severe core damage event.

Assessments of the environmental releases for severe core damage events are based upon the integrated systems analyses carried out for the IDCOR reference plants. In these analyses, specific design features were found to control the ultimate releases to the environment. For example, in a large dry containment, the hold-up within the primary system and in the containment was demonstrated to be a most important aspect of the accident progression. So much so that the other details of the accident sequence had little influence on the ultimate release of the environment. In addition, the analyses for the BWR Mark III design demonstrated that the scrubbing of fission products in the suppression pool was the dominant physical process determining the ultimate releases to the environment. As a result, the specific physical configurations for the different designs are highlighted and designs of similar character are analyzed for a similar capability of fission product retention. In this regard, the specific accident sequences identified for the reactor system must be considered and these are carried out by an integration between the systems analysis and the approximate fission product release evaluations.

This approach to individual plant evaluations has been presented to the NRC staff and has received their tentative endorsement. The methodology for the two elements of these evaluations was completed in July 1985, and reviewed with the NRC staff, the IDCOR Steering and Policy Groups, and also the ACRS. These methods are being applied to the four IDCOR reference plants to provide a validation of the approach. In this effort, the specific interest will be in whether the approximate methodology is sufficient to evaluate the fundamental features of the reference plants. While this test is somewhat circular in character, it does provide for an internal check of the methods before their application to other systems. This will be completed by March 1986.

The IDCOR IPE methodology will be applied to three additional plants, including a BWR Mark II system, a Combustion Engineering plant with a large dry containment, and a B&W NSSS with a large dry containment. This extension of the methodology will provide an example of the implementation for the methods that can be reviewed by the industry (owners' groups and individual plant owners) and will also be presented to the NRC staff. In 1986, the IDCOR Steering Group plans to seek NRC approval of this methodology as an acceptable way to examine existing plants and demonstrate their acceptability with respect to the severe accident issue. IDCOR anticipates NRC approval to be documented in a letter to licensees specifying the requirements for qualifying individual plants.

SOURCE TERM REDUCTION AND EMERGENCY PLANNING

Source terms, based on TID-14844 and WASH-1400, are pervasive in regulatory requirements which affect many aspects of plant design and operation, siting, and emergency planning. A sound technical basis for more realistic source terms is needed to define the benefits of source term reductions in improving emergency planning, or other regulatory areas should the industry or the NRC decide to pursue them.

The tasks being performed in this area was listed above in the section on the IDCOR Program for 1985.

IDCOR's analyses of the four reference plants found several major effects that reduce source terms. These include:

1) Retention of volatile fission products in the primary system due to their release from the fuel and recondensing or settling on cooler surfaces with the primary system.

2) Chemical forms of the fission products, particularly cesium and iodines, the increase their retention because of their low vapor pressures and high solubility in water. Virtually no elemental iodine or cesium are calculated to occur, which is opposite from TID-14844 assumptions.

3) No occurrence of early containment failures from pressurized state. This allows time for fission product laden aerosols to settle on the surfaces. Once on surfaces, material has been shown to remain there in the event of containment depressurization.

4) Retention of fission products by the large amounts of available water within the primary system and containment.

5) Retention of fission products in secondary buildings, primarily by aerosol settling.

As noted earlier, the source terms are lower than previous estimates, including the Reactor Safety Study. Also, releases to the environment, if this occurs at all, generally occur a long time after accident initiation.

Although all themochemical calculations indicate that C_sI and C_sOH would be the dominant chemical species, preliminary (unpublished) experiments performed at Sandia National Laboratories indicate that C_sI may decompose in the presence of stainless steel and radiation and could release elemental iodine. Cesium appears to remain on the surface. We are waiting for the results of confirmatory experiments. Meanwhile, we intend to start preliminary evaluation to determine what influence this effect has on iodine transport in reactor accident sequences.

IDCOR will document the present source terms and identify emergency planning improvements, such as graded response and longer public notification times, that can be derived form them.

Several additional areas are also being investigated further because they could affect present source term values. Among these are:

• Chemical reactions of fission products. (1) Tellurium can react with zirconium and remain with the core debris during pressure vessel melt-through and be released ex-vessel during concrete attack rather than being released at the time of initial fuel melting or be retained in the primary system on surfaces. (2) Lanthanum and other refractories may form oxides during core-concrete interactions that are more volatile than forms assumed by IDCOR.

• Uncertainties in containment failure. Early containment failure and depressurization can cause larger source terms. The NRC calculates greater generation of hydrogen than IDCOR and predicts early failure of ice condenser containments due to hydrogen global burning. IDCOR analyses predict continuous hydrogen burning enabled by natural circulation of air in containment; no early failure is predicted.

• Water pools existing over the debris bed may dry out in certain accident sequences and allow higher fission product release rates. Small scale experimental evidence suggest debris beds may not be quenched when water is added as IDCOR has predicted. However, the NRC has ignored (1) the effects of debris dispersal, which would result in thinner debris beds, (2) the fraction of debris initially participating in concrete attack, and (3) the long times over which the fuel remaining in the vessel, after initial vessel failure, would enter the cavity.

IDCOR will then improve source term models. Two basic areas are being studied that could lower source terms further. First, models are MAAP that control heat transfer from the primary system are being refined, including additional nodalization and radiative heat transfer losses. Second, better knowledge of chemical forms may also reduce the present source terms as well as increase them as discussed above. This is possible because IDCOR ignored the potential for reaction of the volatile fission products with the steel surfaces of the primary system which would form less volatile forms of the fission products. Utilizing this observation would substantially reduce the amount predicted to revolatize and be released through the containment breach.

IDCOR is also studying other means of reducing source terms, primarily through operator actions and plant design. For example, based on the potential release of fission products from debris beds, the operator may reduce releases significantly if he can maintain a pool of water over the debris bed. Actions, such as containment venting, may alter the timing of release and induce transport paths, such as through suppression pools, that enhance aerosol retention. IDCOR anticipates that a number of such means will be identified that will reduce source terms if implemented.

Further desired changes in emergency planning procedures will be assessed to determine if further research on source term reduction would be justified. This would preclude expenditures to support further reductions having little useful impact.

Finally, if so justified, IDCOR will determine further practical improvements which could reduce source terms and will document their technical bases.

SUMMARY

The IDCOR technical program is complete and documented in 48 technical reports and a Technical Summary Report. The results of the IDCOR program show that present generation plants, which comply with existing regulations, can tolerate a broad spectrum of severe accidents and will provide adequate public protection. Thus, major retrofits to designs or regulations to further account for severe accidents are not warranted. However, a few questions remain open; IDCOR and the NRC are pressing toward closure of these questions during 1985 and 1986.

Work is underway to reach the IDCOR objectives added in 1985. The methodology for individual plant evaluations has been developed and is being verified against seven plants. IDCOR is evaluating improvements in source term technology and applying it to emergency planning.

REFERENCES

1. Buhl, A. R., "IDCOR: The Decision Pathway for Resolution of Severe Accident Issues," Paper presented at the American Nuclear Society Conference on Government and Self Regulation of Nuclear Power Plants, Williamsburg, Virginia, October 20, 1982.
2. Buhl, A. R. and M. H. Fontana, "IDCOR - The Technical Foundation and Process for Severe Accident Decisions," Paper presented at the AIF Conference on Emergency Policies, Programs, and Issues in Reactor Licensing and Safety, New Orleans, Louisiana, September 18-21, 1983.
3. Buhl, A. R., M. H. Fontana, and H. A. Mitchell, "IDCOR - Supporting the Technical Foundation and the Decision Process for Source Term Reduction," Paper presented at the ANS Executive Conference on Ramifications of the Source Term, Charleston, South Carolina, March 10-13, 1985.
4. Buhl, A. R., J. C. Carter, M. H. Fontana, and H. A. Mitchell, "The IDCOR Program, Severe Accident Issues, Individual Plant Examiniation, and Source Term Developments," Paper presented at the Atomic Industrial Forum Conference on New Directions in Licensing, Dallas, Texas, May 19-22, 1985.
5. Fontana, M. H. and A. R. Buhl, "Improving Our Understanding of Nuclear Power Plant Response to Severe Accidents: Summary of IDCOR Results," Paper presented at the Fifth International Meeting on Thermal Nuclear Reactor Safety, Karlsruhe, Federal Republic of Germany, September 11, 1984.
6. Fontana, M. H., "The Industry Degraded Core Rulemaking Program: IDCOR - An Overview," Paper presented at the American Nuclear Society International Meeting on LWR Safety Assessment, Cambridge, Massachusetts, August 28 - September 1, 1983.
7. Advance Notice of Rulemaking: 45 FR 65474, October 2, 1980, Nuclear Regulatory Commission.
8. Severe Accident Policy Statement: 50 FR 32138, August 8, 1985, Nuclear Regulatory Commission.
9. Sears, C. F., "IDCOR Source Term Issues," Paper presented at the ANS Topical Meeting on Fission Product Behavior and Source Term Research, Snowbird, Utah, July 15-19, 1984.
10. Fontana, M. H., Asselin, S. V., Buhl, A. R., Dougherty, E. M., Fuller, E. L., Fuller, J., Mitchell, H. A., Moore, R. D., Satterfield, R. M., Standifer, P., and Stroupe, E.P., IDCOR Program Plan, Technology for Energy Corporation, November 1981. Available from AIF.
11. Fontana, M. H., Buhl, A. R., Fuller, E. L., Mitchel, H. A., Asselin, S. V., Stroupe, E. P., Carter, J. C. Meyer, K. A. Satterfield, R., and Fritts, G. A., IDCOR Technical Summary Report - Nuclear Power Plant Response to Severe Accidents, Technology for Energy Corporation, November 1984. Available from AIF.

TRENDS AND NEEDS IN REACTOR SAFETY IMPROVEMENT

M. C. Leverett

Electric Power Research Institute

ABSTRACT

The Three Mile Island accident produced a surge of interest in understanding the technology of nuclear reactor accidents. Most of the resultant research and development has been focused on what happens after the accident starts, with less extensive work on accident prevention. It is pointed out that probabilistic risk analysis is an effective tool for discerning where to apply accident preventive work, and it is recommended that each nuclear power plant should have a level one probabilistic risk assessment, primarily for reasons of protection of the owner's investment in the plant.

KEY WORDS: Safety, Nuclear, Reactor, Risk, Probabilistic, Assessment, Prevention, Accident, Scram, Frequency

Introduction

The safety of the public against accidents in nuclear power plants has been a preoccupation of both the industry and the regulatory authorities from the very first. Even the earliest plants had redundant safety systems. Additionally, because the primary requirement is that the reactor be kept cool, special means of assuring that the reactor could be cooled in spite of any possible failure of its normal cooling system or loss of integrity of its connected piping were provided. Large reservoirs of water, for heat absorption, were provided and connections to effectively infinite heat sinks such as likes, rivers or oceans were made. Additionally, each reactor was enclosed in a containment structure, designed to prevent the release of fission products to the environs if, in spite of the already elaborate measures to prevent an accident, one should occur anyhow.

On the other hand, in these early years, interest in knowing in detail what would happen in an accident was not strong. It was considered acceptable to make some probably overly safe assumptions regarding the kind and amount of fission product release in a hypothetical accident. For example in the 1960s, the Ergen Committee, a group of highly knowledgeable technical experts from both the national laboratories and the industry, gave serious consideration to the question of what kind of research and development was needed for assurance of safety. A principal conclusion was that the most productive efforts would be those directed to prevention of accidents; efforts directed to understanding what would happen in an accident or to mitigating its effects would be less rewarding and vastly more complex and difficult. This attitude persisted rather generally for a number of years, and little progress in understanding accident progression and effects was made.

The Reactor Safety Study (Nuclear Regulatory Commission, 1975) (WASH 1400) did develop some insights to the events which might occur in a severe reactor accident. But, aside from considering some gross aspects of the mechanisms of an accident, WASH-1400 again used conservative assumptions in lieu of a detailed understanding of the progression of an accident.

From the Reactor Safety Study results, one could have estimated that, in a population of 100 reactors, the chance of a core melt accident by the end of the twentieth century would be about 15%, but that the fraction of the reactor fission product inventory escaping from the plant would probably be quite small. As we all know, such an accident did occur, at the Three Mile Island Unit 2, in an unexpectedly short time. However, it is important to note that the accident was, as predicted, of a type in which minimal fission product release occurred; that is, the public was adequately protected against it.

It has been suggested that the history of events in nuclear reactor safety might have been significantly different had the Ergen Committee taken a more far-sighted view and recommended research on accident progression and mitigation. The question is, of course, unanswerable. One opinion is that the attitude of the nuclear reactor community at that time was predominantly that "it can't happen here" and that no committee could be expected, by itself, to produce a radical change in that attitude. Even today, one suspects that there is, in some quarters, a feeling of relative complacency.

The TMI-2 accident sent a major shock throughout the industry worldwide. A core-melt accident, which had been only a theoretical concept, suddenly became a harsh reality with far reaching political and economic effects. It is the purpose of this paper to provide an assessment of the trends in reactor safety since the TMI-2 accident, and to comment on the needs in that field as I see them. My comments will fall under the general headings of the mitigation and understanding of reactor accidents and the prevention of reactor accidents. I add that, although I have had the benefit of association with many groups in the industry, my opinions are my own. They may or may not be shared by others.

Accident Mitigation and Understanding

TMI-2 produced a large surge of interest and of research and development programs on understanding the physics, chemistry and engineering involved in a nuclear reactor accident. In almost no time at all, R&D programs on reactor accidents sprang up all over the country. Workers were shifted quickly from other programs, some of them moribund programs anyhow, and whole new R&D organizations were created within weeks of the accident. The output from these organizations was quick in coming and has continued at an increasing pace ever since. Prominent in this flow of information is a tremendous proliferation of computer codes, some very detailed and some quite global. A particularly good example of the latter is the Modular Accident Analysis Program (MAAP) code produced by the Industry Degraded Core Group (IDCOR). MAAP considers primarily those variables which substantially affect the outcome of an accident sequence, and is based on relatively simple models of physical processes using straightforward physical principles and established correlations. MAAP can portray the entire history of a given accident sequence, starting with the initiating events, and progressing through evaluation of the quantity, type and timing of fission product release from the containment. Although MAAP has not reached the age of veneration, its use is growing. Many other computer codes have been developed also. Except for MAAP, however, these cover either just limited portions of an accident progression, such as fuel damage or molten core/concrete interaction, or they attempt to follow the course of an accident by using such codes sequentially. For reliable results, the individual pieces of a large accident analysis code must be interactive just as are the physical processes themselves. Transferring outputs from one piece to the next by hand is slow and likely to give erroneous results. MAAP is an integrated code.

TMI-2 caused a tremendous burgeoning of experimental work on reactor accidents also. Much of this work has been very useful as a means of validating the computer codes and, in some cases, correcting or confirming hypotheses regarding particular physical processes or chemical reactions. For example, the chemical forms of the fission products after release from the fuel are now much better known than before. It is now generally conceded that iodine appears as cesium iodide, not as elemental iodine as assumed in WASH-1400. The distinction is important because under accident conditions cesium iodide forms an aerosol in air. Aerosols can agglomerate and settle out or be retained on solid or liquid surfaces in the containment, whereas elemental iodine is a vapor and does not experience these removal mechanisms. Similarly, some EPRI-managed experiments on hydrogen combustion in large open structures resembling reactor containments were done and gave a great deal of useful information on the pressures, temperatures and dynamics of hydrogen deflagrations. Experiments on the manner in which reinforced concrete containment structures would fail under excessive pressure were conducted by EPRI also and showed that as the pressure inside a concrete containment rises, cracking, not catastrophic failure, occurs. As the cracks enlarge, they will permit the pressurizing gas or vapor to escape, thus preventing further increase in pressure. One could cite many other examples of experimental work which has been helpful, or even essential, to an understanding of the progression of events during various types of reactor accidents.

The extent of the analytical and experimental work done, in what has come to be called the source term program, since the TMI-2 accident in 1978, is hard to estimate precisely. But it must surely have occupied the attention of many hundreds of professionals each year, and it is still continuing. From an external perspective, the question is sure to rise "For how long should this type of work, on this scale, go on? When will we have learned what we really need to know?" One is reminded of Goethe's story of the "Sorcerer's Apprentice" who was unable to recall the magical phrase to shut off the flow of water which, in his half-educated state, he had magically started. In this case, of course, we are speaking of source term people, not sorcerers, although in their achievements, there may be some resemblance. Obviously, the question of how much is enough should not be answered arbitrarily. Even at this late date there are some important source term questions to be answered. What is needed is a crisp statement of those questions and what it will take to answer them. A decision to do more work than is necessary to answer those questions should be made, if at all, on some basis other than its value to the source term program, such as intrinsic scientific interest or value to other programs. The tendency to continue or expand R&D programs beyond any evident need is frequently observed, particularly in large, powerful organizations.

However, one may properly conclude that the additional understanding of what transpires in a core melt accident which has been acquired since TMI-2 has been highly beneficial, and that such understanding would have been impossible were it not for the large amount of experimental work which has been done. Most of this work shows that the former estimates of the consequences of reactor accidents have been significantly overstated.

Accident Prevention

The pieces of analytical and experimental work to which I have alluded above are quite various in their character, but they share one common characteristic: they are all aimed at attaining a better understanding of severe reactor accidents or of how to mitigate their consequences. For example, the MAAP computer code as well as they myriad of other codes of smaller scope is invaluable for predicting in outline what would happen in an accident and, therefore, how to mitigate its effects. Certainly it is necessary, if one cannot prevent accidents, to understand how to deal with them. But, even more certainly, it is necessary to do whatever is possible to prevent an accident in the first place.

Before going further with the discussion of accident prevention, the question of the need for better accident prevention should be touched upon. Insofar as the protection of the public is concerned, history is reassuring. In the only reactor accident of record in this country, no fatalities occurred and no member of the public sustained identifiable radiation injury. Estimates of the probability of an accident in which radiation exposure of the public would be expected show that the requirements of the Nuclear Regulatory Commission are met with considerable margin to spare. The NRC itself has recently issued a policy statement on safety against severe reactor accidents (Nuclear Regulatory Commission, June 27, 1985) which says in part "On the basis of currently available information, the Commission concludes that existing plants pose no undue risk to public health and safety, and sees no present basis for immediate action on generic rule making or other regulatory changes for these plants because of severe accident risk." It is clearly indicated that, insofar as the public is at risk, existing plants are safe enough.

Unfortunately, from the point of view of the owner of a nuclear power plant, there is still an uncomfortable degree of financial risk. An accident like TMI-2, which did not harm the public, would be nonetheless financially catastrophic for many a utility and would probably have industry-wide consequences of the most severe type. Without elaborating on this aspect, it is clear that a lowering of severe accident risk is highly desirable from the owner's point of view. Let us therefore consider how accident probability might be reduced and, briefly, what is being done about it.

Happily, our historical statistical basis for measuring the frequency of reactor accidents is almost nonexistent. At the time of the TMI-2 accident, the U.S. industry had accumulated about 500 reactor years of operating experience. Since that time, the industry has accumulated roughly an equal amount of reactor operating experience, so that one might say that the indicated accident frequency is about one per one thousand reactor years, and decreasing. But to base any conclusion on such a scant statistical base is clearly self-deluding. Hence, some other, less direct indicator of the probable frequency of such an accident must be sought. One possibility would be to use actual events which, although they did not result in any core damage, nonetheless produced serious concern among reactor safety professionals. There have been several such events since

TMI-2, but their number too is small, and in some cases, it is not clear whether a particular event should be classified as worthy of serious concern or not. One is, therefore, inclined to look for some other better-defined indicator of the possible beginnings of accident sequences.

One such indicator is the frequency of scrams, i.e., unintentional automatic shutdowns of the reactor. By themselves scrams are not unsafe, but a scram is an operational transient which may put demands on both the normal operating systems and engineered safety systems. A scram (or infrequently, failure to scram) is always part of an accident sequence. Moreover, scrams cause loss of operating time and hence are economically highly undesirable unless actually necessary. Unintentional scram frequency is, therefore, one way of measuring potential departures from planned, safe operation.

A perusal of scram frequency data for 1984, based on scrams per 1000 hours of operation at power levels above 15% of plant rating, shows some interesting facts.

Table I

Country	Scrams per 1000 hours critical	
	BWR	PWR
U.S. (1984)	1.0	0.4-1.8*
West Germany (1983)	0.4	0.2
Sweden (half of 1984)	0.2	0.7
Japan	0.01	NA

*Depending on manufacturer and model.

The contrast in Table I between U.S. and other countries' experience is striking and not at all favorable. In looking for possible causes of the unfavorable U.S. record, it is observed that there is a wide range of performance among the U.S. plants. For example, although the BWR average scram frequency was 1.0 per 1000 hours above 15% power, 7 of the 30 U.S. BWRs had no scrams at all of this type in 1984. Although the corresponding average PWR scram frequency was 0.84, 6 of the 53 U.S. PWRs had none.

It might reasonably be suspected that a relatively new plant would naturally have a higher scram frequency. The data show this to be true, and if one omits the plants which were first commercial in 1984, the 1984 BWR average frequency drops to 0.57 and the 1984 PWR average frequency per 1000 hours above 15% of rating to 0.69. These numbers are still on the whole poorer than those for the foreign countries listed in Table I.

In an effort to arrive at a better understanding of the causes of unintentional scrams, I have analyzed the U.S. scram reports for a period of several months in 1985. During this period, there were 84 unintentional scrams reported. Their causes break down as shown in Table II.

Table II

Causes of 84 Unintentional Scrams in U.S. Reactors

Cause	% of Total Scrams
Personnel Error	21
Incorrect Written Procedure	6
Mechanical Failure	15
Electrical Failure	29
Unknown Cause	29

In eight of the "unknown cause" scrams (9% of the total), the scram occurred while testing was underway, and two (2% of the total) scrams appeared to have been associated with maintenance work. It thus appears that electrical failures and personnel errors account for about half of the unintentional scrams, but no one cause stands out clearly.

The facts are cited to show that there is, on the average, a lot of room for improvement in plant operations and hence, by implication, in overall safety. They also indicate roughly where improvement efforts should be targeted.

In an effort to define more sharply the areas where sizable reductions in the calculated probability of severe accidents could be made, the IDCOR program set up a task with this specific objective. (Industry Degraded core Rulemaking Program, September 1984). Risk analyses for 11 plants were studied. As a broad generality, it was found that there were no practical design changes of even moderate cost that would produce a decrease in core damaging accident probability, which decrease could not be approached by making better use of systems already present in the plants. For example, use might be made of existing non-safety grade sources of water which were not part of the hypothetical accident. In a few cases, it was found that system modification, such as automating boron solution injection in BWRs, did reduce the calculated frequency of certain accident sequences sufficiently to appreciably reduce the overall calculated accident frequency.

These findings were at first surprising, but then it was realized that, through industry and regulatory efforts, many of the more easily achievable accident prevention measures have already been incorporated. It is concluded that additional practical reductions will probably be made in small increments, by improvements in procedures, training and plant-specific modifications, most of which will be minor. These measures will, little by little, reduce scrams and associated initiating events. Table I implies that there is ample possibility for such reductions, and the 1984 scram record of 13 plants with zero scrams at powers above 15% shows that the capability for marked improvement does exist in the U.S. nuclear utility industry.

These facts are not news to the nuclear power industry. Particularly through the efforts of the Institute of Nuclear Power Operations (INPO), there are organized improvement programs in the areas indicated in Table

224

II. For example, it is now commonplace to find that operators must spend about one-sixth of their time in training and retraining. Furthermore, equipment histories, aimed at identifying troublesome equipments, are being kept in some degree for each plant and for the industry as a whole. These programs are, in a sense, reactive since they tend to address problems which have already occurred.

At present, there appears to be less acceptance of the idea that one should also seek to identify, in advance, those procedures, systems and components whose failure could lead to hitherto unsuspected accident sequences. The most effective tool for this purpose is the Probabilistic Risk Assessment (PRA). While several plants have done PRAs, they are presently in the minority, and their number is not increasing very rapidly.

From the point of view of accident prevention, what is needed is what is called a "Level 1 PRA." A complete PRA starts with the events which initiate accidents and follows each sequence through core damage, reactor vessel failure, containment failure, fission product release to the environs and concludes with the assessment of potential property damage or injury to the public. A Level 1 PRA carries the analysis only through the core damage stage; thus it includes the initiating events plus those actions which can occur to prevent core damage but not the subsequent stages. From the point of view of the reactor owner, a severely damaged core represents a financial risk so large that it may be catastrophic, even without further damage to the plant. The owner's risk can, therefore, be adequately assessed by the use of a Level 1 PRA.

A Level I PRA provides a systematic, disciplined way of identifying potential accident sequences and quantifying their probability. Only with such information can one intelligently decide where to put his accident prevention effort. Of course, a PRA is not perfect. In particular, <u>one should be wary of a PRA result which says that there is no safety problem</u>. The possibility of overlooking accident initiators or system interactions is always present. <u>On the other hand, when a PRA says that there is a safety problem, that warning should be heeded</u>. These two statements have been suggested as the "first and second laws of PRA."

As earlier stated, PRAs are not perfect. Clearly, their reliability is a direct function of the reliability of the input to them. One of the most questionable types of input to PRAs is that of human reliability. The actions of plant operators in an emergency are difficult to predict. One principle which seems rational and has not yet been found wanting is that relatively strong reliance can be placed on a person's doing what he has been trained to do. The degree of truth in this principle is clearly dependent on the adequacy of his training, but one of outstanding developments of the last seven years is the intensification of nuclear operator training. About one-sixth of an operator's time is spent in training or retraining, using elaborate and expensive simulators, and it appears that the training is rigorous and effective within the scope of the operating procedures up which it is based. These procedures themselves have undergone a major transformation in the last few years, in that they are now largely symptom oriented. Rather than requiring that the operator diagnose what is going on, the procedures increasingly instruct the operator directly in what action to take in response to a given set of control room instrument readouts. This change is a distinct improvement. However, the existing procedures customarily stop short of covering what to do when core damage is actually proceeding. Some expansion of the procedures to cover core damaging sequences is desirable.

Some further thoughts on PRAs are in order:

- The principal value of a PRA accrues to the individuals who do it, in terms of the better understanding of the plant which they acquire. Thus, while a company may need to retain an outside PRA expert as an advisor on PRA techniques, as much as possible of the actual work should be done by utility employees. An externally done PRA deprives the owner of much of what he is paying for.

- A PRA is of little or no value until its results have been applied in the plant in the form of plant modifications or changes in training or procedures. A PRA on the shelf will not prevent accidents.

- PRA results can be useful as guides to decisions on R&D project priorities. Clearly, priority should be given those R&D projects which have the largest effect on safety, and that effect can be determined by introducing the probable result of the R&D into the PRA calculations.

- PRA results can be useful as guides to needed revisions of procedures or training.

- PRA results can highlight areas of needed maintenance improvement.

- PRAs permit management to make rational judgments (cost versus benefit) of proposed plant modifications or procedures.

- Regrettably, it is possible to use the doing of a PRA as a means of delaying a needed and obvious safety improvement. Such misuse must be guarded against.

My advocacy of doing a Level 1 PRA is likely to raise the question of whether the IDCOR generic applicability (or Individual Plant Evaluation) methodology takes the place of a PRA. Most people would probably regard the IDCOR IPE methodology as adequate for IDCOR's purpose, i.e., for determining quickly and economically whether existing plants clearly need major design or other modifications for the purpose of assuring public safety against severe reactor accidents. But there appears to be a predominant body of judgment that, in the long run, it will be prudent to do a Level 1 PRA too, in order to have additional assurance that subtle but important problems have not been overlooked and to realize the other benefits of going through the PRA process. Additionally, it is possible that achieving the extra measure of safety, necessary for financial protection of the owner's investment, over and above that already present and adequate for the protection of the public, will involve more detailed analysis than that provided by the IDCOR IPE. For these reasons, it is my judgment that both the IDCOR IPE and a Level 1 PRA should be done on each plant.

Conclusions

Marked progress has been made since the TMI-2 accident in the understanding of the progression of a nuclear reactor accident. An efficient accident scoping code (MAAP) has been developed, and numerous more detailed supporting codes of smaller scope are becoming available. With a few exceptions, adequate understandings of the physics, chemistry and engineering of accidents in light water reactors are available.

The combination of low accident probability, extensive engineered safeguards and containment provides adequate assurance of public safety.

However, an uncomfortable degree of financial risk to reactor owners' investments remains, since an accident which leaves the public harmless may still result in effective loss of that investment plus large cleanup costs plus far reaching effects on the rest of the industry. A reduction in accident probability is therefore necessary.

The accomplishment of such a reduction will probably be through a combination of many individually small improvements in procedures, training and plant modifications. Probabilistic Risk Assessment (PRA) is the most logical technique for identifying the areas where such improvements will be fruitful, and a PRA should be done on each plant.

That reduction in accident probability is within the capabilities of the industry is indicated by the excellent no-scram performance of both some U.S. and many foreign nuclear power plants.

REFERENCES

1. Commission Policy Statement on Severe Accident and Related Views on Nuclear Reactor Regulation. U.S. Nuclear Regulatory Commission, June 27, 1985.
2. Reactor Safety Study. WASH-1400. U.S. Nuclear Regulatory Commission, 1975.
3. Technical Report 9.1R, "Preventive Methods to Correct Sequences of Events Prior to Core Damage, Rev. 1," Industry Degreaded Core Rulemaking Program. September 1984.

A VALUE-IMPACT APPROACH FOR REGULATORY DECISION MAKING:

AN APPLICATION TO NUCLEAR POWER

Pamela F. Nelson*, William E. Kastenberg** and
Kenneth A. Solomon***

*Instituto de Investigaciones Electricas
**University Of California, Los Angeles
***The Rand Corporation

ABSTRACT

This paper presents an extended value-impact methodology which aids
decision makers in ranking various alternative actions for reducing the
risk associated with nuclear power reactors. It extends the state-of-the-
art value-impact methodology by using the Analytic Hierarchy Process
(AHP), a formalized decision making tool for ranking various alternatives
based on judgment. The method has been applied to a value-impact study of
the implementation of either a vented-containment system or an alternative
decay heat removal system as a means for reducing risk at the Grand Gulf
nuclear power plant. A ranking of several policy actions which could
reduce the economic risk of nuclear power is performed herein. The
results of this analysis show that the method provides considerable
insight to the solution of topics of interest in the decision making area
of nuclear power risk management.

KEY WORDS: Risk assessment; Decision analysis; Analytic Hierarchy Process
(AHP); Nuclear reactor regulation; Cost-benefit; Value-impact

1. INTRODUCTION

Decisions regarding Light Water Reactor (LWR) safety involve
processing large amounts of information. Major decisions require input
from experts in technical, economic and political areas, as well as from
those who have some interest in the future of nuclear power; these
interested parties are called stakeholder groups and include the Nuclear
Regulatory Commission (NRC), electric utility, ratepayers, investors, and
the Public Utility Commission (PUC). Therefore, a method is needed to
organize the decision maker's thinking process and to include data, both
quantitative and qualitative. The purpose of this paper is to provide a
formalism for structuring complex decisions in such a way as to
incorporate subjective judgment in a quantifiable procedure.

The method proposed to accomplish this objective is the Analytic
Hierarchy Process (AHP) developed by T. L. Saaty (1977). The AHP handles
qualitative as well as quantitative factors in an organized structure,
which allows for the use of multiple attributes. Although this formal
analysis cannot be guaranteed to improve decision making, it can clarify a

decision by making explicit the assumptions on which the decision is based.

The purpose here is to investigate the use of the AHP method in multiple criterion decision making in the nuclear industry. The goal is to derive weights for a set of policy actions in order to determine the most important alternative with respect to the objective of insuring the future of the nuclear industry. Importance is usually judged according to criteria which may be the objectives themselves, or measurable qualities of alternatives, as well as intangible qualities of alternatives. The weights reflect the importance of both quantitative and qualitative criteria, named attributes herein. The arrangement of the attributes into levels and these ranked one above another defines the hierarchical structure.

The methodology developed in this study is described briefly below, it requires that the decision maker compare attributes two at a time in order to determine how important one is relative to the other. The series of comparisons is called pairwise comparisons (PWCs). This data is analyzed by the largest eigenvalue approach. In this paper, the AHP method shall be used in an iterative approach to discover the most effective policies to assure the nuclear industry's future.

2. METHODOLOGY

The Analytic Hierarchy Process (AHP) is used to organize problems within a framework that allows for interaction and interdependence among factors. It still enables the decision maker to consider them in a simple and logical way, and to determine the relative importance of each attribute. The AHP, like many other decision methods, consists of 1) identifying alternatives, and 2) generating information on the outcomes of alternatives. Unique to the AHP is a third step which allows for assessing the preferences of the decision maker and stakeholders. This is accomplished by translating a series of paired comparisons into weights for the attributes in the hierarchy. These weights determine the contribution of each alternative to the objective. The method is described below, in terms of types of attributes to use, how to construct the hierarchy, and the evaluation of the AHP. A description of the mathematics in the AHP is provided in References 1, 2, and 3.

2.1 The Attributes

The attributes making up the hierarchy may be quantitative and qualitative; that is, measurable by some method, or only qualifiable through some measure of judgment. Potentially measurable attributes such as risk reduction may be quantified through Probabilistic Risk Assessment (PRA) methods. In addition, less tangible effects such as changes in public opinion regarding nuclear power are considered decision attributes. These attributes may be evaluated through questionnaires. If a value-impact analysis. is to be performed, the attributes consist of costs and benefits of the alternatives. If the analysis is to include stakeholder groups, the attributes consist of the stakeholders and their objectives. While there is no restriction as to the number of attributes allowed, it is more efficient to restrict the number of attributes to nine per level; it has been found that more than this would be too many for the decision maker to compare (Miller, 1956).

2.2 The Hierarchy

The AHP consists of dividing the decision into attributes which are organized into a structure called the hierarchy. Figure 1 is provided as an illustrative example. The top level of the hierarchy is concerned with choosing the best plant for a particular electric company. The bottom level includes the three alternatives to be considered: nuclear plant, fusion plant, or coal plant. The remaining levels of the hierarchy consider the time frame, in level 2, and the importance of cost, energy demand, feasibility and public opinion, in level 3. The fourth level contains measurable attributes of the plants, i.e. capital costs, experience with the technology involved, etc.

2.2.1 Guidelines

Some guidelines have been developed in this study. Figure 1 shall be used to illustrate these recommendations for structuring the hierarchy. A hierarchy is complete when each level connects to all elements in the next higher level. The placement of the levels should be such that the relation between a given level and the one above explains why the attributes of the level are important, the level below explains how the attributes on the given level may be achieved; the intermediate level should link the adjacent levels. Furthermore, it is convenient to place any quantifiable attributes on the level directly above the alternatives.

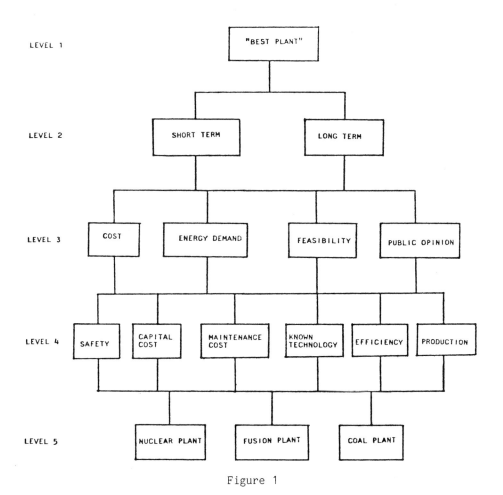

Figure 1

Sample Hierarchy

231

For example, consider level 4 in the sample hierarchy in Figure 1. This level contains the measurable attributes of the alternatives, safety, capital cost, maintenance cost, known technology, efficiency, and production. How these are achieved is through implementation of the alternatives, in the level below. Why they are important is to obtain information about cost, energy demand, feasibility, and public opinion, in level 3, and to relate the alternatives to the attributes in level 3 through level 4, for which data exist. More details on how to structure a hierarchy can be found in Reference 2.

In addition to providing a tool for analysis, the hierarchy is a representation of the decision maker's thinking, and the decision maker should devote sufficient time to the structuring step and review of the suggested structures. Once the hierarchy has been established, the evaluation is conducted.

2.3 Evaluation

In order to quantify the hierarchy, a comparison is made for each pair of attributes in a level with respect to each attribute on the higher level with which they are linked. These pairwise comparisons (PWCs) result in a ranking number which assesses the degree of importance or the likelihood of one attribute over.another, and is reflected in a scale of nine units developed by Saaty (Saaty, 1977). In this scheme, a "1" reveals equal importance and a "9" absolute importance of one attribute over another; the intermediate numbers are shown in Table 1. The process of assigning values for the pairwise comparisons translates subjective judgment into a numerical ranking of the attributes in each level. Finally, the values for the pairwise comparisons are arranged into a matrix form, and matrix manipulation yields the relative values of the alternatives in the bottom level with respect to the objective defined for the assessment.

Especially important in the analysis of nuclear regulatory decision making is the way in which stakeholders' interests are included. Stakeholder groups include the regulatory organisms, the electric utilities, the ratepayers, the investors, nuclear opponents such as intervenor groups, etc. Although each group may have a stake in the outcome of the decision, the group's opinion may or may not affect the decision. For a very technical choice, the knowledge and expertise may lie with the utility; for a decision regarding whether or not to pursue further risk reduction, which ultimately involves the question of how safe is safe enough, the stakeholders may prove to be extremely important, each playing a different role in the economic, political, social and technological areas.

Special emphasis can be placed on the integration of varying opinions into decisions in two ways. First, a number of people may be asked the questions necessary to quantify the hierarchy, and second, stakeholder groups' objectives may be included in the hierarchical structure. The first approach is suitable for establishing a consensus and evaluating the sensitivity of extreme opinions; the latter approach has been found to be more helpful when the stakeholders have some control in the outcome. The geometric mean was found to be the best way to represent the collection of results as a consensus. In this manner, the extreme values did not distort the results as can be the case when using the arithmetic mean. One way to handle digressing opinions is to perform sensitivity studies using the extreme values as input to the hierarchy. If the ordinal ranking of the alternatives is changed in any of the cases, further work is required to resolve the inconsistency.

Table 1. Descriptions for the five point scale

Description	Rating
A & B "are equally important" "equally contribute" "equally perform"	1
A "is somewhat more important than" B "contributes somewhat more than" B "somewhat outperforms" B	3
A "is strongly more important than" B "strongly contributes more than" B "strongly outperforms" B	5
A "is demonstrably more important than" B "very strongly contributes more than" B "very strongly outperforms" B	7
A "is absolutely more important that" B "absolutely contributes more than" B "absolutely outperforms" B	9
B "more important than" A	reciprocals

Source: NUREG/CR-3447

Finally, if a level is to be incorporated into the hierarchy which contains the stakeholder groups, the next level down should contain a set of independent objectives for each group. This approach works best in a planning application of the AHP. In the case that the actors have some control over the outcome, the AHP is very useful in determining policies which may be incorporated in order to achieve some desired future. For this approach, the importance of the groups must be assessed with respect to each of the criteria above. An example of this use of the AHP follows.

3. APPLICATION: POLICY CHOICE

This example illustrates the use of the AHP as a planning tool; the goal of the application is to rank policies which, if implemented, could direct the nuclear industry toward a desired future. The costs of implementing such policies are not included here and will be the subject of a future paper. Given the costs, a value-impact analysis could be performed as a way to compare the value-impact ratios of implementing a policy and backfitting a system, in order to prioritize the many options for improving nuclear power plant safety.

The AHP is used in an iterative process in this example. First, a hierarchy is constructed in such a way as to determine the weighting of several scenarios given the stakeholders, their objectives, and the future they project. This is the first forward hierarchy; the results of which are used in the next step, the construction of the backward hierarchy. In the backward process, the objective on the top level is set as the desired future as opposed to the projected future as in the first forward process. The solution of the backward hierarchy informs which policies, on the bottom level, would have to be employed by the stakeholders in order to achieve the desired future. Finally, another forward hierarchy is constructed similar to the previous forward hierarchy, except the objective is now a projected desired future. This is because the top-ranked policies from the backward process are inserted as stakeholders' objectives, in addition to those in the first forward hierarchy, in order to test the effect on the ranking of scenarios.

3.1 First Forward Hierarchy

The weighting of the stakeholder groups in level 2 in Figure 2 was obtained from the responses to a questionnaire, in the form of PWCs, ie the participants compared each pair of stakeholders with respect to their importance to the future of nuclear power. Then, the geometric mean of the resulting eigenvector was used to best express a concensus. Of course this weighting is subject to change. The objectives of the stakeholders are located on level 3; the priorities of the objectives were taken from a study performed for an electric company in Reference 2, for which the stakeholders' priorities were solicited. It was necessary to construct 15 3x3 PWC matrices in order to compare the scenarios' impacts on each objective in level 3 above. The first of the scenarios is a continuation scenario of the present status of the industry, which means that the present short term policies would be pursued. The second scenario indicates pursuing alternative forms of energy other than nuclear, such as coal. The third scenario is to pursue and plan for an assured industry; this is described as being financially stable, able to satisfy the energy demand, and prestigious. Finally, the matrix multiplication is performed and the results are indicated in the figure. The evaluation of the hierarchy ranks the diversification scenario above the others given the objectives of the stakeholder groups which are specified in the figure.

3.2 Backward Approach

Given the insight and structure of the forward hierarchy, the backward hierarchy was developed and is shown in Figure 3. Although diversification was found to be the most likely scenario in the forward process, an assured industry is assumed to be the more desired future, and is thus located on the first level. In addition to this change from the first forward hierarchy, this hierarchy determines the effectiveness of some suggested policies in achieving the desired scenario, an assured industry. The attributes of an assured industry, financial stability, satisfaction of energy demand, and prestige, are located on the second level of the backward hierarchy. The importance of the three are taken to be equal; the weightings may be varied in order to check sensitivity. The third level contains problems associated with achieving the desired scenarios. A few are briefly described here. Lack of safety incentives indicates that there exists little motivation for self regulated modification by the utility. Equity investor problems contain the investors' concerns of receiving steady, high returns. Excessive regulation refers to the utility's costs of disproving the necessity of a proposed NRC modification for the reactor. Next, the stakeholder groups that can affect the problems are included in the fourth level in order to model their ability to do so. The bottom level contains the policies which are introduced in order to test their effectiveness in reaching the desired scenarios in level 2.

234

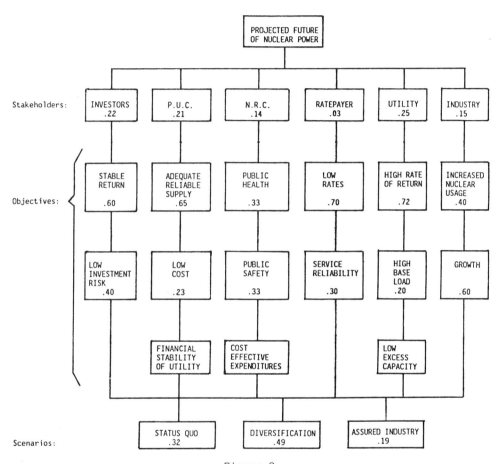

Stakeholders:

| INVESTORS .22 | P.U.C. .21 | N.R.C. .14 | RATEPAYER .03 | UTILITY .25 | INDUSTRY .15 |

Objectives:

| STABLE RETURN .60 | ADEQUATE RELIABLE SUPPLY .65 | PUBLIC HEALTH .33 | LOW RATES .70 | HIGH RATE OF RETURN .72 | INCREASED NUCLEAR USAGE .40 |

| LOW INVESTMENT RISK .40 | LOW COST .23 | PUBLIC SAFETY .33 | SERVICE RELIABILITY .30 | HIGH BASE LOAD .20 | GROWTH .60 |

| FINANCIAL STABILITY OF UTILITY | COST EFFECTIVE EXPENDITURES | LOW EXCESS CAPACITY |

Scenarios:

| STATUS QUO .32 | DIVERSIFICATION .49 | ASSURED INDUSTRY .19 |

Figure 2

First Forward Hierarchy

235

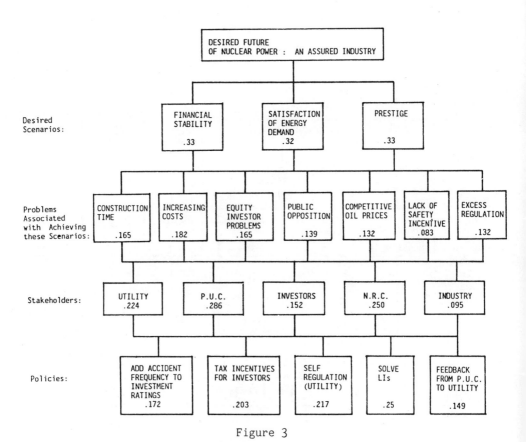

Figure 3

Backward Hierarchy

The policies employed here are derived form a previous study for which a digraph method was used to model the relationships between stakeholder groups and policy actions (Nelson, 1985). These policies are compared with respect to their effect on the stakeholder groups on the level above. The rest of the levels are compared following the usual AHP procedure. The final rankings for each level are shown in Figure 3; these show that solving Licensing Issues (LIs), increased self-regulation, and tax incentives are the preferred policies. These policies are discussed next.

3.2.1 The policies

The policies were introduced from a logical extension of the digraph method in a previous study. In this study, financial issues were found to strongly influence the future of a nuclear power company. For this reason, investors were considered important stakeholders, especially those with investments in companies with nuclear plants under construction. Therefore, several of the policies generated include goals to improve investor perception which could alleviate some of the financial pressures of today. The policies were generated through solving a digraph system which includes the stakeholder groups and major attributes which may influence the nuclear industry, such as accident frequency goal, nuclear companies' investment ratings, and licensing time. Then, for instance, licensing time was decreased to detect the overall effect on utility expenditure. A large effect constitutes a policy suggestion, such as solving licensing issues. Also, arcs were introduced where the influence of one attribute on another was found to be negligible, generating several policy suggestions. For example, decreasing plant accident frequency had little effect on investment ratings; an arc was introduced between these two attributes which generated a large cost decrease thus suggesting that those investing in plants with low accident frequency receive a tax break. The preferred policies obtained from the backward process are discussed below; implementation is beyond the scope of this study.

Solving licensing issues

Solution of Licensing Issues (LIs) by the NRC was introduced as a policy to reach the desired scenario of an assured industry. Because licensing delays increase plant costs, this issue is directly related to economic issues. Licensing issues are not directly related to protecting the health and safety of the public. They include issues related to increasing knowledge, certainty, and understanding of safety issues in order to increase confidence in assessing levels of safety; improving or maintaining NRC capability to make independent assessments of safety; establishing, revising and carrying out programs to identify and resolve safety issues; documenting, clarifying, or collecting current requirements and guidance; and improving the effectiveness of the review of applications.

Increased utility self regulation

This is suggested as a way in which to increase safety incentives and decrease costs. Three suggestions are found in the industry. 1) A utility "good practice manual" has been suggested by the Office of Nuclear Reactor Regulation (Speis, 1984). The manual would include potential actions not passing a cost-benefit test, which the NRC believes the utilities should implement voluntarily. NRC action to encourage such an effort could be proposed as a commission action, perhaps in a safety-goal context. 2) A "five or ten year plan" could be established which would propose the implementation plan for self-regulated reactor modifications (Nandy, 1984). This would decrease both NRC regulation and disagreement over generic issues not applicable to a specific reactor. 3) An "integrated living schedule," first suggested by the Delian Corporation in 1983, consists of a continuing process of selecting and scheduling plant betterment activities in order to optimize the allocation of resources (Delian Corp., 1983). It would encompass either plant modifications initiated by utilities or backfits mandated by the NRC.

Tax incentive

Tax rates for investors in an electric utility could be based in part on the reactor's accident frequency. This could be modelled after tax incentives created for energy conservation in the past. In addition, including accident frequency in investor ratings could further influence investors, which in turn provides safety incentives for the utilities.

3.3 Second Forward Process

A second forward hierarchy was constructed which incorporates the insight obtained from the backward process. The first step is to recalculate the weights of the stakeholder groups as shown in Figure 4. This is done by multiplying the final ranking of the policies by the ranking of the stakeholders in the backward process and normalizing to one. In this, the NRC and the PUC are the most influential in implementing policies to achieve the desired scenario. The policies from the backward approach are incorporated in the third level of the hierarchy, which represents the objectives of the stakeholders. Finally, the possible scenarios are ranked again. This time, however, due to the changes in objectives and weighting of the important groups, an assured industry has resulted as the more likely scenario.

4. CONCLUSION

An attempt has been made to introduce and rank policies which could increase the outlook of the nuclear power industry. The AHP is employed in an iterative approach to rank the policies in such a way as to attain a desired future for the stakeholders. First, the forward hierarchy was used to determine the plan of action to follow given the future projected by the present state of the nuclear industry; the results indicate diversification. Next, given that an insured future for pursuing nuclear power is desired, a backward hierarchy was used to indicate the policies necessary to achieve this goal. The policies are directed toward increasing investor perception through solving Licensing Issues which speeds up the licensing process, providing incentive for the electric utility to decrease accident frequency through tax incentives, and increasing utility self-regulation to decrease unnecessary expenditures. Finally, a second forward hierarchy is constructed to see the effect of implementing the policies on the decision of which scenario to pursue; in this case, pursuance of a strong nuclear future is ranked highest given the implementation of the suggested policies. The backward hierarchy could be evaluated again, adding more policies or changing the weights, in order to detect the sensitivity in the results of the second forward hierarchy. Of course, this is a static analysis; further study is necessary in order to include changes in the industry in time.

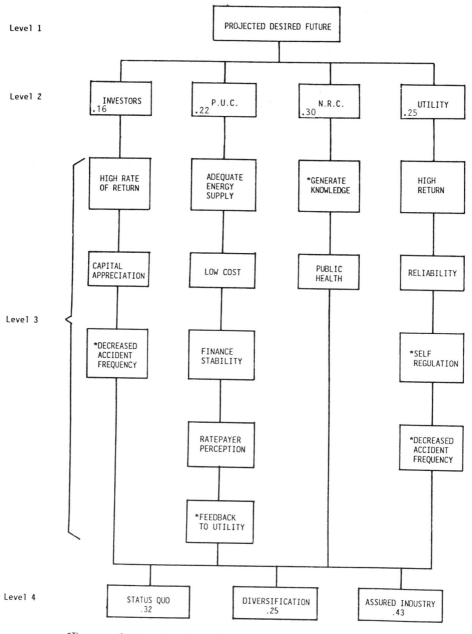

Level 1

PROJECTED DESIRED FUTURE

Level 2

INVESTORS
.16

P.U.C.
.22

N.R.C.
.30

UTILITY
.25

Level 3

HIGH RATE
OF RETURN

ADEQUATE
ENERGY
SUPPLY

*GENERATE
KNOWLEDGE

HIGH
RETURN

CAPITAL
APPRECIATION

LOW COST

PUBLIC
HEALTH

RELIABILITY

*DECREASED
ACCIDENT
FREQUENCY

FINANCE
STABILITY

*SELF
REGULATION

RATEPAYER
PERCEPTION

*DECREASED
ACCIDENT
FREQUENCY

*FEEDBACK
TO UTILITY

Level 4

STATUS QUO
.32

DIVERSIFICATION
.25

ASSURED INDUSTRY
.43

*These are the new stake holder objectives
obtained from the backward process

Figure 4

Second Forward Hierarchy

The strengths of the method have been highlighted in the paper. The flexibility and ease of use are central to its desirability. Its ability to incorporate non-quantifiables, compare incommensurables, include stakeholders' opinions, and obtain numerical rankings from qualitative comparisons is especially useful in regulatory decision making.

The weaknesses of not only the AHP but of all decision methods is their inability to solve a problem. Decision methods rather provide a structure for thinking. In the AHP specifically, a hierarchy which is developed to study decision alternatives is not a unique structure; it is highly dependent on expert opinion. Finally, the method is excellent for clarifying a problem, displaying the decision process, and performing sensitivity analysis; however, it is not suited for determining quantitative criteria.

4.1 Future Work

As mentioned, further study is needed to incorporate the costs of the policies in order to prioritize implementation of various policies and backfits according to their value-impact ratios. Future work is needed in the development of standardized hierarchies for decisions involving similar attributes, in addition to better defining the limitations of the AHP. Better techniques for including uncertainty in the AHP could increase the applicability of this method. Further study of the AHP could prove useful to regulatory and utility planning. The major task yet remaining is to implement the AHP in regulatory decision making.

5. REFERENCES

1. T.L. Saaty, "A Scaling Method for Priorities in Hierarchical Structures," J. of Math. Psychology, v. 15, 1977, pp. 234-251.
2. T.L. Saaty, The Analytic Hierarchy Process, McGraw-Hill International Book Company, New York, 1980.
3. W.E. Vesely et al., "Research Prioritization Using the Analytic Hierarchy Process," NUREG/CR-3447, BMI-2106, August 1983.
4. G.A. Miller, "The Magical Number Seven Plus or Minus Two: some Limits on our Capacity to Process Information," Psychological Review, Vol. 63, March 1956, pp. 81-97.
5. P.F. Nelson, "An Extended Value-Impact Approach for Nuclear Regulatory Decision Making," Master's Thesis, University of California, Los Angeles, March 1985.
6. T.P. Speis, Director, Division of Safety Technology, NRR, U.S. NRC, "Decision-Making Utilizing Cost-Benefit Analysis," Memorandum for H.R. Denton, Director, NRR, U.S.NRC, March 30, 1984.
7. Private conversation with Mr. Fred Nandy, Southern California Edison Company, September 1984.
8. Delian Corporation, "The Living Schedule' Concept: A White Paper for Industry," prepared for NSAC/EPRI, issued by the Atomic Industrial Forum, August, 1983.

IMPROVING AUTOMOTIVE SAFETY:

THE ROLE OF INDUSTRY, THE GOVERNMENT, AND THE DRIVER

Kenneth A. Solomon* and Susan Resetar**

Engineering and Applied Science Dept.*
System Science Dept.**
Rand Corporation, Santa Monica, CA

ABSTRACT

This paper identifies three groups that can improve automotive safety. The three groups are the automotive industry by designing into cars such safety devices as seat belts, roll bars, or air bags; the government by taking such measures as improving road conditions, enforcing seat belt usage laws, or enforcing stricter anti-drunk-driving laws; and finally, the driver by modifying driving habits such as wearing seat belts and not driving while intoxicated.

Of the seven strategies we define for improving automotive safety, this paper argues that "as low as reasonably achievable" (ALARA) is the most applicable risk reduction strategy within the context of improving automotive safety. By applying the ALARA principle to past and proposed safety improvements, we demonstrate that the most lives saved per dollar spent would occur if drivers modified their driving habits.

KEY WORDS: Automotive, Safety, Regulation, Design, Driver habit, Air bags, Seat belts, and Drunk driving

PREFACE

This paper is written in briefing format and is intended to serve two purposes. First, it was presented at The International Society of Risk Analysis meeting (October 1985, Washington, D.C.), and second, it supports a Rand Graduate Institute course and a University of California at Los Angeles tutorial entitled *Risk and Uncertainty in Public Policy Decisions.*

The paper examines alternative means of improving automotive safety.

1. OBJECTIVES

The purpose of this paper is to attain the following four objectives:

- Review generic risk reduction, or safety improvement, goals;
- Select one particular goal to examine in detail;
- Apply this goal to improving automotive safety; and
- Discuss how three distinct groups can implement this goal.

The goals will be discussed later. With regard to our fourth objective, the three groups that can implement our selected goal are industry, the government, and drivers themselves. Industry can improve safety by adding protective devices such as seat belts and air bags to automobiles [1-8]. Government can improve safety at each of three levels: federal, state, and local administrations [2, 3, 6-12, 13].

Each level of government must play its respective role to the fullest to attain the highest possible automotive safety standards. For example, the state must maintain highways and roads sufficiently. State and local law enforcement agencies must strictly enforce laws against speeding, moving violations, and drunk driving. Judicial systems must strictly punish lawbreakers to prevent recurrent offenses as well as to deter prospective offenders. Last, each driver can influence safety through good driving habits. Buckling seat belts, obeying speed limits, and not driving while intoxicated are several positive habits that will improve automotive safety [2, 3, 6-8, 14-17].

2. DEFINITIONS

Identifying Alternative Risk Reduction Goals

Although the safety level of any technology can always be improved, there is no unique approach or philosophy for making such improvements [18-20]. Several prior studies have identified a number of distinct philosophies for reducing risk associated with various technologies. Seven measures to reduce risk and achieve specific safety levels are discussed below [18]. Imbedded within this discussion are examples specific to automotive safety.

What Are Some Alternative Risk Reduction Goals?

Minimizing maximum accident consequence is one method to reduce the risk associated with automobile operation. For example, we can eliminate all accidents involving a large number of fatalities in a single transportation event. This could be achieved, for example, by preventing all fully occupied buses from driving on any highway or road. Because the maximum number of passengers on board a bus could be 50 or 60, the worst possible accident would cause the death of 50 to 60 people. This particular philosophy seeks to reduce total risk by minimizing the maximum number of people that could be killed in any single accident. Another application of this philosophy is to require that not more than two people occupy any one car at a time, and that cars be positioned far enough apart to eliminate the possibility that two cars could ever by involved in an accident. We would minimize the maximum number of fatalities per accident to four in this case. Of course, this is neither a realistic nor a feasible risk reduction goal when applied to automotive safety. The impracticality of trying to reduce the number of people riding in any one vehicle at a given time outweighs any benefits gained.

Minimizing the probability of occurrence for the most probable types of accidents is a second method of improving safety which thereby reduces risk. Because rear-end collisions are a common type of accident, an extreme application of this approach would seek to eliminate all rear-end collisions [2, 3, 9-13]. To fully ensure that all rear-end accidents are eliminated we would have to permit only one car on the road at a time, an obviously impracticable solution. A more practicable one requires the use of center-mounted, high positioned brake lighting. Use of such a light would reduce rear-end collisions by more than half [2, 3, 10-12] and avert as many as 1800 fatalities per year. We would also try to identify other types of common accidents to reduce their probability as well.

Minimizing the total accident risk is a third risk reductional goal. Risk is defined as the probability of an event times the consequence (or outcome) of that event integrated over all negative events. Therefore, as we apply this goal to automotive safety we find that we need to reduce both the total *number* and the *intensity* of accidents (i.e., limit both the total number of buses on the road and the number of passengers per bus).

Eliminating all accidents is a fourth risk reduction goal that appears to be unattainable in any context, however it is applied. Enforcement of the Food and Drug Act's Delaney Clause has prevented the use of any carcinogenic food additive [18]. Presumably this would eliminate the incremental cancer risk that we derive from using food additives. However, within the context of automotive safety, the only way to eliminate all occurrences of property damage, injuries, and fatalities would require that no automobile is every permitted to operate.

Requiring those who partake in the benefits to take proportional share of the risk is a fifth risk reduction goal. Applying this broad goal to automotive safety, we find this is exactly what happens. For example, the more miles one drives per year, either as a driver or passenger, the greater one's probability of being involved in an accident [2, 3]. When this goal is applied to other aspects of automotive safety it becomes complicated. Risks and benefits are not always comparable. The risk of injury to passengers of small cars is greater than the risk to those in large cars. However, the benefits of smaller cars are different. Smaller cars offer better fuel economy--a benefit that may compensate for the higher risk of injury.[1]

Minimizing the socially perceived risks is risk reduction goal number six. These are risks *perceived* to be large, but are not technically or quantitatively large [18-20]. For instance, suppose a passenger bus with 40 occupants falls off a 100-foot cliff, and there are no survivors. This is socially perceived as far worse than 40 individual, fatal accidents. By eliminating all spectacular or well-publicized events we minimize the socially perceived risk. Another example of minimizing this risk is to eradicate all fire-related automobile accidents, regardless of whether or not the fire caused the fatality. While we may perceive this risk reduction measure as socially desirable, it may in fact be costly to implement, and may not reduce the annual number of fatalities.

Reducing risk to as low as reasonably achievable (referred to here as ALARA) is our seventh risk reduction goal. Application of the ALARA goal to industry, government, or individual drivers required a fixed budget to reduce the total accident risk to *as low as reasonably achievable.*

Table 1 summarizes these seven risk reduction goals.

Which Goal Makes the Most Sense?

We will deduce which one of the seven goals makes the most sense when applied both to general situations and to the specific issue of automotive safety. First, Goal 1 (minimize the probability) and Goal 2 (minimize the

---

[1]It is interesting to note that passengers of sports cars have a more severe injury and fatality rate than their counterparts in larger cars [14]. Yet, sports cars are far less likely to cause an accident [18].

consequence) are contained in Goal 7, the ALARA Goal. Therefore, we will not lose anything by eliminating Goal 1 or Goal 2 as long as we still consider the ALARA Goal.

Minimizing total risk, Goal 3, is really a special case of the ALARA Goal. In this special case, there is not budgetary constraints. We minimize total risk without considering how much it costs to minimize such risks and there is not risk/cost tradeoff.

Goal 4 seeks zero total accident risk. The only way to completely. avoid all automobile accidents is to eliminate all vehicles from the road. Obviously, this solution is not practicable when applied to Automotive safety, even though it may have been for carcinogenic food additives (Delaney Clause).

Table 1

ALTERNATIVE RISK REDUCTION GOALS

---

(1) Minimize the maximum accident consequence (e.g., eliminate accidents involving large number of mortalities in a single event).

(2) Minimize the probability of the more probable accident types (e.g., determine the rear-end collisions are a probable type of accident and reduce their frequency).

(3) Minimize total accident risk (e.g., for all types of automotive accidents, reduce the product of their frequency and outcome).

(4) Reduce total accident risk to zero (e.g., zero fatalities per year and zero injuries per year (i.e., eliminate the automobile).

(5) Share risks and benefits equitably (e.g., the more miles you drive per year, the higher the risk you take).

(6) Minimize socially perceived risks (e.g, eliminate spectacular accidents such as a bus falling off a 100-foot cliff)

(7) Reduce risk to ALARA (e.g., for a fixed budget, reduce total accident risk to a low as possible.

Minimizing socially perceived risks is also difficult to attain (Goal 5 includes removing large-scale or spectacular accidents). In addition to being difficult to attain, this philosophy does not have a predictable payoff. We have illustrated that total risk may remain unchanged (recall the 40 passenger bus accident versus the 40 individual accidents). In fact, Goal 5's application could result in a substantial increase of total risk if different types of accidents are traded off against one another [18-20].

As we have discussed, Goal 4 (sharing risk proportionately with benefit) is implicit in any automotive design issue.

Finally, we feel the ALARA Goal makes the most sense. By definition it is intended to provide the most safety at the smallest dollar cost.

Why ALARA?

Let us examine ALARA more carefully and try to understand why it is a sensible goal for the automotive safety application. Realistically speaking, our society is constrained in expenditures and budgetary resources. Therefore, we cannot spend an infinite amount of money to avoid a fatality. currently, approximately 50,000 fatalities and hundreds of thousands of injuries result each year from automobile accidents. If everyone drove a Sherman tank at a speed of 3 mph or less, these statistics would be reduced substantially (but not likely eliminated). On the other hand, the costs associated with this scenario are insurmountable. This example illustrates how impractical it is to eliminate risk without regard to budgetary constraints. Therefore, as long as we drive there will be a finite probability of a fatality. As another example of minimizing risk without a budget constraint imagine eliminating air-travel risk. This would mean that all cross-country travel by aircraft would stop. If someone needed to travel from Los Angeles to Washington, D.C., the traveler would be forced to take a slower, safer means of transportation such as a train. But for some people, safer means of transportation do not compensate for resource costs (such as time lost). Consequently, this does not efficiently allocate resources.

From these examples the ALARA risk reduction goal is clearly the most sensible. When speaking of automotive safety we want to minimize risk of injury, death, or property damage but budget constraints do exist. By using the ALARA Goal we achieve our goal while considering resource costs.

Before applying the ALARA principle to automotive safety and design, we must emphasize the fact the *there is no unique definition of ALARA* as it is applied to improving automotive safety. We can conceive of at least three rather distinct, operational definitions.

(1) For a fixed societal expenditure, we can maximize automotive safety--reduce the risk of driving to as low as possible;
(2) For some prescribed level (accepted standard) of safety, we can spend whatever it takes to achieve that; or
(3) We can weigh the marginal costs of reducing risk against the marginal benefits that result. The optimal decision is to add automotive safety measures until the benefit of the safety measure is equal to, or exceeds, its cost. However, this approach requires that the value of human life be explicitly stated.

We do not contend that any one of these three is better than the other two, but, for the purpose of our demonstration, we have elected to pick the first operational definition.

Assuming a fixed societal expenditure, how do we maximize automotive safety? We propose that a specific way of implementing such a measure would be to enforce the most cost-effective measures first. We would see the highest payoff-in terms of improved safety--at the lowest dollar cost [6]. A good example of this is a mandatory seat belt law which will be discussed later in more detail.

Defining Roles in Improving Safety

As discussed earlier, three groups can control the safety of automobiles--the industry, the government, and the driver. The industry could add seat belts or air bags or make other design changes to improve safety. At the state level, the government could improve highway conditions and add road signs, the police and law enforcement agencies could provide stricter enforcement of drunk-driving and speed limit laws, and the judicial system could more stringently penalize offenders. Last, the driver could improve driving habits in many ways such as by reducing speed and using a seat belt at all times. Associated with each of these actions is a cost. For these examples, cost is in the form of dollars expended or time lost. Whoever pays these costs is determined by the measure taken.

We find that some issues are rather distinct in terms of who can control safety; the voluntary maintenance of one's automobile is clearly the driver's prerogative. Other issues are hybrid; that is, a combination of the government, or the industry, or the driver exercises some control. An example of a hybrid issue is seat belt use. The industry puts the seat belt in the car and the driver elects to wear it. Figure 1 succinctly summarizes the interrelationship between industry, law enforcement agencies, and the individual driver.

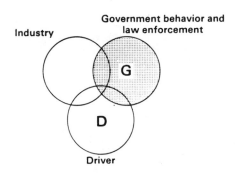

Figure 1. Defining industry/law enforcement/driver role in improving safety: a typical issue.

In some states, law mandates the use of seat belts. In the specific cases of child restraint seats and seat belt use there is a move toward mandatory use. In the State of California, and a number of other states, the parent (or any other person) driving with a child under 4 years old is obligated to keep that child restrained in a state approved car seat while riding in an automobile. In addition, a number of Air Force bases, including Kirkland Air Force Base in Albuquerque, New Mexico, require the driver and all passengers to wear seat belts while driving on base even though the speed limit seldom exceeds 30 miles an hour. Anyone caught without their seat belt will be fined.

3. ANALYSIS

Costs of Risk Reduction

Before discussing our analysis, we must define *reduced risks* for automotive design and the *costs* associated with reducing them. Reducing risks, improving safety, and increasing benefits are equivalent events. An increased benefit may be a decreased probability of incurring death or severe injury. Improved safety can be accomplished in a number of ways' and each method of improving safety has its own cost and benefit implications. It is up to the policymaker to determine which methods have the optimal mix of cost and benefit.

One measure of policy effectiveness is the number of fatalities averted per year. Before 1974, the speed limit on U.S. highways was 65 to

70 miles per hour and statistics showed in average of 55,000 deaths annually. When the speed limit was reduced to 55 miles per hour during the 1974 gasoline crisis, we saw a rapid decline in the number of fatalities per year to approximately 45,000. Currently, the number of fatalities has leveled to around 50,000 per year. Therefore, we see a reduced risk or increased benefit associated with a particular action. The benefit is the lower probability of death and the action is decreasing the speed limit. As we can see, there are additional benefits associated with this action--a lower probability of both severe injury and extensive property damage. Furthermore, because there are fewer accidents, there are fewer investigations by insurance companies, less compensation by insurance companies, and so on, resulting in even more dollars saved. Changing the speed limit will give rise to costs in the initial public announcement campaign, replacement of road signs, and law enforcement.

What are the costs of taking measure to reduce risks? The first thing that we want to consider is who is responsible for the cost. There is a cost to the industry for installing seat belts and other safety devices on cars, but that cost is very typically passed on to the consumer by adjusting the purchase price of the car. The consumer pays an incremental amount for each safety device that is added. Clearly, there is a cost associated with improving roads, adding road signs, and enforcing driving laws. This is a cost to the government that is passed on to the taxpayers. Commercials on television or on billboards that say "buckle up," don't drive while intoxicated," and other such public service announcemelts may be paid for by large companies and organizations. In a sense, a public service announcement is something that the consumer or the taxpaper ends up paying for in the form of higher product costs or tax benefits enjoyed by the organization offering the commercial.

Approximate Dollars Spent per Averted Fatality

In Tables 2A through 2E we list a number of measures that can be taken to reduce the risk associated with automobiles.[1] In some instances, we have identified the number of fatalities, injuries, and occurrences of property damage that are reduced. Also, we have compared the estimated benefit of implementing the measure, with the cost of putting the measure into place. We will discuss a few of the examples shown.

---

[1] Symbol definitions for Tables 2A through 2E are as follows:

G = Government has primary control over safety improvements measure.
D = Driver has primary control over safety improvement measure.
I = Industry has primary control over safety improvement measure.
ΔF = Decrease in fatalities per year should safety measure be implemented on all cars.
ΔI = Decrease in injuries per year should safety measure be implemented on all cars.
ΔC = Decrease in accident dollar cost per year should safety \measure be implemented on all cars.
ΔS = Cost of implementing measures per year, industry-wide.
S/averted fatality = Cost per averted fatality measured in thousands of dollars.

Measure		Benefits			Cost Δ＄	＄/averted fatality (thousand ＄)
		ΔF	ΔI	ΔN		
Stronger drunk laws	G	Up to 25,000	100,000+	200,000?	Billions	50
Stronger seat belt laws	G	Up to 15,000*	100,000+	0 or small	Billions	200
Voluntary seat belt	D	Up to 28,000**	200,000+	0 or small	Billions	100*
Roll bars — Jeep	I	100's	1000's	0 or small	100's millions	1000
Bumpers — 2.5/5.0 mph	I	0	~0	20% reduction	25% reduction	∞
Child car seat	G	500***	1000's	Small	Billions	100
Rear light	I/G/D	1800	60% reduction	60% reduction	1.29 billion	30
1966-1970 auto equip.	I					260

*50% effect.
**90% effect.
*** 4 yrs.

*Public service commercials

Table 2B

Measure		Benefits			Cost Δ＄	＄/averted fatality (thousand ＄)
		ΔF	ΔI	ΔN		
Steering column +	I					200
Airbags	I	6,000-9,000	300% reduction			640
Tire inspection	I/D					800
65 mph to 55 mph limit	G/D	7,000-10,000	~100,000			50
Rescue helicopters	G	10's				130
Passive 3 pt. harness	I					500
Passive torso belt	I					220
Driver ed.	G/D	100's				180
Highway maintenance	G G					40

Table 2C

| Measure | | Benefits | | | Cost | $/averted fatality |
		ΔF	ΔI	ΔN	Δ$	(thousand $)
Signs	G	1000's				68
Guard rail improvement	G	100's				68
Skid resistance	I	~500				84
Bridge rails	G	250-500				92
Wrong way entry	G	250+				100
Impact absorbers	G	1000's				216
Break away signs	G	500+				232
Median barrier improvement	G	1000's				456
Clear recovery	G					586
Remove trucks	G	1,250				very large

Table 2D

| Measure | | Benefits | | | Cost | $/averted fatality |
		ΔF	ΔI	ΔN	Δ$	(thousand $)
Remove large cars	G	10,000's				very large
Eliminate all auto fires	I	250				1000's +
Eliminate all auto fires, rear end only	I	100				1000's +
Standard 301	G	100's				200
Pink cars	G/D	1000's				5 (?)
Anti-skid brakes	I			10%		
Tube tire vs. non tube	D/G			360%		50 (?)
Recap tube vs. non tube	D/G			480%		50 (?)

Table 2E

Measure		Benefits			Cost Δs	$ averted fatality (thousand $)
		ΔF	ΔI	ΔN		
Tube vs. recap tubeless	D/G			260%·		50 (?)
Depth of tread	D/G			200%·		50 (?)
Lights on in day	D/G			Δ15% in front end		
Reflective plates	G			13% in rear end		
Mud flaps	D			1.3%		

As stated previously, there are approximately 50,000 fatalities per year due to automobile accidents [2, 3]. One-half of these result because at least one of the drivers involved was driving while intoxicated [6]. Imagine if all drunk driving was eliminated, by some fortunate method. We could prevent up to 25,000 fatalities and hundreds of thousands of injuries per year. Based on estimates by Solomon, Batten, and Phelps [6] the cost of such a measure might be approximately $50,000 per fatality averted.

An innovative and practical method to deter driving under the influence of alcohol has taken in Midwest City, Oklahoma, by implementing a "scarlet letter" approach [21]. Specifically, when a driver has been convicted of driving while intoxicated he or she makes a choice between spending 30 days in jail or agreeing to flaunt an ostentatious bumper sticker stating the the driver has been convicted of drunk driving, and asking other vehicle operators to report any odd or erratic driving to the police. Drivers who choose to "wear the scarlet bumper sticker" may not park outside of any bar or liquor store and must display it for a full six months; any violators of these simple rules risk being sent to jail for 30 days.

On the other hand, let us examine a measure that improves driving habits *voluntarily*, such as seat belt use. If this measure proved 90 percent effective, as many as 28,000 lives might be saved. The financial campaign (the public service commercial associated with it) could cost only $100,000 per fatality averted [6]. Another measure, a law *requiring* seat belt use, may save an many as 10,000 to 15,000 lives [6]. This assumes that the law was only about 50 percent effective in increasing seat belt use. We estimate that the cost of implementing such a measure might be $200,000 per fatality averted.[2]

The State of New York implemented a mandatory seat belt law in December 1984, and began enforcement on January 1, 1985 [22]. This move already has proved very effective, leaving many officials stunned at the dramatic decrease in fatalities. By the end of January this year, the State of New York documented its lowest motorist fatality statistics since 1926. And, the 15 percent of New York drivers who previously used their seat belts on a regular basis increased to a remarkable 70 percent.[3] A total decrease in fatalities of 27 percent was recorded in New York State after the first three months of 1985 [23]. Figure 2 relates the occurrence of fatalities and use of seat belts.

Officials believed that passage of the mandatory seat belt law would go largely ignored [22], but fines of $10 to $50 for failure to use a seat belt have proven an effective way to decrease fatalities. The increase in the percentage of seat belt users proves that adherence to the law, though considered a great annoyance by most drivers, is not an inconvenience too great to be overlooked in hopes of not being caught. The public is now showing support for the law. After seeing the actual statistics, appreciation for the benefits gained (reduction of serious injuries and fatalities, lower insurance rates, and a feeling of making a positive move to reduce their own risk) are clearly outweighing any inconvenience.

Even though the fines incurred from noncompliance are minimal, the measure remains cost-effective because enforcement agencies are not going out of their way to seek out every offender. Rather, almost all of the 4,500 offenders cited in January had been initially stopped for another violation [22]. The automotive industry has contributed about $15 million to help pass these laws to avoid costly design reformations to include air bags and implementation which they have long fought to avoid.

After observing statistics in Canada and Great Britain, countries which have enforced the mandatory seat belt law for several years, researchers note that the automobile operators most likely to be involved in a serious or potentially fatal accident are also those least prone to adhere to the seat belt law [22]. Hopefully, continued stringent enforcement of these laws will eventually conform the views of those motorists who still may tend to defy the law by showing the further decline in the number of highway fatalities.

---

[2]Reference 14 suggest that if everyone used seat belts, we might see a reduction of about 10,000 fatalities per year. Reference 6 speculates that up to 15,000 fatalities might be averted.

[3]Estimates from the U.S. Department of Transportation state that national seat belt use averages 15 percent, and that 100 percent compliance would mean a 50 percent reduction in serious injuries and fatalities [22].

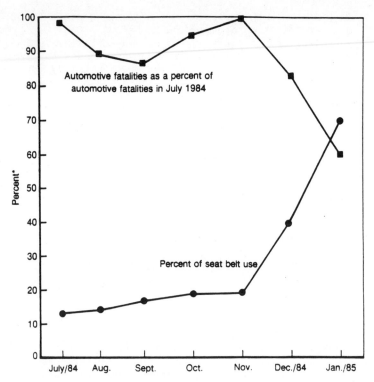

Figure 2.   Fatalities and use of seat belts.   "Percent" refers both to
seat belt use and to fatalities.   For seat belt use it refers to
the percentage of drivers who wear seat belts; this figure varies
from 15 percent use in July 1984 to 70 percent use in January
1985.   The percentage of fatalities is measured relative to 100
percent in July 1984, so that, for example, in January 1985 fatalities were reduced to 60 percent of what they were in January
1984.   Source: [22]

We can look at some examples where the industry has made design
changes, thereby reducing fatalities and injuries.   The installation of
roll bars on utility vehicles (jeeps) has eliminated hundreds of
fatalities per year at a cost of hundreds of millions of dollars. The cost
per fatality averted is one the order of a million dollars [6].   Another
industry design change, bumpers that prevent damage to cars if accidents
are below 2.5 mph for rear bumpers, or 5 mph for front bumpers, generally
does not reduce the number of fatalities. This makes sense because we
would not expect any fatalities in an accident under 5 mph.   Also, the
improved bumper design probably did not reduce the number of severe
injuries by very much, but there was clearly a reduction in property
damage.[4]   Based on estimates in [13] there is a dramatic dollar savings in
repair costs associated with improved bumper design.   These savings can be
represented as a percentage savings relative to 1972 designs.   Model 1973
cars were the first to have the 2.5/5.0 mph bumpers.   The savings in

repair costs are clearly a function of the relative sizes and weights of the bullet car and the impacted car. Table 3 illustrates the percentage savings across all sizes and weights from 1973 through 1978.

In another case, if the government required nationwide that children under 4 years of age use child restraint seats, then the number of deaths for children under 4 years old would be reduced by 500 per year, at a minimum. The cost of enforcing such a law would be millions of dollars and we might see about a $100,000 cost per fatality averted. All would agree that this was very cost effective. Unfortunately, only a few states presently enforce the use of child car restraints.

A number of studies have considered the effect of having a rear brake light at approximately the height of the bottom of the car's rear window. Several concluded that as many as 50 or 60 percent to all rear-end accidents could be reduced by using this rear light.[5] The number of fatalities reduced might be as many as 1,000 to 2,000 per year and the cost of implementing such a system could be as high as a billion dollars. So, we see that dollar cost per death averted is $30,00 per year. Again, such a measure would be very cost effective.

Table 3

REPAIR COST SAVINGS FROM
1973 IMPROVED BUMPER DESIGN

Year*	Percent Savings
1973	4 to 17
1974	21 to 35
1975	8 to 26
1976	19 to 33
1977	1 to 32
1978	4 to 24

*Compared with 1972 models.

---

[4]Before 1973, roughly 20 percent more accidents were reported. This 20 percent corresponds to those accidents resulting in damage in rear-end and front-end bumpers for impacts under 2.5 mph and 5 mph, respectively. The 1978 design improvement eliminated most of these claims.

[5]Reference 16 credits at 66.6 percent reduction in rear-end crash probability, and states that the cost of the average rear-end accident would be reduced from $1,041 to $398. References 11, 12 estimate that 1,200 fatalities per year would have been averted if all passenger cars were equipped with such a light. They further estimated that nearly 150,000 injuries could be averted, and that insurance companies could save perhaps $1.31 billion in 1979 alone.

We can look at a number of other entries on Tables 2A through 2E and demonstrate by example how the cost per averted fatality was estimated. The use of air bags on all cars (roughly 100 million cars), which would clearly be a design change, could save as many as 6,000 to 9,000 lives per year, and could reduce injuries by 300 percent. Because air bags might cost up to $1,000 per car to install, the cost per fatality averted could be as high as one or two million dollars. If we assume that air}bags cost $1,000 per car to install and, in one year, they are installed in all cars manufactured in that year (roughly 10 million cars), then the cost to install air bags in all cars manufactured in one year would be Table 3

$$(\$1,000 \text{ per car})(10 \times 10^6 \text{ cars}) = \$10 \times 10^9,$$

or 10 billion dollars. Because 10 million cars represent about 10 percent of the total number of cars on the road, then perhaps 500 lives could be saved per year. If we further assumed that each car with air bags had a life expectancy of 10 years, then during the lifetime of these 10 million cars perhaps 5,000 lives could be saved. Then the cost per averted death could be estimated at

$$\frac{(\$10 \times 10^9)}{5 \times 10^3 \text{ lives}} = \$2 \times 10^6/\text{life } ^6$$

Some studies suggest that if air bags were used on all cars (about 100 million in the United States) then some number substantially less than 5,000 lives could be saved and, hence, the cost per death averted would be substantially greater than two million dollars.

Further, the use of air bags may, in fact, increase risks in a number of ways:

- They may provide a false confidence and cause people who would otherwise wear seat belts not to wear them. (The air bag is designed to work in only frontal-type crushes, and people not waring seat belts in other types of crashes could be more severely injured, or even killed, if they neglected to wear seat belts.)

- Air bags have been known to fail, even in fatal crashes.
- When the air bags function properly, they may by their very nature induce specific injuries. Since air bags are designed to expand within one-fortieth of a second, the additional amount of energy that must be managed immediately following a frontal impact is increased. This increased energy, by its very nature, may cause injury. For example, the unrestrained child learning against the windshield before a frontal collision could be thrown back instantaneously as the air bag explodes.

- The propellants used in air bags may be carcinogenic. If air bags are installed in all cars on the road, we might expect to have to dispose of roughly twenty million canisters (2 per car for 10 million cars) of carcinogenic propellant per year.

If we perform an extremely conservative calculation of the worth of

---

[6]These terms are stated in scientific notation. The term 10×10^9" translates to ten billion dollars; the term "5 \times 10^3 lives" translates to 5,00 lives; and the term "$2 \times 10^6/\text{life}$" translates to two million per averted fatality.

air bags, we might disregard the negative features of air bags discussed;
we might assume that air bags installed on 100 million cars would save
10,000 lives per year, and that air bags would cost only $640 per car to
install. Using these very conservative assumptions, we would estimate a
cost per averted death of $640,000--still a high number.[7]   The use of air
bags would be considered far less cost effective than the use of child
restraint seats.

These tables list a number of other measures that could be taken by
government, industry, or drivers, stated in dollars per averted
fatality. Cost per averted fatality ranges from as low as $30,000 to as
high as several million dollars.

What the Automobile Industry Has Done to Improve Safety

Figure 3 divides measures that have actually beel implemented from
those that have not. It also illustrates cost per death averted and
whether the measures are predominately controlled by industry, government,
or drivers. For measures actually implemented, we find that approximately
$150,000 to $600,00 per fatality averted has been spent by the auto
industry. These measures include: adding skid resistant properties to
the braking system, improving steering columns, adding additional rear
reflectors, and offering a three point harness seat belt.

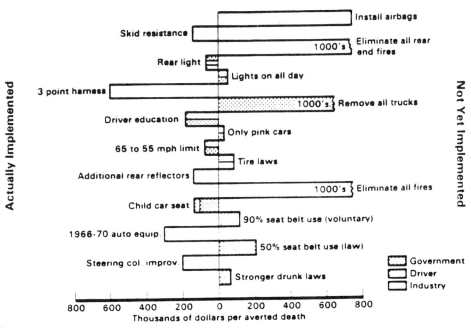

Figure 3. Measures implemented by the automotive industry to improve safety

---

[7]It is interesting to note that if air bags were used in
conjunction with much stricter anti-drunk-driving laws, the cost
per averted fatality for air bag use would increase, since many
of the accident-causing drunk drivers would be no longer on the
road.

To look at what several state governments have spent to reduce the number of fatalities per year we consider the law requiring child restraint seat use. The cost of implementing child care seat laws to these states is approximately $100,000 per fatality averted. Other possible measures subject to government control are reducing the speed limit from 65 to 55 mph and mandating the use of the high, center-mounted rear brake light. Each measure would cost on the order of $30,000 to $50,000 per death averted.

If we compare measures that were actually implemented with those that have not been implemented, we see a rather interesting contrast. Of those not yet implemented, we can divide the measures into two general categories: those that are very expensive to implement (millions of dollars per fatality averted), and those that are relatively inexpensive to implement (typically, $50,000 to $200,000 per fatality averted). Of those that are very costly, three of the four fall on the industry's shoulders; these are (1) to eliminate specifically, rear-end fires in automotive accidents, (2) to eliminate all fires in automotive accidents, and (3) to install air bags. The fourth, to remove all trucks from highways, falls on the regulatory branch of the government.[8]

On the other hand, for relatively modest costs a number of fatalities could be prevented. Such fatality-averting measures might include, stronger drunk-driving laws[9] or a requirement that headlights be on all day. The former requires government action, and to a lesser extent, driver action. The latter is more a function of driving habit, but in fact could also be a function of law enforcement agencies. Both would save a fatality for approximately every $50,000 expended.

Take what seems to be a ridiculous situation, requiring that all cars be pink. We find that the cost of implementing such a measure would be fairly modest relative to the number of lives saved. This is partly due to the belief that pink cars are least likely to be involved in accidents. In all fairness, this is a correlation as opposed to a causation. That is to say, it is not because they are pink that they are involved in fewer accidents; it is that perhaps people who drive pink cars tend to be more cautious. In any event, if we took the information rather

---

[8]While trucks account for 6 to 8 percent of total freeway mile use, they contribute to as many as 50 percent of the fatalities due to rear-end collisions [16]. A typical accident involves a car rear-ending a slow-moving truck on a freeway.

[9]Implementation of such a measure as stronger drunk-driving laws may have significant social costs associated with it such as increased police patrols, busier courts, larger jails, and so on. The issue of how to implement stronger drunk-driving laws will be the subject of a forthcoming paper.

literally and did not assess it carefully, we might facetiously say that if everyone drives pink cars, the cost of reducing the number of annual fatalities is rather modest.

A number of other measures could be taken by the government and drivers which, if implemented, would cost a rather modes amount of money to prevent deaths.

4. IMPLICATIONS

The $10,000,000 Menu

How many lives can be saved for a $10,000,000 expenditure? Another way of comparing risk reduction measures is to consider that we have only a limited amount of money to spend. Suppose you had ten million dollars. There are several ways in which to spend this money, and each way determines a different number of fatalities that could be averted.

Figure 4 summarizes seven ways to save lives given a fixed resource of ten million dollars. In Case One, you would mandate that all automobile fires be eliminates, and you can spend ten million dollars in a lump sum to eliminate these deaths. Each ten million dollar expenditure will prevent approximately one death. We have already seen a 300 percent reduction in fire deaths when Federal Vehicle Safety Standard (FMVSS) 301 was implemented. This standard, FMVSS 301, dictates certain test requirements that cars and trucks must satisfy. These standards reduce the probability of fire. An example is that passenger cars must be able to withstand a 30 mph frontal barrier impact with fluid loss of less than 1 ounce per minute. Case Two, a situation that has been implemented, reduces the speed limit from 70 or 65 miles an hour to 55 miles an hour. Each ten million dollars expended will buy you approximately 200 averted deaths. In Case Three, stricter enforcement of seat belt laws, each ten million dollars will buy you approximately 50 averted deaths. To some extent, that has been implemented in New York State and on several Air Forces bases. In Case four, stronger drunk-driving laws, each ten million dollar expenditure will buy you perhaps 200 averted deaths. We have seen stronger and stronger drunk-driving laws being implemented over the past few years. Case Five, child car seat enforcement, suggest perhaps 100 averted deaths for each ten million dollar expenditure. child car seat laws are required as of mid-1984 in 7 states. Air bags, Case Six, will buy about 12 averted fatalities, and pink cars, Case Seven, might buy 2,000 for each ten million dollars expended.[10]

---

[10]As discussed earlier, the use of pink cars is only correlated with reduced accidents, and does not likely reduce accidents themselves. People who drive pink cars may be more careful drivers. Also, if all cars were pinks, we may not expect much of a decrease in accidents.

Case 1:	Eliminate all death by fire ~about 1 averted death
Case 2:	Reduce speed limit from 65 to 55 mph ~about 200 averted deaths
Case 3a:	Seat belt enforcement law ~about 50 averted deaths
Case 3b:	Voluntary seat belt use ~about 100 averted deaths
Case 4:	Stronger anti-drunk laws ~about 200 averted deaths
Case 5:	Child car seat ~about 100 averted deaths
Case 6	Install airbags ~about 12 averted deaths
Case 7:	Buying only pink cars ~about 2,000 averted deaths

Figure 4.   The $10,000,000 menu: Save as many lives as you can.

The Bottom Line

Industry has, in fact, implemented a number of cost-effective measures to date. Changing driving habits and stricter law enforcement will lead to more cost-effective means of saving lives.

While the means of implementing measures to improve safety is beyond the scope of this presentation, it suffices to say that more effective and stricter law enforcement against drunk drivers and people who fail to use seat belts and child restraint seats will provide the greatest benefit per dollar spent.

The decision by the State of New York to enforce the mandatory seat belt law is a direct and effective step in improving safety on our highways. Enforcement in New Jersey, Illinois, Michigan, and Missouri for seat belt use will begin this summer, and 32 other states are considering instating such a law. Should the implementation and enforcement spread nationwide, a great number of fatalities will be averted in the future. Hopefully, law enforcement agencies will be influenced enough by the statistics of deaths averted to enforce this law stringently. And, agencies hopefully will go after the drunk driver with a rigid campaign to help rid our highways of another great hazard--a hazard over which the drinker has sole control--to provide more complete safety for law-abiding motorists.

REFERENCES

1.   "Use of Air Bags Ordered by Dole," *Los angles Times,* Michael Wines,
         July 13, 1984, pp. 1, 14.
2.   *Fatal Accident Reporting System 1981,* United States Department of
         Transportation, National Highway Traffic Safety Administration,
         Washington, D.C.

3. *Fatal Accident Reporting System 1980@*, United States Department of Transportation, National Highway Traffic Safety Administration, Washington, D.C.

4. *Safety Air Cushion Expenditure/Benefit Study*, John Z. DeLorean, prepared for Allstate Insurance, Northbrook, Illinois, March 18, 1975.

5. Statement of William Haddon, Jr., M.D., Public Hearing on Occupant Crash Protection, Alternative for Passenger Cars, given before Brock Adams, Secretary of Transportation, Washington, D.C., April 27, 1977.

6. Solomon, K. A., C. L. Batten, and C. Phelps, "How Safe Is Reasonable?" *Automotive Engineering and Litigation*, Volume 1, in G. A. Peters and B. J. Peters (eds.), Garland Law Publishing, New York, 1983.

7. *Fatal Accident Reporting System 1976*, United States Department of Transportation, National Highway Traffic Safety Administration, Washington, D.C.

8. *Accident Cause Analysis*, Cornell Aeronautical Laboratory, PB-212-830, NTIS, July 1972.

9. *Fuel System Integrity*, Federal Motor Vehicle Safety Standard 301-75.

10. *Decade of Research to Vehicle Rear Lighting*, University of Illinois, Champaign, HS-021577, August 1979.

11. "An Extra Brake Light Cuts Rear-End Collisions in Half," Highway Loss Reduction Status Report, 15:9, in *Property and Liability Insurance Index*, Vol. I, Issue 4, June 10, 1980.

12. "High, Center-Mounted Brake Lights Proposed," High Loss Reduction Status Report, in *Property and Liability Insurance Index*, Vol. II, Issue 2, February 9, 1981.

13. *Rear-End Collisions Reduced*, Society of Automotive Engineers, New York, Voevodsky Association, Inc., August 1979.

14. *Small Car Safety in the 80's*, National Highway Traffic Safety Administration.

15. Proceedings of the 9th Stapp Car Crash Conference, University of Minnesota, Minneapolis, October 20-21, 1965.

16. Papers presented at the National Road 1972 Monograph Safety Symposium, Canberra, University of Australia, Melbourne, 1972.

17. Solomon, David, *Accidents on Main Rural Highways Related to Speed, Drive, and Vehicle*, United States Department of Commerce, July 1964.

18. Salem, S. A., K. A. Solomon, M. S. Yesley, *Issues and Problems in Inferring a Level of Acceptable Risk*, The Rand Corporation, R-2561-DOE, August 1980.

19. Solomon, K. A., and P. F. Nelson, *An Evaluation of Alternative Safety Criteria for Nuclear Power Plants*, The Rand Corporation, #?, June 1982.

20. Solomon, K. A., and S. Abraham, "The Index of Harm: A Useful Measure for Comparing Occupational Risks Across Industries," *Journal of Health Physics*, Volume 38, March 1980, pp. 375-381.

21. "Bumper Sticker or Jail," *National Enquirer*, April 23, 1985, p. 29.

22. "New Yorkers Buckle Up, Live Longer," *Los Angeles Times*, April 8, 1985.

23. "Deaths Drop 27% After N.Y. Seat Belt Law," *Los Angeles Times*, May 1, 1985.

SELFISH SAFETY OR REDISTRIBUTED RISKS? TRADE-OFFS AMONG AUTOMOBILE

OCCUPANTS' ACCIDENT FATALITY RISKS

Hans C. Joksch
Dr. rer. pol., rer. nat.
Principal Scientist
Mid-America Research Institute, Inc.
Hartford, Connecticut 06105

Stuart F. Spicker
Professor of Community Medicine
and Health Care (philosophy)
Division of Humanistic Studies in Medicine
Department of Community Medicine and Health Care
School of Medicine
University of Connecticut Health Center
Farmington, Connecticut 06032

Donald F. Mela
Retired Head
Mathematical Analysis Division
National Highway Traffic Safety Administration
Washington, D.C.

1. INTRODUCTION

For a long time it has been known that large cars are safer than
small cars. Recently, this has been widely publicized by The Car Book
(1980), published by the National Highway Traffic Safety Administration
under President Carter's administration, and in publications of the
Highway Loss Data Institute (HLDI, 1981), some findings of which were
cited by General Motors Corp. in newspaper advertisements in 1982.

The Car Book states that: "Of the automobiles currently on the road,
a 4000 pound car is twice as safe as a 2000 pound car (p. 18)." Several
graphs are offered to support this summary statement. A reader of the
HLDI reports (and of the GM advertisements) will immediately recognize
that the 19 car models with the best insurance injury claim experience
(i.e., the lowest) are larger and heavier than the 17 models with the
worst experience--3500 pounds versus 2200 pounds. Readers of these
publications receive a clear message that buying a heavier car will reduce
fatality and injury risk in a crash.[1] If automobile manufacturers believe
that lower injury and fatality risk is a selling point for their cars--as
is reflected by the General Motors advertisements--they should have an
incentive to produce heavier cars; on the other hand, the higher cost of
heavier cars and the Corporate Average Fuel Economy standard which
implicitly favors lighter cars counteract this incentive. Consumers have

261

a choice among many manufacturers' products, and manufacturers attempt to influence it, of course. If manufacturers and/or consumers should tend to promote or elect the purchase of heavier cars, then certain consequences--including important ethical ones--follow. We intend to pursue these consequences in what follows.

2. THE CRASH INJURY AND FATALITY RISKS FOR OCCUPANTS OF LIGHT AND HEAVY   CARS: THE EMPIRICAL BASIS

2.1 Structuring the Problem

One must first note that occupant injuries or deaths-per-vehicle-year reflect (1) the effects of vehicle miles driven per year, (2) occupants per vehicle, (3) the accident risk per mile of travel, and (4) the risk of injury or death in an accident. The first two factors do not depend on the vehicle; the third depends more on the driver and the environment but may be influenced by vehicle factors; only the last depends strongly on the vehicle (and also on the accident severity, e.g., as measured by impact speed). Therefore, the occupant injury and fatality risk in an "average" crash is the best measure of the car's safety, except in those cases where a car might have a definitely higher accident risk.

The weight of a car plays very different roles in single car in contrast to multivehicle accidents. In single car accidents, where a car hits a fixed object, or rolls over, there is no physical reason why a heavier car should be safer than a lighter one (except in situations where a heavier car could break an obstacle that results in a "softer landing").

Empirical data reveal that the injury and fatality risk in a single vehicle crash depends relatively little on car weight; the effect is probably indirect because heavier cars tend to be larger, and larger cars can better absorb the impact. In car-car crashes, however, weight plays an important and direct role: the changes in velocity that the two cars experience are proportional to the weights of the cars--the lighter car experiencing the greater change of velocity. This change of velocity has been found to be the single most important variable influencing the occupant injury and fatality risk. Empirical investigations have shown the strong effects of car weight in car-car collisions. Collisions between cars and trucks are similar to collisions between cars, but the stiffer and higher frame of trucks further complicates the analysis. Although multicar collisions are similar to collisions between two cars, we shall restrict our discussion to the most common types: (1) single car accidents, and (2) car-car collisions.

2.2 Quantitative Relations

The effects of the weights in tw car collisions on the occupant injury risk were first quantified in the early 70's (D. Mela, 1974). This relation shows that the injury risk for occupants of a car of weight w (in 100 lbs.) colliding with a car of weight w' is proportional to

$$\exp(-.05w + .02w')$$

More recently, H.C. Joksch (1983) reviewed all the available information on injury and fatality risk in car crashes and found that a formula of this structure still gave an adequate representation of the data, though the exact shape of the relation may be somewhat different, and individual car models may deviate, because characteristics other than weight also play a significant role. For the fatality risk, Joksch found the relation

$$\exp(-.07w + .055w').$$

For the fatality risk in single car accidents, the relation is much less certain:

$$\exp(-.02w)$$

gives an adequate representation of the empirical data. One should note that this relation is nearly the same as in collisions between two cars of the same weight, w=w'. This is plausible because a collision with another car of the same weight is equivalent to a collision with a fixed object; it would be exactly equal, if the coefficients were slightly different:

$$\exp(-.07w + .05w').$$

We will use this relation for conceptual clarity. This equation can then be written as follows:

$$\exp(-.02w)*\exp(-.05w + .05w').$$

The first factor represents the intrinsic crashworthiness of the car of weight w and the second factor is the advantage or disadvantage it has when colliding with a car of weight w'. If we look at the corresponding equation for the other car, then

$$\exp(-.02w')*\exp(-.05w' + .05w).$$

We see that the effect of the weight difference on the second car is exactly the inverse of its effect on the first car. Whereas the first factor reflects a true reduction of injuries or deaths, the second factor simple reflects shifts to deaths and injuries from heavier to lighter cars. A closer look, however, reveals that this is not just a simple shift: If the second factor serves to reduce the risk for the occupants of heavy cars to one half, then it doubles that for occupants of light cars. This amounts to the sacrificing of two lives in order to save one. The first factor, however, reduces this effect. To illustrate these relations, we shall consider three cars with weights of 2000, 3000, and 4000 lbs., respectively. This describes most of the present range of weights. Table 1 reflects the fatality risks relative to that in a collision between two 3000 lb. cars.

Table 1

Illustration of Relative Car Driven Fatality Risks
in Collisions of Two Cars and in Single Car Accidents

Weight of Victim's Car (lbs.)	Weight of Other Car (lbs)			Single Car
	2000	3000	4000	
2000	1.22	2.01	3.32	1.22
3000	.62	1.00	1.65	1.00
4000	.30	.50	.82	.82

2.3 Modeling the Overall Effect of Car Variety

To study the overall effects of having cars of different weights on the road, and the effects of shifts in "car population," we shall assume a car population composed of three types of cars, with the proportion p, q, and r for the light, medium and heavy cars, respectively. Hence, p+q+r=1. We shall also assume that the probability of accident involvement is independent of car weight, and that cars in accidents are randomly mixed. We can then say, 'the proportion p*p' of crashes involves two light cars; '2*p*q' a light and a medium weight car, etc. The total}number of occupants killed is a quadratic function of p,q, and r: t=1.22pp + 2.63pq + qpq + 3.62pr + 2.15qr + 0.82 rr. Since only two of these proportions are independent, one may represent the vehicle mix in a plane, as in Figure 1.

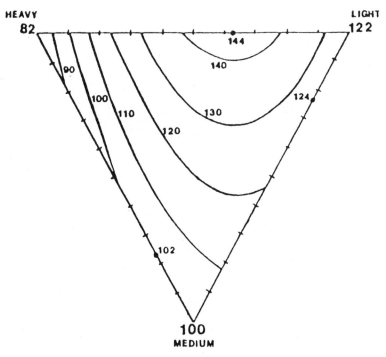

Figure 1.   Total occupant deaths in car-car collisions as functions of the composition of the car population. Each potential mix of the three car classes (heavy--4000 lbs.; medium--3000 lbs.; light--2000 lbs.) is represented by a point in the triangle, the corners representing fleets of all heavy, all light, and all medium cars. Curves of constant numbers of total deaths are shown. The numbers are total fatalities relative to that for a fleet of all medium-weight cars.

Each corner of the triangle represents a car population which consists of only one type of car; a population with one-third of each of the three types is represented by the point in the center of the triangle; a population of one-half heavy and one-half light cars is represented by the midpoint on the upper edge.

The absolutely minimal number of deaths occurs in a fleet of all large cars (82). The absolutely largest number, however, does not occur for a fleet of all light cars: it occurs at a point at the upper edge of the triangle which represents about one-third large and two-thirds light cars. To illustrate the implications of this in some detail, let's assume a fleet which corresponds to the point (on Figure 1) with the highest number of fatalities - 144. This point, then, represents 63% of light cars and 37% of heavy cars. If there were not the interaction of car

weights in crashes, then there would be (.63 * 122) 77 deaths in light
cars, and (.37 * 82) 30 deaths in heavy cars. The total number of deaths
would be 107, of which 72% occurred in light and 28% in heavy cars.
However, the difference of car weights in collisions increases total
fatalities by 38, which is equal to 36%; this also alters the
distribution: 88% of those who die were in light cars; and only 12% of
those who die were in heavy cars.

Imagine a fleet of all light cars (viz. upper right corner): If an
owner would replace his light car by a medium or heavy car (without adding
a car to the fleet)[2], this would shift the point which represents the car
population to the left or lower left. The situation is similar if several
owners do this. Except if this shift is very large, the result is an
increase in the total number of deaths.

Figure 2 describes the results of a more detailed analysis. If the
fleet is represented by a point right of the line A, then a small shift
from light to medium cars (leaving the proportion of heavy cars unchanged)
results in an increase in the total number of deaths. A shift from light
to heavy cars (leaving the proportion of medium cars unchanged) leads to
an increase in the total number of deaths, if the starting point is right
of line B. Similarly, line C is defined for a shift from medium to heavy
cars.

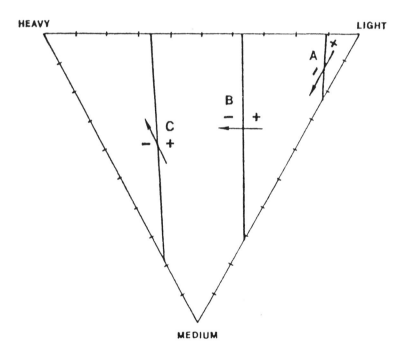

Figure 2. Changes in total occupant deaths in car-car collisions resulting
from changes in the car mix. A change in the car mix in the
direction of the arrows increases deaths on the right sides of
the lines dividing the triangle and decreases them on the left
sides of the lines.

If someone shifts from a lighter to a heavier car, he will reduce his
own fatality risk. However, from this model we must draw the conclusion
that this does not necessarily reduce the number of total fatalities.
Depending on the current composition of the fleet, he may so increase the

risk to others--in cars lighter as well as heavier than his--that overall there will be an increase in the total number of deaths in car-car collisions. On the other hand, someone shifting to a lighter car will increase his or her own fatality risk, but may so decrease that of others such that the number of total fatalities decreases. Whether this condition will actually prevail depends upon the exact composition of the current automobile fleet. Figure 2 illustrates how different the results of a shift in the composition of the fleet can be, depending on the initial position of the fleet.

The model has to be modified slightly if one includes single car accidents. They contribute the terms

$$1.22p + 1.00q + .82r$$

to the total number of deaths. Since about the same number of car occupants die in single car accidents as in multivehicle accidents, we may combine the models so that for a fleet of all medium cars half of the deaths occur in single vehicle accidents and half in car-car collisions.

The results of this model are shown in Figure 3. The overall pattern of the function of total deaths is similar to that in Figure 1; however, the function is much "flatter." There is one difference as is shown in Figure 4: there is no dividing line corresponding to line A in Figure 1, here a shift from light to medium cars will never increase the total number of deaths.

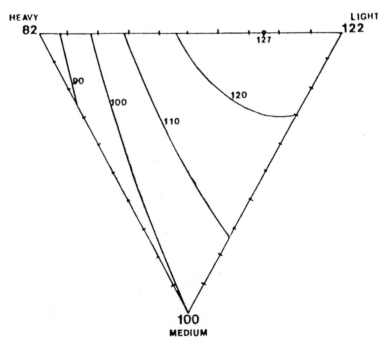

Figure 3. Total occupant deaths in car-car and single-car collisions. Each potential mix of the three car classes (heavy--4000 lbs.; medium--3000 lbs.; light--2000 lbs.) is represented by a point in the triangle, the corners representing fleets of all heavy, all light and all medium cars. Curves of constant total deaths are shown. The numbers are total deaths, relative to that for a fleet of all medium cars where half of the deaths occur in single-car and half in car-car accidents.

266

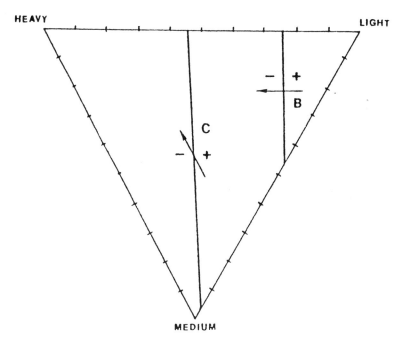

Figure 4. Changes in total occupant deaths in car-car and single-car accidents resulting from changes in the car mix. A change in the car
mix in the direction of the arrows increases deaths on the right
sides of the lines dividing the triangle and decreases them on
the left. A change from light- to medium-weight cars will always
reduce total deaths.

In short, our model shows that someone might decrease his own
fatality risk by shifting from a lighter to the heavier car. One certain
consequence of this choice is that is will increase the fatality risk for
certain other car occupants and possibly to such a degree that the total
number of deaths will also be increased.

2.4 Limitations of the Model

Though our model probably offers a realistic, qualitative picture of
the real automobile accident world, the numerical results may not be quite
accurate, for a few reasons: First, the empirical relations are based on
the experience of 1980 and earlier car models; second, the relation that
exists between weight and risk is probably far more complicated than our
model reveal; third, though the effect of weight is always manifest in
car-car collisions, other factors also play a role in energy management in
crashes. Finally, the real automobile fleet is composed not of three
types of cars, but of many, thereby covering a rather wide range of
automobile weights.

3. AUTOMOBILE CRASHWORTHINESS: REGULATING MANUFACTURES AND INFORMING CONSUMERS

3.1 The Role of the Federal Government

The effects of vehicle weight disparities upon total crash losses and
upon individual risk illustrate quite well the difficulty of many of the

267

problems faced by the National Highway Traffic Safety Administration (NHTSA) in carrying out its mission to reduce the overall losses from highway crashes. A prerequisite to action is to understand and describe the problem. It is not easy to isolate the effects of weight and size, in part because of the large number of factors that can work to raise or lower the crash and injury rates for any vehicle type, and in part because of the difficulty and expense of collecting and processing the necessary quantity and quality of data. Nevertheless, we do have a quantitative description, a mathematical model based upon accident data, that reveals some rather large effects, and for that reason may be adequate to support some decisions.

After obtaining a useful description and understanding of the problem, NHTSA must determine the actions that may diminish the problem and attempt to implement those that meet the criteria of cost and effectiveness. An additional very heavy constraint, as many programs to increase safety belt usage have shown, is acceptability to the driving public. In most cases, NHTSA's response to a perceived major safety problem will consist of one or more of the following:

(1) disseminate consumer information (a) so that vehicle users can act to reduce their own risks, and (b) to use the power of publicity to bring pressure on manufacturers, (legislators, officials responsible for roads, traffic control, driver licensing, etc.) to take helpful actions;

(2) issue mandatory regulations or directives requiring present or future action by the recipients, e.g., motor vehicle safety standards, recalls, etc. The desired results of these actions are changes in human behavior and/or engineering changes in vehicles or in the road and traffic control systems.

3.2 Concern about Light Cars

Interest in the safety effects of car size arose from two principal concerns. First, since the early 60s many persons believed that publishing safety statistics such as accident and injury rates for each make and model of passenger car could force manufacturers to pay more attention to design for safety as a result of market pressure from informed consumers. The latest published NHTSA annual report reaffirms this belief:

The Consumer Information Regulations require motor vehicle manufacturers to submit to the agency, and make available to first and prospective automobile purchasers, information on stopping distance, uniform tire quality grading, and truck camper loading. This information is an outgrowth of the Congressional mandate under the National Traffic Motor Vehicle Safety Act of 1966, and the agency's belief that an informed marketplace is the key to improving safety and performance of various domestic and foreign automobiles. (U.S. DOT, 1985)

Today, thousands of people buy the privately published successor to The Car Book (published under the same name and in similar format) which includes vehicle fatality rates, and the Highway Loss Data Institute continues to publish statistical compendia showing the incidence of collision and injury claims and expenses by make and model for most passenger cars and utility vehicles. Since basic physical considerations show that vehicle size and weight have large effects on these rates, it was desirable to get some quantitative description of these effects in order to ensure fair comparisons.

Most published compendia of make-model comparisons have grouped the vehicles by weight class, although other criteria such as wheelbase serve a similar purpose. This reduces, but does not completely eliminate, the distorting effects of differences in weight and size. For example, Joksch (1983) indicates that the probability of fatal injury in a crash for vehicle occupants in two-car collisions increases about 7 percent with each 100 pound decrease in vehicle weight. Hence, if one groups together vehicles within an interval of 600 pounds, the probability of fatal injury in a two car crash should be about 50 percent greater for occupants of the lightest vehicles in the range than it is for occupants of the heaviest vehicles in the range, and the fatality rates for the vehicles should vary accordingly. In single-vehicle crashes, were weight is a less important factor, the difference is 13 percent. So, if there are equal numbers of occupants exposed to single-vehicle and two-car crashes, the maximum variation in the 600-pound interval would be (50+13)/2=31 percent. (This ignores, however, the effects in crashes involving an automobile and a larger vehicle such as a truck, bus or van.)

The preceding comment raises immediately the question of fairness in comparisons. The weight variations within a class are probably not the principal source of variation in injury rates. Most analysts would agree that vehicle exposure (e.g., who drives the vehicle, when, where and how far, under what road and traffic conditions) is the most important determinant of accident and injury rates. How much of the differences among various make and models within a weight class can be accounted for by weight and exposure differences among the vehicle groups? What are the consequences of erroneous information to consumers and for the manufacturers?

The fuel shortages in 1973-4 and 1979 were the other major factor that created interest in the safety effects of car size. One way of improve fuel economy is to reduce the vehicle weights. In the absence of some countervailing effects, this will result in higher injury rates for occupants of the down-sized vehicles. So this became a matter of some concern to NHTSA and was the incentive for additional work on the problem (Mela, 1974). The empirical relationship arrived at between the injury probabilities for drivers in two-car crashes and the vehicle weights implied that the weight disparities among the passenger cars at that time raised the overall fatality rate in two-car crashes by about 6 percent (Joksch, 1974) over the rate that might be expected in an automobile population, all of whose cars had the same weight as the average weight in the actual car population (Mela, 1975). This 6 percent increase is about the same as would be expected to result from a 200-pound decrease in the average car weight.

Thus, if we consider the major problem to be increases in the overall risk level, then the major contributor is the large reduction in average vehicle weight that has been taking place. Weight disparities, on the other hand, primarily reallocate the risks among the vehicle users. Because one person's purchase of a heavy car can reduce his risk of serious injury in a two-car crash, while increasing the risk for the occupants of the other car, the overall effect in two-car crashes is second order; the net increase in risk is a different between an increase for one group of persons and a decrease for others. Therefore, the ethical implications of the weight disparities assume more importance.

The best way to put this in perspective is to compare the changes in risk levels due to differences in vehicle size with those that result from other factors affecting risk. For example, safetybelt wearers reduce their probability of fatal injury in a crash by about 50 percent. To put

it more dramatically, the non-belt wearer has increased his risk by a
factor of 2. The same increases in risk would result from weight changes
of 950 pounds in two car crashes and 3400 pounds in single vehicle
crashes. So, for most car buyers, the decision to wear or not to wear a
belt is likely to have more effect on their risk of injury than the
decision to "step up" to the next larger and heavier size class of cars.
However, for seatbelt users--and seatbelt use is increasing with the
passing of seatbelt laws--car weight remains the factor most strongly
influencing fatality rate.

3.3 The Protection of Others

The Federal Motor Vehicle Standards are intended to enhance the
safety of occupants of the vehicles to which they apply, although, to the
extent that the standards effect a reduction in multi-vehicle crashes,
they can also add to the safety of other road users. All crash-prevention
standards (series 100 of the Federal Motor Vehicle Safety Standards) fall
into this category. The crash-phase injury prevention standards (series
200) protect with one exception[3] the occupants of the vehicles to which
they apply. Rear-underride guards for heavy trucks to protect occupants
of cars colliding with trucks have been considered, but truckers objected
because of the additional weight and consequent fuel consumption. None of
the standards have a negative effect upon the occupants of other vehicles
with one possible exception: the third high-mounted brake light. It has
been established that vehicles equipped with this configuration of rear
lights are less likely to be struck from the rear by a following
vehicle. But, under some circumstances, it appears that the following
vehicle will be more likely itself to be struck from the rear,
particularly if the following vehicle is not equipped with the high-
mounted tail lamp.

Concerning consumer information, the original edition of The Car Book
might well have had a negative effect on the occupants of light cars. The
Car Book clearly advertised the merits of heavier cars without mentioning
their effect on the occupants of lighter cars. Should government encourage
those who can afford it to buy heavy cars? The authors of The Car Book
apparently thought so. The government has an alternative, which is
implemented in the New Car Assessment Program. This program tests new
cars occupied by instrumented dummies in barrier crashes. These
correspond roughly to collisions with a car of the same weight. The
results of these tests reveal the purely protective characteristics of a
car design without the effect of its weight; thus, the results are not
biased toward heavier cars. On the other hand, the results of these crash
tests are of limited usefulness for assessing the fatality risk in real
world crashes: a light car which compares well with other light cars can
still have a higher fatality risk than a heavier car which ranks only
average.

4. AUTOMOBILE OCCUPANT DATALITY RISKS: THE ETHICAL IMPLICATIONS

4.1 Motor Vehicle Fatalities: The Ethical Issues

The conceptual world of technological, environmental, and risk
assessment and analysis, though heavily dependent upon the sophisticated
theories of the various decision sciences is, nevertheless, inhabited by
additional, yet unacknowledged, theoretical ghosts. One of the central
dimensions of philosphical reflection is ethical analysis; indeed, some
unacknowledged theoretical ghosts (with practical bearings of their own)

are the often presumed and assumed ethical justifications for various practices which affect us all in our daily lives. Furthermore, in our time, philosophy has itself become "applied," given the attention that moral philosophy has given to the science and practice of medicine, for example. But ethical analyses of other actions beyond the multi-faceted health-care context are also warranted these days.

For a long time, attention to automobile accidents and death had been concentrated on the driver and his or her role in accident causation. In the early 1960s, popular and governmental attention was refocused on the automobile and its role in the causation of injury and death. This led to the establishment of the National Highway Traffic Safety Administration, which had the authority to regulate automobile characteristics. Special emphasis was placed not only on preventing motor vehicle accidents, but also reducing the risks of injury and death in these accidents.

More recently the formation of local grass-roots organizations reflects continuing concern over motor vehicle deaths. They again emphasize changing driver behavior and competence by way of legal and educational approaches. Organizations like Mothers Against Drunk Driving (MADD) have been formed with at the very least symbolically reinforce the value of life-saving goals and the urgency of saving lives. Many of MADD's members had a young person killed by a drunk driver and thus their efforts are directed to the saving of lives and to reducing injuries to automobile occupants. All too often attempts at preventive measures have merely symbolic significance. This has led many to conclude that our society does not place a very high value on human life. Is this state of affairs a true reflection of the way citizens in our society dis-value life? We think not.

There are, of course, standard reasons for inferring that we do not value lives as such: (1) by saving lives through improvement of automobiles and/or road conditions, we do not know ahead of time whose lives will be saved; in a sense they remain anonymous; (2) lives lost in actual automobile accidents are usually strangers--although a particular death affects us when we know the persons involved, are touched by the loss of someone dearest to us, or perhaps have been at the scene. Generally, of course, we read about strangers; statistically, we hear the annual or holiday-weekend death tally. Apparently, we are not too moved by such generalizations, statistical and otherwise, and thus we are in danger of a loss of motivation to see the facts for what they are, and to effect changes that would reduce the number of automobile fatalities. We have had only two choices: change individual driving behavior or change the highway system. Since the establishment of the National Highway Traffic Safety Administration, modification of the vehicle has become a third option. Whereas prior strategies emphasized the prevention of accidents, the regulation of vehicles emphasized even more the reduction of the risk of injury or death in accidents, not from accidents. However, they are aimed at protecting the occupants of vehicles to which they apply; they do not provide protection to occupants of other vehicles. That heavy or stiff vehicles increase the risk for the occupants of other vehicles has been recognized in the technical literature; however, publications such as those noted in our Introduction which implicitly recommend heavier vehicles ignore this aspect.

The most obvious effects of structural differences are that heavier and larger cars have lower occupant injury and fatality risks than smaller and lighter cars. However, heavier cars also increase the injury and fatality risks in cars with which they collide.

Thanks to the careful research efforts of many persons, we today are in a much better position to formulate the principal ethical issues raised by the distribution of car-occupant driver injuries and fatalities.

Having reviewed the empirical conditions, we shall now direct our attention to three independent yet related ethical issues which arise on the basis of the general significant <u>disequities</u> which are implicit in the present automobile fleet.

Before turning our attention to the three ethical issues raised by our present practices, it may be useful to mention the three principal characters on our stage: <u>buyers</u> are free to select from a wide range of automobiles, including a wide variation of weight and wheelbase on the new and used car market; <u>manufactures</u> can produce a wide range of cars, domestic and foreign, and advertise their characteristics; and the <u>government</u> can regulate certain aspects of the automobiles through the Federal Motor Vehicle Safety Standards and the Corporate Average Fuel Economy standards. The insurance industry, of course, is a major influence in the context of automobile accident compensation for injuries to persons and property. By setting premiums it can encourage or discourage the choice of certain automobiles. We shall not explore this influence here, however.

4.2 The First Question: Consumer Conduct

The first question, then, is both ethical and legal, since we can ask whether our society should allow this citizens to drive automobiles that are so heavy compared to the lighter and medium-weight cars, that they place the drivers of the lighter cars at a significantly higher risk of fatality than the drivers of the heavier cars. The question is legal in the sense that it can be read as: "Should it remain legal to drive very heavy cars which place others in the lighter cars at serious risk of fatality in car-car accidents?" It is fair to read the question in legal terms, since driving automobiles and other vehicles is already legally governed. Moreover, we need not dwell here on licensure, registration, or safety standards for vehicles on U.S. roads, except to say that (1) the <u>driver's</u> "right" (privilege?) to drive is strongly regulated under police powers, which permit a state to restrict licensing; (2) the right to use a given vehicle is also subject to licensing regulations. Again, (3) there is no right to drive a particular vehicle; only those satisfying state and federal requirements may be used on public roads.

But we are not here asking the legal form of the question; we are asking the <u>moral</u> one: given the facts before use, is it morally justified for us to continue to allow the wide disparity of automobile weights which we currently experience on our roads? Again, is it ethical to purchase a new or used car of heavy weight, which in fact means that the purchaser-- selecting from manufacturers' offerings to the public--not only purchases additional personal safety, but, in addition, "purchases additional personal safety, but, in addition, "purchases" a greater likelihood that he or she will kill occupant drivers of lighter cars in car-car accidents? Here it is important that we be clear. We are <u>not</u> suggesting that we blame drivers, manufacturers, or sellers of heavy automobiles; we are simply raising the ethical issue of obligation or non-obligation, given the fact that by respecifying what weight range of automobiles we permit on our roads, we would reduce the disparities in occupant fatality risks and possibly even the number of deaths of occupants of car-car accidents. But first we must determine whether a new obligation exists; only then can we rationally discuss where the obligation, if it exists, lies. Even if this empirical evidence becomes available to the public, and is repetitively announced via the popular media, would new automobile purchasers avoid buying heavy automobiles? As long as there are heavy cars on the road, and others are buying heavier new cars, a rational buyer will buy the heaviest car he can afford for his own protection. There are, of course, other possible scenarios--e.g., the petroleum fuel crisis of a few years ago where, clearly, lighter cars were preferable. We should keep one fact in mind--that although new, heavy cars are generally more expensive than lighter cars, persons of modest and limited means can and do often purchase heavy automobiles; they usually buy used cars and the oldest used cars are generally quite heavy. So the issue of the heavier automobile owner's advantage in contrast to the lighter automobile driver's disadvantage is <u>not</u> equivalent to the rich taking undue advantage of the indigent. In the future, however, the situation will change-- heavier cars will be driven by the well-to-do, except if they opt for light, more expensive specialty cars. Disequities can be engendered without casting one socio-economic group over or against another--the rich over or against the indigent. In fact, this makes our current problem even more interesting, for it tends to equalize responsibility among automobile owners, whatever their means. For if we can show that the problem lies with the range of choices of car purchasers in general, then any solution--e.g., change of purchasers' behavior, manufacturers' decisionmaking, or sales promotion--will find everyone equally responsible. We should keep in mind, of course, that sellers of automobiles and automobile manufactures and workers also are occupant drivers--indeed, a greater percentage of these groups are drivers than are, for example, minors below legal driving age, the elderly infirm, and the handicapped.

Unfortunately, if we agree that we ought to equalize the risk that occupant drivers take with regard to their lives, the consequences are as serious as they are various. For example, we may decide it is morally proper to continue to allow persons to purchase lighter automobiles so that they assume any additional risk they take on a <u>voluntary</u> basis, "voluntary" in the best sense of the term--they are informed, competent, uncoerced, and freely elect to purchase these smaller, lighter cars. In so doing, if things remain as they are, those drivers can remain free to take a greater risk of death in car-car accidents. But should we continue to allow persons of whatever means to purchase heavier automobiles and by so doing purchase a powerful instrument to radically increase their changes of participating in the killing of those drivers in the smaller vehicles? One answer could be as follows: "Yes, if you allow the purchase of greater-risk-of-death smaller vehicles, then it is consistent to allow the purchase of heavier vehicles by those who prefer them. This is how things stand today. On the other hand, one might argue that though it is morally permissible to allow persons to take greater risks with <u>their</u> lives, retaining a democratic and libertarian ideal, it is not morally permissible to allow persons to purchase a greater likelihood of killing others than being killed: The distinction is one between <u>freely taking a risk with one's own life</u> and <u>freely buying a decisive advantage over others to further secure one's own life</u>. The problem is virtually without analogy, since the interaction of both light and heavy car owners is almost unique in our social intercourse and commerce. It is almost impossible to discover a context analogous to automobile/occupant interactions in which there is virtually no escape from each other in very risky situations. The two groups are on common turf. This common turf-- "the commons" as it was dubbed by political philosophers--should begin to signal to us that we might have obligations to each other, and that present disparities in purchases of various car weights should not be permitted to continue: for those who drive the heavier automobiles put the

lighter-automobile drivers at great disadvantage, but by purchasing less
diverse cars we can significantly reduce discrepancies between the
fatality risks of occupants and drivers of different cars.

4.3 The Second Question: Manufacturer's Conduct

Do all automobile manufacturers whose automobiles operate on U.S.
roads (including all manufacturers of imported foreign automobiles) have
an obligation to protect drivers in automobiles other than the automobiles
each manufacturer produces? Is there an obligation for each manufacturer
to be critical of the weight of cars made by other manufactures? Why,
after all, does each automobile manufacturer invest in improving the
safety and life-reserving features of its own particular make or makes?
It appears from the fact that all automobile manufacturers conduct safety
studies and continue to redesign their automobiles, that they tacitly
endorse the goal of reducing fatality risks to occupant drivers. It does
not appear that they would benefit from further lectures on their
obligations to the public. Moreover, there is no obvious evidence that
manufacturers feel obliged to extend safety considerations to the
occupants of other cars. At least the General Motors advertisements can
be interpreted to the contrary. For they contrast the low risk in heavy
cars (primarily GM products) with the high risk in lighter cars (primarily
Japanese imports) without mentioning that the high risk for light cars is
to some extent due to the presence of its own heavy cars on the road.

On the positive side, it makes little difference what automobile
manufacturers and suppliers intend so long as the purchasers on the demand
side insist on reducing their risk of a fatal accident. Moreover, a great
deal of money is already expended on the part of automobile manufacturers
to influence the purchase of their own products. We are convinced that a
dramatic difference in fatality risks could alter purchasers' behavior, if
purchasers were deeply convinced that fatal accidents can happen to
them. However, most drivers tend to believe (albeit unjustifiably) that
they can avoid fatal accidents; they tend to weigh crashworthiness
relatively lightly and other factors like economic, engineering and
aesthetic ones more heavily. Nevertheless, the fatality risk plays a role
at least in some buyers' decisions. The most dramatic differences are
between the heaviest and the lightest cars, and it is therefore easier for
manufacturers to advertise the advantages of heavier cars than to
demonstrate any differences between more comparable cars. Considering
this, no manufacturer has a motive to reduce the weights of his cars in
order to reduce the occupant fatality risk for other manufacturers' cars
(though other considerations, such as price or fuel economy, may motivate
the manufacturer to do this). Indeed, making his cars lighter will make
them less attractive to some safety-conscious buyers.

Thus, as long as there is no assurance that other manufactures will
not reduce the weights of their cars, a manufacturer will fare best if he
keeps his cars as heavy as possible, considering the other effects of
weight. Only cooperation among manufactures could eliminate the
competitive obstacle to reducing car weights insofar as this would reduce
their "aggressivity" attitude toward other cars. Cooperation among
manufacturers, however, may be difficult, since anti-trust regulations are
complex. Here, in all likelihood, government intervention might be
needed.

By working with one another and legally responding to the intent of
the anti-trust laws, all automobile manufacturers can take a further step
in the direction of fulfilling already-stated obligations to the public,
who purchase and drive their vehicles.   Before you warn us of the Federal

anti-trust laws which prohibit conspiracy among manufacturers, consider the moral point first. After all, if it is clearly for the public good that such an agreement is to be suggested to government by all manufacturers, then there may well be a way--given that no manufacturer is to take financial and market advantage of the others--to create a new range of automobile weights that would, in the end, decrease discrepancies in automobile occupant fatality risks.)

4.4 The Third Question: The Role of Government

This leads us to or last question: Should the U.S. government regulate the weight range of all vehicles used for domestic, non-commercial purposes?

When regulating car weight, the government has to consider obvious concerns. Cars for more occupants have to be heavier than those for fewer persons. Also, there are trucks on the road, where weight cannot be much reduced without affecting the trucks' main purpose. Thus, instead of regulating weight directly, compensatory regulations may be preferable: if a heavy vehicle has a "less aggressive" (or, positively states, "more forgiving") structure, it may have the same effect as a light vehicle on others. Another qualification for regulation might be to require much higher qualifications for licensing drivers of heavy vehicles; though they still increase the fatality risk of other vehicle occupants (given that an accident occurred), a lower accident risk may serve to compensate this.

There already exists implicit government regulation of car weight. Weight is an important factor in automotive fuel economy, and the Corporate Average Fuel Economy Standard tends to decrease the average weight of a manufacture's car models. However, it does nothing to decrease discrepancies: one manufacturer's models may be of similar weights, another manufacturer may produce very light and very heavy models, thus achieving the same average.

Again, should all importers and U.S. manufacturers/sellers be required to change their automobile designs, given that auto weight is related to many other automobile features, including safety features? For those persons of libertarian persuasion, of course, the answer is "No, regulation by government intervention is intrusion," they retort, "and such action should be viewed with disdain--since it inhibits the liberty of buyers and sellers to choose among auto vehicles according to their own personal preferences." Even if one decides that the government should not regulate automobile weight, a related question remains: Should manufactures be allowed to publicize and advertise the safety record of heavier cars without also publicizing the fact that much of the safety is gained with a reduction of safety to others.

This ethical and political question is not new, of course. It is the age-old problem of attempting to construct a moral theory of welfare, which on the one hand reduces the de facto risks to people who drive on U.S. roads, while at the same time it does not advocate coercing citizens by instituting additional regulations which restrict their free choice. Can risks, like the risk of death incurred by auto travel in car-car collisions, be redistributed and/or reduced without affecting the freedom of individuals? If we wish to advocate and maintain a so-called "minimal state," how are we to "manage" or "control" risks like the risk of fatality to occupant drivers? Moreover, if we agree to work to equalize the taking of risks on our roads, who will monitor this behavior? Who will provide protection to those in clear need of and with a right to such protection?

In seeking a reconstruction of the requirements which directly bear on the range of automobile weights and wheelbases, we have little confidence that the public at large will sacrifice and restrict their preferences; further, we do not think that auto manufacturers, domestic and foreign, will take the initiative, either. It seems that one purpose of government in a democratic polity--perhaps the most essential end--is that it offer its citizens protection from non-trivial risks and dangerous forces, both foreign and domestic.

5. SUMMARY

The basic facts are well established: occupants of heavier cars face a lower injury and fatality risk in accidents than occupants of lighter cars. However, this advantage is to a large extent due to the fact that, in car-car collisions, they primarily collide with lighter cars. In these collisions, the occupants of heavier cars are better off than in collisions with cars of the same weight, and occupants of lighter cars are worse off than in collisions with cars of the same weight. In a first approximation, the advantage of heavy and the disadvantage of light cars is just redistributing the same total number of deaths among the occupants of different car classes.

In a second approximation, however, the total number of deaths will vary with the composition of car fleet. If the presence of heavier cars reduces the total number of deaths, it can be argued that this makes the uneven distribution of deaths among car classes acceptable. However, it is possible, depending upon the exact composition of the vehicle fleet, that the presence of heavier cars increases the total number of deaths.

Buyers selecting cars under safety aspects will buy the heaviest cars they can afford, thus trading off their fatality risk against that of buyers who can afford only lighter cars.

If manufacturers tried to appeal to safety-conscious buyers, they would offer the heaviest cars compatible with market price and fuel economy standards, thus enabling buyers to select heavier cars, thereby perpetuating the uneven distribution of traffic deaths.

In reality, the situation is not that extreme: safety is only one of many considerations when buying a car. Buyers who cannot afford the heaviest car on the market and who use seatbelts have no other way to protect themselves against the higher fatality risk caused by heavier cars.

The only entity able to change this distribution is the federal government (and to a lesser extent, state governments, by taxing vehicles and requiring special driver licenses). The most direct approach would be to set standards for automobile weight. This might narrow the range of weights; however, a sizeable range may remain, depending on legitimate car characteristics. Indirect approaches might involve standards requiring features which compensate for the effects of greater weight, or by state governments imposing more stringent licensing standards for drivers of heavier cars, which might reduce the accident involvement risk and thereby reduce total fatalities which result from collisions with heavier cars.

Depending on the current composition of the fleet, and the exact relations between fatality risk and automobile weight, reducing weight discrepancies could even have the additional effect of reducing total fatalities.

Given the banality and emptiness of ideals that govern daily life on our roads, can any death realized in such a way be anything more than senseless, undeserved, and without redemption?

NOTES

1. Actually, these publications present the injury or fatality risk per-car-year (without regard to how much the car is used during a year) not the risks per-crash-involvement.
2. A point we owe to Paul Milvy, Ph.D., which he made during the discussion.
3. See FMVSS-211, which prohibits "winged projections" on wheelnuts, wheelcovers and hubcaps to preven injury to pedestrians and bicyclists.

REFERENCES

Automobile Insurance Losses/Personal Injury Protection Coverages (Claim Frequency Results by Size of Claim: 1978-1980 Models), Research Report HLDI, I 80-1, September 1981, Washington, D.C., Highway Loss Data Institute.
Car Book, December 1980, U.S. Department of Transportation, National Highway Traffic Safety Administration.
Joksch, Hans C., August, 1974, "A Simple Formula to Estimate the Impact of Vehicle Weight Distribution upon Deaths in Two-Car Crashes,"--CEM Working Note 526, Hartford, Connecticut, Center for Environment and Man, Inc.
Joksch, Hans C., 1983, "Light-Weight Car Safety Analysis: Phase II, Part II--Occupant Fatality and Injury Risk In Relation to Car Weight," Hartford, Connecticut, Center for the Environment and Man, Inc.
Mela, Donald F., 1974, "How Safe Can You Be in a Small Car?" in Proceedings of the Third International Congress on Automotive Safety, San Francisco, National Motor Vehicle Safety Advisory Council, Vol. II, pp. 48-1 to 30.
Mela, Donald F., 1975, "A Statistical Relation Between Car Weight and Injuries," U.S. Department of Transportation, National Highway Traffic Safety Administration, Technical Note, DOT--HS-801-629.
U.S. Department of Transportation National Highway Traffic Safety Administration, May, 1985, Motor Vehicle Safety, 1983, DOT--HS-806-731.

FIRE RISK ASSESSMENT AND MANAGEMENT

George V. Alexeeff

Weyerhaeuser Company
Longview, WA 98632

ABSTRACT

Approximately 18 test methods have been developed to examine the
acute toxicity of thermal decomposition products produced in fires.
However, the information obtained from these tests has not be integrated
into a fire risk assessment. This paper presents a fire risk assessment
methodology with the goal of enhancing risk management. The five steps
presented are: (1) Hazard identification; (2) Calculation of the
probability of human exposure to the smoke from a material; (3)
Determination of the magnitude of the expected exposure for humans; (4)
Determination of the toxic effects that may be caused by the smoke; and
(5) Estimation of the likelihood of toxic injury resulting to humans in a
fire. A concentration-time product method for estimating exposure was
found most appropriate for comparing the toxicity of decomposition
products with each other and to pure gases.

KEY WORDS: Combustion toxicology; fire risk; risk assessment; fire
           hazard; smoke hazard.

INTRODUCTION

Smoke and fire present a great hazard to life in accidental fires in
occupied structures. Fire risk assessment predicts and characterizes the
potential adverse health effects associated with human exposures to smoke
from burning materials. This is an important step in helping society set
risk management priorities to reduce loss of life due to fires. In
practice, and in the absence of specific standards of guidance, scientists
active in combustion toxicology are frequently asked to make assessments
of a product's potential for contributing to risk. This paper discusses
current practices in fire risk assessment and suggest future improvements.

HAZARD IDENTIFICATION

Approximately 5 to 6 thousand people in the United States annually
die from fire and smoke inhalation. Smoke presents a greater hazard to
life than heat or any other factor in a fire, according to fatality
studies conducted on victims who survived less than 6 to 12 hours post-
exposure (Birky et al., 1979; Zikria et al., 1972). To place the risk of
death by fire and smoke inhalation into perspective, estimates for annual
mortality rates in the united States for a number risk can be considered
(Engineering and Public Policy (et al., 1983). In terms of mortality
attributed to toxic agents, smoke poisoning from fires is a greater cause

of death than poisoning by solid or liquid, venomous animal bites, or food toxins. Based on mortality rates, the annual risk of an individual dying in a fire is approximately 1 in 37,000 (i.e., U.S. population of 220,000,000 divided by U.S. fire fatality rate of 6000 = 36,660).

In addition to mortality, smoke can produce a number of other sublethal effects. Smoke can produce sensory irritation and narcosis, both of which may result in incapacitation. Further there may be chronic effects of smoke inhalation which would be of concern to fire fighters.

Most natural and synthetic substances produce carbon monoxide and carbon dioxide during combustion. Other toxic gases which may be present in a fire are hydrogen cyanide, hydrogen sulfide, hydrogen chloride, hydrogen fluoride, hydrogen bromide, ammonia, nitrogen oxides, sulfur oxides, acrolein and other hydrocarbons. The chemical content of the smoke is dependent on the substance being burned, temperature, oxygen availability, presence of flame and other factors.

Using GC-MS, Woolley and Fardell (1982) identified a large number of decomposition products present in smoke from wood and from polyurethane. However, in practice, combustion toxicity test methods primarily restrict their chemical measurements to carbon monoxide, carbon dioxide, hydrogen cyanide and hydrogen chloride. Although there are a number of reasons for this restriction, it can bias interpretation of results.

HAZARD CHARACTERIZATION

Gases and vapors have been compared on the basis of 30-minute LC_{50}'s (Alexeeff and Packham, 1984a). As reported, the relative range of toxicity for pure gases/vapors represents a scale of almost four orders of magnitude. The most toxic gas/vapor reported was hydrogen cyanide (4.5 mg/L • minutes) while the least toxic gas/vapor reported was 1-bromohexane (16500 mg/L • minutes). At least 17 methods used to determine the combustion toxicity of home furnishings and building materials have been reported (Alexeeff and Packham, 1984a). The results of these tests were reported in a variety of formats and physical units. The quantification of toxic potency such as LC_{50} (median lethal concentration), EC_{50} (median effective concentration), or time-to-effect varied from test to test. Even when considering the LC_{50} endpoint, there were differences in the derivation of the value; one method reports it as initial sample weight in grams (Alarie and Anderson, 1979 and 1981), others as initial sample weight divided by volume of air in the system (Levin et. al., 1982; Kimmerle and Prager, 1980; Hilado and Huttlinger, 1983), and still others as the sample weight volatized divided by the volume of the system (Alexeeff and Packham, 198-4b; Gad and Smith, 1983). None of the methods estimated the exposure concentration experienced by the test animals or described the variability in smoke concentration throughout the test.
In contrast to pure gases/vapors, the potency of smokes had a reported range of only 2 orders of magnitude using the University of Pittsburgh (UPT) combustion toxicity test (Alarie and Anderson 1979 and 1981; Alexeeff and Packham, 1984). The most toxic smoke reported was from PTFE resin (32.0 mg/L • minutes) while the least toxic smoke was produced from Douglas fir (2647.5 mg/L • minutes). Thus, when the relative toxicity of smokes are compared to those of pure gases/vapors, the smoke produced in fires falls in a relatively narrow but toxic range.

After a fire begins, smoke production will continue to increase until the fire is extinguished or the fuel is consumed. An individual may be exposed to the smoke at any stage of the fire and for almost any length of time. Most fires that threaten human safety occur in residential structures. Consequently, the smoke content will be a result of the mixture of materials present in the location of the fire.

Casualties in fires include a higher casualty rate for young children and senior citizens than for the general population (Purser, 1985). The ability to escape from a fire depends upon one's physical ability, the state of the fire, knowledge of a safe escape route, the presence of incapacitating combustion products and the behavior of the individual. A number of these factors were undoubtedly influential in the recent loss of life in a haunted house fire (Bouchard, 1985).

QUANTITATIVE RISK ASSESSMENT

Two primary approaches have been undertaken to quantify the risk of a fire. One approach can be designated the hazard test approach. That is, developing a single test that would provide toxicologic information on which a trained scientist could estimate the relative risk of a material. The assessment of risk would involve the scientist's interpretation of the estimated exposure to the smoke or the nature of the toxic effect. The second approach involves development of a computer model which incorporates a number of empirical and physical attributes of the material under study. The first approach has primarily been used, however present computer fire models are becoming more sophisticated and more widely accepted.

In the hazard test approach a number of materials are examined and then the results are then ranked or placed into categories. Alarie and Anderson (1981) ranked materials on the basis of their performance relative to wood. The materials they studied fell into three categories: A- as toxic as wood, B- more toxic than wood, and C- much more toxic than wood. There are at least two applications of the hazard test information. First, a limit could be established and materials that failed to meet the limit would be rejected. Second, using categories of toxic hazard, safety factors could be established, and suggested usage of the material would be dependent of the results of other fire tests or the specific application of the material. However, the appropriateness of any decision made based on the hazard test approach is dependent on how well the test method chosen simulates the fire scenario(s) of concern.

The primary difficulty with the hazard test approach is that it appears that the outcome is dependent on the test chosen. To illustrate this, the LC_{50}'s reported for Douglas fir are presented for six test methods in Table 1. Comparison of their values indicate that the toxicity of smoke produced by Douglas fir may differ by up to a factor of five among test methods. The reasons for this range of results may be that the different test methods present test animals with effectively different exposure conditions. The test methods subject test specimens to different temperature profiles; a flame may or may not be present; and the oxygen availability at the site of combustion may also be different. These factors can change the animals' exposure to the smoke both qualitatively and quantitively by influencing the analytical composition, the analytical profile, and the rate of sample weight loss (i.e., the resulting smoke concentration).

The importance of estimating the exposure observed by the animals is indicated in tests conducted using a radiant furnace and a 200-L static exposure chamber. As with any static combustion toxicity system, the smoke concentration will increase until the sample stops burning. Animals were exposed to the smoke from the start of combustion until 30 minutes.

Table 1

LC$_{50}$'s Reported for Douglas Fir Smoke in Various Test Systems

METHODS	LC$_{50}$'s (mg/L)
CMIR[a]	21.5 - 43.0
USF[b]	22.4
Cup Furnace[c]	27.6 - 45.3
Radiant Furnace[d]	59.9 - 101.6
Dupont Methane Flame[e]	> 82.8
UPT[f]	106 (63.8 g)

[a]Gad and Smith, 1983

[b]Hilado and Huttlinger, 1983

[c]Levin et al., 1982

[d]Alexeeff and Packham, 1984

[e]Williams and Clarke, 1982

[f]Estimated from Alarie and Anderson, 1979

Smoke production curves produced by the radiant furnace are shown in Figure 1 for polyvinyl chloride, Douglas fir, acrylic rug, rigid polyisocyanurate foam, and flexible polyurethane foam. These curves indicate that different materials reached 90% of their final concentration from 3 to 25 minutes into the test. A similar phenomenon would be expected in other static test systems.

Another factor found to influence the results of combustion toxicity tests is the form of the test specimen. Presently, the form of the test specimen is primarily defined by the dimensions of the test systems' furnace. The influence of sample form was studied in a radiant furnace system. Figure 2 depicts the smoke production curves for three Douglas fir test specimens of equal weight (15g) but in different forms; the three forms were shavings, a 7.6 x 7.6 x 0.6 cm piece, and a 3.3 cm cube. When Douglas fir was tested as a solid cube as compared to shavings, there was a dramatic decrease in the rate of smoke production, in the final smoke concentration (20% lower), in total smoke exposure (40% lower) and in the CO production (60% lower exposure).

A constant smoke concentration was not observed in a dynamic system. In the UPT method, a quantity of test sample was placed into a Lindberg furnace programmed to increase its temperature at 20° C per minute (Alarie and Anderson, 1979 and 1981). The total air flow was 20 LPM. In this dynamic test system, the smoke produced from the sample was diluted with air, moved past the animals and then was removed from the system. Sample weight remaining data on 45 materials plotted against furnace temperature have been published in the literature. From these curves smoke production versus time curves were generated and the areas under the curves were estimated (Alexeeff and Packham, 1984a). As in a static system, the smoke concentration experienced by the animals was dependent on the burning rate of the sample which was a function of temperature. However, in contrast to static systems, the smoke concentration did not accumulate since it was transferred out of the chamber. Consequently there are a number of influential factors still to be examined and taken into consideration in combustion toxicity test systems, and there is a need to standardize the reporting methods of the systems.

A number of approaches have been taken to model the potential threat of life in a fire scenario. These include experimental models (Alarie et. al., 1983; Packham and Crawford, 1984) and mathematical models such as a probabilistic model (Cohn, 1982), a state transition model (Williamson, 1981), a fire and smoke transport model (Jones, 1984), and egress time models (Cooper and Stroup, 1984; Engler et. al., 1983). The state of the art of mathematical modeling was recently reviewed by Underwriters Laboratories Inc. (1983).

A number of these modeling programs utilize toxicity data to estimate hazard (Engler et. al., 1983; Jones, 1984). However, the data was generated from tests designed to satisfy the hazard test approach. Thus the data is a hazard value and not a clear toxicity value. Furthermore, since the hazard tests have not been standardized and appear to generate dissimilar values for the same material, the use of results from a single test may be misleading.

A problem with simply utilizing a hazard value in a mathematical model is that the toxicity of the smoke from a decomposing material in many cases is dependent on the how much of the material has already decomposed. Using the radiant furnace test method we found that the production of carbon monoxide from wood is very much dependent on how much of the sample has already charred (Figure 3). Thus if one is modeling a fire the toxicity of the smoke produced in the early phases may be much different from the toxicity of the smoke of the later phases. Conse-

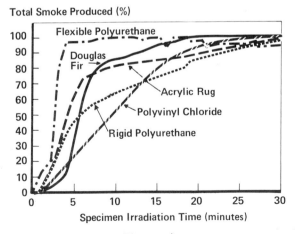

Figure 1

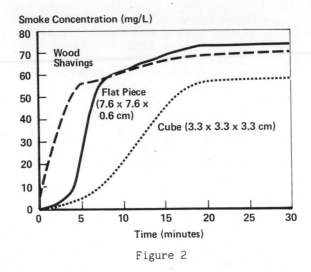

Figure 2

quently, the use of smoke toxicity data in risk assessment requires that it be generated and presented in a format that is more compatible with the exposure data.

One complicating factor is that Ct products associated with any given response vary as a function of concentration. That is, for short acute exposures, Haber's law (i.e., the product of the concentration of a toxicant and the exposure time is a constant) is not a constant. However, one can conduct a few experiments until the relationship is sufficiently defined to allow interpolation.

Full-scale fire tests and/or fire growth computer modeling, such as

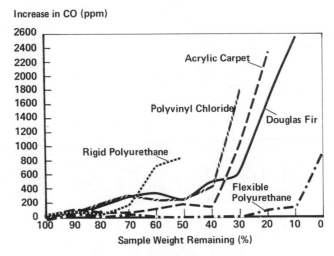

Figure 3

that developed by Smith (1974) can be used to estimate the magnitude of an expected exposure to smoke (or specific toxicants) due to the contribution of a single material. A smoke accumulation curve can be developed which includes information on time and concentration of smoke. The area under the smoke concentration-time curve can be integrated to obtain a Ct product.

As discussed above, the small-scale toxicity tests produce their own smoke concentration-time curves, which may or may not be similar to those of large-scale tests. Thus an ideal combustion toxicity test system would expose animals to a constant toxicant concentration for the entire exposure duration. The toxicity data from the test system at a number of concentrations could then be used to estimate the toxicity of the fire and the smoke concentration is changing. However, none of the above tests has been shown to produce constant smoke concentrations and this may not be possible for a low cost test apparatus. A currently feasible alternative to providing constant exposure concentrations is a careful calculation of the exposure by integration of the material's smoke concentration-time curve to obtain Ct products. Traditionally, smoke concentration has been defined as the mass of material lost from the sample per unit of air into which it is distributed and diluted (Kaplan et. al.], 1983; Packham and Hartzell, 1981). Using this definition, the smoke concentrations produced by combustion toxicity test systems can be calculated from continuous sample weight loss measurements to obtain Ct products (Figure 4). The Ct products can be calculated from the variable exposure concentrations observed in combustion toxicity testing and they provide a reasonable estimate of dose. These qualities make the Ct product an attractive input parameter for risk assessment protocols.

To project the possibility of a toxic injury occurring, human responses must be predicted from a constantly changing environment. This could be accomplished by exactly matching animals test exposures to expected human exposures, but it would require a large battery of tests to cover the range of scenarios possible. Another approach would utilize the Ct products as described above for the toxicity test methods and the expected human exposure (i.e., from fire modeling). I propose that $L(Ct)_{50}$ data be developed (or existing data be reanalyzed) for smoke from materials. Using a fractional approach one could determine what exposure would produce the effect.

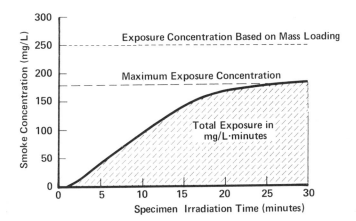

Figure 4

Hartzell et. al. (1985) have worked on a similar approach using carbon monoxide and hydrogen concentrations. They focused on a time-to-effect endpoint, and calculated fractional effective doses at various timepoints. The fractional $L(Ct)_{50}$'s were summed to determine at what time in the fire the effect would occur.

The final correlation of effects obtained using laboratory animals to those expected for humans under actual fire conditions requires the integration of comparative physiology data and clinical observation of smoke inhalation victims. Further it needs to be decided what effect is to be estimated. Instead of using the $L(Ct)_{50}$, it may be more prudent to extrapolate to an $L(Ct)_{10}$ or $L(Ct)_{01}$.

FIRE MANAGEMENT APPROACHES

Current fire management strategies have focused on information, extinguishment and regulation. Generally these strategies have not been developed as a result on knowledge on risk assessment. Information has been presented to public through various media to follow safe practices. Further the use of the smoke alarm now provides detection information for the consumer to escape from a fire in its early stages. The use of sprinklers have provided a means to extinguish fires in their early stages, thus preventing property damage and injuries. An elaborate system of fire codes are present on both state and local levels. In particular, the State of New York is currently considering establishing a data bank on the combustion toxicity of materials based on the UPT method.

Recent trends currently indicate that civilian mortality in the United States due to residential fires has declined from 6,015 in 1978 to 4,075 in 1984 (Carter, 1985). Further advances in risk assessment will provide more information on the nature of fire and the important factors involved in fire hazard. Hopefully, the information obtained from these risk assessment will suggest new strategies to reduce the number of injuries and deaths that occur as a result of fire.

REFERENCES

ALARIE, Y. C. and ANDERSON, R. C. Toxicologic and acute lethal hazard evaluation of thermal decomposition products of synthetic and natural polymers. Toxicol. Appl. Pharm. 51: 341-362 (1979).

ALARIE, Y.C. and ANDERSON, R. C. Toxicologic classifications of thermal decomposition products of synthetic and natural polymers. Toxicol. Appl. Pharm. 57: 181-188 (1981).

ALARIE, Y.C., STOCK, M.F., MATIJAK-SCHAPER, M. and BIRKY, M.M. Toxicity of smoke during chair smoldering tests and small scale tests using the same materials. Fundamental Appl. Toxicol. 3]: 619-626 (1983).

ALEXEEFF, G. V. and PACKHAM S.C. Evaluation of smoke toxicity using concentration-time products. J. Fire Sci. 2: 262-379 (1984a).

ALEXEEFF, G.V. and PACKHAM S.C. Use of a radiant furnace fire model to evaluate acute toxicity of smoke. J. Fire Sci. 2: 306-320 (1984b)

BIRKY, M.M., HALPIN, B.M., CAPLAN, Y.H., FISHER, R. S., McALLISTER, J.M., and DIXON, A.M. Fire fatality study. Fire Materials 3: 211-217 (1979).

COHN, B.M. Formulating acceptable levels of risk. Fire Risk Assessment ASTM STP 762, G.T. Castino and T.Z. Harmathy, Eds. American Society of Testing and Materials, pp. 28-37 (1982).

COOPER, L.Y. and STROUP, D.W. Calculating available safe engress time (ASSET) - A computer Program and Users Guide. National Bureau of Standards (U.S.), NBSIR 82-2578 (1982).

ENGINEERING and PUBLIC POLICY/CARNEGIE-MELLON UNIVERSITY GRADUATE RESEARCH METHODS CLASS. On judging the frequency of lethal events: A replication. Risk Anal. 3: 11-16 (1983).

ENGLER, N., MIDDLETON, V.E. and MACARTHUR, C. The effects of exposure to heat and toxic gas during evacuation. Proceedings Calif. Conf. Product Toxicity 4: 61-95 (1983).

GAD, S.D. and SMITH, A.C. Influence of heating rates on the toxicity of evolved combustion products: results and a system for research. J. Fire Sci. 1: 465-479 (1983).

HARTZELL, G.E., PRIEST, D.N. and SWITZE, W.G. Modeling of toxicological effects of fire gases: 11. Mathematical modeling of intoxication of rats by carbon monoxide and hydrogen cyanide. J.Fire Sci. 3: 115-128 (1985).

HILADO, C. J. and HUTTLINGER, P. A. Screening materials by the NASA dome chamber toxicity test. Proceedings of the California Conference on Product Toxicity, Milbrae, California, USA, 4: 20-6 (1983).

JONES, W.W. A model for the transport of fire, smoke and toxic gases (FAST). National Bureau of Standards (U.S), NBSIR 84-2934 (1984).

KIMMERLE, O. and PRAGER, F.K. The relative toxicity of pyrolysis products. Part II. Polyisocyanurate based foam material. J.Combus. Toxicol. 7: 54-68 (1980).

LEVIN, B.C., FOWELL, A.J., BIRKEY, M.M., PAABO, M., STALE, A., and MALEK, D. Further development of a test method for the assessment of the acute inhalation toxicity of combustion products. NBSIR82 - 2532. National Bureau of Standards (U.S.) Gaithersburg, Maryland (1982).

PACKHAM, S.C. and CRAWFORD, M.B. An evaluation of smoke toxicity and toxic hazard of electrical nonmetallic tubing combustion products. J. Fire Sci 2, 37-59 (1984).

PURSER, D. How toxic smoke products effect the ability of victims to escape from fires. Fire Prevention, May 1985, 29-32 (1985).

SMITH, E.E. Models for evaluating fire hazard. J. Fire Flammability 5: 1979 (1974).

UNDERWRITERS LABORATORY INC., Survey of the state of the art of mathematical fire modeling. For Society of Plastics Industry, Inc., File NC554, Project 82NK1618, (1983).

WILLIAMS, S.J. and CLARKE, F.B. Combustion product toxity: Dependence on on the mode of product generation. Fire Materials 6: 161-162 (1982).

WILLIAMSON, R.B. Coupling deterministic and stochastic modeling to unwanted fire. Fire Safety J. 3]: 243-260 (1981).

WOOLEY, W.D. and FARDELL, P.J. Basic aspects of combustion toxicology. Fire Safety J. 5: 29-48 (1982).

ZIKRIA, B.A., WESTON, A.B., CHODOFF, M., and FERRER, J.M. Smoke and carbon monoxide poisoning in fire victims. J. Trauma 12: 641-645 (1972).

USA MANAGEMENT OF FIRE RISK

Ganapathy Ramachandran

Head, Operations Research and Systems Studies Section
Fire Research Station, Borehamwood, Hertfordshire
WD6 2BL, England

ABSTRACT

Management of fire risk in a building involves three stages - risk evaluation, risk reduction and risk transfer. Statistical and economic techniques have been developed for analysing problems encountered during these stages. These methods and the data needed are reviewed in this paper with some examples illustrating their application.

Fire risk can be expressed as the product of two factors - probability of fire starting and probable damage in a fire. The first factor can be reduced by fire prevention measures aimed at identifying and eliminating major sources of ignition. The second factor can be reduced by fire protection devices such as structural protection, detectors and sprinklers and by fire fighting by fire brigades. Depending on their perception of and attitude to fire risk, the public may be persuaded to adopt some of the fire prevention and protection measures through education, publicity campaigns and economic incentives. Some measures may have to be enforced through regulations, legislation and standards.

By adopting suitable prevention and protection measures a property owner can bear himself (self-insure) part of the risk especially that associated with small fires. The part of risk associated with large fires can be transferred or disposed of through insurance which converts an uncertain loss into a known cost, the insurance premium. The premium decreases with an increase in the level of self insurance (deductible). This interaction between fire protection and insurance is discussed in the paper within a framework provided by Decision Theory and Utility Theory.

KEY WORDS: Fire Risk, Prevention, Protection, Insurance, Probabilities, Decisions, Utilities.

1. INTRODUCTION

Fires, particularly large ones, destroy life and property. In addition, some fires could cause consequential losses such as loss of production, profits, exports and employment and necessitate extra imports. In order to reduce the national wastage due to fires, individuals, organizations and the government have a clear duty to manage or control the risk posed by fire.

Management of fire risk in a building involves three main stages - risk evaluation, risk reduction and risk transfer. The first stage is concerned with identifying all possible causes leading to the occurrence of fires and evaluating the probable loss in the event of a fire breaking out. If the loss is of an unacceptable level removal of some or all of the causes should be considered as the first step in a risk reduction procedure. Since it may be difficult to eliminate all the causes it will be necessary to install in a building fire protection devices which reduce the extent of damage in the event of a fire. The risk then has to be re-evaluated taking into account the steps taken towards removal of cause and reduction of damage. If the reduced risk is small enough to be accepted the property owner may decide to bear the losses himself (self-insurance); otherwise, the risk may have to be insured (risk transfer). A risk can also be self-insured for losses less than a certain level (deductible) and insured for losses greater than this level.

Statistical techniques based on data provided by real fires have been developed for analysing problems encountered during the different stages of fire risk management.[1] These methods include the concept of probability distribution of fire loss[2] and the theory of extreme order statistics for modelling large losses.[3] Point schemes[4], fault trees[5] and stochastic modelling[6] are other methods considered for fire risk assessment. All these methods are reviewed briefly in this paper.

The public are generally persuaded to adopt some of the fire prevention and protection measures through education and publicity campaigns. Some measures may have to be enforced through regulations, legislation and standards. But the effectiveness of these strategies depends very much on the public perception of and attitude to fire risk[7] and human behavior in a fire[8]. These human aspects of fires have been reviewed in a recent paper of Ramachandran[9]. This interaction between fire protection and people is explained in this paper with the aid of a few examples.

Adoption of some of the fire safety measures is also promoted through economic incentives. Fire protection devices such as sprinklers qualify for government grants, tax-allowances and reductions in fire insurance premiums. By installing such devices in his building a property owner can take a risk in accepting a high level of self insurance and obtain a further reduction in insurance premium. This interaction between fire protection and insurance is discussed in this paper within a framework provided by Decision Theory and Utility Theory.[10]

2. RISK EVALUATION

2.1 Risk Identification - General Factors

This procedure involves a physical inspection of a building and enumeration of all possible sources of ignition, materials contributing to fire spread and the presence or absence of fire protection devices. A discussion with people in the building would also be necessary. It would be worthwhile to design a detailed form or questionnaire incorporating all the items affecting fire risk including the special factors mentioned in Section 2.2.

The causes or sources of ignition can be classified into two broad

groups - human and non-human. The first group consists mainly of children
playing with fire, eg matches, careless disposal of matches and smokers'
materials, misuse of electric and other appliances and malicious ignition
which is difficult to eliminate. The second group includes defects in or
faulty connections of appliances using electricity, gas and other fuels.
The appliances may be further classified according to cooking, space
heating, central heating and other uses. This group also includes causes
such as mechanical heat or sparks in industrial buildings, natural
occurrences and spontaneous combustion. Some materials in a building
could be ignitable even by a low energy smouldering source, eg latex foam
and finely powdered rubber. The nature and number of ignition sources and
materials would vary from one part of the building to another. In an
industrial building, for example, three major parts can be identified -
production, storage and others (offices etc).

Fire protection measures could be classified as structural (part of
the building structure) or installed. The former includes fire resistance
of walls, floors and ceilings, compartmentation (sub division into fire
compartments), fire doors, external staircases and other means of
escape. Sprinklers, automatic fire detectors and roof vents are major
installed fire protection devices. Portable fire extinguishers,
hosereels, buckets of water or sand and fire blankets are examples of
minor devices; training is necessary in the use of these methods. Fire
instruction notices and fire drills are equally important fire safety
measures.

2.2 Risk Identification - Special Factors

Buildings of certain types could have special fire risk factors, eg
hospitals, schools, old folks homes. Some people in residential buildings
and offices may be invalids. Industrial buildings have special risks
associated with the manufacturing processes and products. For example, a
number of resins are made by highly exothermic reactions. Processing of
highly flammable liquids and cellulose nitrate and the use of highly
flammable solvents and monomers are other examples occurring in the paint,
ink and resin manufacturing industries. In the textile industry,
cellulosic fibres in particular and all fibres to some degree produce
dense smoke during extinguishment by interaction of water spray with the
intermediate combustion products. In synthetic fibre production the
quantities of solvent involved and the recovery of them present a
considerable hazard of conflagration. In the chemical process industry
the properties and behavior of materials can radically change when they
are subjected to high pressures and temperatures. They may also be
present in large quantities.

2.3 Risk Evaluation

Since it is difficult to control all the factors affecting the
occurrence and spread of fire in a building it would be realistic to
evaluate fire risk in probabilistic rather then deterministic (exact)
terms. The probable loss during a period can be expressed as the product
of the following two components[1]

(i) the probability of fire starting during the period
(ii) the probable extent to which a fire, having started, will spread or
cause damage.

2.3.1 Probability of Fire Starting

The probability of fire starting depends on the nature and number of
ignition sources present in the building. For estimating this probability

it is necessary to analyse data for a group of buildings with similar fire risks since fire in a particular building is a rare event. Statistical studies reviewed by Ramachandran[1] show that the probability of fire starting is given by

$$F(A) = KA^{\alpha} \qquad\qquad (1)$$

where A is the total floor area of the building and K and α are constants for a particular group (risk category) of buildings. F(A) is usually expressed on an annual basis. Values of K and α for major groups of buildings are available for UK[11] and in actuarial studies carried out in some European countries.[12]

Equation (1) gives the probability due to any cause and is the sum of probabilities of fire starting in different parts of a building due to various causes. Without carrying out costly surveys it is difficult to estimate directly the probability due to a particular cause in a particular part. An indirect estimate is given by the product of equation (1) and the conditional probability that the fire is due to the particular cause and part given that the building is involved in fire. The conditional probabilities reflect the relative or comparative risks due to different causes and parts and can be estimated from group statistics such as those available nationally for UK[13] - see Table 1 for example. The conditional probability due to, say, smoking materials in the store/stock room is 0.0129 (= 15/1162). For a textile factory of total floor area 2500 sq. meters, with K = 0.0075 and α = 0.35, equation (1) gives a value of 0.116. Then, for this factory, an estimate of the annual probability due to smoking materials in the store/stock room is 0.0015 (= 0.0129 x 0.116). As explained in Section 3, this procedure enables the re-evaluation of the probability of fire starting in the light of fire prevention measures adopted in the building

2.3.2. Probable damage in a Fire - Extent of Spread

If life loss is to be reduced, a fire should be confined to item or material first ignited, or at least to room of fire origin. For evaluating the extent of spread estimates of probabilities are required for the following four classifications:

(a) confined to item or material first ignited
(b) spread beyond material but confined to the room of fire origin
(c) spread beyond room but confined to the building of fire origin
(d) spread beyond building of fire origin.

Such probabilities can be obtained from UK National Fire Statistics[13] for different materials, sources of ignition and parts of fire origin. Estimates of floor area destroyed by fire are also available for fires which occurred since 1978.

2.3.3 Probable Damage in a Fire - Duration of Burning

The duration of burning is another measure of extent of spread which is useful in problems concerning detection, evacuation of a building and fire brigade operations. UK Fire statistics[13] provide estimates of duration of burning, T, as the sum of the following five periods:

T_1 - ignition to detection or discovery of fire
T_2 - detection to calling fire brigade
T_3 - call to arrival of brigade at the scene of fire
T_4 - arrival to the time when fire is brought under control by brigade
T_5 - control to extinction of fire.

For the first period T_1 an estimate is provided according to the following classification:

    (i)   discovered at ignition
   (ii)   discovered under 5 minutes after ignition
  (iii)   discovered between 5 and 30 minutes after ignition
   (iv)   discovered more than 30 minutes after ignition.

The growth of fire is practically negligible during T_5 and hence only the periods T_1 to T_4 need to be considered in a statistical investigation.

Based on experimental and scientific evidence it can be assumed that

$$A(T) = A(0) \exp(\theta T) \tag{2}$$

where

    $A(T)$ = floor area damaged in T minutes after ignition
    $A(0)$ = floor area initially ignited
    θ = fire growth parameter.

The exponential model in equation (2) gives an estimate of the area likely to be damaged if fire burns for T minutes before being controlled or extinguished. An application of this model is discussed in Section 3 dealing with risk reduction. The model also provides an estimate of "doubling time"

$$d = (1/\theta) \log_e 2 \tag{3}$$

which is the parameter generally used for characterizing rate of fire growth. This is the time for fire to double in size and is a constant for the exponential model. For example, if it takes 5 minutes for the area damaged to increase from 20 m^2 to 40 m^2 it will also take only 5 minutes for the damage to increase from 40 m^2 to 80 m^2 and 80m^2 to 160 m^2 and so on. Estimates for doubling times for some materials are available from experiments carried out in UK, USA and other countries. Estimates for this parameter based on fire brigade statistics are also being obtained and analysed for comparing them with experimental results.[14]

2.3.4 Financial Loss

According to Ramachandran[2], Shpilberg[15] and other authors mentioned in these two papers financial loss (x) in a fire has a skewed probability distribution and in general the variable z (= log x) has a distribution of the "exponential type." Among these distributions normal for z or log normal for x has been recommended widely for modelling fire insurance claims. Exponential for z or Pareto for x is another model considered by some actuaries.

It is a simple statistical problem to estimate the parameters of the fire loss distribution if figures are available for the entire range of possible values of the loss. But loss data are generally available only for large fires for carrying out risk analysis at the national or industry level. Although these fires are of economic importance they constitute only a small percentage of the total number of fires and represent the tail of the distribution. For estimating the parameters from the tail, Ramachandran has developed models based on the theory of extreme order statistics.[3] An application of these methods is discussed in the next section.

The expected loss and other parameters for a particular building with insured value V can be estimated by regarding the probability distribution of loss for the building as a truncated version of the global distribution for losses in all buildings belonging to that particular risk category[3]. An application of this method supported by actuarial studies[12] reveal that the expected loss is given by

$$L(V) = CV^\beta \tag{4}$$

where C and β are constants for a risk category. If we assume that the value (V) is spread uniformly over the floor area of a building, it follows from equation (4) that the expected area damaged is given by

$$D(A) = C^1 A^\beta \tag{5}$$

where A is the total floor area of a building and C^1 a constant. Values of C^1 and β are available for major groups of buildings in the UK[11].

2.3.5 Point Schemes

Point schemes[4] reviewed by Ramachandran[16] constitute a simple technique for fire risk evaluation and include the method formulated by the National Bureau of Standards for Care Buildings[17]. The oldest point schemes are the tariff systems of insurance companies for determining insurance premiums. The following formula is generally proposed:

$$R = \frac{P.A}{N.S.F} \tag{6}$$

where R is a measure of risk. The P factors include fire load, combustibility, potential ground surface area of a fire, building height and the tendency to produce smoke, toxic and corrosive gases; these characterize the inherent hazard of the building. A is an activation factor and represents the tendency for a fire to start while N refers to "normal" fire precautions such as fire brigade and water supplies. The S factors are concerned with "special" protective measures such as detectors and sprinklers and F denotes the fire resistance of the building.

The factors in the numerator of equation (6) are those which cause or enhance fire risk and those in the denominator promote fire safety or mitigate fire risk. For a given building all these factors are enumerated and points assigned to them to reflect their relative contribution. The object of this exercise is that for given values of numerator factors which depend on the risk which is being considered, the values of denominator factors need to be adjusted by choosing suitable protection measures so that R is below a specified value. Allocation of points is based on common sense, expert judgment and practical experience. In some schemes points are calculated by a responsible authority by following consultation with experts in the field, eg Delphi Method.

2.3.6 Fault Trees

The fault tree requires the specification of an unwanted event (the

294

top event) and an analysis is carried out of the ways in which this top event can occur. This is generally done by working backwards from the top event and finding what faults and what conditions can cause the top event, working backwards from each of these, which in effect become new secondary top events, to a final set of basic events or conditions whose probabilities are known or may be judged with confidence.

Figure 1 is a simple example, the undesirable top event being fire spreading beyond a room (origin) protected by sprinklers. The events in the tree are connected by AND gates in which all the constituent events have to be present or OR gates in which any one of the constituents needs to be present to cause the occurrence of the specific top event. For example, fire can spread beyond the room of origin (top event) only if the entire room is involved in fire and sprinklers did not extinguish the fire. A probability of 0.95 has been assigned to the former secondary top event due to the fact that there is a 0.05 probability that the entire room will not be involved even if fire spreads beyond all the materials in the room. The latter secondary top event could arise due either to the non operation of sprinkler head or to the failure of an operating sprinkler in extinguishing the fire. The ignition of the material of fire origin can be due to any one of the three causes specified. It is assumed that other causes are absent in this room. The probabilities are combined using the multiplication theorem in the case of AND gates and addition theorem in the case of OR gates.

The fault tree in Fig 1 describes the situation of ignition and spread given that the room has been involved in a fire; the probabilities for the three causes of ignition are "conditional probabilities" as described in Section 2.3.1. In a complete risk evaluation the probability of the top event has to be multiplied by the probabilities of fire starting in the room and in the building. If sprinklers extinguish the fire starting in the room (with a probability of 0.80) there will be no spread beyond the room which will be a "success." There is, however, a 0.20 chance that sprinklers may not extinguish the fire as a result of which fire may spread beyond the room. Spreading beyond a room may also be due to the failure of the building structure constituted by wall, floor, ceiling and door; the probability of this event has not been considered in the example.

A simple but useful way of employing the fault tree method is to explore the influence of various controllable factors in a known situation in which a fire of substantive magnitude has occurred. Beard[18] used the Coldharbour Hospital fire as a base and estimated the improved safety that might have been obtained by changing a number of factors that could have influenced the course of the fire. Other examples include spillage of liquefied petroleum gas at an LPG terminal[19] and risk of a multiple fatality fire in a CLASP type building[20].

2.3.7 Stochastic Modelling of Fire Spread

Deterministic models[21] provide fixed (hundred per cent probability)

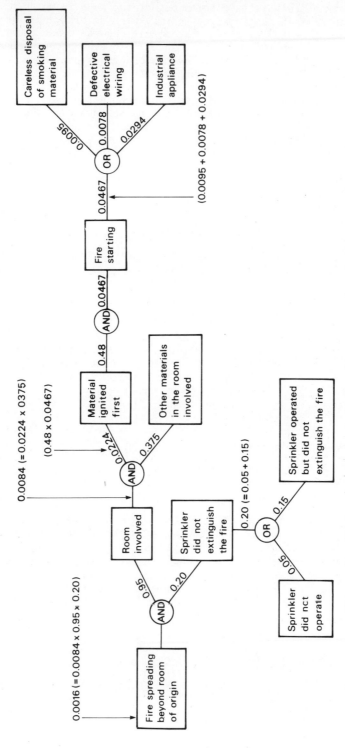

Figure 1. Fault tree analysis for a fire spreading beyond room of origin.

assessments of fire spread assuming that factors affecting the spread will behave exactly as determined by scientific theories and experiments. But the development of a real fire (as distinct from an experimental fire) is influenced by a diversity of materials, differences in their arrangement and environmental changes such as in temperature, air pressure, wind velocity and humidity. Some of these factors cannot be controlled and hence the spread of a real fire needs to be treated as a probabilistic phenomenon.

In a recent paper, Ramachandran[6] has discussed a State Transition Model for describing the progressive stage of fire development (and extinguishment) within a room. This model is consistent with data furnished by fire brigades in the UK for fires extinguished in each state during each time period since ignition. The states relate to the three fire spread categories (a) to (c) described in Section 2.3.2. The fourth state is an "absorbing" state involving extinguishment or burning out of fire. It has been explained in that paper how approximate values can be obtained for a probability distribution of duration of burning in each state and for probabilities of transition from one state to another. The transition probabilities have been evaluated as functions of time (since ignition). Four materials ignited first in the bedroom of a dwelling have been used as examples.

Berlin[22] used measurable criteria such as heat release rate and air temperature to define six realms (states) for residential occupancies - non-fire state, sustained burning, vigorous burning, interactive burning, remote burning and full room involvement. The states defined by Aoki[23] are based on physical extent of spread and his analysis is somewhat similar to that of Ramachandran.[6] Williamson[24] introduced a State Transition Model for analysing and reporting the results of experiments performed under conditions resembling actual fire conditions. In the models mentioned above the transition probabilities have been regarded as constants.

The results for each type of room in a building can be used as inputs to depict fire spread between rooms in the same or different floors. Network Theory has been considered by some authors transforming a building into a network with rooms as nodes; the links between nodes represent possible paths for fire spread. Ling and Williamson[25] include the element of time and probability for each link as well as the containment of fire by fire resistive building elements. Elms and Buchanan[26] have described the development of a computer-based technique for analysing the spread of fire through a multi-compartment building.

3. RISK REDUCTION

3.1 Probability of Fire Starting

For a particular building in a risk category an estimate of the conditional probability (given a fire) for the ith cause in the jth part of the building is given by

$$\ell_{ij} \, P_{ij} \tag{7}$$

where P_{ij} is the probability for this cause and part revealed by figures of the kind shown in Table 1 and discussed in Section 2.3.1. The parameter ℓ_{ij} will be assigned the value 0 if the ith cause is totally absent in the jth part of the building considered for risk evaluation. If the cause is present, ℓ_{ij} should be given a positive value depending on the extent to which this cause can be responsible for starting a fire in the jth part. Taking smokers' materials as an example, it should be possible to determine for group as a whole a quantitative measure, S_{ij}, denoting the exposure of, say, storage area to risk of fire from such a cause. S_{ij} may be the total number of cigarettes etc. consumed by all smokers per day, per floor area. A similar quantity, s_{ij}, should be evaluated with respect to the consumption of smoking materials in the storage area of the particular building considered. Then the ratio s_{ij}/S_{ij} is an estimated value of the parameter ℓ_{ij} for this building. It will be necessary to adjust this ratio to take into account factors such as smoking lobbies and publicity measures taken to make people aware of the risk of fire due to smoking materials.

The rating of the parameter ℓ_{ij} has to be somewhat subjective with its accuracy depending on the extent and accuracy of relevant information used in the calculations. Each possible cause or source of ignition in each part of the building should be identified and its ℓ_{ij} value estimated. The aggregate probability of fire starting for the building is then

$$F\ (A)\quad \sum_i \sum_j \ell_{ij} P_{ij} \tag{8}$$

where $F\ (A)$ is the "global" value given by equation (1).

In regard to non-human causes, those due to electricity, for example, can be eliminated or reduced by such measures as rewiring and checking periodically electrical appliances in the building and connections to these articles. In industrial buildings, high hazardous areas should be equipped with flame-proofed electrical fittings and electrical bonding to reduce the possibility of an electrostatic discharge. The use of insulating materials such as plastic bags which can build up a high electrostatic charge should be avoided. In some areas, the risk due to mechanical sparks can be reduced by the use of non-sparking materials for tools. Plasticised PVC used as insulation on wiring of electronic equipment is not only combustible but it emits hydrochloric acid during combustion and this acid can cause appreciable corrosion damage. It will be prudent to install glass insulation or to coat the insulation with sodium silicate, in parts of equipment subjected to heat. In fire prevention literature several methods of reducing the ignition hazard have been recommended for different types of buildings. But it is difficult to evaluate quantitatively the reduction in the probability of fire starting due to such measures.

3.2   Probable Damage in a Fire - Structural Fire Protection

The safety of a structure against fire is ensured by providing structural elements of an appropriate fire resistance so that in the event of a fire they continue to perform their design function. The fire resistance of an element is measured by its endurance in terms of time in a standard furnace test. This form of protection will be effective only if the fire resistance exceeds the "severity" of a given fire which, for a given room, varies with the quantity of combustible material (fire load), the area of ventilation and the dimensions of the room. For any specified fire resistance value, there is a finite probability the fire "severity" will exceed it, leading to failure of the fire resistance; this is a conditional probability given that a fire has occurred. Baldwin[27] showed that, for office buildings, this probability is given by exp(-0.04 R) where R is the fire resistance in minutes. This probability should be multiplied by the expected loss D, if the failure of the structure occurs, which is the sum of expected property loss, other monetary losses and loss of life and limb. Reliable data were not available for estimating D and hence Baldwin treated this parameter as unknown in his investigation. Carrying out a cost-benefit analysis, he found that, for justifying a fire resistance of 60 minutes, D should be at least 50 times the initial building cost.

Fire doors kept in the closed position would be expected to reduce the damage in a fire. Accurate estimation of the reduction is not possible because of lack of data on this form of protection. However, an analysis of a small sample of large fires (each costing more than £10,000) indicated that fire doors could prevent costly fires from becoming costlier[28]. In industrial buildings the reduction in loss in a large fire is likely to be of the order of £30,000 at 1965 prices.

It is very difficult to estimate the reduction in damage due to other forms of structural protection such as compartmentation and provision of escape routes; this is partly due to lack of data. No studies appear to have been carried out on these aspects.

3.3 Probable Damage in a Fire - Sprinklers

Sprinklers are widely used particularly in industrial and commercial buildings with high financial value at risk since they are capable of extinguishing fires if they operate satisfactorily. Research studies also indicate that sprinklers could reduce life loss in residential buildings. The use of sprinklers in these buildings is gaining importance particularly in the USA.

Rogers[29] applied the extreme value technique (generalized least square) developed by Ramachandran[3] to large property losses in a number of industries and trades. He assumed specifically that fire loss has a log normal probability distribution. Table 2 contains some interesting results obtained by Rogers for average loss in all fires (estimated from large losses). It is apparent that sprinklers reduce the loss expected in multi-storey buildings to a considerable extent. The survivor probability distribution for the textile industry is shown in Figure 2.

For purposes of illustration Ramachandran[1] applied both the methods, generalized least square and maximum likelihood, to large losses in a branch of the textile industry. He estimated the parameters of the fire loss distribution assuming that the distribution is log normal. Both the methods gave similar results. Using Rogers' results, Ramachandran[10] estimated that, for a multi-storey textile factory with a financial value at risk of £2.5 million at 1984 prices, the expected property loss per fire would be £11,000 if sprinkled and £88,500 if not sprinkled.

The investigation by Rogers[29] revealed that sprinklers reduce the probability of financial damage exceeding a large value. Sprinklers also reduce the probability of fire spreading beyond item and room of fire origin[1].

Table 1. Spinning and doubling industry – Places of origin of fires and sources of ignition.

Sources of ignition	Production and Maintenance		Assembly	Storage Areas		Other areas	Miscellaneous Areas	Total
	Dust Extractor (not cyclone)	Other areas		Store/stock room	Loading bay packing dept.			
A. Industrial appliances (i) Dust extractor								
Electrical	14	3	-	-	-	-	-	17
Other fuels	12	-	-	-	-	-	-	12
(ii) Other appliances								
Electrical	6	111	-	-	-	-	-	117
Other fuels	-	22	-	1	-	-	2	25
B. Welding and cutting equipment	-	10	-	6	-	-	7	23
C. Motor (not part of other appliance)	-	7	-	-	-	-	-	7
D. Wire and cable	1	12	-	-	-	-	2	15
E. Mechanical heat or sparks								
Electrical	27	194	-	-	-	-	-	221
Others	52	387	-	2	-	-	-	441
F. Malicious or intentional ignition	-	9	-	3	-	-	3	15
Doubtful	-	13	-	7	-	-	-	20
G. Smoking materials	2	29	1	15	1	-	7	55
H. Children with fire eg. matches	3	4	-	12	2	4	5	30
J. Others	4	29	2	3	2	-	12	52
K. Unknown	11	78	-	14	-	-	9	112
Total	132	908	3	63	5	4	47	1162

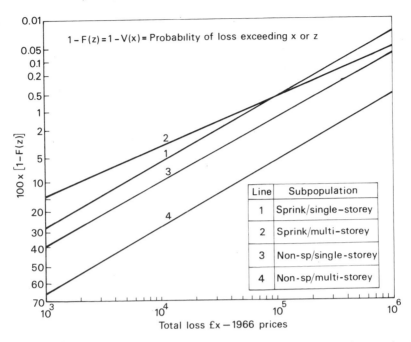

Figure 2.   Cumulative distribution function of fire loss for each class in the textile industry.

Table 2.   Average loss per fire at 1966 prices (£000).

	Sprinklered single storey	Sprinklered multi-storey	Non sprinklered single storey	Non sprinklered multi-storey
Textiles	2.9	3.5	6.6	25.2
Timber and furniture	1.2	3.2	2.4	6.5
Paper, printing and publishing	5.2	5.0	7.1	16.2
Chemical and allied	3.6	4.3	4.3	8.2
Wholesale distributive trades	–	4.7	3.8	9.4
Retail distributive trades	–	1.4	0.4	2.4

3.4 Probable Damage in a Fire - Detectors

In Section 2.3.3 it was mentioned that the expected damage (in terms of floor area) in a fire has an exponential relationship with duration of burning (T). It follows from this model (equation (2)) that T and hence the damage will be reduced if any of the component periods T_i (i = 1 to 4) is reduced. T_3 known as "attendance time" can be reduced by increasing the number of fire stations or resiting some of the existing ones. T_4 (control time) can be reduced by improving the fire fighting strategies of brigades.

A fire detected soon after ignition will be in its early stage of growth when fire fighting commences and hence can be controlled quickly. A reduction in T_1 would therefore shorten T_4 as well thus reducing T and the damage to a considerable extent. An automatic fire detection system is designed to achieve this saving. In addition the period from detection to calling the fire brigade (T_2) can also be reduced by linking the detector directly to the local fire brigade. A pilot application of this model[30] to fires in the textile industry indicated that a detector system, if it operates satisfactorily, can reduce the property damage by 63 percent and this saving will increase to 72 per cent if the system is directly connected to the local fire brigade. A later investigation[31] showed a clear need for providing means of early detection in storage premises and buildings without first-aid fire fighting facilities.

3.5 Risk Reduction - Role of the Government

A government is concerned mainly with the protection of life. In the UK the following major legislative and policy elements are directed towards that end:

   (i)   Fire Precautions Act
  (ii)   Building Regulations
 (iii)   Health and Safety at Work etc Act
  (iv)   Other statutory provisions relating to particular occupancies
   (v)   Consumer protection legislation
  (vi)   Standards for electric and other appliances, materials etc
 (vii)   Fire cover by fire brigades
(viii)   Education and publicity campaigns
  (xi)   Fire research

A detailed discussion of the measures mentioned above is beyond the scope of this paper. However, a few points and examples are worth mentioning particularly those concerned with the part played by the UK Fire Research Station. The FRS has carried out several investigations the results of which have been included in the Building Regulations. Since the British Standard on the fire propagation test, BS 476, was issued the Station has provided the performance index requirements for internal linings. Research on fires associated with electric blankets and bedwarmers showed that a change from asbestos insulation of heating elements to plastic insulation could increase the fire hazard though making blankets safer in respect of electric shocks; this led to considerations and discussions by BSI Committee on electric blankets. Investigation of fire problems of multi-storey car parks led to a relaxation of the Building Regulations and work on dust explosions resulted in a major change in the classification of dusts under the Factories Act. The work of FRS on the leakage of both hot and cold smoke around smoke doors will form the basis of an International Organization for Standardization test for these doors which is needed to complement established tests for the fire resistance of doors.

Other research studies of special interest include fires associated with electric cooking appliances, kerosene burning appliances and television sets and fire hazard of expanded polystyrene tiles. Examples of development work include laser beam detection and a computer controlled fire detection system which is currently going through a pilot stage. Other examples are concerned with tests on loft insulation, combustion products and toxicity.

Analyses of fire statistics have given considerable assistance in identifying and assessing fire risk. Recent statistical studies include influence of weather conditions and socio-economic factors on the incidence of fires in dwellings; these are aimed at identifying residential premises with fire risk higher than normal. The old and the impaired constitute a high proportion of fatal casualties. They are especially vulnerable to fires involving space heating and smokers' materials (igniting upholstery, bedding and other textile materials). These people should be provided with home visits by fire and social service personnel offering advice and practical help on ways of removing domestic fire hazards. There is also in the middle age ranges a high incidence of non-fatal casualties from fires involving cooking oils and fats. This suggests a need for the development of a cooking medium which would present less of a fire hazard if misused. The selective attack mentioned above and other suggestions for an optimal approach to fire risk management by the government are contained in a Consultative Document on Future Fire Policy[32].

4. HUMAN ASPECTS

The human aspects of fires[9] should be taken into consideration for a successful and effective implementation of government strategies aimed at reducing fire risk. A few of these are summarized in the next two sub sections.

4.1 Attitude to Fire Risk[7]

People differentiate fires into two groups: fires which are due to faults of those in the household with responsibility to prevent such events and fires where blame and responsibility lie outside the household. People are unwilling to spend much money in reducing the first group of fires but feel strongly about the second group. People should 'take care' is the recommendation for the first group and technical 'fix-its', either physical (eg non-inflammable wall linings) or procedural (eg more tests), for the second group. For dwelling fires people prefer informational strategies like more television and newspaper advertisements and school classes rather than the 'fix-it' strategies. For fires in upholstery due to careless disposal of cigarettes the preference is in the following order - more publicity, warning labels on furniture, non-inflammable furniture and installation of smoke detectors. A decision about the amount of money to be spent in reducing risks depends on what ought to be done and the cost of difficulty of carrying out prevention measures.

4.2 Human Behavior[8]

The main conclusions are as follows:

1. The behavior of an individual can be modified according to the role in which he sees himself (ie head of house, hotel guest, shopper or staff member) and whether the role is part of a strong hierarchy. Confusion would result if the fire intelligence and action flow conflicted with the normal hierarchy.

2. The earliest clues to fires are often strange noises rather than flame and smoke. Early behavior is characterized by uncertainty, misinterpretation, indecisiveness, seeking for confirmation.

3. Fire protection aids such as fire escapes and fire extinguishers are rarely used.

4. In the stress of a fire people often act inappropriately and rarely panic or behave entirely irrationally. Such a behavior, to a large extent, is due to the fact that information initially available to people regarding the possible existence of a fire and its size and location is often ambiguous or inadequate.

5. Lengthy delays can occur before people realize there is a fire. Even when people suspect that there is a fire they are reluctant to do anything until they have checked, after which they will often try unsuccessfully to extinguish it rather than raise the alarm or escape.

The conclusions mentioned above have broad implications for policies concerned with building (fire) regulations and fire safety legislation which are designed to minimize the likelihood of 'panic' and to reduce the possibility for people being trapped in the fire compartment. It is possible that the same overall objectives of reducing loss of life and injury could be more effectively achieved with less disturbance to the building users and probably for the same or reduced capital costs, if the regulations were reorientated to increase the likelihood of informed decisions being made by people in fires. The findings also have implications for fire prevention education and publicity, training and escape and building design.

It is very clear that timely and convincing communication of the location and spread of fire to building occupants would be of great benefit in preventing serious cases of unsuccessful behavior in fires, which although rare, have led to most of the major fire legislation to date. It is therefore necessary to seek ways to modify human behavior through better communication in order to promote rapid, orderly and safe evacuation of the building. With this objective in view research is currently being carried out to assess the effectiveness of all methods of raising fire alarms through automatic means.

5. RISK TRANSFER

5.1 Fire Insurance

The uncertain or risky situation posed by fires can be handled in two ways. Firstly, as discussed in Section 3, the frequency of fires and the losses in fires which do occur can be reduced by adopting suitable fire prevention and protection measures. Secondly, fire risk can be disposed of by transferring it through insurance which converts an uncertain loss into a known cost, the premium payable at a certain date.

Fire protection measures such as sprinklers reduce not only the expected loss in a fire, but also the probability of loss exceeding a large value. Hence insurance firms offer substantial reductions in insurance premiums for buildings equipped with sprinklers. In addition, sprinklers qualify for government grants and tax allowances. Hence a property owner can recover the cost of sprinklers in about six years[33]; this period is considerably less than the life of a building. The insurance premium discount for detectors is considerably less than the discount for sprinklers.

5.2 Deductible

A deductible can be defined as the participation of the insured in a
loss up to a certain limit agreed on in advance. When a deductible is
introduced in a fire insurance contract, it is hoped that the insured will
show greater interest in adopting loss prevention and reduction measures
since he has to bear himself the entire amount of any loss up to the
deductible level D. For a loss L greater than D, his liability is limited
to D since he will receive the difference (L-D) from his insurer. As an
inducement the insured gets a reduction in the premium towards a
deductible; the premium decreases with increasing levels of the
deductible. When a deductible is applied the insurer will not have to
settle and pay small losses which obviously relieves him of considerable
amount of work.

The deductible level which a property owner can accept depends on the
level of fire protection adopted by him and the probability distribution
of loss under such a protection. By considering all costs and benefits
involved the property owner can decide on a level of D which is economical
to him.

5.3 Decision Tree

A property owner is confronted with various fire protection measures
from which he has to choose a measure or a combination of measures which
is cost-effective[34]. The various options available to him can be
represented by the branches of a Decision Tree emanating from decision
forks - see Fig 3 for example. The effects of the decision are
represented by the branches coming off probability forks. The costs
associated with each option are then estimated and where a chance effect
occurs, weighted according to the probability of the chance effect. He
will then choose the option with the minimum total cost of fire protection
and insurance. A cost may be the actual cost or disutility (Section 5.4)
expressed in cost equivalents.

5.4 Utility Theory

An insurance premium will be greater than the expected loss estimated
by the risk analysis described in the previous sections. This is due to
the fact that an insurance firm regards the expected damage as 'risk
premium' to which two types of 'loading' are added - a 'safety loading' to
cover the uncertainty attached to the damage and an additional loading
towards the firm's operating costs including profits. Hence a property
owner strictly following the expected value approach will come to the
decision that 'no insurance' is a cheaper option than 'insurance', full or
partial with a deductible. Such a person is 'risk-neutral' in the sense
of putting equal weight on each pound of loss or gain. But most property
owners would be keen to avoid risk and adopt a risk-averse attitude. Any
owner, generally, would be a risk-preferrer towards small losses and risk-
avoider for large losses. Such risk preferences can be quantified by
applying Utility Theory.

Disutility, the negative counterpart of utility, is the appropriate
term to be used in an analysis concerned with fire loss, cost of
protection and insurance. Disutility would be low for small fires and
single death fires and high for large fires and multiple death fires.
From the national point of view it is important to consider not only the
number of deaths but also whether they occur singly or as a result of
catastrophies involving many deaths. A large fire might seriously disrupt
or even bankrupt a business or industrial activity; this unpredictable

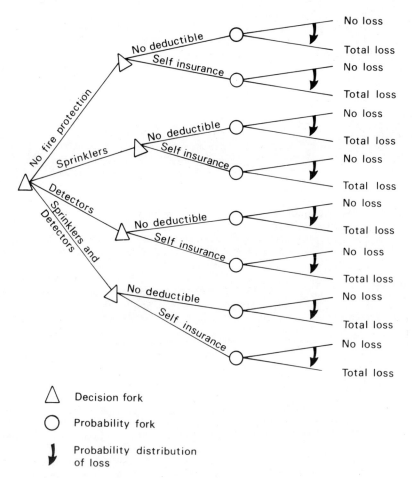

No fire protection
No deductible
Self insurance
No loss
Total loss
No loss
Total loss

Sprinklers
No deductible
Self insurance
No loss
Total loss
No loss
Total loss

Detectors
No deductible
Self insurance
No loss
Total loss
No loss
Total loss

Sprinklers and Detectors
No deductible
Self insurance
No loss
Total loss
No loss
Total loss

△ Decision fork

○ Probability fork

↓ Probability distribution of loss

Figure 3. Decision tree for investment in fire protection and/or insurance.

risk cannot be covered adequately by a consequential loss insurance policy. The activity should be protected from such an event although it has a low probability of occurrence. For this purpose, more money than the expected loss should be spent on fire protection and insurance. But how much more should a property owner or an industrial firm spend or be willing to spend? This amount depends on factors such as the assets of the property owner (or firm) and the extent of his risk-aversion. This problem has been discussed by Ramachandran[10].

ACKNOWLEDGMENT

This paper is Crown copyright and forms part of the work of the Fire Research Station, Building Research Establishment, Department of the Environment. It is contributed by permission of the Director, BRE.

REFERENCES

1. G Ramachandran. "Statistical Methods in Risk Evaluation." Fire Safety Journal, 2, 125-145 (1979/1980).
2. G Ramachandran. "Extreme Order Statistics in Large Samples from Exponential Type Distributions and their Application to Fire Loss" in G P Patil et al. (ed.s) Statistical Distributions in Scientific Work, Vol 2, (D Reidel Publishing Company, Dordrecht, Holland, 1975), 355-367.
3. G Ramachandran. "Properties of Extreme Order Statistics and their Application to Fire Protection and Insurance Problems." Fire Safety Journal, 5, 59-76 (1982).
4. M. Gretener. "Attempt to calculate the fire risk of industrial and other objects." Third Industrial Fire Protection Symposium, Eindhoven, Holland, October 1968.
5. G Ramachandran. "Probability Modelling." Seminar on Cost Effective Approach to Fire Safety, LIFE 84, Olympia, London, April 1984.
6. G Ramachandran. "Stochastic Modelling of Fire Growth." Fire Safety Science and Engineering. ASTM STP 882. T Z Harmathy, Ed. American Society for Testing and Materials, Philadelphia, 1985, 122-144.
7. C H Green, R A Brown and R W Goodsman. "Injury or death by fire: How people rate their chances." Fire, 77 (957), 44-48, 1985.
8. D Canter. "Studies of Human Behaviour in fire: Empirical results and their Implications for Education and Design." BRE Report. Building Research Establishment, Fire Research Station, Borehamwood, Herts WD6 2BL, 1985.
9. G Ramachandran. "The Human Aspects of Fires in Buildings - A Review of Research in the United Kingdom." Fire Safety Science and Engineering. ASTM STP 882. T Z Harmathy, Ed. American Society for Testing and Materials, Philadelphia, 1985, 386-422.
10. G Ramachandran. "The Interaction between Fire Protection and Insurance." Proceedings of B V D Seminar on Fire Prevention Concepts. Brand-Verhutungs-Dienst, Zurich, March 13, 1984.
11. R Rutstein. "The Estimation of the Fire Hazard in Different Occupancies." Fire Surveyor, 8 (2), 21-25, April 1979.
12. G Banktander. "Claims Frequency and Risk Premium Rate as A Function of the Size of the Risk." ASTIN Bull., 7, 119-136, 1973.
13. Fire Statistics United Kingdom, Home Office, London, 1983.

14. G Ramachandran. "Exponential Model of Fire Growth." First International Symposium on Fire Safety Science. National Bureau of Standards, Gaithersburg, Maryland, October 7-11, 1985.

15. D C Shpilberg. "Risk Insurance and Fire Protection; a Systems Approach, Part 1; Modelling the Probability Distribution of Fire Loss Amount." Factory Mutual Research Corporation, Norwood, Massachusetts, Tech Rep. No. 22431 (1974).

16. G Ramachandran. A Review of Mathematical Models for Assessing Fire Risk." Fire Prevention, 149, 28-32, 1982.

17. H E Nelson and A J. Shibe. "A System for Fire Safety Evaluation of Health Care Facilities." Report MNSIR 78-1555. National Bureau of Standards, Gaithersburg, Maryland, 1978.

18. A N Beard. "Applying Fault-Tree Analysis to the Coldharbour Hospital Fire." Fire, 71 (885), 517, 1979.

19. D J Rasbash. "Analytical Approach to Fire Safety." Fire Surveyor, 20-34, August 1980.

20. Project Work of Department of Fire Safety Engineering. University of Edinburgh.

21. S Kumar. "Mathematical Modelling of Natural Convection in Fire - a State of the Art Review." Fire and Materials, 7, 1, 1-24, 1983.

22. G N. Berlin. "Managing the Variability of Fire Behaviour." Fire Technology, 287-302, 1980.

23. Y Aoki. "Studies on Probabilistic Spread of Fire." Research Paper No. 80. Building Research Institute, Tokyo, Japan, 1978.

24. R B Williamson. "Fire Performance under Full-Scale Test Conditions - A State Transition Model. Proceedings of the Sixteenth Symposium (International) on Combustion, 1357-1371. The Combustion Institute, Pittsburgh, 1976.

25. W C T Ling and R B Williamson. "The Modelling of Fire Spread Through Probabilistic Networks." Work sponsored by the Nuclear Regulatory Commission at the Lawrence Berkeley Laboratory Under Contract No W7405-ENG-48 through US Department of Energy, Washington DC, 1981.

26. D B Elms and A H Buchanan. "Fire Spread Analysis of Buildings." Research Report R-35. Building Research Association of New Zealand, Judgeford, New Zealand, July 1981.

27. R Baldwin. "Economics of Structural Fire Protection." Current Paper 45/75. Building Research Establishment, Fire Research Station, Borehamwood, Herts, England, 1975.

28. G Ramachandran. "Fire Doors and Losses in Large Fires." Fire Research Note No. 690. Fire Research Station, Borehamwood, Herts, England, 1968.

29. F E Rogers. "Fire Losses and the Effect of Sprinkler Protection of Buildings in a Variety of Industries and Trades." Current Paper 9/77. Building Research Establishment, Fire Research Station, Borehamwood, Herts, England, 1977.

30. G Ramachandran. "Economic Value of Automatic Fire Detectors." Information Paper IP 27/80. Building Research Establishment, Fire Research Station, Borehamwood, Herts, England, 1980.

31. G Ramachandran and S E Chandler. "The Economic Value of Fire Detectors." Fire Surveyor, 13 (2), 8-14, 1984.

32. "Future Fire Policy: A Consultative Document." Her Majesty's Stationery Office, London, 1980.

33. D Schofield and A Parnell. "Cost Effective Fire Protection." Building, 113-115, January 1975.

34. G Ramachandran. "Economic Aspects of Fire." Workbook, International Conference on Flammability, University of Surrey, Guildford, England, March 1985, 38-45.

EDUCATION OF THE PUBLIC ABOUT POTENTIAL HEALTH AND

ENVIRONMENTAL EFFECTS ASSOCIATED WITH HAZARDOUS SUBSTANCES

Maria Pavlova

EPA - Region II
26 Federal Plaza Room 737
New York, NY   10278

A program is proposed to educate the public at the community level about potential health and environmental effects associated with exposure to hazardous substances. The program will complement and enhance the efforts of Community Relations Programs, which are required under the Comprehensive Environmental Response, Compensation, and Liability Act. The first stage will be an information needs assessment accomplished through discussions with citizens, a study of the community, and examination of existing sources of information. Based on this information, the next stage will be the preparation and dissemination of educational materials to explain the potential environmental and health risks in terms the people can understand and apply in the context of their community. The final stage will be a community-specific evaluation of the materials and program. Particular emphasis will be given to educating the public about what risk assessment means and how it is done. Such a public education program should allow citizens to take an active, informed role in the local decision-making process. In addition, educated citizens are more likely to take measures to monitor and protect their health and thus avert the occurrence of environmentally related disease.

KEY WORDS: Risk assessment, risk management, Community Relations Program, remedial response, environmental hazards.

There is a growing awareness among American communities about environmental hazards. This awareness is being expressed by citizens who are banding together to act in response to actual or potential environmental hazards in their local communities. EPA has recognized this awareness and the role of the public. When a remedial response is initiated under the Comprehensive Environmental Response, Compensation, and Liability Act (CERCLA), better known as Superfund, a Community Relations Program is required to encourage two-way communication between the people of the community and the Government Agencies involved (Fig.1).

However, environmental and health risk assessment, phases of the remedial response, and jurisdictional responsibilities of Federal, State, and local Government Agencies are extremely complex and the citizens may not have the knowledge to apply the information they receive to their specific situation. This knowledge gap between the scientists and regulators and the public needs to be filled.

A program to educate the public about potential health and environmental effects associated with hazardous substances/wastes can facilitate the resolution of an environmental problem. When citizens are informed, they can participate usefully in the local government's decision-making processes. Studies of the effects of health education show that informed citizens tend to be aware of measures they can take to improve their health and that they do actually take such measures. Therefore, education of the public is a positive contributing factor to the prevention of environmentally related disease (Fig. 2).

THE COMMUNITY RELATIONS PROGRAM

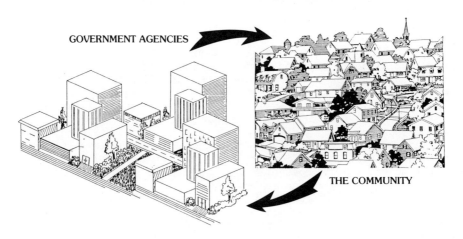

Figure 1

Educating the public in risk assessment is not an easy task. Scientists and regulators have difficulty in communicating with the public about risk because the information is often scientifically complex, highly technical, and quite uncertain. People expect scientists to give answers in the form of facts, but in risk assessment there are no definite answers and the facts are relative. People expect regulators to protect them, but such actions must be balanced against other costs and benefits to society. Therefore, there is a problem with what we are communicating, and there is a problem with how effectively we are communicating.

In communicating risk, two separate components can be considered: risk assessment and risk management (Fig. 3).

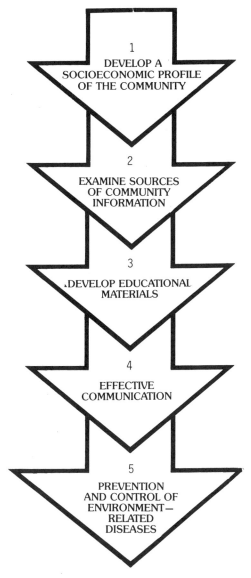

Figure 2

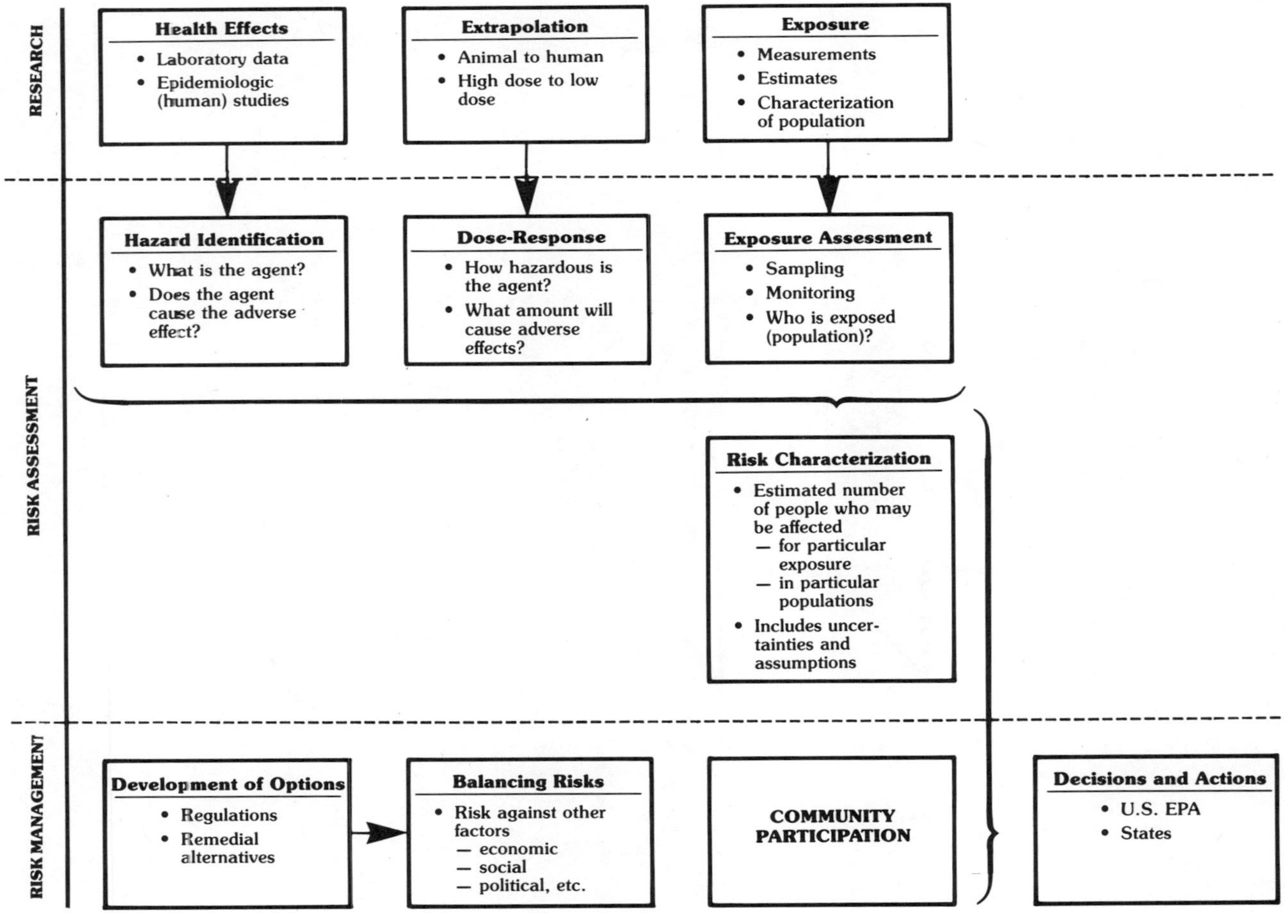
RESEARCH
Health Effects
• Laboratory data
• Epidemiologic (human) studies
Extrapolation
• Animal to human
• High dose to low dose
Exposure
• Measurements
• Estimates
• Characterization of population
RISK ASSESSMENT
Hazard Identification
• What is the agent?
• Does the agent cause the adverse effect?
Dose-Response
• How hazardous is the agent?
• What amount will cause adverse effects?
Exposure Assessment
• Sampling
• Monitoring
• Who is exposed (population)?
Risk Characterization
• Estimated number of people who may be affected
— for particular exposure
— in particular populations
• Includes uncertainties and assumptions
RISK MANAGEMENT
Development of Options
• Regulations
• Remedial alternatives
Balancing Risks
• Risk against other factors
— economic
— social
— political, etc.
COMMUNITY PARTICIPATION
Decisions and Actions
• U.S. EPA
• States

Figure 3

Risk assessment is the characterization of the potential adverse health effects of human exposure to environmental hazards. Risk assessment can be divided into four major steps.

The first and most easily recognized step is hazard identification. This is the process of determining whether exposures to an agent can cause an increase in the incidence of a health condition.

The second step is dose-response assessment, the process of characterizing the relation between the dose of an agent administered or received and the incidence of an adverse health effect in exposed populations and estimating the incidence of the effect as a function of human exposure to the agent.

Another step in risk assessment is exposure assessment, which is the process of measuring or estimating the intensity, frequency, and duration of human exposure to an agent currently present in the environment or of estimating hypothetical exposures that might arise from the release of new chemicals into the environment.

The final step is risk characterization--the process of estimating the incidence of a health effect under the various conditions of human exposure described in exposure assessment.

Even with these well-defined steps, though, there is still uncertainty. Risk connotes chance and where there is chance, uncertainty is always involved. This is no different in risk assessment where uncertainty is inevitable.

Given the usual limitations on the nature and extent of information available, one can never say exactly how many people will be affected by a particular pollutant, or how severely. It is, however, the task of risk assessment to make the most credible statements possible, reducing uncertainty as much as possible, and making explicit whatever uncertainty remains.

Risk management, on the other hand, is the combination of judgment and analysis that uses the results of risk assessment to come to a decision about environmental action. Individual risk management decisions may be seen as balancing risk against available resources. However, the system as a whole is set up to balance risk against risk. Fundamentally, priorities are assigned to different risks, and decisions are made so that the total amount of harm prevented is maximized.

Risk management has a number of elements including

- Development of options such as regulations and remedial alternatives

- Consideration of political, social, economic, and scientific implications involved in selecting appropriate responses

- Inviting community participation in development of appropriate responses

- Decision making and action taking based necessarily on value judgments of acceptability of risk and reasonableness of cost.

Once risk in the environmental sense is understood, one must then examine how risk can be effectively communicated.

In this context, communication is the flow of information among the scientists, policymakers, and the public. Without the smooth flow of information, there is disruption that affects the process of protecting the public from environmental hazards.

As stated above, the importance of communication is explicitly recognized in the Community Relations Program required under Superfund. The Community Relations Program is intended to provide open channels for two-way communication between the Government Agencies responsible for clean-up and the community. A Community Relations Plan is prepared to correspond to the stages of the remedial action. For example, when a remedial investigation is undertaken, the community relations techniques might include the preparation and dissemination of fact sheets and progress reports; the holding of briefings, workshops, public information meetings, and news conferences; the establishment and maintenance of an information repository in an easily accessible place in the community, such as the public library.

All of these community relations activities are appropriate and useful, yet there is still a problem with how effectively risk is being communicated.

A pilot program has been initiated in EPA Region II to improve communication of information about risk at the local community level. The program is intended to educate the public about

- The nature of the problem in their community

- Why the various phases of the remedial response are necessary

- How risk assessments are performed and what the information means in terms of the local community

- Which Federal, State, and local Government Agencies are responsible for managing specific aspects of the situation

- Required activities under CERCLA, including alternatives for clean-up and preventive activities.

Such a public education program at the local community level can enhance, complement, and reinforce the efforts of Community Relations Programs.

While a generic model is proposed, it should be emphasized that the essential element of this program is that it will be specifically tailored to each community and will take into account

(1) The existing level of knowledge in the community

(2) Specific information needs identified by the citizens

(3) Details of the potential or actual exposure and its health impact

(4) Socioeconomic characteristics of the community.

The purpose of this program is to develop a strong linkage--in the form of communication--among the community and its local government and State and Federal governments, industry, health professionals and educators.

The first stage will be an information needs assessment. We will go into the community, talk to people, and try to find out all we can about the community and its specific environmental health concerns. We will talk to the citizen activists--those who are involved in the environmental issue--and others in the community, elected officials, industry and labor leaders, teachers, and health professionals.

We will try to find out such things as the level of interest in and knowledge of exposure and risk issues, the major concerns and information sought, the perceived credibility of the various Government Agencies, and the sources of the citizens' knowledge (Fig. 3). A socioeconomic profile of the community will be prepared to characterize the community in terms of income, education, occupation, age, sex, etc. All of this information is very important to the next phase, the development of educational materials.

Finally, the sources of the community's information will be examined. It is expected that the most important source will be the local media, particularly the local newspapers. Local newspapers will be examined to determine extent of coverage of the environmental problem and any bias in reporting. From all this information about the community, we expect to learn that the people will have an interest in the environmental problem but their understanding may be limited, especially in relation to health and environmental risk assessment. Therefore, the next step will be to develop educational materials to explain the subject in terms that the people can understand and apply in the context of their community.

What must be remembered is that although risk assessment involves complex scientific exercises, it is simply an effort to understand what the problem is, which is precisely what the public wants, as well.

It may not be possible to communicate, to a scientists' satisfaction, the nature and degree of risk to the lay public. However, it is possible to give people the information they need in a form they can understand. The following factors need to be communicated:

(1)   Health and environmental risk assessment involves complex hazard identification steps, such as studies of dose-response relationships, exposure assessments, and risk characterization

(2)   The results of these steps are expressed as probabilistic outcomes, still involving uncertainties

(3)   EPA has established risk assessment guidelines that require extensive peer review and scientific consensus

(4)   Risk management requires the balancing of various risks against social concerns through the application of complex risk-benefit analyses.

In addition to communicating information about risk assessment, information should also be communicated on the regulatory responsibilities of the various government jurisdictions and the technical requirements of the remedial response/feasibility study.

315

This information will be translated into language understandable to the lay public and at an appropriate reading level for the community. The materials developed will be pretested with the assistance of volunteers from the community. This information will be communicated through fact sheets, flyers, audiovisual materials, lectures, press releases, and other forms. In addition, a handbook will be compiled of local community resources to tell the people who to contact about what. Local community networks will be used to disseminate the information.

Communication is a two-way process; therefore, the final phase in this program will be a community-specific evaluation of the materials and program. A survey will be fielded to attempt to detect changes in the extent of the people's knowledge and understanding. Comments and suggestions will be actively solicited from the community.

The findings from the evaluation will be used in subsequent local education efforts in other communities so that as the program progresses, the education materials will be continually refined and improved. The materials will be maintained and made available to anyone interested.

Such a public education program will serve to improve communication of information on risks. Effective communication will enable citizens to take a more informed role in the local decision-making process. Effective communication will ensure that environmental exposure situations do not become emotion-laden crises of confrontation.

The combination of increased knowledge about risk and effective communication techniques, achieved through education of scientists, policymakers, and the general public, can be a major factor in the prevention and control of environmentally related disease.

THE ROLE OF LIABILITY PREFERENCES IN SOCIETAL TECHNOLOGY

CHOICES: RESULTS OF A PILOT STUDY

Robin Cantor, Steve Rayner and Bob Braid

Energy Division
Oak Ridge, Tennessee 37831

ABSTRACT

At the 1984 Annual Meeting of the Society for Risk Analysis, Steve Rayner presented a paper that challenged the conventional wisdom of risk management research. In that paper, he argued that resolving the question, "How safe is safe enough?" is less important in making societal technology choices than "How fair is safe enough?" Adopting the fairness question as the concern of risk management would imply that the process of technology choice should recognize explicitly the preferred principles different parties hold with respect to obtaining consent from those affected by the risks, distributing the liabilities, and justifying trust in the relevant institutions. This paper discusses a recent empirical pilot study which explored the fairness hypothesis in the context of nuclear power.

Individual interviews and focus groups were conducted to examine whether or not preferred principles for liability distributions were consistent with those suggested by the cultural characteristics of the constituency. The results suggest that for this type of societal technology choice, violation of these preferred principles may be a major source of the conflict between different constituencies. Additionally, the study contributes towards the development of a new approach in risk management that combines the cultural model of risk perceptions with the decision-theoretic approaches found in economics and psychology.

KEY WORDS: Risk management, Technology choice, Fairness hypothesis, Liability Preferences

I. INTRODUCTION

In a recent article, Shafer and Tversky argue that the analytical design used by a researcher to examine probability judgements should reflect such seemingly exogenous considerations as the problem of interest, the body of evidence, and psychological aspects of the individuals being studied (Shafer and Tversky, 1985). A major point of their argument is that in all types of measurement, the analytical design selected will ultimately affect the measurement and the quality of the design will depend on its ability to provide "accurate answers to questions of central interest" (p. 310).

We believe that their arguments are equally relevant for the current debates regarding analytical approaches in risk analysis and risk management. Last year, during the SRA meeting, Steve Rayner presented a paper that criticized the conventional approaches in risk perception and management on the grounds that they all too often treat the social considerations of the problem as a tedious exercise tacked on to the end of the formal analytical work (Rayner, 1985). This practice has biased much of the work to concentrate on answering the question, "How safe is safe enough?" and thus, argue about estimates of probabilities and the magnitude of consequences from unlikely events. Instead, Rayner argues, because risk is a way of classifying a whole series of complex interactions and relationships between people, as well as between man and nature, societal technology choice problems should be debated on the basis of issues of trust and equity. The appropriate question to be answered by research in these problems is "How fair is safe enough?"

This challenge to the conventional wisdom of risk management research reflects the observation that designs based on the definition of risk as a matter of probabilities and magnitudes do not provide satisfactory answers to questions of central interest. However, challenging the conventional wisdom is itself a challenge to construct an alternative design based on the fairness hypothsis that can be used for problems of societal technology choice.

This paper presents a pilot study which used such a design and explored the fairness hypothesis in the context of nuclear power technologies. The next section discusses the study and the problem of constructing a framework for analysis which could address questions consistent with our hypothesis. This is followed by a section describing the design in greater detail. The fourth section presents some major results of the case studies used in the research and the last section suggests how our framework could be used in the development of a new approach to risk management problems.

II. THE PROBLEM

The problem we selected to use in this exploratory research was the issue of the market acceptability of new nuclear-power reactor technologies with so-called passive safety features. These included for example, the PIUS and the modular high-temperature gas cooled reactor. This analysis was part of a larger program of evaluating these concepts on engineering, economic, and regulatory criteria (Trauger et al., 1985). As only one segment of the program, we were responsible for the analysis of the market viability of these technologies within the 2000-2010 time period.

There are several aspects of the problem that made it a good candidate for an approach based on the fairness hypothesis. First, the experience of the current generation of nuclear technology would suggest strongly that the viability of the future concepts will not depend solely upon their technical plausibility and projected economic feasibility. If this experience has taught us anything, it has taught us that large public and private expenditures on research, demonstration and manufacture of new reactors cannot be justified on technical criteria alone. Second, nuclear power has been engulfed in a long list of social and technical issues that are likely to haunt any concept that is part of the nuclear family. Finally, because the primary use imagined for these technologies is base-load electricity supply, without evidence to the contrary, we can expect that their attributes and shortcomings will be debated in a regulatory and political environment similar to what we know today.

These aspects of the problem imply that, like the current generation of the nuclear technology, future concepts will be characterized by social conflicts over their use and management of their risks. To answer the viability question, we need an understanding of these conflicts, their implications, and possible resolutions. Societal technology choices of this type are typically examined by concentrating on conflicts over the safety issues, and thus, perceived probabilities and magnitudes. An analytical framework consistent with this view might focus on questions about probability judgements, alternative risks, and feelings regarding catastrophic consequences.

In contrast to this approach, our concept of risk management requires that the analysis explicitly recognize the social issues of trust and equity, and thus, incorporate ethical, political, legal, cultural and economic comparisons of various constituencies and their liability preferences. Consequently, our framework focused on questions about the preferred principles different parties hold with respect to obtaining consent from those affected by the risks, distributing the liabilities, and justifying trust in the relevant institutions. For the purposes of this pilot study, we limited the scope of the analysis to three constituencies: the utilities, state public utility commissions (PUCs), and public interest groups critical of nuclear power.

III. RESEARCH DESIGN

Given the focus outlined above, an important aspect of the analytical framework is to explicitly recognize sources and channels of social conflict that arise over the equity and trust issues when societal technology choices are made. The first step in this process is to identify the constituency that provides the occasion for conflict by being the primary user of the technology. In this case, this constituency corresponds to the electrical utilities.

In order to analyze the utility demand for new reactor technologies, we examined the preferences for different reactor characteristics on the basis of information about a utility's decision-making process for new capacity. Because of the nature of the problem, we decided that the best way to project what the systems planners might recommend in the year 2010 is to look at the process rather than to conduct an attitude survey of the present incumbants of systems planning departments. A method was designed to investigate the criteria used to select new capacity, the types of employees participating in capacity decisions, the data sources and modelling techniques applied, and the alternatives considered in a particular utility's process of capacity choice. Concentrating on these factors allowed a long-term view of how preferences for specific technical characteristics would be formed. The underlying premise of the method is that the process of decision making ultimately influences how alternative technologies are valued by the utility. If the process differs among utilities, presumably their preferred choices will also differ.

To obtain the information about the decision-making processes, extensive interviews were conducted with a cross section of systems planning personnel and executives of five utilities. These utilities control generating systems that range from medium to large and operate in the southeast, mid-alantic, southwest, and west. One utility was not investor-owned. All of them currently own a nuclear power plant. Finally, in addition to these five, limited interviews were conducted at two large municipal utilities.

The decision-making research established the criteria that each utility would generally prefer to use in decisions to build power plants. However, this represents only one part of our problem. The other equally important part is concerned with the potential social conflicts arising from these decisions. The sources of conflict are grounded in the constraints exercised by PUCs and interest groups on utility decision making. The channels through which these conflicts are routed are the regulatory and legal processes established for such purposes as power plant construction approval, technology licensing, and electricity rate determination.

One approach to examine the fairness hypothesis is to observe the public display of the arguments about risk from each constituency and then relate the arguments to specific preferences regarding the trust and equity issues. However, because risk arguments are carefully framed so as to be successful in the particular public forum in which they are made and the adversarial nature of these confrontations often forces the arguments to the extreme, it is difficult to extract a meaningful translation.

We sought to avoid these biases by conducting direct interviews with members of the PUCs and public staffs about their roles in the capacity choice decision. The PUC's role in the market place is generally to approve the need, site, technological option, and apportionment of financial responsibilities for building a plant. Depending on state legislation, PUCs may have a number of subsidiary responsibilities that affect plant certification and that give them considerable flexibility in fulfilling their primary responsibilities. Because of these regulatory powers, these state agencies effectively hold a potential veto over the commercialization of any nuclear technology. Thus, to appreciate their perspective on the trust and equity aspects of risk, PUCs must be thoroughly understood regarding their legislative mandate, regulatory philosophy and procedures, analytical skills, and the degree of access of all parties to the state regulatory process.

The role of public interest groups in relation to the construction and operation of nuclear plants was analyzed through focus group discussions which were held in each state. Public interest groups were selected for study because of their ability to place major hurdles in nuclear licensing activities. Opinions were sought from members of a variety of environmentalist and anti-nuclear organizations on matters relating to confidence in institutions associated with nuclear power, the manner in which liabilities from potentially hazardous technologies are distributed within society, and the problems associated with obtaining legitimate societal consent for such technologies. Preferences for specific principles to be followed in societal technology choices regarding consent, liability, and trust were obtained by presenting realistic examples of technology choice problems. We directed the group to discuss alternative solutions for each example which generally led to a related discussion of the safety risks of nuclear power. We found using the examples to initiate a number of such discussions rather than a single one about the risks of nuclear power to be a helpful tool to discourage groups from simply reiterating the arguments they would normally use in a public debate.

IV. RESULTS OF THE ANALYSIS

Several important results emerge from the analysis that we believe have implications for the current state of risk management research as well as the future market for new nuclear technologies. To be brief, we will present only the results that are more relevant for evaluating the fairness hypothesis approach.

Examining the perspectives of the major constituencies on the basis of the technology choice and not the technological risks, indicated that their predominant concerns about risks were fundamentally different. For the utilities, the risk from the decision is investment risk, i.e., the risk that the costs of plants will not be fully recovered from ratepayers. This is not to say that utilities are not concerned with health and safety risks, however, they view them as part of the technical design which is licensed by regulators. State PUCs are concerned with economic risks that might arise either because costs are incurred that were not anticipated, utilities fail to perform as expected, or demand fails to grow at a rate that warrants new capacity. Their concern for health and safety risks is incorporated into their general concern that, from the public's point of view, the plant's costs will outweigh the benefits. In contrast, the public interest groups focus almost entirely on health and safety risks, pointing out that because these risks are imposed by one group and inevitably fall unevenly on others, they cannot be treated as acceptable under any circumstances. For them, a risk that threatens an individual's health is a risk that cannot be spread equitably. Such incompatibilities in the type of risk being addressed by each constituency make the search for solutions considerably more difficult.

The analysis of the PUCs and public interest groups reveals that these constituencies conceptualize basic nuclear issues differently. We contend that the ways in which they differ suggest implicit agenda of interest for the constituencies that make it difficult for them to understand the fears or objections of others. The different ways of conceptualizing problems are indicated in three critical regulatory concerns, as shown in Table 1.

Table 1

Different Emphases of PUCs and Interest Groups on Parallel
Problems of Utility Capacity Additions

Problem	PUC Emphasis	Interest Group Emphasis
need for the plant	need for power	consent of affected parties
who pays for plant	allocation of costs	distribution of liabilities
management of the technology	management prudency	institutional trust

In regard to the basic question of the need for the plant, the PUCs frame the issue as primarily a forecasting problem that simply requires the utility to present adequate data and justification that the power will be needed when the plant becomes operational. Many PUCs have also become involved in judging whether the utility has selected the correct technological option to meet the demand forecast. While intervenor groups must contest the issues on these terms, the more important philosophical question in intervenors' minds is the need to secure consent of the parties affected by construction and operation of a nuclear plant. Rather than delegating responsibility to regulatory bodies to decide if the plant is needed, intervenors would prefer to decide, perhaps by popular referendum, if people want the plant.

The second important concern is that of who pays the costs of the plant. PUCs view this concern as primarily a financing one with some overtones of equity frequently intervening in the decision. If the utility can demonstrate that its construction costs were reasonably incurred and not the result of poor management, then costs of the plant will be allowed in the rate base and consumers will pay for the plant. If some construction costs are found by the PUC to be unwarranted, then the normal procedure is to pass those costs along to stockholders rather than ratepayers.

The decisions about whether or not costs are warranted require detailed analyses and are highly technical. Intervenors tend to view concerns associated with costs of the plant in broader ethical terms. While intervenors will address the issue of paying for the plant on the PUC's terms because the regulatory process requires it, intervenors would prefer to focus on the more basic issue of who bears the various safety, economic, and managerial costs in society resulting from the plant and who enjoys the benefits and how can the costs and benefits be shared equitably.

The last important concern is that of management of the nuclear enterprise. PUCs focus on issues associated with management prudency. Management prudency admittedly lends itself to vagueness and regulatory expansiveness and has evolved in recent years into a catch-all category of issues that facilitates greater regulatory intervention into utility management. PUCs frequently appear to approach management prudency issues from technical bases in the sense that technical problems may have been created or made worse by mismanagement. Also implied is the belief that use of the correct data and analytical techniques will produce the appropriate response if management is carrying out its responsibilities and that inappropriate responses may well indicate management imprudence.

Intervenors conceive the management concern to be not merely a judgement of the utility's qualifications but, also, a questioning of the regulators' qualifications as well. Ultimately, there is the question of whether nuclear technology can, indeed, be managed safely. Intervenors demonstrate a strong consensus that the technology is simply too complex to oversee and that nothing can be done to alter this inherent flaw. Their view of the regulators is that such agencies are too sympathetic to the industry and are not to be trusted.

Thus, in respect to the concern of managing the nuclear enterprise, PUCs tend to view the issues in narrower terms that allow regulators to address specific management problems frequently in technical contexts. Intervenors expand the scope of management beyond the utilities to include any institutions that are responsible for nuclear technology. Their trust in these institutions is nil -- managers, regulators and the technology itself are parts of the nuclear problem.

These results support the propositions regarding implicit agenda of

Rayner's model of institutional cultures of risk management (Rayner 1984). We see that process is the domain of the regulators, and their objective is the adherence to that process, regardless of the outcome it produces. This objective suggests an implicit agenda for system maintenance. On the other hand, intervenors are concerned with achieving an outcome that is consistent with their anti-nuclear goals. Adherence to process is irrelevant. Their concerns are broad and directed at policy level questions for which regulatory environments are not well-suited. Their implicit agenda calls for a new social and political order that would make the current distribution of resources more equitable. Indeed, intervenors in a very real sense are fighting legislative battles in regulatory proceedings.

V. SUMMARY

We have presented the design and results of a pilot study which explores the question "How fair is safe enough?" The results of this study are intended to help evaluate whether or not this is a meaningful question for risk managers to ask. We believe that the approach uncovers the risk conflicts between constituencies that are rooted in disagreements over principles for consent, liability, and trust and thus, provides unique and valuable information to the decision makers.

As our example illustrates, the problem of finding a risk-management solution to satisfy all constituencies is a difficult one. However, both greater understanding of the liability issues and the processes of policy debates could be enhanced by this kind of approach. Further research into the trust and equity aspects of risk can benefit from using the approach for other examples of societal technology choice and risk management. As examples of relevant problems, we are exploring conservation investments, hazardous waste management, and innovative medical practices.

Further research in this area could also provide important contributions to the decision-theoretic approaches of economics and psychology that are often used in problems of risk managenment. We see these contributions occurring at both the micro- and macro-levels of analyses where models of decision making are applied. At the micro-level, as an alternative to using directly preferences regarding the probabilistic concept of risk, we suggest using the decision maker's preferences for principles of consent, liability, and trust as underlying determinants of derived risk perceptions.

Finally, for a broader level of analysis which must mesh together the preferences of several constituencies, exploring each constituency's preferences for these principles would help risk managers construct meaningful possible solutions to be offered in public forums. Such a practice might enhance the negotiations between constituencies in these open debates by avoiding the insults to strongly held principles that occur because offered solutions fail to reflect these considerations.

REFERENCES

Rayner, Steve, 1984, "Disagreeing About Risk: The Institutional Cultures of Risk Management and Planning for Future Generations," in S. Hadden (ed), Risk Analysis, Institutions, and Public Policy, Port Washington, New York: Associated Faculty Press.
Rayner, Steve, 1985, "Learning From the Blind Men and the Elephant, Or Seeing Things Whole in Risk Management," in Vincent Covello et al.

(eds), <u>Uncertainty in Risk Assessment, Risk Management and Decision Making</u>, New York: Plenum Press, (in press).

Shafer, Glenn and Amos Tversky, 1985, "Languages and Designs for Probability Judgment," <u>Cognitive Science</u> 9, 309-339.

Trauger, D. et al., 1985, <u>Nuclear Power Options Viability Study, Vol. III, Nuclear Discipline Topics</u>, ORNL/TM-9780/3, Oak Ridge: Oak Ridge National Laboratory.

PUBLIC PERCEPTION OF RISK IN DEVELOPING TECHNOLOGIES:

A CASE STUDY OF A BUSINESS COMMUNITY IN MANHATTAN

S. Basheer Ahmed and M. Peter Hoefer

Lubin Graduate School of Business
Pace University
New York, NY   10038

ABSTRACT

A random sample of selected graduate classes (in an MBA program) was drawn to determine their feelings on five developing technologies: nuclear energy, nuclear weapons, robotics, genetic engineering and global mass communications. The population from which the selection was made is over eighty percent full-time employed in the New York City area and had recently been exposed to courses in probability and statistics.

In each technological area respondents expressed their feelings about the probability of occurrence of "worst case" and "least worst case" events associated with each technology. A brief scenario describing example events was included in the questionnaire.

Mean responses showed most concern for the nuclear areas (energy and weapons) and little concern for possible negative effects associated with robotics. Demographically, significant differences in overall expressed concern were noticed between sexes as well as among certain income brackets.

KEY WORDS: Risk perception, Nuclear energy, Nuclear weapons, Global mass
           communications, Genetic engineering, Robotics

INTRODUCTION

The introduction and growth of new technologies may be correctly described as being "exponential" in nature; there are a rapidly increasing number of technologies, and changes in recently introduced technologies are also rapid.[1] Some new technologies are mere passing fancies, while others will have a far reaching effect upon the world in which we live.[2]

----

[1]Perrow, Charles. Normal Accidents: Living with High Risk Technologies, New York: Basic Books, 1984.

[2]Schwing, Richard, and Walter Albers, eds. Social Risk Assessment: How Save Is Safe Enough? New York: Plenum Publishing Corp., 1980.

Whether a society is receptive to a new technology or not may drastically affect future generations of that particular group in a physical as well as psychological sense. This means it is extremely important to know as to whether or not a society accepts a new technology as an integral part of economic growth. However, the question of whether a society will accept an important new technology is often not answered by a purely rational decision-making procedure, but rather upon how the society itself perceives the technology.

Because of the influence "perception" can exert upon a decision-making process. we felt it could be important for us to gather and interpret data on how a particular group perceives the risk involved with certain developing technologies. Being conveniently located at an urban campus of a large graduate business school, we felt that we were privy to a homogenous group that is not politically naive. For this reason we designed an experiment to determine how this group "perceives" the risk involved with certain important developing technologies.

METHODOLOGY

We developed a questionnaire that would measure how a group of people perceive the risk associated with certain new technologies. Naturally, certain attributes of the group being studied had to be considered while designing our experiment. The group we studied is a collection of MBA students at a large, urban graduate business school: Pace University's Lubin Graduate School of Business. Hence, all subjects possess at least a baccalaureate degree (from various institutions). Moreover, since more than 80 percent of the people enrolled in this program (there are over 5,000 of them) are part-time students, we assumed most of them work full-time somewhere near our New York City campus. Finally, since our experiment was designed to question the subjects on their subjective feelings about the probability of an event, we limited our subjects to students who were enrolled in classes who had already completed an elementary course in probability as a prerequisite (or to students enrolled in that course, at a time after subjective probability had been introduced). With this in mind, we restricted our study to randomly selected Management Science courses offered in the Graduate School of Business. We collected the data during the middle months (May-October) of 1984.

CHARACTERISTICS OF THE RESPONDENTS

The next problem was to decide which demographic information was pertinent to the study along with which developing technologies should be included in the study. Considering demographics first, prior to any formal gathering of data, we believed our university to be mostly Caucasian, male, "middle class," urban residing, between twenty-five and thirty years old, with a Judeo-Christian background. We were interested to see if we could determine any difference in perception among age groups, income levels, sexes, or places of residence. For that reason, questions on those demographic areas were built into our study.

DESIGNING THE EXPERIMENT

Considering technologies, it was obvious we wanted to include the very controversial topics of nuclear energy and nuclear weapons. We considered other developing areas and decided our interests also included robotics, generic engineering, and global mass communications. Hence, we began this study desiring to measure how mostly urban, educated, middle-class, northeastern Americans perceived the risk involved in five technologies:

1. Nuclear energy
2. Nuclear weapons
3. Robotics
4. Genetic engineering
5. Global mass communications

We defined the work "risk" pragmatically in the questionnaire itself by suggesting two risky events associated with each technology. The first suggested a "low risk" event which we called a "worst case" event. The second suggested a "high risk" event which we called a "least worst case" event. Listed next are the "worst case" and "least worst case" events associated with the five technologies (time frames are defined by the phrase "in the foreseeable future"):

1. Nuclear energy. Either because of an engineering or an operational error or because of terrorist sabotage, a major accident will occur causing either: (a) disruption in the lives of people living nearby a power plant (least worst case) or (b) large scale injuries and loss of lives (worst case).

2. Nuclear weapons. Whether by design or not, nuclear warheads are exploded somewhere in the world, causing either: (a) environmental damage and international tensions (least worse case) or (b) a nuclear holocaust (worst case).

3. Robotics. A megalomaniac group will be able to seize the control of a large enough portion of the robot population of a country, thereby either: a) dominating that nation economically (least worst case) or (b) seizing complete control of that country (worse case).

4. Genetic engineering. Whether by accident or design, a genetically engineering "unnatural" biological element will be released into the atmosphere causing either: (a) minor illness and panic among the members of local community (least worse case) or (b) large-scale sickness and death such as has not been observed since medieval times (worse case).

5. Global mass communications. Through mass control of global media, an individual or a a group will be able to sufficiently control the whims and desires of a large group of people, resulting either: (a) in the capture of a large portion of an economic marketplace (least worst case) or (b) the exertion of political control over a society (worst case).

Moreover, we hoped to be able to see if we could discern any differences among these perceptions between specific demographic areas.

We further designed our study to measure an individual's perceived risk associated with a technology by having that individual assign a subjective probability to the occurrence of hypothetical "negative" events associated with that technology. To make the elicitations simple, we asked the subjects to respond with two subjective probabilities for each technology: One for the probability of a "worst case" event, the other for the probability of a "least worst case" event. Thus, each subject was asked to provide us with two numbers on a scale of zero to ten (we used an integer scale) for each of the five technologies.

DATA ANALYSIS

In this section we present the data gathered in our study. In all,
161 subjects, attending six randomly selected Management Science courses,
responded to our questionnaire. The first set of questions related to the
place of residence, sex, age, annual family income, religion, and
education of the respondents. The respondents were then asked to express
a subjective probability associated with the risk perceived by them in the
five modern technologies: nuclear energy, nuclear weapons, robotics,
genetic engineering, and global mass communications.

In each technological area the subjects expressed their feelings
towards the dangers associated with that technology by answering two
questions. Each response is their expressed "coded" probability (the
numbers given must all be divided by ten to form a usual probability
distribution) of posqible negative events associated with the technology:
the first number relates to a "least worse case" event; the second number,
to a "worse cast" event. All numbers were expressed on an integer scale
from zero to ten (zero implies an impossible event; ten, a certain
event). Not all subjects responded to all questions.

The demographic data of all the respondents is presented in Table 1.
As can be seen, the subjects are mostly urban, male, Christian, between
eighteen and twenty-nine years of age. It is also interesting to note
that almost 50 percent of those polled have average incomes of $30,000 and
above.

Table 2(a) presents the mean responses to the "least worst case"
negative events caused by a particular technology, ranked from largest to
smallest. Table 2(b) presents the same results for the "worst case"
situations. It is clear that this group of subjects perceives nuclear
energy as being the riskiest of the give technologies, using our form of
measurement. On the other end of the spectrum, relatively little concern
is expressed for possible dangers from the use of robotics.

What is worth noticing is the switch in the ordering of nuclear
weapons with global mass communications in Tables 2(a) and 2(b); there is
more concern expressed for a "minor" catastrophe with nuclear weapons,
whereas for a "major" negative event greater concern is expressed for
global mass communications.

Tables 3(a) through 7(b) present the mean responses of Table 2(a) and
(b) broken down demographically.

Objective analysis of the data in Tables 3 through 7 provides some
interesting results. Robotics is of least concern to all groups of
subjects listed. In the "least worse case" scenario, depicting situations
causing negative (but not devastatingly negative) events, on the average
all groups perceived nuclear energy (in most cases) or nuclear weapons as
the riskiest technology. In the "worst case" scenario, depicting the most
negative types of events associated with each technology, global mass
communications replaces nuclear weapons in standing alongside nuclear
energy as causing most concern.

Objective intergroup comparisons also provide us with the following:

-   For "worst case" scenarios, the urban sample expressed a higher mean
    risk perception than the suburban sample in all five technologies.

Table 1

Demographic Data - All Subjects

Residence:	Urban	65%
	Suburban	35%
Sex:	Male	64%
	Female	36%
Age:(years)	Under 18	0%
	18-29	70%
	30-39	29%
	40-49	1%
	Over 49	0%
Average Family Income: (Dollars):	0-9,999	5%
	10,000-29,999	46%
	30,000-59,000	32%
	Over 60,000	17%
Religion:	Christian	69%
	Jewish	17%
	All Others	14%(includes almost 6% atheist)

Table 2(a)

Subjects Ordered Mean Responses - "Least Worst Case"

Nuclear Energy	6.10
Nuclear Weapons	5.76
Global Mass Communications	4.85
Genetic Engineering	4.53
Robotics	1.91

Table 2(b)

All Subjects Ordered Mean Responses - "Worst Case"

Nuclear Energy	4.28
Global Mass Communications	4.03
Nuclear Weapons	3.40
Genetic Engineering	2.52
Robotics	1.08

Table 3(a)

Ordered Mean Responses by Residence - "Least Worse Case"

Urban (65%)		Suburban (35%)	
Nuclear Energy	6.14	Nuclear Weapons	6.18
Nuclear Weapons	5.48	Nuclear Energy	6.04
Global Mass Comm	5.06	Genetic Eng	4.52
Genetic Eng	4.52	Global Mass Comm	4.41
Robotics	2.10	Robotics	1.60

Table 3(b)

Ordered Mean Responses by Residence - "Worst Case"

Urban(65%)   Suburban(35%)

Global Mass Comm	4.40		Nuclear Energy	4.18
Nuclear Energy	4.28		Nuclear Weapons	3.19
Nuclear Weapons	3.46		Global Mass Comm	3.15
Genetic Eng	2.57		Genetic Eng	2.34
Robotics	1.21		Robotics	.89

Table 4(a)

Ordered Mean Responses by Sex - "Least Worst Case"

Male(64%)   Female(36%)

Nuclear Energy	5.80		Nuclear Energy	6.63
Nuclear Weapons	5.53		Nuclear Weapons	6.14
Global Mass Comm	4.52		Global Mass Comm	5.42
Genetic Eng	4.28		Genetic Eng	4.89
Robotics	1.90		Robotics	1.96

Table 4(b)

Ordered Mean Responses by Sex - "Worst Case"

Male(64%)   Female(36%)

Nuclear Energy	4.25		Global Mass Comm	4.54
Global Mass Comm	3.72		Nuclear Energy	4.34
Nuclear Weapons	3.35		Nuclear Weapons	3.51
Genetic Eng	2.56		Genetic Eng	2.46
Robotics	1.20		Robotics	.91

Table 5(a)

Ordered Mean Responses by Age - "Least Worst Case"

18-29 years (70%)		30-39 years (28%)	
Nuclear Energy	6.17	Nuclear Energy	5.96
Nuclear Weapons	5.81	Nuclear Weapons	5.59
Global Mass Comm	4.86	Global Mass Comm	4.76
Genetic Eng	4.72	Genetic Eng	4.07
Robotics	1.95	Robotics	1.78

Table 5(b)

Ordered Mean Responses by Age - "Worst Case"

18-29 years (70%)		30-39 years (28%)	
Nuclear Energy	4.37	Nuclear Energy	4.16
Global Mass Comm	4.08	Global Mass Comm	4.11
Nuclear Weapons	3.25	Nuclear Weapons	3.80
Genetic Eng	2.68	Genetic Eng	2.22
Robotics	1.12	Robotics	1.01

Table 6(a)

Ordered Mean Responses by Average Family Income - "Least Worst Case"

$0-9,999 (5%)				$10,000-29,999 (46%)	
Nuclear Energy	6.00			Nuclear Energy	6.23
Global Mass Comm	5.86			Nuclear Weapons	5.63
Nuclear Weapons	5.00			Global Mass Comm	5.17
Genetic Eng	4.57			Genetic Eng	4.59
Robotics	4.00			Robotics	1.83
$30,000-59,999 (32%)				Over $59,999 (16%)	
Nuclear Energy	6.02			Nuclear Weapons	6.44
Nuclear Weapons	5.62			Nuclear Energy	5.92
Global Mass Comm	4.30			Genetic Eng	4.80
Genetic Eng	4.18			Global Mass Comm	4.38
Robotics	1.56			Robotics	2.44

Table 6(b)

Ordered Mean Responses by Average Family Income - "Worst Case"

$0-9,999 (5%)				$10,000-29,999 (46%)	
Global Mass Comm	4.83			Nuclear Energy	4.59
Nuclear Energy	3.00			Global Mass Comm	4.54
Nuclear Weapons	2.43			Nuclear Weapons	3.64
Genetic Eng	2.17			Genetic Eng	2.79
Robotics	2.00			Robotics	1.21
$30,000-59,999 (32%)				Over $59,999 (16%)	
Nuclear Energy	3.75			Nuclear Energy	4.60
Global Mass Comm	3.44			Nuclear Weapons	3.76
Nuclear Weapons	2.98			Global Mass Comm	3.08
Genetic Eng	2.02			Genetic Eng	2.52
Robotics	.56			Robotics	1.52

Table 7(a)

Ordered Mean Responses by Religion - "Least Worst Case"

Christian (69%)		Jewish (17%)	
Nuclear Energy	6.23	Nuclear Weapons	6.35
Nuclear Weapons	5.79	Nuclear Energy	6.12
Global Mass Comm	4.89	Genetic Eng	4.64
Genetic Eng	4.52	Global Mass Comm	4.04
Robotics	2.83	Robotics	1.69

Table 7(b)

Ordered Mean Responses by Religion - "Worst Case"

Christian (69%)		Jewish (17%)	
Nuclear Energy	4.29	Nuclear Energy	4.08
Global Mass Comm	3.92	Global Mass Comm	3.81
Nuclear Weapons	3.33	Nuclear Weapons	3.48
Genetic Eng	2.44	Genetic Eng	1.88
Robotics	1.05	Robotics	.85

- In the "least worst case" scenarios, the women sampled expressed a higher mean risk perception than men in all technologies but robotics; in the "worst case" scenario, the women expressed a higher mean than men in all technologies except genetic engineering and robotics.

- For "worst case" scenarios, the 18-29 year-old age group expressed higher mean levels of perceived risk than the 30-39 years old age group for all technologies.

Applying statistical inference to our data base also led to some significant results. The X^2 test for statistical independence was used to determine if there was any dependency in the responses relating one technology to another technology regarding risk perception. The tests reveal no dependency among any pairs of technologies except in the case of nuclear energy and nuclear weapons. In the case of nuclear energy and nuclear weapons, we found statistical dependency exists in the rating of these two technologies in both the "worst case" and "least worse case" responses. This provides us with some statistical evidence that the fears associated with nuclear power are closely linked with the fears an adversity of nuclear weapons. The correlation coefficients of .419 ("least worst case") and .584 ("worst case") between responses rating nuclear energy and weapons also shows a relatively strong relationship between these two variables (all other correlation coefficients between pairs of variables were considerably less).

Also, significant at the 5% level were differences in mean perceptions between men and women subjects in nuclear energy and global mass communications for the "least worst case" situations.

CONCLUSION

This study shows how much our graduate business students are concerned with the risk accompanying the development of some new technologies. They perceive the riskiest technology as being nuclear energy. Concerns are also high for nuclear weapons (especially in a "least worst case" scenario) and global mass communications (in a "worst case" scenario). For nuclear weapons, it is possible that most people perceive the danger associated with them, but have some faith in the concept of "deterrence" and hence assign a relatively low probability to the occurrence of a widespread nuclear war. Concerning global mass communications, it is possible many people believe the "worst case" scenario to be already in widespread existence; namely, dictatorial governments using mass communications to support their dictatorships.

COMMUNITY RISK PERCEPTION: A PILOT STUDY

Branden B. Johnson and Bradley Baltensperger

Department of Social Sciences
Michigan Technological University

ABSTRACT

Hazard identification studies have tended to test only one explanatory model at a time. Preliminary results of a pilot study intended to compare the relative explanatory power of two personality, two bounded rationality, and three "social construction of risk" models of hazard perceptions are reported.

KEY WORDS: risk perception, hazard perception, personality, bounded rationality, social marginality, community

Hazard perception studies have generally assumed concerns about potential hazards are based on (1) emotion and personality, (2) bounded rationality, (3) "objective" reality, (4) cognitive biases. Recently, "social construction of risk" theories have been proposed as well (Johnson and Covello, forthcoming). Eventually, hazard identifications will be seen as some combination of these factors. But at present most researchers test hypotheses appropriate to only one model at a time; the relative validity of different hazard identification models cannot be examined through this approach. This paper is intended to stimulate comparative testing of models and hazards by reporting preliminary results of a pilot study done by the authors. Although the results are not conclusive, they suggest lines of attack for future research.

RESEARCH DESIGN

Because this was a pilot study, with limited money and time, we focused our attention on models which could be examined in a simple and straightforward fashion: two personality models (risk arousal and locus-of-control), two bounded rationality models (knowledge and experience), and three social construction of risk models (social marginality, political views, and community connectedness). All statistical relationship between variables reported below are significant at the .05 level or better.

The study site was the Torch Lake area of the Keweenaw Peninsula in Michigan's Upper Peninsula. Tumors have been found in Torch Lake fish, the state department of health advised against eating lake fish in 1983, and the lake has been placed on Superfund lists pending research results on the tumors' causes (possibly copper tailings) and human health implications. Other hazards include heavy snow (15-foot annual average),

337

nuclear waste (a nearby area is being considered as a national high-level waste repository), and group homes for the mentally retarded. Residents' exposure to automobile, prescription drug, airplane, and cigarette hazards is much like that of other Americans; they are probably less exposed to nuclear power plant hazards (none is located within about 350 miles).

The population of interest was Torch Lake area registered voters, 2293 (87%) of the 2649 eligible adults. Telephone interviews with a random sample of 127 were completed by student interviewers in June, 1985. From that sample, 47 respondents were selected for face-to-face interviews conducted by the authors from July 24 to August 19. Our sample was somewhat biased toward the better educated: 1980 county high school completion rates were 61% for males and 65.4% for females; our overall figure was 89%. Our sample was comparable to the population in age and sex. Information on hazard knowledge and experience was collected almost entirely from the second sample; other variables were measured in both interviews.

RESULTS

Hazard Ratings. Respondents in the large sample were asked to rate the benefits, risks, and acceptability to society of eight items (see Table 1) on a scale from 0 (e.g., no benefit) to 9 (e.g., great benefit). Median benefit and acceptability ratings were high for automobiles, drugs, and airplanes, and low for cigarettes, nuclear and toxic waste facilities; the reverse was true for risk ratings. The relative rankings for five common hazards are similar to those obtained for perceived benefits and risks by Slovic et al. (1980). Benefits and acceptability ratings were positively correlated for all hazards; risks and acceptability were negatively correlated for all hazards except automobiles. Benefits and risks were also negatively correlated for all hazards.

Ratings for nuclear power plants and toxic waste disposal facilities were strongly correlated--benefits ($r=.30$), risks ($r=.37$), and acceptability ($r=.62$)--suggesting a dread dimension might have been tapped, as in Slovic et al. (1980). The correlations among automobile and airplane ratings (.46, .38, and .51) are plausible, since both were found to be familiar hazards by Slovic et al.

Risk ratings were elicited in both interview waves for three hazards, in order to test their reliability over the 4-11 week gap. Nuclear power risk ratings were moderately correlated ($r=.40$), but automobile ratings were not correlated ($r=.08$). To appropriately measure "experience" with snow in a heavy-snow area, we asked for risk ratings of "major winter storms" in the second interview instead of for "snow"--there was no correlation ($r=.10$) between them. It is striking that an emotion-laden issue like nuclear power appears to evoke stable risk ratings, whereas ratings of familiar hazards seem to fluctuate. The very prominence of nuclear power as an issue may have given people a chance to come to a firm conclusion--on whatever basis--about its risk. By contrast, automobiles and snow may be seen as just part of life rather than as explicit hazards, and so rating their risks is an unfamiliar task yielding volatile results.

There was a moderate correlation ($r=.40$) between assessments of trends in overall safety of life during the past 50 years and the next 50 years, suggesting an optimist-pessimist dimension. People who saw life as becoming less safe in the last 50 years were somewhat more likely to rate automobile risks high ($r=.23$). The less safe the future was expected to be, the higher the risks ($r=.28$) and the lower the benefits ($r=-.18$) and acceptability ($r=-.19$) of toxic waste facilities were rated; this again

338

TABLE 1

Hazard Rating

Item	Benefits[a]	Risks[a]	Acceptability[a]	Benefit-Acceptability[b]	Risk-Acceptability[b]	Benefit-Risk[b]
Automobiles	9	4	9	.35***	.01	-.13
Nuclear Power Plants	4	7	4	.64***	-.44***	-.44***
Prescription Drugs	9	4	7	.54***	-.22**	-.33***
Airplanes	9	3	8	.48***	-.20**	-.20**
Toxic Waste Disposal Facilities	5	7	4	.45***	-.38***	-.41***
Cigarettes	0	9	0	.39***	-.36***	-.15*
Group Homes	7	1	7	.42***	-.40***	-.37***
Snow	6	2	6	.51***	-.29***	-.32***

N=122-127

a   Median ratings on a 0-9 scale (e.g., no benefit-great benefit)

b   Pearson correlation coefficients

* $P \leq .05$

** $P \leq .01$

*** $P \leq .000$

suggests some "dread" dimension, though it is striking that nuclear power plants did not correlate significantly with future risk assessments.

Pearson correlations were calculated between automobile ratings and self-reported seatbelt use, cigarette ratings and self-reported smoking, and toxic waste disposal facility ratings and self-reported eating of Torch Lake fish. The only significant relationships were those between smoking and cigarette benefit (r=.46) and acceptability (r=.25) ratings. The low positive response (19.8%) to the question "Do you ever eat fish from Torch Lake?," and low seatbelt usage--on a four-point scale, 10.2% of 127 respondents said they "always" wore one, 18.1% said they did so "most of the time"--may have obscured any attitude-reported behavior correlations on these items.

These seatbelt use responses were collected just before the Michigan mandatory seatbelt use law went into effect (July 1, 1985). Responses from our sample of 47 to the same question after that date were highly correlated with the pre-law responses (r=.63); those reporting using belts "sometimes" or "never" dropped from 32 to 11 of 46. While post-law belt use was not significantly related to second-wave automobile ratings, it was correlated with fewer perceived benefits to automobiles (r=.37) and with support for the state mandatory-use law (r=.40).

Personality. Personality and emotion have been linked to hazard identifications by several researchers (e.g., Sims and Baumann, 1972; Simpson-Housley et al., 1978; Johnson and Tversky, 1983). Others have criticized this approach or had null findings (e.g., Schiff, 1977; Simpson-Housley et al., 1982; Brown et al., 1983a,b; De Man et al., 1984a,b). An "arousal-seeking" scale was constructed by Mehrabian and Russell (1974); we selected from it eight items oriented specifically to arousal from "risk" and asked respondents to rate their agreement with them on a 6-point scale.

Factor analysis identified three statements--all concerned interest in "frightening" or "dangerous" activities--loading highly (.68 to .79) on the first factor (which explained 23.2% of the observed variance). We conservatively used the sum of the responses to these three statements as our only measure of risk arousal. People "aroused" by risk were significantly more likely to find airplanes "acceptable," expect the future to be safer than the present, and favor local siting of a nuclear power plant, but the Pearson correlations were low (about .15). No other variables were significantly correlated with the "risk arousal" score, nor were automobile ratings correlated with agreement that "I enjoy driving very fast."

Locus-of-control (LOC) scales (Rotter, 1966) measure the degree to which people feel they exercise control over their lives. There may be three LOC factors: belief in chance, expectancy of control by powerful others, and perceived mastery over one's own life (Levenson, 1974). Our scale used 18 items from Levenson's 24-item scale. Behavior-specific LOC items may be more predictive of behavior than general ones (Huebner and Lipsey, 1981), so "getting cancer" and Levenson's "car accident" statements were added for comparison of specific and general LOC scales' Ability to predict automobile, nuclear, and toxic waste risk perceptions.

Factor analysis identified three factors which together explained 42.4% of the variance. Three statements in Factor 1 (with factor loadings greater than .7) tapped internal locus-of-control, three in Factor 2 tapped a "powerful others" dimension, and two in Factor 3 tapped a "chance" dimension. Summary scores for each LOC dimension were used as independent variables to predict hazard ratings; the highest Pearson correlations are reported below.

The more internally-oriented a person was, the more he or she was likely to oppose local siting of a nuclear waste facility (r=.21) and express an intention to move out of the community if one was built there (r=.25). Those attributing control to powerful others saw higher risks from airplanes (r=.17), a standard "involuntary" hazard, and said they would move out if a chemical waste facility was built locally (r=.26). Those who saw chance as ruling their lives were more likely to oppose a local group home and to say they would move if a local chemical waste disposal facility was built (r=.24).

Internalization of control over being in an automobile accident was correlated with finding automobiles riskier, less beneficial (r=.31) and less acceptable. A view that accidents are the other driver's fault was correlated with perceiving high automobile benefits (r=.24); scores on the chance-automobile statement were not significantly correlated with automobile ratings. Internalization of cancer causes ("Whether I get cancer depends mostly on my own actions") was correlated with favoring local siting of a nuclear power plant, nuclear waste facility (r=.30), or chemical waste facility, perceiving high benefits from nuclear power and low risks from toxic waste disposal facilities. Correlations for these "specific" LOC statements are slightly better than those for the overall scores.

Hazard Experience and Knowledge. "Bounded rationality" studies emphasize the individual's (limited) knowledge or experience of the hazard and of the range of coping actions as determining perceptions and behavior. Despite some empirical support for this model (e.g., Burton et al , 1978; Lichtenstein et al., 1978), there has been strong criticism of it (e.g., Hewitt, 1983; Sims and Baumann, 1983; Sorenson, 1983). Measures of knowledge of nuclear power were adapted for this study from Kuklinski et al. (1982). Knowledge questions were also formulated for nuclear waste, water pollution, hazardous chemical wastes, and automobiles. Experience variables were constructed for automobiles, snow, and water supply.

Lichtenstein et al. (1978) found that knowing someone who had died from the hazard was correlated with risk ratings. We found no such correlation for automobiles, or for how recently the respondent had been involved in an automobile accident, and reported personal injuries were too few to run a correlation. Being the driver in the most recent accident was confusingly correlated with rating automobile benefits lower (r=.36) and with opposing the new state mandatory seatbelt use law (r=.33). The correlation (r=.31) between the respondent having been in an automobile accident at some time and lower perceived risks is also counter-intuitive (unless experience teaches that accidents are not as bad as they are thought to be).

Most measures of experience with snow hazards (e.g., property or health damage) had too few positive responses to allow analysis. There was no correlation between the time since the remembered "worst year" for major winter storms locally and hazard ratings. There was a small negative correlation (r=-.26) between the time since a major storm last caused "serious problems" for the community and higher risk ratings for such storms.

Preliminary analysis of the summary knowledge scales revealed that the more knowledgeable people were about nuclear power, the lower they rated its risks (r=.15) and the more favorable they were to local siting of a nuclear plant (r=.17). Nuclear waste knowledge was not significantly correlated with toxic waste or nuclear waste facility ratings. Automobile knowledge was significantly correlated only with its acceptability rating (r=.17); other hazard ratings, including reported seatbelt use, were not correlated with this knowledge. Hazardous waste knowledge was negatively correlated with perceived "danger" from local water pollution (r=-.33), suggesting some association of degree of knowledge and concern about Torch Lake pollution. Our measure of water pollution knowledge was correlated with unwillingness to move out of town if a chemical waste disposal facility was built locally (r=.37). Knowledge appears somewhat important in hazard identifications, but its import varies by hazard.

Social Marginality. Some researchers have begun to develop "social construction of risk" theories which assume that hazard identifications are born of everyday social interactions (see Johnson and Covello, forthcoming). Rogers (1985:499) found that "women, the less educated, and particularly young adults [18-29] tend to estimate risk at higher levels and be less likely to find, at least nuclear, risks acceptable." He attributed this to these respondents' marginal location in the social structure. We included gender, education, and age among our socio-demographic variables, as well as income, employment, and marital status.

In contrast to Rogers' (1985) findings, neither age nor education was related to any hazard ratings. Women did rate nuclear power's risks higher (r=.24), as Rogers found, as they did the benefits of automobiles (r=.33) and airplanes (r=.32), but there were no other significant correlations with gender. Of the other indicators of social marginality, lower income was correlated only with high perceived risk from group homes (r=.21). Umemployment in the respondent's family during the past three years was correlated with perceived drug benefits (r=.25) and cigarettes' risk (r=.35), but negatively with cigarette acceptability (r=-.26). Current unemployment of the respondent correlated with lower perceived benefits (eta=.29) but higher acceptability (eta=.24) of airplanes. Unemployment also correlates not only with greater agreement that there is a local pollution problem (eta=.25), but also with favoring cleanup of local pollution even if it meant settling for somewhat higher unemployment (eta=.28)! Our results only partly confirm Rogers' marginality hypothesis for hazard identifications.

Political Variables. Starr (1985) contends that public acceptability of risks is dependent more on public trust in hazard managers than on quantitative measures of such risks. Political variables used in this study included participation in political activities, trust in various political actors, and political ideology.

These were not significantly correlated with most hazard ratings. Exceptions included a link between local electoral activity and perceived cigarette benefits (r=.23), and between self-reported conservative ideology and acceptability ratings for toxic waste disposal facilities (r=.25) and snow (r=.21). Ratings of government's ability to cope with nuclear power plant safety (N=47) were positively correlated with nuclear power's acceptability (r=.28), consistent with Starr's (1985) hypothesis that hazard acceptability is related to confidence in hazard managers. No significant correlation was found between local government ratings for coping with snow and automobile hazards and these hazards' ratings.

Community Connectedness. Community connectedness measures have been implicated in some hazard identifications (e.g., Preston et al., 1983; Fowlkes and Miller, forthcoming). Social interaction variables used in this study include membership in local organizations and various expressions of commitment to the community.

To our surprise, membership in local organizations was quite low: the only organization type to which a majority (76.2%) belonged was a church, and a plurality (37%) of the sample belonged to only one organization. The number of group memberships per person (and thus presumed social linkages in the community) was not significantly correlated with hazard ratings.

Connectedness was also tapped through several attitudinal variables. These were not highly intercorrelated except for "feel responsible for what happens to my community" and "feel capable of influencing decisions on local issues" (r=.33). Neither were they significantly correlated with most hazard ratings.

CONCLUSIONS

We have yet to compare the power of alternative hazard identification explanations directly. These conclusions are highly preliminary and subject to severe constraints--our analysis is still in its early stages (several of our measures of community connectedness and political views have not yet been analyzed, which may account for their generally poor showing), the difficulty of defining and measuring a concept (particularly problematic for "knowledge" and "experience"), the small and perhaps atypical sample, and the relatively narrow range of hazards examined. It is clear that the power of each model to explain hazard perceptions, though non-zero, is moderate at best (though correlations of .30 are typical for inter-attitude survey research) and some of the reported correlations appear counter-intuitive. Because considerable variance in benefit, risk, and acceptability assessments remains unexplained by these individual models, hazard perception model comparison must be a top priority for future research. Explanation may depend upon development of a composite model utilizing the complementary features of various approaches.

REFERENCES

Brown, Jennifer, Joyce Henderson, and Jane Fielding, 1983a, "Differing Perspectives on Nuclear Related Risks: An Analysis of Social Psychological Factors in the Perception of Nuclear Power," University of Warwick, England: Operational Research Society, September 27-30.

Brown, Jennifer, Terence Lee, and Joyce Henderson, 1983b, "Public Perception of Nuclear Power," London: British Psychological Society, December 19-20.

Burton, Ian, Robert W. Kates, and Gilbert F. White, 1978, The Environment as Hazard, New York: Oxford University Press.

De Man, Anton, Paul Simpson-Housley, and Fred Curtis, 1984a, "Trait Anxiety, Perception of Potential Nuclear Hazard, and State Anxiety," Psychological Reports 54:791-794.

De Man, Anton, Paul Simpson-Housley, Fred Curtis, and David Smith, 1984b, "Trait Anxiety and Response to Potential Flood Disaster," Psychological Reports 54:507-512.

Fowlkes, Martha R. and Patricia Y. Miller, forthcoming, "Chemicals and Community at Love Canal," in Johnson and Covello.

Hewitt, Kenneth (ed.), 1983, Interpretations of Calamity, Boston: Allen and Unwin.

Huebner, Robert B. and Mark W. Lipsey, 1981, "The Relationship of Three Measures of Locus of Control to Environmental Activism," Basic and Applied Social Psychology, 2:1, 45-58.

Johnson, Branden B. and Vincent T. Covello (eds.), forthcoming, The Social Construction of Risk, New York: Reidel.

Johnson, Eric J. and Amos Tversky, 1983, "Affect, Generalization, and the Perception of Risk," Journal of Personality and Social Psychology, July, 45:1, 20-31.

Kuklinski, James H., Daniel S. Metlay, and W. D. Kay, 1982, "Citizen Knowledge and Choices on the Complex Issue of Nuclear Energy," American Journal of Political Science, November, 26:4, 615-642.

Levenson, Hanna, 1974, "Activism and Powerful Others: Distinctions Within the Concept of Internal-External Control," Journal of Personality Assessment, 38:377-383.

Lichtenstein, Sarah, Paul Slovic, Baruch Fischhoff, Mark Layman, and Barbara Combs, 1978, "Judged Frequency of Lethal Events," Journal of Experimental Psychology: Human Learning and Memory, 4:6, 551-578.

Mehrabian, Albert and James A. Russell, 1974, An Approach to Environmental Psychology, Cambridge, Massachusetts: MIT.

Preston, Valerie, S. Martin Taylor, and David C. Hodge, 1983, "Adjustment to Natural and Technological Hazards: A Study of an Urban Residential Community," Environment and Behavior, March, 15:2, 143-164.

Rogers, George O., 1985, "On Determining Public Acceptability of Risk," in Chris Whipple and Vincent Covello (eds.) Risk Analysis in the Private Sector, New York: Plenum, 483-504.

Rotter, J., 1966, "Generalized Expectancies for Internal Versus External Control of Reinforcement," Psychological Monographs, 80 (1, Whole No. 609).

Schiff, Myra, 1977, "Hazard Adjustment, Locus of Control, and Sensation Seeking: Some Null Findings," Environment and Behavior, June, 9:2, 233-254.

Simpson-Housley, Paul, G. Lipinski, and E. Trithardt, 1978, "The Flood Hazard at Lumsden, Saskatchewan, Residents' Cognitive Awareness and Personality," Prairie Forum, 3:175-188.

Simpson-Housley, Paul, Robert J. Moore, Patricio Larrain, and Danny Blair, 1982, "Repression-Sensitization and Flood Hazard Appraisal in Carman, Manitoba," Psychological Reports 50:839-842.

Sims, John H. and Duane D. Baumann, 1983, "Educational Programs and Human Response to Natural Hazards," Environment and Behavior, March, 15:2, 165-189.

-------, 1972, "The Tornado Threat: Coping Styles of the North and South," Science, 176:1386-1392.

Slovic, Paul, Baruch Fischhoff, and Sarah Lichtenstein, 1980, "Perceived Risk," in R. C. Schwing and W. A. Albers, Jr. (eds.), Societal Risk Assessment: How Safe is Safe Enough?, New York: Plenum.

Sorenson, John H., 1983, "Knowing How to Behave Under the Threat of Disaster: Can It Be Explained?," Environment and Behavior, July, 15:4, 438-457.

Starr, Chauncey, 1985, "Risk Management, Assessment, and Acceptability," Risk Analysis, June, 5:2, 97-102.

SOURCES OF CORRELATION OF EXPERT OPINION -- A PILOT STUDY

J. M. Booker, M. A. Meyer, and H. F. Martz

Los Alamos National Laboratory
Los Alamos, New Mexico 87545

Expert estimates are relied upon as sources of data whenever experimental data is lacking such as in risk analyses and reliability assessments. Correlation between experts is a problem in the elicitation and use of subjective estimates. This pilot study seeks to identify the sources and structure of interexpert correlation and to discuss some of its ramifications. Until now, there has been no data that identify sources of correlation. Data were gathered using questioning techniques from ethnography and educational psychology. The results of this pilot study indicate that the key to correlation is in the way that people solve problems.

KEYWORDS: Subjective Judgment, Expert Opinion, Correlated Estimates, Problem Solving, Bootstrap

1. INTRODUCTION

This pilot study seeks to identify sources of correlation in expert estimates to provide useful information to managers and others who work with expert judgments. Identifying sources of correlation aids in solving problems associated with correlated estimates such as in aggregating multiple estimates and in obtaining the best coverage of the true value.

There has been much speculation about possible sources of correlation between estimates of experts but little evidence to identify a source. One speculation is that the theoretical orientations individuals learn during their education may be a source of correlated estimates. Other speculations are that the individuals' shared work experiences may lead to correlation. This research proposed and tested these common speculations as well as two additional ones: the process that the individual uses to solve the problem, and the length of time since the individual has worked on a similar problem. In addition, two factors were tested for their affect on the individual reaching the "correct" answer: the complexity of the problem, and the individual's problem-solving process.

The target population for the pilot was a group of 18 statisticians who were asked text-book statistical problems. The statisticians were questioned on their professional backgrounds and problem-solving processes using intensive interviewing techniques borrowed from ethnography and educational psychology. Data on human behavior can be expected to be fuzzy and, therefore, difficult to analyze.

The results indicate that a major source for the correlation among experts could be found in the processes they use to solve a problem. Experts using the same process, or path, tend to arrive at the same answer. No evidence was found to support the common speculations that there is some commonality in the experts' professional backgrounds (i.e., schooling or common work experience) to cause correlated estimates. The individuals' problem-solving paths included their assumptions about the nature of the problem and some algorithm or rule of thumb that required calculation. The paths that included simple and easy to remember algorithms most frequently led to the correct answer. Such paths are referred to as "straight pathways."

2. THEORETICAL BACKGROUND

Interexpert Correlation

Although expert opinion is commonly used as data, the question of sources of correlations between experts has not been studied (Dalkey 1975). Yet, there has been speculation as to the sources of correlation. For example, Baecher (1979) uses the term schools of thought to explain the correlation he found in the expert estimates on seismic hazards. He was able to group the experts into three schools according to their answers but could not explain this grouping because the experts had been anonymous.

Some authors seem to interpret correlation as a positive trait and others, as a negative one. Some view correlation as desirable, as an indication of consistency, reliability, and accuracy. They tend to eliminate outliers and value homogeneous expert populations (Comer et al. 1984). They may also find positive merit in not being able to link experts' estimates to their age, experience, or organization (Meyer 1982). Expert correlation is tacitly viewed as negative by those who place a high value on the diversity of opinions. For example, correlation could be viewed as evidence that the problem has not been considered from enough perspectives to obtain a quality answer (Seaver 1976); that the experts are making one major and probably highly conservative assumption (Ascher 1978); or that the experts are unconsciously following one person's view (Janis 1972). Outliers are not eliminated under this interpretation because diversity, rather than consistency, is valued.

A few authors have assumed that significant correlations exist and have investigated means for aggregating expert estimates. A primary reference on dependent estimation errors in a Bayesian context is Winkler (1981).

Factors Affecting Individual's Problem Solving

This paper does not place a positive or negative value on interexpert correlation but simply seeks to understand its causes. Because literature on causes of interexpert correlation was lacking, the authors reviewed literature on factors influencing individual's problem solving. This literature was used to postulate factors which could be sources of correlation (the subject's background, the recency of his exposure to the problem, and the algorithm he uses to solve the problem) and which could impact on the accuracy of the subject's estimates (the algorithm used and the complexity of the problem).

A previous study by the authors failed to indicate any correlation between an expert's solution and his age, position on the project, years of experience, job satisfaction, or professional degree (Meyer et al. 1981).

However, some other studies propose that traits which humans have in common may influence their problem solving. In particular, humans possess memory limitations (Hogarth 1980) that affect their reconstruction of events and their equations for solving problems. For this reason, the recency of the subject's experience in working a similar problem was postulated as a source of correlation.

A number of studies had shown that the problem itself has an effect on the answers given. For example, Tversky and Kahneman (1981) have shown that the presentation of the decision task influences the individual's response. In another study, the complexity of the questions seemed to have some impact on the answers (Comer et al. 1984). There seemed to be an increase in variance between answers for those questions that had been rated as more complex. These studies imply a link between the question itself and the answers that are selected.

Some studies have shown that the individual's problem-solving techniques influence his answer. For example, if individuals are instructed or assisted in breaking a problem into its component parts and in solving the parts, they give more accurate answers than do those who have not used this problem-solving technique (Hayes-Roth 1980; Armstrong 1975). The assumptions that individuals make are also likely to influence their answers. Ascher (1978) determined that one of the major sources of inaccuracy in forecasting future possibilities, such as markets for utilities, lay in the forecaster's failure to extrapolate sufficiently from present patterns.

Matz (1981) has approached the correlation between the individual's problem-solving path and answer by examining the errors made by the individual. She has proposed that problem-solving errors can be explained as a result of reasonable but unsuccessful attempts to adapt old knowledge to new situations. The present study elicited the subjects' algorithms for solving the problems because these studies indicated that the algorithms might be a source of correlation and estimate accuracy.

To elicit information on the subjects' algorithms, a technique from educational psychology was used in combination with one from ethnography. The educational psychology technique involves having the subjects think aloud. The ethnographic technique is a means of intensively questioning individuals while minimizing the observer's bias. This technique is an iterative one whereby the subjects are repeatedly asked questions that are rephrasings of their previous answers.

This study's model of how people solve problems evolved from the above-mentioned literature and the subjects' responses. Individuals were viewed as selecting some algorithm to solve the problem based on their perception of the problem and what they thought they could remember. Their algorithms were procedures such as an equation or a set of operations that they intended to go through to reach a solution. Sometimes they remembered a simple algorithm or rule of thumb that could be applied to the problem. Other times, the subjects could only think of a more complex algorithm for solving the question. Often they would begin to execute this algorithm only to find that they could not recall it in its entirety. This population typically turned to visualization techniques to get an approximation of the information that they needed to solve the problem.

These algorithms plus any assumptions that the subjects made regarding the nature of the problem or the working of the algorithms were labeled "paths." These paths correlated to the answers given. For example, in question 2 on correlation, subjects' answers were clustered along four paths (Table I). Some assumed that the correlation was large and then used algorithms based on the relationship that sample size is small so the correlation does not have to be large to be significant (path 1). Others made no initial assumption and used no algorithm other than their attempt to visualize tables to determine where the correlation would be significant (path 2). Some assumed that the correlation was small and used algorithms based on the relationship that sample size is large so the correlation must be large (path 3). Some assumed that the correlation was small and used the same algorithms as described in the first path.

3. QUESTIONNAIRE DESIGN

Five classic, text-book statistical problems were asked. The subject areas of these problems were chi-square goodness of fit, Pearson sample correlation coefficient, random numbers, central limit theorem, and analysis of variance -- multiple comparisons tests. (The questions can be found in Booker and Meyer, 1985).

TABLE I

CLUSTERING OF ANSWERS BY PATHWAY FOR QUESTION 2

	("Straight") Path 1	Path 2	Path 3	Path 4
Assumptions That the correlation is...	large	not considered	small	small
Algorithms As the sample increases, the correlation...	does not have to be large	is not considered	has to be large	does not have to be large
Answers	4 8 8 8 9	12 15 15 17 18	5 5	20 23 25 27 27 39

Two types of questions were asked to identify sources of correlation: (1) those on the experts' professional training and experience, and (2) those on how they solved the problem. The first type included questions on the subject's background such as where he went to school, where he worked, and for how long. The background questions were to provide information for matching individuals by school or work experience should education or common experience prove to be sources of correlation. To further investigate work experience as a source of correlation, three populations of the statistics group were interviewed: current members, new members, and ex-members who maintained contact.

The second type of questions were asked because of the literature on problem solving and the authors' previous experience (Meyer et al. 1981; Meyer et al. 1982). Each subject was asked to think aloud while solving the problems. To obtain the necessary information, the subject was frequently queried about his thoughts, using an ethnographic technique. The question information that the subject used in solving the problem (cues), his assumptions, and algorithms were all recorded in detail.

In addition, the subjects were asked when and where (school or work) they had last worked on a similar problem. The duration of each interview was also recorded. It was thought that the amount of time spent might relate to problem-solving style or accuracy because the more time consuming methods of problem solving have this effect (Hayes-Roth 1980). The average interview lasted 59 minutes with a standard deviation of 14.

4. ANALYSIS OF RESULTS

Sources of Interexpert Correlation

It is always difficult to reduce highly qualitative data, and this task was compounded by not knowing, in advance, which factors were sources of correlation. For this reason, factor analysis was first used to investigate the structure of the independent variables (the subjects' problem-solving paths and professional backgrounds). Many of these variables were correlated to each other, which means that they reflected similar information. The background variables (14) were trimmed using the factor loadings from a factor analysis and principles from judgment theory. The resulting set of independent variables included variables characterizing the number of years in the Statistics Group at Los Alamos National Laboratory, the number of years of statistical training, the percentage of current work involved in "text-book" types of problems, whether the respondent's degrees were in statistics, and whether the respondent was currently a member of the Statistics Group at Los Alamos.

General linear models and categorical analysis were used to investigate the relationships between the pathways and background information and the answers. The sole purpose of these analytic procedures was to produce a set of variables that highly correlated to the answers. This set would then be considered as a source of correlation.

The results of the linear models on the final set of independent variables quickly indicated that many of the pathway characteristic variables provided good sources of correlation to the answers (Table II). These pathway variables accounted for a large percentage of the total best model's variation. In question 1, the pathway variables accounted for 48% of the 78% variation, in question 2, for 60% of 68%, in question 3 (part A), for 38% of 38%, in question 4, for 73% of 78%, and in question 5, for 60% of 68%. By contrast, the background factors, the duration of the interview and the recency of experience, were not suitable for predicting the answer. At best only a few variables such as the percentage of the subject's current work on text-book problems, were ever significant and then only for one of the total questions (at a 95% level of significance).

In examining the results of the linear models, a new hypothesis was tested to attempt an explanation of why subjects chose certain pathways. The hypothesis was that aspects of subjects' profession backgrounds led them to select particular paths, and thus indirectly determined the answers. However, no supportive evidence for this hypothesis was found.

Accuracy Study

Many studies have investigated the accuracy of experts' estimates in both real and experimental situations. For example, a recent study by Martz et al. (1985) confirmed that people are unable, in experimental situations, to give accurate percentile estimates. Although the goal of the current study was not one of testing subjects' ability to give correct answers, that aspect was explored because of the strong connections between pathways and answers.

Table II

SUMMARY OF PILOT STUDY RESULTS

Variables	Emerges as a Source of Correlation*	Correlates to Accuracy
Subjects' pathways (Assumptions) (Algorithms)	6 out of 6** questions	6 out of 6 "straight" pathways
Subjects' Education Degree in Stat.	None	None
Work Experience Stat. group member	None	None
Years in Stat. group	None	None
Percentage of current work on text-book problems	1 out of 6 questions	1 out of 6 questions
Recency of Experience	1 out of 6 questions	None
Duration of Interview	1 out of 6 questions	1 out of 6 questions
Question Complexity	Not testable	6 out of 6 questions
Years in Statistics	None	1 out of 6 questions

*Significant at a 5% level (i.e., with at least a 95% chance of being a source)
**Five basic questions were asked but question 3 had two distinct parts.

More correct answers were given on questions that had been rated as simple. The questions were rated on five characteristics to gauge their simplicity: 1) familiarity of formulation, 2) availability of algorithms, 3) need for assumptions, 4) number of acceptable answers, and 5) post survey variation.

Each of the questions was rated on these five characteristics, and these ratings were summed. The more complex the question, the higher the sum. A general linear model, using the per cent of correct answers as the dependent variable and the sum of the number of complex features as the independent variable, showed that more correct answers were indeed given for the simpler questions.

Aggregation of Expert Estimates

In using expert opinion data, the analyst needs a way of combining all the expert information into a single estimate representing a central measure (e.g., mean or median) with an estimate of the dispersion or range of the values (e.g., a variance or confidence interval). Previous studies (see Martz et al. 1985) have used many elaborate estimators to combine the individual estimates. The results presented here suggest that one way of combining the expert estimates is to use the information on the solution pathways because this correlates to the answers.

If pathways correlate to particular answers, which pathways predict the acceptable answer? In all questions, the pathways that led to the acceptable answers were the paths where subjects used simple, easy to remember, rules of thumb that, when applied to the problem, produced answers that did not conflict with their intuition. These pathways were labeled "straight" pathways. The "straight" paths can be identified without knowledge of the acceptable answers. The answers from the experts following the "straight" pathways can be used to formulate central measure estimators that can better predict the acceptable answers. If the medians from "straight" pathways are used as the aggregation estimator, the correct or acceptable answer is covered in all five of the questions. If, instead, the medians from all the data are used, the correct answer is only covered in two of the five questions.

For questions 2 and 4, bootstrap sampling can be used to illustrate the coverage of the correct answers by medians because these answers are in the form of continuous variables. Bootstrap simulation and sampling procedures provide methods of obtaining confidence intervals and variance measures when the distribution of the data is unknown (Efron 1979). These methods are most helpful for small samples and for data that is fuzzy (containing uncertainties). Bootstrap distributions for the mean, median, and geometric mean for questions 2 and 4 were formed using (1) all the data, and (2) the data from subjects using the "straight" pathways. Fig. 1 illustrates the resulting distributions of the medians of question 2.

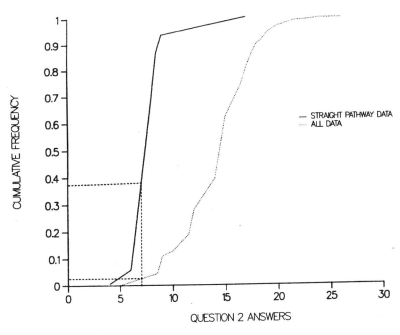

Figure 1
Bootstrap Medians For Question 2

The empirical cumulative distribution plotted in Fig. 1 represents the medians for all the data (solid curve) and for the "straight" pathway data (dashed curve). The correct answer is marked for each curve by the dashed line intercepting the appropriate percentile of the distribution. The all-data median does not cover the correct answer even with an interval covering 95% of the distribution. However, the correct answer is covered with a 95% interval when the "straight" pathway data is used.

5. CONCLUSIONS AND RECOMMENDATIONS

Experts' estimates were found to correlate to the experts' problem-solving techniques and not to any features of their professional backgrounds. The paths that experts used to reach solutions included algorithms and assumptions. Assumptions and algorithms were found to correlate to the answers because they are integral parts of the path. In addition, paths were found to relate to the accuracy of the answers. "Straight" paths, and therefore the assumptions and algorithms which composed them, led to the acceptable answers.

From these conclusions, a few recommendations can be offered in eliciting expert opinion:

1. The experts should be provided with the correct algorithm, if one is available, and with any assumptions that they should make. If these components of problem solving are provided, the experts are less likely to make errors resulting from incorrectly remembering the algorithm, trying to apply an inappropriate algorithm, or making an unacceptable assumption.
2. The experts should be requested to explain their thinking, in detail, and this information should be recorded. There are two advantages to having a record of the experts' thoughts. First it can be used to explore sources of correlation or to select the answers from the pathways that shows the fewest obvious errors. Secondly, it allows the expert's understanding to be monitored.

The next step of this research will be to verify the above-mentioned results and to examine why experts select particular pathways to solution.

ACKNOWLEDGEMENTS

Financial support for this work was provided by the Division of Risk Analysis, Office of Nuclear Regulatory Research, Nuclear Regulatory Commission. The support and cooperation provided by the individuals in the Statistics Group of Los Alamos National Laboratory is gratefully acknowledged.

REFERENCES

Ascher, W. (1978), Forecasting: An Appraisal for Policymakers and Planners, John Hopkins University Press, Baltimore, MD.

Baecher, G. B. (1979), "Correlations Among Experts' Opinions" Unpublished manuscript, Massachusetts Institution of Technology, Boston, MA.

Booker, J. M., and Meyer, M. A., "Sources and Effects of Correlation of Expert Opinion," Los Alamos National Laboratory, Los Alamos, NM., 1985, LA-UR-85-1879.

Comer, M. K., Seaver, D. A., Stillwell, W. G. and Gaddy, C. D. (1984), "Generating Human Reliability Estimates Using Expert Judgments," NUREG/CR-3688, SAND84-7115, Sandia National Laboratory, Albuquerque, NM.

Dalkey, N. C. (1975), "Toward a Theory of Group Estimation" in <u>The Delphi Method</u>, H. Linston and M. Turnoff (eds.), Addison-Wesley, Reading, MA.

Efron, B. (1979), "Bootstrap Methods: Another Look at the Jackknife," Annals of Statistics, 7 pp. 1-26.

Hayes-Roth, B. (1980), "Estimation of Time Requirements During Planning: Interactions Between Motivation and Cognition," N-1581-ONR, Rand Corporation, Santa Monica, CA.

Hogarth, R. (1980), <u>Judgment and Choice: The Psychology of Decisions</u>, Wiley-Interscience, Chicago, IL.

Janis, I. C. (1972), <u>Victims of Group Think: A Psychological Study of Foreign Policy Decisions and Fiascos</u>, Houghton Mifflin, Boston, MA.

Martz, H. F., Bryson, M. C. and Waller, R. A. (1985), "Eliciting and Aggregating Subjective Judgments - Some Experimental Results," Proceedings of the Tenth Annual SAS Users Group International Conference SAS Institute Inc., Cary, NC.

Matz, M. (1982), "Towards a Process Model for High School Algebra Errors" in <u>Intelligent Tutoring Systems</u>, D. Sleeman and J. S. Brown (eds.), Academic Press, New York, NY.

Meyer, M. A., Booker, J. M., Cullingford, H. C. and Peaslee, A. T., Jr., (1981), "A Data-Gathering Method for Use in Modeling Energy Research, Development and Demonstration Programs," in <u>Energy Programs, Policy and Economics: Alternative Energy Sources IV</u>, 8, pp. 421-430, Ann Arbor Science, Ann Arbor, MI.

Meyer, M. A., Peaslee, A. T., Jr., and Booker, J. M. (1982), "Group Consensus Method and Results," LA-9584-MS, Los Alamos National Laboratory, Los Alamos, NM.

Seaver, P. A. (1976), "Assessments of Group Preferences and Group Uncertainty for Decision Making," Social Science Research Institute, University of Southern California, Los Angeles, CA.

Tversky, A., and Kahneman, D. (1981), "Framing of Decisions and the Psychology of Choice," Science, 211, pp. 453-458.

Winkler, R. L. (1981), "Combining Probability Distributions from Dependent Information Sources," Management Science, 27, pp. 987-997.

WHY GOOD RISK ANALYSTS HAVE TROUBLE WITH PUBLIC COMMUNICATIONS-

A QUANTITATIVE ANALYSIS

Raymond Johnson* and W. Larry Petcovic**

Communication Sciences Institute*

Advanced Communication Techniques**

ABSTRACT

Effective risk management requires effective communications. the communication strengths and limitatiols of over 300 health risk analysts, in the radiation protection profession, have been analyzed by the Myers-Briggs Type Indicator. This indicator measures the magnitude of our preferences for gathering data by SENSING(S) or INTUITION(N), for making decisions by THINKING(T) or FEELING(F), for how we relate to others by JUDGING(J) or PERCEIVING(P), and for how we get our energy by EXTRAVERSION(E) or INTROVERSION(I). Profiles for these risk analysts show a strong preference to INTJ. They tend to be self confident, decision makers, practical, orderly, logical, outstanding in research and as executives, hard workers, high achievers, organizers, and pragmatic strategists. On the other hand, they can also be very independent and single minded. They may ignore the views of others and may appear unemotional, cold, demanding, critical, reserved, and determined. They may neglect social rituals and may not like to waste time in idle dialogue or play. This paper will analyze how an awareness of Myers-Briggs Type can be used to develop effective approachs to communication and risk management.

KEY WORDS: public communications, communication style, Myers-Briggs Type Indicator (MBTI), radiation, radiation protection, risk management, and risk analysts.

INTRODUCTION

Since the beginning of the nuclear age, the radiation protection profession has experienced difficulties in communicating about radiation issues. During emergencies these communication problems are compounded as an anxious public seeks assurance of their safety. At such times, most radiation protection professionals would rather avoid communications that may involve confronting other peoples' anxieties, especially when they perceive the public's fears as technically unfounded and irrational. Unfortunately, while our ability improves for estimating potential health risks from radiation, our ability to communicate what we know is not keeping up with the technology.

What we have tried over the years to improve our communications has largely been a matter of simplifying and clarifying radiation concepts and

using analogies with other sources of health risks. This approach is
mainly a one way communication of information from radiation experts to
hopefully achieve understanding by the public. While this transfer of
technical data is necessary and helpful, and may result in some level of
technical understanding, it is not a sufficient basis for public
decisions. The public also makes decisions on the basis of feelings and
perceptions of health risks that go beyond technical understanding.

This is about the point where most radiation prodessionals back away,
except for a few who seem to have a natural talent for communication
(often honed by hard trial and error experience) and a few who are still
striving to develop more effective approaches. Several health physicists
in the latter category, form the Baltimore-Washington Chapter of the
Health Physics Society, began a study in 1983 of communication needs in
radiation protection. This study originated as a project of the Public
Information Committee, chaired by the first author, and is still ongoing
as a project of the Communication Sciences Institute. Out of this study
have come a series of three day workshops to provide radiation
professionals with practical communication skills to meet their needs.
These workshops are now built around a concept of communications called
the Johnson - Petcovic Synchronized Communication Model. This paper will
consider the first two elements of this Model; namely understanding
ourselves and understanding our audience, as a source of insight into why
radiation professionals have trouble communicating especially during
emergencies.

Myers-Briggs Type Indicator

A powerful tool for understanding ourselves and our communication
style is the Myers-Briggs Type Indicator (MBTI). This is a 166 question,
multiple-choice, test based on concepts defined in the 1920's by a Swiss
psychologist, Carl Jung (Ju23). The MBTI was developed in the 1940's as a
practical means of measuring Jung's concepts of psychological type by two
Americans, Isabel Myers and her mother, Katharine (My62). The MBTI is now
a widely used instrument for management and organizational development,
team building, and communication training (My80).

The MBTI measures the strength of our natural preferences in four
areas:
1) Where we get our energy - by EXTRAVERSION (E), from interacting with
people, activities, and things; or by INTROVERSION (I), from inner
reflection, ideas, and private time.

2) How we gather information - by SENSING (S), using our 5 senses for
specific, detailed, factual, concrete data; or by INTUITION (N), seeing
patterns, relations, possibilities, and the big picture.

3) How we make decisions - by THINKING (T), using logical analysis, laws,
consistency, and objective criteria for what is true; or by FEELING (F),
using personal values, other's concerns, harmony, compassion, and
sentiments for what is good.

4) How we relate to the world - by JUDGING (J), striving for conclusions,
planning, and scheduling to reach closure; or by PERCEIVING (P), enlarging

our awareness, keeping options open, being spontaneous, open ended, and resisting closure.

Since January 1985, the first author has administered the test to 307 professionals in radiation protection; including health physicists, scientists, nuclear engineers, lawyers, physicians, educators, managers, technicians, and public information specialists involved in communicating with the public, radiation workers, and coworkers about radiation issues.

The measured preferences of this group are as follows:

Category	PERCENT PREFERENCE Rad. Prof.	Public
E	37	75
I	63	25
S	42	75
N	58	25
T	77	50
F	23	50
J	66	50
P	34	50

These results show that the overall preference of radiation professionals is for I, N, T, and J. This particular combination of preferences is one of 16 possible combinations of Myers-Briggs Type and represents only one percent of the average population. The INTJ preference is typical for scientists. As INTROVERTS, they are not people oriented and are less likely than EXTRAVERTS to be communicators. As INTUITIVES, they are comfortable in the world of abstract concepts and theories. As THINKERS, they prefer to make decisions on the basis of logical, rational, analysis, and as JUDGING types they prefer to lead systematic, orderly lives, and make schedules and plans to reach closure on all issues.

INTJ's tend to be self confident, independent, pragmatic, loyal to their organizations, skeptical, critical, determined, single-minded, and stubborn. They are original thinkers, builders of systems, appliers of theoretical models, and natural brainstormers open to new concepts. They are strategists with a concern for consequences, efficiency, and completion. They are organizers, hard workers, and high achievers, who are stimulated by difficulties. They look for coherence and consistency, are capable of great drive, and they are outstanding in research and as executives.

The distribution of preferences for the radiation protection profession is shown as percentages in the following Myers-Briggs Type Table. The numbers in the left corner of each block are percentages for the average population. This table is based upon 307 MBTI profiles, including 55 women.

Myers-Briggs type Table - %

ISTJ		ISFJ		INFJ		INTJ	
21		2		4		17	
6		6		1		1	
ISTP		ISFP		INFP		INTP	
5		2		5		7	
6		6		1		1	
ESTP		ESFP		ENFP		ENTP	
1		1		5		8	
13		13		5		5	
ESTJ		ESFJ		ENFJ		ENTJ	
9		1		3		9	
13		13		5		5	

     This Table shows that 6 types (ISTJ, INTJ, INTP, ENTP, ESTJ, and
ENTJ) make up 71 percent of the radiation protection profession. In
contrast,}5 other categories that make up 51 percent of the public (ISFJ,
ISFP, ESTP, ESFP, and ESFJ) include only 7 percent of the radiation
profession. These data show that professionals in radiation protection
tend to have preferences that are quite different from the average
population. These preferences are the basis for each person's choice of
profession (or job function) and also are the source of difficulties in
communication, particularly with those whose preferences are different.
Without an MBTI understanding of differences in attitudes, beliefs,
values, data gathering, and decision making, our preferences tend to be
seen as wrong by persons with opposite preferences. Such perceptions of
wrongness are the reason for most conflicts and breakdowns in
communication on our jobs and in our homes.

     Concern for such perceptions was the basis for Isabel Myers' 50 -
year effort to develop and apply the MBTI. In 1980 she published "Gifts
Differing" (MY80) to show how our natural preferences represent gifts and
strengths that may be used to complement the gifts and strengths of
others. She wanted us to appreciate our special gifts and those of others
as a source of understanding to reduce friction and to improve
communication among all types of people. (See the Health Physics Society
Newsletter for a discussion of the special gifts of radiation
professionals (Jo85a)).

Temperament Types

Another way to appreciate the uniqueness of·radiation professionals is to look at the four 2-letter combinations of preferences called TEMPERAMENTS (Ke78). Our temperament is determined by our special combination of preferences that dominate or modify everything we do in ways that are as recognizably ours as our signature. Our temperament is that inner motivation that guides our lives to repetitively seek a uniform style of living that we must satisfy regularly in the same way that we have to satisfy hunger. The table below shows the four temperament groups.

PERCENTAGES

TEMPERAMENTS	Rad. Prof.	Public
NT	41	12
SJ	33	38
NF	17	12
SP	9	38

The primary temperament for the radiation profession is NT (41%) which represents only 12 percent of the average population. The quest for NTs is for competence, and their style is visionary. They are powerful conceptualizers and responsive to new ideas. They hunger for knowledge and are challenged by riddles. They want to understand concepts and may learn by arguing. They are authority counterdependent, i.e. they push against the rules and authority. Their Achilles' heel is incompetency - they cannot stand incompetency in others (or themselves). To NTs everything needs testing for competency and NTs determine the criteria. They tend to be critical of others and themselves about "not measuring up." NTs also tend to be game players and can miss what is immediately important. They like the complex and theoretical and may not be inclined to give simple answers. They can appear impersonal and aloof and may not express appreciation. They like to start more than to finish projects. (See Jo85b for more details on the other temperaments).

NTs may have difficult in communicating with other temperaments (88 percent of the public) when they think of them as incompetent, overly sensitive, illogical, to structured, or unthinking. NTs especially tend to argue with SJs. They can be impatient with others whose future vision, imagination, or grasp of complex subjects is less than theirs.

Preferred Style

Everyone has a primary communication style that they prefer to use. The preferred style will either be based upon one of the functions for gathering data (SENSING or INTUITION) or upon one of the functions for decision making (THINKING or FEELING). Because we repeatedly use our favorite function in communication, that function will likely be much better developed than the other three functions. Therefore, we will be most skillful and most comfortable using our preferred style and this style will be the "wavelength" for our best communication. Two people will communicate with the greatest probability of success when they are both on the same "wavelength."

The communication problems that most of us face can be attributed to relying solely upon our preferred style even when it is different from that of the person with whom we wish to communicate. Since most people do not know of their own style or that of others, they naturally go with their own primary preference and hope for the best. However, the chances are small that any two people at random will have the same primary communication style, as we will see below.

The MBTI provides a quantitative measure of our preferred first, second, third, and fourth approaches for communicating with others as shown in the following table.

COMMUNICATION STYLE PREFERENCES

% Rad. Prof. / % Public

	1st	2nd	3rd	4th
T	56 / 25	21 / 25	12 / 15	11 / 25
N	25 / 12	33 / 12	17 / 38	25 / 38
F	10 / 25	13 / 25	47 / 25	30 / 25
S	9 / 38	33 / 38	24 / 12	34 / 12

The preferred communication style of the radiation protection profession (56 percent) is the logical, rational, analytical THINKING approach. This approach is not the first preference for 75 percent of the public. If the radiation experts turn to their next highest preference for primary style (25 percent for INTUITION), that approach will miss 88 percent of the public who prefer not to communicate on that "wavelength." Most of the public prefer SENSING (76 percent) as their first and second approach to communication. This approach is the first preference for only 9 percent of the radiation profession. (For more details on how to determine your primary style see Johnson (Jo85c) and Yeakley (Ye82).

Least Preferred Style

While it may be helpful to know that our communication strengths come from our primary style, it is also helpful to realize that our greatest weakness involves our fourth or least preferred communication style. Our least preferred style uses our least developed and least controlled function. For the radiation protection profession, FEELING and SENSING are the least preferred functions (see the style chart above). For these people, these two functions will often be expressed in ways that are immature, infantile, unadapted, and "inferior" according to von Franz (vo71).

Our communication problems arise when someone attempts to communicate with us on our least preferred wavelength. This may very well happen during radiation emergencies when someone approaches us on a FEELING or emotional basis seeking sensory (SENSING) data to relieve their anxieties. They are then asking us to function in our most uncomfortable domain. Our inferior functions are also slow. For example, if you ask a THINKING type what they are feeling, they will usually have no idea and may take a long time to get in touch with their feelings or any one elses. In contrast, the primary THINKING style comes spontaneously and is immediately available for response.

We will feel threatened and vulnerable when someone addresses our "inferior" function. We will become touchy and defensive in that area. For example, INTUITIVES may find themselves exasperated when their health risk assessments are challenged by SENSING demands for more concrete, factual, tangible, and detailed data, especially when the data are scarce or uncertain. In such cases, the INTUITIVE wants to say, "Take my word, I am the expert, believe me." But, that is not enough for SENSING types and the INTUITIVES find their credibility and competence in question.

The inferior function also comes out unbidden during crises or times of stress and may inject any number of dark possibilities. For example, a normally down-to-earth, realistic, SENSING type may suddenly start worrying about all kinds of imagined consequences of radiation exposures. This is typical of negative inferior INTUITION. The SENSING type's perception of health risks than becomes clouded by the invasion of the inferior INTUITION's fearful visions. Persecution ideas creep in and he begins to get sinister premonitions of illnesses or other misfortunes that may befall him.

Primary INTUITIVES will also have trouble in areas involving their inferior SENSING function. For example, INTUITIVES may exceed their reasonable limits both psychically and physically because they are not tuned in to the needs of their body. They are also inclined to suffer great vagueness where facts are concerned. INTUITIVES are prone to pass over an amazing number of facts and just not take them in. And then, when suddenly confronted by facts in an emergency, they may make completely erroneous deductions.

The primary THINKING types tend to spend their whole lives settling problems, organizing projects, and stating things in clear logic, and only late in life do they ask themselves what they have lived for and then get in touch with their inferior FEELING function. The unconscious and undeveloped FEELING of these types may also come out under stress in barbaric or fanatic outbursts that overwhelm the person. All sudden conversions have this quality (vo71). The inferior FEELING makes black and white judgments, love or hate, is easily misled by others, and makes judgments on values rather than facts.

Primary FEELING types will dislike having to use their inferior THINKING function, especially if asked to think about philosophical principles or abstract concepts. Because THINKING is neglected, it tends to come out as primitive thinking judgments with cynical negative qualities. In a crisis, a normally friendly FEELING type can suddenly become a block of ice. Dark thoughts of illness, death, and tragedy spring to mind like a momentary cold draft. Little wonder that such types may want to avoid taking time to think, and may adopt other people's THINKING judgments without checking out the basis for themselves. Their inferior THINKING is easily overwhelmed with too much detail or too many facts. So they latch on to one or two thoughts and race ahead imposing these thoughts on the facts.

People are easily influenced in the area of their inferior functions and are prone to make mistakes in these areas. In contrast to their primary function where they feel strong, broadminded, and flexible, in their inferior area they get fanatical and touchy, and tend to make sudden emotional responses, particularly when under stress, without knowing why. Propaganda can make use of the people's ordinary suspicions against others arising out of the inferior function. Thus, primary SENSING-FEELING types may be easily influenced to doubt the intuitive intellectual types representing government bureaucracy or private industry during emergencies. Radiation experts using their primary INTUITIVE-THINKING style may be readily perceived as insensitive and trying to cover up the facts.

Those who oppose nuclear technology know the value of emotional appeals to the inferior function. They know better than to argue with radiation professionals in their INTUITIVE-THINKING domains where they are strongest. Instead, they argue in the SENSING-FEELING domains where these professionals tend to be weakest. This is primarily why radiation professionals are so continuously frustrated by the antinuclear movement (and probably vice versus).

To be Effective

To improve your odds for successful communication about health risks, you will do best to use the preferred communication style of your audience. You may have to adjust your own style for this purpose. If your listener prefers INTUITION, then talk with them in terms of patterns, the "big picture," connections, future possibilities, imagination, innovation, creativity, hunches, various implications, and meanings. If they prefer FEELING, then talk in terms of personal values, people, sentiments, motives, caring, harmony, affirmation, appreciation, compassion, trusting, and conclusions about what is good. When your listener prefers SENSING, talk in terms of specifics available to the five senses, practical/factual details, the present moment, what is realistic, measurable, grounded, literal, and what makes sense. If you are talking with a THINKING type, then use your best logical, rational, analytical approach to present an objective, impersonal argument based on law and evidence to draw conclusions on what is true.

If you do not know you MBTI type or that of the other person, then review the characteristics of each style preference above for clues. When you have no data on your audience, remember that 75 percent of the public are SENSING types. So the SENSING approach may be a good one to start with. If they are in a people oriented job, then try a FEELING approach first. if they are in the radiation protection field, then use your THINKING style first. Most people will give you clues on how they "think" or "feel" so you can adjust accordingly. In any case, be prepared to shift gears if your first approach is not working. Keep in mind that although our INTUITION and THINKING preferences are most important for doing well in our jobs for determining radiation health risks, these preferences may not be our best approach for communicating what we know about health risks to the general public.

REFERENCES

Jo85a   Johnson, R. and L. Petcovic, 1985, "Your special Gifts," The Health Physics Society Newsletter, August 1985, pp. 9-12.
Jo85b   Johnson, R. and L. Petcovic, 1985, "Health Physicist's Temperaments," The Health Physics Society Newsletter, September 1985, pp. 13-14.
Jo85c   Johnson, R. and L. Petcovic, 1985, "When In Rome," The Health Physics Society Newsletter, October 1985, pp. 14-16.
Ju23   Jung, C. G., 1923, "Psychological Types," (New York: Harcourt Brace Publishers).
Ke78   Keirsey, D. and M. Bates, 1978, "Please Understand Me - Character and Temperament Types," (Del Mar, California: Prometheus Nemesis Books).
My62   Myers, I. B., 1962, "The Myers-Briggs Type Indicator," (Palo Alto, California: Consulting Psychologists Press).

My80   Myers, I. B. and P. B. Myers, 1980, "Gifts Differing," (Palo Alto, California: Consulting Psychologists Press).

vo71   von Franz, M. and J. Hillman, 1971, "Jung's Typology," (Dallas, Texas: Spring Publications, Inc.).

Ye82   Yeakley, F. R., 1982, "Communication Style Preferences and Adjustments as an Approach to Studying Effects of Similarity in Psychological Type," Research in Psychological Type, 5, p. 30-48.

TIME BUDGET ANALYSIS AND RISK MANAGEMENT: ESTIMATING THE

PROBABILITIES OF THE EVENT SCHEDULES OF AMERICAN ADULTS[1]

Norman P. Hummon, Linda Mauro and George O. Rogers

Department of Sociology and University Center for Social
and Urban Research
University of Pittsburgh

ABSTRACT

   Comprehensive risk management must account both for the exposure and
consequences of risks. Time budget analysis focuses on the activities and
location of people, which are directly related to potential exposure, and
consequences of risk. The analysis of the distribution of daily activities
allows risk analysts to adjust exposure likelihoods for the changing
population distribution over the course of a 24 hour period. In addition,
time budget analysis allows the risk analyst to account for shifts in
potential consequences associated with location of people at various times
of the day. This paper examines three significant aspects of time budget
analysis and risk management. First, the direct exposure rates to ongoing
hazards as a function of the amount of time spent at risk (e.g. in an
automobile, or airplane, or outdoors in a neighborhood adjacent to an
uncontrolled hazardous materials site). Second, the effect on the
likelihood of exposure to and severity of consequences for relatively
sudden events (e.g. toxic chemical spills, radioactive leaks, other
airborne risks transmitted via the plume-exposure pathway, tornadoes,
earthquakes and flash floods). Finally, the effect on risk management
through effective emergency management is directly related to location and
activity of people at various times of the day (e.g. likelihood of warning
receipt, probable evacuation flow dynamics, and likelihood of inadvertent
adaptive location).

KEY WORDS: Time Budget, Risk Management, Exposure, Consequences,
Emergency Management

----

   [1] This research was partially supported by The Federal
Emergency Management Agency (Cooperative Agreement No. EMW-K-
1024). This report has not been reviewed by FEMA and in no way
reflects the view and policies of the Agency. The authors accept
full responsibility for the contents herein and gratefully
acknowledge the support, comments and criticisms offered by
colleagues at the University of Pittsburgh and the Annual Meeting
of the Society for Risk Analysis.

INTRODUCTION

Risk management is concerned with the problem of describing the relation between a risk generating phenomenon and a human population. The characterization of this relation is particularly useful when it accounts for both space and time. Examples of temporally and spacially distributed hazards abound: Dangerous weather systems impact specific geographic locations during particular seasons of the year and times of the day. Nuclear power plants reside at specific locations, and power lines follow identifiable routes. This relation between a risk generating phenomenon and a human population can be conceptualized as several stochastic processes (Rowe 1977, Lowrance 1976, Shrader-Frechette 1985). One is concerned with the likelihood of a risk generating event, (eg. the likelihood of a tree falling in the forest). Another concerns whether, given such an event, it would impact the human population (eg. given that a tree falls, the likelihood that it would hit someone). And finally given the event and the impact, what is the distribution of consequences. This paper concerns the second set of probabilities and their estimation.

The approach used to estimate these probabilities is based on a simple idea; probabilities can be estimated from data on how and where people spend their time. For example, the probability of whether a person will be at home at 6:15 PM can be estimated from the time and activity logs that comprise the foundation of time use research. In fact, time budget analysis allows the risk analyst to describe the activity profile for the entire day in terms of the best point and interval probability estimates for an incredibly detailed range of activities. This paper highlights the use of time budget data in risk management.

Three Types of Uses are Highlighted:

1. Estimating direct exposure and dose rates due to ongoing hazards (eg. being outdoors in neighborhood adjacent to an uncontrolled hazardous materials site, being indoors subjected to "indoor pollution," or outdoors exposed to ultraviolet rays of the sun with its possibility of skin cancer).

2. Estimating exposure, dose and potential severity of relatively sudden hazardous events (eg. being located in an area subjected to a toxic chemical spill, being indoors when an earthquake or tornado occurs, being outdoors during a radiation leak at a nearby facility).

3. Estimating the likelihood of effective emergency management in terms of emergency planning and the dissemination of warning, potential for (other inadvertent) adaptive/maladaptive locations, and potential for adaptive response.

Time Budget Surveys

In 1975, the Survey Research Center at the University of Michigan administered a time budget survey to a national probability sample of U.S. households (Robinson 1977). The same households participated in a second panel of the same survey in 1981 (Juster et al, 1983). In the 1975 survey, 1519 households were surveyed, which included 1519 respondents and 887 spouses. In 1981, attrition in the panel reduced the sample sizes to 620 households, with 620 respondents, and 376 spouses. The 1981 survey added the time budgets of children in the households.

A comparison of 1975 with 1981 results indicates that the attrition in sample sizes caused little, if any, bias in the results. Controlling for demographic variables indicates that the time budgets of U.S. households were amazingly stable over this period of time. The results in this study are from an analysis of the 1981 panel data.

For both the 1975 and 1981 surveys, four waves were administered, one during each season of the year. For each wave, respondents and spouses were asked to construct a one day (24 hour) log of his or her activities. The log describes the set of all activities the person engaged in during the previous day. Over the four waves of each survey, respondents reported on their activities for two weekdays, and two week end days. The 1975 survey contains 7207 person-days of data and the 1981 contains 3350 adult-days and 881 children-days.

Most of the published reports of these University of Michigan data are based on an aggregated "synthetic week" (Stafford and Duncan 1978 and 1980, Stafford 1980). The two weekdays and two weekend days are combined and weighted to estimate how Americans spend time over an annual average week. For many types of studies, such data are well suited. However, for risk analysis, the synthetic week approach does not provide enough detail about the daily schedules of people. Therefore, this analysis developed a different data structure better suited to risk analysis.

The Period-Activity Data Structure

The raw time log records contain, in part, the following items: respondent identification number, day of week, month, date of interview, activity code (ie., a typology of 233 detailed activities), time activity began, time activity ended, secondary activity code, and elapsed time for activity. Typically, about 30 records describe the activities for a respondent for each day. These raw data are processed in two ways to form a period-activity data structure.

The Michigan time budget activity codes cover 233 detailed activity types. The detail is illustrated in terms of a few examples. Activities in the home, such as meal preparation, are coded in terms of several categories, including meal preparation -- cooking, meal preparation -- clean-up, and meal preparation -- other. Travel activities are comprised of travel to and from work, in search of employment, to and from shopping and to and from day care facilities, to name but a few. Both primary activities, those dominating a particular period, and secondary activity, those being conducted in the background while other activities are undoubtedly conducted, use these detailed activity codes.[2] To use these time budget data in risk management, these detailed data are collapsed from 233 activity codes to 11 broader categories reflecting some major risk management situations. Specific risk applications are best treated in terms of their unique exposure-dose-consequence profiles and their associated time budget implications. The collapsed activity codes are: 1) at home--asleep, 2) at home--active, 3) at work, 4) watching TV, 5) listening to the radio, 6) at neighbor's home, 7) not home--indoors, 8) shopping for goods and services, 9) at home--outdoors, 10) not at home--outdoors, 11) in transit.

---

2. A secondary activity is one that is engaged in at the same time as a primary activity. An example is listening to the radio (secondary) while eating dinner (primary).

These eleven categories[3] describe the kinds of places where people conduct their daily activities. They maintain the distinction of being home or away from home, being indoors or outdoors, and being active or asleep. Also, these broader categories of the daily activities are a mutually exclusive and exhaustive re-categorization of the 233 detailed codes. Interest concerning specific risks may not entail exhaustive categories, but for our purposes this seems most appropriate. Finally, because sleep time is both such a dominant activity in a person's time budget, and because it is a primary consideration risk management, it is maintained as a separate activity.

The second part of the raw record processing involves aggregating time spent in individual activities into composite activity time in the 11 categories during a period of the 24 hour day. Twelve two hour periods were used for this aggregation. Thus for each respondent in each wave, a data record was computed that described the number of minutes spent in the 11 category codes during each of 12 periods of the day. This means period-activity record contains 132 time use variables, plus other variables describing the day, the respondent, and household characteristics.

Analysis of the Period Activity Data

The most dominant feature of the average annual time budget is being at home asleep. Comprising 34.8 percent of an individual's total daily time on average, being home asleep is heavily concentrated in the midnight to 6am period, secondarily in the 6am to 8am and 10pm to 12 midnight periods. For the five two-hour periods beginning at 10pm, the average amount of time spent sleeping at home in each two-hour period is 50.3, 88.1, 94.4, 90.8 and 52.7 percent respectively. This seems to reflect a daily pattern of the typical household. In fact it is what one might expect, but the implication for risk management rests in the amount and sequence of the sleep activity.

The second most dominant feature of the annual time use budget is the time being active in the home. This primary activity comprises 23.9 percent of the typical day. Together, in-home active and asleep categories account for 58.8 percent of the total daily activity of adult Americans. The third most dominant daily activity is work. Working comprises another 11.1 percent of the average total time budget. Concentrated during daylight hours (ie. 8am to 5pm), at its peak periods work comprises 25.8 percent of the period between 10am and 12 noon. Taken jointly these three primary activities comprise 69.9 percent of an average person's daily routine. Figure 1 presents the annual average time use budget for all eleven primary activities.

---

[3]. For some analyses, codes 6, 7, and 8 were combined into a more general not home, indoors, category.

While the remaining categories, taken jointly comprise 30.1 percent
of the total time budget, separately none of the remaining categories
account for more than 10 percent of a typical person's total time.
Watching television accounts for the majority of the remaining time, at
8.1 percent. Compressed primarily within the 8pm to 10pm period, and
secondarily within the two-hour period before and after prime-time
viewing, watching TV is the forth most dominant daily activity.
Considering almost all TV viewing is conducted in the home, all activities
in the home comprise 66.9 percent of the daily budget. Adding the amount
of activity conducted outdoors at home and in neighbor's home, 72.7
percent of the daily activity takes place in the residential
neighborhood. This underscores the use of residential population data as
the foundation for risk management issues concerning exposure, severity,
consequences, and emergency mitigation. However, the more detailed time
budget analysis builds more precise daily location/activity into the
exposure/consequence quantification.

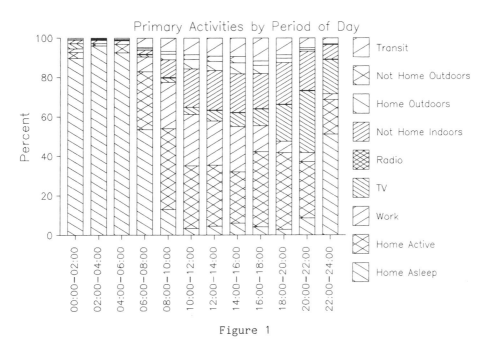

Figure 1

Annual Average Time Use Budget

Electronic media, including radio and television exposure, account
for slightly more of the daily activity, however, when secondary media
exposure is considered. The media "window" expands from 8.3 to 12.7
percent of the average daily time. This analysis suggests that nearly
13.0 percent of the average daily activity is exposed, either through
primary or secondary activity to the electronic media of TV or radio.
Figure 2 highlights the media exposure window which is critical in
connection with emergency warning--alerting and notification. As a
primary activity, radio provides very little warning potential, the
maximum exposure as a primary activity is during the 6am to 8am period,
and is only 0.3 percent. As a secondary activity, radio provides about a
4 percent exposure across the working hours of the day, with a peak of 4.8
percent in the 8 a.m. to 10 a.m. period. Radio listing falls off in the
evening, when television, as a primary activity predominates. TV offers
an 8.1 percent coverage as a primary activity, which increases to 10
percent when taken as a primary and secondary activity. During Day-light
hours (ie. 8 a.m. to 6 p.m.) TV accounts for 2.4 percent of the primary
activity. However, it provides 5.9 percent coverage during the same
period as a primary and secondary activity.

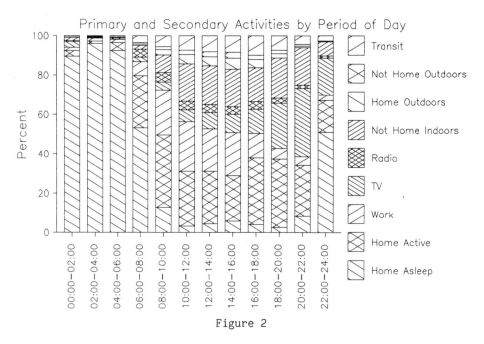

Figure 2

Annual Average Time Use Budget

Activity conducted away from home indoors accounts for 11.4 percent
of the typical day. This activity is comprised of 3.7 percent in
neighbor's home, 3.5 percent shopping and 4.2 percent in other indoor
locations away from home. While shopping seems to be concentrated in the
early afternoon periods, other indoor activities away from home seem to
increase through the day-light hours, tapering off after 10pm.

Transportation activities comprise 5.6 percent of the average
individual's day. Being in transit is concentrated in the day-light

hours, steadily increasing from 6am, and reaching its maximum during the evening rush hour. Furthermore 15.4 percent of the time in transit is exposed to the electronic media, presumably the radio.

Low-level Ongoing Hazards

The use of time in specific places, within specific areas, undertaking particular activities is directly related to exposure to ongoing hazards. Because the average adult American spends so much time at home, the exposure within the home is fundamentally important. The World Health Organization task force suggested guidelines to control only a handful of the more common indoor pollutants. The suggested standards covered, formaldehyde, asbestos, carbon monoxide, carbon dioxide, nitrogen dioxide, and sulfur dioxide (Johnson 1983). Radon in homes accumulates from underground sources hidden from the occupants (Nero 1985), but arsenic is usually airborne (Albert 1985, Patrick and Peters 1985, Baird et al 1985). While the situation is often difficult in work environments, it is often no better at home (cf. Johnson, 1983, Raloff 1985, Hicks 1984). Often the detection of indoor pollution, which is frequently made worse by weather tight buildings, known as the "tight building syndrome," is complicated by relatively poor detection systems (Michaels 1984).

Working outdoors also has its problems. Construction and maintenance crews, farmers and ranchers and year-round workers in the frozen food industry must be concerned about the amount of time spent in the cold (Polakoff 1982). Exposure to ongoing hazards in individual settings may be estimated on the basis of time budget data. For example, an estimated 500,000 U.S. homes contain urea formaldehyde of varying concentrations (Johnson 1983). When divided by the 82.4 million households in the U. S. this represents a crude exposure rate of $6.07 * 10^{-2}$. But refining this estimate by the 66.9 percent of the time spent in the home yields an estimated exposure rate of $4.06 * 10^{-2}$. If we are only concerned with sleep or bedroom exposure, we might estimate the probability of exposure as a function of proportion of households and proportion of time at home asleep, yielding and exposure rate of $2.11 * 10^{-2}$. We can also be less concerned if we find a linkage between day light hours, and in-home pollutants (e.g., should we find that solar heat releases some noxious gas into the home). Because 44.6 percent of the period between 8am and 4pm being spent in the home, the refined exposure rate is $2.83 * 10^{-2}$. Furthermore such gas can dissipate prior to the concentrated exposure associated with evening and night-time occupation. The relatively basic time budget analysis presented here demonstrates the potential exposure as serious. It also flags the importance of within household variations in concentrations of ongoing hazards. Certainly airborne toxin with respiratory exposure pathways are particularly harmful indoors where the most time is spent. The percent of time by period of the day and eleven activities is presented in Table 1.

In Silva et al (1985), an activity systems model is developed to estimate potential exposure related to 60hz electrical fields adjacent to long-distance high voltage power lines. Using time budget data, the model simulates the activities of farmers and others who engage in outdoor activities near high voltage power lines. By combining the electrical properties of the transmission line with the activity data, estimates of annual kilovolts/meter-hour are generated.

Sudden Impact Hazards and Emergency Management

Exposure rates for more sudden hazards may also be estimated as a function of the time-space distribution available in time use data. The consequences of sudden impact hazards such as earthquakes, tornados, flash floods and toxic chemical spills are directly related to how we use our time. For example, mid-day earthquakes are likely to have more human consequences in large cities than night-time or weekend events of similar size. This results from the daily migration of the workforce in communities to and from work locations. Tornadoes, floods other hazards impacting residential areas during night-time or weekend hours will threaten many more people than the same hazard during work-day periods. The risk of shipping toxic chemicals through some areas may be reduced by scheduling such activities to take advantage of time use information -- the associated catastrophic potential may be reduced.

The distribution of human populations may be estimated on the basis of time use data. Emergency planners may begin to anticipate the kinds of problems presented by emergencies occurring at different times of the day, and days of the week. Time budget analysis shows that the often dreaded night time disaster may prove less ominous than anticipated. While darkness no doubt hampers mitigation efforts, households are most likely to be together at home during these periods. In as much as households prefer to take emergency mitigation actions together, (Rogers and Nehnevajsa 1984, Mileti et al. 1975), the family unit is already united and can concentrate directly on adaptive emergency response.

In addition to the relative advantage of inadvertently being in a comparatively safe location during the impact of a sudden impact hazard, emergency management is enhanced by a thorough understanding of the time budget implications for dissemination of the warning message, notification of appropriate emergency activity, and the likelihood of adaptive mitigative action. The window provided by the electronic media is directly related to an emergency manager's ability to disseminate emergency warning to potentially impacted communities. The relatively limited media window during the day-light and dead-of-night hours underscores the need for alerting systems to get people "tuned in" to their radios and televisions. Planning for the late-night dissemination of warning is greatly enhanced through the probabilistic modelling of the processes and an appreciation of the proportion of the population awake during the affected periods. A detailed analysis of the contagion of the warning in the dead-of-night hours based on the proportion of the population awake, the likelihood of arousal among those sleeping, the likely dissemination of warning within households, the likelihood of inter-household contact, household size, and age distribution has been developed to provide emergency management insight for nuclear power plant emergency plans (Nehnevajsa 1985).

CONCLUSIONS

This paper has highlighted a few uses of time budget data and analysis for risk management. The more global categories of activity used here were designed to demonstrate the overall usefulness of the time budget approach to risk management. Three important aspects of risk management are highlighted; 1) the estimation of exposure to ongoing hazards, 2) estimating the probability of exposure to the catastrophic potential of more sudden hazards, and 3) examining emergency management implications of population distribution throughout the day.

While the rich data base provided by the time budget approach has been aptly demonstrated, the depth of the risk management potential has been but touched upon. Specific risk potentials will require detailed analysis of particular activities, the distribution among people, geographic location, day of the week, season of the year and time of day. Time budget data provide such richness and depth in part because they reflect action; not merely attitudes bearing on acceptability, but action reflecting varying degrees of acceptability. Perhaps in this vein time budget data may be used to provide foundation for public perception of risk and its associated acceptability. In any event, daily exposure to hazards of various kinds may be appropriately traced through time budget data. Through careful examination of daily time budgets, legislators, regulators, and risk managers may better focus: a) attention on hazards with the most significant exposure-consequence implications, b) appropriate and effective standards may replace blanket assumptions of safety, c) risk mangers may focus limited resources on issues of great catastrophic potential, and d) emergency managers may better prepare for the most likely event-exposure-consequence chains, by taking advantage of likely daily activities in specific locations. For it is through these actions that risk managers can earn the public's confidence and trust, so much a part of effective risk management.

We have taken a positive view about the potential usefulness of time budget data and analysis for risk management applications; however, some caveats are required. Most of the applications we have discussed have not been tried in practice. Hence, only a few risk assessments have been based on time budget analyses, to our knowledge, and these have been covered herein. Most of what we have presented remains untried, and therefore must be subjected to the validation of real applications. While our analysis suggests that the time budgets of adult Americans are very similar across demographic groups, seasons of the year, and other variables, it is certainly possible that subpopulations may exhibit quite distinct time budgets, and are too infrequently represented in the Michigan data base to influence the overall results, or to be analyzed as a separate group[4]. For example, the time budgets of farmers are somewhat different from other working subpopulations, because farmers work longer hours than most other Americans (Silva et al 1985). In summary, we believe our suggestions will prove to be a valued contribution to risk management, while understanding that much more needs to be done.

REFERENCES

Albert, R., "Health Risks Associated with Arsenic Exposure," Paper presented at the 1985 Annual Meeting of the Society for Risk Analysis, Alexandria, VA, October 7 to 9, 1985.
Baird, B. N. R.(et al.), "Public Judgement of Environmental Health Hazard: Two Studies of the ASARCO Smelter," Paper presented at the 1985 Annual Meeting of the Society for Risk Analysis, Alexandria, VA, October 7 to 9, 1985.
Hicks, J. B. "Tight Building Syndrome: When Work Makes You Sick," Occupational Health and Safety, January 1984, p. 51-56.
Johnson, G. "Air Pollution: The 'Inside' Story," Industry Week, May 2, 1983, p. 45-50).

---

[4]. In analyses not reported here, we have learned that the time budgets of adult Americans do not vary greatly when we compare seasons, men and women, young, middle aged and the elderly for the eleven types of activity considered here. We are continuing these analyses to discover the variables that significantly modify the structure of time budgets.

Juster, F. T., et al, "1975 - 1981 Time Use Longitudinal Panel Study", The University of Michigan, Institute for Social Research, Survey Research Center, Ann Arbor, 1983.

Lowrance, W. W. Of Acceptable Risk: Science and the Determination of Safety, William Kaufmann, Inc. Los Altos, CA, 1976.

Nero, A. V. Jr., "Risk and Policy Implications of Indoor Exposure to ^{222}Rn Decay Products and Other Indoor Pollutants,"Paper presented at the 1985 Annual Meeting of the Society for Risk Analysis, Alexandria, VA, October 7 to 9, 1985.

Michaels, D. "Workforce Valuable In Tracking Syndrome" Occupational Health and Safety January 1984, p. 34-57.

Mileti, D. et al., Human Systems in Extreme Environments, Institute of Behavioral Science, University of Colorado, Boulder, 1975.

Nehnevajsa, J., Personal Communication regarding research in preparation for hearings in connection with the Shearon-Harris Nuclear Power Facility, NC, October 1985.

Patrick, D. and W. Peters, "Exposure Assessment in Setting Air Pollutions Regulations: ASARCO, Tacoma, Acase Study," Paper presented at the 1985 Annual Meeting of the Society for Risk Analysis, Alexandria, VA, October 7 to 9, 1985.

Polakoff, P. L. "Warming Up for Cold Weather Work" Occupational Health and Safety October 1982, p. 23-25.

Raloff, J. "Is Air Pollution Worse Indoors than Out?" Science News Vol. 128, p. 198, 1985.

Robinson, J. P., How Americans Use Time: A Social-Psychological Analysis of Everyday Behavior, Praeger Publishers New York, NY, 1977.

Rogers, G. O. and J. Nehnevajsa, Behavior and Attitudes Under Crisis Conditions, Government Printing Office, Washington D. C., 1984.

Rowe, W. D. An Anatomy of Risk John Wiley and Sons, New York, NY, 1977.

Shrader-Frechette, K. S. Risk Analysis and Scientific Method: Methodological and Ethical Problems with Evaluating Societal Hazards, D. Reidel Publishing Co., Boston, MA, 1985.

Silva, M., L. Zaffanella, and N. Hummon , "An Activity Schedule Systems Model to Estimate Public Exposure to Hz Electric Fields," IEEE Transactions on Power Apparatus and Systems, Volume PAS-104, Number 7, July, 1985.

Stafford, F., "Women's Use of Time Converging With Men's", Monthly Labor Review, December, p. 57-59, (1980).

Stafford, F. and G. J. Duncan, "The Use of Time and Technology by Households in the United States," Research in Labor Economics Vol 3, p. 335-375, (1980).

Stafford, F. and G. J. Duncan, "Market Hours, Real Hours and Labor Productivity" Economic Outlook USA, Autumn p. 74-76, (1978).

INFORMATION UTILIZATION IN THE FORMULATION OF HAZARDOUS WASTE FACILITY

SITING REGULATIONS: A METHOD OF RESEARCH FOR ORGANIZATIONAL LEARNING

Jeannette M. Trauth

University of Pittsburgh
Pittsburgh, PA

ABSTRACT

The demand for siting new hazardous waste disposal facilities has grown nationally during the past decade while opposition to these facilities has also increased. At the heart of this controversy is the issue of risk. The meaning of risk in this context is subject to various interpretations. The task of resolving these controversies has been left to the states. This paper discusses the problem of defining risk in the context of hazardous waste facility siting regulations, and proposes a method of research for analyzing the process by which risk is defined and the implications of this process for organizational learning.

KEY WORDS: Defining Risk, Risk Acceptability, Organizational Learning, Hazardous Waste Facility Siting

INTRODUCTION

The problem of hazardous waste management·has frequently been referred to as "the single most threatening environmental issue facing the country," (U.S. General Accounting Office, 1982:8) or the "environmental problem of the century" (Epstein et al., 1982:37). These characterizations of the problem are an acknowledgment of a serious predicament which this issue poses for a modern industrial society. On the one hand, society has come to depend on products and processes which require the ever-increasing use of complex and dangerous chemicals that must somehow be safely disposed of after they are no longer useful. However, in spite of the increasing demand each year for new hazardous waste disposal facilities (HWDF) to be built, there has been continuous opposition to the location of these facilities in almost every community across the nation.

At the heart of this siting controversy is the issue of the risks posed by these facilities to the communities in which they would be housed. The meaning of the concept of risk in this context is subject to various interpretations by all those who have a stake in the outcome of the decision. In particular, there have been disagreements over the proper boundaries of the risk debate (that is, the breadth and nature of risk in this context), as well as disagreements about what is an acceptable level of risk for a community to bear from these facilities.

The task of resolving these siting controversies has been left to the states; who, for the most part, have responded to these issues by developing regulations which codify what the states consider are acceptable levels of risk from a proposed HWD facility to any given community. In the course of developing the regulations governing the location of these facilities, the states have been guided in their decision making by certain norms, strategies and assumptions which are descriptive of and provide an explanation for their overall behavior (Schon, 1983:117).

Given that the problem of decision making in this area is fraught with uncertainties and incomplete information due to continuous changes in the technological, economic, and political environments which affect hazardous waste disposal, those responsible for developing HWDF siting regulations are presented with a difficult situation. Decision makers are not only confronted with the need to consider multiple and sometimes conflicting perspectives on this issue, but they must also remain ready to respond to the continuous challenges brought about by a changing environment which may require a rethinking of their theories-of-action; that is, the standard operating assumptions, strategies and norms which guide their decision making on risk. The question remains whether or not states have the capacity to cope with a changing environment regarding risk and thus make the necessary adaptations that are required for an organization to learn and therefore to survive and flourish.

The Theoretical Debate

There is a debate currently taking place among scholars of risk analysis and policy making regarding the proper scope and nature of the concept of risk. Traditionally, risk has been defined as, "a compound measure of the probability and magnitude of adverse effect. Thus a statement about risk is a description of the likelihood and consequences of harmful effect" (Lowrance, 1980:6). This approach to the definition of risk has been widely accepted in the past, but is currently being challenged by a growing number of scholars who say that it is not comprehensive enough to address issues which do not easily lend themselves to quantification and measurement. It has been asserted that the conventionally-accepted definition of risk, while appropriate for an engineering-type approach to risk, is inappropriate and, "misleading at the broader, more intractable, level of risk management" (Rayner, 1984:4). Along these lines, Nelkin and Pollak have also pointed out that when risk is being discussed within the context of controversial technologies it is not always viewed, "as a problem to be solved, but as a controversial question requiring dialogue and negotiation" (1979:313).

These scholars and others have pointed out the need for a new emphasis in the approach to defining risk. Fischhoff et al., have noted that because

> the definition of risk.. is inherently controversial, [that is]
> the choice of definition can affect the outcome of policy
> debates, the allocation of resources among safety measures, and
> the distribution of political power in society..., a highly
> flexible general approach to defining risk [is necessary]
> (Fischhoff et al., 1984:124).

An approach is needed which is more responsive to multiple and, perhaps, different meanings of risk grounded in different sets of values.

Hadden, (1984) states that the decision making process regarding technological risk has been dominated by technical considerations to such an extent that various political considerations have been considered illegitimate. In particular, decision makers have tended to overlook the importance of gathering information on the meaning of risk from those who are directly affected by it in favor of gathering more analytical information.

> Domination of the risk analysis field by economists, psychologists, and toxicologists has caused this simple truism to be lost in a forest of strategies for measuring risks and treating them efficiently. Issues that are redistributive, that are based on technical information that is characterized by uncertainty, and that affect individuals' own health and quality of like are issues that must forever be political. Refinements of political institutions should therefore be designed <u>to improve participation of affected parties and to elicit relevant information--in other words, to perfect the process by which all public decisions are made</u>...(Hadden, 1984:17). Emphasis added.

Defining risk differently can lead to alternative ways of thinking about the acceptability of various risks (Fischhoff et al., 1984). For instance, Rayner (1984) has pointed out that although public acceptance of risks has always been

> framed in terms of differential perceptions of probabilities... the choices between those probabilities are incomprehensible to most of the public and...I would guess that the truth is that the public doesn't care about probabilities in choosing between two courses of action when the differences in probability are so small as they are in most of the risk-management decisions that policy makers currently face (Rayner, 1984:8).

Starr (1984) has pointed out that what people are concerned about is trust. Societal acceptability of risk depends on its confidence in the capability of its institutions to manage various risks rather than on rigorous, scientific assessments. What is being underscored by all of these writers is the need for changes in the approach to risk assessment, that is, changes in the process by which decisions are made about the scope and nature of risk.

The Meaning of Risk in the Hazardous Waste Context

It has been noted that there are at least three questions which concern the public most when it is confronted with a situation involving societal risk.

1. Is the procedure by which collective consent is obtained for a course of action acceptable to those who must bear its consequences?
2. Is the principle that will be used to apportion liabilities for an undesired consequence acceptable to those affected?
3. Are the institutions that make the decisions that manage and regulate the technology worthy of fiduciary trust? (Rayner, 1984:9).

Judging by the type of issues that have been raised regarding the risks from hazardous waste disposal facilities, the above questions accurately summarize the scope of public concerns. Although the reasons for opposition to HWD facilities vary from community to community, they generally include some combination of the following factors.

1. Fear and uncertainty...about the safety of these facilities.
2. Both real and perceived impacts from facility construction and operation activities (noise, traffic, public service burdens, risks and aesthetic impacts etc.)...

3. A fear that property values will drop...
4. ...[A] perceived stigma associated with becoming a 'hazardous waste dump.'
5. ...[Distrust [of] industry and government's ability to assure the long run safety of these facilities.
6   ...[Inability] to fully comprehend the extent of the costs, risks and benefits associated with these facilities, and thus how they should appropriately respond to a proposal.
7   ...[The suitability of the site including] soil permeability, seismic stability, groundwater contamination and alternative uses· for a site.
8   ...[A biased] siting process [favoring developers at the expense of local citizens]...
9. The types of wastes to be treated or disposed of...
10 The information provided to communities is viewed as insufficient or too technical for them to confidently make a decision (Clark-McGlennon, 1980:6).

"Opposition to the siting of hazardous waste management facilities...is in part a consequence of conflicting perceptions of how best to manage the risks associated with hazardous waste" (Elliott, 1984:397). In most states, local citizens' interests and perceptions of the problem differ from those of other stakeholders-namely, regulatory agencies, hazardous waste generators, and operators of treatment and disposal facilities. Those who have been arguing on behalf of the siting and construction of new treatment and disposal facilities have often utilized the following types of arguments to neutralize the opposition of their critics. It is often said that the risk from HWD facilities is no greater than the risks from other commonly-accepted industrial operations and therefore, these types of facilities should not be feared. A corollary statement that is also often put forth is that because individuals often voluntarily engage in activities that are far more riskier than living near a hazardous waste treatment or disposal facility, it is illogical for them to oppose the siting of such a facility in their community. Thus, involuntary risk is equated with voluntary risk. Finally, it is often argued that opposition to hazardous waste facilities is based on irrational fears and lack of information and education about such facilities; and that once opponents are educated about the technological safety of the facility they will no longer oppose the siting process.

Many of those who have been arguing in favor of the immediate siting and construction of hazardous waste treatment and disposal facilities, often have not been speaking the same language of risk as their opponents. Gaming research has shown that citizens involved in hazardous waste facility siting issues, "are concerned with a richer array of risk management options" than was previously realized (Elliott, 1984:398). That is, laypeople are often more concerned with strategies of risk management which emphasize risk detection and mitigation versus risk prediction and prevention. The former strategies stress such issues as:

> If hazardous conditions develop, do we have the means to detect these changes? If so, will that data be collected and scrutinized so as to detect changes quickly? If serious hazards are detected, do we know how to reverse the dangers and the negative impacts? Will these mitigation measures be applied with sufficient speed and skill to be effective? (Elliott, 1984:398).

Previous approaches to risk management have not focused on these types of issues. Rather, risk management has traditionally dealt with the risks from hazardous waste facilities by means of improving systems for predicting and preventing problems from occurring, and relying on technological control mechanisms rather than on social control mechanisms (Elliott, 1984).

A Proposal for Research

The very nature of the theoretical debate regarding the meaning of risk provides a compelling reason to examine the process by which risk has been defined in the context of developing hazardous waste facility siting regulations. The states have the primary responsibility for determining what the risks are from HWD facilities and what are acceptable levels of risk for individuals and communities to bear. Given the variation in the meanings of risk and the fact that in this issue area continuous changes are occurring in the technology, economics and politics of hazardous waste management, the following question needs to be researched. How have the states responded to the need for a dynamic decision making process regarding the definition or risk?

The subject of the present research is a comparative analysis of the process by which risk has been defined in the hazardous waste facility siting regulations of Pennsylvania (by the Department of Environmental Resources-DER), and New Jersey (by the Department of Environmental protection-DEP), to determine whether or not learning has occurred within these two organizations during the process of developing the siting regulations.

At the present time, approximately one-half of the states have regulations governing the siting of HWD facilities. States such as Pennsylvania and New Jersey are among the largest generators of hazardous waste and as such, have the greatest need for new disposal facilities to be located and constructed. In response to this need Pennsylvania and New Jersey passed comprehensive legislation in the early 1980's governing the management of hazardous wastes. This legislation called for the respective states to develop criteria and standards for siting HWDFs and to review and amend these criteria on a regular basis.

The development of the siting criteria and standards (which were finalized as departmental rules and regulations) was an iterative process which took place over the course of five years in Pennsylvania and two years in New Jersey. Decision makers in each of these states initially drafted siting criteria (e.g. wetlands, flood hazard areas etc.) which reflected their respective departments' assumptions about what they considered were the greatest risks from hazardous waste disposal facilities to the surrounding areas in which they would be located. The initial siting standards, were a measure of an acceptable level of risk from a proposed facility to any given criterion.

Once the initial siting criteria and standards were drafted, the states allowed a public comment period. The comments represented a variety of individual and organizational views of risk; some of which, were based on an entirely different set of norms, strategies and assumptions than those used by the states. Following this period of public input, the DER in Pennsylvania and DEP in New Jersey considered the comments and revised the initial siting criteria and standards. This process was repeated in each state until final siting regulations were approved -- in August, 1985 for Pennsylvania in September, 1983 for New Jersey.

A Method of Research for Organizational Learning

There are several major questions which research on organizational learning addresses: Has learning occurred, or is it occurring? If so,

what kind of learning is involved? Is it organizational? What is its
quality? (Schon, 1983; Argyris and Schon, 1974). To study these types of
questions, it is necessary to have access to at least three interrelated
phenomena.

1. Organizational theory-in-use at Time 1
2. Organizational inquiry
3. Organizational theory-in-use at Time 2

An organization's theory-in-use is implicit in the norms, strategies
and assumptions that govern its regular task performance. Thus, an
organizations' theory-in-use may be inferred from the way in which it
detects and corrects errors (Schon, 1983). In order to tell whether there
has been a change in theory-in-use, it is necessary to identify and
describe two successive states of the theory-in-use. In order to tell
whether the change is attributable to organizational learning, it is
necessary to study the process of inquiry that mediates the shift from one
state of theory-in-use to the next.

For organizational learning to occur, the organization must first
engage in a process of inquiry; which has been described as a combination
of "thinking and doing" (Schon, 1983:121). Organizational inquiry is
preceded by the occurrence of some phenomenon (in this case, the input
from the public hearings) which triggers the organization to, "...reflect
on previously unquestioned assumptions, gather new information, experiment
with new patterns of action, or argue over conflicting interpretations
rooted in different values" (Schon, 1983:121).

Although there are different types of organizational learning, Schon
(1983) draws a distinction between two types; both of which involve the
restructuring of an organization's theory of action. One involves changes
only in an organization's strategies whereas, the other involves a change
in both the organizations' strategies of action and the underlying
norms. This research will determine whether, and to what extent, the
various revised drafts of the HWDF siting criteria reflected change in the
respective states' theories of action. That is, any change in their
norms, strategies and/or assumptions.

How states have responded to challenges to their operating
assumptions and norms during the course of preparing the siting
regulations may indicate their capacity for learning and suggest ways to
improve it. Whether or not states have the capacity for organizational
learning is important in this context because it will affect the states'
ability to update and revise the siting regulations on an ongoing basis as
changes occur in the technology, economics and politics of hazardous
waste.

REFERENCES

Argyris, Chris and Donald A. Schon, 1974, Theory in Practice: Increasing
    Professional Effectiveness, San Francisco: Jossey-Bass Publishers.
Clark-McGlennon Associates, 1980, Negotiating to Protect Your Interests:
    A Handbook on Siting Acceptable Hazardous Waste Facilities in New
    England, Boston: Clark-McGlennon Associates.
Elliott, Michael L. Poirier, 1984, "Improving Community Acceptance of
    Hazardous Waste Facilities Through Alternative Systems for Mitigating
    and Managing Risk," Hazardous Waste v.1, no. 3, pp. 397-410.
Epstein, Samuel S., Lester O. Brown and Carl Pope, 1982, Hazardous Waste
    in America, San Francisco: Sierra Club Books.

Fischhoff, Baruch, Stephen R. Watson and Chris Hope, 1984, "Defining Risk", Policy Sciences, v. 17, pp. 123-139.

Hadden, Susan G., 1984, "Introduction: Risk Policy in American Institutions," in Risk Analysis, Institutions, and Public Policy, edited by Susan G. Hadden, New York: Associated Faculty Press.

Lowrance, William W., 1980, "The Nature of Risk", in Societal Risk Assessment: How Safe is Safe Enough?, edited by Richard C. Schwing and Walter A. Albers, Jr., New York: Plenum Press.

Nelkin, Dorothy and Michael Pollak, October 1979, "Consensus and Conflict Resolution: The Politics of Assessing Risk", Science and Public Policy, pp. 307-318.

Rayner, Steve., October 1984, "Learning From the Blind Men and the Elephant, or Seeing Things Whole in Risk Management," (Paper presented at the 1984 Society for Risk Analysis Conference, Knoxville, Tennessee).

Schon, Donald A., 1983, "Organizational Learning" in Beyond Method: Strategies for Social Research, edited by Gareth Morgan, Beverly Hills: Sage Publications.

Starr, Chauncey, October 1984, (Presentation given at the 1984 Society for Risk Analysis Conference, Knoxville, Tennessee).

U.S. General Accounting Office, 1982, Environmental Protection: Agenda for the 1980's, Washington, D.C.: Government Printing Office.

PUBLIC JUDGMENT OF AN ENVIRONMENTAL HEALTH HAZARD:

TWO STUDIES OF THE ASARCO SMELTER*

Brian N. R. Baird*, Timothy C. Earle** and
George Cvetkovich***

University of Wyoming*
Battelle Seattle Research Center**
Western Washington University***

ABSTRACT

Results from two studies focusing on public risk judgment concerning the ASARCO Smelter in Tacoma, Washington are reported. The first study examines the factors affecting risk judgment among persons directly exposed to emissions from the smelter. Two public samples were studied, one composed of participants in public hearings and one generated by a telephone sampling of the general population of Tacoma. For these public groups, risk judgments and risk tolerance were closely associated with judged benefits of the hazard source, among other factors, and not with level of technical information about the hazard nor to residential distance from the smelter. The second study employed college students as subjects in a "simulated hazard" where subjects were instructed to respond " as if they lived in an area of Tacoma affected by the smelter." Where the primary purpose of the first study was substantive, that of the second study was methodological, exploring the use of a longitudinal panel design to study risk judgment. Data were collected from the same subjects at three points in time, a week separating the first from the second and the second from the third. Information about the hazard was made available to subjects during the breaks between sessions. In each testing period, subjects provided information on judgments of risk, on their information seeking behavior and on risk mitigation. These data were used to test and revise a structural model of the effects of information on risk judgment and risk mitigation.

KEY WORDS: Risk Judgment, Risk Communication, Hazard Information, ASARCO
Smelter

The public information activities undertaken by the Environmental Protection Agency as part of the hazard management process for the ASARCO smelter in Tacoma, Washington, provided a rare opportunity to study the effects of formal risk estimates on public risk judgments. Two such studies are described in this report. The first study is a field study,

----

*This research was supported in part by the Technology Assessment and Risk Analysis Program of the National Science Foundation and the Division of Civil and Environmental Engineering of the National Science Foundation under Grant PRA-8312309.

examining the factors affecting risk judgments among persons directly
exposed to emissions from the smelter. The results of this study raise
doubts about the direct effects of formal risk estimates (i.e.,
calculated, scientific or technical estimates of the ill effects of a
hazard). The second study is a laboratory study, exploring the factors
affecting the use of hazard information by college-student subjects acting
as if they were residents of Tacoma. A local earthquake hazard is used as
a comparison case to help demonstrate those conditions that lead to the
seeking out and use of hazard information.

FIELD STUDY

INTRODUCTION

    Other participants in this symposium have addressed the many
technical problems associated with estimating and attempting to manage the
risks of the ASARCO smelter. The complexity of those problems and the
uncertainties that accompany them would in themselves make determination
of the best course of regulatory action a difficult task. In the ASARCO
case, as in most risk management cases, the technical and scientific
difficulties are compounded by complex social questions and by the legal
and ethical right of the affected public to have an influence on the risk
management process.

    From a social science perspective the ASARCO case presented a unique
opportunity for research. It raised the difficult questions of risks
versus benefits, and, at the same time, involved a natural population of
potential subjects who were directly exposed to the risks and had an
opportunity to influence their level of exposure. Along with these
characteristics, the Environmental Protection Agency's efforts to
publicize its formal risk estimates and proposed controls made it possible
to examine the effects of such information on public reactions. In light
of the other papers describing elements of the formal risk estimation
process, this paper will emphasize findings relating to the effects, or as
the case may be, the lack of effects of formal risk estimates on public
opinions and risk tolerance.

Method

    The findings to be reported here are based on data collected from
questionnaires distributed at the EPA-sponsored public hearings in Tacoma,
and from a concurrent systematic telephone survey of persons living within
a twelve mile radius of the smelter. A total of 347 completed
questionnaires were collected at the hearings, an estimated 80% of the
hearing attendees who were residents of the affected area. Two hundred
and sixty-six persons completed the telephone survey.

    Questionnaire items were essentially the same for both the hearing
and phone samples. They were designed to measure such variables as
respondents' informal risk estimates, judgments of the risks versus
benefits of the smelter, voluntariness of the risk exposures,
environmental ideology, and factual knowledge of the formal risk estimates
and proposed regulations. A variety of demographic factors were also
examined, the most important of these including distance of residence from
the smelter, length of residence in the area, age and family member
employment at the smelter.

    In the data analyses all of the variables just described were
considered in relation to respondents' attitudes toward additional

controls for the smelter given the possibility that such controls might
lead to the smelter's closure and the resultant loss of jobs. Based on
their attitudes toward additional controls, respondents were identified as
either More Tolerant (less controls) or Less Tolerant (more controls) of
the smelter risks.

Results and Discussion

In reporting the study's results, data obtained from respondents at
the hearing must be distinguished from data obtained from the telephone
survey. Because respondents who attended the hearings showed themselves
to be more interested and informed about the ASARCO issue, and in view of
the fact that many in this group provided input directly to the EPA,
results from the hearing will be given more attention here. At the same
time, however, it is important to keep in mind that because the hazard in
question affected all of the residents of the area, not just those who
attended the hearings, the opinions of the general population also warrant
attention. Thus, along with the main findings from the hearing, key
findings from the telephone survey will also be reported where
appropriate.

Because the purpose of the hearings was to obtain public input about
the need for additional pollution controls for the smelter, it is
appropriate to consider first how respondents felt about this question.
Table 1 presents the results of two questions, the first asking simply if
additional pollution controls were favored for the smelter, the second if
additional controls were favored if it meant the smelter might have to
close and jobs would be lost. As can be seen in the table, the explicit
reference to the possibility of plant closure and job loss produced
notable changes in the response percentages for both hearing and phone
survey respondents. While a majority of those at the hearing still
favored additional controls even if they might lead to closure, among
phone survey respondents the weight of opinion shifted from a plurality
support for controls to a plurality in opposition. The different
responses to the two questions illustrate the importance of the jobs
versus health question on public risk tolerance. The differences between
the opinions of hearing and phone survey respondents suggests that input
received at such public hearings may not be representative of the
sentiments of the public at large.

Turning to factors that may have shaped the opinions just examined,
Table 2 presents selected correlational results from the Hearing data,
showing the 9 items having the highest correlations with risk tolerance as
reflected in desires for additional controls. Consistent with what we
have just seen, respondent's judgments of the relative costs versus

Table 1

Attitudes Toward Additional Pollution Controls

	Support additional controls (no mention of closure)			Support additional control (if closure might result)		
	Yes	No	Don't Know	Yes	No	Don't Know
Hearing	58%	34%	8%	51%	42%	7%
Phone	40%	29%	30%	32%	47%	21%

Table 2

Correlation With Risk Tolerance

Item	Pearson r*
Harmful effects vs benefits of smelter	.863
Do you think the smelter is a health hazard	.818
"Real risks" (in S's judgement) are higher or lower than EPA estimates	.807
Personal immunity to cancer caused by ASARCO emissions	.525
Voluntarines of exposure to ASARCO emissions	.470
Should standards be based on affordability	.454
Personal immunity to general environmentally caused cancer	.387
Agencies should not wait for certainty before acting to reduce risks	.386
Costs versus benefits of pollution controls in general	.374

*All correlations presented are significant at less than the .001 level.

benefits of the smelter provided the best predictor of tolerance for the smelter risks. As one would expect, those who rated the benefits as greater than the risks were more willing to tolerate the existing risk levels, while those who viewed the risks as greater than the benefits were more likely to demand further risk reductions.

Just behind cost-benefit judgments, tolerance for the smelter risks is most closely related to three items associated with subjects' "informal" risk judgments. The first of these asked for subjects' impressions of whether or not the smelter is a "health hazard." The second reflects subjects comparisons of their personal estimates of the smelter risks with the formal EPA risk estimates. The third item tapped the process of personal risk denial.

For present purposes, the most interesting element of all three items as well as the risk benefit item just examined is that they show informal risk estimates to be perhaps the key variable in shaping risk tolerance.

Lest this conclusion sound self reflexive, it is important to realize that in the ASARCO case, as in most "real world" risk management situations, people evidently do not experience the question as that of tolerating one level of clearly specified statistical risk versus another higher or lower statistical risk. Instead, they ask themselves what they think the existing risk is from a specific hazard and if they will tolerate the risk or would like it lowered. Thus, peoples' informal judgments of a risk will naturally have a profound impact on their tolerance for that risk "as they estimate it."

Because informal risk estimates are shown to have such an important influence on risk tolerance, it is appropriate at this point to consider the relationship between informal estimates, tolerance, and factual knowledge of formal estimates and regulations. Table 3 presents the response percentages for two questions demanding factual knowledge. The first asked respondents to give the EPA's estimate of the lifetime risk of arsenic-causing lung cancer among the 1000 people living nearest the estimate was actually 2, but answers ranging from 1 to 5 were scored as correct. The second item asked respondents simply to indicate whether or not proposed regulations would establish an ambient air standard for arsenic.

Examining this Table, the first thing to note is that in spite of the extraordinary efforts the EPA made to inform the public, and notwithstanding the fact that the purpose of the hearings was to obtain public comment on the risk estimates and proposed regulations, barely half of the respondents demonstrated accurate knowledge of the risk estimate, while less than forty percent were knowledgable about a key element of the proposed regulations. The corresponding figures from the telephone survey are not shown in Table 3, but they reveal the vast majority of the public to have been virtually ignorant of the factual information. Only 9% of the telephone survey respondents provided a risk estimate within the range scored as correct, while only 12% correctly indicated that the proposed regulations would not establish an ambient air standard.

In the case of the telephone survey results it is immediately apparent that factual information probably exerted little influence on people's attitudes toward the smelter risks. If scarcely anyone in the general public knew what the formal risk estimates were, those estimates could not have been an important factor in shaping their informal risk estimates or tolerance decisions. The situation is somewhat different for

Table 3

Results of Factual Knowledge Questions
for Hearing Respondents

| | Risk Estimate Question | | Regulation Question | |
	Correct	Incorrect(1)	Correct	Incorrect
Less Risk Tolerant	62%	38%	47%	53%
More Risk Tolerant	41%	59%	26%	74%
Overall Percentage	52%	48%	37%	63%

1. Percentages cited as incorrect include those who gave incorrect anwers as well as those who did not answer or selected the Don't Know response option.

2. Chi square analyses reveal the differences between MT and LT groups to be significant at less than the .001 level for both questions.

respondents at the hearings, but the conclusion is similar.

Looking again at Table 3, it can be seen that the percentage of knowledgable respondents is significantly higher among Less Tolerant than among More Tolerant respondents. Yet simply noting that greater percentages of one group were knowledgeable than another does not indicate whether factual information or lack of it was a key factor in shaping tolerance. A better insight into this question is gained from strength association measures when knowledge items are compared with the risk tolerance item. In this case the association between knowledge and tolerance is not found to be strong. The squared correlation coefficient between the tolerance and formal risk estimate item was .04, while another measure of association, Asymmetric Lamda, with tolerance dependent on knowledge of the risk estimate was only .125. Thus, knowledge of the factual information was not found to be closely related to or highly predicative of risk tolerance, and it seems improbable that such information had a large effect on shaping the opinions of most respondents.

Considering the time, energy, and money that were devoted to establishing and publicizing the risk estimates and proposed regulations in the ASARCO case, policy makers may find it disheartening to discover that such information played at most a relatively small role in shaping public reactions. The next questions that need to be asked then are: Why was the information about formal risk estimates not more important? and, If formal risk estimates and regulatory information do not influence public reactions to risk what does?

To account for the non-effects of factual information it is possible to identify three contributing factors which became apparent during the course of the present study. These are, first, a general lack of knowledge of the factual information, second, difficulties the public faces in trying to make sense of whatever information was known, and third, the influence of non-informational characteristics on shaping reactions to factual information.

The first reason for information's lack of impact has already been mentioned, that is, information cannot influence people's decisions unless it is known, and most people know very little about formal risk estimates. Confronted by this finding it would be possible, but unfortunate, to simply write it off as evidence of ignorance or apathy on the part of the public. A preferable response is to ask what factors contribute to the apparent lack of knowledge.

For example, it may be that in cases such as this people consciously or unconsciously choose not to become informed lest information threaten their established beliefs and raise the possibility that they might feel a need to change their opinions or, more threatening still, change such important parts of their lives as where they live or work. If this is the case, apathy and ignorance are not at the root of the problem; fear of change, uncertainty or responsibility are. An alternative possibility is that people want to be informed, but the selected means of informing the public were not appropriate to the task. This would be analogous to a marketing problem with the formal information as the product (see Earle and Cretkovich, 1984).

Turning from the problem of not having information to the closely related problem of not understanding information, the present study indicates that an important contributor to the non-effects of information is the fact that normal people do not know what to make of the language and numbers of formal risk analysis. While professional scientists and administrators become accustomed to the principles, statistics, and language of risk analysis, to most people such things are meaningless at best and frustratingly confusing at worst. This was revealed in the ASARCO case through responses to open ended questions asking what could be done to better inform the public. Comments such as "Cut out the Jargon!!", were frequently scribbled angrily in the space provided below this question. Other evidence that formal risk estimates are apart from normal public thinking comes from responses to telephone survey requests to indicate the EPA risk estimates. In response to this question it was not uncommon for people to offer comments such as "Oh, I don't think the risk is very high. Maybe only about 10 or 15% of the people will get cancer because of the smelter." It is obvious to members of the risk analysis community that such informal risk estimates are several orders of magnitude greater than the levels which are debated as acceptable bases for policies, but the fact that some members of the general public are able to view such extreme risks as "not very high" reveals just how alien risk analysis and the magnitude of the probabilities it involves are.

The final process to be discussed here concerns how people who do know the formal risk estimates interpret those estimates and make their tolerance decisions in relation to them. This process reflects the other side of the coin of information's non-effects. Much as information cannot affect people's reactions unless it is known, when people are equally knowledgable of formal risk estimates, but still react differently to the risks, the risk estimate information alone cannot be the key variable shaping the different reactions.

One of the ways this is demonstrated is in the finding that although only 52% of the hearing respondents knew the correct figure for the EPA's risk estimate, 96% of the respondents offered an opinion about the accuracy of that estimate, and only 22% considered it to be roughly correct. Thus, whether they knew what the formal estimate was or not, most people were willing to offer an opinion about its accuracy, and even among knowledgeable respondents, only a small minority considered the formal estimates to be correct. In such circumstances it is not surprising that knowledge of the formal estimates had little effect on risk tolerance. Instead, it appears that other factors, such as respondents' attitudes toward health, jobs, industry, the environment, ethics, the EPA, and perhaps to statistics themselves, shaped both how they made informal judgments of the risks and how they reacted to information about the formal risk estimates.

LABORATORY STUDY

Results from the field study described above indicate that, in the ASARCO case, scientific hazard information had little effect on public judgment and tolerance of health risks. In this section of our report we describe a laboratory study that was designed in part to identify factors that may contribute to increasing the impact of scientific and other hazard information on public risk judgments and on risk mitigating and reducing behaviors.

Method

The aim of our research procedures was to simulate in a controlled setting the essential elements of public risk judgment processes. One central element of risk judgment is that it is a dynamic process. That is, an individual's risk judgment at a particular point in time is the result of preceding events, particularly experience with the hazard in question and the processing of information about that hazard. Also, subsequent events and information may modify an individual's judgment of risk. In order to capture the dynamic character of risk judgment processes, a longitudinal research design must be used. A panel design was used in this study, with the same group of 132 subjects providing data at three points in time. This type of design facilitates a causal analysis of the relations among the variables measured. We can therefore identify which factors, if any, lead to increases in risk judgments, for example, or information seeking and risk mitigation activities.

One week separated the first wave of data collection from the second and the second from the third. The 132 subjects were recruited from the subject pool of the Psychology Department of Western Washington University. At the end of the first two data collection sessions, information regarding the two hazards under study (the ASARCO smelter and the seismic hazard in Whatcom County, Washington, the location of WWU), was made available on an optional basis to the subjects. The information consisted, for example, of reproductions of Tacoma News Tribune articles on the ASARCO case (detailing EPA's role, etc.) and pamphlets describing the local seismic hazard and how to deal with it. Subjects were instructed that they were free to take or leave the information provided; they were also free to seek out any other information they desired during the weeks separating the data collection sessions.

In responding to the questionnaires, subjects were asked to roleplay their responses to certain items. With regard to the Whatcom County earthquake hazard, respondents were asked to "respond as an individual (yourself) living in a single-family house located somewhere in the general WWU area of Bellingham..." For the ASARCO hazard, subjects were instructed to "respond as if you lived in an area of Tacoma that is affected by the emissions from the ASARCO smelter. Aside from where you live, all other aspects of your life would remain the same: <u>You should</u> <u>respond as you would if you lived in an area affected by ASARCO...</u>" Measures designed to evaluate these simulation procedures indicated that they were effective.

The contents of the questionnaires were derived from our dynamic model of risk judgment (Earle and Cvetkovich, 1983). In brief, this model includes subject background variables (e.g. scientific training), risk judgment variables (described below), hazard information variables (e.g. information seeking and information content) and risk mitigation variables (e.g. what has or should be done to reduce the effects of the hazard). The risk judgment variables were derived from the work of Fischhoff and his colleagues (Fischhoff, Slovic and Lichtenstein, 1983; Fischhoff, Watson and Hope, 1983) who make two basic points: 1) there is no single definition of risk suitable for all problems (and this is true for both scientists and the public); 2) the choice of definition in any individual case is a political one, in the sense that it expresses someone's values about the importance of different adverse effects.

Risk is thus multidimensional and variably defined both within and among individuals. And, further, risk is just one of several factors considered by individuals when making risk decisions. People don't ordinarily judge abstract levels of risk. Instead, they engage in risk decisions, choosing among several alternatives (among employment opportunities, for example). Risk is only one among several possible significant aspects of the alternatives. The other important aspects may include costs and benefits, each of which is also, of course, subjectively defined. Application of this approach to a "real-life hazard" would

require a preliminary determination of an acceptable general structuring
of the risk decision for the particular hazard and group of respondents.
This laboratory study is the first use of these procedures. The research
process was simplified somewhat, therefore, through the provision of
general, pre-structured sets of judgments for the two hazard cases.

To illustrate the item-generation process, an outline of the major
risk decision aspects is given in Table 4. This general structure was
adapted to the two hazards. With ASARCO, for example, items referring to
the morbidity of workers were included; none were included for the
earthquake hazard. Aside from such necessary differences, the items
referring to the ASARCO hazards were the same as those referring to the

Table 4

Risk Decision Aspects Used in Item Generation

Risk

    Mortality
            Self
            Others
                  General Public
                  Workers
                  Future generations

    Morbidity
            Self
            Others
                  General Public
                  Workers
                  Future generations

    Knowledge of hazard
            Self
            Science and government
    Dread of hazard
            Self
            Others

Benefits

    Economic
            Self
            Others
    Non-economic
            Self
            Others

Costs

    Property damage
    Income loss

Environmental effects

    Plants and animals
    Non-living environment

Table 5

Risk Decision Variables Included in Analysis

Endogenous variables

Risk

ASARCO	Mortality/morbidity: Self
	Mortality/morbidity: Other
Earthquake	Mortality/morbidity: All

Benefits

ASARCO	Benefits: All
Earthquake	Benefits: Economic
	Benefits: Non-economic

Information seeking

(Same for both hazards)

Risk mitigation/reduction

(Same for both hazards)

Exogenous variables

Scientific background

Attitude toward science/technology

Attitude toward government

Concern in hazard information

seismic hazard. Examples of the ASARCO items are: "How likely is it that some employee of ASARCO will die as a result of emissions from the smelter?" (Risk-mortality-others-workers.) Answered on a five-point scale ranging from Very Unlikely to Very Likely); "To what extent do you gain economically by living in an area exposed to emissions from the ASARCO smelter?" (Benefit-economic-self. Answered on a five-point scale ranging from No Economic Gain to Great Economic Gain.).

Results and Discussion

Results on a selected subset of variables are reported here, with focus on the effects of hazard information on risk judgments and risk mitigation activities. The variables analyzed are listed in Table 5. These variables were derived form the original questionnaire items through a factor analysis data reduction procedure. All of the questionnaire items relating to risk, for example, were factor-analyzed to determine the number and make-up of the risk dimensions generated by the respondents. With respect to the ASARCO case, four factors were generated: mortality/morbidity: self; mortality/morbidity: other; knowledge of the hazard; and dread of the hazard. (Note that only the first two of these factors are included in the present analyses). In the case of the earthquake, only three factors emerged due to subjects distinguishing less between themselves and others on mortality/morbidity than they did with the ASARCO hazard. A similar situation occurred with the benefit items. For ASARCO, subjects related all of the items to a single benefits dimension while dividing benefits into economic and non-economic for the earthquake. These simple results demonstrate the important basic idea that different types of hazards may be classified or otherwise dealt with cognitively in significantly different ways. Knowing how particular individuals classify specific hazards may point the way to improved hazard communication.

The variables in Table 5 are divided into endogenous and exogenous. The endogenous variables are the "dependent variables" in our structural equation models of the risk judgment process. The exogenous variables are the "independent variables." since our models cover three time periods, an endogenous variable that is "dependent" in Wave I will be a predictor variable for later endogenous variables. An endogenous variable can also be both dependent and a predictor. In addition to the risk and benefit variables, the endogenous variables for the present analysis also include information seeking (a measure of the time and effort spent obtaining information about the hazard) and risk mitigation/reduction (a measure of the number of steps subjects say they or the government have taken plus the number of steps subjects say they or the government should take).

Four exogenous variables are included in this analysis: scientific background (a measure of the science courses completed in high school and college); attitude toward science and technology (a high score on this variable indicates a negative attitude); attitude toward government (a high score indicates a negative attitude); and concern in hazard information (a measure of the level of concern experienced by a subject as the result of processing information about the hazard). This last exogenous variable, concern, is a key variable in our analyses since it sums up the emotional impact on subjects of the information they have sought out and used. Estimates of the relations between this variable and the other variables in the model provide an indication of some of the effects of hazard information on hazard-related judgments and behaviors.

The relations among the variables in our models were estimated using the LISREL procedure developed by Joreskog and Sorbom (1981). The parameter estimates for our model of the ASARCO case are given in Table 6. The endogenous variable names are coded in this way: MMO = mortality/morbidity: other; MMS = mortality/morbidity: self; BEN = benefits: MIT = risk mitigation/reduction activities; and INFO = information seeking. The exogenous codes are: SCI = scientific background; STA = attitude toward science and technology: GOVA = attitude toward government; and CON = concern in hazard information. The parameter estimates for our model of the earthquake case are given in Table 7. The endogenous codes are: MMA = mortality/morbidity: all; EBEN = economic benefits; and NBEN = non-economic benefits. The remaining codes are the same as in the ASARCO model. In both models, the numerical suffixes indicate the wave on which the variable was measured.

Many points of comparison can be made between the ASARCO model and the earthquake model. It can be noted, for example, that the background variables (SCI, STA and GOVA) were important predictors of mortality/morbidity judgments in the ASARCO case but not in the earthquake case. In the ASARCO model, subjects with stronger scientific backgrounds and positive attitudes toward science/technology and government tended to give lower judgments of mortality/morbidity. These individuals apparently believed that the ASARCO hazard could be well managed by government officials, and their scientific training contributed to their faith in that management. The earthquake, on the other hand, was apparently seen as an "unmanageable" hazard, with judgments of mortality/morbidity independent of the activities of technologists and government officials. While such substantive findings in comparisons between the two models are intriguing and suggestive, they will not be pursued in this report. Our focus here is primarily methodological, with the aim being to demonstrate a method by which the effects of hazard information can be studied.

One method of demonstrating the effects of hazard information in these risk judgment models is to compare a model that includes estimates of the parameters associated with the information variables with a model that sets those parameters equal to zero. For the ASARCO case, this comparison can be seen in Table 6 in the two columns of R^2s, one for a model with hazard information (the variables INFO and CON) and one for a model without. The decrease in R^2 as the result of information removal demonstrates its effects. See, for example, MIT1 which goes from an R^2 of 0.19 to 0.00. Similar comparisons can be made in Table 7 for the earthquake case. Removal of hazard information effects from the earthquake model, however, results in relatively small decreases in R^2s. It can be concluded, then, that hazard information had significant effects in the ASARCO case but not in the earthquake case.

The comparison of R^2s between models is not a very clear way of demonstrating information effects because the effects become hidden in the changes in the variables over time. A more dramatic demonstration involves the calculation of the total effects of information content on each of the endogenous variables over time. These total effects are given in the final columns of Tables 6 and 7. There are two key sets of comparisons here. The first is on the MIT variables: For ASARCO, concern had significant effects on mitigation activities; concern had no effect on MIT for the earthquake. (Interestingly, benefit judgments predict MIT for the earthquake.) The second set of key comparisons is on the INFO variables: In both cases, information seeking was strongly affected by concern in hazard information. It seems, therefore, that concern about a hazard will lead to the seeking and use of hazard information, and the concern generated by that information will tend to lead to risk mitigation/reduction activities when the hazard is considered to be manageable.

SUMMARY AND CONCLUSIONS

Two studies of the effects of hazard information on risk judgments have been described. The first was a field study of the ASARCO smelter case in Tacoma which demonstrated that formal EPA risk estimates had little effect on the risk judgments or tolerances of persons living in the affected area. The second study was a laboratory study that demonstrated a method for the studying of hazard information effects over time. By comparing the risk judgment models for the ASARCO and earthquake hazards, it was shown that hazard information can have strong effects on hazard-related judgments and behavior.

394

Table 6

ASARCO: LISREL Maximum Likelihood Parameter Estimates
(All t-values greater than 2.0)

Dependent Variable	Predictors	R^2	R^2 (Without Hazard Information)	Total Effects of Concern
MM01	SCI (-0.21), STA (0.20), GOVA (0.33), CON (0.26)	0.25	0.25	0.26
MMS1	MMS1 (0.43), STA (0.22	0.28	0.28	0.11
BEN1		0.00	0.00	0.00
MIT1	CON1 (0.43)	0.19	0.00	0.43
INFO1	MIT1 (0.17), CON1 (0.40)	0.25	-	0.48
MM02	MM01 (0.46), STA (0.21), CON (0.35)	0.45	0.36	0.46
MMS2	MMS1 (0.16), MM02 (0.37), INFO2 (0.20)	0.28	0.27	0.29
BEN2	BEN1 (0.63)	0.39	0.39	0.00
MIT2	MIT1 (0.40), CON2 (0.42)	0.36	0.27	0.60
INFO2	MMS1 (0.26), CON2 (0.45)	0.27	-	0.48
MM03	MM01 (0.25), MM02 (0.59), INFO3 (0.24)	0.64	0.58	0.47
MMS3	MMS2 (0.53), MM03 (0.24), CON3 (0.14)	0.46	0.49	0.40
BEN3	BEN1 (0.24), BEN2 (0.46), CON3 (0.25)	0.40	0.40	0.00
MIT3	MIT1 (0.33), MIT2 (0.20), MM03 (0.24), CON3 (0.25)	0.40	0.36	0.63
INFO3	INFO2 (0.38), CON2 (-.28), CON3 (0.63)	0.48	-	0.53

395

Table 7

Earthquake! LISREL Maximum Likelihood Parameter Estimates
(All t-values greater than 2.0)

Dependent Variable	Predictors	R^2	R^2 (Without Hazard Information)	Total Effects of Concern
MMA1		0.00	0.00	0.00
EBEN1	MMA1 (0.33), GOVA (-0.27)	0.18	0.18	0.00
NBEN1	EBEN1 (0.40)	0.16	0.16	0.00
MIT1	EBEN1 (0.27)	0.08	0.08	0.00
INFO1	CON1 (0.35)	0.12	-	0.35
MMA2	MMA1 (0.59), INFO2 (0.17), CON2 (0.21)	0.50	0.44	0.28
EBEN2	EBEN1 (0.43)	0.18	0.18	0.00
NBEN2	NBEN1 (0.40), MMA2 (0.14), EBEN2 (0.28), INFO2 (0.16)	0.36	0.35	0.11
MIT2	MIT1 (0.45), NBEN2 (0.27)	0.30	0.29	0.03
INFO2	CON2 (0.42)	0.17	-	0.43
MMA3	MMA2 (0.78), CON3 (0.10)	0.62	0.64	0.32
EBEN3	EBEN1 (0.20), EBEN2 (0.28), MMA3 (.12), NBEN3 (0.48)	0.60	0.61	0.10
NBEN3	NBEN2 (0.58), MMA3 (0.20)	0.42	0.46	0.13
MIT3	MIT2 (0.58), NBEN3 (0.20)	0.44	0.44	0.04
INFO3	INFO2 (0.32), CON3 (0.49)	0.40	-	0.52

The question, then, is why there were no information effects in the field study while there were large effects in the laboratory study. There no doubt are many reasons for this, including aspects of methodology, etc. We wish to emphasize another set of factors, however. These factors are developed elsewhere (Earle, 1984) and present a useful guide to effective hazard communication. In brief, hazard information will affect hazard-related judgments and behavior when: a) individuals are involved (interested) in the hazard; b) they are motivated (i.e. concerned) to process information; and d) the information available meets their

Figure 1

A Conceptual Framework for Integrated Risk Management at the Local Level

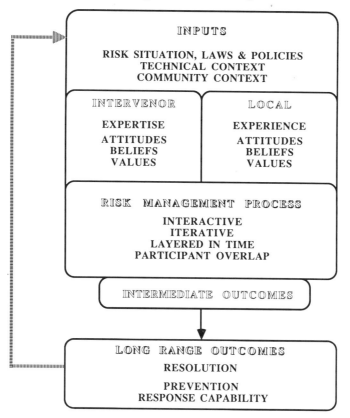

individual needs (i.e. there are large individual differences and customized information is necessary). With respect to the field study, we know that the persons at the public hearings were involved and motivated. It would seem, therefore, that the formal EPA risk estimates failed to affect the public because of information processing difficulties: How is a person in Tacoma to integrate such a formal estimate into her/his risk decision processes?

In noting the "non-effects" of the formal EPA risk estimates, it must be emphasized that we are not claiming that all EPA risk management activities had no significant effects on public risk judgment in the ASARCO case. Results from the laboratory study suggest that government risk management activities outside the realm of formal risk estimates can have strong effects on public risk judgment. These "informal" risk management activities affect public confidence in the government's ability to manage, and this confidence may, in the long run, be more significant for public risk judgment than formal estimates of risk.

REFERENCES

Earle, T. C., Risk communication: A marketing approach. Paper presented at NSF/EPA workshop on risk perception and risk communication. Long Beach, CA, Dec., 1984.

Earle, T. C. and Cvetkovich, G. Risk judgment and the communication of hazard information: Toward a new look in the study of risk perception. BHARC (400/83/017). Battelle Human Affairs Research Centers, Seattle, Washington, 1983.

Jöreskog , K. G. and Sorbom, D. LISREL V: Analysis of Linear Structural Relationships by Maximum Likelihood and Least Square Methods. Chicago: National Educational Resources, 1981.

RISK ASSESSMENT AND RISK MANAGEMENT: A SURVEY OF RECENT MODELS

D. Krewski* and P. L. Birkwood**

*Health and Welfare Canada, Canada   K1A 0L2
**University of Ottawa, Canada   K1N 9B5

The rational management of health and environmental risks ideally requires a well defined structured approach in order that risk may be dealt with in a complete and equitable fashion. In this paper, formal models of the process of risk assessment and risk management which have been proposed in the literature in recent years are reviewed. Common elements amongst these models are identified, and the potential impact of these approaches on practical decision making is examined.

KEY WORDS: Risk Assessment, Risk Management, Hazard Identification, Risk
           Estimation, Risk Evaluation.

INTRODUCTION

In recent years, growing public awareness has led to increased concern over potential risks to human health and the environment. Controversy surrounding health risk has often been fueled by sensational media reports concerning the pending dangers of adverse lifestyles, food additives, drugs, pesticides, and contaminants in air, water, and the general environment.

The selection of environmental hazards for government attention has often been handled in an ad hoc fashion in the past, usually in a reactive manner rather than as part of a carefully planned strategy. Issues which attract the public's interest have often been the focus of societal resources, at the expense of more serious but less popular problems.

Despite the pressures on regulatory agencies to respond to external initiatives and shifting priorities, several factors indicate the need for a more pragmatic approach to the management of health risks. These include the desirability of balancing risks and benefits across society in an acceptable way and the need to consider societal priorities other than human health. The need for an orderly and systematic approach to risk management is further supported by the existence of resource constraints, which prevent maximum control of all risks.

A number of formal models for risk assessment and risk management have been proposed in recent years. These models are of great value in clarifying the main elements of risk assessment and risk management, and have served to establish a well defined framework within which risk may be addressed.

In section 2 of this article, we discuss the different models which have been proposed in the literature. These models are then compared and a number of common elements identified (section 3). We conclude with a brief discussion of the key components of the models and their role in understanding and improving the overall process of risk assessment and risk management (section 4).

RISK ASSESSMENT AND RISK MANAGEMENT

Scientific Committee on Problems of the Environment (SCOPE)

The first formal model of the risk assessment and management process appears to have been formulated by SCOPE (Whyte & Burton, 1980). They outlined a three stage risk assessment process consisting of risk identification, risk estimation and risk evaluation. The first step involves recognizing that a hazard exists. A quantitative estimate of the magnitude of the associated risk is then prepared by scientifically determining its characteristics. This is followed by an evaluation of the significance and acceptability of risk probabilities and consequences. Following risk assessment, some decision regarding whether or not to intervene takes place. This is informally termed "risk management."

National Research Council (1983).

The NRC (1983) model consists of two stages: risk assessment, and risk management. Risk assessment refers to the use of a factual base to define the health effects of exposure of individuals or populations to hazardous materials or situations. The information obtained at this stage may be used to set priorities for regulation and for further toxicity testing. Risk management consists of the development of and selection regulatory options.

Risk assessment is subdivided into four components: hazard identification, dose response assessment, exposure assessment, and risk characterization. Hazard identification is the determination of a cause-effect relationship between a particular chemical and a decline in health status using epidemiological studies of human populations, animal bioassay data, mutagenicity tests, and examination of molecular structure. Dose response assessment involves examination of the relation of the magnitude of exposure and probability of occurrence of the health effects in question using extrapolation methods for high to low doses and for animals to humans as the primary research tools. Exposure assessment involves study of the extent of human exposure before or after application of regulatory controls. Risk characterization includes hazard identification, dose response assessment and exposure assessment, and involves a description of the nature and magnitude of human risk, including attendant uncertainty.

At the risk management stage, regulatory options are developed and evaluated. Selection of a particular regulatory option involves consideration of the public health, economic, social, and political consequences of implementation. Other factors of significance include the technical feasibility of the proposed solution, desired level of control, ability to enforce regulations, uncertainty in scientific data and the corresponding inferential bridges used to fill gaps in knowledge, and the public perception and level of information.

The implementation of one specific course of action requires efficient resource utilization, and should be accompanied by communication to affected parties regarding the reliability of the information used to make the decision, trade-offs, the values applied, and the relation of these factors in arriving at a specific policy.

400

The NRC model was subsequently adopted by the United States Environmental Protection Agency (1984) with no significant structural or definitional changes.

The Royal Society

The Royal Society model (Royal Society Study Group, 1983) is composed of only two stages: risk assessment and risk management. The former is further subdivided into risk estimation and risk evaluation.

Risk assessment is the general term used by the Royal Society to describe the study of decisions having uncertain consequences. Risk estimation refers to identification and estimation of the probability and magnitude of the consequences of a hazardous event. Risk evaluation is the complex process of determining the significance or value of the identified hazards and estimated risks to those concerned with or affected by the proposed decision. Embedded within this stage are the interrelated processes of developing alternative courses of action and decision analysis. These components take into consideration public awareness and perception, the acceptability of risk, and the analysis of risks, costs, and benefits. These latter factors include consideration of the level of justifiable risk, economic and technical feasibility, and resource requirements.

Based on this evaluation of risk, risk management is the making of decisions concerning risks and their subsequent implementation. Decision making itself involves consultations between industry, government, the public, and other special interest groups affected by the decision. Implementation of a decision, its monitoring, evaluation, and revision, are considered integral part of the process.

Interdepartmental Committee on Toxic Chemicals (ICTC)

The ICTC model developed by the Interdepartmental Working Group on Toxic Chemicals (1984) represents an elaboration of the SCOPE model. The first step in the process is hazard identification based on case reports, epidemiological studies of human populations, and toxicological experiments conducted in the laboratory. Another potential approach for the identification of chemical risks is a comparison of molecular structure and biological activity with that of known toxicants.

The next step is to obtain an estimate of the magnitude of the risk in question. This involves the statistical analysis of epidemiological and toxicological data to determine the level of risk associated with specific hazards and to establish acceptable criteria for exposure to environmental hazards. This process is subject to considerable uncertainty and may require strong assumptions, as in the conversion of animal pesults to the human situation.

The first step towards selecting a strategy for dealing with a given environmental risk is the development of a number of alternative courses of action. Available options can range from advisory to economic to strict regulatory control. In order to ensure a consistent approach to risk management, the set of options selected for further evaluation should be compatible with existing environmental health program objectives and remain cognizant of any overall risk management policy guidelines.

The decision as to the most appropriate course of action depends on a host of factors, including a balancing of health risks against health benefits in some cases. Consideration may also be given to the public's perception of risk, which may not always correspond to the actual risk determined by objective analysis. The technical feasiblity of each proposed course of action should be demonstrated, including the ability to enforce any proposed regulations. Economic effects are often important in evaluating alternatives, both in terms of program-related costs and the impact on productive output. Socio-political factors involving equity considerations and repercussions at the international level should not be overlooked.

Implementation of the selected risk management strategy will usually require some commitment of resources and should be accompanied by attempts to communicate the nature of the chosen control mechanism to all affected parties. Once the control mechanism is in place, continued monitoring is recommended. Continual evaluation and review of new health risk information may suggest modification to the risk management strategy currently in place.

World Health Organization (WHO)

The WHO (1985) considered a four stage process comprised of hazard identification, risk estimation, risk evaluation, and risk management. The process as a whole is influenced by a number of participating bodies including scientists, industry, special interest groups, the public, media, and politicians.

Hazard identification requires the collection of chemical, toxicological, ecotoxicological, clinical and epidemiological data. In addition, extrapolations from animal to man and from high dose/short time to low dose/long time may be required to evaluate the health effects. Toxicity and exposure information are obtained at this first stage.

Risk estimation characterizes the extent of harm and the probability of its occurrence. This stage utilizes the information gained in hazard identification, and exposure information, to predict the severity, extent, and distribution of the increased incidence of disease, disability, or defects caused by exposure to a hazard.

The risk evaluation stage involves comparative analysis between the risk in question and accepted risks, voluntary risks, and other risks, as well as examination of the acceptability of the risk in question. The latter process involves consideration of political factors, public perception, and industrial and public liability.

The risk management stage consists of decision making with a view to reducing or eliminating the risk in question. Decision making must take into account cultural, socio-economic, and political factors, and the type and nature of the risk in question. The possibility of reducing or eliminating the risk through control measures, technology changes, prevention or reduction of exposure, and product substitution must be considered in terms of feasibility, costs/benefits and magnitude and distribution. The decisions resulting from such analysis form the basis for regulatory action.

Other models

Various individuals and regional organizations have also proposed models for risk assessment and risk management. Baram's (1981) framework consists of six steps: hazard identification, risk measurement, risk management options selection, economic and technical feasibility analysis, ordering of risk management initiatives, and deployment of risk management options.

Lave's (1982) model contains eight stages: hazard identification, risk assessment, identification of regulatory alternatives, decision analysis, regulatory decision, legal or political challenge, implementation, and monitoring. This model closely resembles that adopted by the ICTC.

Rodricks & Tardiff (1984) consider only two broad stages: risk assessment and risk management. The former is subdivided into three phases: hazard identification and evaluation, dose response evaluation, and identification of conditions of exposure. The latter stage also consists of three phases: examination of alternative courses of action, decision analysis, and implementation.

The model developed by the Ontario Advisory Council on Occupational Health and Occupational Safety (1984) is divided into four stages: hazard identification, risk estimation, risk evaluation (development of alternative actions, and decision analysis), and risk management (implementation).

Shrader-Frechette's (1985) framework includes three stages: risk identification, risk estimation, and risk evaluation. Although the framework lacks a risk management stage, its three stages closely parallel those of the SCOPE model.

COMPARISON OF MODELS

The models for risk assessment and risk management presented in section 2 follow the general framework devised by Whyte & Burton (1980), although the degree of similarity and level of detail presented in each of the models varies. In addition to delineating the steps comprising the risk assessment and risk management process, each model distinguishes between the scientific and extrascientific components of the overall process. A comparison of the major models examined in section 2, using the general framework established by Whyte & Burton is provided in Figure 1.

With the exception of the Royal Society model, each of these models explicitly designates hazard identification as the initial step. The NRC/EPA model emphasizes the use of scientific research as the basic tool for identifying risks. Several models correctly refer to this initial phase as hazard identification rather than risk identification since the probability of an adverse effect occurring is generally not calculated at this stage. In current usage, the term hazard is used to describe the nature of the adverse effect, whereas risk involves both hazard and the probability of its occurrence (Kaplan & Garrick, 1981).

With the exception of the Royal Society model, there also appears to be general agreement that hazard identification should be followed by risk estimation. (The Royal Society includes both hazard identification and risk estimation in their definition of risk estimation, but does not clearly identify these as distinct sequential steps.) In the NRC/EPA framework the term risk characterization is effectively equivalent to risk estimation.

All models cite the use of toxicological and epidemiological data as the primary sources of information for health hazard identification and risk estimation (Office of Technology Assessment, 1981). In the case of chemical hazards, structure/activity analysis may also be used.

As with the original SCOPE model, all models then proceed to some form of risk evaluation. At this stage, scientific method is subsumed by

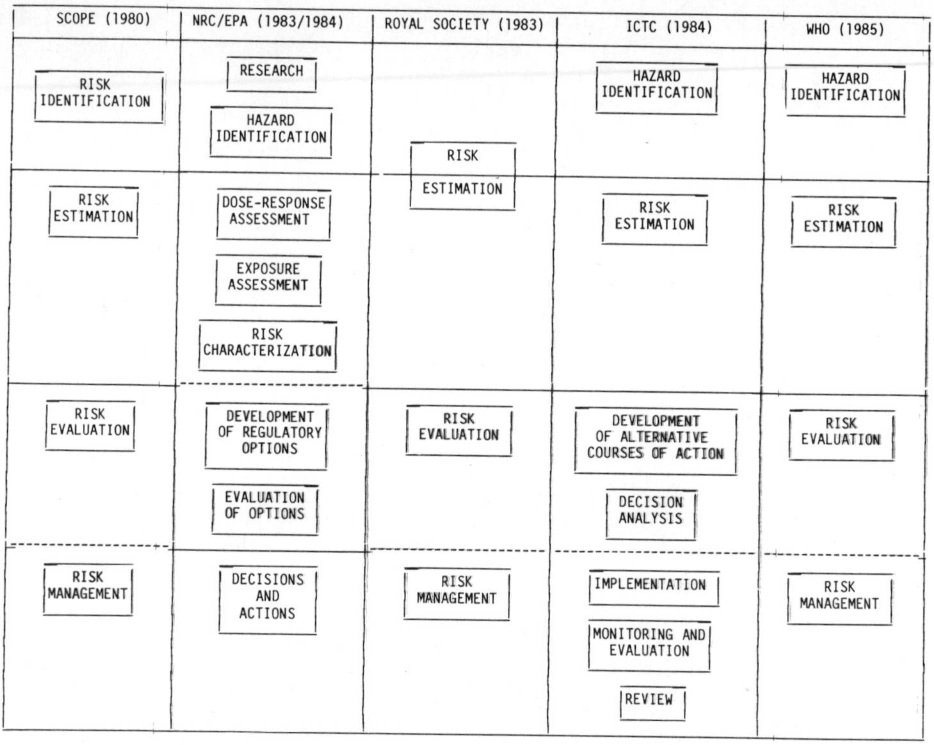

SCOPE (1980)	NRC/EPA (1983/1984)	ROYAL SOCIETY (1983)	ICTC (1984)	WHO (1985)
RISK IDENTIFICATION	RESEARCH HAZARD IDENTIFICATION	RISK ESTIMATION	HAZARD IDENTIFICATION	HAZARD IDENTIFICATION
RISK ESTIMATION	DOSE-RESPONSE ASSESSMENT EXPOSURE ASSESSMENT RISK CHARACTERIZATION		RISK ESTIMATION	RISK ESTIMATION
RISK EVALUATION	DEVELOPMENT OF REGULATORY OPTIONS EVALUATION OF OPTIONS	RISK EVALUATION	DEVELOPMENT OF ALTERNATIVE COURSES OF ACTION DECISION ANALYSIS	RISK EVALUATION
RISK MANAGEMENT	DECISIONS AND ACTIONS	RISK MANAGEMENT	IMPLEMENTATION MONITORING AND EVALUATION REVIEW	RISK MANAGEMENT

Figure 1

A Comparison of Models for Risk Assessment and Risk Management
(dotted line indicates division between risk assessment
and risk management)

public policy considerations. The subsequent models are generally
described in more detail than is the scope model, and with the exception
of the Royal Society model, differentiate between identifying
alternatives, and the decision analysis tools used to choose amongst
them. Alternative options may be of an advisory, economic or regulatory
nature, and many factors need to be considered in selecting a preferred
management strategy. These include the use of formal economic tools for
program evaluation (Torrance & Krewski, 1985), tempered by the public's
perception of the risk involved as well as prevailing socio-political
factors. Again, although not highlighted as distinct components, similar
considerations are included within the Royal Society's risk management
phase.

The final stage, informally termed risk management in the SCOPE
model, involves the implementation of the control strategy selected. Each
of the models, except the NRC/EPA, and WHO models, I stresses the need for
risk monitoring and follow-up, with a view to modifying the risk
management strategy currently in place should this be considered in
appropriate. All models, except the SCOPE model also stress the
importance of communication at the implementation stage so that affected
parties are properly informed as to both the risks and risk management
strategy adopted.

One point which remains obscure is the location of the division between risk assessment and risk management. The original SCOPE model seems to consider risk assessment as encompassing both the scientific enterprises of hazard identification and risk estimation as well as the more politicized function of risk evaluation. In this model, the term risk management is thus reserved for the final implementation and follow-up stage. This point of view is also adopted in the Royal Society, ICTC and WHO models. The NRC/EPA, on the other hand, define risk assessment as consisting only of hazard identification and risk estimation.

Taking into account differences in terminology, all models essentially agree on the division of the scientific and social aspects of the risk assessment and risk management process. Hazard identification and risk estimation are clearly in the scientific realm, whereas risk evaluation and risk management fall within the domain of social decisionmaking. Thus, the responsibility for risk analysis rests largely with the scientific community, whereas those responsible for the establishment and implementation of risk management decisions play the leading role in extrascientific matters (Ruckelshaus, 1983).

Although there is general agreement that the risk assessment/ management framework can be divided into scientific and policy concerns, Davis (1983) maintains that both science and values play a role in risk assessment and that the steps in the risk control process are more interactive than sequential. During the risk assessment process, analysts may overlook hazards, deem them unimportant, or ignore them because they are difficult to assess. Decisions are often influenced by judgments or policy due to gaps in scientific information.

CONCLUSIONS

In this article, we have reviewed the major models for the risk assessment and risk management process. All of these models reflect the basic elements of original SCOPE model (risk identification, risk estimation, risk evaluation, and risk management) as described by Whyte & Burton (1980). Subsequent models more correctly refer to the initial step as hazard rather than risk identification, reflecting the fact that risk estimation requires a quantitative rather than qualitative description of adverse health effects.

Although all models involve scientific and public policy considerations, the only model which equates these two dimensions with those of risk assessment and risk management is that of the NRC/EPA. In the remaining models, the social evaluation is included in the risk assessment phase, leaving only the implementation of the chosen control strategies to the risk management phase.

The application of the models of risk assessment and risk management discussed here, to practical decision making situations should facilitate identification and clarification of the many important considerations in the complex process of risk assessment and risk management. This is particularly true of some of the more recent models which describe the component steps in detail, including the distinctive development of a range of viable risk management options and the criteria and tools to be applied in choosing among these options. Other considerations which may otherwise be overlooked include the need for continual monitoring and review as well as communication of information on risks and risk decision to all affected parties.

REFERENCES

Advisory Council on Occupational Health and Occupational Safety (1985). Advisory Memorandum 85-I, Criteria and Alternative Approaches for the Control of Hazardous Substances and Agents in the Workplace, Part I: Identification of Criteria, Ontario.

Davis, J. C. (1983). Science and policy in risk control. In: Risk Management of Existing Chemicals. Chemical Manufacturer's Association, Government Institutes, pp. 13-21.

Interdepartmental Working Group on Risk-Benefit Analysis (1984). Risk-Benefit Analysis in the Management of Toxic Chemicals. Agriculture Canada, Ottawa.

Kaplan, S. & Garrick, B.J. (1981). On the quantitative definition of risk. Risk Analysis 1: 11-28.

Krewski, D., Clayson, D., & McCullough, R.S. (1982). Identification and measurement of Risk. In: Living with Risk: Environmental Risk Management in Canada. (I. Burton, C.D. Fowle & R.S. McCullough, eds). Institute for Environmental Studies, Toronto, pp. 7-23.

Lave, L.B. (ed) (1982). Quantitative Risk Assessment in Regulation. Brookings Institution, Washington, D.C.

National Research Council, Committee on the Institutional Means for Assessment of Risks to Public Health (1983). Risk Assessment in the Federal Government: Managing the Process. National Academy Press, Washington, D.C., pp. 196-203.

Rodricks, J.V. and Tardiff, R.G. (1984). Conceptual basis for risk assessment. In: Assessment and Management of Chemical Risks. American Chemical Society, Washington, D.C., pp. 1-12.

Royal Society Study Group (1983). Risk Assessment: A Study Group Report. Royal Society, London., pp. 22-23, 149-184.

Ruckelshaus, W.D. (1983). Science, risk and public policy. Science 221: 1026-1028.

Shrader-Frechette, K.S. (1985). Risk Analysis and Scientific Method. D. Reidal Publishing, Boston., pp. 15-48.

Torrance, G. & Krewski, D. (1985). Economic evaluation of toxic chemical control programs. Submitted.

United States Environmental Protection Agency (1984). Risk Assessment and Management: Framework for Decision Making. EPA 600/9-85-002, Environmental Protection Agency, Washington, D.C.

Whyte, A.V. & Burton, I. (eds) (1980). Environmental Risk Assessment. Wiley, New York., pp. 10-14.

World Health Organization, Working Group on Health and the Environment (1984). Risk Assessment and Its Use in the Decision Making Process for Chemical Control. ICP/RCE 903(28), World Health Organization, Geneva.

World Health Organization (1985). Risk Management in Chemical Safety. ICP/CEH 506/m01 56881. World Health Organization, European Regional Program on Chemical Safety, Geneva.

ECONOMIC THEORY OF COMPENSATION RULE DESIGN FOR

PROBABILISTIC INJURIES

Louis A. Cox, Jr.

Arthur D. Little, Inc.
Massachusetts Insitute of Technology

ABSTRACT

An important recent development in the theory of social risk
management has been the systematic exploration of the roles of private
information and incentives in the design of insurance policies,
compensation rules, tort liability standards, and regulatory provisions.
Such mechanisms attempt, among other things, to motivate economic agents
to allocate their risk avoidance efforts so as to minimize the total
social costs of risk bearing. This paper presents a unifying framework,
based on this perspective, for designing risk management mechanisms.
Namely, the designer must choose a rule that will cause potential injurers
and victims to choose "desirable" behavior in strategic equilibrium.

The main objectives of this paper are: (1) To show how much
mechanisms as product liability, insurance rating schemes, administrative
compensation programs, and health and safety regulation can be brought
within a common economic framework and analyzed according to a common set
of normative design principles; (2) To show how differences in the costs
and availability of information to different parties such as regulators or
economic agents (e.g., the ability of injured parties to identify their
probable injuries ex post and ex ante) can both explain and predict the
types of risks for which regulation is likely to be the most effective
management strategy, and the types for which alternatives such as tort
law, insurance, or related instruments such as fines or injunctions, are
likely to be more appropriate; and (3) to identify potential roles for the
social decision maker in enhancing the efficiency of risk management.

KEY WORDS   Social decision analysis, risk management, alternatives to
            regulation, second-party and third-party risks, rights

1. INTRODUCTION

This paper considers the problem faced by a monolithic "social
decision maker" (SDM) concerned with managing the risk from a risky
(accident-generating) economic activity. For concreteness, we will assume
that the activity is production of a consumer product, which potentially
threatens employees in the production process, consumers of the product,
and neighbors who may be put at risk from "externalities" generated by the
production activity. The SDM seeks to assure that continued operation of
the activity is in the public interest, in the vague sense that "its
benefits outweigh its risks": otherwise, he is empowered to shut it down.

2. A SIMPLE ACCIDENT MODEL

Formally, a production process may be thought of in terms of a "production function" mapping flows of inputs (capital and labor) per unit time into flows of outputs (consumer products, pollution) per unit time. At the consumer end, use or consumption of a product over time produces a flow of value to the consumer. In addition to these deterministic flows, both the production and consumption activities may entail risks, i.e., occurrences of untoward events such as illnesses and injuries whose arrivals occur at random (and possibly not at all) in the activity stream.

A simple static model useful for representing this situation supposes that the producer has a <u>control technology</u> available to him, represented by a pair $[c(x),p(x)]$, where x is his level of "care", $c(x)$ is the dollar cost to him of taking care level x, and $p(x)$ is the probability that a potential victim (consumer, employer, or neighbor) will suffer an injury when care level x has been taken. Only one potential victim at a time is considered.

Despite the evident simplifications in this model, it and its extensions lead to a number of useful insights into the problems of risk management and into the potential roles that the SDM can play. In the remainder of this paper, we analyze the voluntary risk management contracts that might emerge between producer and potential victims in the absence of the SDM, and investigate how the SDM can intervene to improve on these voluntary contracts.

3. PRIVATE CONTRACTING AS A MODEL FOR MANAGING SECOND-PARTY RISKS

We define a "second-party" risk as one arising from a voluntary economic transaction between two agents, such as from sale of a product to a willing (though perhaps ignorant) buyer, or from an employment agreement.

3.1 Contract Negotiation Between Perfectly Informed Parties

A. A Distributive Bargaining Model of Negotiation

In the simplest case, neither party can directly control risk, except by refusing to participate in transactions whose terms are unacceptable to him given his information. Risk to the potential victim (consumer or employee) is adequately characterized by a pair (p,D), where p is the probability that he will be injured if the transaction is consummated and D is the magnitude of the damage if injury occurs. Both players are assumed to be risk neutral, with D being measured in dollar terms. This is oversimplified since we are concerned with health and safety risks, but is warranted by the fact that most of our results are negative; extensions to more general utility functions can easily be made.

A contract in this context is a pair (w,L), where w is the ex ante monetary transfer (selling price) between the parties and L is the ex post payment to be made by the producer to the victim in the event of an accident (a form of "provider insurance", "worker's compensation", or "producer liability".) Because of the assumption of risk neutrality, a contract (w,L) between a consumer and producer, for example, is evaluated by both parties at the time of contracting as equivalent (indifferent) to a contract $(w - pL, 0)$ with compensation being paid ex ante rather than ex post. The two parties may thus be seen as actually negotiating over the single quantity $w - pL$.

The dollar economic value of the labor-power or consumer product transferred in a transaction is assumed to be v to its receiver and c to its original owner. Henceforth, we shall use the producer-consumer example throughout our discussion of second-party transactions; all results, however, apply equally well to the employer-employee relationship. The possible expected gains from trade, evaluated at the time of contracting, are thus v -c -pD, which we assume to be positive. The terms of the contract, w - pL, allocate this potential social surplus between the two agents, with the producer's surplus being w - pL - c and the consumer's surplus being v - pD - (w - pL).

In the absence of an SDM, we assume that private contracting on w - pL between the two parties is the only mode of risk management. The mechanism of negotiation is assumed to be alternating offers and counter-offers of proposed w - pL amounts. The potential consumer or employee is assumed to open the negotiations, and the first offer made by one party that is accepted by the other is implemented. Bargaining costs per period are assumed to be fixed and to differ for the two players.

B. A Solution to the Distributive Bargaining Problem (Rubinstein, 1982)

To predict the outcome of this contract negotiation process it is necessary to use modern game-theoretic concepts. Specifically, we define a strategy of a player to be any (possibly randomized) decision rule specifying the offer to be made by him at any time (when it is his turn) as a function of the sequence of offers and counteroffers that he has observed so far. A pair of strategies (f,g) for the producer and potential victim, respectively, is a Nash equilibrium pair if neither player can increase his expected payoff by unilateral deviation from his strategy, given that the other player dos not deviate. Thus, f is a "best response" against g, and conversely. For example, any division of the social surplus could be a Nash equilibrium, if each player could credibly commit himself to accepting nothing else.

The strategy pair (f,g) is said to be a perfect equilibrium if, after any sequence of offers generated during the bargaining, f and g are still in Nash equilibrium from that point on. Thus a player's threats to take an action (such as permanently walking away from the bargaining table if his demands aren't met) that it is common knowledge that he would regret actually having to carry out are ruled out as "noncredible", and may not be used as part of a perfect equilibrium.

The concept of perfect equilibrium as a model for bargaining between rational players can be applied to the w - pL negotiation game. If each player's preferences are stationary, continuous, and exhibit a weak form of impatience -- three concepts made precise in Rubinstein, 1982 -- and are common knowledge, then a unique perfect equilibrium solution exists to this negotiation problem.

RESULT 1: (Rubinstein, 1982): Under the above assumptions, the producer and the potential victim will immediately agree to a contract in which the player with the lower bargaining costs captures essentially all the expected gains from trade.

For example, if w is fixed by market conditions and negotiation is over L alone, then the unique perfect-equilibrium outcome requires the producer to immediately accept either full liability or (virtually) no liability.

Here, and throughout the paper, we omit formal and precise statements and proofs in the interest of brevity. We shall, however, try to make clear the intuitive meaning and scope of each result presented. Exact results are given in the references, and in most cases the extensions and adaptations required for the current context are straightforward.

Result 1 implies that, left to themselves, the producer and his potential victim will agree on a lopsided allocation of risk reflecting relative bargaining strength. (If the producer has lower bargaining costs, he will accept his one-period bargaining cost for liability, but we assume that this is trivial.) Although possibly inequitable, this outcome is Pareto-efficient. It is achieved without costly haggling, and the full potential social surplus is actually obtained and allocated between the two players. There is no role for the SDM in improving ex ante efficiency, although (s)he may which to intervene to prevent one party from appropriating a disproportionate share of the expected gains from trade, or to prevent inequitable ex post allocations of risk.

3.2 Contract Negotiation with Private Information

A. Inefficiency of Negotiated Contracts

We can extend the preceding model by allowing one or both players to have private information. Such extensions destroy the efficiency conclusion of Result 1, however. For example, suppose the producer knows the "risk" of his product (or process), captured by the probability p of an accident, while the potential consumer (or employee) knows only that p is equally likely to be "safe" (p = 0.1) or "dangerous" (p = 0.9).

Let the amount of the producer's potential liability L be limited to some maximum amount, L*, e.g., by a wealth or corporate liability constraint, and assume that the contract (w,L*) gives both players positive expected payoff for p = 0.1, but that it gives the consumer negative expected payoff for p greater than 0.3, for example. Then even if the producer knows that the produce is "safe" (p = 0.1), he has no credible way of signalling this to the consumer. For whether p = 0.1 or p = 0.9, he will make the same claims to convince the consumer that it is "safe", perhaps blaming any subsequent accidents on exceptional bad luck. Knowing this the consumer, for whom p = 0.5 is unacceptable, will not buy the product. Thus, even if potential gains from trade exist, there is no practical way for the two parties to achieve them without outside assistance.

This illustrates the following rule, which holds with great generality:

RESULT 2: (Samuelson, 1984; Chatterjee, 1985): Private information creates inefficiency in private negotiations and distributive bargaining.

This inefficiency result extends to many contexts, including competitive markets in which producers have private information about product safety. If safer products are more costly to produce but impossible to signal, for example, then "bad" producers will drive "good" ones out of the market, and the entire market may collapse as consumers cease buying products which are no longer high - safety on average (Shapiro, 1982, and references therein.)

Private information can make it impossible to reach a mutually beneficial contract even if one exists, as in the above example, or can impose dead-weight costs on the players during the negotiation process. To avoid these (sometimes prohibitive) costs, players may find it advantageous ex ante to commit themselves to negotiation procedures (such as first-and-final offers) that put positive probability on an impasse even when gains from trade exist in principle. The "efficiency" of any particular contract negotiation process must be judged separately from the standpoint of each player's ex ante expectations based only on his private information at that time, and from the standpoint of the information that he ends up having after the process has concluded.

B. One-Sided Control of Risk (Harris and Raviv, 1978; Shavell, 1982)

The same sorts of conclusions emerge when the producer has a control technology $(p(x),c(x))$ available to him, and can choose from an entire range of x values ("care levels"). This is the situation in the above example if, instead of only knowing p, the producer gets to choose it, again assuming that lower p's require greater costs. Again, the producer will always have an incentive in any one-shot transaction to choose a low x value, and so the consumer, knowing this, will not buy from him.

Even if producer liability L is not exogenously constrained, efficient contracts can not in general be designed when x is private information. For let (w,L) by any contract. The expected payoff to the producer is then $A(x) = w - c(x) - p(x)L$, while the expected payoff to the consumer is $B(x) = v - w - p(x)(D - L)$. In principle, a Pareto-efficient outcome requires that the producer choose x to maximize the sum $T(x) = A(x) + B(X) = v - c(x) - p(x)D$ and that this surplus (which is independent of w and L) then be allocated between the two players. However, in fact, the producer seeks to maximize $A(x)$ given the allocation determined by the contract (w,L). That is, he will choose x such that $A'(x) = 0$, rather than so that $T'(x) = 0$ (where we assume that $[p(x), c(x)]$ is such that each of these first-order conditions identifies a unique interior maximum.) Only if L = D will these first- order conditions coincide, so that in solving his own problem -- maximization of $A(x)$ -- the producer will also be maximizing social surplus $T(x)$. We can summarize this observation as

RESULT 3: A Pareto-optimal contract requires that the risk neutral producer fully "insure" the consumer by paying him an amount L = D equal to the damage that he suffers if an accident occurs. Any other choice of L will, under appropriate assumptions about the control technology $(p(x),c(x))$, (e.g., that first-order conditions determine a unique internal maximum) induce the producer to choose a value of x that is either too great or too small.

With this result in mind, it becomes clear that whenever the producer is able to negotiate for himself a value of L less than D, he will also end up putting in too little care to maximize total social surplus, $T(x)$.

A stronger result holds when D, the amount of damage to the consumer if an accident occurs, is an ex post jointly observable random variable whose distribution $F(D;x)$ is stochastically decreasing in x. Suppose we allow the consumer to choose any contract terms $(w, L(D))$, with the producer's sole right being to refuse to participate in a contract that gives him negative expected utility. In economic terminology, the consumer acts as a "principal" and the producer as his "agent" (Harris and Raviv, 1978; Shavell, 1982).

Given any acceptable contract, $(w, L(D))$, the producer will choose x to maximize his own expected utility. Assume that $c(x)$ displays increasing marginal costs and is continuous in x, that both players are risk averse, and that the control technology $(F(\bullet;x),c(x))$ is common knowledge. A Nash equilibrium in this context is found as follows. For any liability rule L = L(D), the consumer can calculate what value of x, say $x^*(L)$, the producer would choose in response to L to maximize his own expected utility. The consumer can also calculate what his own expected utility would be, given the producer's "best-response" level of care, $x^*(L)$. He will therefore choose a liability rule L^* such that $x^*(L^*)$

gives him a higher expected utility than x*(L), for any other liability rule L. The pair (L*,x*(L*)) is a Nash equilibrium: each player's choice (of L for the consumer, and of x for the producer) is a "best response" to the other's.

To understand the effects of private information, we can compare the efficiency of the Nash equilibrium outcome when x and D are both jointly observable, denoted by [L*(x,D),x*(L*)], with the Nash equilibrium outcome when only D is jointly observable, [L*(D),x*(L*)].

RESULT 4: In the above situation, if x and D are both jointly observable, than an ex ante Pareto-efficient liability rule will have the form L*(x,D) = 0 for x greater than x', L*(x,D) = L*(D) for x less than x', i.e., the payment made from the producer to his victim is zero if he has not been "negligent" (used a level of care less than some level x' specified in the contract), and depends only on the amount of damage, but not on his care level, if he has been negligent.

RESULT 5: In the above situation, the producer takes less care when x is his private information than when x is publically observable, i.e., x*[L*(D)] is less than x*[L*(x,D)].

RESULT 6: In the above situation, both the producer and his potential victim have lower ex ante expected payoffs (utilities) in the Nash equilibrium outcome when x is private information than when x is jointly observable.

This implies that having x private information unambiguously damages welfare. it is an illustration in the principal-agent context of result 2: that ex ante Pareto-efficient outcomes can not in general be implemented as strategic equilibria of contracts arrived at by agents with private information.

RESULT 7: Suppose that x is "partially" jointly observable, in the sense that some variable s that is correlated with x is jointly observable. (For example, x might be the producer's actual level of "care", and s might be the number of dollars that he budgets for product safety research.) Then both players' expected payoffs can be improved by making the liability rule depend on s, i.e., by using a liability rule of the form L(s,D) instead of L(D).

C. Two-Sided Control of Risk (Holmstrom, 1982; Kambhu, 1982; Cooper & Ross, 1985)

Finally, suppose that both players have some control over risk, that both are again risk neutral, and that each player's level of "care" is his private information. The producer's payoff from a contract (w,L) when he uses care level x and the consumer uses care level y is A(w,L,x,y) = w - c(x) - p(x,y)L. The corresponding payoff to the consumer is B(w,L,x,y) = v - w - b(y) - p(x,y)(D - L), where b(y) is the consumer's cost function for his "cost", assumed like c(x) to be increasing and convex (increasing marginal costs). We also assume that b(0) = c(0) = 0. The risk function p(x,y) is assumed to be smoothly decreasing and convex (diminishing returns to care) in each argument.

The Nash equilibria corresponding to different liability rules L can be analyzed as above by considering the "best response" functions x*(y;L) and y*(x;L) giving each player's optimal (expected payoff-maximizing) level of care, given the other's level of care and the liability rule being used. Where these "response curves" intersect, the players' care levels, say x* and y*, are in Nash equilibrium. Under appropriate assumptions about the control technology, [p(x,y),c(x),b(y)], e.g., that x and y have complementary effects on reducing p(x,y), it can be shown that the response curves x*(y) and y*(x) will intersect exactly once, establishing the existence of a unique Nash equilibrium.

RESULT 8: In the above situation, with two-sided control over risk, there is no value of L that will induce both players to choose jointly Pareto-optimal levels of care as a Nash equilibrium.

In other words, as in the principal-agent context, it is impossible to implement a Pareto-efficient outcome as a Nash equilibrium of some liability rule when x and y are private information. This result holds no matter how L is determined--whether by negotiation, by the consumer alone, or by an outside SDM. The conclusion depends on specific technical assumptions, however, such as that x and y are continuous control variables, rather than having only a few discrete levels.

RESULT 9: In the above situation, ex ante Pareto efficiency can sometimes be improved by allowing each player to commit himself to paying a fine if an accident occurs (where by a "fine" is meant any payment that goes outside the system. For example, destruction of one's property would constitute a "fine" in this sense, but a payment by one party to the other in the event of an accident would not.)

By committing themselves to pay fines if an accident occurs, the players can signal to each other their intentions to take enough care so that payment will very probably not be necessary. As in the case of one-sided information, budget constraints or other limitations on contingent payments can make such signalling impossible and reduce Pareto efficiency, either by preventing a contract from taking place, or by causing to few or too many resources to be spent on risk avoidance. "Too much" defensive expenditure occurs when one party spends resources on risk reduction, even though the other has lower marginal costs of risk reduction, because the cheaper risk averter can't be trusted to spend to reduce risk.

Result 9 illustrates again the conflict between ex ante and ex post efficiency when players have private information. Clearly, it is inefficient for players to pay a fine after an accident occurs, when they have already taken due care to reduce its risks. Yet unless they can commit themselves ex ante to pay such penalties in the event of an accident, they will not be able to trust each other to take due care (and in fact will have incentives not to), so that a contract may become impossible or inefficient. Keeping payments within the system by redistributing the fines between the players would undermine their incentives to take care and the signalling value of the precommitment to pay penalties. Similar results apply to any number of players.

4. POTENTIAL ROLES FOR THE SDM IN MANAGING SECOND-PARTY RISKS

Understanding the weaknesses of voluntary contracting as a method of managing second-party risks suggests several potential roles for the SDM in improving the efficiency of risk management. Important roles suggested by the foregoing analysis include the following:

- The SDM as Equity-Promoter: As already suggested, the SDM may wish to intervene in private negotiations to prevent one party from exploiting its superior bargaining strength (or its superior information about transaction risks) to take unfair advantage of the other. OSHA standards for workplace safety, CPSC and FDA standards

for consumer products, as well as right-to-know and duty-to-disclose
legislation and regulations may be seen in this light as devices to
prevent exploitative behavior in second-party transactions.

- **The SDM as Information Provider/Signaller**: When the producer has
control technology $(p(x),c(x))$, the SDM can establish a minimum level
of x by fiat, i.e., through (enforced) regulation. Knowing that this
minimum level of x is guaranteed by the SDM may give potential
consumers the assurance they need to engage in mutually beneficial
transactions with vendors of risky products. In addition to outright
regulation (setting x levels), the SDM can also signal information
through certification, licensing, and grading programs -- a role
played by government agencies such as USDA and FDA.

  Still a third way in which the SDM can fill the informational gap
  between agents that might otherwise prevent mutually beneficial
  transactions is by providing for ex post determination of care levels
  after an accident occurs. By making care levels publicly
  observable after the fact, the SDM can allow ex ante compensation
  rules with improved efficiency, i.e., rules of the form $L(x,D)$ (or
  possibly $L(s,d)$ if the SDM's ex post assessment is imperfect),
  inducing Nash equilibria that are Pareto-superior to any achievable
  through private contracts of the form $L(D)$. (See Results 6 and 7.)
  This informational role may, in practice be filled to some extent by
  the courts, by insurance companies, and by agencies such as the FAA
  that conduct inquiries into who was "at fault", and to what extent,
  in causing an accident.

- **The SDM as Terms-Setter**: Potentially prohibitive private negotiation
costs can be alleviated by having the SDM set the terms of "implicit
contracts" that agents are required to abide by. Much of tort law
can be interpreted as a set of implicit contracts that avoids the
necessity of costly explicit contracting in everyday activities and
transactions. Rather than having the parties negotiate compensation
rule L, the SDM (or the courts, in practice), can set L based on the
equilibrium strategic behavior (care levels) that he expects it to
induce.

  If x is not observable to the SDM, however, then Result 5 still
  holds, with the SDM now playing the role of the principal, and he can
  design no rule that will induce a Pareto-efficient level of care as a
  Nash equilibrium.

- **The SDM as Budget Constraint Breaker**: The effects of individual
budget constraints on limiting an individual's ability to signal his
high care levels has been mentioned several times. If x is
observable to the SDM, then he can signal high levels of x to
potential consumers by providing extensive, publically observable,
liability insurance to the producer, if it is known that he acts as
an expected profit-maximizing insurer.

  The SDM can also serve as a sink for "fines". The producer, for
example, can precommit himself to pay a penalty (possibly in excess of the
damage to the consumer) if an accident occurs, and the SDM can collect
these payments and use them elsewhere in society -- perhaps to operate the
insurance role just described. Thus, the potential gains mentioned in
Result 9 can be achieved without wasting any of society's resources. In
each individual transaction, penalty payments effectively pass out of the
system, but overall, they are used to finance social insurance and other
beneficial public activities. Everyone, including the participants in the

original transaction (who gain by being able to signal) gain from this scheme. This suggests and effective combined role for the SDM in providing liability insurance (a signalling role) with adjustable premiums (a "fining" role) for accidents.

In summary, because voluntary contracting tends to be inefficient when individuals have private information, the SDM has a chance to improve on the resource allocations that pairs of individuals could obtain by themselves. Three primary avenues for intervention are (i) the regulatory approach, in which he directly sets and enforces levels of care, x and y, to be used by the parties; (ii) the tort law approach, in which he sets liability or compensation rules, e.g., L(x,y) (depending on what he can observe) that will motivate the parties to take due care in strategic equilibrium; and (iii) the administrative approach, including social insurance, in which the SDM sets or collects fines and makes payments or provides insurance, both to give agents appropriate risk-avoidance incentives to allow them to signal high care levels, and to maximize their expected welfares from participation in an economy of risky transactions.

The SDM can play other roles in managing second-party risks, for example, through his ability to effectively randomize compensation payments (arguably one role of the courts), or to exploit the positive externality of statistical stabilization across many independent risky transactions to provide personal health and safety insurance. The roles summarized above, however, illustrate principles that are useful for classes of risks that can not be well addressed by contracting. These are discussed in the following section.

5. THIRD-PARTY AND OTHER RISKS

Many risks arise not out of voluntary transactions between a potential injurer and a potential victim, but out of production or sale risk externalities. Important examples include:

- The health and safety risks to local populations from the operation of a chemical plant or a nuclear reactor. We call such risks, imposed by an activity on potential victims without their consent (and perhaps without their knowledge) "third party risks". A special case are public risks, in which the risk-imposing activity is sanctioned by public or collective choice (as in the case of some hazardous facilities).

- The risks to sensitive individuals from a new drug that is safe and beneficial to most consumers, but dangerous to a few. (The externality here is that protecting the few sensitive members of the population, if there is no way to screen them, may deprive others of the benefits of the drug.) This is a "heterogenous response" risk. Heterogenous responses are also important in occupational populations.

- The risk created by multiple producers, or by the interaction of multiple products or risk factors (e.g., the health risks of the combined pollutants from multiple sources, or the cancer risks from consumption of Saccharin.) This is an example of a distributed risk, in which it is not possible even in principle for the victim to identify a single party as the cause of his injury, either before or after the fact.

A compensation rule for a third-party risk specifies what payments must be made by a producer to or on behalf of his neighbors as a precondition for his continued participation in the activity. (A payment "on behalf of" the process's neighbors would take the form of risk reduction and mitigation expenditures by the producer, which can be thought of as payments made "to" the neighbors in terms of increased safety.) A similar definition applies to heterogenous response risks. Compensation rules for distributed risks (and perhaps for some public risks) require a specification of how compensation costs should be allocated among multiple responsible injurers, e.g., through tax-funded social insurance programs, and will not be considered in this paper.

5.1 The SDM as Rights-Assigner

In second-party negotiations, failure of the parties to reach a mutually beneficial agreement implies that the risk-producing transaction will not take place. The "right" of each participant not to have "unacceptable" risk-cost-benefit combinations imposed up him is thus automatically protected by his ability to veto any proposed agreement. Rights are more complicated in the third-party case, where the right of the producer to produce (and perhaps of his consumers to have him produce) must be balanced against the neighbor's right to be protected from imposed risks.

To cut through some of this complexity, the SDM can allow the producer and neighbor to negotiate privately over the amount of compensation to be paid by the producer (and perhaps indirectly by his consumers through increases in product price) to or on behalf of the neighbor if production is to continue. Only if no negotiated settlement is achieved will the SDM impose a solution. Then the problem of compensation rule design for the SDM reduces to the problem of choosing a "no-agreement" point for third-party negotiations. This role is also played by courts when they provide the no-agreement outcome for out-of-court settlement negotiations <u>after</u> an accident or injury has occurred.

An SDM or judge typically has at least the following goals in designing default compensation rules:

(i) <u>Economic efficiency in individual cases.</u> If the producer and neighbor in a specific case are thought of as negotiating over "ownership" of a production right, then economic efficiency requires that the one who values it more highly should end up with it, i.e., that production continues only if its value to the producer (and his customers) exceeds the value of non-production to the producer's neighbor(s).

(ii) <u>Economic efficiency on average</u>. The court wishes to design compensation rules that will induce efficient ex ante risk avoidance behavior and efficient out-of-court settlements in cases that never come to court. Since most cases in the United States are settled out of court, this is an extremely important objective in practice.

(iii) <u>Protection of individual rights</u>. The compensation rule used should respect the initial allocation of rights to produce or to be protected from production externalities, respectively. Pre-assigned or court-determined rights automatically establish the no-agreement point for private third-party negotiations, and the court merely has to enforce them. How rights should initially be assigned is a separate, difficult subject, involving entitlement dynamics such as differences in the allocation of production rights according as the producer moved in before or after his current neighbors.

Unfortunately, these goals are in general incompatible.

RESULT 10: (Samuelson, 1985) When the producer and neighbor have private information about the value of the production right to themselves, no initial preassignment of rights can guarantee economically efficient negotiated outcomes.

The reason is that ownership of a production right is here assigned before learning who values it most highly. If private values for production rights were common knowledge, and if there were no effective budget constraints or transaction costs, then the initial assignment of rights would not compromise long-run economic efficiency. Whichever party, producer or neighbor, valued the production right most highly would end up owning it or purchasing it ("Coase's Theorem".) In a world of private information, however, private bargaining is not efficient (Result 2), and Coase's Theorem no longer applies.

5.2 The SDM as Social Arbiter

Instead of passively pre-assigning rights and allowing private negotiations to take care of third-party risks thereafter, the SDM can actively serve as an arbiter in cases where out-of-court settlement negotiations fail to lead to agreement. We assume that the SDM hears many such cases and enforces a consistent rule or set of rules in each, mapping statements of preferences, beliefs, abilities, and so forth by the producer and neighbor into an amount of compensation (possibly zero) to be paid by the producer to or on behalf of the neighbor for production to continue.

RESULT 11: (Myerson and Satterthwaite 1983): When players have private information about their preferences and beliefs (including beliefs about each other's preferences and beliefs), there may be no compensation rule mapping player statements into enforced settlements that will induce the players to make statements that will produce a Pareto-efficient settlement.

Implicit in this result is an assumption that the players are strategically rational, i.e., that they will make statements that are in "Bayesian Nash equilibrium" with each other. In other words, neither player believes that he can increase his own expected payoff by changing his own statement to the SDM (judge), given his beliefs about the judge's compensation rule and about the other player's statement.

RESULT 12: To achieve increased economic efficiency averaged over all cases, the SDM may have to enforce settlements in individual cases that risk violating case-specific economic efficiency.

For example, if the SDM expects the neighbor to exaggerate the value of non-production to him, he may allow the producer to make a compensation payment that is less than the neighbor's stated minimum acceptable amount. But this risks having production continue even when the disbenefit to the neighbor really does exceed the benefit to the producer (and his consumers.) Conversely, the SDM may sometimes shut down activities that would have been left open if all private information were made public.

RESULT 13: (Crawford, 1985): The agents in an economy can often agree on a set of compensation rules, to be implemented by the SDM, before learning their private information (e.g., before learning who will play what roles in future cases) that gives greater expected payoffs to all participants than any set of rules that they would be able to agree on after learning their private information.

For example, agents may all be able to gain on average by agreeing to accept inefficiently great (e.g., bankrupting) punitive damages for certain types of accidents, if the deterrent effects of the agreement allow everyone to be assured that such accidents will be very rare. (Here, we assume that the control technology is such that it is impossible or uneconomic to eliminate accidents altogether. Whether these expected gains translate into actual gains for each individual over his lifetime, or whether some individuals suffer ex post inequitable losses, depends on assumptions about the number of independent transactions that each individual participates in over his life in which the compensation rules play a direct or implicit role. Result 13 implies that cost-risk-benefit analysis of one case or decision at a time may not always provide the most fruitful perspective for public risk management decisions: it is the efficiency and equity of the <u>process</u> averaged over all cases, rather than of each outcome that it generates, that must be judged.

6. CONCLUSION

This paper has examined several possible roles that a hypothetical monolithic social decision maker (SDM) could play in managing the risks from economic activities. Table 1 summarizes possible roles under different information conditions -- assumptions about who knows what when.

Our observations suggest that the design of compensation rules as a unifying approach to several aspects of risk management is apt to be fruitful for political economists interested in social risk management. It should be clear from this initial discussion, however, that there are important aspects of compensation rule design that require further research. For example, if the control technology is known to the producer but not to the SDM, or if, as is likely in some "toxic tort" cases, the control technology is not known to anyone, then the design of ex post compensation rules raises special difficulties. Personal or socially subsidized insurance, which we have not considered here, may be the most appropriate mechanism for risk management when the incentive and information roles provided by compensation rules are inapplicable -- e.g., because the SDM and the economic agents involved have insufficient knowledge of the control technology, or because risks are "distributed", with individual agents being unable to control them except through collective action.

Finally, this essay has suggested that the most appropriate perspective to take in designing compensation rules may be the "participatory" or "process" perspective, in which the SDM, or the agents in society acting collectively outside the context of any particular case, choose compensation rules that are expected to induce efficiency-maximizing behavior on average (though at its expense in certain individual cases). Whether this perspective, which contains elements of the Rawlsian conception of justice as well as catering to economic efficiency, can in fact be reconciled with deontological compensation principles remains to be seen.

Table 1

Potential Roles for the SDM in Social Risk Management
as a Function of Information Conditions

Producer's Level of Care, x, Known To				Potential Role for SDM	Risk Management Methods for Filling Roles	
---SDM---		-Consumer-			Regulatory	Non-Regulatory
Ex Ante	EX Post	Ex Ante	Ex Post			

1.	✓	✓	✓	✓	Equity Promotor	Set x to "fairly" divide expected gains from trade.	Set L (courts)
2.	✓	✓	X	✓	Exploitation Preventer	Enforce "Right-to-know" and "duty-to-warn" legislation.	
3.	✓	✓	X	--	Signaller/ Information Provider	Set and enforce standards (x≥x') (Regulation)	Underwrite liability (Insurance) Inspect, license, grade, certify
4.	✓	✓	X	--	Permit more efficient signalling by breaking budget constraints	--	Provide liability insurance; collect "fines" and penalties (Insurance)
5.	X	✓	X	X	Permit more efficient contracts.	--	Allow L(x, D) instead of L(D) (Courts)
6.	X	X	X	X	Incentive Provider	--	Set L(D)

Third Party Risks

- Rights Assigner
- No-agreement point setter
- Social arbiter and rules enforcer

Key

✓ = Information Known
X = Information Not Known
-- = Information May Be Known Or Unknown

REFERENCES

Chatterjee, K., "Disagreement in Bargaining: Models with Incomplete Information", Chapter 2 in A. Roth (ed.) <u>Game-Theoretic Models of Bargaining</u>, Cambridge University Press, Cambridge, MA, 1985 (in press).

Cooper, R., and T. W. Ross, "Product Warranties and Double Moral Hazard", <u>The Rand Journal of Economics, 16</u>, 1, Spring, 1985, 103-113.

Crawford, V.P., "The Role of Arbitration and the Theory of Incentives", in A. Roth (ed.) <u>Game-Theoretic Models of Barganing,</u> Cambridge University press, Cambridge, MA, 1985 (in press).

Harris, M., and Raviv, A., "Some Results on Incentive Contracts with Applications to Education and Employment, Health Insurance, and Law Enforcement", <u>American Economic Review, 68</u>, 1, 1978, 20-30.

Holmstrom, B., "Moral Hazard in Teams", <u>Bell Journal of Economics, 13</u>, 2, Autumn, 1982, 324-340.

Kambhu, J., "Optimal Product Quality Under Asymmetric Information and Moral Hazard", <u>Bell Journal of Economics, 13</u>, Autumn, 1982, 483-492.

Myerson, R., and M. Satterthwaite, "Efficient Mechanisms for Bilateral Trading", <u>Journal of Economic Theory, 29</u>, 1983, 265-281.

Rubinstein, A., "Perfect Equilibrium in a Bargaining Model", <u>Econometrica, 50</u>, 1, 1982, 97-109.

Samuelson, W., "Bargaining under Asymmetric Information", <u>Econometrica, 52</u>, 1984, 995-1005.

-- "A Comment on the Coase Theorem", forthcoming in A. Roth (ed.) <u>Game-Theoretic Models of Bargaining</u>, Cambridge University Press, Cambridge, MA, 1985 (in press).

C. Shapiro, "Consumer Information, Product Quality, and Seller Reputation", <u>Bell Journal of Economics, 13</u>, 1, Spring, 1982, 20-35.

Shavell, S., "On Liability and Insurance", <u>Bell Journal of Economics, 13,</u> 1, Spring, 1982, 120-132.

RIGHT TO KNOW AND BEHAVIORAL RESPONSES

TO HAZARD WARNINGS*

W. Kip Viscusi* and Wesley A. Magat**

University of Chicago (Visiting) and Northwestern
University*, Fuqua School of Business, Duke University**

ABSTRACT

Survey data on consumer and worker responses to labels for hazardous products suggest that there are many rational aspects to economic behavior, particularly with respect to precautions. Nevertheless, there is evidence that consumers may overreact to low probability events. In addition, assessed risk perceptions appear to be quite sensitive to the framing of risk-related survey questions. The format in which the risk information is presented on labels is also instrumental.

KEY WORDS: labeling, right to know, framing, and information

1. INFORMATION AS A REGULATORY POLICY

In recent years labeling has become an increasingly popular regulatory approach to controlling the dangers from hazardous products. The Environmental Protection Agency (EPA) administers a long-standing program for labeling pesticide formulations, and the agency was given the power under the Toxic Substances Control Act (TOSCA) to use labels as a mechanism for controlling the hazards from other toxic chemicals. The Food and Drug Administration (FDA) sets labeling requirements for the ingredients of food and drug products. The Occupational Safety and Health Administration (OSHA) recently promulgated an extensive and costly chemical labeling program to protect workers. The Federal Trade Commission (FTC) has promulgated labeling regulations for products such as home insulation, textile wearing apparel, and used automobiles. The Consumer Product Safety Commission (CPSC) included labeling requirements in its lawnmower and CB antenna rules.

In addition, many states and cities have also launched initiatives in this general area. Most of these policies are directed at hazards arising in the workplace. In some instances, the risks involved affect the community at large. In these instances, the need to inform consumers of the risks so that they can take appropriate action hinges on the type of concerns explored in our consumer information survey.

Particularly for chemical hazards and other health risks, the general heading under which these policies have been placed is the "right to know" designation. Although this phraseology has popular appeal, we will not delve into the issue of whether individuals have or should be given the right to know the risks to which they are exposed. We will, however, address whether it is _efficient_ for individuals to have this information, and we will investigate the efficiency gains that are achievable under these right-to-know policies. For concreteness, we will discuss chemical labeling efforts, since they are the target of much of the right-to-know movement and the focus of our research.

Relative to other regulatory alternatives for controlling hazardous chemicals, labels possess two strong advantages. First, they allow chemical users with different preferences towards risk, different needs for the products, and different usage rates to select the combination of risk, product efficacy, and usage rates that is best for each of them. If individuals are "fully rational," giving them more information will only enhance their welfare. They can choose to leave their actions unaltered, or they can modify their actions in the presence of the new information if that is desirable. The principal exception to this welfare-enhancing property of information is that added information about risks that we cannot alter may create anxiety and welfare losses that outweigh the value of information for decision-making. In the usual case, however, more information is preferable to less. This property no doubt has contributed to the widespread advocacy of right-to-know policies by consumer groups.

The choice in governmental contexts is usually different since there the principal policy alternatives to inaction are informational policies or more direct, choice-limiting alternatives, such as restricting the uses of the chemical. The flexibility of informational policies differs from that of the standard-setting approach, which forces every consumer to face the same level of risk. The labeling alternative is more consistent with freedom of individual choice than standards or other policies dictated by a regulatory agency.

Notwithstanding the many appealing aspects of labels, little is known about their effectiveness in altering precautionary behavior. To increase our knowledge of the properties of labels we undertook surveys of consumer and worker responses to labels that we will review briefly here.

2. FRAMING AND FORMAT EFFECTS

Framing Risk Issues

Ideally, one would like to inform consumers that with no precautions they will face some additional probability X of injury from product usage and that with precautions they will lower the risk to some value Y. They can use this information to decide whether or not to buy the product and, if they purchase it, which precautions to take.

Presenting risk information in such a straightforward manner is unlikely to be effective, however. Most fundamentally, the true risks are not well understood. Not all injuries are reported to poison control centers or to other government agencies, and information on the frequency of use of different products is not easy to obtain. For chemical hazards of a long-term nature, there may also be fundamental shortcomings in our knowledge of the properties of different chemical exposures. Even if the government agency understood the overall average risk, the user-specific risk would not be known. Individuals differ both in terms of the effectiveness of their precautionary actions and in their susceptibility to different exposures. Young children, for example, are often likely to face a greater cancer risk from a given level of carcinogenic exposure than are adults.

A second barrier to presenting probabilistic risk information is that evidence such as that in Kunreuther et al. (1978) suggests that individuals have difficulty processing risk information of that type, particularly regarding low probability events. The difficulties that arise can be illustrated with respect to seemingly modest changes in questions designed to elicit individuals' risk assessments.

In Viscusi and O'Connor (1984) the authors elicited workers' risk assessments for their current jobs and for jobs altered by the introduction of a new chemical. The technique used was to present respondents with a linear scale from very safe to very dangerous, with an arrow that marked the riskiness of the average U.S. private sector injury and illness rate. Workers then assessed the risk of their jobs by marking on the scale their current job's risk.

The responses appeared to be generally reasonable. Workers assessed their job risks as being almost twice as large as the published accident rate for the chemical industry, which tends to exclude chemical risks and captures primarily accidents. As a result, the survey responses are quite plausible in view of the notorious under-reporting of the chemical hazards associated with such positions. What was most striking were the risk assessments for the subsample of workers who were told that the chemicals with which they now worked would be replaced by sodium carbonate, thus eliminating the chemical-induced risk of their jobs. For this group the average risk assessment was identically equal to the published accident rate for the chemical industry, which should be expected since the BLS statistics primarily reflect such non-chemical hazards.

Far less reassuring results were obtained in the study by Viscusi and Magat (forthcoming) of consumers' risk perceptions for bleach and drain opener. To ascertain the value of individuals' risk assessments for the four injuries in this study, we asked respondents to scale particular risks relative to those faced by an average household. This procedure was adopted because of the very low level of the annual risks -- on the order of one accident per 50,000 households, or one accident per 150,000 people. An alternative procedure that we considered was to present respondents with a linear risk scale, but this was not feasible because of the small level of the risk involved and the difficulty in finding meaningful reference points. The procedure we selected instead was to inform consumers of the true average risk and then to ask them whether or not they believed they faced above average risk, below average risk, or the same risk as the average.

The results in Table 1 are quite striking. In all cases very few consumers -- about 3 percent or less -- consider their households to be above average in risk. Roughly half of all households consider themselves to be about average in riskiness, and the other half consider themselves to be below average in risk. It is noteworthy that the major outlier in terms of risk perceptions is child poisonings from drain openers, as 65 percent of all households view themselves as being below average in this risk. This is by far the most severe risk in the sample, as burns to the throat may cause the permanent loss of use of the child's esophagus. Consumers appear to be particularly optimistic that this very adverse event will not occur.

Table 1

Relative Risk Assessment

	Distribution of Relative Risk Ranges		
	Above Average	Average	Below Average
Drain Opener Risks			
Hand Burn	0.03	0.46	0.51
Child Poisoning	0.03	0.32	0.65
Cleaning Agent Risks			
Chloramine Gas	0.03	0.50	0.46
Child Poisoning	0.02	0.57	0.40

The high degree of optimism among consumers is not unprecedented in studies of risk perception. Interviews on automobile driving behavior by Svenson (1970) suggest that most drivers view themselves as being among the most skillful and safe drivers in the population. Similarly, a study of consumer risks by Rethans (1979) found that 97 percent of all consumers believe that they were either average or above average in their ability to avoid accidents from bicycles and power mowers. This high fraction of people who believe that they are relatively safe suggests that there may be some overoptimism in individuals' risk perception when these questions are asked in relative terms.

The framing of these risk assessment questions appears to be of fundamental importance. For the chemical worker results discussed above, which utilized a linear scale, the responses were more reasonable. Other researchers have also not observed a pattern in which risks are all underassessed. Lichtenstein et al. (1978) have found that individuals overassess small mortality risks and underassess large mortality risks -- a result that is shown in Viscusi (1984) to be consistent with a rational Bayesian learning process. These studies did not find systematic overoptimism in risk perceptions. As a result, the risk perceptions that actually drive individual behavior may not necessarily be biased, but when asked to make relative risk judgments, it may be that consumers do have an overoptimistic perception of their own relative ability to avoid the risk.

A simple modification in the manner in which risk perception questions are asked consequently produces widely varying results. These findings suggest that the success of efforts to provide risk information is likely to be quite sensitive to the manner of information transfer. One cannot simply provide information and ensure that it will be processed reliably and acted upon. The manner of information provision will greatly affect what the ultimate impact of the information will be on individual welfare.

These concerns suggest that many of the policies that include, for example, detailed lists of chemical contents may not be successful. What is needed is the provision of risk information that can be understood by consumers and workers and which can be used in a reliable fashion to promote better decisions.

Format Effects

One important dimension of information transfer is the format in which the information is provided. The importance of format arises in other contexts as well, such as in the energy audit analysis of Magat, Payne, and Brucato (1984). In our consumer labeling study, we examined the effects of different labeling formats on the precautionary actions of a group of 368 consumers interviewed at a mall intercept in Greensboro, North Carolina.

In the case of both bleach and drain opener, a label purged of risk information was included to assess the effect of the absence of hazard warnings on behavior. For each product we also included more than one format for which risk information was provided to ascertain the effect of information format on risk-averting behavior.

For the bleach, three different formats were examined. The first format was patterned after the current Clorox label. The second format used was based on the Kroger brand of bleach, called Bright, which organizes the risk information in what we believed to be a more effective manner. Finally, we included what we called the Test label developed in cooperation with our colleagues James Bettman, John Payne, and Richard Staelin. This label organized information on the nature of the risk and the appropriate precautions in a systematic fashion and featured it prominently on the label.

A similar approach was used in the case of drain opener, except in that instance we used only one existing label to augment the No Warning and Test label experimental treatments. The market-based label was patterned after the Drano and Red Devil Lye labels, which featured the risk information quite prominently.

The results obtained suggest that information and the format in which it is presented are consequential. In all cases involving the bleach label, the Test label performs best in terms of inducing consumers to take precautions to avoid the key hazards. The danger of mixing the cleaning agent with either toilet bowl cleaner or ammonia-based cleaners is that chloramine gas will form. This toxic gas is a leading cause of poisonings among adults. In the absence of a hazard warning, 17 percent of all respondents would take this precaution. The Clorox and Bright labels have a modest effect on the toilet bowl mixing behavior, increasing the proportion of consumers taking precautions to 23 and 32, respectively, and the Test label more than doubles the proportion of subjects who would undertake this precaution, increasing it to 40.

The likelihood of storage in a childproof location is enhanced in all cases by the label, with the Test label being most effective as it increases the childproof storage propensity by 33 percent. The Bright label was least effective, raising the storage propensity by only 8 percent. On average, the Test label creates an awareness of the key risks among over one-tenth of the population that would not otherwise have been reached with existing labels.

In the case of drain openers, there was also evidence of differential performance of the labels, but in this case the Test label did not perform as well as the label on the existing product (Drano). The risks of drain opener appear to be well-known to consumers even in the absence of a warning on the label. The majority of the subjects (63 percent) would wear gloves even in the absence of the warning and would also store the product in a childproof location (57 percent). The Drano label increases the propensity to undertake such precautions by 19 percent in the case of wearing rubber gloves and by 11 percent in the case of storage in a childproof location. In contrast, the Test label has roughly half this effectiveness.

The general spirit of these results is also borne out in more sophisticated statistical analyses that distinguish the effect of labels per se from the role of personal characteristics, such as education. Format effects are clearly of consequence. Labeling policies, such as OSHA's, that leave the choice of the format to the firm's discretion, may not fully exploit the advantages from providing formatting guidelines for effective labels.

3. VALUING THE HEALTH EFFECTS

Research such as that discussed above can be used to ascertain how the frequency of precaution-taking will increase in the presence of risk information. Much more problematic is ascertaining the willingness to pay to avoid these injuries. In an effort to assess their magnitude we used two techniques. For the first of these, contingent valuation (see Cummings, Brookshire, and Schultze [1984] for a review), we asked consumers how much they would be willing to pay per bottle of bleach or drain opener to reduce various risks by a small amount. The second approach, conjoint analysis (see Green and Srinivasan [1978] for a review), used a series of price-risk combinations to elicit the magnitude of this trade-off.

The amount consumers would be willing to pay to reduce the injury rate by one for every 2 million household users is substantial. In the case of contingent valuation, the willingness to pay per bottle is $.15 for chloramine gassings, $.27 for child poisoning from bleach, $.06 for hand burns from drain opener, and $.18 for child poisoning from drain opener. The conjoint analysis responses are consistently greater -- up to ten times as large for drain opener hand burns.

Because of the low level of the probabilities involved, even a small additional willingness to pay per container for a safer product translates into a large valuation. For example, the implied value of a hand burn from drain opener is $120,000.

In all likelihood, these findings provide an excessive measure of individuals' actual valuation of the health outcomes. In particular, the values appear high relative to estimated values for mortality risks. We do, however, believe that the survey results, although perhaps irrational, accurately reflect how individuals will react to low probability events. Whether these numbers should be used in a benefit-cost analysis is more questionable.

The high valuation numbers do, however, suggest that individuals may overract to low-probability events. The individuals have difficulty with small probabilities is not a novel result. What is intriguing is that there is often an overaction in terms of the risk-dollar trade-offs implied by individual behavior. The limitations to rationality in this instance are systematic and in a common direction.

4. CONCLUSION

Rather than approaching informational policies in terms of whether individuals have a right to know, we have asked the somewhat different question of whether it is efficient for them to know. The typical labeling policies urge consumers to undertake particular precautions, but they may not heed these warnings and when they do there is an offsetting disutility of precautions. In this instance it is particularly important to assess whether, on balance, increased precautionary behavior is desirable.

Overall, the task of conveying risk information is by no means straightforward. Seemingly minor changes in the manner in which the information is presented can have a substantial influence on its ultimate effect. Although informational strategies have many attractive features, notably their flexibility with respect to individual differences in the desirable level of precautions, they are also fraught with difficulties. Additional research on the design of information transfer mechanisms will enhance the effectiveness of these policies and allow us to better assess the net benefits of information provision as a regulatory alternative.

REFERENCES

Cummings, Ronald G., David S. Brookshire, and William D. Schultze, 1984, "Valuing Environmental Goods: A State of the Art Assessment of the Contingent Valuation Method," Draft Report to the U.S. Environmental Protection Agency.

Green, Paul E., and V. Srinivasan, 1978, "Conjoint Analysis in Consumer Research: Issues and Outlook," Journal of Consumer Research, Vol. 5 (September), pp. 103-123.

Kunreuther, Howard, et al., 1978, Disaster Insurance Protection: Public Policy Lessons, New York: Wiley-Interscience.

Lichtenstein, S., P. Slovic, B. Fischoff, M. Layman, and B. Combs, 1978, "Judged Frequency of Lethal Events," Journal of Experimental Psychology, Vol. 4, pp. 551-578.

Magat, Wesley, John Payne, and Peter Brucato, 1984, "Information Provision as a Regulatory Alternative: The Case of Residential Energy Conservation," Working Paper, Duke University Center for Study of Business Regulation.

Rethans, A., 1979, An Investigation of Consumer Perceptions of Product Hazards, University of Oregon doctoral dissertation.

Svenson, O., 1981, "Are We All Less Risky and more Skillful than Our Fellow Drivers?" Acta Psychologica, Vol. 47, pp. 143-148.

Viscusi, W. Kip, 1985, "A Bayesian Perspective on Biases in Risk Perception," Economics Letters, Vol. 17, pp. 59-62.

Viscusi, W. Kip, and Wesley Magat, forthcoming, Learning about Risk: Economic Responses to Risk Information, Cambridge: Harvard University Press.

Viscusi, W. Kip, and Charles O'Connor, 1984, "Adaptive Responses to Chemical Labeling: Are Workers Bayesian Decision Makers?" The American Economic Review, Vol. 74, No. 5 (December), pp. 942-956.

MEASURING BENEFITS FOR AIR QUALITY FROM SURVEY DATA

Edna T. Loehman

Department of Agricultural Economics
Purdue University

ABSTRACT

The purpose of this paper is to discuss how to model benefits for changes in air quality based on economic theory. Two different willingness to pay responses are studied - willingness to pay to avoid loss of air quality and willingness to pay to obtain improvements in air quality. Observations of willingness to pay were obtained from a survey; survey results were used to develop and compare models for these two types of responses. Differences in the estimated response functions indicate that preferences regarding gains and losses may be generated by different preference models, i.e. obtaining gains may be a "luxury" whereas avoiding losses may be a "necessity."

KEY WORDS: benefits, air quality, economics, willingness to pay

Introduction - the Need for a Benefit Function

The measurement of benefits for environmental goods has been the subject of a large number of studies (Cummings, Brookshire, and Schulze give a recent review). The need for benefit measurement arises because of the need to compare benefits to costs in policy analyses of government environmental regulations. The purpose of this paper is to discuss how to model benefits for changes in air quality based on economic theory. Here, "willingness to pay" is used as an indicator of individual benefits associated with a change in air quality because this is a measure of demand for air quality. Two different willingness to pay responses are studied - willingness to pay to avoid loss of air quality and willingness to pay to obtain improvements in air quality. Observations of willingness to pay were obtained from a survey; survey results were used to develop and compare models for these two types of responses.

This paper considers how such benefit measures can appropriately be related to air quality as functional relationships. That is, rather than simply obtaining averages of willingness to pay, the information on the survey was used to estimate a functional relationship between willingness to pay and air quality measures. The advantages of having such a functional relationship are: it may be used to infer benefits for the study area for air quality changes other than those on the survey; it may be used to infer benefits for geographic areas other than the given study area if it can be assumed that individuals in different geographic areas will have similar preferences regarding tradeoffs between income and air quality. Model specification also requires consideration of how to include socioeconomic data (such as income) in the appropriate way.

The benefit function is developed to be a function of air quality characteristics (namely visibility and health characteristics) rather than being in terms of ambient air quality levels. There are two reasons. First, for a survey of air quality values, air quality characteristics are more readily described than physical measurements of air quality. Second, the relationship between characteristics and ambient levels may vary by geographic area (e.g. the relationship between visibility and ozone may be different in areas with different humidity conditions). Thus a model in terms of characteristics, when combined with appropriate phsical models, has broader application than a model in terms of physical measurements.

Below, we discuss how to specify a benefit function for air quality and and present results of analysis of a survey performed for EPA in the San Francisco Bay area.

Economic Theory Basis for Benefit Measurement

One method of estimating benefits associated with changes in air quality would be to obtain a relationship between health effects associated with air pollution and levels of air quality (e.g. the work by Lave and Seskin); benefits are then evaluated by placing a value on health effects. Although past work has utilized this method, recent methods of benefit measurement have used other methods to allow inclusion of other types of benefits (such as visibility benefits). Benefits have been measured using two predominant methods: "hedonic" methods based on market data (usually property values) and surveys of willingness to pay. These methods are based on different types of of observations regarding willingness to pay. However, both methods use the underlying assumption that persons making choices involving tradeoffs between income and air pollution levels recognize the effects of pollution on health, visibility etc.

Economists have traditionally preferred the use of market observations compared to information obtained from a survey since such information is based on actual choices. In fact, survey studies of willingness to pay have also been called "contingent valuation" to indicate the hypothetical nature. However, several comparative studies of hedonic and contingent valuation methods have supported the validity of the latter approach by showing that average survey responses yield willingness to pay values which are similar in magnitude to the values produced by the market analysis (see Cummings et al. and Loehman et al.).

With the hedonic method, changes in property values are related to a physical measure of pollution. Since health and visibility are described by physical measures which are correlated (e.g. ozone and coefficient of haze), the hedonic method cannot be used to obtain separate values for health and visibility. Since one concern here is to obtain benefit values separately for health and visibility characteristics (rather than obtaining benefits for ambient air quality levels), the survey approach is preferred.

Regardless of the source of data regarding willingness to pay, there is a common body of economic theory which is the basis for benefit measurement. The economic basis for benefit measurement of nonmarket goods (such as air quality) is similar to microeconomic theory of demand for market goods (see Loehman, 1985). Individuals are assumed to have well-defined preferences over both market goods and nonmarket goods and these preferences are represented by a utility function. Preferences, prices, and budget constraints determine choices; observations of choices (such as willingness to pay) then reveal underlying preferences.

The indirect utility function is used to represent the resulting level of satisfaction achieved by an individual after constrained choices are made:

$$\bar{U}(M,Y,p) = \underset{x}{\text{Max}}\ U(x,Y)$$
$$\text{s.t. } p\ x \leq M$$

where $\bar{U}(.)$ denotes the indirect utility function, $U(.)$ denotes the utility function, x denotes consumption of market goods at prices p, Y denotes the level of nonmarket goods such as air quality (exogenously given), and income M.

The dual of the utility maximization problem is expenditure minimization subject to achieving a given utility level; the expenditure function expresses the resulting expenditure.

$$\mu(\bar{U},Y,p) = \underset{x}{\text{Min}}\ p\ x$$
$$\text{s.t. } U(x,Y) \geq \bar{U}$$

where $\mu(.)$ denotes the expenditure function.

"Willingness to pay" for air quality is defined as the difference in the expenditure for alternative levels of air quality holding utility constant at certain levels. The two types of measures, payment to avoid worse air (WTP^e) and payment to obtain better air (WTP^c), are defined by:

$$WTP^c = \mu(U^0, Y_0, p) - \mu(U^0, Y_0 + y, p)$$
$$WTP^e = \mu(U^1, Y_0 - y, p) - \mu(U^1, Y_0, p).$$

In the case of obtaining better air, WTP^c is the maximum that would be paid from income to achieve the same utility level as initially (U^0) before the air quality change. In the case of avoiding worse air, WTP^e is the decrease in income which would be equivalent in utility terms to a decrease in air quality; the corresponding utility level is a worse level (U^1). (Willingness to accept measures may be similarly defined but are not the subject of this study.) The functional relationship between WTP and nonmarket good changes is called a bid curve. The size relationship between alternative willingness to pay measures depends on the slopes of the indifference curves.

In order to estimate a functional relationship for these willingness to pay measures, a functional form for the relation must be}specified. One method to determine a form would be to assume a form for the indirect utility function, derive the corresponding expenditure function, and use it to define the resulting willingness to pay measures. Here, the forms assumed are:

$$\bar{U}(M,Y,p) = M + \alpha_1(S)\ \ln(Y_1) + \alpha_2(S)\ \ln(Y_2) + \gamma\ln(Y_1)\ \ln(Y_2) - f(p);$$
$$\mu(\bar{U},Y,p) = \bar{U} - \alpha_1(S)\ \ln(Y_1) - \alpha_2(S)\ \ln(Y_2) - \gamma\ln(Y_1)\ \ln(Y_2) + f(p);$$

The terms α_i and γ describe the tradeoffs between money income M and air quality characteristics; Y_1 and Y_2 denote measures of visibility and health characteristics. Since such tradeoffs may also depend on socioeconomic factors, α_i are specified as linear functions of socioeconomic characteristics (S); $\alpha_1 > 0$ and $\alpha_2 > 0$ are assumed. Regarding the interaction of health and visibility, it may be assumed that either these goods are independent or they interact positively ($\gamma \geq 0$) in the utility function; that is, increased health should lead to no decrease in the enjoyment of visibility.

The derived functional form for WTP^C is then:

$$WTP^C = \alpha_1(S)\ln(1 + \rho_1) + \alpha_2(S)\ln(1 + \rho_2) + \gamma\ln(1 + \rho_1)\ln(1 + \rho_2)$$

where ρ_i represent percent increases from the initial air quality. In order to compare the relative sizes of the two WTP values, the functional form of the model fitted for WTP^e was the same as for WTP^C except the percents ρ_i represent decreases instead of increases.

Study Area and Survey Design

The study area was the San Francisco Bay area. To develop a sampling scheme, all 946 census tracts in this area were initially classified as to socioeconomic type using cluster analysis; to limit the sample size for the study, only tracts with "normal" density of population and single family owner occupancy were included in the sample design. Using two categories for age of residents and three income categories, six types of tracts were identified according to socioeconomic conditions. The area was further subdivided into 5 types (A,B,C,D,E) by air quality characteristics, by location (East and West Bay, and by urban and suburban types). The combined classification system yielded forty-two types of tracts (not all possible combinations were present). One tract was randomly chosen from each type (with selection probabilities proportional to population) for a total of forty two tracts. For the survey, ten respondents were then chosen randomly from each tract; 412 usable survey responses resulted. (The same design was used for a comparative hedonic study. More details about the study are available in the full report by Loehman et al.)

For the categorization of air quality, cities in the Bay area were classified according to two visibility categories (good and fair visibility) and three health categories (good, fair, and poor health); only five combinations were represented - the good visibility, poor health category was not present. Air quality data for these areas were used to develop information concerning visibility and health characteristics given to repondents.

Table 1 summarizes information given to respondents concerning air quality in each of the five air quality areas plus one area which was worse than any in the Bay area. Each area was described in terms of health and visibility characteristics. Visibility was described in terms of days with visibility at three levels (clear, moderate, poor). Photographs were used to represent these levels pictorally for three different typical scenes in the Bay area. These levels correspond to greater than 10 miles visibility, 6-10 miles visibility, and below 6 miles visibility. Health characteristics were described in terms of days of different health types based on the PSI index developed by EPA. Respondents were told what types of health symptoms might be expected to occur for each type of day for persons with different health conditions.

Respondents were asked to make pairwise comparisons of air quality in their area with another and then state their willingness to pay per month - either to avoid the situation in a worse area or obtain the situation in a better area. Respondents could bid any dollar amount per month but were given a list of possible amounts ranging from $0 to "more than $100" as suggested amounts; it was stated that the money would go to the Bay Area Air Quality Management District to improve air quality in all areas.

Table 1

Characteristics for Air Quality Comparisons

Area

	A	B	C	D	E	F*
VISIBILITY						
Non-Polluted Days	330	265	330	265	265	205
Moderate Days	20	70	20	70	70	100
Poor Days	15	30	15	30	30	60
HEALTH						
Good Days	294	294	232	232	191	161
Moderate Days	70	70	130	130	150	140
Unhealthful Days	1	1	3	3	20	50
Very Unhealthful Days	0	0	0	0	4	12
Hazardous Days	0	0	0	0	0	2

*Fictitious Area added to provide greater air quality variation

Results

A regression analysis based on the specification above was used to estimate a functional relationship for willingness to pay responses; the same functional form was used for both types of willingness to pay responses. Table 2 summarizes the estimation results. Under "visibility" are listed socioeconomic factors which interact with visibility to affect willingness to pay. Included were location shifters (market area and urban/suburban), income (CINC), and a measure of perceptions of air quality (Q7GD). It was hypothesized that persons who believed air to be cleaner than others in their air quality area would pay less to obtain changes. Variables hypothesized to interact with health characteristics include existing health level (HI), smoking habits (SMKI), an index of the respondent's belief in the occurrence of health symptoms associated with the PSI index (RI), income, and location.

It was hypothesized that persons with worse existing health would be willing to pay more than persons with better health because they would be more affected by changes in air quality. Also, persons who do not believe they would be at personal risk should be willing to pay less than respondents who believe they would experience the health symptoms associated with the PSI index. For both health and visibility, it is assumed that persons with higher income would pay more.

Also included was a term to test for interaction effects between visibility and health. Correction terms to account for some differences between air quality in the respondent's location and information given on the questionaire are denoted by CORR; information given on the questionaire regarding air quality was given with less variation than in the actual conditions in order to simplify the questionaire design.

Table 2

Monthly Willingness to Pay Regression Models

Variable	Obtain Better		Avoid Worse	
	WTP^c_G	WTP^c_B	WTP^e_G	WTP^e_B
VISIBILITY (α_1):				
Q7GD	-10.81	-4.67	-8.45	-2.66
	(-2.02)	(-2.05)	(-1.19)	(-1.33)
CINC	.00074	.00032	.00097	.00023
	(3.54)	(3.55)	(3.42)	(3.84)
URBAN	-9.45	-2.67	-12.39	-8.38
	(-.91)	(-.60)	(-.65)	(-1.03)
MKT1	29.85	11.80	-6.34	3.79
	(3.65)	(3.43)	(-.53)	(1.24)
HEALTH (α_2):				
HI	.0050	.0041	.0095	.0024
	(1.25)	(1.71)	(2.64)	(2.88)
SMKI	.0259	.0120	.065	.01843
	(1.71)	(1.36)	(3.93)	(4.57)
RI	1.34	.7687	1.6888	.5567
	(1.64)	(1.61)	(1.85)	(2.50)
CINC	.00066	.00038	.00052	.00014
	(4.33)	(4.28)	(2.69)	(3.69)
URBAN	--	--	-30.01	-3.27
			(-3.15)	(-1.38)
MKT1	8.89	7.44	36.42	4.80
	(1.48)	(2.03)	(4.55)	(2.74)
CORR (Vis.)	14.57	13.97	14.09	4.15
	(3.39)	(3.27)	(2.77)	(.83)
CORR (Health)	12.03	10.51	23.64	13.99
	(4.23)	(3.74)	(6.28)	(2.96)
VISIBILITY (γ)	-67.61	-17.16	66.57	5.52
& HEALTH	(-2.48)	(-2.35)	(1.97)	(2.67)
Adj R^2	.0601	.0756	.1649	.1580
N	571	571	800	800

$\underline{WTP_G}$: ρ_1 = %Δ Good visibility days
$\quad\quad\quad \rho_2$ = %Δ Good health days

$\underline{WTP_B}$: ρ_1 = %Δ Moderate or poor visibility days
$\quad\quad\quad \rho_2$ = %Δ PSI2

t values in parentheses are t values

Because it was not known how respondents integrate information given on the questionaire into a subjective scale of air quality, two different measures of air quality change were tested in estimating the functional relationship. For one type, air quality was measured in terms of percent changes in "good" days; for the other, air quality was measured in terms of changes in "bad" days. These alternative models are denoted by the subscripts "G" and "B" in Table 2; PSI2 denotes the average PSI for an area weighted by the percent of not good days.

The most surprising result to be noted from Table 2 is that quite different socioeconomic factors are significant for the "obtain better" and "avoid worse" models. Consistent results are obtained for each model regardless of whether air quality change is measured as a percent change in good days or in bad days. More specifically, coefficients of health related interaction variables (health index, smoking, and risk belief) are positive and significant in the case of avoiding worse air (as expected) but are not significant in the case of obtaining better air. The coefficient of the visibility perception variable is negative (less would be paid by those who believe air to be better) and significant for the "obtain better" relationship but not significant for the "avoid worse" relationship.

Also, the coefficient for the health-visibility interaction term is positive as expected for the "avoid worse" model and is significant; however, it is significant and negative for the "obtain better" model. Thus, respondents would pay more than the separate values for visibility and health combined in the "avoid worse" case and less than the separate values in the "obtain better" case. (Of course, the size of the coefficient is different for the different pollution measures.)

Another observation is that while neither fit is very good, as is common in survey studies, the regression fit is much better for the "avoid worse" model than for the "obtain better" model. (The same people gave responses for both types of willingness to pay questions.) The inference can be made that there was not as much discrimination among willingness to pay responses for varying air quality levels in the "obtain better" case. In terms of R^2, the model based on change in the level of "badness" provides a better fit for willingness to pay to obtain better air; the change in the level of "goodness" provides a better model for willingness to pay to avoid worse air.

To compare the relative sizes of alternative predictions of willingness to pay and see the size of the interaction term, the models were evaluated for 1, 7, and 30 day changes in visibility and health. Table 3 compares the results of the alternative models using socioeconomic conditions and existing air quality for one air quality area. Resurlts indicate that the two different models (avoid worse and obtain better) give different bid predictions even for small changes in air quality. The effect of the interaction term is to change the combined bid by about ten percent. The measurement of air quality changes in terms of "good" or "bad" also produces different numerical values.

Conclusions

The purposes of this research were to demonstrate how to specify a benefit function for air quality changes and to study the relationship between two alternative benefit measures (willingness to pay both in terms of gains and losses in air quality). Results indicate that these two willingness to pay measures may not be derived from the same preference model. That is, there may be a different basis for response (e.g. a different utility function) for the two types of willingness to pay questions. Reasons for this conclusion are:

1) the estimated models are different in terms of the socioeconomic factors which are significant;

2) the interaction term is of opposite sign for the gain and loss
    models;

3) the estimated models are quite different in terms of the
    explanation power of the model;

4) the estimated bids for small changes are different for gains and
    losses.

This conclusion is consistent with the observation of Kahneman and
Tversky in different context that people may respond differently when
avoiding losses or obtaining gains. Here, the reason may be that better
and worse air could be viewed as different types of goods. That is, when
one decides to live in a certain geographic area, one implicitly accepts
the status quo and associated tradeoffs; any improvement in conditions is
then a "luxury" good. However, any deterioration has not been accepted so
that avoiding a worse condition may be a "necessity" good.

In light of the small sample size for this study relative to the many
sources of variation, the need for additional studies of this type is
clear. Rather than being concerned with testing whether survey reponses
are valid, new studies should be concerned with specification and
measurement issues. Because of the apparent differences in behavior
concerning gains and losses and questions concerning the subjective
evaluation of air quality, cooperation of economists and psychologists is
needed for such studies.

Table 3

Comparison of Model Values, Monthly Willingness to Pay
Area B, West Bay Suburban

	Visibility			Health			Combined Days		
	1	7	30	1	7	30	1	7	30
	(Good Days)			(Good Days)			(Good Visibility/ Good Health)		
WTP^e_G	.05	.34	1.43	.21	1.50	6.15	.26	1.88	8.27
WTP^c_G	.15	1.04	4.34	.11	.80	3.30	.26	1.81	6.93

	Visibility			Health			Combined Days		
	1	7	30	1	7	30	1	7	30
	(Mod. or Poor Days)			(Moderate Days)			(Mod. or Poor Visibility/ Moderate Health)		
WTP^e_B	.07	.53	2.05	.22	1.49	7.06	.30	2.06	9.76
WTP^c_B	.16	1.11	4.30	.39	2.55	10.69	.55	3.53	13.23

WTP^e_G = Avoid loss of good days.
WTP^c_G = Obtain increase in good days.
WTP^e_B = Avoid increase in polluted days.
WTP^c_B = Obtain reduction in polluted days.

REFERENCES

Cummings, Ronald G., David S. Brookshire, and William D. Schulze, <u>Valuing</u>
    <u>Public Goods: An Assessment of the Contingent Valuation Method</u>,
    forthcoming, Rowan & Allenhead, March 1986.
Kahneman, David and Amos Tversky, "Prospect Theory: An Analysis of
    Decisions Under Risk", <u>Econometrica</u> 47(2): 263-291, March 1979.
Lave, Lester B. and Eugene P. Seskin, "Acute Relationships Among Daily
    Mortality, Air Pollution, and Climate", in <u>Economic Analysis of</u>
    <u>Environmental Problems</u>, ed. E.S. Mills, National Bureau of Economic
    Research, Columbia University Press, New York, 1975.
Loehman, Edna T., "Exact Measures of Welfare for Nonmarket Goods: Some
    Conceptual and Empirical Issues", Staff Paper 84-1, Department of
    Agricultural Economics, Purdue University, September 1985, 42 pages.
Loehman, Edna T., David Boldt, and Kathleen Chaikin, <u>Measuring the</u>
    <u>Benefits of Air Quality in the San Francisco Bay Area</u>, Office of
    Policy Analysis, Office of Policy, Planning, and Education, U.S.
    Environmental Protection Agency, Washington, DC, October 1984, 272
    pages.

THE VALUE OF LIFE SAVING:

LESSONS FROM THE CIGARETTE MARKET

Pauline M. Ippolito*

Federal Trade Commission

ABSTRACT

This paper reports the results of a study of the cigarette market designed to measure what consumers are willing to pay for increased life expectancy. The spread of information on the health effects of smoking has dramatically transformed the cigarette market in the last 30 years. Using survey evidence on consumer beliefs together with reductions in cigarette demand gives a direct estimate of consumers' valuation of safety. The average "value of life" is estimated to be $460,000 (1985$), but consumers are found to differ considerably in their valuations. Moreover, there appears to be a skewness to the value of life distribution; the median value of life is approximately $380,000, compared to the mean of $460,000.

KEY WORDS: Value of life, information, cigarettes, beliefs, safety policy, risk.

I. THE CIGARETTE MARKET

There is probably no market in America today that has been more affected by consumer reactions to health information than the cigarette market. Over the last 30 years, the continual flow of information to consumers on the dangers of smoking has no serious competition as an explanation for the dramatic switch to safer smoking habits. The number of people who smoke today and the types of cigarettes they smoke are very different from what would have been expected on the basis of the market's behavior before 1952, when the first Readers' Digest and Consumer Report articles began appearing on the hazards of smoking. Moreover, there is a wealth of data available on the cigarette market, including survey data on consumers' beliefs about the risks of smoking. These features make the cigarette market an ideal candidate to measure how much consumers are actually willing to give up for an increase in life expectancy.

---

* The views expressed in this paper are those of the author and do not necessarily reflect the positions of the Federal Trade Commission or of any individual Commissioner. I am indebted to Gerard Butters, Richard Ippolito and Paul Portney for helpful comments on an earlier draft.

A. The Consumer's Decision To Smoke Cigarettes

When a consumer makes the decision to smoke a particular type of
cigarette, he presumably judges the enjoyment of smoking to be greater
than the perceived costs. These costs are of two types: the direct money
cost of cigarettes and a perceived health cost based on the individual's
beliefs about the hazards of smoking. Moreover, the consumer must choose
a type of cigarette. Here again the tradeoff is enjoyment versus
safety. In general, higher "taste" cigarettes are also higher risk
cigarettes, since the components of smoke that contribute to taste also
add to the health risk. Nicotine is a convenient index of both taste and
risk.[1]

Over the last 30 years, consumer perceptions of the health cost of
smoking have changed substantially. This change is responsible for a
large reduction in the demand for cigarettes and for a substantial switch
in the type of cigarette smoked. These reactions allow us to measure how
much consumers willingly gave up for the expectation of longer lives.

B. The Cigarette Market in 1980

The best recent evidence on consumer beliefs about the hazards of
smoking is a nationally projectable U. S. survey conducted by the Roper
Organization for the Federal Trade Commission in November 1980. Because
of this evidence on consumer beliefs, 1980 was used as the base year for
this study. In the survey, individuals were asked to judge the
truthfulness of an assertion that 30-year-old pack-a-day smoker had a
lower life expectancy than a comparable non-smoker. Those who answered in
the affirmative were then asked how many years of life were lost on
average. The survey results are shown in Table 1.

While these results are suggestive of consumer knowledge of
smoking   risks, some problems are evident. For instance, 30 percent of
the population (and 40 percent of smokers) deny that smoking affects life
expectancy. Yet, these responses are directly contradicted by the
individuals themselves in other parts of the survey and by overall market
response behavior.[2] Notwithstanding these shortcomings, the survey
results suggest several qualitative features of current consumer knowledge
on smoking.

First, on average, individuals do not appear to underestimate the
risk of smoking. Even taking the survey at face value, and ignoring non-
responses, beliefs about the life loss have an average value of
approximately 3.5 years lost, which closely corresponds to epidemiological
estimates.[3] More realistically, if those who responded that smoking had
no life expectancy effects are placed in the 0-2 year category to adjust
for the response bias, the average belief rises to 4.67 years. Second,
the belief distribution is not symmetric. While a greater number of
people underestimate the life loss of smoking, those who do overestimate,
do so by a greater margin on average. Third, consumer beliefs show a
relatively wide variance, enough to suggest that differences in beliefs
are an important determinant of behavior in the cigarette market.

According to surveys conducted by the National Center for Health
Statistics (HHS (1982)), approximately 33 percent of the adult population
smoked cigarettes in 1980. Cigarette production statistics indicate that
per capita consumption was 195 packs per year.[4] Nicotine content by brand
and variety and corresponding market share data (FTC (annual) and Maxwell
(1981)) indicate that the average cigarette sold in 1980 had approximately
1 milligram of nicotine. Nearly 30 percent of cigarettes sold had less

TABLE 1

Consumer Beliefs About the Life Expectancy Cost of Smoking, 1980[1]

Estimated life expectancy loss from smoking[2] (Years)	Survey Response Distributions (Percent)		
	Total	Smokers	Non-smokers
Zero	30.4	40.9	24.7
Less than 2	5.2	5.6	5.0
2-4	11.9	13.3	11.3
4-6	15.5	14.2	16.2
6-8	10.0	8.0	11.0
8-10	10.7	6.2	13.1
More than 10	4.6	2.7	5.6
Don't know how much[3]	11.7	9.1	13.1
Total	100.0	100.0	100.0

Source: Roper Survey, November 1980.

1 In 1980, the Federal Trade Commission asked the Roper Organization to include a number of smoking questions in their 1980 random survey. The survey included 1005 individuals, including 339 smokers, reflecting the national smoking rate.

2 Individuals were asked whether a 30-year-old person reduces his life expectancy if he smokes at least one pack a day for life. If answered in the affirmative, the respondent was then asked to estimate the life expectancy cost.

3 These individuals said they thought that smoking reduced life expectancy but were unable to assign a particular number of years to the loss.

than .75 milligrams of nicotine and about 13 percent had more than 1.25 milligrams.

C. The Cigarette Market That Would Have Existed in 1980 Without Health Information

If there had never been disclosures about the health effects of smoking, the 1980 cigarette market would have been very different from the one just described. While it is always somewhat precarious to attempt predictions of the world that might have been, the cigarette market is one where such predictions can be made with some confidence. In most respects, the cigarette market was on a stable path prior to the health discoveries. There was a strong growth trend in the incidence of female smoking, a more modest growth in male smoking, and virtually no change in the product itself for the twenty-five years before the first disclosures. Using standard statistical techniques and data from the HHS surveys covering 1947-1975, it has been estimated that if there had been no health information, approximately 54 percent of the adult population would have smoked and per capita consumption would have been 586 packs per year by 1980.[5]

Finally, the market share of the different nicotine-type cigarettes is projectable from simple historical evidence. Prior to 1953, a few non-filter cigarettes with very similar nicotine contents dominated sales for over twenty-five years (Maxwell (1975)). The sales-weighted nicotine content of cigarettes sold was virtually stable from 1926 to 1953. Even when new brands entered, their nicotine content was essentially the same as those already in the market. Therefore, it seems reasonable to assume that absent the health concerns, nicotine content would have remained constant and virtually all cigarettes would have had the same nicotine content. Using FTC and Maxwell data, the nicotine content of these no-information cigarettes is put conservatively at 1.49 milligrams.

This basic description of smoking behavior in 1980 with the health information and what it would have been without the health information[6] is shown in Table 2. From these estimates it is clear that consumers have reacted dramatically as their beliefs about the health risks have changed. By 1980, per capita consumption had fallen to approximately 50 percent of its projected level and the average nicotine content of cigarettes had been reduced by at least one-third. As more consumers become convinced of the risks of smoking, demand should fall still further and the distribution of cigarette types should continue its trend towards low tar/low nicotine cigarettes.

II. LESSONS FROM THE CIGARETTE EXPERIENCE

What can be learned about consumers' willingness to pay for longer lifespans from this reaction in the cigarette market? In a recent study (Ippolito and Ippolito (1984)), estimated reductions in individuals' demands for cigarettes were compared with their changed beliefs about the life expectancy effects of smoking.[7] Since the reductions in demand were the direct result of the changed beliefs, they provide a clear measurement of how much consumers were willing to pay (in reduced smoking pleasure or more technically, in reduced consumer surplus) to increase their life expectancy. More specifically, the vertical shifts in consumers' demand curves reveal their perceptions of the dollar value of the hidden health cost of smoking. Using the adjusted Roper survey as a measure of consumers' beliefs, this health cost translates directly into a "value of life" measure.

TABLE 2

Available Evidence About Smoking Behavior
With and Without Health Information, 1980.

Smoking Behavior	Without Information	With Information
Per capita cigarette consumption (packs per year; 18 years old and over)	386*	195
Percent of population smoking (18 years old and over)	54.2*	32.5
Elasticity of cigarette demand	-0.48*	-0.48*
Nicotine content per cigarette smoked (milligrams)		
Mean	1.49*	0.996
Standard Deviation	0.00	0.34

Source: The numbers not marked by an asterisk are data reported by or calculated from published sources in 1980. The numbers marked by an asterisk are estimates of what smoking behavior would have been in 1980 if cigarette-health disclosures had never been made available. All data sources are described in the text. Detailed estimations are in Ippolito and Ippolito (1984).

Three types of consumer differences were accounted for in the study: differences in beliefs (taken to be reflected by the adjusted Roper survey), differences in the underlying taste for cigarettes, and differences in the "value of life" itself. These last two factors in the cigarette reaction were estimated as part of the study by assuming particular functional forms for the underlying distributions of tastes and values of life and then finding the distribution parameters that best fit the aggregate reaction.

A. Consumers Differ in Their Willingness to Pay For Safety

The average "value of life" for the population estimated from the cigarette reaction is approximately $460,000 (1985 dollars).[8] This implies that on average individuals are willing to pay up to $460 to reduce the risk of death by 1/1000 or up to $46 to reduce the risk of death by 1/10,000.[9]

This estimate is in the lower range of those in the literature. It is based on a cleaner situation from which to measure the willingness to pay for safety -- one where there is a direct connection between the observed behavior and the risks to life. Moreover, the study corrects for possible errors in consumers' beliefs about the risks in question and for differences in consumers' valuations of safety. That these improvements in study methodology lead to lower estimates than many in the literature suggests that more serious attention must be given to these issues and to the potential bias they introduce into measures of the "value of life."

While the average willingness to pay for safety is interesting in its own right, it obscures a potentially important variation across the population. This study was specifically designed to estimate the distribution of consumers' valuations of safety. The estimated population density is shown in Figure 1. It is apparent from the figure that consumers vary greatly in their preferences. While the mean "value of life" is $460,000, a substantial portion of the population has values significantly above or below this average. The standard deviation of the estimated distribution is approximately $350,000 or about $350 to remove a 1/1000 risk of death. This variation in willingness to pay for risk reduction suggests that selection problems may indeed color estimates drawn from cross-section data. For instance, those who continued to smoke in 1980 were estimated in this study to have an average value of life that is approximately half that of non-smokers, that is, approximately $275,000 versus $550,000 (1985 dollars).

Equally significant is the decidedly skewed nature of the distribution. More than 40 percent of the population is not willing to spend even $335 to eliminate a 1/1000 risk of death, but 20 percent of the population is willing to spend more than $670 to remove the same risk. These figures reflect the relatively large portion of the population concentrated in the lower ranges of the willingness-to-pay distribution; and the smaller portion of the population in the more skewed right tail of the distribution.

This result probably comes as no surprise to those who have attempted to market safety; some consumers are willing to pay a sizable premium for safety, but a relatively large portion of the population is not. In particular, this estimate implies that a majority of the population (nearly 65%) would not be willing to pay the estimated mean of $460 to eliminate a 1/1000 risk of death. If these results are valid, this distribution has important implications for marketers and for safety policy.[10]

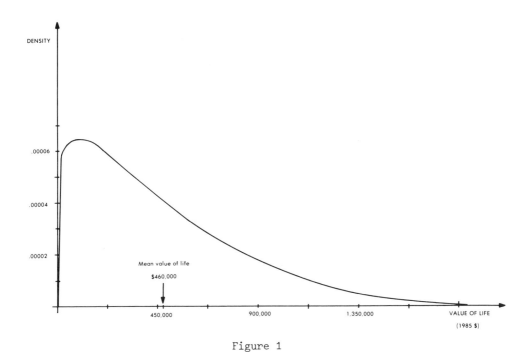

Figure 1

Estimated Value of Life Density Function from Cigarette Market Reaction

TABLE 3

Smoking Reaction to Health Information By Type of Smoker, 1980

Individual's Smoking Rate Without Information (Packs/day)	Average Reduction il Smoking Rate With Information1 (Percent)		Percent Who Quit Smoking
	Including Those Who Quit	Those Who Continue to Smoke	
1	80%	44%	65%
2	60	38	37
3	44	33	16
4	29	27	3

Source: Estimates of cigarette consumption based on Roper survey of beliefs about smoking health hazards and aggregate cigarette consumption data from USDA and HHS sources (see text).

1 Reduction in smoking rate does not account for the related adjustment in the type of cigarette smoked. Virtually all who continued to smoke in 1980 also reduced the tar and nicotine content of the cigarettes they smoked.

445

In the regulatory arena, for instance, this skewed distribution implies that mandatory safety standards that are consistent with consumers' average willingness to pay for safety will seem excessive to the majority of the population, but will be decidedly too weak for those who value safety highly. This factor makes labeling and other information approaches to safety regulation more attractive, since the information approaches allow greater freedom for the market to satisfy widely varying safety preferences. Similarly, in liability matters, standards of care that are based on less than the average willingness to pay for safety might be appropriate; this is especially true if there is a defense based on a lower price relative to otherwise similar items on the market or on disclosure of relative safety features of the product.

B. Underlying Consumer Characteristics Affect Overall Reactions to Health Information

In estimating the underlying taste for smoking (before health concerns), it was found that consumers who had a "high taste" for cigarettes also had a lower sensitivity to price changes.[11] Thus, while all consumers reacted to the health information, light smokers reacted more than heavy smokers. This helps explain why on average current smokers consume nearly as many cigarettes as smokers in the past.

Table 3 shows the estimated reduction in the smoking rate of different types of smokers caused by the change in beliefs about smoking. Those who would have smoked 1 pack a day without the health information reduced their smoking by 80% on average. This reduction came from two factors: 65% of 1 pack-a-day smokers quit smoking altogether and those who continued to smoke reduced their rate by 44% on average (that is, to a little more than half a pack a day). In contrast, those who would have been 4 pack-a-day smokers reduced their consumption by only 29% (that is, to about 2.8 packs per day). This reduction is a combination of the 3% who quit smoking and a reduction of 27% for those who continued to smoke.

This result illustrates the importance of underlying demand characteristics in predicting the consumer response to health information. Other things equal, consumers with a higher demand elasticity will respond more to new health risks. The overall pattern of consumer reaction thus depends directly on the distribution of price sensitivity across the consuming group, as well as on consumers' ability to absorb the information and on their valuation of the safety itself.

In particular, the effectiveness of hazard warnings (or other information policies) cannot be judged solely by whether all groups of consumers have reacted similarly to the information One should expect instead that some groups of consumers will put a relatively greater value on the consumption of the hazardous product and will therefore reduce their consumption less in response to the warnings. For instance, even if the saccharin labels are working perfectly, consumers for whom overweight problems are a serious health issue will probably cut their saccharin consumption by less than other consumers -- for them, low calorie food products may simply be more valuable than for the average consumer.

C. Most Consumers Do Absorb Significant Health Information: Differences Remain Across Groups

One of the clear lessons from the cigarette experience is that most consumers will absorb significant health information that affects them (and will act on this new information). Measuring consumer beliefs is always a difficult exercise, subject to many problems of survey design. Nonetheless, the pattern of responses to a wide variety of questions about the health hazards of smoking strongly supports the view that most consumers are aware of the fundamental cigarette health issues. Knowledge seems weaker on some of the particulars of the health risks and across some subgroups of the population, but the general health concern appears to have been absorbed quite well.

On the basic issue of whether smoking is "hazardous to health," for instance, a 1978 Roper survey done for the Tobacco Institute (FTC 1981) found that only 5% of the population responded "Smoking isn't hazardous" and only 4% responded "Don't know." Even smokers had a high level of acknowledgment on this issue with only 8% responding "Smoking isn't hazardous" and only 5% responding "Don't know."

The more specific question of whether a 30 year old who smokes at least a pack a day reduces his life expectancy is a good illustration of the general pattern of the more specific survey results (Roper 1980). As shown in Table 4, the population as a whole reports a somewhat lower (but still high) level of knowledge of this fact: 69.7% of the population chose "know" or "think it's true," 22.1% chose "don't know if it's true," and 7.8% chose "know" or "think it's not true." Smokers and non-smokers show a distinctly different pattern, with smokers reporting significantly less knowledge of this fact.[12]

Beliefs about smoking's effects also generally differ by income and education level. The results for the life expectancy question for different income groups are shown in Table 5 and are typical of the survey responses generally. Overall, higher income and education groups appear to have absorbed the health information about cigarettes more completely than lower income or education groups. Only 3% of those earning more than $25,000 per year responded that they "know" or "think it's not true" that life expectancy is reduced. Seventy eight percent responded that they "know" or "think it's true." In contrast, for the lowest income group (under $7000 per year), the corresponding figures were 17.7% for "know" or "think it's not true" and 53.2% for "know" or "think it's true."

This relationship between beliefs and income or education is consistent with reported smoking behavior. Surveys show that individuals in higher income and education groups are less likely to smoke cigarettes (Roper 1980 or HHS 1979) and are more likely to smoke low tar and nicotine cigarettes when they do smoke (HHS 1981).

It is plausible that the reported differences in beliefs are directly responsible for the observed differences in smoking behavior. This is the approach taken in measuring the value of life above. It is also possible, however, that higher income and education groups place greater value on safety, and for this reason, have been more attentive to the particulars of the health information; if so, different concerns for safety have led to the formation of different beliefs about the risks. Similarly, the fact that higher income and education groups have absorbed the health information more completely may reflect a relative efficiency in processing information or it may reflect information flows that have somehow have been directed towards these groups.[13] These are potentially fruitful areas of research that have not been explored to date.

III. CONCLUSION

In the last 30 years, the cigarette market has been dramatically

TABLE 4

Consumer Beliefs About Life Expectancy Effects of Smoking, 1980

Smoking Reduces Life Expectancy[1]	Survey Response Distribution (Percent)		
	All	Smokers	Non-smokers
True	69.7	59.0	75.2
Don't Know	22.1	26.8	19.7
Not True	7.8	13.8	4.5
No Answer	.5	.3	.6

Source: Roper Survey, November 1980.

TABLE 5

Consumer Beliefs About the Life Expectancy Effects of Smoking, By Income Group, 1980

Smoking Reduces Life Expectancy[1]	Income Group Response Distributions (Percent)			
	<$7,000	$7-15,000	$15-25,000	>$25,000
True	53.2%	65.8%	73.2%	78.2%
Don't Know	28.2	24.7	20.1	18.4
Not True	17.7	9.1	6.7	3.0
No Answer	.8	.4	-	.4

Source: Roper Survey, November 1980.

[1] Individuals were asked whether a 30 year-old person reduces his life expectancy if he smokes at least one pack a day. Responses were "Know it's true", "Think it's true", (grouped as "true" in the table), "Know it's not true", "Think it's not true", (grouped as "not true" in the table), and "Don't know if it's true", and "No Answer."

transformed by the spread of information on the health effects of smoking. There is considerable evidence that consumers have absorbed much of this information and have acted on it. Virtually nobody in the United States today smokes the type of cigarette that had dominated the market for 25 years before the health discoveries. Compared to the world that would have been without the health information, by 1980 the portion of the population that smoked cigarettes was 40 percent lower, per capita consumption was 50 percent lower, and the average nicotine content of cigarettes was at least one third less.

Based on the evidence in the cigarette market, the need for government imposition of direct safety regulation (as opposed to the provision of safety information) appears to be less than often supposed. Information has been quite effective in changing consumers' beliefs about smoking and has led most consumers to alter their consumption patterns appropriately. Moreover, because consumers are found to differ substantially in their valuation of safety, uniform safety standards result in too much safety for many consumers and too little safety for others. In those cases where regulation may still be justified, the best estimate of the mean "value of life" from this study is approximately $460,000 (in 1985 dollars) and under a number of sensitivity tests stays under $1 million.

Finally, a common complaint about efforts to measure the value of safety and its use in safety policy can be clearly addressed with the cigarette experience. It is often argued that "value of life" estimates are too low for policy use, because low income individuals' ability to pay for safety is too strong an influence in the estimates. The willingness to pay for safety measured in the cigarette market is free of these income concerns -- once informed of the potential hazard, individuals must pay an out-of-pocket cost to expose themselves to the risks of smoking. The fundamental point of all value of life studies -- that individuals are willing to pay only limited amounts for safety -- may be more convincing to skeptics when drawn from studies where income does not limit individuals' choices.

NOTES

[1] The amount of nicotine in a cigarette is highly correlated with the other components of cigarette smoke (FTC), e.g., the amounts of tar and carbon monoxide, the components most directly linked to the health effects of cigarettes. The "taste" of cigarettes is generally tied to the amount of smoke in each puff, and thus, is also linked to the amount of tar, nicotine and carbon monoxide. Nicotine, in particular, seems to cause the pleasurable physiological effects on the brain that makes smoking attractive. The general technology for increasing the safety of cigarettes is to dilute the smoke in each puff through a variety of techniques, thus creating the link between "taste" and safety.

[2] For instance, in the same survey, only 2.9 percent of the population and 5.1 percent of smokers denied that smoking causes lung

cancer, a widely acknowledged fatal disease. Moreover, aggregate data shows that while 40 percent of smokers may say that smoking does not cause early death, only seven percent persisted in smoking non-filtered cigarettes in 1980 (Maxwell (1981)).

[3] Based on smoking surveys and subsequent follow-ups upon the death of respondents, several studies have estimated the effects of smoking on life expectancy.} The estimates are generally based on the consumption of pre-information nicotine content cigarettes. Standardizing to the same intensity levels, the results range from 2.3 years to 4.8 years of expected life lost for lifetime pack-a-day smokers (Hammond (1967), Ippolito et al. (1979), and U.S. Department of Health, Education and Welfare (1979)).

[4] The HHS surteys also contain quantity information, but these responses are known to be seriously biased. When compared to sales figures, it is clear that consumers significantly underestimate the amount they smoke when responding to surveys.

[5] A more detailed discussion of these estimates is available in the appendix to Ippolito and Ippolito (1984). When extrapolated to 1980, other studies of per capita consumption in the cigarette market are generally consistent with the predictions here (see Hamilton (1972), Ippolito et al. (1979), Klein et al. (1981) and Porter (1985)).

[6] In characterizing these projections as pertaining to the market without information, it is assumed that prior to 1952 consumers were generally not aware of the life-threatening risks to smoking. To the extent that these risks were known, the "value of life" estimates below are biased low.

[7] To the extent that consumers were reacting, in part, to other newly discovered health costs of smoking, the estimated "value of life" is biased high, since it includes these other health costs. The estimate also does not treat smoking as an "addiction." Studies show that there are physical withdrawal effects to smoking, but that these effects are significantly reduced within a week of quitting (Krasnegor 1979). Empirical estimates to test whether the addictive characteristics of smoking are significant in explaining aggregate smoking behavior suggest that they are not. If the addictive characteristics of smoking were important in the aggregate, it would follow that after 1964 (the date of the first Surgeon General's Report), the reduction in start rates would have been proportionally larger than the corresponding reduction in overall participation rates; that adjusting for other factors, pre-1964 starters would smoke either more cigarettes or higher nicotine content cigarettes than post-1964 starters; and that post-1964 quit rates would be lower for older smokers than for younger smokers. Available empirical evidence rejects these hypotheses (Ippolito et al. (1979)). If there is a one-time cost of changing smoking behavior, our estimated value of life is biased low by that amount; however, it is unlikely that this cost is large enough to affect the order of magnitude of the estimates.

[8] A more detailed description of the theory and estimating procedure is outlined in Ippolito and Ippolito (1984) where the estimates are expressed in 1980 dollars. The Consumer Price Index was used to inflate these 1980 estimates (conversion factor is 1.28).

This estimate assumes that consumers discount the future only to account for the risks of survival. If there is an additional subjective discounting of the future above and beyond the risk of survival, these estimates would increase somewhat. For instance, if there is an additional (real) discount rate of 1.25%, then the estimated mean "value of life" would increase by about 10 percent to $505,000. For added discount rates of 2.5 percent and 5 percent, the estimates increase to approximately $560,000 and $765,000 respectively.

Similarly, the estimate is based on regression coefficients that are subject to statistical uncertainty. Using the 95% confidence bounds on the regression coefficients that underlie the estimates in Table 2 to determine the sensitivity of the estimates, the mean value of life is bounded between $276,000 and $844,000.

Finally, the estimate is based on the adjusted Roper survey where those who denied any life expectancy effect were placed in the lowest response category of 0-2 years of life lost. Alternative adjustments where these individuals were placed in a 0-1 year category or in a 0-1/2 year category were decidedly inferior in fitting the aggregate data.

[9] A variety of studies have used labor markets to estimate the wage premiums attached to risky occupations as a means of estimating the value of safety. These studies, which generally assume that workers are correctly informed about the risks, use highly aggregated industry-level data to attempt to isolate the safety effect from the variety of other factors that determine wages. The studies generate "value of life" estimates ranging from approximately $505,000 (Thaler and Rosen) to about $3,500,000 (Brown) in 1985 dollars. See Bailey (1980) and Blomquist in Jones-Lee (1982) for reviews of this literature. Moreover, because these studies estimate the market price of risk, it is impossible to determine whether these estimates represent "value of life" figures for individuals with above or below average valuations of safety.

[10] A recent British survey which asked individuals directly about their willingness to pay for safety (rather than estimate it from actual market behavior) found the same type of skewed distribution, though with substantially higher values of life (Jones-Lee et al. (1985)).

[11] In particular, the individual's demand for cigarettes was specified as $Q=r-cP/r$ where P is price per pack, Q is quantity of packs purchased per year, c is an estimated constant and r is a "taste" parameter that varies across individuals and reflects income and other individual-specific factors that affect consumption. Simpler demand specifications where individual specific factors did not affect price sensitivity (such as $Q=r-cP$) were decidedly inferior in fitting the aggregate data.

[12] Certainly these results are colored by some degree of response bias where both smokers and non-smokers rationalize their choices, but the differences seem large enough to suggest a real difference in beliefs.

[13] For instance, the cigarette ad ban on electronic media has the effect of reducing the amount of advertising for low tar and nicotine brands that lower income groups are exposed to, since they are more intensive users of these media. Most of the information on the health effects of smoking has appeared in print media.

REFERENCES

Bailey, Martin J. 1980. Reducing risks to life. Washington, D.C.:
    American Enterprise Institute for Public Policy Research.
Federal Trade Commission. Annual. Report of tar and nicotine content.
    Washington, D.C.: Federal Trade Commission.

Federal Trade Commission. 1981. Staff report on the cigarette advertising
    investigation. Washington, D.C.: FTC.
Hamilton, James L. 1972. The demand for cigarettes, advertising, the
    health scare and the cigarette advertising ban. Review of Economics
    and Statistics. 39:401-411.
Ippolito, Pauline M. and Richard A. Ippolito. 1984. Measuring the value of
    life saving from consumers reactions to new information. Journal of
    Public Economics. 25:53-81.
Ippolito, Richard A., Denis Murphy and Donald Sant. 1979. Consumer
    responses to cigarette health information. Staff Report to the Federal
    Trade Commission. Washington, D.C.
Jones-Lee, M. W. Editor. 1982. The value of life and safety. Amsterdam:
    North-Holland.
Jones-Lee, M. W. et al. 1985. The value of safety: results of a national
    sample survey. The Economic Journal. 95:49-72.
Klein, Benjamin, Kevin Murphy and Lynne Schneider. 1981. Government
    regulation of cigarette health information. Journal of Law and
    Economics. 24:575-612.
Krasnegor, Norman A. Editor. 1979. Cigarette smoking as a dependent
    process. National Institute on Drug Abuse Research Monograph 23.
Maxwell, John P. 1975. Historical sales trends in the cigarette industry.
    Richmond, Virginia: Maxwell Associates.
Maxwell, John P. 1981. Historical sales trends in the cigarette industry.
    New York: Lehman Brothers Kuhn Loeb Research.
Porter, Robert H. 1985. The impact of government policy on the U.S.
    cigarette industry. In Empirical Research in Consumer Protection
    Economics. Pauline M. Ippolito and David S. Scheffman, Editors.
    Washington, D.C.: Federal Trade Commission.
U.S. Department of Health and Human Services. Annual. The health
    consequences of smoking. Washington, D.C.: GPO.

VALUING FOOD SAFETY[*]

Tanya Roberts

United States Department of Agriculture
Washington, D.C. 20005-4788

ABSTRACT

This paper reviews methods for assessing the economic costs of foodborne disease and estimates the annual costs of salmonellosis and campylobacteriosis. These foodborne diseases cause intestinal disturbances in approximately 4.1 million Americans annually. Annual medical costs and lost wages from salmonellosis and campylobacteriosis are estimated at $1.4 to $2.6 billion. Inclusion of the economic value of leisure time lost and other factors would increase these cost estimates.

Chicken was associated with 9.5 percent of the outbreaks of salmonellosis reported in 1981, and fresh chicken may cause half of the cases of campylobacteriosis. Irradiation is one method proposed to reduce the incidence of these diseases caused by chicken. Irradiation is estimated to have a favorable benefit/cost ratio of between 2.2 to 4.2. Estimated net benefits range between $186 to $498 million annually.

KEY WORDS: food safety, foodborne disease, salmonellosis, campylobacteriosis, food irradiation, benefit/cost analysis.

Two major outbreaks of foodborne disease occurred this year in the United States. One was an outbreak of salmonellosis from contaminated milk that infected approximately 18,000 persons. The other was an outbreak of listeriosis caused by contaminated soft cheeses that resulted in approximately 100 deaths. These outbreaks are noteworthy because of the unusually high incidence and potential economic implications. These outbreaks illustrate that modern sanitation and processing have not eliminated foodborne disease.

Although some diseases such as typhoid fever have decreased markedly, other foodborne diseases are thought to be increasing (Kamplemacher, 1985). The reasons are diverse and range from practices on the farm to the kitchen: Greater concentration of animals in larger production units permits easier transmission of disease from one animal to the other. The considerable geographic movement of animals and birds can spread disease

---

[*] The views expressed here are those of the author and not necessarily those of the U.S. Department of Agriculture.

across the countryside. Today the use of improperly processed animal byproducts and wastes in animal feeds can introduce and perpetuate disease cycles. Concentration of animal slaughter in fewer and larger plants increases the possibilities for cross-contamination between carcasses (Schwabe, 1985, pp. 552-3; Snoyenbos, 1985). An increased number of distribution stages means more mass production of food and the greater inherent possibilities of improper heating and refrigeration -- two of the most common contributors to foodborne disease in meat and poultry (Bryan, 1980). People are traveling more and eating more exotic foods and being exposed to a greater variety of foodborne hazards. Finally, the organisms themselves have been evolving. They are adapting to modern food processing and are more able to survive (Archer, 1985). Also, they are developing resistance to human drug therapies (Holmberg, et. al., 1984).

Another factor is our changing life styles--eating more of our meals away from home where additional health risks from further handling of food and improper preparation may occur. The 20 percent of the meals consumed outside the home (Consumers, 1985) caused 68 percent of the foodborne disease outbreaks reported in 1981 (CDC, 1983). Conversely, the 80 percent of the meals consumed at home caused only 32 percent of the reported foodborne outbreaks. But perhaps this is an unfair inference to make because of the severe underreporting of foodborne disease and perhaps the greater likelihood that food poisoning at home will go unreported, undiagnosed, or misdiagnosed.

The severity of recent foodborne disease outbreaks and the accompanying publicity have renewed interest in developing estimates of the economic costs of these outbreaks and identifying and quantifying food safety management techniques. This paper discusses several of the practical difficulties with making such estimates: (1) valuing the growing number of sectors associated with a foodborne disease outbreak, and (2) estimating the costs of control The specific foodborne diseases evaluated here are salmonellosis and campylobacteriosis, both intestinal diseases of mild, but occasionally life threatening, severity.

Methodology

Foodborne disease costs can be classified into 3 categories: individual, industry and public (Table 1). The individual's costs associated with illness and death include medical resources used, loss of wages or productivity during sickness, reduction of leisure time choices during the illness and recovery, and pain and suffering. The costs to the industry or firm found responsible for the outbreak may include the value of product recalled, reduction in future demand for the product due to reputation damage, plant cleanup, and liability awards[2]. Public costs include investigation, surveillance and possibly part of the cleanup expense.

Traditionally, only the easily monetizable, direct costs have been estimated, namely the medical costs and wages (or productivity) lost during an illness. However, averting behavior costs (behavior designed to avoid or reduce the risk of illness) can be a significant cost item and, in fact, may swamp the traditional medical and productivity costs. A recent Resources for the Future study of the contamination of a water supply addresses the willingness of the public to pursue a variety of measures to avoid illness--boiling water, travelling to another community to obtain water, and purchasing bottled water (Harrington, et. al., 1985).

Table 1

Social Costs of Foodborne Illness

Costs to individuals

   Medical costs

   Income or productivity loss

   Pain and suffering

   Leisure time cost

   Averting behavior costs

   Risk aversion costs

   Travel cost

   Child care cost

Industry costs

   Product recall

   Plant closings and cleanup cost

   Product liability costs

   Reduced product demand

Public health surveillance costs

   Costs of investigating outbreak

   Costs of maintaining disease surveillance

   Cleanup costs

455

Averting behavior by the public can result in diet and consumption expenditure changes that affect sales and revenues of the involved industry. An opinion survey by the National Pork Producers Council found that 40 percent of the surveyed consumers claimed that they had reduced their consumption of pork because of health concerns about salt and 17 percent claimed decreased poultry consumption because of disease concerns (Weise Research Associates, 1984). Of course, opinion surveys by themselves don't provide empirical evidence of actual reductions in consumption and impacts upon industry revenues.

Finally, the costs to firms in the industry and the public are typically excluded from cost estimates, although Ewen Todd has found they are often significant components of foodborne outbreak costs (Todd, February 1985 and July 1985).

Evaluation of Costs of Illness

The three components of the cost of illness estimate are the number of persons affected, the severity of the illness, and the costs associated with that severity:

o Estimated Disease Incidence. All diseases are typically underreported. By looking at outbreaks of foodborne illness, epidemiologists have found that only 1 in 75 or 1 in 100 salmonellosis cases are reported (Smith and Blaser, 1985). Rather than just rely on reported cases, estimates of the total U.S. incidence are used.

o Severity of Illness. The range of illnesses caused by the diseases considered here vary from essentially unnoticeable to life-threatening. Among other things, the impact depends on the number of microbes ingested and on the efficiency of the individual's immune system to fight off the diseases. However, fatalities can occur in relatively normal human adult hosts (Smith and Blaser, 1985). Costs have been estimated for three disease severity levels--mild, moderate, and deadly.

o Cost of Illness. Secondary data sources (updated to 1985 prices) are used for the cost estimates. Often these costs are derived from surveys of people involved in an outbreak of foodborne disease. Generally, they are confined to medical costs and wage losses and re underestimates.

Evaluation of Death

Traditionally, deaths have been evaluated traditionally by the human capital method which measures the individual's contribution to productive output. The income stream that would have been produced by the individual is collapsed into a present value for that production at today's prices.

$$\text{Human Capital Method} = \sum_{t}^{T} \frac{L_t + H_t}{(1 + i)^t} \text{ , where}$$

T = remaining lifetime
t = a particular year
L_t = labor income in year t
H_t = value of nonmarket time spent on homemaking services
i = social discount rate; opportunity cost of society investing in life-saving programs

The human capital method only places a value on what the individual produces for society.

456

From the perspective of the individual and consumer demand theory, a life ought to be valued by what the individual is willing to pay to avoid a particular risk of death. The individual's non-labor sources of income are included as resources to pay for risk reduction along with wages. Even more important are the nonmarket activities that may be of more value to the individual than his/her income loss. These include pain and suffering, loss of leisure time, and aversion to risk.

$$\text{Revealed Preference Willingness to Pay Method} = \sum_t^T \frac{B_t}{(1 + \rho)^t} \, \alpha, \text{ where}$$

- T = remaining lifetime
- t = a particular year
- B_t = benefits of living = $L_t + NL_t + NM_t + P_t$, where L_t = labor income, NL_t = nonlabor income, NM_t = nonmarket activities and leisure, P_t = premium for pain and suffering
- ρ = individual rate of time preference
- α = risk aversion factor

Historically, the range of value of life of estimates resulting from the willingness to pay method has been large (Landefeld and Seskin, 1982).

A hybrid approach attempts to bridge the gap between the two methodologies (Landefeld and Seskin, 1982). The adjusted willingness to pay/human capital approach includes only measurable economic losses associated with death. It is based on after-tax income from labor and nonlabor sources, discounts at the individual's rate of return after taxes, and includes risk aversion shown by investment in life insurance, security systems, etc.

$$\text{Adjusted Willingness to Pay/Human Capital Method} = \sum_t^T \frac{Y_t}{(1 + r)^t} \, \alpha, \text{ where}$$

- T = remaining lifetime
- t = a particular year
- Y_t = after-tax income = $L_t + NL_t$, where L_t = labor income, NL_t = nonlabor income
- r = individual's opportunity cost of investing in risk-reducing activities
- α = risk aversion factor

Perhaps most important, data exist for estimating with this methodology.

Costs of Salmonellosis and Campylobacteriosis

Two of the most prevalent foodborne diseases in the United States are salmonellosis and campylobacteriosis which annually cause intestinal disorders in an estimated 2 million and 2.1 million persons, respectively (Holmberg, 1985). The most extensive data on costs of illness come from the Centers for Disease Control (CDC) survey of a 1976 salmonellosis outbreak in Colorado (Cohen, et. al., 1978). These data are used to estimate the medical costs, productivity losses, and miscellaneous costs for mild cases ($230) and moderate cases ($1,290) (Table 2). The incidence of moderate salmonellosis cases is conservatively assumed to be those 40,000 salmonellosis cases reported annually to CDC (Holmberg, 1985). The mild cases are the remainder, or 2.0 million estimated salmonellosis cases minus the 40,000 reported cases which equals 1,960,000 mild cases.

Table 2

Annual Cost Estimates for Salmonellosis, United States (1985 prices).

Item	Number of cases	Cost per case	Total cost	
			low	high
	thousand	dollars	million $	
Moderate severity	40	1,290	51.6	
Mild severity	1,960	230	450.8	
			502.4	
Loss of life	2	85,800[a]	171.6	
		351,500[b]		703
Total cost			673	1,205

[a] Based on human capital value method.
[b] Based on the adjusted willingness-to-pay/human capital method.

For campylobacteriosis, the same costs are used because of the similarity of the course of the diseases (Seattle, 1985)(Table 3). The U.S. incidence for moderate cases is based on a study in Denver for the low estimate (Smith and Blaser, 1985) and the high estimate is based on a Seattle study (Seattle, 1984). Mild cases are the residual of the 2.1 million cases.

Death's are evaluated by using the CDC estimated death rate of one in a thousand for these diseases (Holmberg, 1985) and the actual age distribution of reported deaths due to salmonellosis (Table 4). The low estimate, $85,800 is based on the present value of life with the human capital method. The high estimate, $351,500, is based on the adjusted willingness to pay/human capital method.

For the medical and productivity categories, U.S. costs for salmonellosis and campylobacterosis are estimated to range from $1.4 billion to $2.6 billion annually (Table 5). Note that while deaths are the largest component of the high estimate, productivity losses are the largest component of the low estimate. This changing position highlights the importance of what assumptions about incidence and severity are made in deriving the estimates and the methodology used to evaluate deaths. Also note the fewer number of cost categories estimated in Table 5 when compared to Table 1 implies that this estimate is quite conservative.

Table 3

Annual Cost Estimates for Campylobacteriosis, United States, (1985 prices).

Item	Number of cases	Cost per case	Total cost low	high
	#	$	million $	
Moderate[a] severity	57,340 or 168,025	1,290	74	217
Mild[b] severity	2,042,660 or 1,931,975	230	470	444
Loss of life	2,100	85,800[c]	180	
		351,500[d]		738
Total cost			724	1,399

[a]   The low estimate is based on the incidence reported in the Denver area (Smith and Blaser, 1985) while the high estimate is based on the Seattle study.
[b]   Total cases of campylobacteriosis are estimated at 2.1 million (Holmberg, 1985).   The moderate cases are subtracted from this number to get the estimated mild cases.
[c]   Based on human capital method.
[d]   Based on the adjusted willingness-to-pay/human capital method.

Table 4

Value of Life for Salmonellosis Fatalities, 1985

Method	Age	Male Deaths	Male Present Value	Male Total Value	Female Deaths	Female Present Value	Female Total Value	Average Value[c]
		#	thousand $		#	thousand dollars:		$
Human capital[1]:	0-4	3	88	264	4	77	307	
	5-14	0	159	0	2	139	278	
	15-24	2	300	600	1	241	241	
	25-44	0	371	0	4	238	954	
	45-64	10	189	1,890	6	144	867	
	65+	20	14	271	27	41	1,107	
		35		3,025	44		3,754	85,800
Adjusted willing- ness to pay/human capital[b]	0-4	3	1208	3,624	4	836	3,102	
	5-14	0	1408	0	2	961	1,922	
	15-24	2	1655	3,309	1	1086	1,086	
	25-44	0	1432	0	4	866	3,462	
	45-64	10	548	5,480	6	410	2,459	
	65+	20	34	680	27	90	2,443	
		35		13,091	44		14,675	351,500

[a] Data from Dolan, et. al., 1980; Vital; Updated to March 1985 dollars.
[b] Data from Landefeld and Seskin, 1982; Vital; Updated to March 1985 dollars.
[c] Value calculated by dividing the total values for male and female by total number of deaths.

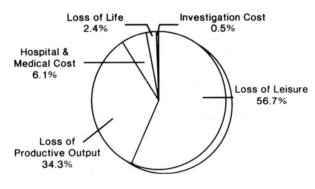

Figure 1

Economic Costs of Human Salmonellosis in Canada, 1982. Source: Curtin

Table 5

U.S. Annual Costs for Salmonellosis and Campylobacteriosis, 1985

Cost Categories	All Cases		
	low		high
	million dollars		
Medical Costs			
Mild Cases	0		0
Moderate Cases & Deaths	91	or	195
Lost Productivity			
Mild Cases a/	921	or	895
Moderate Cases a/	27	or	59
Deaths-Human Capital or Adjusted Willingness to Pay/Human Capital	352	or	1,441
Miscellaneous costs b/	6	or	13
TOTAL	$1.4 to 2.6 billion		

a This is a low estimate because it leaves out the value of homemaking.
b Miscellaneous costs include transportation, child care, other laboratory tests, finding new jobs.

Source: Data from Morrison and Roberts, 1985.

A Canadian study has also estimated costs of human salmonellosis and included two additional categories: loss of leisure and investigation (Curtin, 1984). The leisure cost is even more important than the loss of productive output, 56.7 percent of the total vs. 34.3 percent (Fig. 1). Some of their key assumptions on valuing leisure time are: there are 5 hours of leisure time available on a working day, 12.5 hours of leisure on a non-working day, and the value of leisure time is the average hourly wage rate (wage rates were calculated for five groups of people: working men 14-65, working women 14-65, working men and women 65+, non-working men and women 14-65, non-working men and women 65+). Productivity and leisure time losses are more important than hospitalization and other medical costs for salmonellosis and campylobacterosis in the Canadian study because the vast majority of the cases are mild and do not require hospitalization or even a visit to the doctor.

However, there are chronic medical syndromes that can follow both diseases that are difficult to quantify in their frequency and severity. For salmonellosis, rheumatoid arthritis is thought to be a common complication (Archer, 1985). Less common complications can affect the heart, the thyroid, the spleen, the pancreas, or even cause blood poisoning (Mossel, 1984). For campylobacteriosis, complications can include arthritis, blood poisoning, or inflammation of the heart, the colon, or the brain (ibid). If effects of these complications were accounted for, the estimates of the medical costs would be higher.

Food Safety Management Options

Pathogens in food are dependent upon three variables according to Mossel's and Stegeman's formula: $N_R = (N_0) (\Lambda^{-1}) (\Delta)$

pathogen pathogens in food	=	contamination in raw product	pathogen reduction during processing	$\uparrow$ or $\downarrow$ in pathogens after processing

Control options for reducing pathogens in food occur at all three points in this formula. Raw product contamination can be decreased by reducing or eradicating animal disease on the farm. One key factor in reducing salmonellosis on the farm is reducing or eliminating Salmonella in the feed. Improved sanitation practices in chicken slaughter and packaging plants could reduce the transfer of fecal matter and pathogens onto chicken meat. At the second stage, a processing technique such as canning or freezing can reduce pathogens. Irradiation has been proposed as a new method of reducing pathogens in raw pork, chicken and beef. Finally, there are procedures which could reduce salomonellosis and other pathogens in commercial and private kitchens. These include cooking to higher or more uniform internal temperatures and adopting better and more effective sanitation practices to keep raw chicken from contaminating cooked chicken or fruits and vegetables which are eaten raw.

Irradiation as a Control Option

Irradiation kills pathogens by interrupting their DNA. Work in the Netherlands by Mulder suggests that a 93 percent reduction in Salmonella-contaminated chicken carcasses can be achieved by an absorbed irradiation dose of 250 krads. A colleague, Rosanna Mentzer Morrison, estimated that irradiating fresh chicken packed at large and medium sized plants in the U.S. would cost $155 million a year. In comparison, the public health prevention benefits of irradiating U.S. fresh chicken to reduce Salmonella are estimated at $48 to 86 million. Chicken was identified as the source of 9.5 percent of the salmonellosis outbreaks reported in 1981 to CDC and 81 percent of the fresh chicken in the United States is packaged at these large and medium sized plants. ($48-86 million = $673-1,205 million x .93 x .095 x .81). In addition, irradiation kills 100% of the Campylobacter (Maxcy, 1983). Chicken was the cause of half of the campylobacteriosis cases in the Seattle study. The benefits for reducing campylobacteriosis by irradiating fresh chicken packaged at large and medium sized plants are $293 to $567 million annually ($724-1,399 million x .50 x .81).

The combined benefits of reducing salmonellosis and campylobacteriosis are $341 to $653 million. The estimated benefit/cost ratio of irradiating fresh chicken then ranges from 2.2 to 4.2, or $341/$155 to $653/$155.[3] Estimated net benefits range between $186 million ($341 minus $155) to $498 million ($653 minus $155).

CONCLUSION

The categories and methods which economists use to estimate the costs involved in foodborne illness have been briefly outlined. The example of estimating benefits and costs of irradiating fresh chicken to reduce salmonellosis illustrates many of the important considerations that must go into making these estimates. For example, the fact that irradiation also eliminates Campylobacter and other pathogens from chicken must be accounted for in benefit estimates.

ACKNOWLEDGEMENTS

I wish to thank Edna Loehman, Clark Burbee, Carol Kramer, and Doug McNiel for thoughtful comments on the paper.

NOTES

[1]Tanya Roberts is an economist with the National Economics Division, Economic Research Service, U.S. Department of Agriculture. The views expressed in this paper do not necessarily reflect those of the U.S. Department of Agriculture.

[2]In adding up costs, care must be taken to assure that product liability costs to firms are not already counted in the estimated pain and suffering costs to individuals.

[3]A number of other issues are overlooked in a benefit/cost analysis. The ratio depends upon what is included in the analysis. Are consumers concerned enough about salmonellosis and campylobacteriosis to be willing to cover the expense of irradiation? Are consumers convinced that irradiation is safe? Also, the estimates assume that these diseases are uniformly distributed throughout plants and not associated primarily with large or small packing plants.

The 250 krad absorbed dose level used in this analysis has not been approved by the Food and Drug Administration. However, Codex Alimentarius, an international cooperative body affiliated with the United Nations has approved doses of up to 700 krads for chicken.

REFERENCES

Archer, Douglas L., "Enteric Microorganisms in Rheumatoid Diseases: Causative Agents and Possible Mechanisms", J. of Food Protection, vol. 48, no. 6 (June 1985)538-45.

Bryan, Frank L., "Foodborne Diseases in United States Associated with Meat and Poultry", J. of Food Protection, vol. 43, no. 2 (1980) 140-50.

Centers for Disease Control. Foodborne Disease Outbreaks, Annual Summary 1981. Issued June 1983. HHS publication No. (CDC) 83-8185.

Cohen, M.L., R.E. Fontaine, R.A. Pollard, S.D. Von Allmen, T.M. Vern and E.J. Gangarosa, "An Assessment of Patient-Related Economic Costs in an Outbreak of Salmonellosis," The New England J. of Medicine, vol. 299 (1978)459-60.

"Consumers Eat Out More in 1985," NRA News Vol. 5, No. 7(Aug. 1985) 36-39.

Curtin, Leo. "Economic Study of Salmonella Poisoning and Control Measures in Canada." Agriculture Canada Working Paper 11/84, August 1984.

Dolan, T.J., T.A. Hodgson, and L.M. Wun, "Present Values of Expected Lifetime   Earnings and Housekeeping Services, 1977", Division of Analysis, National Center for Health Statistics, HHS (1980).

Field, R. A., F. C. Smith, D. D. Dean, G. M. Thomas and W. A. Kotula, "Sources of Variation in Bacteriological Condition of Ground Beef," J. of Food Protection, vol.40, no. 6 (June, 1977) 385-388.

Harrington, Winston, Alan J. Krupnick, and Walter O. Spofford, Jr. "The Benefits of Preventing an Outbreak of Giardiasis Due to Drinking Water Contamination," ELI/EPA Seminar, Washington, D.C. 18 July 1985.

Holmberg, Scott D., Enteric Diseases Branch, Divisions of Bacterial Disease, Centers for Disease Control, HHS, letter to Tanya Roberts, April 24, 1985.

Holmberg, Scott D., Michael T. Osterholdm Kenneth A. Senger, and Mitchell L. Cohen, "Drug Resistant Salmonella from Animals Fed Antimicrobials", New England J. of Med. vol. 311, no. 10 (Sept. 6, 1984) 617-622.

Kamplemacher, E.H., "Benefits of Radiation Processing to Public Health", paper presented at IAEA/FAO/WHO Symposium, San Diego, Fall, 1984.

Landefeld, J. Steven, and Eugene P. Seskin, "The Economic Value of Life: Linking Theory to Practice", Amer. J. of Public Health, vol. 72, no. 6 (June 1982)   555-565.

Kraus, Nancy Nighswonger, "Taxonomic Analysis of Perceived Risk: Modeling the Perceptions of Individual and Representing Local Hazard Sets," Ph.D. Dissertation, University of Pittsburgh, 1985.

Maxcy, R. B. "Significance of Residual Organisms in Foods After Sub-sterilizing Doses of Gamma Radiation: A Review," J. of Food Safety, 5 (1983) 203-211.

Morrison, Rosanna Mentzer and Tanya Roberts, "Food Irradiation: Technical, Regulatory, and Economic Considerations", Draft for the Office of Technology Assessment, May 1985.

Mossel, D.A.A., "Intervention as the Rational Approach to Control Diseases of Microbial Etiology Transmitted by Foods," J. of Food Safety, vol. 6 (1984) 89-104.

Mossel, D.A.A. and E.F. Drion, "Risk Analysis: Its Application to the Protection of the Consumer Against Food-transmitted Disease of Microbial Aetiology", Antonie van Leeuwenhoek, 45(1979) 321-3.

Mossel, D.A.A. and H. Stegeman "Irradiation: An Effective Mode of Processing Food for Safety," Paper presented at the IAEA/FAO International Symposium on Food Irradiation Processing, Washington, D.C. (March 4-8, 1985).

Mulder, R. W. A. W. Salmonella Radicidation of Poultry Carcasses, PhD. Dissertation, Agricultural University, Wageningen, The Netherlands, 1982.

Schwabe, Calvin W. Veterinary Medicine and Human Health. 3rd ed. Williams Wilkins: Baltimore, 1985.

Seattle - King County Dept. of Public Health, Communicable Disease Control Section. "Surveillance of the Flow of Salmonella and Campylobacter in a Community", USHHS Contract No. 223-81-7041. August, 1984.

Smith, Gordon S. and Martin J. Blaser, "Fatalities Associated with Campylobacter jejuni Infections", J. of the Amer. Med. Assoc., vol. 253, no. 19 (May 17, 1985) 2873-5.

Snoyenbos, H.G. (ed), Proceedings of the International Symposium on Salmonella (Amer. Assoc. of Avian Pathologists: Kenneth Square, PA) 1985.

Todd, Ewen C. D., "Economic Loss from Foodborne Disease and Non-illness Related Recalls Because Of Mishandling by Food Processors", J. of Food Protection, 48(July 1985)621-633.

Todd, Ewen C. D., "Economic Loss from Foodborne Disease Outbreaks Associated with Foodservice Establishments", J. of Food Protection, 48 (Feb. 1985) 169-180.

Vital Statistics of the United States, 1979: Volume II - Mortality, Part
    A. U.S. Dept. of Health and Human Services, Public Health Service,
    National Center for Health Statistics (Hyatsville, Maryland), 1984.
Wiese Research Associates, Inc., "Consumer Reaction to the Irradiation
    Concept", prepared for the U.S. Department of Energy and the National
    Pork Producers Council, March 1984.

THE COCHRAN-ARMITAGE TEST

FOR TRENDS OR THRESHOLDS IN PROPORTIONS

S. Stanley Young

Statistical and Mathematical Services
Lilly Research Laboratories

ABSTRACT

The Cochran-Armitage test for trends or thresholds in proportions.
Young, S. S. (1985) Society for Risk Analysis, 1985 Annual Meeting. the
Cochran-Armitage (C-A) test (1954, 1955) is widely used as a test for
linear trends in proportions in the analysis of long term rodent
studies. Implicit in the use of this test is the assumption that the dose
response pattern is known. Although in practice the dose response pattern
is often assumed linear on a log dose scale, this test can be used to test
for nonlinear dose response patterns. The effect of the choice of
different dose response patterns is examined using hypothetical and actual
examples of tumor data in rodents. The choice of a particular dose
response pattern can greatly influence the p-value from the C-A test. As
an alternative to the usual C-A test, a sequential testing procedure,
similar to the Williams-t (Williams, 1971, 1972), is suggested. Under the
assumption of a threshold model, this procedure gives improved testing and
estimation and leads to better inferences.

KEY WORDS: Cochran-Armitage test, Bioassay, Thresholds, Trends, DDT,
TDE, DDE

INTRODUCTION

It is common practice in toxicology experiments to give increasing
doses of a compound to groups of animals and to compare their response to
the response of animals in an untreated group. Experimenters are
interested in the progressive nature of any induced toxic phenomenon.
They are also interested in does that are without effect (or with effects
that are so small as to be considered unimportant). Typically, many
responses are measured in each animal. Progressivity of a dose response
is often used to help assess whether an observed group response is
treatment related or random. For example, a statistically significant
response at a low dose, unconfirmed at higher doses, would usually be
considered indicative of a false positive result.

It is often stated, see for example the Report of the NTP Ad Hoc
Panel on Chemical Carcinogenesis Testing and Evaluation (1984), that a
trend test is more powerful than multiple tests of each treated group
versus the control; trend tests gain this advantage since numerous tests

are replaced with a single test. However, there are some disadvantages to trend tests. They usually do not address the question of a "no-effect" dose. Also there is an implicit assumption that the shape or the form of the dose response curve is known.

The purpose of this paper is to examine the Cochran-Armitage (C-A) test (1954, 1955) for trends in proportions with regard to its implicit assumption of a known dose response pattern. A threshold test alternative to the usual C-A test is given. Numerous examples are included for three reasons. First, p-values for the same data vary greatly depending on the form of the test. Second, a number of data sets offer empirical evidence for thresholds. Third, computations are exemplified.

METHODS

The Cochran-Armitage trend test can be computed as the square of Z, given below:

$$Z = \frac{\Sigma \, d_i(x_i - p^*n_i)}{(p^*q^*(\Sigma n_i(d_i - \bar{d})^{**}2))^{**}0.5}$$

where

i = index for treatment group,
    0 control, 1 low dose, etc.
x_i = the number of tumor bearing animals in group i
n_i = the number of animals in group i,
d_i = selected to match the expected dose response,
N = Σn_i
p = $\Sigma n_i / N$
q = $1 - p$
$\bar{d}$ = $\Sigma n_i {}^* d_i / N$.

Z is approximately normally distributed with a mean of 0 and a variance of 1. Negative Z-values indicate a decreasing trend in the proportions; positive Z-values indicate an increasing trend. The d_i are selected by the experimenter to match the expected dose response curve. They are often chosen as 0,1,2 etc to match a dose response that is presumed linear on a log scale.

EXAMPLES: HYPOTHETICAL DATA

To examine the influence of the selection of d_i on the C-A test, several examples were constructed. Three examples are given in Table 1. These three examples were constructed to have doses placed in three different ways on a sigmoid dose response curve. See Figure 1. Example (a) has the low dose on the initial flat portion of the sigmoid curve. Example (b) has the low dose in the "linear phase" of the dose response and Example (c) has both the two treated groups on the upper flat portion of the dose response curve. For each example, the C-A z-values and corresponding p-values are given for three different sets of d_i. The first set of d_i, (0,0,1), is constructed to match doses that are located at control, lower plateau, and higher plateau. The second set of d_i, (0,1,2), assumes a linear response. The third set of d_i, (0,1,1), models control and both treated groups on the upper plateau of a sigmoid curve. It is obvious from Table 1 that the z-value and corresponding p-value are greatly influenced by the choice of d_i. The more closely the choice of d_i corresponds to the observed dose response pattern, the larger the z-value and smaller the p-value.

Table 1

Results of Cochran-Armitage Test for Constructed Examples
of Tumor Data for Different Sets of Di, See Figure 1

Example	Dose Group 0	Dose Group 1	Dose Group 2	C-A di	Z Value	P Value
(a)	0/50	0/50	10/50	001	4.629	0.000002
				012	4.009	0.00003
				011	2.315	0.010
(b)	0/50	5/50	10/50	001	2.887	0.002
				012	3.333	0.0004
				011	2.887	0.002
(c)	0/50	10/50	10/50	001	1.698	0.045
				012	2.942	0.002
				011	3.397	0.0003

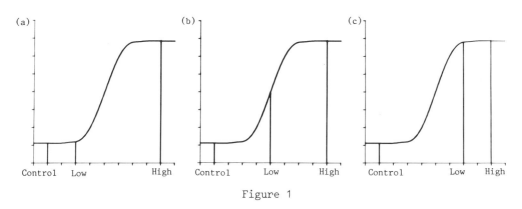

Figure 1

Dose Placement on a Signoid Response Curve

EXAMPLES: REAL DATA

Two examples are now given of mouse experiments conducted within
Lilly Research Laboratories. For Study 1, Table 2(a) gives the survival
at one and two years and the incidence of animals with proliferative
hepatic lesions: hyperplasia, adenoma, or carcinoma. Survival is given
to indicate that early deaths in the treated groups did not produce the
decline in hepatic lesions. Table 2(b) gives the results of C-A tests for
several sets of di. For both males and females a simple test of control
versus treated (0,1,1,1) is unimpressive. A test assuming the doses are
linearly spaced on the dose response curve (0,1,2,3) is significant for
both males and females and indicate a decrease with increasing dose. A
set of di that matches the apparent threshold nature of the dose response

for each sex gives an even smaller p-value. The latter di were selected by looking at the observed dose response and so the choice of di is subject to post hoc criticism.

Table 2

Lilly Study 1 in Male and Female Mice

(a) Survival at one and two years and the incidence of proliferative hepatic lesions.

Dose Group	Males			Females		
	Survival 1 Year	Survival 2 Years	Liver Lesions	Survival 1 Year	Survival 2 Years	Liver Lesions
0	59/60	53/60	19/60	59/60	47/60	5/60
1	60/61#	52/61#	22/61#	59/59#	48/59#	5/59#
2	60/60	48/60	20/60	60/60	51/60	2/60
3	59/60	51/60	9/59*	58/60	47/60	0/60
4	60/60	54/60	10/60	60/60	57/60	1/60

\# Animal missexed.
* One animal lost for evaluation.

(b) Cochran-Armitage trend test using different sets of di

Sex	Dose Group					C-A di	Z Value	P Value
	0	1	2	3	4			
Males	19/60	22/61	20/60	9/59	10/60			
(%)	31.7	36.1	33.3	15.3	16.7	01234	-2.81	0.997
						01111	-0.98	0.836
						00011	-3.40	0.9997
Females	5/60	5/59	2/60	0/60	1/60			
(%)	8.3	8.5	3.3	0.0	1.7	01234	-2.61	0.995
						01111	-1.69	0.955
						00111	-2.80	0.997

For Study 2, Table 3(a) gives the survival at 12 and 22 months and the incidence of animals with proliferative hepatic lesions. Again, survival is given to indicate that animals in the different groups were equally at risk so that increased survival did not produce the increase in hepatic lesions. Also note that the increase in liver lesions was not associated with a decrease in survival. Table 3(b) gives several C-A tests for males and females. For both males and females a simple test of control versus treated is not significant. Tests assuming the doses are linearly spaced on the dose response curve are significant for both sexes and indicate an increase with increasing dose. A set of di that matches the apparent threshold nature of the dose response gives an even smaller p-value. This set of di was selected by looking at the observed dose response and is again subject to post hoc criticism.

Table 3

Lilly Study 2 in Male and Female Mice

(a) **Survival at 12 and 22 months and the incidence of proliferative hepatic lesions.**

	Males			Females		
Dose Group	Survival 12 Months	Survival 22 Months	Hepatic Lesions	Survival 12 Months	Survival 22 Months	Hepatic Lesions
0	108/120	44/120	10/120	107/120	38/120	0/120
1	69/ 80	31/ 80	6/ 80	72/ 80	21/ 80	0/ 80
2	64/ 80	17/ 80	7/ 80	71/ 80	17/ 80	0/ 80
3	67/ 80	35/ 80	18/ 80	68/ 80	27/ 80	2/ 80

(b) Cochran-Armitage trend test using different sets of di

Sex	Dose Group 0	1	2	3	C-A di	Z Value	P Value
Males (%)	10/120 8.3	6/80 7.5	7/80 8.8	18/80 22.5	0123 0111 0001	2.78 1.29 3.54	0.003 0.099 0.0002
Females (%)	0/120 0.0	0/80 0.0	0/80 0.0	2/80 2.5	0123 0111 0001	2.05 1.00 2.65	0.020 0.159 0.004

Table 4(a) gives the incidence of urinary bladder neoplasia of female mice treated with 2AAF in animals that survived 18 or 24 months, Littlefield, et al. (1979). The incidence of neoplasia in the three lowest doses is essentially equal to that of control animals. A positive dose response appears to begin at 60 ppm. A formal test of threshold for this data set is given in Table 4(b) and will be described later.

A final example is a composite experiment on three structurally related compounds, DDT, DDE and TDE, see Figure 2. DDE and TDE are metabolites of DDT. These compounds, each at two dose levels, were run together in an experiment by the National Cancer Institute, Report 131 (1978). Table 5(a) gives the incidence of liver carcinoma for this experiment. Table 5(b) gives the results of several C-A tests. A test of control versus treated is significant. A test of linear trend has a substantially smaller p-value. A C-A test for a threshold followed by a linear trend followed by a plateau has an even smaller p-value. The decrease in p-values can be taken to indicate progressively better models of the dose response. A formal test of threshold for this data set is given in Table 5(c) and will be described next.

Table 4

NTP Study in Female BALB/c Mice Treated with 2AAF,
Killed at 18 or 24 Months, Littlefield et al (1979).

(a) Urinary bladder neoplasia

Group	Dose (ppm)	Bladder Incidence	Neoplasia Percent
0	0	2/ 784	0.26
1	30	4/2473	0.16
2	35	3/1434	0.21
3	45	2/ 828	0.24
4	60	6/ 684	0.88
5	75	4/ 578	0.69
6	100	30/ 291	10.31
7	150	162/ 251	64.54

(b) Results of threshold test, see Figure 3.

Test	"Control" Incidence	Percent	"Treated" Incidence	Percent	z Value	p Value
0 vs 1	2/ 784	0.26	4/2473	0.16	-0.531	.798
0,1 vs 2	6/3257	0.18	3/1434	0.21	0.180	.429
0-2 vs 3	9/4691	0.19	2/ 828	0.24	0.296	.384
0-3 vs 4	11/5519	0.20	6/ 684	0.88	3.199	.001
0-3 vs 4,5	11/5519	0.20	10/1262	0.79	3.421	.00031

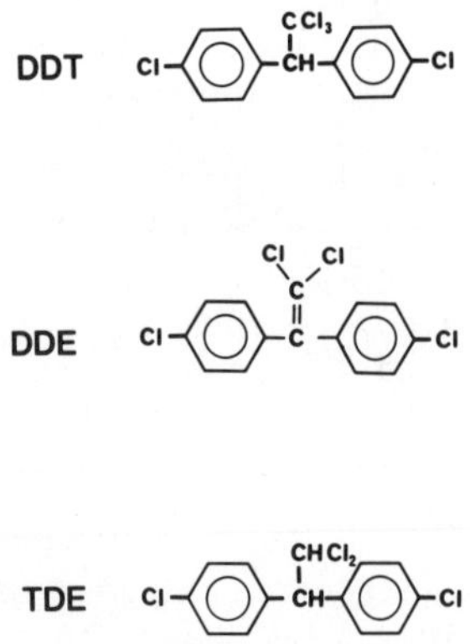

DDT

DDE

TDE

Figure 2

Structure of DDT, DDE and TDE

Table 5

NCI Studies on DDT, DDE and TDE in Male B6C3F1 Mice.

(a) Liver carcinoma

Group	Treatment	Liver Carcinoma Incidence	Percent
0	Control	4/56	7.1
1	22 ppm DDT	1/49	2.0
2	44 ppm DDT	1/48	2.1
3	148 ppm DDE	7/41	17.1
4	261 ppm DDE	17/47	36.2
5	411 ppm TDE	12/44	27.3
6	822 ppm TDE	15/50	30.0

(b) Cochran-Armitage trend test using different sets of di

C-A d_i	Z Value	P Value
0111111	2.22	1.3×10^{-2}
0123456	5.25	7.6×10^{-8}
0001222	6.06	9.3×10^{-10}

(c) Results of threshold test, see Figure 3.

Test	"Control" Incidence	Percent	"Treated" Incidence	Percent	z Value	p Value
0 vs 1	4/ 56	7.1	1/49	2.0	-1.22	.889
0,1 vs 2	5/105	4.8	1/48	2.1	-0.79	.786
0-2 vs 3	6/153	3.9	7/41	17.1	2.99	.002

473

The C-A test can be modified to give a statistical testing procedure similar to that of Williams (1971, 1972). The pattern of the test is given in Figure 3. The approach is to first test the control vs the low dose. If the result is significant then there is evidence of a problem: the low dose is an effect level (EL). If the low dose does not differ significantly from the control, then the low dose and the control are combined and used to test the next dose. This procedure is continued until an effect dose is found or all the dose groups have been considered. Dose levels below the effect level are considered to be no-effect levels (NOEL).

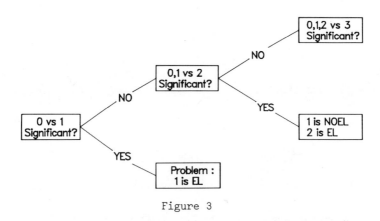

Figure 3

Schematic for the Application of a Williams Type Test to Binomial Data

Threshold testing is applied to the 2AAF and DDT composite data sets and the results are given in Tables 4(b) and 5(c). In both cases no effect levels are determined.

There are two practical aspects of the threshold method that deserve comment: control of experiment-wise error rate and allocation of animals to groups. First, it is common practice in any multiple comparison procedure to adjust the α-level of the statistical test so that a specified experiment-wise error rate is maintained. The greater the number of statistical tests, the more extreme the test statistic must be before significance is declared. The determination of critical values can be difficult. Two aspects of the threshold test can be used to simplify computation of critical values. The first aspect is a question of experimental intent. Often it is the intent to establish a no-effect level. Dose levels are set so that if the low dose is a no-effect level safety is considered assured. In this case, the control versus low dose comparison can be made at the nominal error rate as the experimental intent is satisfied if that test is not significant. The second aspect is that the construction of the test assures statistical independence of the step-wise statistical comparisons. Each sequential test can be formulated as a polynomial and the polynomials are orthogonal. For example, for a control and three treatment groups

	Group			
Comparison	0	1	2	3
0 vs 1	-1	1	0	0
0,1 vs 2	-1	-1	2	0
0-2 vs 3	-1	-1	-1	3.

The independence of the comparisons allows a simple determination of a per-comparison critical value that assures a specified experiment-wise error rate. Critical z-values for the threshold test are eiven in Table 6. The first row, only one treated group, can be used if establishment of one no-effect level is the only issue. The other rows give critical z-values if a specified experiment-wise error rate is to be maintained. It should be pointed out that if the premise of the test is correct -- threshold exist -- then adjustment for multiple comparisons does not make sense. Once a no-effect level is declared, safety is assured. Correction for multiple comparisons only makes sense if, even while using a threshold model, safety is not considered assured unless all tests are not significant. Anyone considering this strategy would be better advised to simply test control versus high (one test) at the experiment-wise error rate.

Table 6

Critical Per-Comparison Z-Values that Maintain a Specified Experiment-Wise Error Rate, One-Tail; for Two-Tailed Testing use 1/2 Experiment-Wise Error Rate.

Number of Treated Groups	Experiment-wise error rate			
	.050	.025	.010	.005
1	1.6449	1.9600	2.3263	2.5758
2	1.9545	2.2390	2.5749	2.8066
3	2.1212	2.3909	2.7119	2.9348
4	2.2340	2.4944	2.8059	3.0229
5	2.3187	2.5723	2.8769	3.0896
6	2.3862	2.6347	2.9338	3.1434

The second practical aspect of the threshold method is how to allocate animals to the various groups. There is much confusion in the literature about "optimal" allocation of animals, see for example Portier and Hoel (1983, 1983, 1984) and Krewski (1983). Much of this confusion can be attributed to an unclear statement of the objective of the experiment.

Once the goal of the experiment is determined, the allocation of animals is straightforward. With a threshold experiment there are two reasonable ways to allocate animals depending upon the goal of the experimenter. First, if the goal is to establish a no-effect level at a particular dose, then the animals should be divided equally between the control group and the dose level, see Table 7. Second, if the goal is to determine where the threshold begins, then there are three questions.

Table 7

Allocation of Animals to a Dose-Response Study as a
Function of the Goal of the Experiment. N. is the Total Sample Size.

Goal	Allocation	Comments
Low dose effect	N/2, N/2, 0,0,etc	Only issue is safety of low dose.
High dose effect	N/2, 0,...,0, N/2	Only issue is toxicity of high dose
Where is threshold	3 Groups: N/4,N/4,N/2 4 Groups: N/8,N/8,N/4,N/2	Maximum power at top dose level
Determine shape	3 Groups: N/4,N/2,N/4 4 Groups: N/8,N/4,N/4,N/8	Maximum power for quadratic response
Control vs several groups	For k treated groups, control group replicated k times the trt group size.	Decreases false positives from aberrant controls

1. How many dose groups?
2. How to space the dose groups?
3. How many animals at each group?

The answer to the third question offers some guidance to the first
two questions; unfortunately answers to questions 1 and 2 depend upon
knowing the shape of the true dose response. If a control and three dose
levels have been chosen, then the optimum allocation of animals is 1/8 at
control, 1/8 at low dose, 1/4 at mid dose, and 1/2 at high dose. The
reason for this allocation is that at each stage of the threshold test it
is optimal to have an equal number of animals in the two groups being
compared. It is well known that the optimal allocation in a two group
comparison is equal allocation of animals. This result is somewhat
disturbing: there is less power to detect a threshold at a particular
level than at the next. The answer to this dilemma is that maximum power
to detect an effect at a particular level is a different goal and as was
mentioned before the best allocation of animals in that situation is 1/2
at control and 1/2 at that level. Note that if the threshold occurs at
the highest dose, then final test of the threshold method will have 1/2 of
the animals combined and tested against the highest dose. This test is
identical to optimum allocation for the question "Is there any effect?"
That test would use two groups: a control and a group at the highest
possible dose. Table 7 gives suggested optimum allocations of animals for
various experimental situations.

The above discussion offers some guidance to the questions of how
many dose groups and how to space them. Fewer dose groups will have more
animals in each dose group (assuming a fixed total number of animals) so
each sequential test will be a powerful as possible. The top dose should
be as high as is reasonable so that maximum response can be observed. The

low dose should be as low as possible commensurate with human exposure, safety factors etc. Intermediate doses should be spaced as far apart as possible. It is often argued that the dose scale be in log units. It is doubtful that increasing the number of dose groups beyond three adds much beyond insurance against misplacement of the dose levels.

DISCUSSION

The Cochran-Armitage trend test requires that the dose response pattern, i.e. the di, be specified by the experimenter. The true dose response pattern must be known for the test to be optimal. It is clear that the choice of di can have a large effect on the test statistic. Unfortunately, the optimal set of di is seldom known until the results are scrutinized. If the dose response is sigmoid, the actual spacing of doses might fall in any of a number of ways. If the actual doses do not fall in a linear portion of the response curve, then the C-A test with linear di will not give a z-value that is as large as that given by a test with a set of di that matches the real dose response.

Several data sets are given where the dose response is nonlinear. In Lilly Study 1, the control and low doses are similar in response and the higher doses give a decrease in response. In Lilly Study 2, the control and two low doses are similar and in the high dose there appears to be an increase in response. Both studies along with the 2AAF and DDT-DDE-TDE experiments can be taken as empirical evidence for the existence of thresholds. The usual application of the C-A test which assumes a linear dose response can be misleading when there is a threshold or nonlinear dose response present.

Although it has been taken on faith by some that thresholds do not exist, this faith is far from universal and a number of recent papers support the existence of thresholds; see for example the book CANCER AND THE ENVIRONMENT, Possible Mechanisms of Thresholds for Carcinogens and other Toxic Substances, Cimino, ed. (1983). Also in an extensive review of the potential carcinogenic risk from formaldehyde, Squire et al. (1984) question the presumption that thresholds can not exist. Matters of faith are not testable, hence are outside the usual scope of science; the proposed threshold test does bring thresholds into the realm of testability.

The DDT-DDE-TDE experiment is included for several reasons. First it is illustrative of how the p-values of the C-A test can change as a function of the di. The p-value can change by eight orders of magnitude over rather reasonable sets of di, Table 5(b). If it is presumed that the compounds are so similar structurally and metabolically that they will be roughly identical in the induction of hepatic tumors, then this data set is illustrative of a sigmoid dose response pattern with a threshold and a plateau. The premise that all three compounds are roughly equal in their ability to induce hepatic tumors is not unreasonable as the nonresponding compound, DDT, has been shown to induce hepatic tumors in other studies, see for example Wahrendorf, 1983. There are few long term studies with enough dose groups to span the entire range of a sigmoid dose response curve. The low doses of DDT, 22 and 44 ppm, appear somewhat protective. In studies in trout, Hendricks et al. (1977), and Sheldon et al. (1984), show that PCB, another enzyme inducer, is protective against induced hepatic tumors.

There are several methods in the literature for addressing the testing of thresholds and the fitting of dose response functions with plateaus. Williams (1971, 1972) gives a method of testing for a threshold that we have modified here for proportions. Anderson and Nelson (1975) give a method of piece-wise linear fitting of a response function so that thresholds and plateaus can be modeled. Both methods are for continuous data, but are easily extended to binomial data. The methods of Anderson and Nelson are aimed at curve fitting whereas the methods of Williams are aimed at hypothesis testing. Daly (1962) gives a method for testing for trends in a contingency table which is the mechanical equivalent of the method given here, but he combines his sequential tests into one composite test. Tukey et al. (1985) have proposed a sequential testing scheme to find a "no-statistical-significance-of-trend" level. Their scheme is for quantitative variables and although it could be extended to binomial data, they do not recommend extension, Ciminera (personal communication). Poon (1980) compares several methods for binomial data.

There are a number of reasonable objectives in the assessment of a dose response. The particular objectives and the methods to be employed should be stated before the conduct of the study. Care is needed in the application of the Cochran-Armitage test; the results are dependent on the particular dose response pattern assumed, i.e. the set of d_i. If a crude indicator of treatment effect is all that is desired, then the Cochran-Armitage test with a linear set of d_i, i.e. 0,1,2, etc, could suffice although a control versus high appears preferable. This test has essentially equal power and makes no assumption on the shape of the dose response. If thresholds are considered possible and no effect levels are of interest, then the threshold test given here appears reasonable. It allows for the determination of "no effect" levels and still has good power for the detection of treatment effects. If curve fitting is of interest, then a method similar to that of Anderson and Nelson appears reasonable. Neither method requires that the complete shape of the dose be known.

There is a final important caveat: All of the methods discussed herein assume that the single response of interest has been identified before the conduct of the study. In the case of long-term rodent carcinogenic studies, assessment of the data often constitutes a survey of several hundred possible tumors rather than an explicit testing scheme. It is not known how curve fitting and hypothesis testing that were designed for a single predetermined response behave when they are applied to several post hoc selected response variables. It is probable that hypothesis testing, by any usual method, is greatly upset and that false positives will result, Muller et al. (1984).

REFERENCES

Anderson, R. L. and L. A. Nelson. "A family of models involving intersecting straight lines and concomitant experimental designs useful in evaluating response to fertilizer nutrients" Biometrics 31:303-318 (1975).
Anolymous. "Bioassay of DDT, TDE, and p,p'-DDE for possible carcinogenicity" NCI Technical Report, No. 131. (1978).
Armitage, P. "Tests for linear trends in proportions and frequencies" Biometrics 11:375-386 (1955).
Board of Scientific Counselors, NTP. Report of the ad hoc panel on chemical carcinogenesis testing and evaluation. U.S. Dept. of Health and Human Services. (1984).
Cimino, J.A. Cancer and the Environment, Possible Mechanisms of Thresholds for Carcinogens and other Toxic Substances. Mary Ann Liebert. New York. (1983).

Cochran, W.G. "Some methods of strengthening the common Chi-Square test" Biometrics 10:417-451 (1954).

Daly, C. "A simple test for trends in a contingency table" Biometrics 18:114-119 (1962).

Hendricks, J.D., T.P. Putman, D.D. Bills and R.O. Sinnhuber. "Inhibitory effect of a polychlorinated biphenyl (Aroclor 1254) on aflatoxin B1 carcinogenesis in rainbow trout (Salmo gairdneri)" JNCI 59:1545-1551 (1977).

Krewski, D., J. Kovar, and M. Bickis. "Optimal experimental designs for low dose extrapolation" In Topics in Applies Statistics edited by T.W. Dwived: Marcell Dekker, New York (1983).

Littlefield, N.A., J.H. Farmer, D.W. Gaylor and W.G. Sheldon. "Effects of dose and time in a long-term low-dose carcinogenic study" Journal of Environmental Pathology and Toxicology 3:17-34 (1979).

Muller, K.E., C.N. Barton, and V.A. Benignus. "Recommendations for appropriate statistical practice in toxicology experiments" Neuro. Toxicology 5:113-126 (1984).

Poon, A.H. "A Monte Carlo study of the power of some k-sample tests for ordered binomial alternatives" J. Stat. Comp. and Sim. 11:251-259 (1980).

Portier, C. and D. Hoel. "Low-dose-rate extrapolation using the multistage model" Biometrics 39:897-906 (1983).

Portier, C. and D. Hoel. "Optimal design of the chronic animal bioassay" J. Tox. Env. Health 12:1-12 (1983).

Portier, C. and D. Hoel. "Design of animal carcinogenicity studies for goodness-of-fit of multistage models" Fundam. Appl. Toxic 4:949-959 (1984).

Sheldon D.W., J.D. Hendricks, R.A. Coulombe, and G.S. Bailey. "Effect of dose on the inhibition of carcinogenesis/mutagenesis by Aroclor 1254 in rainbow trout fed aflatoxin B1" J. Tox. and Envir. Health 13:649-657 (1984).

Shirley, Eryl A. C. "The comparison of treatment with control group means in toxicology studies" Applied Statistics 28:144-151 (1979).

Squire, R.A. and Cameron, L.L. "An analysis of potential carcinogenic risk from formaldehyde" Regulatory Toxicology and Pharmacology 4:107-129 (1984).

Tukey, J.W., Ciminera, J.L. and Heyse, J.F. "Testing the statistical certainty of a response to increasing doses of a response to increasing doses of a drug" Biometrics 41:295-301 (1985).

Wahrendorf, J. "Simulatneous analysis of different tumor types in a long term carcinogenicity study with scheduled sacrifices" JNCI 70:915-921 (1983).

Williams, D.A. "A test for differences between treatment means when several dose levels are compared with a zero dose control" Biometrics 27:103-117 (1971).

Williams, D.A. "The comparison of several dose levels with a zero dose control" Biometrics 28:519-531 (1972).

DEVELOPMENT OF THE NON-DIMENSIONAL METHOD OF RANKING RISKS

John C. Chicken* and Michael R. Hayns**

J. C. Consultancy Ltd and*
John C. Chicken Consultancy GmbH
United Kingdom Atomic Energy Authority**

ABSTRACT

This paper presents a critical review of the progress made in the development of the risk ranking technique. The aim of the development of the technique has been to produce a method of making a comprehensive assessment that takes into account the technical, economic and socio-political factors involved in determining the acceptability of a risk.

The paper examines: the data available for ranking acceptability, the ranking of the Moss Morran and Eemshaven projects, the efficacy of the technique in its present state of development and the future uses for the technique.

KEY WORDS: Risk Ranking, Overall Acceptability Assessment

1. INTRODUCTION

This paper examines the practical problems associated with applying the method of ranking the acceptability of risks which was described in a paper presented at the 1984 Annual Meeting.[1] The incentive for developing the technique is to produce a unified, non-emotive, non-dimensional, easily understood way of describing the acceptability of risks. In the following the application of the technique to ranking two projects is examined.

The factors that have to be considered are grouped under the headings of technical, economic and socio-political, the rank of each project being determined by integrating the acceptability scores of each group of factors. The scores allocated are an assessment of the acceptability and uncertainty of each factor. Table 1 shows how the scores are related to the ranking and the type of control action likely to be associated with each level of ranking.

The problems involved in ranking acceptability are examined in three steps which are: the data required, ranking the acceptability of the British Moss Morran and the Dutch Rijnmond projects and assessing the efficacy of the technique. Finally, the general uses and future development of the technique are examined.

2. DATA FOR RANKING

Each group of data has quite different characteristics.

481

Table 1

Definition of Rank Acceptability and Control Action

RISK RANK	ACCEPTABLITY OF PROPOSAL	TOTAL SCORE ALLOWABLE FOR EACH RANK	MAXIMUM ALLOWABLE SCORE FOR EACH RANKING FACTOR (TECHNICAL, ECONOMIC, AND SOCIO-POLITICAL	CONTROL ACTION REQUIRED
1	UNLIKELY TO BE ACCEPTABLE	6 - 12	4	UNLIKELY ANY POSSIBLE
2	ONLY ACCEPTABLE IF RISK CAN BE REDUCED	4 - 6	3	ADMINIS-TRATIVE AND ENGINEERING
3	YES SUBJECT TO CERTAIN ACTION	>2 - 4	2	ENGINEERING
4	YES WITHOUT RESTRICTION	0 - 2	1	NONE

The technical group of data is essential to the evaluation of the acceptability of a risk. In one definitive technical study of risk, (NUREG 1050), a clear indication of the uncertainty associated with such data is given by statements that: estimates of the frequency of nuclear reactor core-melt may differ by two orders of magnitude and that estimates of the likelihood of operator error may deviate by an order of magnitude.[2] The magnitude of these uncertainties led to the following interesting conclusions about the usefulness of quantitative risk assessment.[2]

"Probabilistic Risk Assessment results are useful, provided that more weight is given to the qualitative and relative insights regarding design and operations, rather than the precise absolute magnitude of the numbers generated.

It must be remembered that most of the uncertainties associated with an issue are inherent to the issue itself rather than artifacts of the Probabilistic Risk Assessment Analysis. The Probabilistic Risk Assessment does tend to identify and highlight these uncertainties, however.

Probabilistic Risk Assessment results have useful application in the prioritization of regulatory activities, development of generic regulatory positions on potential safety issues and the assessment of plant-specific issues. The degree of usefulness depends on the regulatory application as well as the nature of the specific issue.

The basic attributes of a Probabilistic Risk Assessment are not highly compatible with a safety-goal structure that would require strict numerical compliance on the basis of the quantitative best estimates of Probabilistic Risk Assessment."

These conclusions draw attention to two very important findings, which are the significance of a risk will not be known accurately and the allowance for uncertainty is not generally adequate so there is a need to develop a comprehensive way of allowing for uncertainty.[2]

Further indication of the range of uncertainty that can be associated with estimates of risk is given by the results of a study of decision making and risk analysis in relation to the siting of liquefied energy gas facilities.[3] The study argued that for most risk estimates the range of uncertainty is at least 10^2 To emphasise that 10^2 may be the minimum range of uncertainty attention is drawn to two figures from the study, which are estimates for the probability of an internal system failure, one is 3.2×10^{-3} and the other is 1.0×10^{-11}. Such a wide difference shows dramatically how great the uncertainty in risk estimates can be.

The conclusion about the technical data that is justified is that the data likely to be available will contain an element of uncertainty. It is in dealing with uncertainty in risk assessment that the ranking technique can be particularly helpful.

We are all conscious of the economic significance of variations in our expenditure. With major projects the variation in cost can be many millions of pounds. In NUREG 1050 it is shown that the total financial risk for a pressurized water reactor ice-condenser plant can be between 5 $\times 10^5$ and 8×10^7 dollars per plant lifetime.[2] The problem was examined further in a study which the US Nuclear Regulatory Commission had made of the socio-economic consequences of nuclear reactor accidents.[4] The study stressed the uncertainties in predicting the economic impact of an accident.[4] Such evaluation of economic losses generally includes an allowance for pain and suffering, which in a way quantifies the emotive factor associated with risk. The variability of economic factors is given by the statement: "We can reduce the risk in any sector provided we are prepared to pay the cost."[5] This exposes the concept of opportunity cost which underlies most economic decisions.

There are clear indications from ref 3 that the authorities responsible for deciding about the acceptability of sites attempt to take into account the need for economic development in the area surrounding a proposed site,[3] but there are no universally agreed ways in which such factors are taken into account and this fuzziness in the economic argument shows the need to evaluate the uncertainty or ambiguity in the data when determining the ranking.

In a study by Chicken of the correlation between expenditure on life saving and the public's perception of risk the following conclusions were drawn, which are relevant to the ranking.[6]

1) The level of expenditure on risk reduction is more related to people's perception of risk than to estimates of the probability of the risk.

2) Policy makers are willing to contemplate higher levels of expenditure to reduce involuntarily accepted risk than for voluntarily accepted risks.

3) The value of life for compensation purposes, including an allowance for pain and suffering, often seems to be put at about £200,000, but there is a considerable range in such valuations.

4) The range of cost of saving an extra statistical life (often referred to as the CSX value) used is from £0 to 2×10^9. For many decision

situations the values used are in the range £10^4 to 10^5.

5) The cost of action to save a life is sometimes higher than the compensation paid for loss of life.

A more recent study of the way human life is valued for various purposes draws attention to the view that life insurance does not really value life but just amounts to saving to provide for dependants or the future.[7] The values of human life reported, in ref 7, range from £1 x 10^3 for a child-proof drug container to £20 x 10^6 for a change in British building regulations.

The conclusion that seems to be justified about the economic data is very similar to the conclusion about the technical data, but there is even greater uncertainty about the data that has to be used, and this must be taken into account in determining the ranking score.

At the heart of assessing socio-political factors is determination of public opinion. Public opinion is fickle and opinions do change and this variability has to be allowed for. Public opinion can be assessed either from the opinions of those active in the field or by polls. Dr. Keyes, a Director of the Westinghouse Electric Corporation, has summarized the roll of polls in the following incisive way:[8] "Certainly, the techniques are not perfect. Sometimes the pollster errs; sometimes, his client. Nevertheless, polling is one of the most important tools available in measuring public attitude on certain issues in order to ascertain the public will which, in the long run, will find expression in the actions of government in a democratic society." One important weakness of polls is that unless they are carefully designed they can give too much emphasis to the views of people who are not concerned with the issues involved.

If there is opposition and it is based on a lack of information or on a misunderstanding of information given, it is possible by judicious publicity and education processes to reduce it, but such processes can take a considerable time.[9]

The conclusion about socio-political data that seems to be warranted is that although a great diversity of views are involved there are survey techniques available that enable opinions to be assessed in a way that indicates the ranking that may be justified.

3. DEMONSTRATION OF THE APPLICATION OF THE RANKING TECHNIQUE

To demonstrate how the ranking technique may be applied in practice two well known cases, Moss Morran and Rijnmond, that have caused a certain amount of controversy were assessed.

3.1 The Moss Morran Facilities and Pipeline

The Moss Morran liquefied energy gas terminal facilities and pipeline was planned as part of the development required to exploit the Brent oil and gas field in the North Sea. There were three main stages in the process leading to outline permission being granted.[3] Stage 1 was Shell and Esso formally lodging planning applications to develop a processing facility at Moss Morran. Stage 2 included the Secretary of State for Scotland calling for the decision to be made at central rather than local government level, a public inquiry into the acceptability of the proposal being held, local government authorities publicising the fact that the planning applications had been lodged and describing the general nature of the proposals, the hazards involved and the environmental impact of the proposals being assessed, and the directors of planning of the local authorities concerned preparing a report on the socio-economic impact of the proposal. The conclusion of Stage 2 was marked by the Secretary of State receiving the report of the public inquiry. Stage 3 started when it was found that the public inquiry had exposed differences in views and concern about the possibility of a vapour cloud being ignited by radio frequency transmissions. The Secretary of State invited written comments on the subject. It was finally concluded from tests that radio frequency transmissions were unlikely to produce sufficient power to reach the minimum required for ignition.[10] In August 1979 the Secretary of State announced he would grant outline planning permission.

The risks associated with the pipeline from St. Fergus to Moss Morran were assessed by the Health and Safety Executive in 1978 and again in 1980 when it was proposed to increase the pipeline size from 16-inch to 24-inch diameter.[11] The assessment showed that the chance of leakage from the pipeline reaching people in the area of the pipeline fell in the range 1 to 4×10^{-6} per year. The report advised: "...the level of risk would not be such as to lead to a recommendation that a Construction Authorization should be withheld on health and safety grounds".

Although consequence analysis calculations were made the results were expressed in qualitative terms like low, very low or extremely low and gave no estimate of the possible number of fatalities.[3] The Action Group estimated that the probability of an individual fatality was 7×10^{-4} per year.[3] The one hazard figure that seems to be very high is the shipping hazard figure, the same figure of 10^{-3} per year appears to have been used in the assessment of the acceptability of Eemshaven, Braefoot Bay and Wilhelmshaven. This apparent statistical anomaly has been adversely commented on in reference 3.

Concern about the safety and risk justification of the Moss Morran site is indicated by the conditions that were attached to the outline planning permissions granted to Shell and Esso.[3] The most important condition from the safety point of view being the requirement that a full hazard and operability audit should be conducted before the facilities are allowed to be commissioned. The importance attached to the audit is indicated by the fact that the Secretary of State decided the audit must be to his satisfaction and not just to the satisfaction of the Health and Safety Executive.[3]

From the information above and assuming that all the planning conditions are satisfied it is considered that the risk ranking that can be justified for Moss Morran is 3. The construction of the ranking is shown in Table 2.

3.2 The Rijnmond Decision

The history of the Rijnmond Decision is complicated and has its origins in the early 1970's when plans were made to import large quantities of liquefied natural gas (LNG) from Algeria.[3] Eight possible sites for the LNG terminal were considered.[3] The two main contenders were Rotterdam and Eemshaven.

The discussion that took place about which was the most acceptable site also took place in three stages.[3] Stage 1 was the period up to the final signing of the contract for the supply of LNG and included the preliminary search for a terminal site. Stage 2 involved the cabinet and several government departments and at this stage it was recognized that siting involved several issues such as energy policy, the environment, safety, land use and regional planning. At the beginning of this round,

Table 2

Ranking Factor Score for Moss Morran

FACTOR	SCORE	JUSTIFICATION
TECHNICAL	2	All the advice, which was a mixture of qualitative and quantitative assessments suggested the proposals were acceptable subject to detailed justification. The installations are similar to those accepted in other parts of the world.
ECONOMIC	1	National Energy Policy required the Brent Oil and gas field to be exploited. The financial risks of the operation were undertaken by private companies and were consistent with the scale of risk they undertook in other parts of their work.
SOCIO-POLITICAL	1	The proposals were accepted at Government level but the Secretary of State made it a condition that he was satisfied with the safety audit. The opposition to the proposals was essentially of a limited local nature.
TOTAL SCORE	4	So risk rank 3 was justified.

Rotterdam was the preferred site and discussions were held with the local authorities, which showed that local authorities, particularly the Rijnmond Public Authority, were likely to apply stringent safety requirements to any LNG terminal. This is why the decision became known as the 'Rijnmond Decision'. Stage 3 ended with a cabinet deciding in favour of Eemshaven. During this period there were formal council debates and public meetings. Local authorities and trade unions were in favour of Eemshaven.[3] The environmentalist groups, Shipowners Association and Electricity Corporation were against Eemshaven.[3] In August 1978 the cabinet announced its preference for Eemshaven primarily on socio-economic and regional industrial grounds and in October 1978 Parliament approved the decision.

The view has been expressed that in part the reason that the decision went in favour of Eemshaven was that the Governor of Groningen was a skillful politician and a long standing member of one of the parties in power.[3] On this basis the final decision appears to have been guided more by political considerations than by consistent government policies.

For a major accident it was predicted that the number of deaths and casualties would be ten times lower for Eemshaven than for Maasvlakte, but such differences are not beyond the errors in such calculations.

On the basis of this evidence both sites justified a rank 3, but the

Table 3

Ranking Factor Score for the Eemshaven Site

FACTOR	SCORE	JUSTIFICATION
TECHNICAL	1	Probability of a major accident put at 5×10^{-8} and the increase of risk of individual death $< 3 \times 10^{-7}$, this is 10 times higher than Maasvlakte and mainly why a lower score than Maasvlakte is justified.
ECONOMIC	1	Benefit to the development of the area. Risk the same as the other site.
SOCIO-POLITICAL	1	The site was accepted. Political support for the site. Trade union support for the site.
TOTAL SCORE	3	So a rank 3 is justified.

score for Maasvlakte was 4 as against 3 for Eemshaven which makes Eemshaven slightly more acceptable. The construction of the Eemshaven ranking is given in Table 3.

3.3 Assessment Of The Ranking

The information available was adequate to show that the ranking technique gives an overall view of the acceptability of a proposal. The process of constructing and justifying the ranking scores exposes very clearly the strengths and weaknesses of the evidence on which the assessment of acceptability has to be based.

The technical factor evidence showed considerable differences between the two cases considered. One very important difference was between the qualitative evidence about risks presented for Moss Morran and the quantitative evidence used to compare the Maasvlakte and Eemshaven sites. If there had only been qualitative evidence about the risks associated with Moss Morran any ranking of acceptability would have been

Table 4

Technical Ranking and the Ashby Criteria

RISK RANK	ACCEPTABILITY	TECHNICAL SCORE MAXIMUM	ASHBY CRITERIA (RISK OF DEATH PER YEAR)
1	UNLIKELY TO BE ACCEPTABLE	4	Unacceptable (one in 1000)
2	ONLY ACCEPTABLE IF RISK CAN BE REDUCED	3	Willing to spend money to reduce risk (one in 10,000)
3	YES SUBJECT TO CERTAIN ENGINEERING ACTION	2	Warnings given (one in 100,000)
4	YES WITHOUT RESTRICTION	1	Acceptable (one in a million)

questionable. There was, however, some quantitative data, which included estimates of pipeline failures, the risk of a shipping accident and estimates of fatalities. Also, it was possible to estimate the order of the risk by comparison with the estimates of the risks made for other similar installations. From the study Kunreuther et al made of four similar plants in four different countries some criticism of the differences in the analyses used in such cases appears justified.[3] The criticism that is common to the Moss Morran and Rijnmond case is that the uncertainty in the calculations involved was not properly dealt with.

The way the ranking of the technical factors agrees with the steps in the Ashby quantitative criteria of risk acceptability is shown in Table 4.[12] Lord Ashby acknowledges that he developed his criteria from some ideas Chauncey Starr expressed.[12]

The assessment of the acceptability of the economic factors associated with the two cases considered is perhaps the weakest part of the exercise as there was not a great deal of direct evidence available. The evidence that was available was somewhat doubtful as it included shadow pricing and was also politically influenced. The assessment of acceptability was based, mainly, on the fact that the installations in some way or other formed part of the national fuel policy of the countries they were built in and that the risks were of a type accepted by the companies involved. If the companies had been unused to dealing with such risks, doubts about the acceptability of the economic factors would have existed.

Scoring of the acceptability of the socio-political factors was in this study somewhat simplified as the ultimate decision was known. However, if the projects were new sampling techniques exist that would given an indication of the attitudes of the relevant populations. Studies have also been made which have identified the basic underlying value structures in different cultural groups.[13] Knowledge of such basic value structures can be particularly helpful in likely public reaction to controversial issues.[13]

The conclusions that seem to be justified about the ranking technique are that: it gives an overall assessment of all the factors that have to be considered in determining the acceptability of a potentially hazardous installation, no other method gives such a comprehensive assessment, and the technique identifies the issues that are likely to generate the most concern.

4. THE CURRENT STATUS OF THE DEVELOPMENT OF THE RANKING TECHNIQUE

Now to examine some of the other uses that have been made of the technique, the problems with the technique and possible future developments.

4.1 Current Uses Of The Technique

Two specific uses of the technique that have been made are to assess the acceptability of the transport of potentially hazardous materials and to assess the current acceptability of buildings for the storage of irradiated nuclear fuel.

In assessing irradiated nuclear fuel transport the technical consequences of possible accidents led directly to assessment of the economic factors. The economic assessment had to take into account the possible potential loss of revenue and the possible claims for compensation. This led to the assessment of the socio-political factors. An accident to a nuclear fuel cargo could have an adverse effect on the nuclear industry and the significance of such an event had to be assessed. The experience gained in this assessment showed clearly how building up the ranking of an activity exposes weak points in the argument and data used and indicates where improvements can most effectively be made.

The ranking made of the acceptablity of a twenty year old nuclear material handling building necessitated consideration being given to the possibility of age defects in the buildings causing risks in addition to the other risks.

These applications of ranking indicate the interest there is in the technique. There is also interest in the development of the technique from government and intergovernment organizations. The attraction they see in the technique is that it presents a genuine comprehensive assessment of the acceptability of a proposal in a way that may help decision makers and eliminate unnecessary public debate about acceptability.

Quite apart from these developments the Dutch Directorate-General of Labour has made use of a simplified form of ranking in the guidance on the classification of hazardous areas in relation to the installation and selection of electrical apparatus where there is a gas explosion hazard.(14)

4.2 Problems With The Ranking Technique

The problems with the technique are mainly associated with the adequacy, relevance and accuracy of the data that has to be used. Ideally for the ranking of proposals to be comparable the quality and comprehensiveness of the data used to rank each proposal should be the same. In practical terms perfect data is rarely available and some compromise has to be made.

For major projects the ranking would, in general, be reviewed several times as they progress from conception to completion. This iterative development and review of ranking enables allowance to be made for: changes in the accuracy of the data, changes that take place in the relative significance of the hazards considered, changes in design, and operational changes.

4.3 Future Developments

It is intended to apply the technique to ranking the acceptability of a wider range of projects including the assessment of the acceptability of a major new project. The testing of the technique will be aimed at determining its efficacy both as a management and as a regulatory tool.

In future applications of the technique it is hoped to develop a more consistent approach to the assessment of the various factors, particularly in the way uncertainty in the data used is allowed for, also it may be that two forms of the technique are required, one for management purposes and the other for regulatory purposes. The two forms of ranking could be linked with management ranking being regarded simply as the first stage ranking and the regulatory ranking as the final ranking.

5. CONCLUSIONS

We believe that the study shows that the risk acceptability ranking technique that has been developed is a useful tool in three important related ways, which are: it has the potential to bring a structure and discipline to the subject, it can be tailored to a variety of management and regulatory evaluation needs, and it can be used for presenting to the public an easily understandable assessment of complex risk issues.

6. REFERENCES

1) Chicken, J. C. and Hayns, M. R., A Multi-Factor Criterion for Risk Acceptability, a paper presented at the 1984 Annual Meeting in Knoxville USA of the Society for Risk Analysis.

2) NUREG-1050, Probabilistic Risk Assessment (PRA) Reference Document, US Nuclear Regulatory Commission, published September 1984, pp 2-6.

3) Kunreuther, H. C. and Linnerooth et al, Risk Analysis and Decision Processes, Springer-Verlag, Berlin, 1983.

4) NUREG/CR-3566 PNL-4911, Socioeconomic Consequences of Nuclear Reactor Accidents, The Nuclear Regulatory Commission, published 1984, pp iii-iv and pp 7.32-7.33.

5) Kunreuther, H. C. and Ley, E. V. (Editors), The Risk Analysis Controversy, An Institutional Perspective, Springer-Verlag, Berlin, 1982, p 116.

6) JCC/CWL/P3, Factors Influencing Expenditure on Risk Reduction, a report prepared by J. C. Consultancy Ltd for the United Kingdom Atomic Energy Authority, November 1983, p 15.

7) RGWP (85) P5 INF, The Evaluation of Life Saving, R. McKeague, a paper presented to the Radiological Guidelines Working Party, March 1985.

8) Keyes, G. B. and Poncelet, C. G., Opinion Sampling : an Essential Tool, published in Acceptance of Nuclear Power, Published by Vulkan-Verlag, Essen, 1979, pp 85-86.

9) Bota, G., The Management of Nuclear Power Dissent, published in Acceptance of Nuclear Power, published by Vulkan-Verlag, Essen, 1979, pp 29-30.

10) Health and Safety Executive Report of the Steering Committee on radio frequency ignition hazards at St Fergus, Scotland, February 1979.

11) Health and Safety Executive Report 'A reappraisal of the HSE safety evaluation of the proposed St Fergus to Moss Morran NGL pipeline', September 1980.

12) Ashby, E., Reconciling Man with the Environment, Oxford University Press, 1978, pp 71-72 and p 99.

13) Swanton, E., Attitudes Towards Risk : A Cross-Cultural Comparison, a paper presented at the Status Seminar on Tasks, Methods and Predictive Power of Risk Research, organized by the University of Bielefeld, November 1980.

14) R no 2E, Guide for the classification of hazardous areas in zones in relation to gas explosion hazard and to the installation and selection of electrical apparatus, Report of the Directorate-General of Labour, First Edition 1980. Published by the Directorate-General of Labour of the Ministry of Social Affairs, Voorburg, Holland, p 15.

DEVELOPING RISK ESTIMATES FOR TOXIC AIR POLLUTANTS THROUGH

PROBABILISTIC RISK ASSESSMENT

Larry J. Zaragoza, David R. Patrick, Robert M. Schell,
Ila L. Cote, Mike Dusetzina, Nancy B. Pate, and Harvey M.
Richmond

U.S. Environmental Protection Agency Research
Triangle Park, North Carolina

ABSTRACT

The Environmental Protection Agency has recently accelerated its
efforts to determine the need to regulate toxic air pollutants. A key
input in determining the need for regulation is the characterization of
estimated public health risks. This paper examines some aspects of the
feasibility of using probabilistic methods for this purpose.

A probabilistic approach provides for the explicit characterization
and consideration of uncertainties in exposure estimates, exposure-dose
relationships, and dose-response relationships in developing health risk
estimates. The methodology under consideration uses available scientific
information in developing the risk estimates. The incorporation of expert
judgment would be used to address limitations and uncertainties in the
available scientific information.

KEY WORDS: probabilistic risk assessment, toxic air pollution.

INTRODUCTION

Late in 1983, former Environmental Protection Agency (EPA)
Administrator William Ruckelshaus made a commitment to Congress to decide,
by the end of 1985, on the need to regulate 20 to 25 potentially toxic air
pollutants. This commitment reflected the Agency's decision to place a
greater emphasis on air toxics and formalized the role of risk assessment
in regulatory decision-making for air toxics. While meeting this
commitment, several aspects of the assessment process were identified for
future improvement. For example, the approach used to support decisions
did not explicitly deal with both the probability of risk and associated
uncertainty in a quantitative manner. This has led to beginning efforts
to improve the presentation of risk and associated uncertainties in order
to better support decisions for potentially toxic air pollutants.

An important part of estimating risk to populations is an examination
and assessment of uncertainties in the information and the models employed
in assessing risks. Once each of these uncertainties is characterized,
they should be examined collectively to estimate risk to populations.
Examples of uncertainty that will affect the population risk estimates
include:

- Uncertainties in extrapolation from animal to man.
- Differences in the sensitivity of population subgroups to exposure.
  Exposures that should be protective of the average member of a population may not be protective of all individuals.
- Uncertainties in the extrapolation to estimated ambient concentrations from the "dose" that is biologically effective.
- Uncertainties in the inputs to and outputs from dispersion modeling.
- Uncertainties in estimating the exposure of subpopulations to a chemical.

This paper describes efforts to evaluate the feasibility of more explicitly addressing uncertainties in order to refine risk estimates and to clarify the bases for regulatory decisions on toxic air pollutants. More specifically, this paper describes the application of risk assessment procedures that employ probabilistic methods. For purposes of this paper, a probabilistic method is defined as one that characterizes probabilities of risk as a function of expected exposures and provides quantitative estimates of the uncertainty associated with the risk assessment.

ASSESSING RISK USING PROBABILISTIC METHODS

The assessment of risk using probabilistic methods uses available information to formulate quantitative estimates of risk. Figure 1 is a flow diagram of a process that might be used to develop probabilistic risk estimates. The model presented in this flow diagram consists of three general steps: assembling health and exposure information, complementing available information with encoding (eliciting probability judgments) from experts, and presenting results.

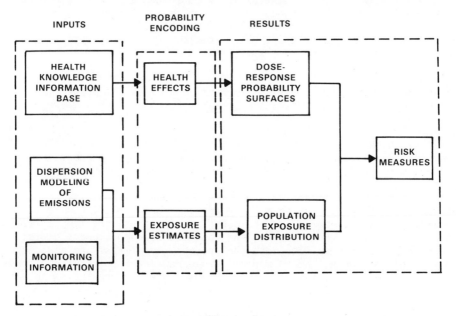

Figure 1

Generalized Flow Diagram for the Development of
Risk Measures Employing Probabilistic Methods

The first input to the model is health information. The desired
result of investigations on the potentially adverse effects of pollutants
is a dose-response relationship for each effect of concern. Such
investigations typically attempt to determine the relationship between
that index of exposure that is most closely related to the response and
differences in the degree of response. In some cases, investigators have
found that biological markers (i.e., measures of exposure involving the
measurement of pollutant concentrations in body tissues or fluids) of
exposure are more closely related to biological responses than air
exposures. Other studies have found that air exposures can be used with
some confidence to estimate the likelihood of human response, especially
when factors such as sensitivity of the population and activity patterns
are considered.

Exposure estimates are usually developed through dispersion modeling
of pollutant emissions or from monitoring data. Because there is a very
limited database of monitoring information on toxic air pollutants as well
as a limited number of monitoring methods with known accuracy and
precision, dispersion modeling is typically the primary approach used to
estimate exposure in risk analyses. In many cases, the Agency has
collected information on emissions from the sources and this information
is used as an input to emissions modeling. In general, greater confidence
may be placed in long-term modeling outputs, because it is more difficult
to define the short-term emission rates and adverse meteorological
conditions than it is to describe average emission rates and typical
meteorological conditions. Additional uncertainty is introduced into the
development of exposure estimates in the inputs used in dispersion
modeling, the monitoring information, and the accuracy and precision of
the models employed.

Other considerations in the estimation of exposure are human activity
patterns and microenvironment to which a population or individual might be
exposed. The present methodology for estimating human long-term exposure
for air toxics is designed to provide relative differences in exposure and
does not provide for the consideration of microenvironments (e.g.,
indoor/outdoor) or activity patterns (e.g., yard work, sleeping). Because
microenvironments and activity patterns may affect both absolute and
relative exposure estimates, a feasibility study is currently in progress
investigating possible refinements to the current exposure analysis
methodology.

Figure 1 also shows that encoding would be used to complement and
build upon available health and exposure information. In any assessment,
there are uncertainties, which may or may not be explicitly identified.
The process of making a decision requires that a judgment be made when
information is uncertain. Although such judgments could be made by the
decision-maker, the objective of encoding (i.e., the elicitation of
judgment from those scientists and technical experts who are most familiar
with the biological and exposure information) is a process that attempts
to utilize the knowledge of individuals most qualified to provide a
quantitative (probabilistic) representation of key relationships that are
uncertain.

There are some aspects regarding the use of encoding that would
appear to be applicable to assessing risks of air toxics. First, the use
of experts is not intended to replace scientific information but rather to
complement that information. Second, it is critical to develop protocols
for encoding probability judgments from experts. Such protocols generally
have the following objectives:

- The selection of experts should attempt to maximize the chance that a balanced set of perspectives are represented in the probability judgments (Feagans and Biller, 1981).
- Providing information to the experts that will participate in the encoding sessions so that the experts will be aware of highlights of the relevant literature (Whitfield and Wallsten, 1984).
- Careful definition that will focus the experts on technical questions and minimize the potential for biases. When differences are found between experts, efforts should be made to determine if those differences are related to differences in assumptions.
- Encoding sessions should be performed so that the preparation of questions and presentation is comparable for experts who respond to the same questions.

At this stage, no decisions have yet been made on the extent to which expert judgment would be used or on the factors that would be used to determine when expert judgment would be employed.

Figure 1 also shows several types of results that are possible using the approach outlined. These are dose-response probability surfaces, population exposure distributions and risk measures. Figure 2 presents a hypothetical dose-response probability surface adopted from Feagans and Biller (1981), which uses concentration for some fixed time period as a measure of dose. Although this dose-response probability surface is only limited to one type of response, a number of different responses may be expected following exposure to a pollutant and should be evaluated and presented as a part of the results of the risk assessment. However, those effects that are considered to be most serious in terms of endangerment to public health or are most likely to occur as a result of exposures in the ambient air are the most appropriate for assessment. Figure 2 also shows the probability of an effect occurring for a defined population increases with increasing concentration. The abscissa shows concentrations that are associated with the estimated threshold for eliciting a response in varying percentiles of the population from the first percentile ($C_e 1\%$) to the entire population ($C_e 100\%$). This figure shows that the variance decreases as concentration is increased. Thus, as one approaches lower concentrations the probability of an effect occurring decreases and the uncertainty that the concentration is the concentration that would elicit a response increases. This conclusion is generally consistent with available data.

The population exposure distribution would show how populations are distributed and would allow for the identification of percentiles of population exposure. An alternative form for characterizing the population exposure distribution would be to characterize the variation in exposure that an individual might be subjected to during different parts of the day.

Risk measures would include those measures that are appropriate for the types of effects characterized with the dose-response probability

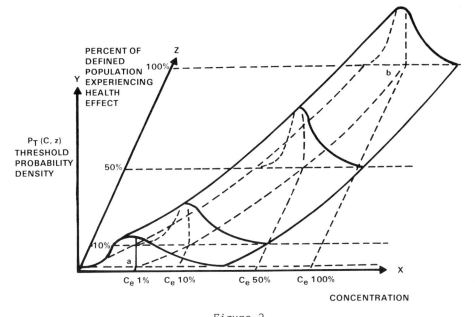

PERCENT OF DEFINED POPULATION EXPERIENCING HEALTH EFFECT

$P_T (C, z)$ THRESHOLD PROBABILITY DENSITY

100%

50%

10%

a

b

C_e 1% C_e 10% C_e 50% C_e 100%

CONCENTRATION

Figure 2

Does-Response Probability Surface

surfaces. Two measures of risk have been most commonly employed in examining risks of air toxics. First, an estimate of risk at the highest exposure to which any individual is exposed from all sources is estimated. This measure is the maximum individual risk. Second, the cumulative risk in cases per year that would result from exposure to populations at risk in the analysis is estimated. This measure is the aggregate risk estimate.

The presentation of the results to those who make decisions is one of the strengths of the approach outlined. Figure 3 shows how exposure and dose-response information might be presented in one figure. It illustrates the cumulative probability distributions of exposure and exposure-response. The probability of eliciting the health effect is based upon biological data and is independent of the cumulative probability distribution of maximum pollutant concentrations in the ambient air. However, the convolution of these two cumulative probability distributions (i.e., the intersection of these two distributions when one is folded over the other) is directly related to the risk of eliciting this effect for the exposures shown. If the distribution of pollutant concentrations were altered by controlling emissions, which would move this distribution to the left, the risk would be reduced.

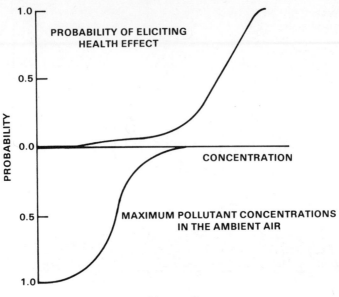

Figure 3

Cumulative Probability Distributions for MaximumPollutant Concentrations
in the Ambient Air and for Eliciting a Specific Health Response. The
Likelihood of Triggering Responses at Some Concentration for any Specific
Health Effect in the Ambient Air Will be Related to the Convolution of
These Two Distributions.

DISCUSSION

Earlier this year the Agency released a strategy for air toxics (EPA,
1985). This strategy outlines different approaches that are to be
employed as the Agency addresses air toxics problems. The strategy
describes how the Agency will determine the need to regulate toxic air
pollutants under alternative control programs. Risk estimates that are
accompanied by some estimate of uncertainty should play an explicit role
in providing decision makers with an improved basis for decisions. The
estimates of uncertainty become particularly useful when making
comparisons between pollutants as the need for regulation and the type of
regulatory program are determined. The failure to consider uncertainties,
either qualitatively or quantitatively, in developing risk estimates could
lead decision makers to have a sense of false confidence in the risk
estimates presented.

The adoption of probabilistic risk assessment methods would almost
certainly prove more resource intensive than non-probabilistic methods
currently in use for several areas including: development of
probabilistic dose-response relationships, development of estimates of
uncertainty, use of experts in encoding, and documentation. Nevertheless,
the use of probabilistic approaches to risk assessment appears feasible
and desirable as a decision making tool such as review of the national
ambient air quality standards (NAAQS) (Jordan et al., 1983).

However, there are several differences in the assessment of risks
between the criteria pollutants and toxic air pollutants that may make it
more difficult to apply this approach in the latter case. For the

criteria pollutants, there are often data on responses of humans to exposures that are expected in the ambient air. This is rarely available for air toxics. There also is typically much more data on criteria pollutants (pollutants regulated under the NAAQS) on exposure, mechanisms of action, as well as differential sensitivity of selected subpopulations. Moreover, there are only six criteria pollutants and there are many more pollutants that will be addressed as toxic air pollutants. Therefore, one the requirements for incorporating probabilistic risk assessment methods into air toxics decisions will be to tailor the approach to the problem. A feasibility study outlining an approach to the use of probabilistic methods for air toxics will be initiated in the near future.

The need for risk assessment information and its role in regulatory decision-making has been raised by other groups concerned with the protection of public health. In general, most alternative approaches used for making regulatory decisions do not explicitly characterize both risk and uncertainty. In some of these methods, health information is used to estimate some specific level of exposure that is expected to be "safe". As such, exposures below the established "safe" level are deemed to be protective, while exposures above that level may be considered to pose unacceptable risks to public health. Examples of such nonprobabilistic methods include the use of Acceptable Daily Intake (ADI) values, which have typically been used to estimate acceptable intakes of contaminants through foodstuffs and drinking water. ADI values are determined based upon toxicological information that may be adjusted for the route of exposure.

Although the ADI approach is accepted as a reasonable tool for many risk assessment purposes, this approach has limitations. On the positive side it allows for a relatively rapid assessment and it is accepted for several purposes within the Agency. However, it has several limitiations including:

- Because this approach typically estimates environmental exposures that either exceed or are lower than ADI values, there is a tendency to weave together risk assessment and risk management. These two processes that should be conceptually and operationally separated.
- Failure to discriminate between varying risk levels and differing effects for alternative exposures and the implication that any exposure exceeding the ADI value would pose an unacceptable risk.
- Differing ADI values that result from alternative approaches used in their calculation. Although such differences may be reasonable, if the basis for the ADI value is not explicitly provided, then the differences in ADI values could appear inconsistent. Efforts are currently underway to identify and resolve differences in ADI values within the Agency.

Alternative approaches to assessing noncarcinogenic health risks is to compare occupational limits with ambient concentrations. Because members of the general population may be expected to be more sensitive to pollutant exposure than the general workforce, occupational limits should not be interpreted to represent safe levels for the general population (Cornish, 1980). Recognizing that general populations, which includes subpopulations, may be more sensitive than the general workforce and that the duration of exposure should be considered in estimating acceptable ambient exposures, some States have applied safety factors to occupational limits in making judgments on ambient air exposures should be protective of public health.

Similarly, approaches currently used to evaluate cancer risks for air toxics do not explicitly characterize risk and associated uncertainty. Such estimates are derived from a unit risk estimate. The unit risk is typically defined as an upper-limit estimate of the additional risk of cancer for an individual breathing a unit concentration (usually one microgram of pollutant per cubic meter) of a pollutant over his or her lifetime (Anderson et al., 1983).

REFERENCES

Anderson, Elizabeth L., and the Carcinogen Assessment Group of the U.S. Environmental Protection Agency (1983). Quantitative approaches in use to assess cancer risk. Risk Analysis 3:277-295.

Cornish, Herbert H. (1980). Solvents and vapors. Chapter 18 In: Casarett and Doull's Toxicology: the Basic Science of Poisons. Second edition. Editors John Doull, Curtis D. Klaassen, and Mary O. Amdur. Macmillan Publishing Co., Inc. New York. p. 468.

Feagans Thomas B., and William F. Biller (1981). A general Method for Assessing Health Risks Associated with Primary National Ambient Air Quality Standards. Strategies and Air Standards Division, Office of Air Quality Planning and Standards. Research Triangle Park, NC.

Jordan, Bruce C., Harvey M. Richmond, Thomas McCurd (1983). The use of scientific information in setting ambient air standards. Environ. Health Persp. 52:233-240.

Whitfield, Ronald G., and Thomas S. Wallsten (1984). Estimating Risks of Lead-included Hemoglobin Decrements under conditions of Uncertainty: Methodology, Pilot Judgments and Illustrative Calculations. Argonne National Laboratory, Energy and Environmental Systems Divisions, Argonne, IL ANL/EES-TM-276.

U.S. Environmental Protection Agency (1985). A Strategy to Reduce Risks to Public Health for Air Toxics. U.S. Environmental Protection Agency, Washington, D.C.

THE HAZARD METER: A CONCEPTUAL HEURISTIC TOOL OF RISK ASSESSMENT

Stephen L. Brown

Commission on Life Sciences
National Research Council[*]
Washington, D.C. 20418

ABSTRACT

This paper suggests that the process of risk assessment attempts to emulate a hypothetical device, a hazard meter, that could directly measure the individual or population risks of a well-defined material, activity, or situation. The meter could be calibrated to read in different units, such as cancer cases per year in the United States, lifetime probability of accidental death for a specified group of people equally exposed to a specified hazard, or annual probability of exceeding a specified severity of catastrophe. Several aspects of the meter that are analogous to the activities of risk assessors are explored. Special attention is given to uncertainty in risk assessment, which is compared to a meter having a thick, fuzzy, or vacillating needle. The utility of the hazard meter analogy in explaining both the objectives and limitations of risk assessment to a lay public is discussed.

KEY WORDS: Hazard measurement, risk assessment, hazard meter, uncertainty analysis.

INTRODUCTION

For the last few years, I have been sprinkling my writings and talks about risk assessment with the idea of a hazard meter. As you will discover as you read this paper, the instrument I have in mind is not yet on the market, and I suspect that it will be a long time arriving there. Yet I think the concept of such a meter has been useful in enabling me to think more clearly about risk assessment, its uncertainties, and the policy implications that arise from using an imperfect tool in risk management. I am equally confident that others can find insights by analyzing risk problems with the hazard meter idea, which I describe for you here.

---

[*]The opinions expressed in this paper are those of the author and do not necessarily represent the position of the National Research Council.

Perhaps the simplest conceptual application of the hazard meter is in judging which of several possible materials is best with respect to potential hazards for human health if used in a certain type of product. Suppose that one had samples of the alternative materials. Assessment of the relative safety of these materials would be very easy if one could use a hazard meter like a meat thermometer, inserting it into each sample and then reading a dial to determine the magnitude of the health hazard, as shown in Figure 1. But of course the units that one wants to be inscribed on the dial are very important in designing the meter. My own bias is that the meter is most useful if it registers annual deaths across the United States, presuming that death is the only (or at least the dominant) health risk of concern. This measure is the national population risk, which I sometimes refer to as "total hazard," in the same sense that we say that automobile accidents kill 50,000 people per year. I discuss other scales later in this article. Figure 2 shows a close-up of what I, dispensing with false modesty, call Dr. Brown's Incredible Hazard Meter. Unlike the meat thermometer, this meter has a logarithmic scale to permit us to measure population risks of very different magnitude--a positive feature because comparisons among vastly different risks are often necessary.

Judging the Hazard

In the example application described above, it is only necessary to rank the safety of the materials tested according to their readings on the

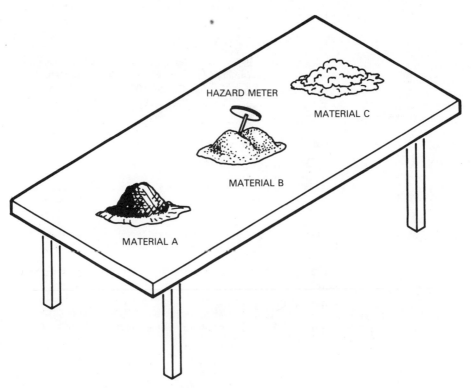

Figure 1.   Ranking alternative materials with the Incredible Hazard
            Meter. Meter directly reads the relative hazards that would
            result from use of the materials in a specified product.

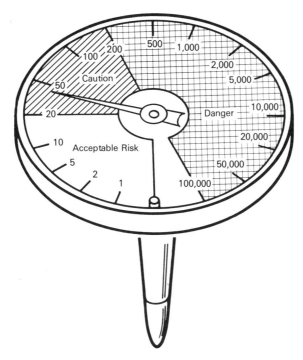

Figure 2.   Close-up of a typical hazard meter. Meter displays annual U.S.
            deaths attributable to hazard. The location of boundaries
            between zones is a social value judgment.

meter. All other factors aside, the material with the lowest reading
would be preferred. (Here I inject the usual disclaimer that there may be
many other technical, social, economic, and political considerations that
will argue for a different ranking.) In other cases, it may be necessary
to decide whether even the material with the lowest reading is too
hazardous to be used in the product; in such cases, one needs indication
of acceptable and unacceptable total hazards, as indicated by the
variously shaded zones of the meter. To be specific, I have made a
personal value judgment that fewer than 20 deaths per year spread over a
population of 240 million (annual risk, less than 10^{-7}) is of relatively
little concern, but more than 200 per year is of considerable concern.
Others might put the danger zone of the meter higher or lower. And if we
knew the risks were concentrated in a smaller, identifiable population, we
would probably place the danger zone lower on the scale. An improved
model of the hazard meter could allow the users to adjust the boundaries
of the zones to suit their own values--hopefully before, not after, they
have taken their measurements.

Measures of Hazard

Notice that this hazard meter is truly incredible. To give a total
hazard reading, it must do both of the tasks of risk assessment: exposure
assessment and effects assessment. Even when the same number of units of
each product are used (or abused) by the same number of people, to
determine exposure we still need to know whether one material is more
volatile than another and whether the number of people exposed to the
materials in the manufacturing processes differs, and so on. To assess

the effects, the meter must be able to estimate the risks of developing a fatal disease from low exposures as well as from higher ones. If it is to be an absolute meter that can indicate the population risks presented by very different hazardous materials or activities, it will need to measure the distribution of exposures over all those people exposed, taking into account the different properties of the exposure conditions: physical, chemical, biological, and perhaps even psychological hazards. If its user needs to consider not just total deaths but also the amount of life-shortening, it will need to measure the age distribution of the exposed individuals. And if there are nonfatal effects, then some sort of weighting of their social signifiaance compared with mortality is necessary to display the hazard information on a single scale.

In some cases, we may wish to measure hazards in several different ways and contemplate the different social responses that could be appropriate. To do so, we need a meter with control knobs that allow us to select different measures of hazard and different populations at risk. The meter shown in Figure 3 can measure not only annual deaths but also the maximum lifetime risk of death by cause among all the subpopulations at risk or the total annual years of life lost in the population. Furthermore, it can accomplish all this for several different populations.

To show other adjustments that might be useful, I have also included a knob that allows one to compare the hazard under current conditions with that under some altered conditions, for example, after a regulation is issued or after a new use for a chemical is introduced. Another knob is quite different. It acknowledges the fact that we don't know very well how to build our meter and allows us to test the sensitivity of our measurements to certain key assumptions, in this case the model for the dose-response relationship. Other knobs can easily be imagined. A very complicated instrument indeed.

Some Analogies

Because the hazard meter is only a heuristic tool rather than a real one, its utility lies in changing the way we think about risk assessment. A few analogies may be useful.

One characteristic of an instrument is its sensitivity. How low a hazard or risk can be detected by a hazard meter? The question is like that asked about instruments for measurement of concentrations. In only a few years, we have developed techniques that can now measure parts per trillion concentrations of certain chemicals, where the most remarkably sensitive measurements had previously been parts per million. We now have risk assessment tools with a sensitivity similar to that of an instrument that can measure perhaps one part in a hundred, but we may need a meter with a sensitivity of one part in a million to satisfy some social concerns. This need for sensitivity lies at the heart of the low-dose extrapolation problem that bedevils many if not most risk assessors.

Closely related is the difficulty in calibration. Any hazard meter design is at best a surrogate; we really do not expect to detect and record actual deaths or other hazard outcomes except in cases, like deaths in automobile accidents, where the association between cause and effect is easily discerned. Thus we need to calibrate the instrument by using it to measure some situations in which we have an independent estimate of hazard. Two types of calibration are possible when the hazard meter is intended to measure annual or lifetime risk in an arbitrary population.

The better calibration comes about when we have human evidence, such

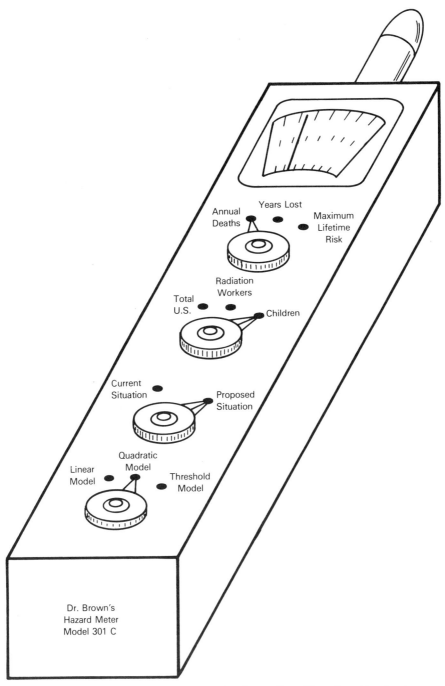

Figure 3. Hazard meter with control knobs. By adjusting the knobs, one can measure hazards in different units in different populations under different conditions. The sensitivity to assumptions about the underlying model can also be tested.

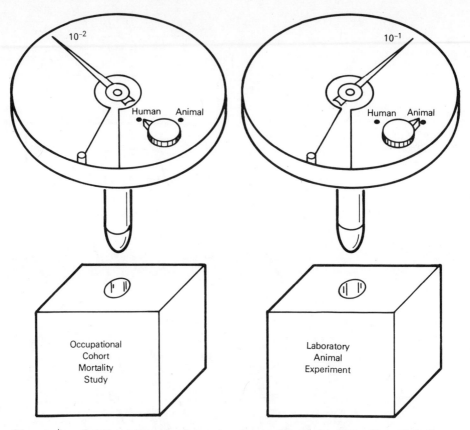

Figure 4. Calibrating the hazard meter. We might know the risk in an occupational cohort or in a group of laboratory animals. Measuring these populations with the hazard meter can help calibrate its scale.

as from an occupational cohort mortality study. Experiments with laboratory animals also provide an estimate of risk, but these need to be translated to human risks. If we knew enough about interspecies extrapolation, we could wire into our meter a switch that would adjust the reading to account for calibration in either human or animal systems, as shown in Figure 4.

Another way to look at the animal experiment is to consider the experiment itself as a surrogate meter. The analogy with real instruments could be use of a thermocouple. We want to estimate temperature, but we really measure electrical resistance and have a relationship between resistance and temperature that has been programmed into the meter.

A final analogy illustrates one of the greatest problems both of risk assessment and of instrumentation: No matter how good the meter, did the technician measure the right thing? An example comes from epidemiology, in which an excess of lung cancer was seen in hematite miners. In light of the lack of confirming observations in other exposures to iron or iron oxides, the explanation probably lies in something other than iron, such as radon and its progeny or possibly a heavy metal in the ore. The difficulty arose not in faulty observations of the health effects, but rather in identifying and measuring the exposure. As a result, the observation of the association between hematite mining and lung cancer could not be used to assess other exposure situations.

Uncertainty

The meter that I have described, of course, is the ideal risk assessor. Real risk assessors try to do more or less what the Incredible Hazard Meter is designed to do, but they are faced with an additional problem: even though they may understand fully (nor nearly so) what information is needed to do their jobs, they never have precise, accurate information in every category. The resulting analysis, however well conceived and conducted, will inevitably contain many uncertainties that make the overall characterization of the total hazard correspondingly uncertain. I can think of two ways to discuss such uncertainty in terms of the hazard meter: the fuzzy needle and the jumpy needle.

The Fuzzy Needle Many of the difficulties in risk assessment originate because we cannot measure many of the needed input data very well. In the case of carcinogenic substances, for example, we usually need both a dose-response extrapolation and an interspecies extrapolation from results obtained in animal experiments to derive risk estimates for humans exposed to low doses of the carcinogen. These measurement difficulties result in a fuzzy picture of the population risks, sometimes involving several orders of magnitude differences among possible outcomes. The analogy is a hazard meter with a fuzzy or thick needle that points only to a general area of the dial--not to a well-defined index mark--as shown in Figure 5. As a consequence, decisions become more difficult to make. If we are comparing the population risks of alternative materials as in the first example, the areas of the dial covered by the fuzzy needle for some of the materials may well overlap, decreasing our confidence in the ranking process. If we are interested in an absolute "acceptable risk" determination, we may be thwarted when the fuzzy needle overlaps "safe" and "dangerous" zones of the dial.

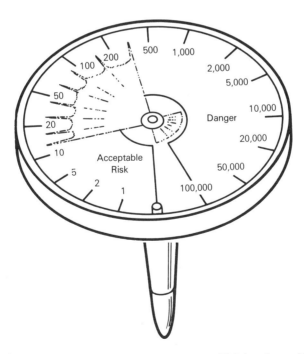

Figure 5.   Hazard meter with a fuzzy needle. Width of needle represents uncertainty of estimation. In example shown, needle is more than a factor of 10 wide and could indicate either definitely acceptable or definitely unacceptable risks.

The Jumpy Needle The second kind of uncertainty comes not so much from lack of acuity but from the lack of predictability about events. If the risky activity is the operation of nuclear power plants, the needle of the meter would ordinarily point to a very low reading, well below my arbitrary cutoff of 20 deaths per year. But in the year of severe accident, it might swing upward toward or into the danger zone. Over a long period, the appearance of the meter would be similar to that of a speedometer of a car moving over rough terrain; the needle would jump back and forth irregularly, and the observer would have difficulty in assessing either the average or maximum readings of the meter and in interpreting their meaning (Figure 6).

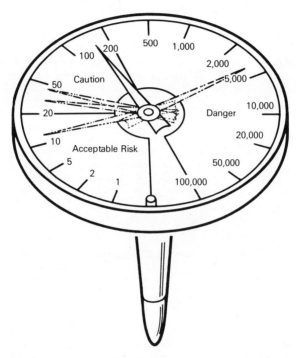

Figure 6. Hazard meter with a jumpy needle. Risk level changes abruptly and unpredictably. Difficult to determine a typical value. As shown, risks can be sometimes acceptable, sometimes clearly unacceptable.

Decision-Making in the Face of Uncertainty If either one or both of these conditions prevails, it is difficult to make a decision on the basis of the meter's reading. We do not know the true value of the total hazard; we can only read the center of the fuzzy needle or the typical position of the jumpy needle, and note the extremes. (If the meter reads on a logarithmic scale, the middle of the needle would show the geometric expectation of the value of total hazards, not the arithmetic expectation, which would probably be higher. The latter might be the proper one to use for policy decisions.)

CONCLUSIONS

If I could build and patent the Incredible Hazard Meter in any of its models, I not only could expect to become modestly wealthy, but I would also probably put a lot of risk assessors on the unemployment line. Rest easy, I have no such plans. However, I do intend to continue using the concept to help structure my own thinking about risk assessment and to encourage those with whom I work to do the same. Using analogies to the hazard meter should allow the risk assessor to decide better what aspects of risk to assess and how to go about it. In particular, the uncertainty analogy can help an assessor decide in advance whether an assessment with available data is likely to be sufficiently reliable to aid in reaching whatever decision is under consideration. The meter analogy may also be useful in explaining to users or even to the public what sorts of questions the risk assessors tried to answer and how they went about doing so. Readers are encouraged to use the hazard meter and to develop further useful analogies.

DECISION ANALYSIS MODELS FOR

RISKS IN THE DISTANT FUTURE[*]

Charles M. Harvey

Dickinson College
Carlisle, PA 17013

ABSTRACT

Cost-benefit and risk analysis studies that model tradeoffs between the present and the distant future by means of present value discounting have been criticized for according the future, and thus future generations, far too little importance. This paper presents an alternative means of modeling tradeoffs between different periods that accords the future far more importance than present value discounting, and that is no more difficult to apply.

KEY WORDS: Present value discounting, importance of the distant future.

1. INTRODUCTION

In formal models for public policy studies in which there are consequences extending into the distant future, preferences are usually evaluated by means of present value discounting. For each year, t = 1, 2, ..., the costs, risks, and benefits are summed over the affected members of society, and these sums are reduced to a single variable x_t that often is measured in monetary terms. Then, preferences among the alternative policies are determined by evaluating each policy's net present value

$$V(x_1, x_2, \ldots) = x_1 + ax_2 + a^2x_3 + \ldots \tag{1}$$

in which $a = (1 + i)^{-1}$ denotes the discount factor corresponding to a social discount rate i. Discussions from a decision analysis viewpoint are in Bell (1974), Fishburn (1970), Keeney and Raiffa (1976), and Meyer (1970), and discussions of the assessment of the social discount rate i are in Mishan (1976), Stokey and Zeckhauser (1978), and Sugden and Williams (1978).

The use of present value discounting places certain restrictions on preferences, e.g., that the importance of future consumption or risk decays geometrically as the separation from the present increases. For costs, risks, and benefits that extend into the distant future and over a number of generations, even modest discount rates i lead to weights a^{t-1} that may be regarded as strikingly undervaluing the future. Consider, for

*This research is supported in part by the National Science Foundation under grant no. SES84-10665.

example, a discount rate of 5% per year and a period t = 100 years in the future. Then, a cost that occurs now is evaluated to be as serious as a cost 130 times as great that occurs in 100 years.

Many people, particularly those concerned with the availability of natural resources and the quality of the environment for future generations, would make value judgments reflecting a far greater importance for the future. This objection has been discussed from a variety of viewpoints, for example, by Fischhoff et al. (1981, p. 112), Lovins (1977), Mishan (1981, pp. xv and 498-505), Owen (1983), and Schulze (1974).

This paper presents an alternative model that is analogous to present value discounting, but that places far greater importance on the distant future. Certain conditions on intertemporal tradeoffs are shown to imply that preferences can be represented by a value function of the form

$$V(x_1, x_2, \ldots) = x_1 + (1/2)^r x_2 + (1/3)^r x_3 + \ldots \qquad (2)$$

in which the parameter r determines society's attitude toward the importance of future periods. The weights $(1/t)^r$ in the model (2) decay much more slowly than the weights a^{t-1} in the present-value discounting model (1), since for any r>0 and any 0<a<1 the ratio $a^{t-1}/(1/t)^r$ converges to zero as t tends to infinity.

Procedures are described by which an assessment of society's tradeoffs between the present and the future can be used to evaluate the parameter r in (2). These procedures are analogous to the internal rate of return method that is used to evaluate the parameter i in (1). Questions of social values that are as simple as possible are shown to imply a specific parameter value for r. By this method, it can be reported in an evaluation study which ranges of social values lead to which preferences among the alternative policies. The value functions and their parameter values will then serve as an unobtrusive technical link between relatively simple value judgments and relatively complex policy preferences. Persons having a stake in the decision will be able to see more clearly how their differing values lead to conflicts in the preferred alternatives, and public decision makers will have useful information for finding an alternative that represents an overall reasonable decision and that is consistent with other public decisions in that it reflects similar social values.

Use of the value function models discussed in this paper is not restricted to those public policy studies in which the amounts x_t, t = 1,2,..., for the alternative policies are known with certainty. Applications are also intended where it is appropriate to assume that society has an attitude of risk neutrality toward the uncertainty involved. Then, the variables x_t may be defined as expected values; for example, x_t may denote the expected net benefit or the expected health effect in period t. Utility function models are discussed in Harvey (1985c) that extend the value function models in this paper and that can be used to model a number of preference issues regarding social attitudes toward risk.

This paper is closely related to the paper Harvey (1986) which also discusses preference conditions that are related to the issue of temporal inequity. These conditions are shown to imply value functions that contain a single parameter q to represent the degree of aversion to temporal inequity as well as a single parameter a or r to represent the importance of the future. The paper Harvey (1986) also contains proofs of

510

the technical results presented in this paper.

2. GENERAL INFINITE-PERIOD MODELS

   A preference model is presented in this section such that tradeoffs
between different times are represented by a value function having the
form of an infinite series. This model may be regarded as a
generalization of the model for present value discounting that was
developed by Koopmans (1960), (1972) using a stationarity condition (see
also Koopmans et al. (1964) and Strotz (1957)).

   Consider a unit of time, e.g., a year, that is sufficiently long for
information gathering purposes and sufficiently short so that the timing
of events within a single unit can be ignored. Suppose that the future is
divided into a sequence of time intervals, i.e., periods, of the form (t -
1, t) , t = 1,2,..., that have unit duration. For each period, t =
1,2,..., the sum of the consequences (costs, risks, and benefits) to an
affected group of individuals will be described by a single variable x_t.
This reduction to a single variable may involve the pricing out of non-
monetary attributes for each affected individual by willingness-to-pay
methods (see, e.g., Jones-Lee (1982) and Kunreuther and Ley (1982)).

   The variables x_t, t = 1,..., are to be defined so that equal amounts
$x_s = x_t$ in different periods s ≠ t have an equal value given that all
preference concerns as to the timing of the amount $x = x_s = x_t$ are
excluded from consideration. For example, x_t might denote the expected
number of fatalities due to a specified cause that occur in period t or
the amount of a natural resource from a given region that will be obtained
in period t.

   Where x_t is measured as monetary amounts, the above criterion implies
that x_t should be defined in terms of dollars (or another currency) at a
fixed time. Often but not necessarily, it will be appropriate to specify
the fixed time as t = 0. If the modeling information on costs and
benefits is expressed in fixed time dollars, then no adjustment for
inflation is needed; if this information is expressed in time t dollars,
then the amounts x_t should be discounted for expected future inflation.
By this approach, beliefs concerning inflation rates can be separated from
value judgments concerning the tradeoffs between different periods.

   The consequences over the future will be described by sequences $(x_1,
x_2, ...)$ of the single-period amounts x_t, and will be called infinite-
period consequences. The set of infinite-period consequences such that
each amount x_t is in a common open interval I will be denoted by C.
Suppose that a standard amount x* in I is chosen that represents a base
amount or a type of equilibrium; typically, x* will be chosen as a no-cost
or no-benefit amount.

   Social preferences among the infinite-period consequences in C will
be denoted by the preference relation >, "is at least as preferred
as." The problem addressed in this paper is to determine a value function
for >, i.e., a function $V(x_1, x_2, ...)$ that represents preferences among
the infinite-period consequences.

   In Harvey (1986), certain conditions (A) - (E) are introduced for the
preference relation >. It is shown that conditions (A) - (D) are
satisfied if and only if there exists an infinite series value function

$$V(x_1, x_2, ...) = v_1(x_1) + v_2(x_2) + ... \qquad (3)$$

511

and conditions (A) - (E) are satisfied if and only if there exists an infinite series value function

$$V(x_1, x_2, \ldots) = a_1 v(x_1) + a_2 v(x_2) + \ldots \tag{4}$$

such that (a) $V(x_1, x_2, \ldots)$ converges if and only if $(x_1, x_2, \ldots)$ is in the set C^* of consequences defined in Harvey (1986), (b) $V(x_1, x_2, \ldots)$ is a value function for the preference relation $>$ on the set C^*, (c) the common component function v is continuous, strictly increasing, and normalized such that $v(x^*) = 0$, and (d) the coefficients a_t, $t = 1, 2, \ldots$, are positive.

3. TYPES OF SOCIAL ATTITUDES

The central concept to be examined in this paper is that of tradeoffs between two periods s and t. For a given cost or benefit w_s in period s, what is the corresponding cost or benefit w_t in period t such that society is indifferent between having w_s in period s and having w_t in period t? How does the corresponding cost or benefit w_t in period t depend on the futurity of the periods s and t, and how does it depend on the base wealth of society in period t?

Definition 1. Suppose that (x^*, x_t) denotes an infinite-period consequence having amounts $x^* = x^*$ and x_t in periods s,t and having standard amounts x^* in the other periods. Consider a change w_s from the standard base amount x^* to the amount $x^* + w_s$ in period s. Let w_t denote the corresponding change from the base amount x_t to the amount $x_t + w_t$ in period t such that

$$(x^*_s, x_t + w_t) \sim (x^*_s + w_s, x_t). \tag{5}$$

Then, w_t will be called the tradeoffs amount corresponding to w_s, and will be denoted by $w_t = f(w_s; s, t, x_t)$. In particular, if the base amount x_t is $x_t = x^*$, then the notation $w_t = f(w_s; s, t)$ will be used.

For example, if society is indifferent between a net benefit of \$40 million (in today's dollars) occurring during the fifth year from now and a net benefit of \$60 million occurring during the tenth year from now, then $w_5 = 40M$ and $w_{10} = f(40M; 5, 10) = 60M$. Note that a tradeoffs function $f(w_s; s, t, x_t)$ is a strictly increasing function of w_s and that $f(0; s, t, x_t) = 0$.

For the preference issue of the relative importance of future periods, three types of social attitudes may be defined as follows:
Definition 2. Consider two different periods s and t, an amount w_s in period s, and the tradeoffs amount $w_t = f(w_s; s, t)$ in period t.

(a) Society will be said to be timing neutral provided that $w_t = w_s$ for any two periods s,t and any amount w_s.
(b) Society will be said to be timing averse provided that $w_t > w_s$ for any two periods s<t and any amount $w_s > 0$.
(c) Society will be said to be timing prone provided that $w_t < w_s$ for any two periods s<t and any amount $w_s > 0$.

Thus, timing aversion is defined as the condition that for positive net benefits w_s and w_t, society is indifferent between a smaller amount w_s in an earlier period s and a larger amount w_t in a later period t. Such preferences appear to be the typical social attitude. The interpretations of timing neutrality and timing proneness are similar.

512

The three attitudes (a)-(c) toward the timing of events are
equivalent to certain types of sequences a_t just as the attitudes of risk
neutrality, risk aversion, and risk proneness are equivalent to certain
types of utility functions. (As a technical observation, it is the
cumulative sequences, $A_t = \Sigma_{s=1}^{t} a_s$, $t=1,2,\ldots,$ that are regarded as
corresponding to utility functions.)

<u>Theorem 1.</u> For a preference model of type (A)-(E):
    (a) Society is timing neutral if and only if the sequence a_t is
constant.
    (b) Society is timing averse if and only if the sequence a_t is
strictly decreasing.
    (c) Society is timing prone if and only if the sequence a_t is
strictly increasing.

    Timing aversion is equivalent to the condition of impatience defined
by Koopmans (1960) (see also Fishburn and Rubinstein (1982)). In the
present context, society will be said to have an <u>impatient</u> attitude toward
waiting provided that for any two amounts x,x' and any two periods s,t, if
$x>x'$ and $s<t$, then the consequence $(x_s=x, x_t=x')$ is preferred to the
consequence $(x_s=x', x_t=x)$. Similarly, society will be said to have an
<u>unconcerned</u> attitude toward waiting provided that these consequences are
indifferent.

<u>Theorem 2.</u> The attitudes toward timing in Definition 2 are equivalent to
the attitudes toward waiting defined above. For example, the attitude of
timing aversion is equivalent to impatience and the attitude of timing
neutrality is equivalent to unconcern.

    A second preference issue is that of the dependence of tradeoffs
between periods on the base levels of consumption or risk in those
periods. This issue can be formulated as the dependent of the tradeoffs
amounts $w_t = f(w_s; s, t, x_t)$ in a period t on the base amount x_t in that
period.

<u>Definition 3.</u> Consider two different periods s and t, an amount $w_s \neq 0$
in period s, and the tradeoffs amounts $w_t = f(w_s; s, t, x_t)$ in period t.
Society will be said to have <u>independent tradeoffs amounts</u> provided that
w_t is independent of x_t.

    Conditions on the dependence of tradeoffs on base amounts are
discussed in Harvey (1986). These conditions as well as that of
independence are equivalent to certain types of functions v in (4).
<u>Theorem 3.</u> For a preference model of type (A)-(E), society has
independent tradeoffs amounts if and only if the component function v is
linear.

4. DEPENDENCE OF TRADEOFFS ON FUTURITY

    In this section, two conditions are discussed concerning the
dependence of tradeoffs between two periods on the futurity of the
periods. The first condition is a slight generalization of the constant
discount factor condition used in cost-benefit studies and of the pairwise
invariance condition in Keeney and Raiffa (1976, p. 480). This condition
is shown to imply the present value discounting function, with
coefficients a^{t-1} as in (1), that was derived by Koopmans from a
stationarity condition. The second condition is new, and is shown to
imply an infinite series value function with coefficients $(1/t)^r$ as in
(2).

Definition 4. Society will be said to have <u>absolute timing preferences</u>
provided that all tradeoffs between two periods s and t depend only on the
(absolute) difference t-s between the periods. Society will be said to
have <u>partial absolute timing preferences</u> provided that for some $w \neq 0$
the tradeoffs amount $f(w;s,t)$ between two periods s and t depends only on
the absolute difference t-s between the periods.

For example, the condition of absolute timing preferences implies
that the tradeoffs between the first year and the second year coincide
with the tradeoffs between year eighty and year eighty-one. Condition (a)
in the following result is used in Section 5 as part of an assessment
procedure whereas condition (b) is simpler conceptually.

Theorem 4. For a preference model of type (A)-(D), the following are
equivalent:
  (a) Society is timing averse, has equal tradeoffs comparisons, and
has partial absolute timing preferences.
  (b) Society is timing averse and has absolute timing preferences.
  (c) There exists an infinite series value function of the form

$$V(x_1, x_2, \ldots) = v(x_1) + av(x_2) + a^2 v(x_3) + \ldots \qquad (6)$$

such that V is as described in (3)-(4) and $0 < a < 1$.

The coefficients a^{t-1} in (6) tend to zero geometrically, and hence
very rapidly, as t increases. This strong discounting of the distant
future has led to criticism of the appropriateness of (6) for public
policy evaluation. A value function (6) can be regarded as a useful
approximation for public policies having consequences that extend over
several years but is questionable when the consequences extend into the
distant future, e.g., over several generations.

For the evaluation of such long-term public policies, the following
condition may be more appropriate.

Definition 5. Society will be said to have <u>relative timing preferences</u>
provided that all tradeoffs between two periods s and t depend only on the
ratio (i.e., the relative difference) t/s between the periods. Society
will be said to have <u>partial relative timing preferences</u> provided that for
some $w \neq 0$ the tradeoffs amount $f(w;s,t)$ between two periods s and t
depends only on the relative difference t/s between the periods.

For example, relative timing preferences implies that the tradeoffs
between the first year and the second year coincide with the tradeoffs
between year fifty and year one hundred, and that tradeoffs between the
first year and the tenth year coincide with those between year fifty and
year five hundred.

Theorem 5. For a preference model of type (A)-(D), the following are
equivalent:
  (a) Society is timing averse, has equal tradeoffs comparisons, and
has partial relative timing preferences.
  (b) Society is timing averse and has relative timing preferences.
  (c) There exists an infinite series value function of the form

$$V(x_1, x_2, \ldots) = v(x_1) + (1/2)^r v(x_2) + (1/3)^r v(x_3) + \ldots \qquad (7)$$

such the V is as described in (3)-(4) and $r > 0$.

The model with a value function (6) will be called a <u>present value</u>

discounting model although this terminology is typically used for the special case in which the component function v is linear, i.e., v(x)=x. By analogy, the new model with a value function (7) will be called a relative value discounting model.

The coefficients $(1/t)^r$ in (7) tend to zero polynomially, that is, as an r-th power of t, as t increases. Such polynomial decay is much slower than the geometric decay in (6) since for any r>0 and any 0<a<1, the ratio $a^{t-1}/(1/t)^r$ converges to zero as t tends to infinity.

Another distinction between the value functions (6) and (7) is concerned with whether preferences change with time. Imagine that society has a value function, either of type (6) or of type (7), in which the parameter a or r is fixed. Consider tradeoffs between the years 2090 and 2095. For a value function of type (6), the society of 1990 has the same tradeoffs between these years as will the society of 2090. For a value function of type (7), however, the society of 1990 is more indifferent to whether an event occurs in 2090 or in 2095 than is the society of 2090. Such a dependence of tradeoffs on the temporal position of society seems to be more representative of actual social preferences.

Consider a public policy study in which the base time from which preferences are being measured is earlier by an amount of b periods than the time at which any policy alternative will begin to have an effect on society. Then, the condition of relative timing preferences with respect to such an earlier base time implies a value function of the form

$$V(x_1, x_2, \ldots) = (\frac{1}{b+1})^r v(x_1) + (\frac{1}{b+2})^r v(x_2) + \ldots \qquad (7')$$

Here, the amount b≥0 will be referred to as a time lag.

Value functions of the form (7') with a variable b+t for time can be regarded as a generalization of value functions (7) with the variable t for time just as utility functions, e.g., of the form u(x) = log(c+x), with a variable c+x for final asset position are a generalization of utility functions, e.g., u(x) = log x, with a variable x for net monetary change.

5. PROCEDURES FOR DETERMINING a_t

In this section, procedures are described for determining a value function for a policy evaluation study in which the issue of the importance of the future is crucial but the issue of temporal inequity is not. In such a study it may be appropriate to use a relative value discounting model with independent tradeoffs amounts. Then, by Theorems 3 and 5, preferences are represented by a value function of type (7) or (7') with v(x)=x. Such a value function can be determined by the following steps:

(i) Verify conditions (A)-(D). The primary task is to choose appropriate summary variables x_t. Preferential independence can be verified by procedures described in Keeney and Raiffa (1976). It is not necessary to verify the condition (E) of equal tradeoffs comparisons since the independent tradeoffs amounts condition below implies (E).

(ii) Verify the condition of independent tradeoffs amounts. An indirect approach is to judge that the issue of temporal inequity is not of sufficient importance to warrant inclusion in the evaluation study. The direct approach is to choose pairs of periods s,t that are representative and amounts x_t, x_t' that differ as much as possible within the range of the study, and to ask whether the tradeoffs amounts $f(w;s,t,x_t)$ and $f(w;s,t,x_t')$ are equal.

(iii) Verify the condition of partial relative timing preferences. This condition is a structural assumption in that it determines the type of preference model to be used. By contrast, the assessment of the parameter r in step (iv) below is a specific value judgment reflecting society's degree of importance of the future.

To verify partial relative timing preferences, first choose a single amount $w \neq 0$ that is convenient to consider. Then, choose a number of representative pairs of periods s,t and s',t' with $t/s = t'/s'$ and ask whether the tradeoffs amounts $f(w;s,t)$ and $f(w;s',t')$ are equal.

(iv) Evaluate the parameter $r>0$. A variety of single tradeoffs assessments are possible, and the analyst should choose one that is readily interpretable as expressing the degree of importance accorded to future periods. One choice is to assess that period m such that society is indifferent between a cost, risk, or benefit of w in period m and a cost, risk, or benefit of $\frac{1}{2}w$ in the first period. This assessment has the advantage that the degree of importance, which is relatively difficult to consider, has a simple preassigned value of one-half, and the period, which is relatively easy to consider, is the quantity to be assessed. The period m will be referred to as the temporal midvalue of the sequence t=1,2,... of future periods.

The parameter r (and the parameter a of a present value discounting model) can be calculated from m by:

TABLE 1

Numerical Examples of Discounting Models

Assessed quantities m	b	Present Value discounting		Relative value discounting	
		a_1/a_2	a_1/a_{100}	a_1/a_2	a_1/a_{100}
12	0	1.065	512.0	1.21	3.6
	5	"	"	1.11	6.7
25	0	1.029	17.4	1.16	2.7
	5	"	"	1.07	3.4
50	0	1.014	4.1	1.13	2.3
	5	"	"	1.05	2.4
100	0	1.007	2.0	1.11	2.0
	5	"	"	1.04	2.0

$$r = \frac{\log 2}{\log(\frac{m+b}{1+b})}, \quad \log a = \frac{-\log 2}{m-1}.$$

Table 1 below provides several examples of coefficients a_t, $t=1,2,\ldots$, that have been calculated from assessed values of m and b by first calculating a parameter r or a. The purpose of Table 1 is not to suggest any particular coefficients a_t as appropriate for applications, but to illustrate the distinctions between present value discounting and relative value discounting that are discussed in Section 1.

If a time lag $b \neq 0$ is included in a model, then b can be regarded either as a constant to be assessed or as a parameter to be calculated from an assessment, e.g., an assessment of tradeoffs between two specified periods. Observe in Table 1 that the larger time lag, $b=5$, leads to ratios a_1/a_t in the relative value models that are closer to the corresponding ratios a_1/a_t in the present value models.

The above steps (i)-(iv) determine a value function of type (7) or (7') with $v(x)=x$. Such a value function can be used to evaluate each of the policies being considered in the evaluation study. A more indirect, and perhaps more useful, procedure is to calculate which of the alternative policies is most preferred for which ranges of the temporal midvalue m. This approach avoids the problematic task of attaining a consensus on the importance of the future, and provide information as to the implications for policy choices of various degrees of importance of the future.

REFERENCES

Aczel, , J. 1966. <u>Functional Equations and Their Applications</u>. Academic Press, New York.

Barrager, S. M. 1980. Assessment of Simple Joint Time/Risk Preference Functions. <u>Management Science</u> 26, 620-632.

Bell, D. E. 1974. Evaluating Time Streams of Income. <u>Omega</u> 2, 691-699.

Bodily, S. E. 1981. Stability, Equality, Balance, and Multivariate Risk. In <u>Organizations: Multiple Agents with Multiple Criteria</u>, J. N. Morse (ed.). Springer-Verlag, New York.

Debreu, G. 1960. Topological Methods in Cardinal Utility Theory. In <u>Mathematical Methods in the Social Sciences</u>, K. J. Arrow, S. Karlin, and P. Suppes (eds.). Stanford University Press, Stanford, California.

Diamond, P. A. 1965. The Evaluation of Infinite Utility Streams. <u>Econometrica</u> 33, 170-177.

Fischhoff, B., S. Lichentstein, P. Slovic, S. L. Derby and R. Keeney. 1981. <u>Acceptable Risk</u>. Cambridge University Press, Cambridge.

Fishburn, P. C. 1970. <u>Utility Theory for Decision Making</u>. Wiley, New York.

Fishburn, P. C. and A. Rubinstein. 1982. Time Preference. <u>International Economic Review</u> 23, 677-694.

Gorman, W. M. 1968. The Structure of Utility Functions. <u>Review of Economic Studies</u> 35, 367-390.

Harvey, C. M. 1985a. Assessment of Preferences by Conditions on Pricing-Out Amounts. <u>Operations Research</u> 33, 443-454.

Harvey, C. M. 1985b. Decision Analysis Models for Social Attitudes Toward Inequity. <u>Management Science</u> 31, 1199-1212.

Harvey, C. M. 1985c. Utility Functions for Infinite-Period Planning. Working paper. Dickinson College, Carlisle, PA.

Harvey, C. M. 1986. Value Functions for Infinite-Period Planning. To appear in Management Science.

Jones-Lee, M. W. (ed.) 1982. The Value of Life and Safety. Praeger Publishers, New York.

Keeney, R. L. 1982. Decision Analysis: An Overview. Operations Research 30, 803-838.

Keeney, R. L. and H. Raiffa. 1976. Decisions with Multiple Objectives; Preferences and Value Tradeoffs. Wiley, New York.

Koopmans, T. C. 1960. Stationary Ordinal Utility and Impatience. Econometrica 28, 287-309.

Koopmans, T. C. 1972. Representation of Preference Ordering over Time. In Decision and Organization, C. B. McGuire and R. Radner (eds.). North-Holland, Amsterdam.

Koopmans, T. C., P. A. Diamond, and R. E. Williamson. 1964. Stationary Utility and Time Perspective. Econometrica 32, 82-100.

Kunreuther, H. and E. v. Ley (eds.) 1982. Risk Analysis Controversy: An Institutional Perspective. Springer-Verlag, New York.

Lovins, A. B. 1977. Cost-Risk-Benefit Assessments in Energy Policy. George Washington Law Review 45, 911-943.

Meyer, R. f. 1970. On the Relationship among the Utility of Assets, the Utility of Consumption, and Investment Strategy in an Uncertain, but Time Invariant World. In OR 69: Proceedings of the Fifth International Conference on Operational Research, J. Lawrence (ed.). Tavistock Publications, London.

Mishan, E. J. 1976. Cost-Benefit Analysis. Praeger Publishers, New York.

Mishan, E. J. 1981. Introduction to Normative Economics. Oxford University Press, New York.

Owen, P. A. 1983. Decisions that Influence Outcomes in the Distant Future. IEEE Transactions on Systems, Man, and Cybernetics 13, 1-10.

Schulze, W. 1974. Social Welfare Functions for the Future. American Economist 18(1), 70-81.

Stokey, E. and R. Zeckhauser. 1978. A Primer for Policy Analysis. W. W. Norton, New York.

Strotz, R. H. 1975. Myopia and Inconsistency in Dynamic Utility Maximization. Review of Economic Studies 23, 165-180.

Sugden, R. and A. Williams. 1978. The Principles of Practical Cost-Benefit Analysis. Oxford University Press, Oxford.

von Weizäcker, C. C. 1965. Existence of Optimal Programmes of Accumulation for an Infinite Time Horizon. Review of Economic Studies 32, 85-104.

TOXIC EFFLUENTS: A SIMPLIFIED PROCEDURE

FOR ASSESSING HUMAN HEALTH RISKS

Joseph G. Bolten*, Paolo F. Ricci** and James F. Stine***

The Rand Corporation*
Santa Monica, California 90406
Electric Power Research Institute**
Palo Alto, California
Pennsylvania Power and Light Company***
Allentown, Pennsylvania

ABSTRACT

This paper presents a simplified methodology for assessing the chronic health risks caused by discharge of toxic pollutants to surface water bodies. The methodology has been incorporated into a microcomputer program (WTRISK) and includes simplified transport models for atmospheric, overland, and surface water media, as well as procedures for calculating exposure rates through alternative pathways and the consequent chronic health risks. The program can be used to make preliminary calculations of potential risks and to estimate the uncertainties in the results. With this information, the risk analyst can evaluate discharge problems and determine where additional data or more detailed analysis are required. The approach has been applied to a case study where an effluent containing selenium was discharged from an existing coal-fired power plant. The analysis found that incremental exposure rates and health risks are negligible and that the simplified approach can be used to assess the bounds on potential risks.

KEY WORDS: Risk analysis, Chronic health risk, Environmental transport Risk assessment, Toxic chemicals, Selenium, Coal fired power plant,

BACKGROUND

The health risks associated with the discharge of toxic pollutants from industrial sources have become the subject of growing concern within industry and government agencies at the federal and state level. Federal legislation to regulate these emissions includes the Clean Air Act, Clean Water Act, and the Resource Conservation and Recovery Act of 1976. In the context of deriving specific environmental regulations, government agencies and industries have recognized the need for a relatively simple approach to calculating the health risks of toxic discharges into the air,

---

Disclaimer: The opinions expressed in this paper are not necessarily those of EPRI or its members.

Although researchers have developed many specific computer models for risk assessment, most of these models are not suitable for first order or preliminary analysis. Currently available codes are generally complex, data-intensive, and expensive to run. They cannot be easily transferred between computer systems or used by people, other than their developers, without lengthy preparation and instruction. Moreover, because they are expensive and difficult to use, these codes may not be suitable for the large-scale sensitivity analyses needed in the initial phases of a study when specific costs and benefits have not been established (Ricci, 1985).

Recognizing the need for a simplified, integrated approach to health risk assessment, the Electric Power Research Institute (EPRI) began supporting the Rand Corporation in the development of such a tool. The goal was to develop a computer model that could be easily applied to a wide variety of effluent discharge problems. The approach considers the chronic health risks associated with toxic emissions to all environmental media, but is directed primarily toward discharges to surface water and associated exposure pathways. Moreover, it is oriented toward the needs of the potential user, easily transferred to other locations and computer systems, and it incorporates existing models whenever possible.

Although developed primarily for the electric utility industry, the program can be used in those situations involving discharges from either a point source or a limited area. It has been applied to two hypothetical case studies and one actual case study of arsenic and selenium discharges from coal-fired power plants. These studies have helped to improve the models and have demonstrated how the approach can be applied to actual situations. The overall approach and details of the computer program and case studies are described fully in Bolten et al. (1983, 1985).

The methodology of the program should be used in preliminary analysis, where its convenience and low cost facilitates rapid and extensive sensitivity analysis. Using the model, the analyst can estimate upper and lower bounds for pollutant concentrations and the consequent exposure rates. These results and others can be used to improve understanding and definition of the problem, eliminate unimportant pathways, and isolate those areas where additional, more intensive research is necessary. Specifically, the models could be used to (1) prepare for regulatory and licensing proceedings, (2) support site selection, (3) prepare environmental impact reports, (4) facilitate long-term environmental planning, (5) study the effect of alternative regulatory formulations, and (6) respond to public concerns about current or future issues.

DESCRIPTION OF THE APPROACH

Risk calculations should be performed within a well-understood context. More specifically, one must first define the existing or base case situation, to serve as a reference for all subsequent risk calculations. Within this context, background pollutant concentrations, exposure rates, and health risks should be determined. With these results, the marginal changes in pollutant concentrations, exposure rates, and chronic health risks for all alternative discharge rates and concentrations can be calculated and compared.

Risk Assessment Framework

As shown in Figure 1, the general risk assessment framework consists of five distinct stages: (1) plant emissions, (2) environmental transport, (3) exposure analysis, (4) toxicology and pharmacokinetics, and (5) dose-

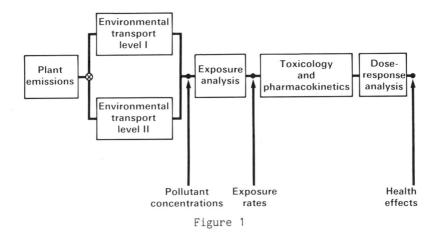

Figure 1

General Analysis Framework

response analysis. To assess the risk associated with emission of a toxic pollutant from a specific source, models, measured data, or a combination of both are used at each stage of the analysis. The framework is designed to permit use of alternative models at the different stages of the analysis, depending on the problem and the specific constraints of the situation. In this paper, we are most concerned with the two alternative levels available in the environmental transport analysis--levels I and II.

Levels of Analysis

The environmental transport analysis takes the rate and concentration of the discharge from the source to each environmental medium and calculates the distribution of pollutant in the environment surrounding the source. As shown in Fig. 1, these calculations can be performed at either of two levels. The Level I calculations use simplified transport models. These models can be set up and operated by people with a basic understanding of transport processes and a knowledge of the particular problem. The models require limited amounts of aggregated data and can be run quickly and cheaply. They are designed to be used with extensive sensitivity analysis of key parameters.

The assumptions and simplifications made in these models may cause them to be less realistic and could lead to significant errors if they are not used correctly. The analyst should be aware of the limitations of the models and data and must realize that these simplified calculations are best used in sensitivity analysis for the purpose of (1) defining the problem, (2) generating upper and lower bounds on results, and (3) investigating the sensitivity of results to variations in inputs and model parameters.

The Level II calculations use the more traditional complex environmental transport models, such as EXAMS, ARM, SERATRA, ISC, and others (Bolten et al., 1983; Onishi et al., 1982). These models, although they may produce more realistic results in specific cases, cannot be run easily and cheaply. They are complex and require specialized knowledge and significant effort for operation on a computer system. They also have extensive data requirements that must be met if the models are to be used to their full advantage. Because of the costs and difficulty of using these Level II models, they are not suitable for extensive sensitivity analysis, particularly at the beginning of a study.

The results of either level of environmental transport analysis will be the distribution of pollutant concentrations in the environment around the source. These concentrations can then be used in the exposure analysis to calculate population exposure rates as a function of exposure pathway, location, and other characteristics. The toxicological and pharmacokinetic analysis of the pollutant should be considered to develop the appropriate health effects from the population data and the calculated exposure rates. Although this approach would normally involve the use of dose-response relationships, in many cases health data or pollutant characteristics may not suffice for this type of analysis and other approaches become necessary.

In addressing a discharge problem, the analyst should follow a specific strategy. The first step is to define the situation, including those factors and alternatives that will be modeled, given the problem and the objectives of the analysis. After collecting relevant data, the Level I transport models should be used to calculate pollutant concentrations, exposure rates, and health risks for the nominal situation and alternatives. This step of the analysis can help the analyst to define the problem more clearly and determine data requirements more precisely. Next, the Level I models should be used in extensive sensitivity analysis involving all stages of the risk assessment process. The results of this step are upper and lower bounds on the concentrations, exposure rates, and health risks. These bounds should provide a quantitative description of the relative importance of different environmental and exposure pathways and allow the analyst to bound the problem accurately.

These results may show that there is no emissions problem (i.e., significant health risk) even under worst-case assumptions. However, if the results do indicate a potential problem or are ambiguous, then more intensive analysis with the Level II environmental models is required. In this case, the Level I analysis provides information to improve allocation of resources to the various aspects of the problem. If the upper bounds determined in the Level I analysis indicate that certain pathways or emissions are not important, subsequent work can concentrate on those areas of the analysis where the Level I results show a problem.

WTRISK Model

To facilitate the process of assessing chronic health risks, we have developed a computer program that can be applied to a wide variety of problems. This program, called WTRISK (WaTeR RISK), includes (1) simplified models for transport in the air, overland, and surface waters; (2) exposure models for all significant pathways; and (3) six dose-response functions. The program allows the user to specify a region in terms of geographic or representative areas with appropriate populations separated by age, sex, or other characteristics. Exposure rates can be calculated by population group, location, and specific pathway for up to five pollutant species simultaneously. Although the species must act independently in the transport and exposure calculations, their effects can be aggregated in the dose-response calculations.

Using WTRISK, an analyst can perform Level I investigations of point source or indirect atmospheric emissions and surface water discharges, including the transfer of pollutant between media. Although the program does not incorporate simplified transport models for saturated or unsaturated groundwater, it does provide for the contamination of surface waters from the groundwater. The atmospheric transport component includes a simple Gaussian plume model and a distributed source model. Surface water transport calculations can be performed for either rivers and streams, or lakes with some thermal stratification. The overland model partitions total pollutant deposition (atmospheric and irrigation) into runoff, infiltration, and retention in surface soil layers.

The exposure analysis section of WTRISK calculates total exposure by intake route for the population surrounding the emission source. The calculation involves summing the exposure from each separate pathway to the three intake modes: inhalation, ingestion, and dermal contact. Inhalation exposure is calculated from the distribution of air pollutant concentrations. Ingestion exposure is determined for consumption of drinking water, atmospheric particulates, aquatic organisms, and animal and vegetable products. Dermal exposure can be calculated for exposure to air pollutants as well as treated or untreated waters.

The health effect calculations use the exposure rate results to estimate the increased risk (over background) of a particular chronic toxic response (or set of responses). To calculate this estimated risk, one must use statistical or statistical-biological models relating the dose presented to a human or test animal to the increased probability of toxic response per unit of exposed population. Because we are concerned with chronic (long-term) rather than acute effects, the code (and its associated methods) are focused on dose-response relationships for chemical carcinogens.[1]

The WTRISK model incorporates six dose-response functions. Parameter values (potency) for these must be supplied to the program, and must be estimated through off-line calculations or obtained from the literature. The six models included in the program are the one-hit, multihit, multistage, Crump, probit, and Weibull models. Because none of these dose-response functions can be said to have a superion molecular and biologic-biochemical basis (Ricci and Molton, 1985), alternative, but biologically plausible, functions should be used whenever possible to provide alternative estimates of the adverse health effects. This is particularly true because some functions generate either high or low response rates for a given dose. Unfortunately, for many of the toxic pollutants, the available data may not be sufficient in quantity or quality to estimate the necessary parameters for some of the more complex models. As a result, the analyst must make use of experience and judgment.

Uncertainty Analysis

Quantitative risk assessment deals with, and has long been plagued by uncertainty. An analysis may have little meaning and questionable value in setting or meeting regulations if its results have an uncertainty of several orders of magnitude. Unfortunately, this may frequently be the case when determining the chronic health effects of toxic pollutants. Even if the overall uncertainty in an analysis cannot be reduced, it is incumbent on the analyst to obtain and portray some measure of it. If the sources of uncertainty in the results can be determined, it may be

---

[1]These models may equally well be used to estimate the prevalence of other chronic diseases such as liver or kidney necrosis, teratogenicity, or fetotoxicity, so long as a threshold is not apparent and the cellular and organism responses are replicated by the dose-response functions chosen (Ricci and Molton, 1985).

possible to improve the analysis in those areas.

The WTRISK program can be used to assess how errors in the input and parameter values required by the various models contribute to the overall uncertainty in results--the health risk. A number of theoretical approaches have been applied to the problem of quantifying uncertainty associated with input and parameter values. Although Cox and Baybutt (1981) address five alternative methods, several others have been discussed in the literature. Eight methods, including (1) analytic techniques, (2) Monte Carlo simulation, (3) response surface analysis, (4) differential sensitivity analysis, (5) confidence intervals, (6) extreme values, (7) linear propagation of errors, and (8) simple sensitivity analysis have been considered in our work (Bolten et al., 1983). Not all of these approaches are useful for the complex problem of risk assessment, and each has relative advantages and disadvantages.

Of these alternatives, five could reasonably be used in risk assessment. These are (1) response surface analysis, (2) differential sensitivity analysis, (3) extreme values, (4) linear propagation of errors, and (5) simple sensitivity analysis. If an analysis is constrained by limited resources, a simple sensitivity analysis is reasonable. In this approach, the analyst makes three point estimates of each parameter (a "best" estimate, a low, and a high value) rather than using a distribution of values. During the investigation, the analyst can observe how changes in the values of each parameter (between the low, best, and high estimates), one at a time, affect the results. For the more sensitive parameters (i.e., those that have greater influence on the net risk), simultaneous changes in two or three parameters can be made. Thus, sensitivity analysis can be considered as informal uncertainty analysis.

It would be much too laborious, in most cases, to perform sensitivity analysis on each parameter or pairs, given their number. To reduce the number of perturbations, the analyst should use the models and data to establish which (among all parameters) meet two conditions: (1) they might significantly affect the results, and (2) their values are not well established and have large uncertainty. These selected parameters can then be perturbed.

APPLICATION TO A CASE STUDY

To demonstrate how the overall risk analysis framework and the WTRISK program could be used, we have applied them to two simplified, illustrative case studies and to one actual case study. The simplified studies, described in Bolten et al. (1983, 1985), considered a hypothetical coal-fired power plant of 500 MWe generating capacity sited near rivers in Washington and Nebraska. These studies looked at discharges of arsenic and selenium into the air, surface water, and groundwater. The actual case study, discussed in Bolten and Resetar (to be published), considers the discharges of selenium into surface waters by a coal-fired power plant in Pennsylvania. The utility (Pennsylvania Power and Light Company) that operates this power plant (the Montour Steam Electric Station) is currently undergoing permit review for the surface water discharges.

The analysis was, by design, limited to the chronic health risks associated with selenium discharged from the waste treatment basin at the Montour plant. The plant, located north of the junction of the West and North Branches of the Susquehanna River, discharges into the Chillisquaque Creek, which subsequently flows into the Susquehanna. Exposure pathways considered in the analysis included the consumption of treated drinking water and fish obtained from the Susquehanna. These two pathways are used by the Environmental Protection Agency in its determination of the water quality criterion for selenium (EPA, 1980a).

Approach

Once the basic problem had been defined and initial bounds were placed on the analysis, the approach used in the Montour case study followed the general procedure developed in the previous two hypothetical cases. The steps in this analysis were as follows:

- Describe Montour water systems, calculate from mass balance analysis the selenium discharge rates, and compare these calculated rates with discharge concentration measurements.
- Specify the base case (nominal discharge rate) and alternatives to be considered.
- Determine the hydrologic characteristics of the affected surface waterways (Chillisquaque Creek and Susquehanna River) and find background selenium concentrations.
- Specify the exposure pathways and collect appropriate data.
- Identify the exposed population for each pathway.
- Define the health effects analysis and method of calculation.
- Use WTRISK (including Level I transport models) to calculate selenium concentrations, exposure rates, and health effects for the base case and its alternatives.
- Perform sensitivity analysis for the transport, exposure, and health effects calculations.
- Refine or revise the analysis as necessary on the basis of all results, including the sensitivity analyses.

Assumptions

The analysis was based on a number of assumptions that simplified the calculations. The primary assumptions, most of which were supported by preliminary analysis, include:

- There is no significant contribution to surface waters from plant selenium emissions in stack discharge or leaching from disposal ponds and landfills.
- Processes removing selenium from surface waters or changing its chemical form can be approximated by first order relationships.
- The exposed population includes only those people who regularly consume either drinking water or fish obtained from the Susquehanna or Chillisquaque downstream from the discharge point.
- The health effect of concern was selenosis rather than cancer.

Because no dose-response potencies have been estimated for selenosis, the health effects calculations were based on the threshold ingestion rate approach described in the Environmental Protection Agency water quality criteria document for selenium (EPA, 1980a). Using literature data, we modeled the distribution of selenium consumption in the population with a log normal probability distribution function. The fraction of the exposed population that might be expected to exceed the selenosis threshold (calculated by the EPA to be 7.0 mg/day), given a particular mean consumption rate and the estimated standard deviation of the distribution, was then calculated. Plant emissions affect the mean consumption rate by shifting the distribution toward higher or lower consumption levels, in turn, changing the number of people that might exceed the threshold. The shifts were also modeled and found not to unduly change the excess risks. The calculated population exposure rates were thus translated into an equivalent chronic health risk. We discuss these results next.

Results and Sensitivity Analysis

In the analysis, the transport calculations were separated from the exposure and health effects work. This permitted the identification of those parameters that affect each aspect of the calculations, as well as the overall risk estimates. The results of the sensitivity studies of selenium transport were used as inputs to the sensitivity analysis of exposure rates and health effects, along with variations in the exposure and health effects parameters. In general, the primary parameters in the analysis were the (1) river flow rates, (2) effectiveness of drinking water treatment processes, (3) ingestion threshold for selenosis, and (4) background level of selenium in the general diet.

The results of the basic calculations and sensitivity analysis of selenium concentrations along the Susquehanna River are summarized in Table 1. These results show that selenium concentrations were not increased significantly in the Susquehanna, the only waterway that both receives plant discharges and affects population exposure to selenium. With long-term mean flow rates (the flows most significantly affecting chronic health risk), selenium concentration increases were negligible. Even under worst-case assumptions (an upper bound), average selenium concentrations along the river increased by less than 10 percent and remained well below the primary drinking water quality standard of 0.010 mg/l. This criterion is based on animal data; the Lowest Observed Effect Level (LOEL) is derived from rat studies.

Table 1

SELENIUM CONCENTRATIONS IN THE SUSQUEHANNA RIVER
(mg/l)

| Case Description | | | Mean Selenium Concentration | | |
Discharge Rate{a}	Removal Rate{b}	River Flow	Chillisquaque Inflow	Harrisburg	Maryland Border
Background Concentration			0.00200	0.00200	0.00200
Permit	Nominal	Mean	0.00201	0.00200	0.00200
Permit	None	Mean	0.00201	0.00200	0.00200
Permit	None	Minimum{c}	0.00228	0.00209	0.00208
Nominal	Nominal	Mean	0.00202	0.00200	0.00200
Nominal	None	Mean	0.00202	0.00201	0.00201
Nominal	None	Minimum{c}	0.00252	0.00216	0.00214

NOTES: {a} Selenium concentrations in plant discharge: Permit level--0.010 mg/l; Nominal discharge--0.017 mg/l
{b} Nominal removal rate coefficient--8.02 x 10(-7)
{c} Worst-case conditions (upper bounds)

Similarly, exposure rates for the 727,000 people in the affected population increased insignificantly over background levels. Background and total selenium exposure rates for the basic analysis and sensitivity cases are summarized in Table 2. As shown in the table, the increase in the worst case was less than 0.15 percent of background exposure levels. In the nominal case, using mean flow rates, the increase was less than 0.002 percent of background exposure.

The health effects associated with these exposure rates depended strongly on both the assumed threshold level and the background consumption rate for selenium. In spite of this dependence, in the analysis of the worst case, the individual lifetime health risk was less than 10(-6), a standard of acceptability often applied in risk assessment and environmental standard-setting approaches (EPA, 1980b). Table 3, which summarizes the results of the health risk calculations, shows the number of people in the exposed population of 727,000 that could be expected to exceed the EPA selenosis threshold of 7.0 mg/day. The table presents the results for both the nominal background exposure rate and for a high background rate used in the sensitivity analysis.

Table 2

SELENIUM EXPOSURE RATES FOR REGIONAL POPULATION
(mg/day)

| Case Description | | | Mean Population |
Discharge Rate	Removal Rate	River Flow	Exposure Rate{a}
EPA selenosis threshold			7.000000
Background exposure rate			0.129317
Permit	Nominal	Mean	0.129320
Permit	None	Mean	0.129321
Permit	None	Minimum	0.129419
Nominal	None	Mean	0.129324
Nominal	None	Minimum	0.129509

NOTE: {a} Exposure rates are expressed to six digits only to show the variation between cases. Actual selenium background exposure rates may differ from calculated values by as much as fifty percent, although the increments associated with plant discharges should not change.

CONCLUSIONS

The potential user of WTRISK or other risk assessment methods should recognize risk analysis is not an exact science that can develop accurate and precise risk estimates. Instead, risk analysis is a quasi- science that can (1) roughly approximate the relative risks of alternative designs, (2) determine the relative sensitivities of calculated risks to uncertainties in input data, and (3) identify weaknesses in the original assumptions. Our risk assessment methodology is based on a particular set of assumptions and is thus subject to limitations and potential problems.

No risk analysis framework or methodology should be used without a thorough understanding of the various models and data, their scientific basis, and their limitations. No one can construct a foolproof package of models that can be properly used by someone unfamiliar with the basic problem and general situation. "Cookbook" risk analysis must not be done. The analyst must have access to adequate information about (1) all models used in the analysis; (2) the operation and characteristics of the emission source and its waste streams; (3) the relevant characteristics of the regional geography, geology, hydrology, meteorology, and agricultural production (if relevant); (4) regional population; and (5) the behavior and chronic health effects of the pollutant. This is basic information, although the level of detail required will vary significantly between problems.

Table 3

HEALTH EFFECTS: NUMBER OF INDIVIDUALS AT LIKELY RISK

| Case Description | | | Expected Number |
Discharge Rate	Removal Rate	River Flow	Exceeding Threshold
Threshold Level = 7.0 mg/day			
Background exposure--0.129317 mg/day			0.0281
Permit	Nominal	Mean	0.0281
Permit	None	Mean	0.0281
Permit	None	Minimum	0.0282
Nominal	None	Mean	0.0281
Nominal	None	Minimum	0.0284
Background exposure--0.256470 mg/day			3.3650
Permit	Nominal	Mean	3.3653
Permit	None	Mean	3.3653
Permit	None	Minimum	3.3737
Nominal	None	Mean	3.3655
Nominal	None	Minimum	3.3813

The simplified approach described in this paper and implemented in the WTRISK program is designed to make the process of data collection and analysis as simple and understandable as possible. The user must always remember his responsibility to use this and other tools in a reasonable and appropriate manner, recognizing the limitations and uncertainties that will be present in his results.

ACKNOWLEDGMENT

We thank Andrea Henderson of Bechtel for her thoughtful review of this paper and her insightful comments.

REFERENCES

Bolten, J. G., P.F. Morrison, and K.A. Solomon, Risk-Cost Assessment Methodology for Toxic Pollutants from Fossil Fuel Power Plants, The Rand Corporation, R-2993-EPRI, Santa Monica, California, June 1983.

Bolten, J. G., et al., Alternative Models for Risk Assessment of Toxic Emissions, The Rand Corporation, N-2261-EPRI, Santa Monica, California, April 1985.

Bolten, J. G., and S.A. Resetar, A Case Study of Selenium Emissions from a Coal Fired Power Plant, The Rand Corporation, N-2387-EPRI, Santa Monica, California, (to be published).

Cox, D. C., and P. Baybutt, "Methods for Uncertainty Analysis: A Comparative Survey," Risk Analysis, Vol. 1, No. 4, pp. 251-258, 1981.

Environmental Protection Agency (EPA), Ambient Water Quality Criteria for Selenium, EPA-440/5-80-070, October 1980a.

Environmental Protection Agency (EPA), "Water Quality Criteria Documents; Availability," Federal Register, Vol. 45, No. 231, pp. 79318-79378, November 28, 1980b.

Onishi, Y., et al., Multimedia Contaminant Environmental Exposure Assessment (MCEA) Methodology for Coal-Fired Power Plants, Vols. 1 and 2, Battelle-Pacific Northwest Laboratories, Richland, Washington, April 1982.

Ricci, P. F., Principles of Health Risk Assessment, Prentice-Hall, Englewood Cliffs, New Jersey, 1984.

Ricci, P. F., and L. S. Molton, "Regulating Cancer Risks," Environmental Science and Technology, Vol. 19, No. 6, pp. 473-479, 1985.

DEALING WITH UNCERTAINTY ABOUT RISK IN RISK MANAGEMENT

Chris Whipple

Electric Power Research Institute

ABSTRACT

Conservative assumptions in risk analysis are shown to be protective of human health when the social costs of misestimation are highly asymmetrical, when risk management actions do not incur significant opportunity costs, when risk management actions do not lead to the substitution of significant new risks, and when risk managers do not compensate for perceived conservatisms when setting standards or making other risk management decisions. An issue central to the effect of systematically conservative assumptions is the ability of risk analyses to distinguish large risk from small risk; here it is argued that conservative assessments can fail to make adequate distinctions. The influence of these factors on the protectiveness of conservative analytical methods is examined.

KEY WORDS: risk, uncertainty, conservatism

> Science tells us what we can know, but what we can know is little, and if we forget how much we cannot know we become insensitive to many things of great importance. Theology, on the other hand, induces a dogmatic belief that we have knowledge where in fact we have ignorance, and by doing so generates a kind of impertinent insolence towards the universe. Uncertainty, in the presence of vivid hopes and fears, is painful, but must be endured if we wish to live without the support of comforting fairy tales.
>
> Bertrand Russell, in the Introduction to A History of Western Philosophy, 1945

INTRODUCTION

Until the last fifteen or so years, efforts to improve health and safety were directed primarily at risks of relatively certain magnitude. The social harm from accidents and diseases such as polio were all too easy to measure. Risks were managed by learning from past mistakes; this is still an essential part of good risk management. But trial and error management is particularly ill suited for many risks of current concern, for example, risks with long latency periods or catastrophic potential.

We now seek better ways to manage risks prospectively, methods which avoid the human costs of a trial and error approach.

Where past experience is not a guide, risk management is more difficult. We have been struggling with several such cases for the past decade: nuclear power, chemical carcinogens, and more recently, biotechnologies. Here, one approach to uncertainty about such risks has been to try to reduce it through research. Substantial resources have been expended to understand these risks, and risk management has been improved by such studies. Despite much effort to estimate risk, where direct human evidence is not available, large uncertainties about risk remain. Research may eventually resolve many questions that now trouble us, and in some cases postponing a decision for research may avoid uncertainty. But many risks are likely to remain uncertain for the foreseeable future.

Estimating the magnitude of risks that cannot be measured directly frequently requires the use of assumptions that cannot be tested empirically. Not only are such risks uncertain, but often the uncertainty cannot be characterized probabilistically. Probability distributions are useful for describing some uncertainties, but this is often not feasible in risk assessment. Often there is no reasonable method even to assign weights to the plausibility of alternative assumptions. Methods have been developed to elicit subjective descriptions of uncertainty; this raises the question of whose estimates to accept.

Recognition of these uncertainties has at times led to the view that risk assessment is a dubious enterprise, too uncertain to be relied upon for risk management decisions. But low level risks are inherently uncertain regardless of the approach taken to their study. This uncertainty is simply more apparent under some approaches to social risk management than others. Given the discomfort that uncertainty causes, it is tempting in some cases to overstate what risk assessment can tell us. The limits to science are imprecise, as are the distinctions between that which is known and that which can reasonably be assumed. For this reason, a technically accurate description of uncertainties is now considered essential in risk assessment.

Risk assessors bridge gaps in knowledge with assumptions. Often there are many alternative assumptions, each scientifically plausible, with no reasonable basis for choosing among them. For example, an analyst must select a dose-response model for extrapolation to low dose risk. Here the recent tradition endorses conservatism in risk estimation as protective of public health. I argue here that conservatism, defined here to refer to the systematic selection of assumptions leading to high risk estimates, is not protective of human health in most situations.

RISK VERSUS UNCERTAINTY

Risk, as generally used by health and safety risk analysts, measures probability and severity of loss or injury. Uncertainty, using the dictionary definition that best describes its use in the risk field, refers to a lack of definite knowledge, a lack of sureness; doubt is the closest synonym. At times, these definitions are confused. Risk and uncertainty are related to the extent that both preclude knowledge of future states, and that both are often described by use of probabilities. But it is important to distinguish whether a lack of predictabiity arises from insufficient knowledge (uncertainty) or from a well understood probabilistic process (risk). The risk associated with a bet on a fair coin toss is precisely known; the risk has no uncertainty, although the outcome of the toss is uncertain. Conversely, the outcome of the administration of an experimental drug is also uncertain, but in such a case the inability to predict may be due more to a lack of information than to what also may be an inherently probabilistic process. The predictability of the result of a large number of trials helps to make the distinction between risk and uncertainty clearer -- for a fair coin toss, we can predict that about half of the results will be heads. For an experimental drug given to a large population, the number of people adversely affected may not be predictable except to within a broad range.

In the case of an experimental drug, the estimated probability that an average individual will experience an adverse effect (or equivalently, the number of people in an exposed population experiencing an adverse effect) might be described by use of a probability distribution. A probability distribution applied to a probability is known as a second story probability (such a distribution describes the relative likelihood that the probability of an adverse effect is a particular value).

Decision analysts and theorists of subjective probability frequently note that the second story probability representation is unnecessarily complex; that such measures can be mathematically collapsed into a single probability. That is, the probability of a probability is a probability. For individual decision making, it may be immaterial what combination of probabilistic processes and information gaps give rise to an estimate of the likelihood of some outcome; it is sufficient to describe the likelihood of an outcome by a probability. However, in the case of social risk management by a regulatory agency, it is often useful to distinguish between risk and uncertainty.

RISK ASSESSMENT POLICY

The recent National Academy of Sciences report Risk Assessment in the Federal Government: Managing the Process (National Research Council 1983) endorsed the concept that scientific questions about the degree of risk posed by some exposure or activity should be separated, to the extent feasible, from the policy questions of what risk management steps should be taken. This report clearly describes how science and policy cannot be entirely separated, and noted that many seemingly scientific issues such as the assumptions made in a risk assessment have direct relevance to management decisions. As seen by the committee which wrote this report:

> The goal of risk assessment is to describe, as accurately as possible, the possible health consequences of changes in human exposure to a hazardous substance; the need for accuracy implies that the best available scientific knowledge, supplemented as necessary by assumptions that are consistent with science, will be applied.

The difficulty arises when there is no scientific basis to select among alternative assumptions. The NAS Committee did not offer a general recommendation for choosing assumptions when this occurs, however it did note that in such cases, it may be appropriate to select the most conservative assumptions (i.e., those leading to the highest estimate of risk).

Carcinogenic risks and their assessment were chosen to illustrate many points in the NAS report cited above, primarily because the approach to these risks has become more standardized than has the estimation of other risks. Assumptions generally thought to be conservative are used by agencies in evaluating potential carcinogens. For example, conservative

531

risk assessment assumptions are used by EPA's Carcinogen Assessment Group to estimate a plausible upper bound for risk; the pausible lower bound is taken to be zero risk except where direct human evidence indicates otherwise. These upper bound risk estimates are based on data from the most sensitive sex, strain, and species of test animal; for the cancer tumor type (often including benign tumors) and site which maximize the estimated potency; transfer of animal results to humans based on the ratio of surface areas, an approach more conservative then scaling by weight; and extrapolation to low dose is based on a dose-response model that exhibits linearity at low doses. The sensitive sex, strain, and species selection is at times justified on the grounds that humans are genetically diverse, widely varying in existing health status, and exposed to many other potentially harmful agents. A recent article (Anderson et al, 1983) provides a good description of carcinogenic risk assessment at the EPA.

IS CONSERVATISM PROTECTIVE?

Does reliance on assumptions producing upper bound risk estimates protect health? The question is analytically tractable. Not surprisingly, its answer depends what assumptions are made. For some seemingly reasonable analytical assumptions, conservatism is protective; for other assumptions, also reasonable, conservatism is not.

Certainly the perception of many risk analysts is that conservative risk assessment assumptions are protective. High risk estimates are associated with stringent standards. An analyst's own sense of responsibility encourages conservatism. Although the social costs of false alarms are acknowledged, to give a false assurance of safety is believed to be far worse. The relative social cost of risk underestimation is taken to outweigh that from overestimation. An analytical case for conservatism is made by Talbot Page (Page,1978), who argues that the appropriate response to uncertain environmental risks is to balance the social costs of false negatives (substances or activities incorrectly thought to be safe) with the costs of false positives (things incorrectly believed to be hazardous). His analysis indicates that the use of this expectation rule seems clearly preferable to approaches aimed exclusively at avoiding either type of risk misclassification (i.e. false positives or false negatives). Page notes that "Application of this approach requires four pieces of information: the cost of a false negative; the cost of a false positive; and the probability of each." Given the difficulty in knowing the probabilities of false positives and negatives, he argues that:

> when the potential adverse effects of an environmental risk are many times greater than the potential benefits, a proper standard of proof of danger under the expected cost minimization criterion may be that there is only 'at least a reasonable doubt' that the adverse effect will occur, rather than requiring a greater probability, such as 'more likely than not,' that the effect will occur. Simple rules of thumb embodied in legal and regulatory institutions may come closer to expected cost minimization than elaborate attempts at quantification.

The interesting feature of Page's analysis is his lack of aversion to uncertainty; uncertain risks are judged on their expectation to the extent it can be estimated and characterized. The rather stringent proposed rule, "at least a reasonable doubt" is consistent with Page's analysis in which it is argued that for most environmental risks, the relative social costs of a false negative (leading to a failure to regulate a hazardous substance) greatly exceed the costs of regulating a safe substance. Among the common characteristics of environmental risk, Page lists modest benefits and catastrophic costs. For substances like food color additives or fluorocarbon propellants, where benefits are easy to forgo or where safer substitutes exist, the "at least a reasonable doubt" rule is appropriate from a cost-benefit viewpoint.

But to find that analytical conservatism is protective requires three premises: (1) that the disparity in social costs between false negatives and false positives is great, (2) that risk management decisions are insensitive to resource constraints and do not incur significant opportunity costs, and (3) that activities or agents identified as hazardous (whether true positives or false positives) can be eliminated without the creation of significant new risks. The potential protectiveness of conservatism also depends on whether risk managers compensate for conservatism in standard setting.

THE SOCIAL COSTS OF ERROR

In his analysis, Page described dichotomous risk decisions and classifications. Substances were carcinogenic or not; when they were misclassified, the resultant errors were false positives or negatives. This representation is a useful way to illustrate how it is socially desirable to balance the costs of errors in managing uncertain risks, and this was Page's objective.

Actual problems are generally not so black-or-white. Current issues often are with a substance's degree of carcinogenic potency, and with the establishment of exposure limits. Under this view, risks and risk management alternatives are continuously variable rather than discrete. It is actually easier to make the case for controlling risk under this continuous perspective, because it is generally harder to justify the ban of a hazardous substance on cost-benefit grounds than it is to justify a marginal reduction. This follows from the common assumption that health benefits are constant per unit of reduced exposure but that as use goes to zero, progressively more valuable social benefits are forgone.

If potency and exposure are variable, the harm from risk assessment errors is less than if they are discrete. A shift in analytic assumptions, for example to the average carcinogenic potency exhibited in several species rather than potency in the most sensitive species, could result in a less stringent standard. But this seems unlikely to lead to a public health disaster or excessive individual risk that one associates with the failure to recognize and control a potent carcinogen. Some risks, such as from biotechnologies or from climatic change do not necessarily follow this characterization. Consider basing exposure standards on assessed risk, using cost effectiveness criteria that appropriately reflect social cost. For exposures at the standard, marginal costs and risks are presumed to be equal. For slightly misplaced standards, due perhaps to small errors in assessing risk, the costs of over (or under) exposure will largely be offset by reduced (or increased) costs of risk control. These costs due to small inaccuracies in the estimation of risk are roughly symmetrical; for large errors, the costs of excessive public health risk and unnecessary regulation will vary.

The social costs from errors in risk estimation would be minimized if mean value estimates were used. Mean value risk estimates reflect the weighted average of all possible risk values. Conservative analysis and upper-confidence-bound estimates lead to overinvestment in risk control, but also to lower risk. At least this is the first-order effect.

Are national health and safety expenditures limited in the aggregate, or are they variable, depending on the outcome of many independent risk management decisions? If risk reduction expenditures are not limited in the aggregate, but are determined on a case-by-case basis, then it is appropriate to consider whether conservatism is protective by considering specific cases. However, if the fraction of GNP allocated for risk reduction is politically constrained, or if some other factor constrains risk management spending in the aggregate, then the collective effect of risk management decisions is the appropriate basis for evaluating whether conservatism serves a useful purpose.

Because risk analysts and agency standard setters generally focus on one risk at a time, this single risk focus is a natural frame of reference. From the perspective of a single risk management decision, analytical conservatism is protective, but at a price. A conservative risk estimate produces lower risk exposures. Here, the potential costs of large errors seem to be asymmetrical to the regulator. Risk reduction costs appear to be bounded, while the consequences of uncertain risk exposures are potentially much greater than these control costs.

An additional factor encouraging conservatism is how decisions might be judged in hindsight. An overcontrolled risk will probably drop from sight once a decision is implemented and control investments made. But an undercontrolled risk, possibly discovered through the identification of victims, is far more disturbing for a regulatory agency.

If risk reductions are limited by resource scarcity, however, the logical objective is to allocate the scarce resource in a way which maximizes social benefits. Opportunity costs, of little concern for a single risk, become important under this viewpoint. Money or regulatory attention spent on one risk is not available for another, so it is important not to waste resources on trivial risks. In this case, conservatism is counterproductive, and risks are increased if resources are shifted from significant risks to small, exaggerated risks. Under this fixed allocation or zero sum case, risk reductions are maximized when the cheapest and easiest risk reductions are given highest priority. Here, conservative estimates shift resources to uncertain risks, increasing expected health consequences.

Which perspective on regulatory resources is correct? Both have their merits. Regulatory agencies actions may be limited by the availability of scientific or administrative resources within their own staffs. But risk management responsibility assigned to the agencies by Congress is fragmented, and suggests nothing in the way of an overall ceiling on risk spending. The bulk of control costs come from producers, not regulatory agencies, so agency budgets are not a direct constraint. But while these expenditures appear to be variable and flexible, dependent on the perceived appropriate action in each case, there may be a political feedback from the regulated parties that limits the amount of money an agency can require to spend. A subtler consideration is that, to the extent that the public finds uncertain risks discomforting, greater expenditures for risk control may be politically feasible if funds are directed to deal with uncertain (and unpopular) risks.

RISK TRANSFERS

Often a regulatory action that reduces one risk will increase another

(Whipple 1985). This is especially prevalent when the particular benefit being obtained is considered essential but all methods for achieving the benefit carry risks. The important issue here is the recognition that the appropriate measure for analysis of a risk-reducing action is the net risk reduction. From this perspective, uneven conservatism in risk assessment can have a perverse effect by leading to the substitution of large risk for a small one. The cyclamate ban, leading to greater use of saccharine, may be a case in which this occurred. (Risks from both subtances are significantly uncertain.) Electricity production is also a good example, because utilities are obligated to provide service. A restriction on coal use can lead to greater oil use; regulatory restrictions on nuclear power can lead to increased use of coal.

In some cases, for example, those involving carcinogens, it may be possible to compare risks with common conservative assumptions and arrive at a reasonable relative ranking. But for dissimilar technologies such as coal and nuclear electricity, the comparison of conservative risk estimates does not include conservatisms common to both estimates. In these cases, conservatism is less useful and less protective than are central estimates or risk.

DO STANDARD SETTERS COMPENSATE FOR CONSERVATIVE RISK ANALYSIS?

Regulatory decision makers may consider the details of the evidence supporting a risk estimate and compensate for perceived biases in analysis. If this is the case, and appropriate adjustments are made, then standards will be the same no matter what risk assessment assumptions are made. In this case, conservative analysis would not lead to more or less stringent standards than would best estimates. It is likely that conservatively estimated risks are discounted in some cases but not in others and it is unlikely that adjustments could be made appropriately and consistently.

In the previous discussion of resource constraints, it was assumed that conservative estimates lead to stringent criteria. But it is apparent that conservatism in risk management need not be achieved through conservative risk assessment assumptions. One could use stringent criteria for allowable risk, and less conservative assumptions for estimating risk, and end up with the current levels of protection.

If greater use were made of this flexibility to vary risk criteria in response to conservatisms in risk assessment, an attractive approach would be to select risk assessment assumptions based on their discriminatory power. Relative risk estimates based on overly conservative assumptions may not distinguish important differences between risk. For example, an increase in benign liver tumors and decrease in leukemias and mammary gland fibroadenomas has been observed in response to test chemicals in the Fischer 344 rat (Haseman 1983). Under present assessment methods, a carcinogen that increases benign tumors at one site but reduces malignant tumors at other sites might have the same assessed risk as one that increases the overall burden of malignant tumors.

CONSERVATISM IN RISK ASSESSMENT: COMMENTS

Even if efforts to be less conservative in risk assessment are accepted, there will be cases where no method for choosing between alternative assumptions is available. About the best that risk analysis can provide when this happens is a collection of estimates based on a range of plausible models. Granger Morgan and his colleages have taken this approach to describe the estimated health effects from sulfur air pollution (Morgan et al,1984).

If less conservative assumptions are adopted for carcinogens, understanding the implications for human health of alternative animal bioassay results takes on added importance. There would be apparent value in conducting a wide variety of animal tests with known human carcinogens as a means of calibrating these experiments. A second consideration, suggested by animal test results (Haseman 1983), is whether certain carcinogens redistribute the tumor burden, whereas others increase total tumor incidence. If this turns out to be the case, it would be beneficial to health to discriminate between the two types of effect. Conservative assumptions about risk are thought to provide protection against uncertainty in risk, although sometimes at an added cost. Much impetus for analytical conservatism comes from the perception that this practice is protective of health. This is the perspective when risks are viewed singly. But conservatism may not protect if reduced exposures to uncertain risks is achieved at the expense of increased exposures to known risks.

Considering the many ways in which a conservative analysis can fail to protect, intentional use of conservative risk estimates is not beneficial to public health. In addition to misallocating scarce resources, conservatism can lead to unwise risk transfers and encourage risk regulators to compensate for perceived conservatisms. When this happens, risk regulation becomes less predictable and more arbitrary.

REFERENCES

Anderson, E. L. and the Carcinogen Assessment Group of the U.S. Environ-
       mental Protection Agency, 1983. "Quantitative Approaches
       in Use to Assess Cancer Risk" Risk Analysis, 3(Dec.):277-295.
Haseman, J. K. 1983. "Patterns of Tumor Incidence in Two-Year Cancer
       Bioassay Feeding Studies in Fischer 344 Rats" Fundemental and Applied
       Toxicology, 3:1-9.
Morgan, M. G., Morris, S. C., Henrion, M., Amaral, D. A. L. and Rish, W.
       R. "Technical Uncertainty in Quantitative Policy Analysis--A Sulfur
       Air Pollution Example" Risk Analysis,4(Sept.):201-216.
National Research Council, 1983. Committee on the Institutional Means for
       Assessment of Risk to Public Health. Risk Assessment in the Federal
       Government: Managing the Process, Washington, D.C., National Academy
       Press.
Page, T. 1978. "A Generic View of Toxic Chemicals and Similar Risks"
       Ecology Law Quarterly 7(2): 207-244.
Whipple, C. G. 1985. "Redistributing Risk" Regulation, May/June.

DEALING WITH UNCERTAINTY IN RISK REGULATION

Chauncey Starr

Electric Power Research Institute

ABSTRACT

The uncertainties in risk analysis are inevitable and cannot be reduced to zero. They arise from the incompleteness of the system modeling, the simplification of sub-system interactions, database errors, the variety of failure initiators, the range of failure consequences, and the prediction of public and individual exposures and doses. The composite uncertainty in the quantification of a single risk makes choosing regulatory criteria difficult. However, alternative systems for providing a specific end function generally have similar types and magnitudes of uncertainty, and a comparison of their mean values of quantitative public risk may disclose their relative risks adequately for regulatory purposes.

KEY WORDS: Uncertainty, risk, regulation

The use of the regulatory process to establish boundaries on public risks is usually presumed to be based on a valid perception of these risks, and of their relative importance in the spectrum of public exposure to all risks.

Let me specify what I mean by risk. Risk is a measure of the potential exposure to a loss arising from the by-products of an activity, with the usual descriptives of what, where, when, who, and how much. The ambiguities associated with this simple definition arise from the variety of the losses that may be incurred (life, life expectancy, financial, property, environmental, etc.), the time periods used for the probability statement (exposure time, latency period, lifetime, annual, etc.), the population exposed (individual, group, regional, national, age sector, etc.), and the quality of the estimate. The calculation of risk involves the product of three separate factors, (1) the probability of an initiating event, (2) the magnitude of the loss-creating outcome, and (3) the resulting size of the loss.

The average person is not likely to develop a balanced perspective of life's spectrum of risks, or of the associated benefits of life's activities. Although risks are real, and often quantifiable in the aggregate -- as with physical accidents -- individual perceptions and attitudes usually are not derived from these realities. Thus, public concern with issues of risk may result in powerful popular movements, but these are rarely a useful guide for the most effective allocation of national resources to increase public health and safety. Providing a

537

better and less subjective guide for this purpose is the objective of risk analysis and regulation.

The regulatory process obviously deals with future events, and thus suffers from the well-known limitations of any prediction. Ideally, risk regulation should be based on a statistically significant history of similar risk events which are reasonably measurable and which disclose the relevant cause-effect relationships. Unfortunately, such a professionally satisfying analytical basis seldom exists, and most risk regulation is unavoidably embedded in large uncertainties. Even when a reasonably verifiable basis exists -- such as with smoking, drunk driving, auto seat belts -- the predicted outcomes of proposed regulatory actions are sufficiently uncertain as to provoke much public argument.

The uncertainties in risk analysis are inevitable and can never be reduced to zero. Consider any system intended by man or nature to function safely under normal conditions. For obvious reasons, the actual operating conditions will vary about the norm in some statistical fashion, and for this discussion assume the usual bell-shaped probability distribution of such conditions. So, the stresses on the system produced during operation will sometimes be below the norm and sometimes above. To operate safely most of the time the system is designed to withstand a stress considerably above the normal operating point, thus providing a "safety factor". The actual ability of the system to withstand stress varies with time about the design level in some statistical fashion due to the usual uncontrollable elements - material variations, aging processes, assembly tolerances, etc. Again, assume a bell-shaped probability distribution for the system strength. We thus have an analytical situation in which the upper tail of the operating stress distribution overlaps the lower tail of the system strength distribution. This overlap area is the failure zone.

It is clear that as long as the tails of the probability distributions extend sufficiently, the overlap failure zone will always exist. Narrowing the probability distributions by (1) greater effort to minimize variations from normal operation, and (2) to strive for "zero defects" in the system, will certainly decrease the probability overlap and thus the frequency of failure, but can never remove the failure zone. In a schematic sense, this explains why "zero risk" is not a rational objective. In a pragmatic sense, this explains why we will always have to deal with uncertainties in projecting future probabilities.

Thus the policy issue is not whether regulation of risk should be withheld until everything is predictable, - an impractical goal - but rather, when the body of evidence is sufficiently strong to clearly justify some regulation, how should the many pervasive uncertainties be taken into consideration.

In this regard, we should recognize that regulations operate at two extremes of public risk. The first is the great body of public exposures which are commonly assumed to be safe (e.g. natural foods) and are occasionally found to represent a hazard requiring regulatory constraints (e.g. aflatoxin in peanut butter). The second is the growing body of public exposures which are commonly assumed to be hazardous, and require regulatory permission for use (e.g., man-made drugs and pesticides). Constraint and permission are thus the two sides of the regulatory coin, but their implementations are quite different. The first is safe until proven guilty, the second is guilty until proven safe. Constraint requires the regulatory agency to prove the risk, whereas permission requires the producer to prove the safety, both beyond a reasonable doubt.

The treatment of uncertainty is thus also implemented at the
extremes. In the case of the commonly safe exposures, constraint is
absent until the risks are well established, i.e., the uncertainty in risk
quantification may be small (e.g., tobacco). For the commonly hazardous
group, permission is withheld if there exists any indication of risk,
i.e., the uncertainty in risk quantification may be large (e.g., PCB's,
dioxin, etc.).

In any risk analysis, the uncertainties arise in each one of the
basic components of the analysis. The first is the completeness of the
model used to represent the system. The core structure of any model
consists of the "?" whose role and system behavior are assumed to be well
understood. These are interwoven with the "known-unknowns" whose
existence is recognized but whose behavior is not well understood.
Omitted from the models are the "unknown-unknowns", elements which are not
recognized as being involved, but nevertheless may become important
factors in a failure sequence.

The second uncertainty arises from the inadequacy of the model's
prediction of system behavior. The dynamics of the relationships among
the many model elements is rarely simple, but it becomes impractical to
include higher-order effects and probability distributions in a
complicated system analysis. As a result, the best one can expect is an
approximate quantitative mean value prediction, and a crude estimate of a
resulting band of uncertainty. The third uncertainty arises from errors
in the data base used in the model calculations. In most issues of public
risk, the data is likely to be of dubious accuracy or incomplete or
difficult to separate from secondary variables. In most models,
quantitative outcomes can be very sensitive to small changes in some of
the relevant data, so the selection of a data base can often determine the
outcome of the model.

The above three sources of modeling uncertainty relate to the
methodology of analysis. As a practical matter, the quantitative
assessment of a public risk involves a sequence of several relatively
independent models. The initial model commonly attempts to predict the
probability distribution of failure of a system during normal operation -
e.g. the collapse of a bridge or a dam, the explosion of a steamboiler,
the blowout of an auto tire, the nuclear core-melt, etc. Such failures
may have many diverse causes such as corrosion processes, or poor
maintenance, or a stressful concentration of several independent events.
A rare-event input model attempts to predict the probability distribution
of failure initiators arising from unusual natural phenomena such as
earthquakes, lightning, hurricanes, tornadoes, and the thousand-year
flood; and from man-made events such as fires, bombs, sabotage, etc. A
third model estimates the magnitude of the physical consequences of the
failures - for example, the amount of water released by a dam failure, or
the chemicals released in a plant explosion. A fourth model is concerned
with the size of the public exposure to these physical consequences - how
many people are involved, and can they be evacuated or protected? A fifth
model covers the individual dose exposure - wet feet to drowning; or lung
irritation to asphyxiation.

This is a typical list of the models needed to predict physical or
physiologic failure probabilities and uncertainties. There is also a non-
technical domain of economic, sociologic, and political factors that
always encompasses the regulatory process. Such factors generally are not
as susceptible to quantified analysis as are the technical factors listed
above, although they may be pragmatically of comparable or greater
importance. It is obvious that in many cases, the quantification of risk

is often overwhelmed by the composite magnitude of the uncertainties. It is important, therefore, to review the value of risk quantification under such circumstances, to establish its area of usefulness.

We should recall that the prime criterion in the choice of a technical system (physical or physiologic) is the successful accomplishment of an end objective. For example, the need for a river crossing leads to a choice of a bridge or a ferry. Or, more commonly, cure of a disease leads to a choice among medical treatments or drugs. In every case, the chosen mode is designed to work, not fail. From this positive perspective, risk quantification serves two functions: first it assists in the disclosure of the comparative risks among available alternatives; second, for any chosen mode, it assists in the comparison of design alternatives within that mode. In either case, it is the comparative risk analysis which makes risk quantification useful. The process raises the probability of successful achievement of the end function, and reduces the public risks from a potential failure of the chosen mode.

The novel contribution of modern risk analysis, based on quantification of system event probabilities and their consequences, is best understood by considering the accepted approaches to risk prior to the middle of this century. Civil engineering structures -- buildings, bridges, dams, etc. -- are classic examples. The historical design objective was to avoid failure of the structure, defined as collapse under expected usage. To provide such assurance, the designers applied a traditional "safety factor." For example, if a rope was tested to hold 100 pounds, a safety factor of 10 would be provided if the maximum load did not exceed 10 pounds. In practice, these safety factors traditionally ranged from a low of 3 to as much as 40, depending on the designers' judgment and the tradition for each type of usage, i.e., steady state, cyclic stress, shock, corrosion, etc. Thus, the safety factor supplied a design umbrella large enough to cover all the areas of the designers' known range of ignorance, i.e., the "known unknowns." The system worked reasonably well, although an occasional structure collapsed because of an "unknown unknown"; for example, the Tacoma bridge collapse caused by unanticipated wind-induced oscillations; or the sinking of the "unsinkable" Titanic by iceberg collision.

The safety factor design approach was socially acceptable at that time. The engineering profession said, "trust us," and the public did. There were no probabilistic risk assessments involving off-design failure analyses, no environmental impact statements, nor any of the other modern trappings of project reviews. The designers' judgment on the choice of safety factors integrated all uncertainties without an explicit justification of the choices. The public risk was implicitly covered by the presumption of safety arising from the design objective of avoiding failure, but risk was never explicitly estimated. When the unforeseen occasionally occurred, it was usually accepted as an "act of God."

The historical approach to the risk management of a short-lived replaceable product which permitted rapid feedback was one of empirical "trial and error," as, for example, with modern autos and modern airplanes. Operating experience was fed back to guide improvements, a process that continues today. The traditional "safety factor" was less important in such product designs, because the feedback process was sufficiently rapid (a few years) to permit improvements needed for achieving a performance target. The collective public risk was initially low, because only a few individuals were involved in the early developmental stages, although individual risks were high.

540

It should be recognized that the "safety factor" and "trial and error" methodologies continue to be pragmatically useful, and are only slowly being supplemented by modern risk assessment approaches in a limited number of publicly pervasive systems. The public penetration of large-scale technologies has become much more rapid than decades ago, so the "safety factor" and "trial and error" method can be very costly both in public health and cost. This is particularly evident with low-level effects which can develop in a large population. Further, some large-scale systems involve so many interdependent components, that the compounding of individual safety factors would make the system inoperable (e.g. air transport). Finally, very rare but high consequence events may require decades or centuries to provide the feedback information for guiding decisions, and each such occurrence may be undesirably costly to public health and safety. It is these considerations that have encouraged the development of modern risk assessment approaches which try to estimate the probability and magnitude of future events. Such risk assessments disclose the system interactions, sequences, and individual component failure probabilities that produce the final estimate of the probability distribution of a public risk. The assessments thus provide a guide to reiteratively altering the system to reduce the public risk. A notable example is the Probabilistic Risk Assessment (PRA) now common in nuclear plant engineering. Thus risk assessment is a powerful tool for reducing the central value (mean) of the probability distribution of a public risk, but it has little influence on reducing the uncertainties. In fact, risk assessment tends to make the uncertainties more evident by disclosing the sensitivity of the mean value to small variations in the database or the model.

Recognizing the technical merit of an analytical projection of future probabilities, the handling of the uncertainties surrounding such projections is a major obstacle to regulations. It is particularly so when the quantification of an isolated single risk is being sought. For some time, many of us have emphasized that the well known Probabilistic Risk Assessment (PRA) of nuclear plants is useful primarily as a guide to comparative analysis of alternative engineering modifications. Extension of the PRA to a quantification of public risk in an absolute sense is very dubious, for the reasons I've already given.

However, if the objective is a comparison of the relative public risk of alternative electricity generation systems (coal, oil, gas and nuclear), such a comparative quantification has usefulness in managerial and regulatory decision making. Because alternative systems for providing a specific end function may have many common modes of uncertainty, or similar magnitudes of uncertainties, in such a comparative framework the central values (the mean) of quantitative public risk estimates may correctly disclose the relative risks of alternative choices, even if the absolute scale remains uncertain.

It has become very evident that the uncertainties surrounding individual projected public risk estimates will always be large. These uncertainties can be disregarded only when the public risk quantification is so low, that even the upper bound of the uncertainty estimate is below a "de minimis" level (e.g. the aflatoxin constraint in food). For larger risks only the comparative risk analysis of alternatives is meaningful.

It should be emphasized that foreclosure of any technical option forces the acceptance of an alternative. The resulting transfer of public risk to that of an alternative should not be disregarded. Our current example is the nuclear power regulatory debate, presently being conducted without a balanced comparison with the risks of the fossil fuel options.

Eventually, a comparative risk analysis of all electricity alternatives must become the basis of a rational regulatory policy. In general, while much may eventually be accomplished to reduce the uncertainties in public risk analysis, the emphasis should be on the use of comparative risk analysis as a means of reducing the influence of uncertainties on the choice among alternatives for providing an end-function.

TOWARDS COST-EFFECTIVE METHODS FOR REDUCING UNCERTAINTY

IN ENVIRONMENTAL HEALTH DECISION PROCESSES

Adam M. Finkel and
John S. Evans

Harvard School of Public Health
Dept. of Environmental Science
and Physiology
Boston, Massachusetts

ABSTRACT

Multiple uncertainties create two major problems in reaching level-of-control decisions in environmental health decision situations: insecurity about when to stop collecting additional information and proceed with the "optimum" control strategy available, and imprecision about how to allocate resources among various possible uncertainty reductions during this research phase. This paper uses statistical decision theory and a computer simulation package to explore the properties of the response surface relating the expected value of perfect information, total uncertainty, and uncertainty in each parameter contributing to overall health risk (e.g., population exposure, carcinogenic potency, etc.). The framework is then applied to the case study of the research and control decisions EPA faced at the ASARCO smelter in Tacoma, Washington.

KEY WORDS: value of information, cancer risk assessment, error propagation, ASARCO arsenic emissions, utility theory.

I: INTRODUCTION

Surrounding all environmental health decision processes is the spectre of uncertainty, which among other effects always promotes a tension between analysis and action. Rarely is this tension more palpable than when the decision-maker is confronted with the task of balancing environmental controls against the public health risks posed by emissions of toxic or carcinogenic substances. When a potential health problem has been identified and a discrete set of control options mapped out, the decision-maker may believe his task is simply to pick the single "best" option from the feasible set. In fact, the range of choices is far broader, for each decision point has associated with it the additional variable "time"-- time that can be spent refining the knowledge of the problem in order to make more secure the wisdom of the ultimate action. Often (though see Section IV below) it is easy to generate a first approximation of the <u>cost</u> of continuing to analyze a risk-benefit problem.

It is, however, not nearly so straightforward to determine the value of additional information, in order to gauge whether the expected rewards of investigation warrant the various costs of obtaining it. More significantly, a truly optimal decision process would not only arrive at the solution that yields the greatest achievable net benefit, but would take the most efficient and expeditious path to that choice-- and for this it is necessary to know how to allocate research efforts to maximize the ratio of the value of new information to its price.

It is our intention to elucidate general truths about the properties of additional information in environmental health questions where uncertainties exist along two or more dimensions. In this paper, we will: 1) summarize the axioms governing value-of-information theory; 2) present the results of computer simulations that explore the relationship between value-of-information, total uncertainty, and uncertainty along individual dimensions; 3) apply these results to a familiar risk management case study (cancer risks due to arsenic emissions from the ASARCO smelter in Tacoma); and 4) describe the refinements we are currently developing to make our model more applicable for analysis of decisions such as those surrounding uncontrolled hazardous waste sites.

II: DETERMINING THE VALUE OF REDUCING UNCERTAINTY

A. Theory of Expected Value of Perfect Information (EVPI)

The value of information is determined with reference to the concept of expected opportunity loss (EOL). Opportunity loss accrues because the decision-maker must at some point select a strategy before the true values of dose and potency are precisely known. Because for each possible value of risk there is an "optimal" strategy defined by the prevailing decision rule (usually the strategy corresponding to the expected value of risk), there may be some cases wherein the choice made under uncertainty does not match the choice that would have been made were perfect information available. Although there are economic and health costs associated even with the locally optimal strategy, additional costs will accrue whenever the true risk falls outside of the range of values for which the chosen strategy is optimal. EOL is thus the integral over all possible values of risk (appropriately weighted by the probability of risk taking on each value) of the extra costs of choosing what is on average the optimal strategy for those cases where another choice would have been superior:

$$EOL = \int pdf(R) \ [C(R)-C^*(R)] \ dR, \tag{1}$$

where $C(R)$ is the cost of the apparently optimal strategy (evaluated at each value of R) and $C^*(R)$ is the cost of the least-cost strategy associated with that same R.

Assuming the analyst could obtain perfect information about risk at some cost, he would then always pick the strategy for which $C(R)=C^*(R)$, and his EOL would reduce to zero. Faced with a decision node where perfect information could be obtained at a cost equal to the EOL under the existing burden of uncertainty, the decision-maker would be indifferent between obtaining the information and making his best guess about control- -therefore, the expected value of perfect information, EVPI, is exactly equal to EOL. Moreover, moving from a state where EVPI=$X to one where EVPI=$Y implies directly that information worth $(X-Y) has been obtained; thus, the upper bound on the value of any incremental amount of new information is simply the difference in the EOL prior and posterior to the analysis.

In our hypothetical scenarios, three strategies always define the range of control choices. Strategy 1 (no additional controls) incurs no control costs but leaves the uncontrolled health risk R unaffected; Strategy 2 incurs some costs but reduces the risk to (1-E)R, where E is the efficiency of the "best available technology" (BAT); Strategy 3 eliminates all health risk for a fixed cost [the marginal cost of this second increment of risk reduction is assumed to be higher than that of Strategy 2]. Figure 1 shows opportunity loss (OL) as a function of risk for a model scenario. Which graph applies depends on the initial choice of strategy, but EOL is always the integrated product of this function and the pdf over risk. Note that OL is always zero in the region where the chosen strategy matches the optimal strategy, conditional on the given value of risk.

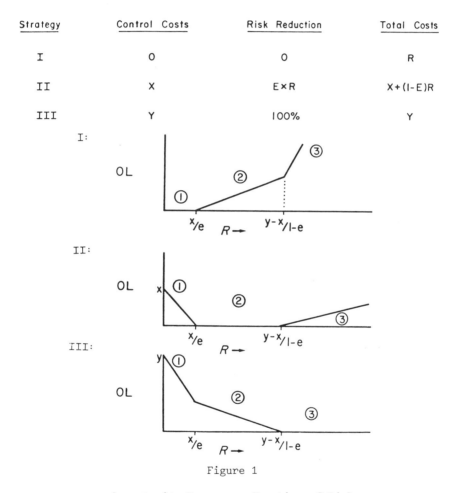

Strategy	Control Costs	Risk Reduction	Total Costs
I	0	0	R
II	X	E×R	X+(1-E)R
III	Y	100%	Y

Figure 1

Opportunity Loss as a Function of Risk

B. Computer Simulation of EOL

We have developed a computer program for the IBM-PC which provides generalizable results about the relationship between uncertainty and value-of-information, using a somewhat restricted set of paradigms for their expositional value. The major flexibilities remaining in this paradigm are the risk in the absence of control, the cost of the risk-elimination option, and the cost and efficiency of the "best available technology" strategy. The pdf for uncertainty in dose or potency could justifiably be drawn from a number of different families, including distributions generated ad hoc by eliciting and pooling the subjective probability estimates of one or more experts (Evans, 1985). We have chosen lognormal distributions primarily because they are simple to manipulate. In addition, many inputs to regulatory processes implicitly assume lognormal variability, most commonly evident in statements that a given estimate is correct "to within a factor of x."

The computer program numerically evaluates equation (1) given a median value for both dose and potency and an assumed geometric standard deviation (s_g) around each estimate. In addition to reporting the EVPI, the program notes the actual ranges of dose values for which each of the three strategies would be optimal if perfect information were available.

C. Theoretical Results

By sequentially varying the geometric standard deviation of both dose and potency over a wide range of possibilities, we were able to discern some of the properties of the response surface relating uncertainty in dose, uncertainty in potency, and value-of-information. The most basic finding concerns the behavior of the surface in the xz and yz planes-- when either uncertainty parameter is held constant, the cross-sections of the response surface are sigmoid in shape. Figures 2 and 3 show this behavior by graphing EVPI at various points and by presenting a contour map of EVPI ismquants, respectively. Essentially, when total uncertainty is very small (s_g of each parameter < 2) and again when it becomes very large (s_g of each parameter > 6), the change in EVPI with uncertainty in dose or potency is relatively small-- the value of marginal improvements in information is often negligible. However, for ordered pairs of s_g(dose) and s_g(potency) yielding moderate to large values of total uncertainty, EVPI can change dramatically following small achievements in uncertainty reduction. For example, Figure 2 shows that it would be worth a maximum of approximately $1.6 million per year ($3.8 million minus $2.2 million) to both improve (s_g) of potency from 5 to 4.5 and improve (s_g) of dose from 3 to 2.5. It is clear that at least for control strategies ordered in this way, by far the most valuable bits of new information are those which enable the decision-maker to increase his confidence that "BAT" is preferred to "closure" for plausible values of risk.

D. Sensitivity Analyses

We then tested the two parameters most likely to influence the response surface. As expected, the spacing of costs for the three strategies strongly affected the appearance of the surface, although the basic shape was preserved in all cross-sections. Lowering the cost of "BAT" from $5 million to $2 million made it the preferred strategy over 3most of the simulations and shifted the location of the steep region of the response surface. This scenario demonstrates another principle of the value-of-information function-- the greatest marginal increases in EOL occur in regions where an unattractive strategy suddenly begins to dominate for a growing region of the pdf over risk.

EVPI (in $1000)

Strategy	Control Cost	Control Efficiency
I	0	0%
II	$5 Million	80%
III	$8 Million	100%

σ_g(DOSE)

σ_g	1	1.5	2	2.5	3	3.5	4	4.5	5	5.5	6	6.5	7	7.5
7.5														5226
7										III			5259	5241
6.5												5299	5278	5260
6						II					5351	5324	5302	5282
5.5										5410	5380	5352	5328	5306
5									4819	5144	5410	5382	5355	5332
4.5								4286	4528	4802	5109	5414	5386	5360
4			I				3924	4080	4279	4503	4758	5043	5358	5392
3.5						2323	3069	3915	4068	4248	4454	4688	4948	5236
3					1173	1685	2295	3000	3801	4034	4198	4386	4597	4832
2.5				441	757	1160	1648	2220	2876	3615	3989	4136	4305	4494
2			79	220	444	750	1134	1593	2126	2732	3411	3942	4073	4224
1.5		.3	16	89	239	466	768	1139	1577	2080	2649	3283	3909	4029
1	0	0	2	43	157	346	608	931	1330	1784	2298	2875	3517	3948

Figure 2

EVPI (in $1000)

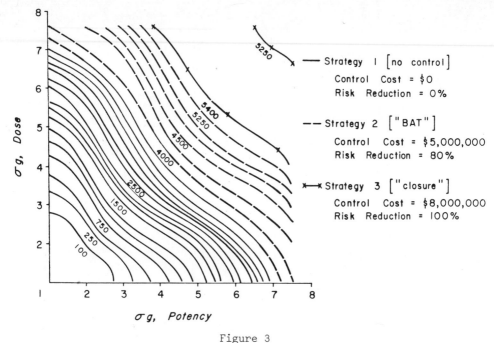

Figure 3

Isoquants of Equal EVPI (in $1000)

The monetary value placed on a statistical death definitely affects
the parameters of the response surface, though not to as dramatic an
extent as might be assumed. When the analysis was repeated with the value
of life placed at $333,333 instead of $1 million per life, the EOL did
decrease at all points, indicating that a decision-maker with this
estimate of the value of life would be less inclined to seek additional
information in every case. The region for which the "no control" choice
was optimal also broadened significantly. However, in a substantial
region of moderate uncertainty in both parameters the EOL for each case
was rather similar. It appears that when one is squarely in the middle of
the range for which the "BAT" strategy is locally optimal, new information
is equally valuable for a broad range of opinion on the value of life.

E. Value of Dose Information

We have to this point been unable to generalize the properties of the
response surface relating expected value of dose information (EVDI) to
uncertainty. This relationship is of particular interest to the
regulator, since reducing uncertainty in dose through ambient or personal
exposure monitoring is generally more feasible in the short-run than
conducting additional generic studies of potency. Our analyses indicate
that EVDI is highly dependent on the relationship between the three
strategies, and on local differences in the gradient of the overall

response surface, and that analysts will therefore need to examine this response surface separately for each decision problem.

III: APPLICATION TO ASARCO CASE

The attempt by the U.S. Environmental Protection Agency (EPA) to explicitly balance the risks and benefits of arsenic emissions at the ASARCO smelter is a useful paradigm not only of the difficulties of including the affected community in the risk-balancing process, but of the role of incremental reduction of uncertainty. In 1983 and 1984, EPA set about trying to apply its newly proposed standard for arsenic emissions to the ASARCO plant, the only facility in the country processing copper ore with high arsenic concentrations (Kalikow, 1984). The situation was ripe for regulation, as EPA's first estimate of the number of cancer deaths among the local population ranged from 1.4 to 22 deaths/yr. Table 1 shows the three control options EPA was contemplating at that time, along with our estimates of the costs and efficiencies of each. In this case, BAT entailed the installation of secondary hoods on the copper converters; the most stringent option, which ASARCO claimed would force closure of the plant, involved limiting the arsenic content of any ore processed to 0.7 weight percent.

Table 1

ASARCO Control Scenario

Control Strategy	Control Cost (10^6/yr)	Risk Reduction Efficiency	Expected Total Cost (10^6/yr)
A - no additional controls	0	0	$\hat{R}$
B - converter hoods ("BAT")	0.92 [a]	75% [b]	.92+ .25$\hat{R}$
C - regulations forcing closure	20 [c]	100%	20

NOTES:

(a) The cost estimate is comprised of $757,000 in annual operating costs ($117,000 of which is increased electricity use) and capital costs of $3.5 million annualized over a 20-year period.

(b) EPA estimates that the hoods will remove 95% of arsenic emissions from the converters. Other fugitive emission sources will be unaffected by BAT. Since these sources account for about 50% of estimated arsenic concentrations near the plant, and about 15% in the remaining areas (where most of the predicted risks accrue), we estimate that the residual risk would be 20% from the other fugitive sources in addition to the 5% residual from the converters.

(c) Plant closure would cause the Tacoma area to lose $20 million annually in goods and services purchased by ASARCO.

In June 1984, ASARCO announced it would shut down its Tacoma plant, citing falling world copper prices and difficulty meeting the state of Washington's standard for SO_2 emissions. Despite this outcome, analysis of the uncertainties surrounding the three strategies and EPA's attempts to reduce them provides a good test case for our computer model of value-of-information.

A. EPA's Dose Calculations

In the summer of 1983, EPA used the Human Exposure Model (HEM),consisting of the ISCLT air dispersion model and the MED-X data base for local population density estimates, to estimate aggregate exposure to arsenic in the Tacoma area. This combination led to an initial median estimate for the total dose to the approximately 368,000 people living within 20 km of the plant of approximately 103,000 persons*ug/m3. However, EPA soon discovered that the uncertainty around this estimate was rather substantial, as actual ambient concentration values supplied by ASARCO indicated that near the plant EPA was overestimating levels by up to a factor of 20 (EPA Region X press release, 1983). In general, the Agency believed at this time that only about half of its predicted values were within a factor of 2 of the true values. Two conditions in particular fostered this lack of precision. First, the ISCLT model does not account for potential fumigation of the plume due to the proximity of Puget Sound (leading to possible underestimation of concentrations) or peculiarities in topography (the smelter is built on the side of a steep hill) that could lead to overprediction in many instances. More significantly, once actual stack tests were conducted and fugitive emissions observed, it became clear that EPA's assumptions about emissions rates overestimated arsenic output from some sources (estimates for the main stack were lowered from 165 tons/yr. to 57 tons/yr., and for the converters from 132 to 17 tons/yr.),but underestimated the severity of other fugitive emissions at or near ground level (these estimates were revised upwards from 14 to 34 tons/yr.). Because very little of the predicted risk was due to contributions from the main stack, and because ground-level emissions are particularly troublesome, these errors tended to balance each other.

In response to these deficiencies, EPA improved their dose model using the new emissions estimates, plant-specific meteorologic data, and a dynamic algorithm that took into account ASARCO's tendency to cut back operations during weather conditions that made it probable the SO_2 standard would be exceeded (EPA, personal communication).

B. Potency Calculations

For their original estimate of the "unit risk" of respiratory cancer due to arsenic inhalation (i.e., the excess lifetime probability of contracting lung cancer if exposed to 1 ug/m^3 arsenic continuously for 70 years), EPA relied on three epidemiologic studies of occupational exposures (EPA, 1984): 1) Pinto et al. (1977), a study of workers at the Tacoma smelter; 2) Lee and Fraumeni (1969), a study of the Anaconda smelter in Montana; and 3) Ott et al. (1974), a study of pesticide workers exposed to arsenate compounds. For each of the studies, EPA fit a relative-risk model to the data, using the linear no-threshold assumption that R (the relative risk) is equal to $1+(B*D/P_0)$, where B, D, and P_0 are the potency of arsenic, the cumulative dose, and the background probability of getting lung cancer (derived from U.S. age-specific incidence data), respectively. After fitting the best regression line through the origin for each of the studies, EPA pooled the three maximum likelihood estimates of relative risk at 1 ug/m^3 by taking their geometric mean, and derived the pooled unit risk by multiplying by $(1-R)*P_0$. This pooled estimate was 2.91×10^{-3}/lifetime, or 4.2×10^{-5}/yr.

Recently, EPA has revised the unit risk estimate (EPA, 1984) slightly upward to 6.13×10^{-5}/yr., making use of new data and concluding that a

linear, absolute-risk model best fit all of the suitable data. Again, EPA
took the geometric mean of the unit risk estimates to establish a single
point estimate.

C. Uncertainty in Dose

In their public statements about the potential risks from ASARCO
emissions, EPA effectively treated the aggregate dose value as having no
uncertainty, the range of expected cancer incidence deriving entirely from
uncertainty in potency (see below). It is evident, though, that both the
initial and final estimates of total dose have significant associated
uncertainty, although substantial improvement was made during the
refinement process discussed above.

We estimate the initial uncertainty as lognormally distributed with
s_g = 3.6; i.e., 95% of the estimated doses for individual population
segments would lie within a factor of 13 above or below the true value.
This is consistent with EPA statements that only half of all initial
predictions were correct to within a factor of two, and the observation
that at least some isolated predictions were in error by a factor of 20.
Formally, we arrived at our estimate for s_g by propagating three lognormal
error processes: 1) modeling error for the ISCLT model when site-specific
meteorologic data is unavailable (s_g=3)(EPA, 1982); 2) imprecision of
emission rates (s_g=1.4); and 3) inability to predict whether the standard
Gaussian plume or the fumigation model is appropriate (s_g=2).

According to EPA (personal communication), once the refined exposure
model and emissions estimates were in place, the range of estimates for a
given ambient concentration value were almost all an order of magnitude or
less in breadth. So, we can assume that 95 percent of the predictions
were within a factor of 3 of the true values, implying an "improved" s_g of
1.7.

D. Uncertainty in Potency

According to EPA, the original unit risk estimate of 4.2×10^{-5}/yr. had
a lognormal uncertainty of s_g = 2.3 surrounding it. EPA derived this
figure simply by calculating the standard deviation of the logarithms of
the estimates from the three epidemiologic studies and
exponentiating. [The revised estimate of 6.13×10^{-5} had no uncertainty
calculation with it, although we used the above procedure and got
essentially the same estimate for s_g.]

We assert that this uncertainty estimate overstates the confidence
with which the potency of arsenic can be known. Several factors not
considered by EPA would be expected to broaden the pdf for potency,
including: 1) lack of certainty about which dose-response function and
which model specification (absolute or relative risk) is biologically
appropriate (Crouch and Wilson, 1981) ; 2) imprecision of exposure
estimates in the occupational cohorts; 3) uncertainty about whether to use
national or state-specific "background" rates in calculating "expected
deaths"; 4) exclusion of variations in human susceptibility from the model
(Finkel, 1985a); and 5) uncertainty about whether measuring cumulative
exposure as simply the product of concentration and duration is
appropriate (Brown and Chu, 1983). Few of these factors are amenable to
quantitative resolution. However, EPA's uncertainty estimate is
undoubtedly a lower bound on the actual uncertainty in potency.

E. Results of Simulation

We then applied our computer routine to the ASARCO scenario outlined
in Table 1. Unlike the hypothetical scenarios, where the median risk was
set arbitrarily at 1 death/yr., the EOL takes on rather large values in
this scenario because the central estimate of the number of deaths is
$(6.13 \times 10^{-5})(103,000) = 6.3$ deaths/yr.

The simulation showed that the assumed value of improved dose
information does depend strongly on what the uncertainty in potency is
taken to be. If we took EPA's s_g for potency as true, our calculations
show that the reduction in s_g(dose) from 3.6 to 1.7 would be worth a
maximum of $720,000 per year (for a net present value of about $10 million
assuming a 5% discount rate and a 20-year time horizon). If, however, the
95% confidence interval for potency is twice as broad as EPA believed
(i.e., $s_g = 3.3$), the same achievement in reducing s_g(dose) takes on a
value of nearly $1.5 million per year. Our estimates of the value of
improved exposure estimates are based on a high value for the social cost
of ASARCO closure, $20 million per year. If instead, we use closure costs
one half to one fourth this large, we obtain even larger estimates of the
value of improved exposure estimates.

According to EPA (personal communication), at least $500,000 was
spent, exclusive of the time spent by EPA staff, to generate the improved
dose information. Thus, it seems that even if the potency of arsenic was
as well-characterized as EPA's initial estimate would indicate, this money
was probably well-spent.

IV. ONGOING REFINEMENTS OF VALUE OF INFORMATION MODEL

We believe that application of this simple value of information model
would yield significant improvements over the haphazard way information-
gathering resources are currently allocated. However, during the next
year we intend to refine our analysis to more closely approximate the
complexity of current environmental health decision processes. We have
identified four areas where added complexity in the model is most likely
to broaden its utility:

• Allowing for uncertainty in estimates of control efficiency.

• More thorough analysis of the many separable sources of uncertainty
in estimates of dose. These include uncertainties in biochemical fate
and transformation, uncertainties in estimating-long range patterns of
land use and behavior of human populations, and uncertainties in the
estimates of the uncertainty inherent in application of environmental
transport models in specific situations of interest.

• Analysis of the costs of obtaining improved risk estimates.
Analysts need to consider not only the direct costs of obtaining
information, but also the social costs and economic inefficiencies that
occur as a result of delays in decision-making.

• Incorporation of "regret theory." Rather than focusing solely on
measures of central tendency of risk and social cost, by incorporating
utility theory we intend to more closely approximate the actual social
costs associated with any specified level of residual risk.

To conclude, we envision that further applied research in this field will lead to development of an analytic tool useful for quickly differentiating situations where slight reductions in uncertainty lead to large social benefits from those where relatively large reductions in uncertainty are of almost no consequence.

ACKNOWLEDGEMENTS

We thank the many talented persons who have contributed to this effort. In particular, Bettina Burbank, Rick Letz and Avis Stiller deserve mention. In addition, we thank Henry Lee of the Harvard University Energy and Environmental Policy Center for his initial support of the work.

REFERENCES

1. Brown, Charles C. and Kenneth C. Chu, 1983. "Implications of the Multistage Theory of Carcinogenesis Applied to Occupational Arsenic Exposure." Journal of the National Cancer Institute, 70, 455-63.
2. Crouch, Edmund and Richard Wilson, 1981. "Regulation of Carcinogens." Risk Analysis, 1, 47-57.
3. Evans, John S., Douglas W. Cooper, and Patrick Kinney, 1984. "On the Propagation of Error in Air Pollution Measurements." Environmental Monitoring and Assessment, 4, 139-53.
4. Evans, John S., 1985. "The Value of Improved Exposure Estimates: A Decision Analytic Approach." Presented at the 78th Annual Meeting of the Air Pollution Control Association (APCA), June 1985.
5. Finkel, Adam M., 1985a. "Modeling the Implications of Lognormally-Distributed Susceptibility to Environmental Carcinogens." Presented at the 78th Annual Meeting of APCA, June 1985.
6. Finkel, Adam M., 1985b. "Setting Appropriate Levels of Carcinogen Protection in Light of Human Susceptibilities and Perceptions." Presented at the International Student Pugwash Conference, Princeton, N.J., June 1985.
7. Kalikow, Barnett, 1984. "Environmental Risk: Power to the People." Technology Review, October 1984, 55-61.
8. Office of Technology Assessment (OTA), 1985. Superfund Strategy, April 1985.
9. Raiffa, Howard and Robert Schlaifer, 1961. Applied Statistical Decision Theory, M.I.T. Press.
10. U.S. Environmental Protection Agency (EPA), 1983a. "Source Contribution to Ambient Air Quality Estimates for Arsenic at the ASARCO Tacoma Smelter," letter from Joseph A. Tikvart to Robert J. Ajax, Aug. 12, 1983.
11. U.S. EPA, 1983b. "New Data on Arsenic Emissions from Tacoma's ASARCO Smelter...," Region X News Release, Oct. 20, 1983.
12. U.S. EPA, 1984. Health Assessment Document for Inorganic Arsenic, Office of Health and Environmental Assessment (EPA-600/8-83-021F), March 1984.

PRIORITIZING HEALTH RISK ASSESSMENTS

Gary R. Rosenblum

Toxicologist
Atlantic Richfield Company

ABSTRACT

Health Risk Assessments are being conducted with increasing
frequency. The stages of a Health Risk Assessment (HRA) are generally
described as Problem Identification, Hazard Assessment, Exposure
Characterization, Risk Analysis, and Risk Management. While much emphasis
is correctly placed on the risk analysis step, the problem identification
stage is often overlooked. When resources to conduct HRA's are limited,
prioritization becomes a key process, especially for corporations faced
with the need to fully assess numerous chemicals. Identifying a list of
chemical candidates for HRA is only a first step that should be followed
by a systematic priority analysis. Data from a priority analysis of
petroleum products and petrochemicals were generated and analyzed. The
data were generated through use of an Integrated Risk Index System, which
was first presented by the author at the 1983 Society of Risk Analysis
Meeting. Conclusions are reached suggesting that the important factors
necessary for informed, defensible prioritization decisions can be
categorized as "inherent," "internal," and "external." The detailed
description of these three factors provide a working guide for generating
informed judgments how best to apply limited resources to assess the
health risks of a large group of chemical candidates.

KEY WORDS: Risk, Prioritization, Health Risk Assessment

Awareness of potential health effects caused by exposure to chemicals
has increased dramatically in the past few years. As a result,
corporations that manufacture, sell, and purchase chemicals are examining
which of the chemicals they handle present health risks to their
employees, their customers, or the public. In a large corporation this
could be an enormous task because the health risks of hundreds of
chemicals may have to be assessed.

Each individual health risk assessment (HRA) is a multi-stage process
consisting of problem identification, hazard assessment, exposure
characterization, risk analysis, options analysis, and finally risk
management. Much emphasis is rightly placed on developing and refining
the risk analysis stage. However, the practical necessity of developing a
systematic approach to the problem identification stage has been somewhat
overlooked.

With large numbers of chemicals to assess, corporations and
regulatory agencies will no longer find it sufficient to simply identify a

list of chemicals requiring HRA. Arranging the chemical candidates for HRA according to a perceived priority is essential. The importance of prioritizing chemicals after identifying them for HRA becomes clear when it is seen that a perfectly conducted risk assessment is not very useful if the assessed chemical is of little importance to the corporation, and limited resources were diverted from the assessment of more appropriate chemicals.

When resources and the time to conduct HRA's are limited, finding the appropriate chemicals to assess becomes a key process of the identification stage, especially for the industrial companies and regulatory agencies faced with the need to assess hundreds or even thousands of chemicals. It would be difficult to specifically define a standard format that would always be successful identifying the appropriate chemicals for HRA. However, it is possible to develop some general principles for prioritizing chemicals for HRA that can be applied in a wide variety of specific situations. I will discuss these principles in terms of developing a systematic method for ranking chemical candidates for HRA.

A well designed systematic method for prioritization will be rapid, consistent, effective with limited data, and defensible. The usefulness of any prioritization system depends on maximizing all these traits. If one is traded off for another, such as reducing defensibility to gain rapidity, the overall effectiveness of the system is reduced.

A rapid prioritization system will rank a list of chemicals in as little time as possible. It is logical to assume that when more time is spent ranking chemicals on a candidate list, less time is spent conducting the HRA's on those chemicals. The system, therefore has to be designed to use time efficiently. It should not be overly complex, but instead, require only a few steps to achieve the placement of a single chemical.

I don't believe that rigorous mathematical formulations are necessary for a rapid prioritization system. When more complex mathematics are used, it seems, a deeper data search is required, which bogs the initial HRA step down in areas that are best left to the more difficult risk analysis step. Finally, the system should be designed to be computerized, for obvious time efficiency reasons.

Consistency is critical for any prioritization system, and without it, the system will be useless. Consistency allows more than one person to use the system, so that tasks can be delegated to different people. It should use a standardized format, so that there is less chance of making an error on any of the operations performed on each chemical.

Consistency can be achieved more easily when a quantitative system is employed. If each chemical can be assigned a score that represents an estimate of its potential health risk relative to the other chemicals on a list, the chemicals can be compared in a consistent manner, and appropriately ranked.

The system must be effective even when the data base for a chemical is limited. The criteria for scoring the chemicals must be developed with the understanding that there will be data gaps. The criteria for scoring the chemicals should be sufficiently flexible to allow professional judgment to substitute for incomplete information.

Consistency will lead to a more accurate prioritization of HRA candidate chemicals, which in turn creates a more defensible system.

Defending a prioritization system could be of major importance to a corporation or government agency, particularly in a courtroom where it might be necessary to explain why risk assessments have been conducted for certain chemicals, and not for others. A defensible system will also provide support for explaining to the management of a corporation why certain chemicals have been singled out for HRA's.

In order to create a rapid, consistent, and defensible system, criteria that will enable the reviewers to quantitatively assess the candidate chemicals need to be developed. I will describe those factors I have found to be well balanced between being simple and quick, and delivering a scientifically accurate representation of relative risk.

There are three groups of factors that are useful in building a successful HRA prioritization system. I call these three groups of factors the Inherent Factors, the Internal Factors, and the External Factors. Within each of these three groups are subfactors, which when assessed and quantified, can be used to rank chemicals for HRA.

The Inherent Factors describe the properties of a chemical which, as a result of interaction with a biological organism, are harmful. There are three types of hazards that can be considered as Inherent Factors when reviewing chemicals for risk prioritization.

One is the health hazard of the chemical. The toxicological data describes the biological response to contact with the chemical, and what amount of the chemical causes that response. A health hazard assessment of a chemical can consist of reviewing human data, animal bioassay data, or short-term animal or in vitro data. Sometimes a structure-activity analysis is also useful.

The physical hazards of the chemical are the next group of Inherent factors to consider. This is a review of the flammability and explosivity of the material, a type of hazard that may sometimes be overlooked in a risk analysis. For instance, a risk analysis of a chemical that is based strictly on carcinogenicity, but does not consider that the material is extremely flammable, may greatly underestimate the potential for that chemical to cause instant harm.

The third set of Inherent factors that are important to review are the environmental properties of a material. The two major categories of interest are bioaccumulation, and adverse ecological effects, which are also sometimes overlooked in risk assessments. A preliminary risk assessment should consider what damage a chemical could do to the food chain, or non-human organisms if they were exposed to the chemical.

The three factors, health hazard, physical hazard, and environmental hazard are termed Inherent Factors because the specific properties of a chemical that will cause it to interact with a specific biological organism in a particular way are inherent to that chemical. These inherent characteristics can be objectively measured by using scientific methods. The ability of a chemical to explode at a particular temperature, or cause cancer in a particular species at a certain dose level, or bioaccumulate in a particular fish at a certain rate can be experimentally tested and scientifically assessed. As factors inherent to the chemical, they are not subject to control or alteration by a corporation or government agency.

Now that the first important factors have been identified, it is necessary to propose criteria that will allow a reviewer to quickly and accurately quantify the relative level of hazard inherent to the chemical. I have used the criteria outlined in Rosenblum et al. (in press) successfully, but there is no reason why these criteria cannot be modified to suit specific prioritization needs.

Criteria were assigned to score six areas of health hazard: acute hazards, subchronic hazards, carcinogenicity, mutagenicity, teratogenicity, and reproductive effects. The actual criteria for each hazard and how they are scored are covered in detail elsewhere (Rosenblum et al., in press).

The criteria allow each type of health hazard to be rapidly reviewed, an assigned a numerical score corresponding to the level of toxicity. Higher scores indicate that the chemical is toxic at lower doses. Weighting can be worked into the system at this point to compensate for what is sometimes considered differing levels of severity among the health hazards. For instance, the carcinogenicity score can be given more weight than the mutagenicity score. The individual scores for each type of health hazard are than combined into a single health hazard score.

A similar process takes place for the physical hazard and environmental hazard review. Chemicals that are more flammable or explosive receive a higher score, as do chemicals that are highly toxic to wildlife or fish, and rapidly bioaccumulate. The result will be three numbers representing physical hazards, environmental hazards, and health hazards, which are then combined into a single "hazard" score.

Each type of hazard would ideally be scored by an appropriately trained individual. A toxicologist would score the health hazards, a fire safety specialist would score the physical hazards, and an environmental biologist would score the environmental hazards. Each could then input their number into a computer program which would store, collate, and calculate the results.

Once the inherent hazards of a chemical have been characterized by numerical scores, it is logical to then characterize the potential exposure to that chemical by a numerical score. it is interesting to contrast the control that a corporation has over either the inherent hazards (minimal) or the potential exposure (significant). A corporation can exert far greater control over potential exposure, which leads me to describe the factors used to characterize potential exposure as Internal factors. The factors are Internal in the sense that the amount of the chemical produced, and how many employees or customers will come in contact with the chemical, are largely based on internal corporate decisions.

It is possible to produce a relatively accurate representation of the potential exposure to a chemical by considering chemical related factors, employee/public related factors, and environmental discharge factors. The chemical related factors score the chemical simply on how much of it is produced. For a prioritization system it is good enough to compare chemicals based on how much is produced, rather than trying to assemble industrial hygiene data which is more appropriate for a full HRA. It does not seem illogical to assume that ten million pounds of a chemical is more likely to result in exposures to more people then ten thousand pounds.

The physical form of the chemical can also be taken into account. Chemicals can also be scored on the basis of whether they are gases, volatile liquids, non-volatile liquids, dusty or powdered solids or non-dusty solids.

It is also important to look at who could be exposed to the chemical. It would be ideal to know exactly how many people could possibly be exposed, but that data is not likely to be readily available. Instead, populations can be identified and a score assigned based on the control the corporation has over a potential exposure. This is done by characterizing the potentially exposed populations as belonging to one of three groups: occupationally exposed through production of the chemical; occupationally exposed through consumption of the chemical; or exposed through public consumer use of the chemical from a finished product.

While exposures to workers may occur in the production of a chemical, a corporation has significant control over the manner in which the chemical is handled. It can measure for the chemical in the workplace. It can provide engineering controls or personal protective equipment. It can adjust worker shifts, and the number of workers exposed. A corporation loses much of this control when the chemical leaves the production facility and goes to an industrial consumer. It can label to warn, and recommend handling procedures, but there is really no way to guarantee or control what will happen to that chemical. As a result, the potential for exposure should be considered increased.

Finally, the least control is exerted over the general public that can be exposed through use of a finished product containing the chemical. How many warning and handling labels are unread? How many inappropriate uses will be found for the product? The industrial consumer is likely to have some training in proper handling procedures. When a chemical reaches the general public, almost all control over the potential exposure is lost.

Reduced control over potential exposure translates into an increased risk of exposure to a larger number of people who will be more heterogeneous for age and sex. Therefore, chemicals with the potential for consumer use should be ranked higher than those in strictly industrial use.

If there is some doubt about precisely categorizing the extent of use of the chemical by each population, then environmental discharge, (another Internal factor) can be considered. If some the chemical is released into the atmosphere, poured into rivers, or eventually buried, there is a possibility of widespread exposure. Considering the route of environmental discharge, if any exists, and approximating how much discharge occurs is useful for gauging and scoring the potential exposure.

The two potential exposure scores I've used consist of estimating the amount of chemical produced, then assessing the populations that use the chemical, and weighting that score with consideration of the potential for exposure through environmental discharge of the chemical. These two scores are then combined into the potential exposure score.

Once the inherent hazards and potential exposure of the chemical are estimated and represented by two numbers, a relative risk estimate can be calculated by multiplying the two numbers, simply based on the concept that risk is a function of hazard and exposure. In fact, an Integrated Risk Index System developed by Rosenblum et al. (in press) was based on that concept.

However, after applying the system to rank chemicals for the development of hazard warnings, it became clear that to provide a system for accurately reflecting a corporation's priorities for HRA, another group of factors had to be considered.

Including another group of factors into the risk prioritization calculation resulted from the realization that corporations do not set priorities and commit resources to HRA in a vacuum. There are extensive, and powerful influences from outside of a corporation that can significantly impact on a risk prioritization decision. These influences, which can be termed External Factors, include commercial importance, government regulation, litigation, and media coverage of a chemical.

While the latter three factors are beyond the direct control of a corporation, the first factor, commercial importance of the chemical, is within the realm of corporate control and has significant impact on corporation HRA decision making. This factor is external in the sense that revenue derived from a chemical depends on its position in the marketplace, and it is becoming increasingly clear that the marketplace is responding to concerns about health risks. It is becoming more common to find certain products being touted as "safer" than a competitor's product.

The External factors that a corporation has little direct control over also can have a major impact on HRA priority. Toxic tort litigation is beginning to be recognized as a potentially major drain on the financial resources of a corporation. Sometimes out-of-court settlements have the effect of suspending scientific judgment of a chemical's actual level of risk. A settlement creates a precedent suggesting that any exposure to the particular chemical involved in the litigation can be harmful. These precedents can provide ammunition for further litigation. The only real defense against future litigation is to control present and future exposures. Increased litigation concerning a chemical can be used as a signal to a corporation that the risks posed by the chemical should be assessed and managed.

Societal concerns about a chemical are eventually reflected by the extent of government activity to characterize and control the chemical's risk. An assessment of External factors should include a review of government activities such as lists of hazardous substances for right-to-know laws, rebuttable presumptions of adverse effects, health effects test rules, and TSCA 8(e) and 8(c) notifications. It is also obvious that a chemical should be considered a high priority if a government agency is already proceeding with risk assessment activities on that chemical.

If government activity concerning a chemical reflects societal concerns about the chemical, what influence shapes society's opinions? Clearly, the news media can play a major role in determining the public's opinion of the health risk presented by a chemical, and it seems logical therefore to consider this as an External factor as well. When public attention is focused on a chemical by the news media, the perceived risk, which in many cases can be as important as the "actual" risk, increases dramatically. Both government activity and toxic tort litigation seem to increase in direct proportion to the extent of the media coverage. The recent media event and subsequent government response concerning ethylene dibromide (EDB) is a classic example of this effect.

The criteria for quantifying the External factors can be flexible, but there seem to be some useful possibilities for scoring the extent of the commercial importance of the chemical, and the influence of litigation, government activity, and the news media. The simplest method to quantify the commercial importance of a chemical is to determine the revenue derived from its sales. This information may sometimes be difficult to acquire, so other means such as number of units sold could be used. It is also not strictly necessary to directly input commercial

560

importance into the risk prioritization process because the "amount produced" factor, which was assessed as part of the potential exposure category, could be considered an indirect measure of a chemical's commercial importance.

Litigation can be scored by considering the number of cases, the number of plaintiffs, and the dollar value of the cases. Government regulation can be quantified by assigning point values to different areas of toxic substance regulation based on the impact the type of regulation could have on the company. Higher values would be assigned to those government activities that occur after an agency has already identified the chemical through their own risk prioritization process. The news media impact can be scored simply on whether the chemical has been covered by local, regional, or national news media, with the highest score going to national coverage. The External factor can then be derived from a summation of these four scores, and can provide a corporation with an indication of whether a chemical can be described as having a "high profile" externally.

Scoring the factors I've identified will result in three numbers: the ratings for relative hazard, exposure, and External factors. The Integrated Risk Index System that I have used for prioritizing a group of petroleum products, and a group of petrochemicals multiplies the hazard score by the exposure score, which leads to an indication of relative risk. An External factor score could then be multiplied by the relative risk score to provide further input into the prioritization process. It seems desirable to input the External factor after the relative risk is indexed in order to better visualize the differences between priority based on "actual" risk, and priority based on "perceived" risk. Also it could be decided to apply the External factor only to the "top ten" of the relative risk list, in order to fine tune the priorities of the clearly high risk chemicals.

This discussion of developing a risk prioritization system is intended as a guide not a blueprint. I have covered what I believe to be the significant factors that should be considered when the risks of a large group of materials must be assessed. It is up to the individual or the corporation to decide which factors are necessary for generating an informed judgment how best to apply limited resources to the risk assessment process. It is hoped that this discussion makes the enormous task of conducting Health Risk Assessments on numerous chemicals easier, more efficient, and more accurate.

REFERENCE

Rosenblum, G. R., Effron, W.S., Siva, J.L., Mancini, E.R., Roth, R.N. (in press) An Integrated Risk Index System, Proceedings of the Society for Risk Analysis, 1983 Annual Meeting, New York.

A DISCUSSION OF SOME OF THE PROBLEMS ENCOUNTERED IN

COMMUNICATING RISK ASSESSMENTS TO DECISION MAKERS*

C. Richard Cothern and William L. Marcus

US Environmental Protection Agency
Washington, D.C. 20460

ABSTRACT

Three general areas where problems occur in the attempt to
communicate risk assessment information to decisionmakers are examined and
discussed. These areas include the language used, the use of uncertainty
and probability concepts and the complex nature of risk assessments.
Possible resolutions discussed relating to these problems include the use
of positive words, more clarity and education.

KEYWORDS: Risk, Assessment, Management, Decisionmaker, Environmental

1. INTRODUCTION

One of the major problems faced daily by scientists in attempting to
communicate environmental risks to risk managers is the use of the
language. Almost all risk managers lack scientific training or
background. There are many important scientific questions that must be
addressed in making decisions concerning environmental contaminants. In
order to assess the situation, the decision maker needs to understand all
the available information. However, there appears to be a gap between
those presenting the information concerning environmental contaminants and
their resulting risks and those who need to understand the importance of
those risks. Some of these gaps are the result of miscommunication and
these aspects are discussed and analyzed here.

There are many factors that militate against effective communication.
The three that are examined here are: language or the lack of clarity and
understanding or the way we speak about risks due to environmental
contaminants, the use of concepts such as probability and uncertainty,
and the lack of background understanding of the complex quantitative
nature of risk analysis.

Our use of language is done often with little thought about how the
receiver (listener) decodes and interprets what is heard. We can,
unknowingly, make the situation worse or distort information by our choice
of words. A simple example of this is in describing the glass half full
or half empty.

---

*The thoughts and ideas discussed here are those of the the authors
and are not necessarily those of the U.S. Environmental Protection Agency.

There are generally two ways to view reality-- either it is exactly black or white or it is grey. Many risk managers live in a grey world but they perceive it as a precise black or white world. To them the number is either 2.756 or 2.757. Doing something is either safe or it isn't. An environmental contaminant is either harmful or not. But reality is a range of safe, harmful or risky. The effect of an environmental contaminant may vary with concentration, characteristics such as sex, and physical factors such as weather, geology and chemistry. It is in the communication of this probabilistic character of reality that we scientists often fail.

An important characteristic of our probabilistic world is its uncertainty. What do we know for sure? Yet we expect definite answers to the question of whether it is safe, acceptable or whether to regulate! The information and data needed to try and answer these questions is not exact and precise. It is an inherent result of the measurement and estimation process that each quantity has some uncertainty or error. All too often this uncertainty is not communicated with the data, especially when communicated serially through several layers of management.

The discussion that follows is far from an extensive survey of problems encountered in trying to communicate risk assessment information to those who make decisions concerning the regulation of environmental contaminants. The situation is presented from the viewpoint of the environmental scientist. What follows are musings, rambling thoughts and some suggestions for improving this communication link.

2. DOES OUR CHOICE OF WORDS MAKE THE SITUATION WORSE?

All too often we choose words to express the results of risk assessment that have negative connotations. The word risk itself connotes a feeling of danger, insecurity and precariousness. For example, we use such bad sounding words as toxic, hazard, chronic, carcinogen (see a suggested list in Table 1).

Using words that are highly mathematical and technical would seem a poor idea in a society that is characterized by being non-mathematical and even to some degree suspicious and afraid of matters mathematical (after all it takes a modern major general in the Pirates of Penzance to be able to understand matters mathematical). Words such as extrapolate, estimate, guesstimate and statistical are far from reassuring. In fact, they connote the idea that we really don't know what is going on. And for those with some mathematical background, the idea of extrapolating a curve into the unknown is somewhere between dubious and a shocking procedure.

Also used in describing a risk assessment are a lexicon of words meant to reassure but that convey definitive negative feelings. Consider words such as: minimal risk, virtually safe dose, maximum tolerated dose, de minimis (non curat lex or the law does not concern itself with trifles). To many this is like being partly pregnant. Their response to such phraseology is to ask if it is safe or not. At this point the person trying to convey risk assessment information needs to realize that little reassurance or information is being communicated by such phrases.

A major misunderstanding for the decisionmaker is the use of statistical terminology in non-statistical analyses. Statistics require measured data points upon which accepted mathematical analyses are performed. These procedures then produce variances of the measured data, 95% confidence levels based on the data, and error terms. Those involved

Table 1

List of Words Used in Describing a Risk Assessment
That Convey Positive or Good and Negative or Bad Connotations

Bad Connotation, Bad Sounding or Negative Words

absolutely	interpretation
acute	judgement
always	law suit
anxiety	lifetime exposure
average	maximum tolerated dose
below regulatory concern	mimimal risk
carcinogen	never
causality	nuclear(e.g. NMR to MR)
controversy	perilous
chancy	poisonous
chronic	precarious
cost	probability
danger	provocation
decision	radiation
di minimis	regulations
dispute	risky
estimation (over- or under-)	scientific
evaluation	statistical
extrapolate	statistics
fear	technical
guesstimate	toxic
hazardous)	uncertainty
insecure	unsafe
	virtually safe dose

Good Connotations, Good Sounding Words, Positive Meaning or Connotation

acceptable	prevention
admissible	reliable
assurance	responsible
benefit	safety
choice	security
confidence (as in 95% confidence level)	stable
common sense	strength
dependable	threshold
faith	tolerable
free	truth
freedom	trust
health	unforced
intact	voluntary
no effect	willing
predictable	zero risk

in risk analyses have borrowed the terminology and applied it to
hypothetical data sets derived from some arbitrarily chosen mathematically
chosen model. This mistakenly gives the decisionmaker the false
confidence that he is dealing with actual statistical data from which the
true number can be determined.

A common mistake is to express risk assessments with absolute words.

Using words like always and never (e.g., the toxic material in the town dump will never reach your well), ultimately leads to suspicion as most people feel that almost anything is possible. The decisionmaker is at one extreme thinking that all health effects are due to some pollutant in his air or drinking water. Expressing a risk assessment at the other extreme by saying it isn't possible does little to allay fears.

Often the very words that have a negative character are used too freely. Constant use of words like anxiety, fear, cancer, controversy, radiation and hazard should be held to a minimum. The proper use of these words should not be avoided or minimized, the point is to tell the whole truth and nothing but the truth.

Society is full or misrepresentations, myths and lies. Ideas such as cancer is always fatal, the nuclear reactor or town dump will not pollute the river and dioxin always does bad things to humans, feed what may be an already high level of fear, anxiety and guilt. Once an official has made the mistake of propagating a lie, he is stuck with these emotions and will likely continue to convey them (see Reference 1 for a recent discussion of the phenomena of lying).

Sometimes we use language to seduce us to accept the unthinkable. In the area of nuclear devices we use words like accident, overkill and arms control to mask a highly deadly force. In risk assessment similarly we have language such as cases averted, excess cases and population risk that are used which often mask the real meaning.

Too often the question of whether a situation is safe arises too late for an education process to be possible. Statements that the level of risk is low (even of the order of 10-6 per lifetime) are not reassuring. The truth must be made clear as soon as it is known or any trust will be destroyed. This trust will likely be best built at the local level since ultimately the local community will likely be the one to deal with risk management.

In order to minimize fear, anxiety and misunderstanding, language should be used that provides a more balanced picture. It might be tempting to misuse words to deceive, but the responsible official seeks to convey the truth. The objective is to avoid words with an unnecessary negative connotation. Examples of words with a positive connotation are given in table 1. Instead of technical jargon such as estimate, why not say this is our knowledge or understanding. It sounds better to say that 'we determined that' instead of 'we estimate that' or 'we conclude that.'

The above discussion is admittedly short and far from comprehensive. However, if those doing and communicating risk assessment information would think some about the words used to express the results, a more balanced picture can be conveyed and some trust can be built.

3. COMMUNICATING THE PROBABILISTIC ASPECT OF RISK ASSESSMENT

We live in a probabilistic world where very little, if anything, is totally certain. Where you are, what you do, when you do it are all things that it may not be possible to describe with exact precision. Why then is it so difficult to comprehend what a probability of one in a million risk is like? What is the response to the question, "Well, is it safe, and if so how safe?" To get some idea of the dimension of this situation first consider the role of probability in our day-to-day

existance. Later in this section possible responses to this question will
be discussed.

Some of our information on non-fatal probabilities are handled in a
qualitative way. Whether our cold will get better or worse will determine
whether we go to work today. What is the likelihood that the car will
start, the boss will be late? We take risks based on our judgement of the
probabilities of these and other events. Table 2 is a short compilation
of daily probabilistic choices most of us make and take for granted.

We are exposed to probabilistic information daily. The weatherman
tells us that there is a 30% possibility of rain tomorrow of our boss
tells us that the chances of our proposal being accepted are one in
four. The stock market involves the use of probabilities based on assets,
sales, past performance, size, etc. What are the odds that it will go up
or down tomorrow? Our insurance premiums are based on the odds of us
dying given our age, sex and general health. These estimates are all
based on experience. For example, physicians are used to telling us that
the odds of the hernia getting worse may be 50% now and higher in the

Table 2

Common Daily Probabilistic Choices

Category	Probability
Weatherman (forecast probabilities)	10% 80%
Bus or train being late	
5 minutes	50%
10 minutes	40%
20 minutes	5%
30 minutes	1%
Airplane	
Takeoff or arrival being late	50%
Medical probabilities	
Inheritable traits (color blindness, Huntington's Chorea, diabetes)	25%
Heart trouble	40%
Breast cancer	20%
Lung cancer	
Smoker (3 packs a day)	60%
Non-smoker	5%
Alarm clock failure	1/365
Car failing to start	1/365
Gambling	
Poker	1/52
Roulette	1/38
Dice	1/6
Lotteries (winning jackpot)	1×10^6

future, or the chance that the hernia will strangulate are 5% over a lifetime. An EKG stress test comes complete with a consent form that estimates the risk of episodes or transient lightheadedness, fainting, chest discomfort, leg cramps of 2 to 3 per 10,000. The chance of a pack a day cigarette smoker getting lung cancer is about 10%.

Even if we know that the odds are against us people generally continue to act as if that was not true. Anyone who has thought about gambling such as the roulette wheel, dice and card games know that the house always wins in the long run.

In making decisions on the quality of life versus death, pulling the plug, or expensive heroic measures, we have to make judgments that involve qualitative measures. The odds of having a child with birth defects increase with the age of the parent. The parents of a child born with birth defects must decide how far they should go in giving medical attention? Should their response be based on medical, ethical or financial information, or on all? How much information in the form of quantitative values do we need for everyday decisions? (for driving, medical treatment, eating, sleeping, working, etc.)

Another problem the health scientist encounters in trying to communicate with decisionmakers is establishing what an adverse effect is and at what level it occurs. All decisionmakers easily grasp that carcinogenicity and death are adverse effects. It is hard to convince decisionmakers that decreases in nerve conduction velocity, or in increase throughout the general population in both diastolic and systolic blood pressure are adverse. There are two classes of toxicological endpoints. The first is the traditional measured endpoint from an experimental group or cohort. The second is these changes produced in the general population.

Changes noted in the general population are major health effects. Most decisionmakers cannot perceive this. Examples of this are the 20 years it has taken to convince people of the causal association between lung cancer and cigarette smoking. A second example is the slight but statistically significant increase in blood pressure as a result of lead exposure. If the blood pressure of people increases with small increases in blood lead levels, then many tens of thousands of deaths, strokes and myocardial infarctions could be avoided by controlling lead exposure.

Subtle traditional toxic endpoints produced in the human population such as enzyme changes, increased red blood cell fragility, or decreased immune system function are hard to determine exactly when they go from statistically significant changes to adverse effects.

We use a limited number of heuristic principles to analyze seemingly complex daily problems. However, the probability or sample size appear to views on probability are dependent on their life experiences and not on reason or logic.

Since the use of probability is a learned skill for the public, the decision maker or anyone, more attention needs to be placed on how to educate in this area. We need to expand peoples' numerical abilities beyond one in a thousand or perhaps into the region of one in a million. This latter level is of the order of the lifetime background risk of fatality due to natural occurrences such as lighting, tornadoes, cyclones, earthquakes, and bee stings.

If risk assessment/risk management is to have any usefulness to the decision maker, the meaning of 10^{-5}/lifetime or 10^{-6}/lifetime must be communicated in a way to be useful next to the social, psychological (perceptional), political and economic consequences of a potential environmental contaminant.

4. UNCERTAINTY

The most straightforward kind of uncertainty is that involving the measurement of the facts themselves. Any measurement contains random and systematic errors. In measuring the length of the table, the yardstick may be worn so that it is less than one yard. This is an example of a bias or systematic error. The smallest measure on the yardstick is a limit to the smallest length difference that can be measured. If several people use the same yardstick to measure the length of the same table, there will be a range of values related to the smalles measure on the yardstick. This latter range is representative of random error or uncertainty.

Another contribution to help the understanding of uncertainty is to point out where we use this concept in our everyday lives. For example, if the speed limit is 55 mph, do all the cars go that fast as an upper limit? We are all aware of a range of speeds around that value due to differences in what our speedometers read, lack of care to maintain the speed or a deliberate pushing of the limit. In any case, most people are aware of an uncertainty of a few mph. Another example of use of uncertainty is when to show up for an appointment or at a dinner party. In some circles it is common knowledge to show up 15 minutes or 30 minutes after the appointed hour for a dinner party. In any case we all have a range of times we find acceptable for being 'late'.

There are many kinds of uncertainty besides the quantitative error related to the measurement and estimation. There can be uncertainty about what people think about the facts and the future consequences of present decisions (3). Other kinds of uncertainties include questions like 'have we included all events and outcomes' and 'is the description mutually exclusive?' (4). If a model is used, there is uncertainty about how well it represents reality.

Any measurement of environmental parameters likewise will contain some uncertainty. In addition, extrapolations of these measurements of specific values to general predictions increases the uncertainties. For example, using the measurements in 1,000 drinking water supplies to estimate the concentrations in all 60,000 public drinking water supplies will involve uncertainty. These kinds of uncertainties are inherent in the measurement system itself and are an inescapable part of reality. However the magnitude of these uncertainties can be estimated.

Communicating the inherent measurement and estimating quantitative uncertainties is often a difficult and frustrating task. All too often, the caveats describing the uncertainty in a standard of level are lost in the use of the number and the number itself is quoted without these caveats. A partial solution to this problem is to express all background information as ranges, reflective of the uncertainty, and only give a single number as the final standard.

One general misunderstanding of the idea of uncertainty is represented by those who want to get more data to reduce the uncertainty. In some cases this is unnecessary. If a lifetime risk estimate were, for example, in the range of 0.00001 and 0.01 extra health effects, most people would agree that this is a quite small value and may not require a regulation in spite of the uncertainty of three orders of magnitude or a factor of 1,000.

Besides trying to educate decisionmakers about the value of knowing the uncertainty quantitatively, the way in which numerical estimates are quoted should be considered. In most high school mathematics courses we all learn about significant figures. With the advent of the hand-held calculator, we can calculate a number to many significant figures. But if the estimation is a range of 0.001 to 100, it makes little sense to quote a single value of 1.239671 as we too often do.

The development of a health-related regulation or standard is a legal and political, as well as scientific, endeavor that requires specific language and in most cases a specific number. Enforcement and the legal process demand a specific numerical value against which to test the situation. But the reality of existing data involves a wide range of uncertainty in any measured or estimated value. Thus there is a conflict between reality and the legal process.

The objective of determining quantitatively the uncertainty in risk assessment information is to characterize reality. Not knowing how far off an estimate can be may be just as bad as not knowing the number at all. An estimate of cost somewhere in the range of $1 to $10,000,000 is very different than one in the range of $100 to $500. The latter case involves more certainty and is likely to be more useful.

5. CAN DIFFERENT RISKS BE COMPARED?

As a way of getting an understanding of what a risk 10^{-4}/lifetime, 10^{-5}/lifetime and 10^{-6}/lifetime, it could be compared to other risks. However, all risks do not have the same characteristics and certain complexities make interpretation difficult. Comparing the risks of ingesting or inhaling an environmental contaminant to that of hang gliding, rock climbing or insect bites raises the issue of which is voluntary or involuntary. Other complexities that make comparison of risks difficult include: natural/manmade, luxury/necessity, old/new, catastrophic/ordinary (5). Because of these complexities it is seldom possible to get a good understanding of a given risk level by comparing it to other risks of the same frequency. Thus, the understanding of a given risk must be done on a case-by-case basis.

Assessing the risk due to an environmental contaminant is only part of the larger picture the decisionmaker is faced with. In communicating risk information we must realize that it is only part of the total picture. Even in the risk analysis itself, it is a danger to think too narrowly. For example, usually just the individual risk rate is not enough information. Also needed are the population risk values, the background risk rate and the risk rate from other contaminants.

Also, the decisionmaker, in an effort to get the 'big picture', can be overwhelmed with detail. There is little problem today in getting detailed information and lots of it. The problem is to limit that going to the decisionmaker to what is pertinent. The risk assessor must organize and display data and information in a concise way that is understandable by the decisionmaker.

6. ARE THERE LIMITS OR BOUNDS ON NUMERICAL COMPREHENSION?

Can we understand the probability as small as 1 in 100, 1 in 1000, 1 in 10,000, ... etc? Is there a point in this sequence beyond which we cannot comprehend? The odds of winning lotteries or giveaways are often listed and can be even less than those listed above. Yet many people take the chance. is this a calculated risk? Do we really understand the risk of 1 in 10,000?

There is a limit to numerical experience that is culturally based. In some primative societies the counting sequence is 1,2,3, infinity. That is, a number larger than 3 is infinite -- all numbers larger than 3 are infinite or beyond comprehension. By analogy, can we understand and make decisions based on risks of 1 in 10, 1 in 100 and 1 in 1,000, but beyond that all risks are called small or negligible? The limits to our understanding of numerical estimates are similarly culturally limited.

Many of us resist estimating times, distances or anything quantitative. It is a well known procedure to an attorney. When asked how often a witness went to the park this year, the response might be that he doesn't know. The attorney then says is it 1,2,10, 100, more than 100? Finally the witness responds, say not more than 100. The attorney then tries to narrow the estimate. We all have this kind of information, but seldom think quantitatively, or need to.

We usually respond negatively to quantitative questions. For example, can you name 20 birds? Your first response is likely, no. But think for a minute and you will soon name more than 20 birds easily. Why the resistance? Likely it is part of our education. We somehow come out of school with a negative view of mathematics and a dislike for word problems (which many of the estimation problems in environmental regulation are). It is this fear of mathematics that leads to our resistance to quantitate or estimate.

The limits to our abilities to handle numerical or quantitative estimates is thus limited by our culture and experience. The only way to alter this situation is through education.

7. DISCUSSION AND CONCLUSION

The three general areas discussed are shown in Table 3, with some possible solutions. The thoughts and ideas cover a range from the specific to the general.

In the area of communicating information concerning the risk due to the environmental contaminants, perhaps the easiest adjustment is to use positive language. For example, use words such as 'range of certainty', 'benefit', and 'predictable', instead of 'uncertainty', 'risk' and 'probability'.

However, these ideas and concepts must be included in any presentation, discussion or analysis. Whether the true risk is called 'range of certainty', 'uncertainty' or 'error', it is reality and to ignore this leaves the decisionmaker with a skewed and simplistic perspective about what is really known.

To transmit the complete picture of scientific and technical knowledge about an environmental contaminant requires some education in the area of quantitative analysis. Whether it is liked or not, the decision maker needs the quantitative tool called probability and statistics. However these concepts are exciting and interesting when properly presented. As pointed out earlier, we use these concepts in our every day life from weather to medicine. What is needed is to put a clear

Table 3

General Problems in Communicating Risk Assessment Information
to Regulatory Decisionmakers and Some Possible Solutions.

Communicate Problem	Potential Solution
language	use words with positive connotation
complex nature of risk assessment information	more clarity and reality in scientific and technical information presented (e.g., use uncertainty)
lack of understanding of concepts such as uncertainty and probabilty	education -- schools -- news media -- use everyday examples

picture of these ideas about reality into the analysis of the risk resulting from environmental contaminants.

Thus, it is the task of the scientist (technical person) to introduce and explain to the decision maker concepts in toxicology, chemistry, meterology, geology and physics, some grasp of Greek prefixes, orders of magnitude and the reality of measurement. These must be done in as positive a manner as is possible because the non-technical decision maker must weigh these considerations when making public policy decisions. Reminding the decision maker of reality is one of the tasks we scientists meet to perform regularly. Using positive ideas such as range of uncertainty and relating that to real world situations to help quantify the range is the step in the education process most often neglected.

REFERENCES

1. M.S. Peck, People of the Lie, Simon and Schuster, New York. 1983.
2. Kahneman, D., Slovic, P. and Tversky, Eds., Judgement Under Uncertainty: Heuristics and Biases, Cambridge University Press, New York, 1982.
3. L. Ashby, "The Subjective Side of Assessing Risks," New Scientist, May 19, pp. 398-400. 1977.
4. Rowe, W.D., Anatomy of Risk, John Wiley and Sons, New York, 1977.
5. D. Latai, D.D. Lanning, and N.C. Rasmussen, "The Public Perception of Risk," in The Analysis of Actual versus Perceived Risks, V.T. Ravello, W.G. Flamm, J.A. Roderick, and R.G. Tardiff, eds. Plenum, New York. 1983.

COMMUNICATING INFORMATION TO RISK MANAGERS:

THE INTERACTIVE PHASE[1]

Rex V. Brown

Decision Science Consortium, Inc.
Falls Church, Virginia 22043

ABSTRACT

Information display and presentation is one of the most serious
problems standing in the way of more extensive and effective use of risk
analysis. Most risk analyses as presented do not clear minimal display
requirements; viz. that the user adequately understands what the analysis
can tell him that is useful for his purposes, and this is why risk
analysis so often fails as a practical aid to decision makers.
Information communication has two phases: "basic," where the essential
information is presented in a preplanned set report; and "interactive,"
where the user calls up additional information as his interest dictates.
This paper discusses methods for performing the interactive phase,
especially through interactive computers, using novel concepts, such as
macro modeling, user override, and plural analysis. The communication
methodology is exercised in the context of two cases: a PRA adapted to an
NRC regulatory decision on whether to require a costly backfit at an
operating reactor; and a computer aid for making lab safety decision,
based on a complex risk analysis model and data base.

KEY WORDS: Risk management, information communication, interactive
           computers, decision aids

1. INTRODUCTION

    An issue of considerable importance to risk analysts and other
decision scientists is how to get across, economically and effectively,
the fruits of their research efforts to decision makers in government and
elsewhere. Communicating risk management information to a decision maker,
such as a regulator, usually has two distinct phases.

    The first is the "basic phase," wherein the communicator sets forth a
minimum set of information that he is satisfied the user will want to
know, and which he can prepare ahead of time. This usually takes the form
of a basic report, which is typically a written document or a formal
briefing. We have addressed elsewhere methods for enhancing this phase

---

[1]Preparation of this paper was supported by the National Science
Foundation, Decision and Management Science Program, under Grant No.
SES84-20732.

which has, in any case, attracted most research attention to date (Brown & Ulvila, 1985).

The second is the "interactive phase," which conveys optional information in response to user needs or interests that emerge after the basic phase. In many cases, this is the more important part of the communication process and may account for the bulk of the time the user devotes to informing himself about the problem at hand. The basic set report may simply play the role of launching a dialogue between user and researcher, which carries the main burden of communication.

The purpose of this paper is to review some approaches to enhancing this latter interactive phase. The object is for the user, with a modest expenditure of effort, to end up understanding what a given body of research information (such as a risk analysis study) has to say that is useful for his purposes (e.g., to make or defend a regulatory decision). The work we will discuss is part of a larger research program on communicating with decision makers, supported largely by the National Science Foundation and by the Nuclear Regulatory Commission. The current findings are summarized in Brown (1985b), which includes references to more detailed project reports.

The objectives of the interactive phase of communication are not essentially distinct from those of the basic phase. However, there are some distinctive thrusts. The prime function of the basic phase is to present findings of the research which are of direct interest to the user (e.g., the probable implications of adopting one action or another); as well as their most obviously relevant determinants (such as baseline risk, for a risk management decision). In the interactive phase, however, one may wish to focus primarily on other facets: "making the black box transparent" (i.e., understanding the argument which drives the main findings); pooling the findings with alternative perspectives the user may have access to on the same issue (including his personal judgment); and integrating the issues addressed with other considerations (e.g., political), which he will need to take into account before he makes a decision.

2. A CASE ILLUSTRATED APPROACH

2.1 Context

We have been developing some techniques, computer-oriented in the main, to help in the interactive phase and have begun to give them operational implementation, in the form of two software prototypes developed for live risk management problems. The first of these is intended to support a one-off regulatory decision for NRC, the other is to support repetitive lab safety decisions at a local level for EPA. For concreteness, we will discuss our ideas in the context of these two cases. Neither of them, it should be pointed out, has yet been used to make real decisions, though both have been partially field tested and have received favorable responses from users and the research community. The technology is certainly still immature.

The first case relates to a decision by the Nuclear Regulatory Commission, specifically the Commissioners acting on the advice of Office Directors, on whether to require a certain "venting" backfit at particular operating reactors (Brown & Ulvila, 1985).

The research information to be communicated, at least in part, deals primarily with the current level of "baseline" risk at the plant, reduction in the risk to be attributed to the proposed backfit, and the cost of installing the backfit. The issues have, in the past, been the subject of major probabilistic risk assessment and related studies, whose relevant implications the decision makers wish to learn.

They have received a basic report (presented in Brown & Ulvila, 1985, as a "sample decision support paper") whose central finding is captured in Figure 1. The rest of the basic report is essentially a clarification and a summary of the rationale behind this finding. The primary message is that the proposed venting backfit has a modestly positive net benefit, if risk reduction is valued at $1,000 per man-rem averted, but there is major uncertainty about this assessment, due mainly to uncertainty in the risk reduction side.

2.2 The Macro Model

At the core of our approach is the "macro model," which is a deceptively simple idea, developed some ten years ago in the context of evaluating nuclear safeguards (Brown & Feuerwerger, 1978). It consists essentially of expressing a target variable of real interest to the user (in this case the net dollar benefit of requiring a venting backfit) as a function of a small number of its high-level determinants. These are few enough in number, typically no more than a score, that the user can work comfortably with them, at a level of aggregation that he can readily relate to. (Figure 1, in fact, shows an extreme form of macro model in that net benefit is expressed as a two term function--the difference between benefit and cost.)

Usually a lower level of aggregation is more useful. In this case, for example, backfit net benefit was expressed as a function of: baseline core melt probability per year; remaining plant life; baseline risks, given core melt (onsite man-rems, offsite and onsite property damage); industry and NRC costs; impact on each of the above due to backfit; and the dollar equivalent of a man-rem averted. (This macro model will be an approximation, but it could be turned into an identity by using residual variables, such as "any other costs" or "any other benefits.") Such a macro model can be used both as an organizing principle for designing and analyzing total research effort, or for exploring the implications of a given research effort, as in the interactive communication phase.

The macro model is usually not obtained as a summary distillation from an existing and finely grained "micro" model, however, since the latter is typically not designed to produce exactly the target variable best suited to the user. Typically, "feeder" models (or analyses) are needed to organize available research material into the inputs required for the macro model; or "bridging" models (or analyses) to adapt the output of already existing models (such as PRAs) into input for the macro model. This need for adaptation was certainly true of the case study in question. For example, available PRAs addressed only the probability of a core melt that was internally initiated. Externally initiated events (such as station blackout) needed to be addressed from some other source, in order to come up with an overall probability of core melt (one of the macro inputs).

Figure 2 shows the main macro model display developed for the backfit decision, as displayed on an interactive PC screen. The complete computerized aid is described in Ulvila and Thompson (1985).

For each of the input variables cited above, there is an assessment consisting of a median estimate and a 90% uncertainty range about where an "ideal" estimate might lie. (The meaning of this concept is discussed in

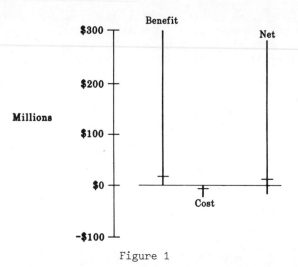

Figure 1

Cost-Benefit of Venting: Expectation and Assessment Uncertainty (90% Range)

Brown (1985a)). The screen also displays implication of these assessments for the target assessment, expressed as a mean and 90% range (on the arguable grounds that, while the median is more readily assessed, the mean is a more useful performance measure). Some intermediate calculations of potential interest are also displayed, such as mean inputs, benefits and costs. The user of the macro model can set (or change) any of the input, and have immediately displayed impact on output and intermediate assessments.

Although structurally simple, the development of this screen requires non-trivial attention to formulation and display from the point of view of user friendliness and to the computational algorithms of uncertainty propagation. Because the format of these assessments was selected for ease of judgmental assessment and verification by the user, they required some bridging with PRA material.

VENTING BACKFIT: INPUTS AND IMPLIED NET BENEFIT

RISKS:	------ Baseline --------			---- Backfit Impact ----		
	Median	90% Ratios	Mean	Median	90% Ratios	Mean
					Reduction Factors	
Core Melt/yr (×10E-4)	.300	.100-10.0	.749	.700	.140-1.35	.633
Plant life: 30 yrs.						
Risks Given Core Melt:						
Offsite man-rems (M)	20.0	.010-3.00	23.7	.500	.800-1.90	.564
$/man-rem: 1000						
Offsite property ($ B)	1.00	.000-6.00	1.74	.500	.800-1.90	.564
Onsite property ($ B)	4.00	.250-2.50	4.55	.980	.990-1.01	.980
COSTS:						
Industry implementation cost ($ M)				3.00	.330-5.00	4.84
NRC implementation cost ($ M)				.200	.250-5.00	.320

NET BENEFIT:	Benefit	− Cost	= Net
Means	$ 40.6 M	− $ 5.1 M	= $ 35.4 M
90% Range	1.1 − 168.9	1.1 − 15.5	13.4-- 159.6

F2 INPUT	F4 INTER	F6 OUTPUT	F1 CALC-1	F3 CALC-2	F5 CALC-3

Figure 2

Macro Model Screen for Backfit Decision

2.3 Plural Analysis

This simple macro model device can be used to perform several distinguishable functions in the interactive communication phase. In particular, it can be used to make transparent the "black box" of the underlying PRA and other research, by showing how the target assessment is related to key determinants.

However, it can also perform more ambitious tasks having to do with integrating the material being communicated with alternative perspectives on the same issues, which we refer to as "plural analysis" (Brown & Lindley, 1982, 1985). For example, it can enable the user to splice in his own judgment (or any other information he may have) by overriding the input assessments he wishes to take issue with (or to test the sensitivity of the output to). It can also be used to help the user pool information represented by the macro model with alternative models and assessments of the same target variable, using the pooling techniques of plural analysis. In particular, it provides a quantified measure of confidence in findings, in the form of a 90% uncertainty range, which can be made to reflect the user's personal confidence in the main areas of analysis (through input 90% ranges). This can be used in weighting alternative assessments (including this one) for pooling purposes.

2.4 Multi-Level User Override

The second case study, dealing with a communication aid for safety decisions, takes the "user override" idea a significant stage further. The underlying research material to be communicated in this case was a very large "micro model," consisting of an extensive technical data base, integrated with a complex risk analysis model and multiattribute utility model. In principle, it will take any chemical substance subjected to a laboratory operation and calculate the relative value of adopting one safety measure or another. The problem with this, as with any general-purpose decision aid designed in advance of any particular decision situation, is that when a decision situation actually arises, the decision aid never exactly fits. It needs to be adapted to the special circumstances. In particular, the substance-operation-safety measure combination may not have been anticipated; and the assessments incorporated in the large "micro" model may not be based on the most relevant information that may then be currently available.

To attempt to address this problem and introduce the necessary flexibility, we developed an elaborate user interface which allowed the user to inspect and override variables at any of a large number of levels within the micro model. The main user override features of the aid are shown in Figure 3 (for a detailed description, see Mendez, et al., 1984a,b). The boxes whose titles are underlined are inputs; those in capitals are outputs; and those which are both capitalized and underlined can be both inputs and outputs. These are the user override variables.

For example, if the substance being analyzed is not on the stored list, a close analogy can be selected (first column of boxes), and its chemical properties displayed (in the second column). These can then be adjusted, in the override mode, for any judged differences and carried through in the model's remaining calculations. Alternatively, at an intermediate level, the user might observe that the calculated probability of upset does not jibe with his experience at this facility, and he may override it. Yet again, the relevant cost of using a fume hood as a safety measure may be higher than the standard cost stored in the data base, because all available hoods are already being used, and so the opportunity cost of a hood is abnormally high. The user may even wish to override stored value judgments; for example, he may not wish to use $1

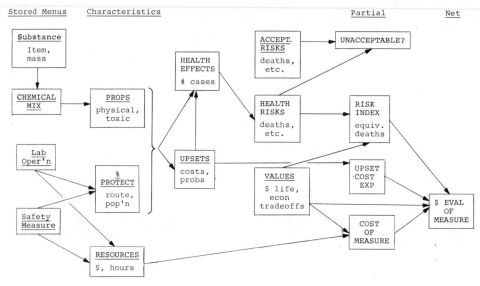

Figure 3

A User Override Model to Evaluate Lab Safety Measures

million as the value of a human life or give the health of laboratory
workers only 1/10 of the weight of the health of the general public (both
of which were default parameters).

In a sense, this user override aid is a generalization of the macro
model. It can be thought of as a macro model which can be specified at
varying levels of depth, and any of the uses to which the macro model can
be put, this override can be put to also. For example, it can be used to
merge plural analyses, including splicing in the user's independent
judgment, at any point in the model where input can be supplied.

3. CONCLUSION

3.1 Design of an Information Management System

Figure 4 recapitulates the various elements discussed above for a
man-model information management system, for the interactive communication
phase. It shows how the primary data base, which may be one or more
extensive studies and/or models is successively transformed and reduced
into a form where it directly answers the user's question. More
important, it shows how the user's judgment (and other data he has access
to) can be introduced at varying points in the transformation in a dynamic
interactive fashion; such that at the end of the interactive phase the
user has extracted from (and incorporated into) the research material
being communicated, what he needs to make a balanced and informed
decision.

3.2 Institutional Issues of Interactive Communication

We have talked as if our information communication tools were to be
used directly by the decision maker/user to selectively dig out and absorb

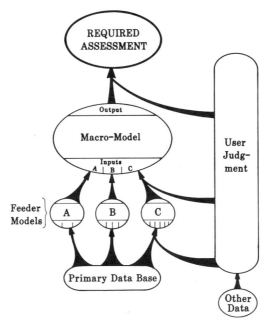

Figure 4

An Information Management System

what he needs from the research material to be communicated. In fact, we
believe that a quite separable role needs to be played, that of the
"communicator," who mediates between the user and researcher.

For the foreseeable future, we see the user needing to interact
directly with the communicator, who answers the user's questions using
whatever data and tools he has available, including, but certainly not
limited to, the computer-oriented aids we have been discussing. Indeed, a
sufficiently skilled and well-informed communicator would not need any
aids at all to be effective, but could draw directly on his own
knowledge. However, we have not yet seen his likes, and he would need
quite unusual talent, training and knowledge. Nor have we seen a user
with sufficient training and leisure to access the data directly or
through computer-aided tools, without the mediation of as competent a
communicator as he can find.

REFERENCES

Brown, R.V., and Feuerwerger, P.H. A macromodel of nuclear safeguard
    effectiveness (Interim Report PR 78-6-80). McLean, VA: Decisions and
    Designs, Inc. March 1978.
Brown, R.V., and Lindley, D.V. Improving judgment by reconciling
    incoherence. Theory and Decision, 1982, 14, 113-132.
Brown, R.V., and Lindley, D.V. Plural analysis: Multiple approaches to
    quantitative research. Theory and Decision, 1985 (in press).
Brown, R.V. Uncertainty and the firmness of assessments: Communicating
    with risk managers. Submitted to Risk Analysis, May 1985a.

Brown, R.V. <u>Presenting risk management information to policymakers:</u>
<u>Executive summary</u> (Technical Report No. 85-4). Report to National
Science Foundation. Falls Church, VA: Decision Science Consortium,
Inc., July 1985b.

Brown, R.V., and Ulvila, J.W. <u>Communicating information to risk</u>
<u>managers: Techniques with examples from nuclear regulation.</u> Volume
<u>I: Main report. Volume II: Supplementary material</u> (Technical Report
No. 85-4). Report to National Science Foundation. Falls Church,
VA: Decision Science Consortium, Inc., July 1985.

Mendez, W., Bresnick, T.A., and Brown, R.V. <u>Laboratories level-of-control</u>
<u>decision aid final report</u>. Washington, DC: ICF Incorporated, 1984a.

Mendez, W., Schwartz, J., and Brown, R.V. <u>Laboratories level-of-control</u>
<u>decision user's manual</u>. Washington, DC: ICF Incorporated, 1984b.

Ulvila, J.W., and Thompson, B.B. <u>A computerized communication aid for a</u>
<u>nuclear backfit decision</u>. Falls Church, VA: Decision Science
Consortium, Inc., July 1985.

THE USE OF RISK COMPARISON TO AID THE COMMUNICATION AND INTERPRETATION OF

THE RISK ANALYSES FOR REGULATORY DECISION MAKING[1]

Lee W. Merkhofer

Applied Decision Analysis, Inc.
Menlo Park, California 94025

ABSTRACT

Risk comparisons can aid communication by providing reviewers of risk analyses with a conceptual "ruler" that helps them to understand and interpret risk analysis results. The pitfalls of using comparative risk information and suggestions for overcoming those pitfalls are presented.

KEY WORDS: Risk Communication, Comparative Risk, and Risk Analysis

INTRODUCTION

The numerical outputs of risk analyses are often difficult for decision makers to interpret. One promising approach for improving the ability of decision makers and others to interpret the results of risk analyses is to provide them with a means for placing estimated risks in perspective. If decision makers who review risk analyses have information on the level of risk associated with other more familiar risks, they possess a conceptual "ruler" that can help them to understand and interpret risk analysis results. For this reason, comparative risk information is an important component of a comprehensive methodology for communicating the results of risk analysis.

The paper describes the results of a brief research task to develop and describe a preliminary methodology for incorporating comparative risk information into the presentation of risk analysis results. To provide background and context, the paper begins with a description of previous attempts to use comparative risk information. The principal criticisms that have been directed at such applications are then summarized. Finally, the elements of a methodology designed to minimize these limitations while retaining the potential benefits of risk comparisons are described. The methodology is illustrated using an example application involving nuclear reactor safety decision making.

---

[1]This material is based upon works supported by the National Science Foundation under grant no. PRA 8413113 (prepared under subcontract to Decision Science Consortium, Inc.). The opinions findings and conclusions expressed in this publication are those of the researchers and do not necessarily reflect the views of the National Science Foundation.

Many analysts have recognized the potential for using comparisons to promote understanding of numerical risk estimates. The risk measure receiving the most attention to risk comparisons is the low-probability event. Most individuals, including most scientists, have little intuitive feeling for probabilities that are less than 10^{-4}. Studies have shown that people have a limited capacity to distinguish small probabilities (e.g., the different between 10^{-5} and 10^{-6}) and to understand the significance of those differences (Sjoberg, 1979). Thus, it is not very helpful simply to tell someone that it has been estimated that the probability of large numbers of fatalities resulting from an accident is less than 10^{-6} per year.

To help convey low probabilities, analysts sometimes compare their estimates with the probabilities of various reference events. These reference events are typically natural risks or technological risks that are relatively familiar to most individuals or of interest because of the attention given to them by the media. Two approaches are available. One is to estimate the extend to which one would have to be exposed to familiar hazards to produce a level of risk equal to the risk whose clarification is desired. The second approach is to locate the estimated risk along a scale of greater and lesser risks. Reference risks serve as benchmarks in this approach.

Most comparisons based on equating risks have focused on the probability of death, one of the risk measures that might be produced by a risk analysis. Wilson (1979), for example, used toxicological and exposure data to reduce a number of familiar activities to a level that would increase an individual's annual chances of death by one chance in a million. He found, for instance, that actuarial statistics may be interpreted to suggest that smoking 1.4 cigarettes or traveling 300 miles by car both appear to increase the annual probability of dying by about once chance in a million. Some of Wilson's other comparisons are summarized in Table 1. Similarly Crouch and Wilson (1982) estimated the length of time required to accumulate an average risk of dying of one in a million from several natural causes and life-style activities. Some examples of their results are provided in Table 2.

The approach based on comparing an estimated risk with greater and lesser risks requires a set of risk benchmarks. Several authors have provided such benchmarks. Crouch and Wilson (1982), for example, estimated the average probability of death per year from several common causes, occupations, and sports. Examples of their results are presented in Table 3. Sowby (1965) provided extensive data on the risks per hour of exposure for various activities and situations. Wilson (1984) recently presented a scale of risks ranging from the clearly unacceptable to the unnoticeable. Figure 1 shows Wilson's scale. Lawless et al. (1984) provided a more refined version of such a scale, reproduced in Figure 2.

Some risk comparisons have used expected reduction in life expectancy rather than probability of death as the unit of measure. An advantage of the loss-of-life-expectancy measure is that it permits risk comparisons to account for the average ages of exposed individuals and permits a more meaningful comparison with risks for which the time lag between exposure and possible death may be long (such as exposures to carcinogens). Cohen and Lee (1979), for example, ordered many different hazards in terms of their expected reduction in life expectancy. Table 4 summarizes some of their estimates, which represent average values for U.S. inhabitants. Reissland and Harries (1979) conducted a comparison of the days of life

Table 1

Risks which Increase the Probability of Death by One Chance in a Million
Source: Adapted from Wilson (1979)

Activity	Cause of Death
Smoking 1.4 cigarettes	Cancer, heart disease
Drinking 1/2 liter of wine	Cirrhosis of the liver
Traveling 10 miles by bicycle	Accident
Traveling 300 miles by car	Accident
Flying 1000 miles by jet	Accident
Flying 6000 miles by jet	Cancer caused by cosmic radiation
Living 2 months in average stone or brick building	Cancer caused by natural radioactivity
One chest x-ray taken in a good hospital	Cancer caused by radiation
Living 2 months with a cigarette smoker	Cancer, heart disease
Eating 40 tablespoons of peanut butter	Liver cancer caused by aflatoxin B
Eating 100 charcoal-broiled steaks	Cancer from benzopyrene
Drinking 30 12 oz. cans of diet soda	Cancer caused by saccharin
Living 5 years at site boundary of a typical nuclear power plant in the open	
Living 20 years near PVC plant	Cancer caused by vinyl chloride (1976 standard)
Living 150 years within 20 miles of a nuclear power plant	Cancer caused by radiation
Risk of accident by living within 5 miles of a nuclear reactor for 50 years	Cancer caused by radiation

expectancy lost by workers in the nuclear industry with estimates derived
for several other industries. Table 5 summarizes their results.

Although risk comparisons are logically distinct from judgments
concerning the acceptability of a risk, most of the above-mentioned risk
comparisons have been coupled with an argument that certain risks were
achieving too much or too little attention. Wilson (1979) commented on
his comparison of one-in-a-million risks by stating, "...these comparisons
help me evaluate risks and I imagine that they may help others to do so,
as well. But the most important use of these comparisons must be to help
the decisions we make, as a nation, to improve our health and reduce our
accident rate." Similarly, Cohen and Lee (1979) referred to their results
(Table 4) by saying, "...to some approximation, the ordering (in this
table) should be society's order to priorities. However, we see several
very major problems that have received very little attention, whereas some

Table 2

Time to Accumulate a One-in-a-Million Risk
Source: Adapted from Crouch and Wilson (1982)

Living in the United States:

Motor vehicle accidents	1.5 days
Falls	6 days
Drowning	10 days
Fires	13 days
Firearms	36 days
Electrocution	2 months
Tornadoes	20 months
Floods	20 months
Lightning	2 years
Animal bite or sting	4 years

Occupational Hazards:

General

Mining and Quarrying	9 hours
Construction	14 hours
Agriculture	15 hours
Transport and Public Utilities	1 day
Service and Government	3.5 days
Manufacturing	4.5 days
Trade	7 days

Specific

Fire Fighting	11 hours
Coal Mining (accidents)	14 hours
Police Duty	1.5 days
Railroad Employment	1.5 days

of the items near the bottom of the list, especially those involving radiation, receive a great deal of attention." Likewise, Sowby (1965) argued that to decide whether or not we are regulating radiation hazards properly, we need to pay more attention to "some of the other risks of life," and Lord Rothschild (1979) has added, "There is no point in getting into a panic about the risks of life until you have compared the risks which worry you with those that don't but perhaps should."

Starr (1969) formalized comparative analysis as a logic for determining risk acceptability in his revealed preference approach to defining "laws of acceptable risk." Starr's approach is based on the assumption that, by trial and error, society has arrived at a nearly optimal balance between the risks and benefits associated with any activity. If this is the case, then historical data can be used to reveal acceptable levels of risk. Starr's analysis of historical data indicated that (1) the public accepts greater risks for beneficial activities; and (2) much greater risks are accepted from risks associated with voluntary activities (e.g., skiing) than from involuntary activities (e.g., air pollution) that provide similar levels of benefit. Thus, Starr concluded,

Table 3

Average Annual Probability of Death From Common Causes,
Occupations, and Sports
Source: Adapted from Crouch and Wilson (1982)

Common Causes:

	Risk per Million Persons[a]
Motor vehicle accidents, total	240.0
Home accidents	110.0
Falls	62.0
Motor vehicle collisions with pedestrian	42.0
Drowning	36.0
Fires	28.0
Inhalation and ingestion of objects	15.0
Firearms	10.0
Electrocution	5.3
Tornadoes	0.6
Floods	0.6
Lightning	0.5
Tropical cyclones and hurricanes	0.3
Bites and stings by venomous animals and insects	0.2

Occupations or Industries:

	Risk per Million Workers[b]
Mining and Quarrying	950.0
Fire fighting	800.0
Construction	610.0
Agriculture[c]	600.0
Stone quarries and mills	590.0
Transport and Public Utilities	370.0
Farming[d]	360.0
Steel worker (accident only)	280.0
Railroad employees	240.0
Police officers, total, in line of duty	220.0
Police officers killed by felons	130.0
Service and government	110.0
Tractor fatalities per tractor	88.0
Manufacturing	82.0
Trade	53.0

Sports:

	Risk per Million Participants[e]
Professional stunting	10,000
Air show/air racing and acrobatics	5,000
Flying amateur/home-built aircraft	3,000
Sport parachuting	2,000
Thoroughbred horseracing	1,000
Lighter-than-air flying	900
Power boat racing	800
Bobsledding	700
Mountaineering	600
Scuba diving	400
Glider flying	400
Football, professional and semiprofessional	400
Ice yachting	100
Spelunking	100
Bicycle racing (registered)	90
Hang gliding	80
Boating	50
Football, college	30
Hunting	30
Swimming	30
Ski racing	20
Football, high school	10
Football, sandlot	2

[a]A risk of 1.0 per million persons means a risk of one in a million (or 1.0×10^{-6}) for each individual in the population.
[b]A risk of 1.0 per million persons means a risk of one in a million (or 1.0×10^{-6}) for each individual in the exposed population. Note that some of these occupations may have less than one million workers.
[c]Includes transport accidents and all agriculture.
[d]Refers to nontransport deaths occurring on farms.
[e]Data provided in this form for easy comparison with the above estimates. Most of these sports have far less than 1 million participants.

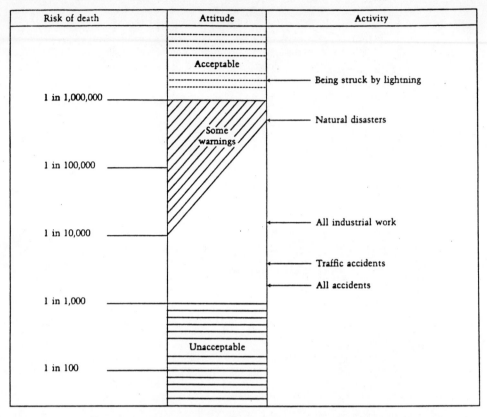

Risk of death	Attitude	Activity

Acceptable

Being struck by lightning

1 in 1,000,000

Some warnings

Natural disasters

1 in 100,000

1 in 10,000

All industrial work

Traffic accidents

All accidents

1 in 1,000

Unacceptable

1 in 100

Figure 1   Regions of Acceptable/Unacceptable Risk Expressed in Terms of
the Probability of Death for an Individual per Year of Exposure
Source: Wilson (1984)

acceptable risk is determined by two factors, benefit and voluntariness.
The well-known graphical display to Starr's findings is reproduced in
Figure 3.

Noting that risk comparisons have often been conducted by analysts
motivated by a desire to create higher public acceptance for low-
probability risks, Keeney and von Winterfeldt (1984) concluded that risk
comparisons have generally been unsuccessful, in part "because the
communicator's motives were mistrusted." Mistrust, undoubtedly, is
largely responsible for the significant controversy surrounding the major
studies that have attempted to compare alternative energy technologies,
especially the Nuclear Regulatory Commission's Reactor Safety Study (NRC,
1975) and Inhaber's comparisons of energy product risks (Inhaber, 1979).
The Reactor Safety Study compared the consequences and frequency of
reactor accidents to natural disasters, such as earthquakes, dam failures,
etc. Figure 4 provides an example of the comparisons. Inhaber's study
was a comparative assessment of the risks of using ten different energy
sources. The study considered both occupational and public health
risks. A total risk was calculated for each technology and compared on
the basis of calculated number of man days that would be lost per megawatt
year of electricity produced. Figure 5 provides an example of Inhaber's
results. Inhaber's reports and subsequent articles and books have sparked

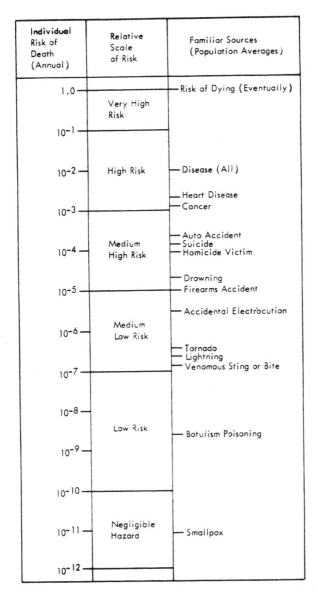

Individual Risk of Death (Annual)	Relative Scale of Risk	Familiar Sources (Population Averages)
1.0	Very High Risk	Risk of Dying (Eventually)
10^{-1}		
10^{-2}	High Risk	Disease (All)
10^{-3}		Heart Disease Cancer
10^{-4}	Medium High Risk	Auto Accident Suicide Homicide Victim
10^{-5}		Drowning Firearms Accident
10^{-6}	Medium Low Risk	Accidental Electrocution
10^{-7}		Tornado Lightning Venomous Sting or Bite
10^{-8}		
	Low Risk	Botulism Poisoning
10^{-9}		
10^{-10}		
10^{-11}	Negligible Hazard	Smallpox
10^{-12}		

Figure 2. Comparative Scales of Individual Risks of Death from Various Causes

Source: Lawless et al. (1984)

intense interest, comment, and analysis, particularly his conclusion that nuclear power carries only slightly greater risk than natural gas and less than all other technologies considered. Criticisms applicable to the above studies' use of risk comparisons as well as the more generally directed criticisms of the use of comparative information in the communication of analytic results are presented in the following section.

Table 4

Loss of Life Expectancy Due to Various Causes
Source: Cohen and Lee (1979)

Cause	Days
Being unmarried--male	3500
Cigarette smoking--male	2250
Heart disease	2100
Being unmarried--female	1600
Being 30% overweight	1300
Being a coal miner	1100
Cancer	980
20% Overweight	900
<8th Grade education	850
Cigarette smoking--female	800
Low socioeconomic status	700
Stroke	520
Living in unfavorable state	500
Army in Vietnam	400
Cigar smoking	330
Dangerous job--accidents	300
Pipe smoking	220
Increasing food intake 100 cal/day	210
Motor vehicle accidents	207
Pneumonia--influenza	141
Alcohol (U.S. average)	130
Accidents in home	95
Suicide	95
Diabetes	95
Being murdered (homicide)	90
Legal drug misuse	90
Average job--accidents	74
Drowning	41
Job with radiation exposure	40
Falls	39
Accidents to pedestrians	37
Safest jobs--accidents	30
Fire--burns	27
Generation of energy	24
Illicit drugs (U.S. average)	18
Poison (solid, liquid)	17
Suffocation	13
Firearms accidents	11
Natural radiation (BEIR)	8
Medical X rays	6
Poisonous gases	7
Coffee	6
Oral contraceptives	5
Accidents to pedalcycles	5
All catastrophes combined	3.5
Diet drinks	2
Reactor accidents (UCS)	2*
Reactor accidents--Rasmussen	0.02*
Radiation from nuclear industry	0.02*
PAP test	-4
Smoke alarm in home	-10
Air bags in car	-50
Mobile coronary care units	-125
Safety improvements 1966-76	-110

*These items assume that all U.S. power is nuclear.   UCS is Union of
Concerned Scientists, the most prominent group of nuclear critics.

Table 5

Days of Life Expectancy Lost as a Result of Hazards in the Nuclear
Industry Compared with Hazards in Other Industries
Source: Reissland and Harries (1979)

	Age (at Beginning of Exposure)				
	20	30	40	50	60
One year at risk in:					
Deep sea fishing	51.4	41.6	31.9	22.8	14.9
Coal mining	5.7	4.6	3.6	2.5	1.7
Coal & petroleum products	4.1	3.3	2.6	1.8	1.2
Railway employment	3.5	2.9	2.2	1.6	1.0
Construction	3.5	2.8	2.1	1.5	1.0
All manufacturing	0.7	0.6	0.5	0.3	0.2
Paper, printing & publishing	0.5	0.4	0.3	0.2	0.1
Radiation work at 50 mSv/year	4.6	2.7	1.3	0.5	0.1
Radiation work at 5 mSv/year	0.4	0.3	0.1	0.1	0
Exposed for remainder of working life to risk in:					
Deep sea fishing	1393.0	923.0	551.0	273.0	80.2
Coal mining	155.0	103.0	61.3	30.4	8.9
Coal & petroleum products	111.0	73.8	44.0	21.8	6.4
Railway employment	95.5	63.3	37.8	18.7	5.5
Construction	93.5	62.0	37.0	18.3	5.4
All manufacturing	20.5	13.5	8.1	4.0	1.2
Paper, printing & publishing	12.0	7.9	4.7	2.4	0.7
Radiation work at 50 mSv/year	68.0	32.0	12.2	3.4	0.6
Radiation work at 5 mSv/year	6.8	3.2	1.2	0.3	0.1

CRITICISMS AND ALLEGED LIMITATIONS OF RISK COMPARISONS

Most criticisms of the use of comparative risk information attack the
implication (either explicit or implicit in the comparisons) that risks
that are small or comparable to risks that are already being accepted
should themselves be accepted. Although intuitively appealing, this
argument often breaks down because the risk comparison compares only one
or two of the many dimensions of risk that are relevant to decision
making. There is ample research demonstrating that people's reactions to
risk depend on a wide range of factors, including not only voluntariness
and benefits, as recognized by Starr, but also catastrophic potential,
equity in the distribution of risks and benefits, whether the adverse
consequences are immediate or delayed, the ease of reducing the risks, and
so forth.

Because the acceptability of a risk depends on more than voluntariness and benefits, when Fischhoff et al. (1979) repeated Starr's
analysis with a wider spectrum of risks, they found greater variability in
the levels of risks that society has accepted than was suggested by
Starr's analysis. As a result, they found that they could obtain results
differing from Starr's depending on the reference risks considered and the
measures of risks and benefits that were used. Figure 6, produced by
Fischhoff and his colleagues, shows a result differing from Starr's,

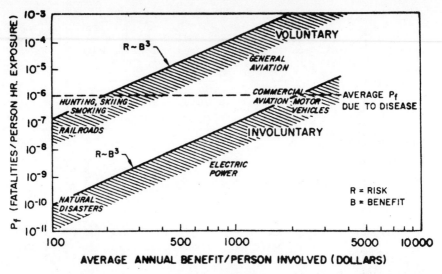

Figure 3. A Comparison of Risk and Benefit to U. S. Society from Various
Sources

Source: C. Starr (1972)

obtained with another set of data and slightly different methods.[2] While
Starr concluded that the acceptability of risk is roughly proportional to
the third power (cube) of benefits, with risks approximately 1000 times
greater being accepted for voluntary activities, Fischhoff and his
colleagues arrived at the different relationship indicated in the figure
(slope = 0.3, correlation = 0.55). Inspection of the data points in
Figure 6 indicates the effect of factors other than voluntariness and
benefits. Smoking is plotted very high in Figure 6, but it is not only a
voluntary risk but also a delayed one, hence presumably more acceptable
than one which is associated with swift death, such as swimming or
hunting. Nuclear power is located below swimming not only because it is
an involuntary risks, but also because it is perceived to be
associated with catastrophic accidents, events which are far more
objectionable to the public than simple personal accidents, such as
drowning.

To avoid the problems associated with comparing unlike measures, the
analyst must take care in selecting and comparing risks. Slovic and
Fischhoff (1982), however, present a number of other criticisms that
cannot be so easily countered. In criticizing Starr's analysis, these
authors note that the method "assumes that past behavior is valid
predictor of present preferences," which may not necessarily be valid.
Thus, the method is "politically conservative in that it enshrines current
economic and social arrangements." Furthermore, they say, the implication

---

[2]Whereas Starr estimated risk in terms of fatality rate per hour of
exposure, Fischhoff and his co-workers simply used annual fatalities.
Also, while Starr measured benefit either by the average amount of money
spent on an activity by a single participant or the average contribution
of the activity to the participant's annual income, the Fischhoff analysis
used total annual consumer expenditure as a measure of benefit.

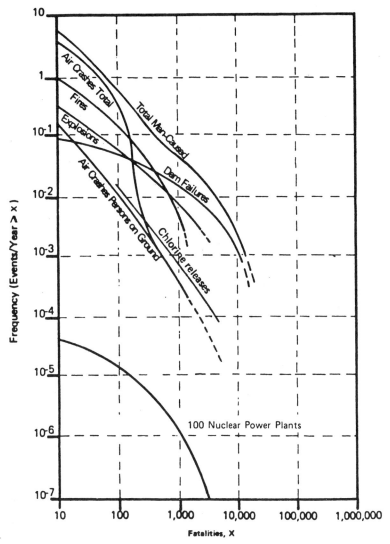

Figure 4. Frequency of Man-Caused Events Involving Multiple Fatalities
Source: Nuclear Regulatory Commission (1975)

that risks that people already accept should be used as a guideline for
decisions about other risks

> ... makes strong (and not always supported) assumptions about the
> rationality of people's decision making in the marketplace and the
> freedom of choice the marketplace provides. It may underweight risks
> to which the market responds sluggishly such as those with a long lead
> time (e.g., carcinogens).

Another criticism of the use of comparative risk information relates
to the influence of the risk measures selected and the format in which
results are presented. To illustrate this point, Whipple (1980) cites
Herman Kahn's description of the response he received to his use of two
ways for expressing the estimated risks of atmospheric testing of nuclear
weapons. Kahn's (1979) estimate was that a thousand cases of bone cancer
or leukemia would result per thousand-megaton bomb exploded, which he also

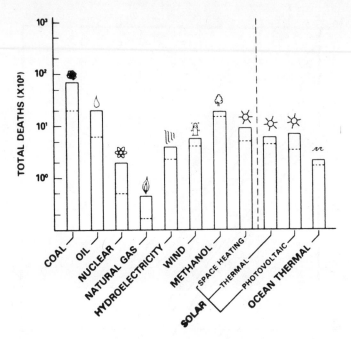

Figure 5.   Total Deaths, Times 1000, per Megawatt-Year as a Function of
the Energy System
Source: Inhaber (1979)

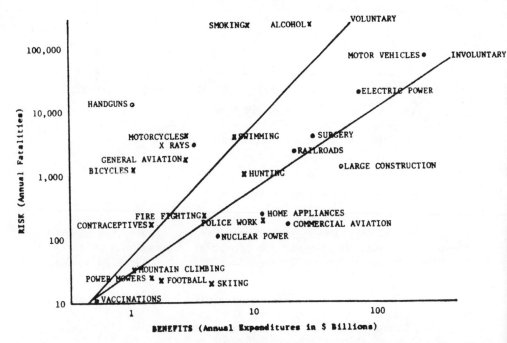

Figure 6.   Another Comparison of Risks and Benefits
Source: Fischoff et al. (1979)

expressed as once chance in 3 million (assuming a world population of 3 billion). Half of Kahn's mail complained, "Why do you mention a thousand? Are you trying to scare people? There's only once chance in 3 million." The other half asked, "Why do you mention one chance in 3 million, are you trying to corrupt the thousand?"

Crouch and Wilson (1984) illustrate how the selection of risk measures can affect a risk comparison. Figures 7(a) and (b) show how two different measures of the risk of accidental death for the U.S. coal industry varied over the 20-year period from 1950 to 1970. One figure seems to suggest that the industry got substantially "safer" during this period, while the opposite conclusions may be inferred from the other. Crouch and Wilson note: "Each measure represents a different aspect of the risk of accidental death, and whether they support or deny any conclusions as to the safety of the coal industry depends, inter alia, upon a definition of 'safety' in this context."

Because of the sensitivity of risk comparisons to the measures used, it is easy to misinterpret results. In Figure 6, for example, police work is more than an order of magnitude below swimming, which might suggest to the casual observer that the latter is more dangerous. Actually, per hour of exposure, police work produces a probability of fatality that is about an order of magnitude higher than swimming, as may be inferred from Tables 2 and 3. Swimming appears higher in Figure 6 because the y-axis for this comparison is expressed in units of total fatalities rather than per unit of exposure. In general, care must be exercised in reducing risks to common units. Expressing risks in terms of expected loss of life expectancy, for example, can be confusing. As Slovic et al. (1980) note,

...although some people feel enlightened upon learning that a single takeoff or landing in a commercial airliner takes an average of 15 minutes off one's life expectancy, others find themselves completely bewildered by such information. On landing, one will either die prematurely (almost certainly be more than 15 minutes) or will not. To many people, averages seem inadequate to capture the essence of such risks.

Another limitation of comparative risk information is the scientific uncertainty associated with the determination of reference risks. As with any other risk assessment, the estimation of risks for reference events requires the use of a model to describe the process which is being assessed and to associate a quantitative measure of risk with it. The typical approach is to propose a plausible model and then to obtain the parameters of that model by fitting it to historical data. Crouch and Wilson (1984) provide the example of the risk of death from automobile accidents. The first step in computing a reference risk for automobiles is to define a suitable risk measure, for example, the U.S. average annual death rate. Figure 8 shows the basic data for the period 1950 to 1978. The model selected by the analyst might be that this measure of risk is roughly constant over time, with random year-to-year variations. "Fitting" this simple model to the data, the analyst would conclude that the average fatality rate per year is approximately 24 per 100,000 with a year-to-year variability (two standard error confidence band) of roughly 20%. By extrapolation, therefore, the analyst would estimate that current risks (i.e., risks at the time that the comparison is being made) are roughly 24 per 100,000, plus or minus about 20%.

Crouch and Wilson point out that there are two sources of error in this estimate. The first is statistical error due to the limited data for parameter estimation. Standard methods of classical statistics are

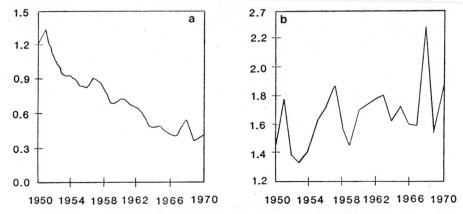

Deaths per million tons output   Deaths per thousand employed

Figure 7. Different Measures Can Create Different Impressions
Source: Crouch and Wilson (1984)

available for estimating confidence bounds and other measures of
statistical uncertainty due to limited data. The second source of error is
the possibility that an incorrect model was chosen to calculate the risk
measure. To illustrate this possibility, Figure 9 shows another risk
measure for summarizing automobile fatality data--deaths per 100 million
vehicle miles driven. An alternative model for estimating risk would be
to multiply an estimated average number of deaths per vehicle mile
traveled by an estimate of the number of vehicle miles traveled. This
would obviously be a preferable model if some change (e.g., gasoline
shortage) dramatically altered automobile use since the time the fatality

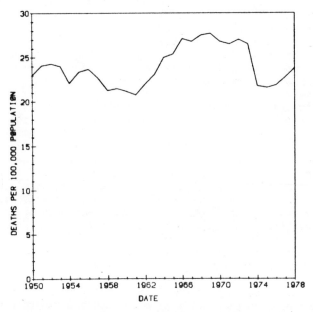

Figure 8. U. S. Motor-Vehicle Accident Deaths, 1950-1970. Deaths per
100,000 Population.
Source: Crouch and Wilson (1984)

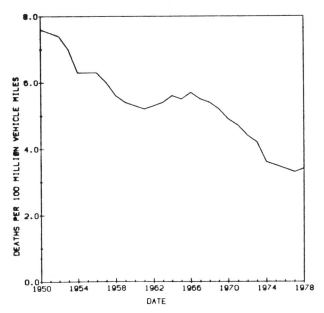

Figure 9.   U. S. Motor-Vehicle Accident Deaths, 1950-1970.   Deaths per 100
            Million Vehicle Miles.
                    Source: Crouch and Wilson (1984)

data had been collected.   Uncertainties due to the possible use of an
incorrect model can only be guessed at by making assumptions, for example,
by assuming that a certain set of models encompasses all possibilities and
exploring the sensitivity of estimated risk levels to the model form
selected.

     Thus, because of lack of sufficient data or the use of inappropriate
models, the reference risks computed for comparisons may be in error.
Studies of psychological factors in risk perception suggest that if two
alternatives present equal risks, costs, and benefits, but one has
considerably more uncertainty surrounding the estimated level of risk,
then most people would prefer the option with the more narrow band of
uncertainty.   Therefore, the uncertainty in estimated risk measures may be
a significant factor to retain in risk comparisons.

     In summary, there are several significant limitations to the use of
comparative risk information: risk comparisons do not provide a simple
rule for risk acceptability, the measures and format selected can easily
alter the impression induced, care must be taken in the conversion of
risks to common units, and the reference measures themselves are subject
to the same sorts of errors and inaccuracies as the risks that are
compared to it.   Despite these important limitations, critics and analysts
alike have recognized that risk comparisons have important characteristics
that make them an attractive means for aiding communication.   Slovic and
Fischhoff (1982), for example, state:

     Comparative analysis has several attractive features.   It avoids the
     difficult and controversial task of converting diverse risks into a
     common monetary unit (like dollars per life lost or per case of
     sterilization or per day of suffering).   It presents issues in a mode
     that is probably quite compatible with natural thought processes.
     Among other things, this mode may avoid any direct numerical reference
     to very small probabilities, for which people have little or no
     intuitive feel.

595

If reasonable care is taken in the design and use of comparative risk information, the method can be an important element of a communication system. The following section describes and illustrates some of the principal elements of a methodology for using comparative risk information as part of a communication package produced to summarize for a decision maker the results of a risk analysis.

ELEMENTS OF A METHODOLOGY FOR USING COMPARATIVE RISK INFORMATION

The above consideration of the strengths and weaknesses of comparative risk information suggest that the technique has considerable potential, but that care should be taken to minimize the likelihood that such comparisons will be misinterpreted by those to whom they are presented. Furthermore, it is apparent that careful design of risk comparisons can considerably enhance the value derived. Five guidelines for effectively using comparative risk information suggest themselves. These are: (1) strive, to the extent possible, for neutral or value-free comparisons, (2) provide the decision maker with multiple comparisons using different risk measures and reference scales, (3) tailor each comparison to illuminate a particular aspect of the risk under investigation, (4) clarify for the decision maker the intent of the comparison and provide a caution against drawing unwarranted conclusions, (5) develop reference events iteratively, allowing for feedback from decision makers to ensure that the most helpful comparisons are provided, and (6) explain any assumptions or uncertainties in the reference risk estimates as necessary to prevent misinterpretation.

Table 6 summarizes these guidelines and indicates the principal objective of each. These and related considerations for the use of comparative risk information are discussed in more detail below. The reader should be cautioned that the displays presented are meant only to illustrate various considerations--the scope of this research task did not include recommending specific reference scales or risk measures for use in risk comparisons. Consequently, the comparisons presented are incomplete and no attempt has been made to optimize them for the example considered. Further research is needed to design and develop the comparative information that would be most appropriate for any given decision setting.

The example providing the context for the discussion is that addressed by Brown and Ulvila (1985a, 1985b). Brown and Ulvila (1985b) consider an analysis of the costs, risks, and benefits of a decision to install a vented containment system in a nuclear reactor. The purpose of backfitting the reactor with this system would be to reduce the probability of containment failure in the event of a core melt.[3] The intended audience for this risk/cost/benefit analysis would be senior decision makers at the Nuclear Regulatory Commission, such as Commissioners, who are assumed to be in the process of deciding whether to require such a backfit. These decision makers have limited time to study

---

[3]Fitting the reactor with a vented containment system involves installing a high-volume, unfiltered vent from the reactor's suppression pool through the turbine building to the atmosphere. The vent is activated at pressures exceeding design limits, and the system would be equipped with a manual shutoff capability to protect against the release of fission products when the suppression pool is saturated and the core degraded.

Table 6

Guidelines for Comparative Risk

Guideline	Principal Objective
Strive for neutral or value-free comparisons, make any value-laden assumptions explicit	Avoid influencing or subverting decision maker's responsibility to make value judgments
Use multiple comparisons based on multiple risk measures	Counter tendency of comparisons to encourage an overly simplified view of the problem
Tailor each comparison to illuminate a particular aspect of the risk	Increase the effectiveness of risk comparisons
Clarify the intent of the comparison and provide appropriate cautions	Reduce the likelihood of misinterpretation
Develop reference events iteratively with decision maker input	Increase the meaningfulness of risk comparisons
Explain all assumptions and uncertainties	Ensure that risk numbers attain a degree of influence commensurate with that which they deserve

the extensive and highly detailed documentation that is typically produced in a cost/risk/benefit analysis. Furthermore, they are unlikely to have the technical and quantitative skills necessary to interpret rapidly and comprehend accurately the many numbers that such an analysis would produce. Thus, methods are needed to improve the communication of risk analysis information to these and similar regulatory decision makers. Providing comparative risk information may assist in this respect.

A key question for the use of comparative risk information within a system for communicating results to decision makers is the appropriate degree of simplification. As noted in previous sections, risk has multidimensional characteristics--it cannot be completely described by any single number. To distinguish various aspects of risk, analysts have proposed using multiple risk measures, including: (1) total expected fatalities, injuries, etc., per year; (2) probabilities of fatality, injury, etc., for typical or representative individuals; (3) probabilities of harm for individuals grouped by occupation, geographic location, etc. (to aid equity considerations); (4) probabilities of catastrophic losses; (5) distribution of risks over time; and (6) qualitative factors, such as voluntariness, controllability, familiarity, anxiety, etc. Some degree of aggregation across these characteristics is essential--detailed estimates for each risk measure with appropriate reference aids and caveats would overwhelm the typical decision maker. Furthermore, strict attention to the distinctions among risks would severely limit the ability of the analyst to select reference risks for comparisons that are familiar and intuitively meaningful. On the other hand, limiting or substantially simplifying analytic detail creates the danger that critical information will be lost and that the decision maker's understanding will suffer.

The use of successive risk comparisons to illuminate different aspects of the risk under investigation provides a useful approach to the problem of achieving an appropriate degree of simplification. With this approach, multiple risk comparisons would be provided, with each comparison involving an aggregation over some characteristics but not others. To help avoid misinterpretation and unwarranted conclusions, the purpose of each comparison would be explained to the decision maker. An advantage of providing multiple risk comparisons is that the inevitable weaknesses of any single scale might be overcome by relying on different scales to accomplish different things. Furthermore, the potential biases that might be introduced by a given risk comparison can be minimized by providing the decision maker with the variety of perspectives that multiple comparisons would achieve.

The first application of comparative information as part of a communication package might be to help the decision maker interpret the small probabilities produced by the analysis. For this purpose, it might be best to select reference risks whose low probabilities of occurrence can be most easily appreciated by the decision maker, without regard to whether the risks are similar along other dimensions. For example, one of the important risk measures produced by the example analysis is the estimate that backfitting the reactor with a vented containment system reduces the probability of prompt fatality due to severe accidents for individuals living within one mile of the plant from a value of 3×10^{-7} to a value of 1×10^{-9}. Because the significance of such small numbers is extremely difficult to appreciate in the abstract, comparing these numbers against a reference scale, such as that shown in Figure 10, might be useful.

Figure 10 places the individual risks of death estimated as part of the analysis into perspective by comparing them with the average risks of dying from other causes. The figure indicates that the best estimate is that backfitting reduces the risk of prompt death for a typical exposed individual from a level comparable to that faced by an average U.S. citizen from lightning to a level comparable to that faced from botulism poisoning. Actual applications, of course, would use reference scales that have been tailored to the problem under study. For example, the reference scales would be composed of risks selected to be most familiar to the decision maker and the estimates would take into account any special circumstances relevant to the particular population under study. Even when the reference risks are carefully selected, however, they will differ among themselves and with the risk being evaluated along many dimensions other than the probability of individual fatality. For this reason, it may be wise to include a caution, such as that indicated in the figure, to warn the decision maker about drawing unwarranted conclusions. Information about the uncertainty in the risk estimates should also be provided.

One of the most significant characteristics of the risk associated with nuclear power in the minds of many people is the catastrophic potential--unlike many of the other risks displayed in Figure 10, which affect one or a small number of individuals at a time, a severe accident at a nuclear power plant can conceivably create a large number of fatalities, injuries, and property losses which are concentrated in time and space. To help clarify the significance of this aspect of risk, it may be helpful to provide the decision maker with a comparison along the lines of that used in the Reactor Safety Study, where the consequences and frequency of severe reactor accidents were compared to those from earthquakes, dam failures, etc., that might also produce multiple fatalities. Figure 11 illustrates one form by which such comparisons

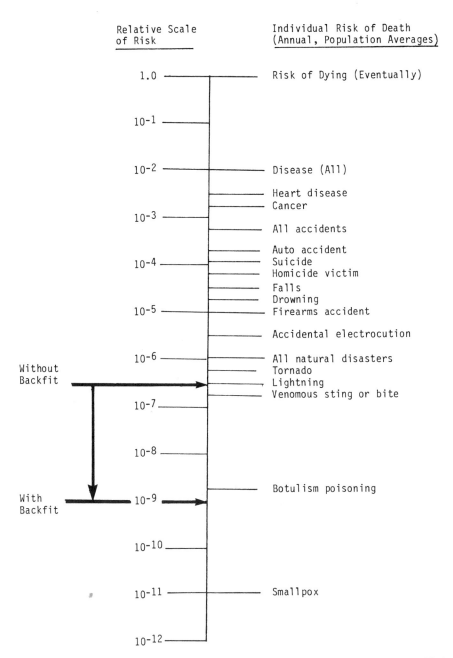

Figure 10. Using Risk Comparisons to Clarify the Reductions in the Risk of Prompt Fatality for an Individual Living within One Mile of the Plant Achieved through Backfitting with the Vented Containment System

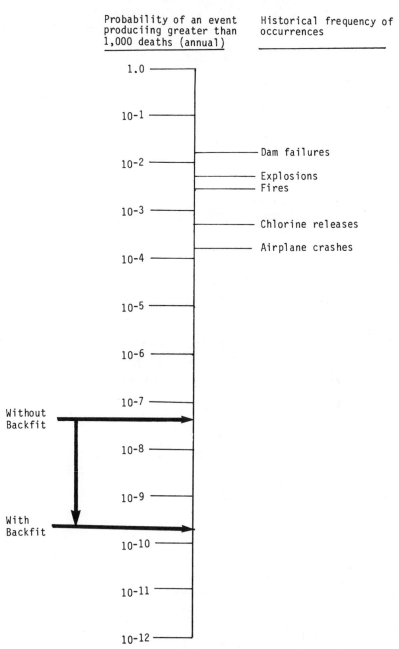

Probability of an event producing greater than 1,000 deaths (annual)

Historical frequency of occurrences

1.0

10-1

10-2 — Dam failures

— Explosions
— Fires

10-3 — Chlorine releases

— Airplane crashes

10-4

10-5

10-6

10-7

Without Backfit

10-8

10-9

With Backfit

10-10

10-11

10-12

Figure 11. Using Risk Comparisons to Clarify the Reduction in the Risk of Multiple Fatalities Achieved through Backfitting with the Vented Containment System

might be made. Comparative information might also be presented in the form of risk profiles (complementary cumulative distributions). Although risk profiles (such as Figure 4) have been criticized as less understandable by a nontechnical audience (Brown and Ulvila, 1985a), they provide more information about the nature of the risk and might be justified if the decision under consideration alters the shape of the risk curve, or, if through an initial effort to become familiar with such curves, the decision maker is comfortable with their use.

In situations where the estimated risk is complicated by latency (time delay in the realization of effects), involuntariness, dread, and other complicating characteristics, developing an intuitive understanding of the significance of the risk can be extremely difficult. In the backfitting analysis, for example, it is difficult to interpret the significance of the estimate that a vented containment system would reduce the risk of latent fatality due to core melt accidents for individuals living within 50 miles of the plant from approximately 10^{-7} to 10^{-10} per year. Interpretation is difficult not only because the numbers are so small, but because the nature of a latent cancer risk is difficult to conceptualize. Understanding might be aided by decomposing this risk reduction and comparing its component parts to other risks. Part of the decrease in latent fatality risk attributed to vented containment is due to a reduction in the likelihood of core melt. According to the backfitting analysis, vented containment reduces the probability of core melt from 3×10^{-5} to 5×10^{-6} per year. These probabilities might be clarified for the decision maker using an appropriate scale for low probabilities similar to that in Figure 10. The other part of the decrease in latent fatality risk is due to the fact that vented containment reduces the severity of core melt accidents (by making the more serious accident sequences less likely).

To help clarify the significance of this effect, a comparison along the lines suggested by Marshall (1982) might be useful. Marshall suggests that latent fatality risks from nuclear power plant accidents can be clarified by comparing them to the risks produced from a program of compulsory smoking. The concept of a compulsory smoking program is suggested for comparison with latent fatality risks from nuclear power plant accidents because both risks involve an uncertain possibility of death from cancer. According to Marshall, the risk from a radiation dose given to an individual at any age may be simulated by supposing that the individual is obliged to smoke cigarettes regularly, starting 10 years after the incident and ending 40 years after the incident. Using Marshall's estimates the reduction in latent fatality risk from a core melt accident produced in the backfitting analysis may be expressed in terms of a compulsory smoking program as follows: Without the vented containment system the probability of a core melt is 3×10^{-5} and, if a core melt should occur, the risk of latent death for individuals within 50 miles of the plant is estimated to be comparable to that which would result if those individuals were obliged to smoke approximately 40 cigarettes (2 packs) per week. With the vented containment system, the probability of core melt would be reduced to 5×10^{-6}. If a core melt should occur, the risk of latent death is estimated to be comparable to that from a compulsory smoking program that required individuals within 50 miles of the plant to smoke approximately 1/4 cigarette per week. Figure 12 summarizes the risk reduction using this comparison. Although the comparison may be criticized for attempting to draw parallels between two very different situations, some decision makers may find that such comparisons provide a level of insight sufficient to justify their use. Again, such comparisons should be accompanied by information concerning the uncertainties in the risk estimates.

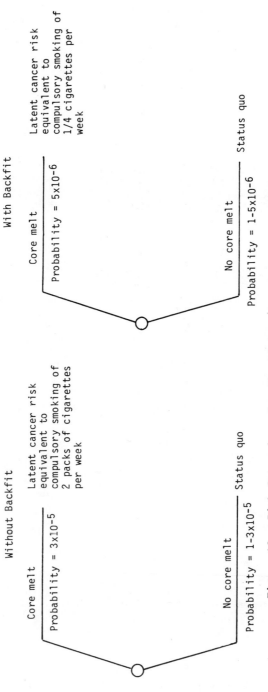

Figure 12. Risk Comparison for Clarifying the Risk of Latent Cancer Fatality Achieved through Backfitting with the Vented Containment System

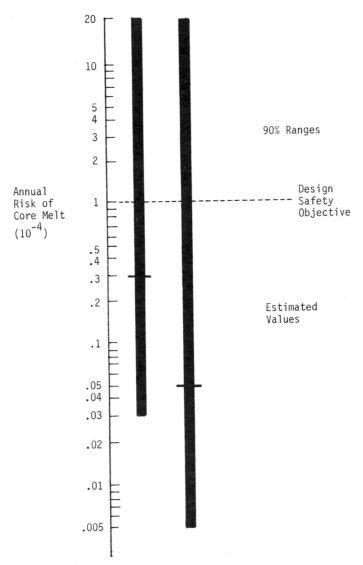

Figure 13. Risk Comparison for Clarifying Estimated Values and 90 Percent Confidence Ranges for the Annual Risk of Core Melt with and without Backfitting the Vented Containment System

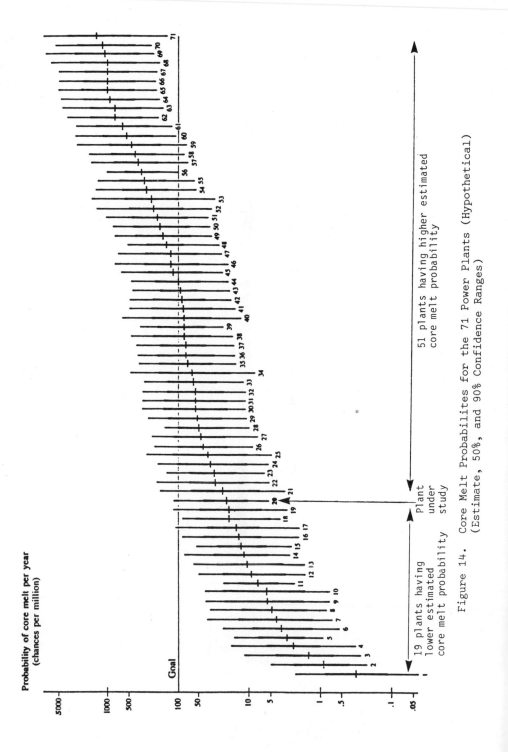

Figure 14. Core Melt Probabilities for the 71 Power Plants (Hypothetical) (Estimate, 50%, and 90% Confidence Ranges)

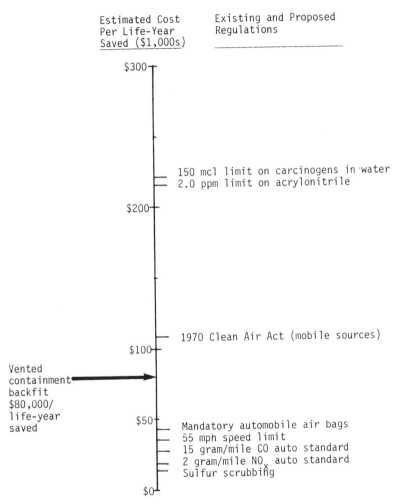

Figure 15. Risk Comparison for Clarifying Cost-Effectiveness Estimated for Backfitting with the Vented Containment System

In addition to using risk comparisons to allow the decision maker to develop a personal perspective on the significance of the numerical risk estimates, risk comparisons can also be constructed to provide an institutional perspective. Brown and Ulvila (1985a, 1985b) suggest several applications that compare risk estimates with various benchmarks that are important to the NRC. Figure 13, for example, compares estimated annual probabilities of core melt with and without vented containment to proposed design safety objectives. The figures uses range bars to indicate the uncertainty in the estimates and is similar to several plots used by Brown and Ulvila. Figure 14 compares the estimated core melt probability and range of uncertainty with similar (hypothetical) estimates for other nuclear reactors. It is also similar to a figure presented by Brown and Ulvila. As illustrated by these latter applications of comparative risk information, whenever the uncertainty in estimates is significant for the risk comparison, it should be conveyed to the decision maker. Figure 15 illustrates one final form of comparison that may help the decision maker achieve an institutional perspective. The figure compares the estimated life-saving cost-effectiveness of the vented containment system with cost-effectiveness estimates for other regulatory decisions that have and have not been taken.

SUMMARY

There is obviously a great deal of flexibility for developing and using comparative risk information. In the absence of empirical tests for the effectiveness of alternative methods, the best strategy for using comparative risk appears to be to proceed with caution. Recognizing the danger that poorly structured risk comparisons can easily mislead, the analyst should take care to explain the limits of any comparisons and emphasize that no particular conclusion needs to be drawn. Perhaps the most important rule governing initial designs is to allow for feedback from decision makers. The reference risks, means, and formats for comparisons should be selected according to the desires and preferences of those who will use them. If initial use is monitored, the effectiveness of various methods of risk comparisons will become more apparent and initial systems will, undoubtedly, be improved upon.

REFERENCES

Brown, R. V., and J. W. Ulvila: 1985a, "Communicating Information for Risk Management: preliminary Appraisal and Guidelines," Decision Science Consortium, Inc., Falls Church, Virginia, February.

Brown, R. V., and J. W. Ulvila: 1985b, "Decision Support Paper: Risk and Cost/Benefit Information Relevant to Vented Containment and Alternative Decay Heat Removal Backfits at Peach Bottom Unit 2," draft, Decision Science Consortium, Inc., Falls Church, Virginia, January.

Cohen, B., and I. Lee: 1979, "A Catalog of Risks," Health Physics 36, 707-722.

Crouch, E. A. C., and R. Wilson: 1982, Risk/Benefit Analysis, Ballinger, Publishing Company, Cambridge, Massachusetts.

Crouch, E. A. C., and R. Wilson: 1984, "Inter-Risk Comparisons," in J. V. Rodricks and R. G. Tardiff (eds.), Assessment and Management of Chemical Risks, American Chemical Society, Washington, D.C.

Fischhoff, B., P. Slovic, and S. Lichtenstein: 1979, "Weighing the Risks," Environment 21 (4), 17-20 and 32-38.

Inhaber, H.: 1979, "Risks with Energy from Conventional and Nonconventional Sources," Science 203, 718-723.

Kahn, H.: 1979, "Symposium/Workshop on Nuclear and Nonnuclear Energy Systems: Risk Management and Governmental Decision Making," February 5-7, 1979, Washington, D.C., the MITRE Corporation, Metrek Division, MTR-79W00335, September.

Keeney, R. L., and D. von Winterfeldt: 1984, "Improving Risk Communication: Insights and Decision Analysis," paper presented at the workshop "Risk Perception and Risk Communication," Long Beach, California, December 10-12.

Lawless, E. W., M. V. Jones, and R. M. Jones: 1984, "Comparative Risk Assessment: Towards and Analytical Framework," Midwest Research Institute, Kansas City, Missouri, Spring.

Marshall, W.: 1982, "Big Nuclear Accidents," paper presented at the International Conference on Nuclear Power Experience, Vienna, September 13-17, 1982, IAEA-CN-42/18, International Atomic Energy Agency.

Nuclear Regulatory Commission: 1975, "Reactor Safety Study," WASH-1400 (NUREG/74/104), Washington, D.C.

Reissland, J., and V. Harries: 1979, "A Scale for Measuring Risks," New Scientist 803, 809-811.

Rothschild, N.: 1979, "Coming to Grips with Risk," address presented on BBC television, reprinted in the Wall Street Journal, May 13.

Sjoberg, L.: 1979, "Strength of Belief and Risk," Policy Sciences 11, 39-57.

Slovic, P., and B. Fischhoff: 1982, "How Safe is Safe Enough? Determinants of Perceived and Acceptable Risk," in Gould and Walker (eds.), Too Hot to Handle, Yale University Press, New Haven.

Slovic, P., B. Fischhoff, and S. Lichtenstein: 1980, "Informing People about Risk," in M. Maziz, L. Morris, and I. Barofsky (eds.), Banbury Report 6, The Banbury Center, Cold Spring Harbor, New York.

Sowby, F. D.: 1965, "Radiation and Other Risks," Health Physics 11, 879-887.

Starr, C.: 1969, "Social Benefit Versus Technological Risk," Science 165, 1232-1238.

Whipple, C.: 1980, "Comparisons of Risk," paper presented at a Joint MURS/NAS Seminar on Risk Assessment and Decision Process, Orsay, France, December 17-19, 1980, Electric Power Research Institute, Palo Alto, California.

Wilson, R.: 1979, "Analyzing the Daily Risks of Life," Technology Review 81, 40-46.

Wilson, R.: 1984, "Commentary: Risks and Their Acceptability," Science, Technology, and Human Values 9 (2), Spring, 11-22.

REGULATORY NEGOTIATION: LESSONS FROM <u>BENZENE</u>

Steven M. Swanson* and James V. DeLong**

Health and Environmental Affairs Department, American
Petroleum Institute*, Murphy & DeLong**
Washington, D.C.

ABSTRACT

Recent efforts by the Occupational Safety and Health Administration
(OSHA) to negotiate an agreement on a revised standard for occupational
exposure to benzene represented an important initiative by the Agency.
Increasingly, the Government is seeking more efficient and effective ways
to establish health and environmental standards, and negotiation is a
promising alternative for promoting this goal. While use of negotiation
in rulemaking proceedings is new, negotiation has been common in other
contexts for many years. It is important, however, not to assume that the
lessons learned in these other contexts can be applied automatically to
rulemaking negotiations. The paper discusses some of the most significant
distinctions among the different contexts in which negotiation occurs.

KEY WORDS: Rulemaking, Rules, OSHA, Negotiation, Mediation, Benzene,
Environment, Health.

INTRODUCTION

In 1978 the Occupational Safety and Health Administration (OSHA)
promulgated a new standard lowering the permissible exposure limit (PEL)
to benzene from 10 ppm to 1 ppm. The revised standard was challenged in
court, and ultimately the Supreme Court ruled against the agency.[1] The
Court rejected OSHA's contention that the applicable law permitted the
Administrator to reduce the standard simply because benzene is a
carcinogen and there is no proven safe level of exposure. The agency had
to show that exposure at current levels creates a significant risk that
would be significantly reduced by the new standard. OSHA's failure to do
this meant that it had not met its statutorily-imposed burden of showing
that the lower standard is "reasonably necessary and appropriate."[2]

---

*This paper expresses only the views of the authors and does not
necessarily represent the position of the American Petroleum Institute or any
of its members.

[1]<u>Industrial Union Dept., AFL/CIO v. American Petroleum Institute</u>,
448 U.S. 607 (1980).

Following this decision, OSHA could have reopened the proceeding to introduce additional evidence on the significant risk point. It chose not to do so, however, and the 10 ppm standard remained in force. In 1983 OSHA received petitions from labor and public interest groups asking it to revisit the issue and lower the PEL.

In the period between the Benzene case and the 1983 petitions the government had developed an increasing interest in the concept of "regulatory negotiation." This is the idea that in some instances an agency might develop regulations through negotiations among all the interested parties (including the agency) rather than through formalized rulemaking processes. The arguments for and against "Reg Neg" are complicated and we will not try to recapitulate them here. Probably the most complete treatment is the 1981 report that Philip Harter wrote for the Administrative Conference of the United States, and anyone wanting to explore the topic in more depth is urged to consult that work.[3] For present purposes the important point is that the idea of Reg Neg was in the air and some OSHA staff members had become interested in its possibilities.

The 1983 petitions asked for not only a revised PEL but for an Emergency Temporary Standard (ETS) as well. OSHA denied the request for an ETS, but in the course of doing so it committed itself to a proceeding to inquire into the need for a lowered PEL. Furthermore, OSHA announced its intention to follow a stringent schedule for the rulemaking. A final rule was to be in place by June 1984.

This was the context in which OSHA suggested to a number of organizations having a stake in the issue that they meet and explore the possibility of negotiating the provisions of a proposed rule that would be acceptable to the parties and to the agency. The parties were interested, and the ensuing discussions continued intermittently from the fall of 1983 to the fall of 1984.

The ultimate participants were:

Labor

- Industrial Union Department, AFL/CIO
- Oil, Chemical and Atomic Workers
- United Rubber Workers
- Steel Workers of America

Industry

- Chemical Manufacturers Association
- American Petroleum Institute
- American Iron and Steel Institute
- Rubber Manufacturers Association

---

[2]Occupational Safety and Health Act, 29 U.S.C. § 652(8).

[3]Philip Harter, "Negotiating Regulations: A Cure for Malaise," 71 Georgetown Law Journal 1 (1982). See also Henry Perritt, "Analysis of Four Negotiated Rulemaking Experiments," A Report to the Administrative Conference of the United States, Sept. 4, 1985 (Draft).

In the end the parties were not able to reach agreement, and so informed OSHA. As of this writing, OSHA has not released a proposed revised benzene standard.

The main point to be made here is that in analyzing the benzene negotiation -- or any other regulatory negotiation, for that matter -- it is important not to be too quick to analogize the process to other, more familiar kinds of negotiations. One frequently hears analogies drawn between efforts to negotiate a benzene standard and:

- Labor negotiations over wages and hours
- OSHA advisory committees and science advisory panels, such as the NSF or EPA's SAB
- Negotiated settlements in environmental litigation

As a general proposition, analogies and models are important and useful. Used appropriately, they can give essential structure to an unfamiliar situation by providing ready-made expectations and behavioral norms. Used inappropriately, however, they can create false expectations that can lead parties seriously astray. In the authors' view, one of the most important lessons of the benzene negotiation is the limited applicability of any of the models listed above.

Explaining the reasons for this requires some additional background on two key aspects of a regulatory negotiation.

The first of these involves a core concept of negotiation theory called BATNA -- "Best Alternative To a Negotiated Agreement."[4] This means simply that each party to a negotiation, before entering an agreement, will have to decide that the result is superior to what it thinks will happen in the absence of agreement. If the party would prefer the alternative to the agreement, then of course it has no incentive to sign.

In most cases, of course, the alternative to an agreement will not be entirely clear. There will be a range of possible outcomes with varying probabilities attached to them. A party's willingness to accept an agreement will depend on its appraisal not only of what will most probably happen otherwise but also of the worst that might happen. One of the benefits of reaching agreement is the guarantee of avoiding the worst, and an important element in a negotiation is the comparative risk preference of the parties. One could speculate that a more risk averse party, all other things being equal, would have a larger appetite for negotiation than a less risk averse party. Thus a risk averse party might enter an agreement even though it estimated that it had, say, a 90% chance of attaining a substantially better result without an agreement if the remaining 10% represented a very disadvantageous outcome.

The BATNA concept had several applications in the benzene negotiation. Looking at the situation objectively, it seems safe to say that each participant had reason to think that negotiation might produce an outcome superior to the outcome the participant foresaw if OSHA proceeded in a conventional manner. In addition, each had to face the fact that some extremely poor possible outcomes could not be totally discounted.

---

[4]Roger Fisher & William Ury, Getting to Yes, 104-11 (Houghton Mifflin Co. 1981: Boston).

All the parties recognized that the alternative to reaching an agreement was an administrative rulemaking proceeding, not the status quo. They also knew that a prudent participant would have to recognize that OSHA would go into such a proceeding with a presumption that the standard should be lowered, given the agency's position of three years before.

At the same time, a prudent participant would recognize that an agency desire to lower the PEL would not necessarily translate into quick action. As a matter of historic fact, OSHA proceedings have tended to be long, and there was no reason not to think that a benzene rulemaking would not follow the pattern. Nor could there be any guarantee that a new standard would survive judicial review. The exact dimensions of the "significant risk" standard articulated in the <u>Benzene</u> case remain unclear, and there was always a chance that the agency could go through a lengthy rulemaking only to be overturned again.

Given these realities, each party had an incentive to give serious consideration to the possibility that negotiations could produce a result superior to its BATNA.

There is an important additional BATNA issue. Historically, the rulemaking process has been poor at identifying possible trade-offs arising from the differing values that affected parties may place on various parts of a rule.

The essence of any bargaining process is that people place different values on different things. In a sales transaction, to take the most elementary example, the seller would rather have the money than the goods while the buyer would rather have the goods than the money.

In a rulemaking context, when the parties are considering the different possible combinations of provisions it is likely that the values they attach to the different provisions will vary. Consider an occupational exposure standard, for example. A union may press for a low exposure limit with no "exceedences" of that level allowed.[5] In fact, the union may think it very important that the average level of exposure be kept down, but not be worried about random exceedences. Industry may press for a higher exposure level with wide latitude for exceedences. In fact, it might not object to the low exposure limit desired by the union if exceedences were allowed.

This is precisely the stuff of which bargains are made, but the parties' true positions are not likely to surface in a rulemaking proceeding, in which each feels compelled to maintain a hardline posture on every individual issue. The rulemaking process may actually produce a combination of provisions representing the least desirable outcome for all parties.

This concept of differential value is important. It means that even if one neglects factors like delay and potential judicial reversal a negotiated agreement can be a positive sum game. In the right circumstances every participant can be better off under the agreement than it would be under a rule imposed by an agency.

----

[5]Exceedences are defined here as periodic excursions above the PEL but less than the short-term exposure limit.

The second important factor in considering the applicability of these other models to negotiated rulemaking is the nature and uses of information brought to bear in the process.

In a negotiation over a proposed rule, information is evaluated by the participants from a number of perspectives.

An obvious consideration is that each party wants to convince the others of the correctness of its own position. No party believes that the others are totally irrational or malevolent. If the unions could convince industry that a lower PEL were necessary to protect workers then industry would stop protesting. Similarly, if industry could convince the unions that a lower standard was a pointless waste of money the unions would stop pressing for it.

It is easy to discount this itch to convert the opposition as naive, but it is an important factor in negotiations. And, one might add, it can have an effect. We all know how often organizations or individuals will adopt an official truth, regarded as so obvious that it is exempt from analysis or reconsideration. To have such truths questioned by an intelligent and articulate adversary can be a valuable educational experience. In the benzene negotiation the participants, positions had hardened in the earlier rulemaking and the litigation that followed it, and it seems likely that all parties emerged from the bargaining sessions with new perspectives.

Another use of information is closely related to the one discussed above. A party might not convince an opponent of the correctness of its views, but it can convince the opponent that the party itself is sincere in these views, and thus not easily budged. Consequently, information is constantly being evaluated in terms of whether it represents the real views of the party presenting it.

In a negotiation such as the one over benzene, information must also be constantly evaluated in terms of its probable impact on the agency. If a representative of a company or a union regards a piece of information as likely to cause OSHA to be moved in one direction or another then the parties must consider this as the bargaining proceeds.

Obviously, scientific information is very important in this context, since the parties know that OSHA will react to it. There are some countervailing considerations that may dilute the purity of the participants' technical presentations, though. All participants have to work with at least one eye on possible court challenges should the negotiation fail. Intermedairies in a negotiation must remain aware that the parties will have a well-founded fear of producing outcomes in a "failed negotiation" that might undermine their case at a later time.

Another potential problem is that a participant may find it difficult to judge exactly the impact a particular piece of information may have on OSHA. The information ultimately provided to the agency decisionmakers flows through a filter of many layers of bureaucracy. This makes it hard for the participants to assess what will influence the decisionmaker, or how much. Consequently, it is difficult for participants to assess precisely the bargaining value of particular information. Also, different evaluations of the same information can lead to a deadlock.

This problem of appraising the value of information is exacerbated in the context of health and safety regulation by the immense uncertainties involved. Almost every aspect of the problem, ranging from the risks presented at particular exposure levels to the costs of compliance with proposed rule provisions, presents substantial and usually irreducible uncertainty. One of the most difficult aspects of rulemaking (or negotiating) in these conditions is developing an appropriate response to the uncertainties that cannot be eliminated.

However, this raises an interesting comparison between formalized rulemaking and negotiation. In rulemaking, an agency will often tend to follow a legal model of decisionmaking in which the agency resolves uncertainties by making "findings of fact" that treat anything that is "more probable than not" as if it were 100% certain, and then bases agency policy conclusions on these supposed "facts." In other words, most of the uncertainty is assumed away.[6] In negotiation, the parties will not agree to such artificial resolutions of uncertainties. Consequently, they are forced to seek solutions that do not depend on eliminating uncertainties and that would be acceptable across a range of possible states of the world. This can result in a more realistic treatment of uncertainty than would emerge from the supposedly more rational process of formalized rulemaking.

A final important kind of information in negotiation concerns the values parties place on the different possible provisions of an agreement. Since such information delineates the bottom line of a party's negotiating position, it will always be exchanged cautiously, and often only by implication. An important part of the negotiation process revolves around a party's making a tentative or partial disclosure of this kind of information and then waiting to see if other participants reciprocate.

Information introduced into the negotiating process is used in all of these contexts at once, which creates a very complex system. Parties are constantly weighing the utility of a piece of information in one context versus another.

These two dimensions -- BATNA issues and information issues -- are crucial to any effort to use other kinds of negotiation as a paradigm or model for Reg Neg. If the proposed paradigm does not correspond with Reg Neg in terms of these two dimensions, its utility as a model is likely to be quite limited.

Analysis of the three models often cited as paradigms leads to the conclusion that none of them is satisfactory.

Labor Negotiations

The most commonly-drawn analogy is between regulatory negotiation and labor negotiations. This analogy is particularly appealing when a

---

[6]For further discussion of this problem of the artificial elimination of uncertainty, see James DeLong, "Informal Rulemaking and the Integration of Law and Policy," 65 Virginia Law Review 257, 346-47 (1979); James DeLong, "How to Convince an Agency," Regulation, Sept./Oct. 1982, at 27, 33-35. See also American Petroleum Institute, Comments on EPA, "Proposed Guidelines for Carcinogen Risk Assessment," 49 Fed. Reg. 46294 (November 23, 1984) (Filed Jan. 22, 1985); American Petroleum Institute, Comments on EPA, "Formaldehyde; Determination of Significant Risk: Advance Notice of Proposed Rulemaking and Notice," 49 Fed. Reg. 21869 (May 23, 1984) (Filed August 3, 1984).

regulatory negotiation involves an OSHA health or safety standard because the principal interests are the same -- management and labor. However, there are a number of crucial differences between the two contexts, and too facile a reliance on the collective bargaining analogy can lead to serious mis-estimates of the situation.

An initial, and important, distinction is that a regulatory negotiation may involve many different participants interlocked in a complex jigsaw of congruent and conflicting interests. A collective bargaining situation usually involves only two parties, the company and the union. The difference has a major impact on both BATNA and information issues.

A particularly crucial dimension of the two-party character of a labor negotiation is that there is no outside agency waiting to act if the parties do not agree. At any given time, the alternative to agreement facing each party is a work stoppage and consequent economic loss, followed by some agreement when one of the parties exhausts its capacity to take punishment. This creates quite a different BATNA structure than exists in the regulatory context.

There is also less room for bargaining over differential values. While the participants in collective bargaining may find some areas that present the prospect of trading off differential values, (work rules versus pay rates versus fringe benefits, for example), for the most part the disagreements involve tangible questions of money. This tends to make the game zero-sum (or even negative sum, if a long work stoppage occurs) and reduces the prospects for finding positive sum outcomes.

The nature and use of relevant information is also rather different. While some of the same considerations apply to collective bargaining as to regulatory negotiation, such as the need to convince the other party that one is serious and committed, many do not. The primary differences are, again, that in a labor negotiation there is no independent entity waiting to act, and scientific information and analysis of uncertainty are of lesser importance.

OSHA Advisory Committees and Science Advisory Panels

The Occupational Safety and Health Act allows the establishment of advisory committees to assist in standard setting. Any advisory committee "shall include among its members an equal number of persons qualified by experience and affiliation to present the views of the employers involved and of persons similarly qualified to present the viewpoint of workers involved...."[7] An advisory committee is also to include representatives of state and federal agencies and outside experts.

On the face of it, such a group might appear to present a reasonable paradigm for regulatory negotiation. In practice, though, OSHA Advisory Committees have been used as scientific advisory committees, concerned with evaluating and advising the Administrator on the scientific information relevant to a standard. Thus they can best be considered together with groups which are more explicitly designated as "Science Advisory Boards."

---

[7]Occupational Safety and Health Act, 29 U.S.C § 656(b).

The process of "negotiation" that occurs in the context of a board of scientific advisors is quite different from regulatory negotiation. While science panels are often put together with an eye to obtaining diverse viewpoints, scientists seek professional consensus, which is a different type of negotiation than the attempt to reconcile competing interests that characterizes the regulatory negotiation process. Scientists are attempting to reach consensus on technical matters according to certain well-defined canons of inquiry. A certain amount of compromise may take place, but the scope for horse-trading is severely limited by the nature of science itself.

In addition, a science panel is not expected to develop a rule which an agency can then propose forthwith. Almost always, it is expected that other considerations, such as cost or technical feasibility, will have to be combined with the scientists' judgment to produce a finished product. (For example, the Science Advisory Board of EPA reviews the agency's risk assessments, but is not asked to comment on the risk management decisions that flow from them.)

Furthermore, a failure of an advisory group to reach agreement does not mean that the agency will automatically act, or decline to act, to the benefit or detriment of the negotiating parties.

In terms of our two axes of comparison -- BATNA issues and information use -- it is difficult to find any significant similarities between science advisory groups and regulatory negotiation. The only point of comparison seems to be that both will, on occasion, make use of scientific information. In fact, if one were to find that the principles applicable to regulatory negotiation were in fact relevant to the operations of a science advisory board, one would be sure that the board was acting as a policy making body, not as a scientific counselor.

Negotiated Settlements in Environmental Litigation

In several respects, this analogy is better than the others. Here, as in regulatory negotiation, if the negotiations fail then an institution with authority over the parties to the dispute will resolve the issue. There is also substantial scope for the interplay of differential assessments of the value of different segments of a proposed settlement and for the development of positive sum games in which everyone is better off than they would be if the authority imposed a settlement. Consequently, many of the same BATNA incentives are at work as aree operating in a regulatory negotiation.

Some of the issues involving the use of information are also similar to those that exist in regulatory negotiation. The parties must assess the potential impact of information on the outside decisionmaker, and must also assess the utility of information in various contexts. There are substantial uncertainties over key issues.

In one respect, this analogy fails -- the issues in a specific piece of environmental litigation are usually more narrow than those in a rulemaking. In a rulemaking, the question is usually, "What should the standard be?" In a lawsuit, the question is more likely to be, "Given the standard that exists as a result of a statute or existing rule, has it been violated and what should happen as a result?" The uncertainties more often than not involve questions of factual proof and timing more than they involve fundamental questions of science, economics, and values. Consequently, there is less scope for compromises that leave both sides better off than they would be under an imposed solution. There is also a considerable difference between the kinds of information relevant to this type of negotiation and the kinds relevant to a negotiation over a rule.[8]

For the reasons stated, none of these oft-suggested paradigms is directly on point. There are, however, enough similarities to create a temptation to analogize between familiar kinds of negotiation and the regulatory situation.

The limits on these analogies must be kept firmly in mind. If regulatory negotiation is to be useful in the future, it is important that everyone interested in it help develop our understanding of the nature and dynamics of the process. Relying on seductive, but only partially applicable, paradigms will lead to unreasonable expectations and disappointments.

The importance of maintaining a realistic view of regulatory negotiation is shown by events since the end of the benzene affair. A lively literature of evaluation has developed, much of it directed at the question of whether the negotiations "succeeded" or "failed." As a matter of fact, there seem to be far more people interested in helping perform the autopsy than ever worked to keep the patient alive.

The end point sought in the benzene negotiation was a draft proposed rule which would then have moved through the normal administrative structure of proposal and final rule. As stated at the outset, the parties were not able to achieve this, and to this extent one could say the process failed.

On the other hand, the parties did work towards some creative solutions to problems in a less adversarial setting than exists in a conventional rulemaking. The understanding of the problems attained during the negotiations will certainly have an impact on the rulemaking proceeding when it finally commences. The efforts during the negotiations were marked by a more cooperative spirit than had characterized some industry/union contacts in the past, and it seems fair to say that all parties achieved a better grasp of the problems and positions of the others. Important lessons were learned about both the regulation of benzene and the process of regulatory negotiation. In all of these dimensions one would have to count the experiment a success.

----

[8]The term "usually" in this paragraph deserves particular emphasis. In some cases, settlement discussions will in fact revolve around the broader question "What should the standard be?" and the process can become very much like a regulatory negotiation. In such a situation the judge may play the role of mediator, albeit a mediator of unusually large authority.

TOWARDS AN ACCEPTABLE CRITERION OF ACCEPTABLE RISK

Paul Milvy

ABSTRACT

   The determination by federal risk managers of an acceptable level of
carcinogenic risk depends upon many factors. Several of the factors are
amenable to objective analysis while others remain largely subjective
and/or culturally determined. The size of the population that is at risk
influences our perception and analysis of what level of risk constitutes
an acceptable risk. The rate of risk and the total or population risk are
often used uncritically or interchangeably to express risk. Yet the rate
of risk and the total or population risk seem to modulate our notions of
what level of risk is perceived as acceptable. This general problem is
explored and an approach for the resolution of this perplexing situation
is suggested and compared to empirical data.

KEY WORDS: Acceptable risk, Population risk Individual risk, Risk
            Management, Carcinogenic risk

   The paradox is a way station to knowledge. It implies some degree of
insight into the way the world is and the way it works.   But the
inability to resolve a paradox attests to the limitations and the
incompleteness of understanding and of knowledge. By begging to be
resolved, the paradox is a reflection of the dichotomy   between
appearance and reality, between our limited knowledge and   our urge to
understand ever more deeply. Perhaps paradoxes confirm that scientific
efforts are squarely placed at the interface of knowledge and ignorance.
To resolve a paradox is to move forward in the never-ending struggle to
understand better the world in which we exist. Paradox is but knowledge
in the making.

---

*Environmental Protection Agency, (WH562A), 401 M Street, SW, Washington,
D.C. 20460. The views expressed are entirely those of the author and do not
necessarily represent those of the US EPA.

The new discipline of risk management abounds in paradox. In this communication I examine one aspect of a central conceptual problem of risk management that has been analyzed many times already. The problem I address is that of "acceptable risk." In the phrase "acceptable risk" there exists a tension between the noun "risk" which in principle can be objectively measured and the adjective "acceptable" that modifies it and is largely subjective. Society's lack of consensus as to the meaning of the term "acceptable" in this phrase leads directly to such questions as "How safe is safe enough?" and "acceptable to whom; those who profit from the risk or those who must endure it?" The concept of a risk sufficiently small or sufficiently safe to be acceptable when compared to other risks to life and limb is straightforward. It is the application of this standard to the real world in which we live and die that has proven so difficult. Attempts to define the term "acceptable risk" illustrate the dilemmas and paradoxes that bedevil regulators and managers of risk. Risk is an objective, quantifiable externality. In principle it is knowable, although the scientific methodologies and armamentaria presently available to estimate carcinogenic risk are not nearly as powerful as we might wish. Of yet greater concern is the recognition that these tools provide no more than a very limited glimpse of the myriad of carcinogenic species that we know must confront us. A recent study by the National Research Council (National Research Council, 1984) provides a sobering perspective regarding the efficacy of present testing methodologies on our ability to identify chemical carcinogens. The NRC estimates that of the more than 65 thousand chemicals in what it defines to be the "select universe" of its study, approximately 48,000 are used in commerce. The study estimates that no toxicity information of any kind is available for about 79% and no carcinogenicity tests have been conducted on 85-90% of these chemicals. In view of the hundreds of new chemicals added annually to the inventory of commercial chemicals, one concludes that fundamentally new technologies must be developed if the fraction of chemicals for which carcinogenic information is available is not to become even smaller. Automated short-term mutagenicity tests that correlate fairly well with animal bioassay studies to predict mammalian carcinogenicity are already a viable option. As the Ames test is improved or as other tests that may complement and/or be superior to it are developed, this would become an increasingly attractive and cost effective approach.

We acknowledge, therefore, that however formidable the obstacles faced by risk analysts may be, in principal cancer risk from man-made carcinogenic chemicals can be measured quantitatively and its impact on mortality evaluated objectively. But it is a different matter to determine empirically or define abstractly a level of acceptable carcinogenic risk that is itself acceptable to society at large. The notion of "acceptability," as already noted, is largely subjective. Dictionary definitions themselves revert to subjective terms to illustrate its meaning. Neither dictionaries nor experts can be expected to agree on this term, nor on the criteria that can best be used to evaluate it.

The public generally does not estimate or evaluate risk objectively (Slovic et al., 1979; Litai, et al., 1983; Corvello et al., 1983; Milvy, 1986). Individuals do not reach decisions regarding personal conduct based exclusively or even in large part on such considerations. But the federal risk manager ignores the public's judgment of acceptable risk levels only at his or her own peril. To suggest that the added incremental risk is very minute, or that it is smaller than the 1.4×10^{-2} lifetime risk of death from automobile accidents, is arguably beside the point. To argue that a reduction in mortality has accompanied industrial progress (e.g. U.S. life expectancy at birth has increased more than 5 years since 1965 and 28 years since 1900) also does not demonstrate that the added risks from new carcinogenic chemicals are acceptable. For it does not demonstrate that a policy more prudent with respect to the management of carcinogens would not have achieved an even more rapid improvement in the nation's health. Finally, it has not generally been demonstrated to be true that the introduction into commerce of a new carcinogenic chemical, by replacing an existing more potent one or by decreasing total mortality in some other way, lowers total risk, although in specific instances this is obviously quite true.

The problem of defining a general algorithm or general approach for establishing levels of acceptable risk remains. It would seem to be largely intractable. Quantitative risk analysis (QRA) tries to diminish the distortions that subjective perceptions of risk introduce into the management of risk. As the methodological and technological weaknesses of QRA are overcome, the analysis of risk becomes more objective and more reliable. But this will not necessarily change the distortions involved in the public's perception of risk. It may be argued that these distortions tend to diminish in time with the dissemination of pertinent information. But these distortions do not result solely from a lack of information. When we look at optical illusions, an Esche lithograph is a case in point, it is not ignorance that leads to the distortions of our perceptions. It is one of the major roles of science to overcome our propensities to distort reality (it has been observed that "were appearance and reality identical there would be no need for science".) Education can go only so far to reduce such dichotomies. Litai, et al., (1983) and Slovic, et al., (1979) have shown, for example, that a voluntary[1] risk that is two or three orders of magnitude higher than an involuntary risk is equally acceptable given similar benefits from each. This is not a distortion of perception in the usual sense: it is an additional dimension or characteristic of the risky activity that influences our attitudes about its acceptability. The acceptability of a risk is a function of more independent variables than just the rate of risk or the absolute risk alone. I do not calculate cardiovascular benefit versus risk of skin cancer while jogging on a sunny afternoon. I may prefer Mozart's string quartets to hard rock, not because the risk of an injury to my hearing is less, but for reasons totally unrelated to risks. Risk quantification can help us to clarify such preferences only marginally, if at all. Individuals consciously and unconsciously assess relevant variables (within certain restraints for which the umbrella term "voluntary" seems largely to apply) and reach decisions. It is clear they can do this "gut calculus" best only when they have full access to the relevant facts, and full freedom to act on these facts. If an item - be it a food, an indoor environmental pollutant, or a workplace chemical - is carcinogenic yet those at risk are unaware of this, the uninformed judgment that is made may be inappropriate. If the risk is not totally voluntary the freedom to make an informed decision is circumscribed.

Several attributes of risk in addition to the quality of being voluntary influence levels of risk perceived as acceptable, as Table I indicates. Two additional factors that effect perception of an acceptable risk level merit attention. We begin by noting two conventional methods for expressing levels of mortality. The rate of risk, often called individual risk, expresses either the number of deaths as a fraction of

---

[1]Slovic et al. (1980) have conjectured that "voluntariness" may be surrogate variable closely linked to other characteristics.

the total number of people exposed and actually at risk or it uses some more convenient denominator, for example, 10^{-4} or 10^{-6} to express this fraction. Thus a cancer risk of 3×10^{-5} implies that three of every 100,000 people will die from cancer that results from exposure to a carcinogen. It indicates an annual risk if this is the annual rate, a lifetime risk if the deaths occur over a lifetime, generally assumed to be 70 years. The alternative approach to expressing risk defines risk in terms of total risk, sometimes called population risk. This expresses the excess mortality arising from the risk in terms of the total number of deaths. If 674 people die from cancer by virtue of exposure to an environmental or industrial carcinogen, this is the risk incurred and no explicit mention of the number of people at risk is made. These two ways to express risk are easily interconverted when the number of people at risk is known. In terms of the regulation of a risk, however, each carries different implications and the germ of paradox exists in these alternative approaches to formulating risk.

The concepts of equity and equality under the law and the dictates of common sense would seem strongly to suggest that the standards of acceptable risk for an individual be independent of the number of people similarly at risk from the same hazard. Yet in the real world this seems not to be the case, as the following examples illustrate. During a 70-year interval 236 deaths from cancer in the United States is often thought of as the bench-mark for the level of acceptable risk from a single man-made carcinogenic chemical.[2] This criterion of acceptable risk is more generally expressed as a lifetime rate. Since the 1984 population of the United States was 236 million these 236 deaths are equivalent to a rate of one in a million, or 10^{-6}. Yet 236 deaths would not be perceived as acceptable if they were to be limited to the workers in a chemical manufacturing plant that employs 250 people, the citizens of a small village of similar population, or some other small and discrete population. In both examples, when viewed from the perspective of the United States, 236 cancer deaths in a total population of 236 million have resulted from the carcinogenic chemical. But these deaths are discrete and localized they are likely to be perceived as a catastrophe; when they are dispersed over time and space, if perceived at all, they are probably considered to be background noise: a negligible, random, uncaused, rather trivial perturbation. In the one case the individuals who die of cancer can be identified with a high degree of statistical confidence. In the other case the 236 deaths, unless the primary tumor is a rare and unique tumor not normally seen in the population at large, are unidentified and unidentifiable. Epidemiologists are unable to separate those who die from these cancers from the total of 32 million cancer deaths that also occur during the 70 years interval. From this example I am persuaded that the criterion of acceptable total risk is somehow dependent on the size of the population that is at risk. But if the size of the total population that is at risk is included, we have implicitly reverted to using the rate of risk.

On the other hand, only a very small chance of even a single cancer death results if the 10^{-6} criterion of acceptable lifetime risk is applied to the factory or village cohort of 250 people.[3] Such a minute

---

[2]One should explicitly add the caveat that this chemical must fulfil some socially beneficial role, as well. How we quantify this requirement does not here concern us.

[3]250 people x $10^{-6} \ll 1$ cancer death. On an annual basis we expect abou two people to die annually in a population of 250. Because of the added 10^{-} risk we now expect 2.000004 annual deaths.

incremental risk of cancer is acceptable from the point of view of incremental mortality.[4] But a 10^{-6} rate of risk is impossible to achieve for each individual while at the same time maintaining a viable economy. It is three orders of magnitude smaller than the white collar fatal accident rate, which is, in turn, significantly smaller than accident rates among blue collar employment categories. The radiologist, the farmer, the carpenter, the short-order cook and the individual cooking meals at home, to name a few classes of people, all are at a risk much higher than 10^{-6} from individual carcinogens (e.g. x-rays, sunlight, sawdust, benzopyrene, and benzopyrene, respectively.) Whether we like this or not, it remains a fact that we can do little to reduce to 10^{-6} each of these small risks that effect small, discrete sub-populations, although a ten-fold reduction is generally technically quite feasible.

I have sought, by the analysis of this example, to make the case that the size of the population in which specific number of cancer deaths occur influences our perception of what constitutes an acceptable level of risk. But it is not only our perception (which connotes a subjective quality) of acceptable risk that is influenced by the size of the population exposed to the hazard. Objective analysis would seem to lead to similar conclusions. No expert would reach the conclusion that, in spite of the fact that most of a small village's mortality is known to result from a single carcinogen, regulatory action is unnecessary because nationwide the number of victims is not in excess of 236 deaths; no greater that is, than a rate of 10^{-6}. This conclusion would be unanimously rejected by company safety officers, hygienists, public interest group advocates, medical epidemiologists and risk managers. These professionals have reached this conclusion using the expertise of their disciplines and consequently their expert judgment takes on an "objective" quality, albeit one that really is no more than a consensus in a Delphic oracle-type exercise. Because it is a human exercise, it is inherently "subjective." The subjective/objective duality of our knowledge never be totally eliminated, but such philosophical nuances can largely be ignored by those seeking rules of thumb for effective management of risk.

In view of the above considerations, we see that as the population at risk becomes larger, the random, accidental, or "uncaused" quality of the cancer deaths seems to become more pronounced. As the population size decreases these deaths are seen by expert and non-expert alike as less random and more causally related to the carcinogen. The random quality is inexorably linked to the population size and both influence the conclusions of our analysis of criteria of acceptable risk. These two risk characteristics are also shown below the dotted line in Table I.

How do the above considerations help to resolve the subjective/objective and the rate of risk/total risk dichotomies that are endemic to the setting of acceptable criteria of risk?

Figure I presents risk as a function of population. The line representing a lifetime rate of risk $R'_L = 10^{-6}$ and the line representing

---

[4] I should emphasize that if 1000 similar factories or small villages each were exposed to the 10^{-6} risk, the population at risk would total 1000 x 250 = 250,000. With this population at risk there is now a 25% chance that a single additional person would die every 70 years. But in the example I am discussing, a single exposed population of 250 is considered.

236 deaths (236 = PR''_L) are both shown as a function of population (P) and of rate of lifetime risk (R_L). I have argued above that neither a constant <u>number</u> of deaths from a carcinogen (Figure 1, Curve A: mortality M' = 236) nor a constant <u>rate</u> of risk (Figure 1, curve B, for which the rate is constant and equals 10^{-6}) can simultaneously satisfy reasonable objective and subjective criteria for acceptable risk. The expressions for curves A and B have been constructed so that they result in the same acceptable risk at P = 236 million, where the curves intersect. As the population at risk decreases the two expressions increasingly diverge, one indicating a criterion for an acceptable risk level that I have argued above is too large, the other too small for the population actually at risk. Curve C, based on the expression $R_L = 0.015/P^{.5}$, represents the geometric mean of curves A and B [$R_L = (R'_L R''_L)^{.5} = .015/P^{.5}$]. By averaging the two more extreme risk expressions, it provides a criterion for acceptable risk as a function of population that represents a reasonable compromise. This criterion of acceptable risk explicitly incorporates the size of the population at risk as an independent variable. However it has been developed with little recourse to empirical data. If it is intended for use in the real world of carcinogenic risk, federal risk management, and public perception of reasonable and safe risk rates it must be compatible with these realities. At the same time it should provide general guidance that can help resolve substantive questions related to risk policy and management.

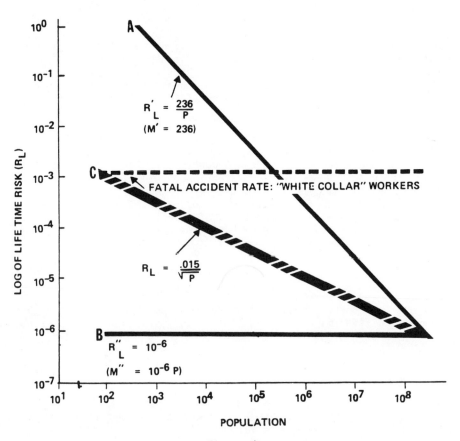

Figure 1

Figure 2 presents data points for 90 circumstances of human exposure to 42 carcinogens and carcinogenic mixtures. These points are plotted on coordinates that indicate the estimated size of the population at risk and the estimated lifetime cancer risks prior to any regulatory action that may have been taken. In this figure those chemicals for which a federal decision was made not to promulgate a regulation to reduce risk are shown by open triangles. The solid squares represent carcinogens for which regulations are currently under consideration or have already been promulgated. The dotted diagonal line is the best fitting straight line for the data shown by the black squares. Its slope is -0.047. The solid line represents the expression $R_L = .015/P^{.50}$ which has been discussed previously.

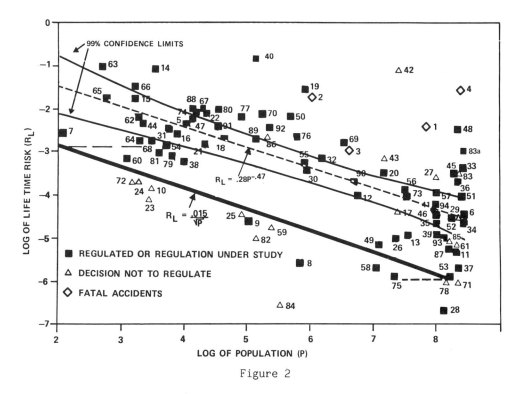

Figure 2

Figure 2 shows 19 hazards for which the decision not to regulate has been made by EPA. Ten of the triangles representing these hazards lie below the $R_L = .015/P^{.50}$ line. Of the nine that lie above the line, the greatest risk is cigarette smoking by men[5], represented by point #42.

---

[5]One might argue that cigarettes are regulated: the packs are required by law to bear four rotating warnings. I have chosen, however, to use a triangle to designate this risk in view of this near minimal regulatory requirement. If the risk associated with this hazard were thousands of times smaller - in the 10^{-4} to 10^{-5} range - I would consider the rotating warnings to be appropriate (e.g. saccharin.) My use of the triangle in effect provides the clue that I perceive this "regulation" to be tantamount to no regulation at all and to be quite inappropriate in view of the magnitude of the risk and its social costs. This in spite of the fact that this carcinogenic risk has a significant voluntary quality associated with it.

1. Accident, fatal - private sector 1982
2.   - mining
3.   - finance, insurance and real
                       estate, 47 yrs. (18-65)
4.   - all, 1982 rate for 70 yrs.

5. Acrylonitrile

6. Alachlor - dietary
7.   - flaggers
8.   - farmers
9.   - ground applicators

10. Amitraz - apple & pears sprayers
11.   - apple & pears consumers
12.   - apple, dietary
13.   - pears, dietary

14. Arsenic - copper smelters - high
15.   - copper smelters - low
16.   - glass manufacturing
17.   - Inorganic, neighboring
                 population average exp.
18.   - maximum exp.

19. Asbestos - occupational
20.   - school; students & teachers

21. Benzene - fugitive emission
22.   - coke by-product
23.   - maleic anhydride
24.   - ethylbenzene/styrene
25.   - storage
26.   - Stage II gasoline market
27.   - urban
28.   - average population exposure - drinking water
29.   - average population exposure - air

30. Beryllium

31. Butadiene,1,3 - occupational

32. Cadmium

33. Captan - food consumption

34. Captofol - food consumption

35. Carbon tetrachloride - urban

(continued)

(continued)

Key to Figure 2 (Continued)

68.   - all workers - TLV based

69. Nickel

70. Nitrosamines - occupational exp. from metal working fluids

71. NTA - public drinking water
72.   - formulators (occupational)

73. PCB - dietary fish

74. Pentachlorophenol - applicators/workers
75.   - air

76. Radiation, ionizing - all workers in medicine
                          and industry
77.   - power reactor workers
78.   - coal-fired boilers

79. Radionuclides - DOE facilities
80.   - uranium mines
81.   - elemental phosphorus plants
82.   - phosphate industry

83. Radon - drinking water

84. Styrene monomer - occupational

85. Tetrachloroethylene - urban population
86.   - dry cleaners

87. Trichloroethylene - urban air

88. Uranium mill tailings - inactive sites
89.   - active sites
90. Vinyl chloride - average exposure for population - air
91.   - max. exposure (occupational)
92.   - workers (occupational)
93.   - average exposure for population - water

94. Volatile Synthetic Organic Compounds

        ─ ── ── Risk - fatal "white collar" accidents (finance,
                     insurance, real estate) for 70 years.
        ─ ── ── ── 10^{-6} risk

*   Source: Milvy, 1986

TABLE I

Characteristics of Risk

Voluntary	Non-voluntary
Delayed	Immediate
Old	New
Necessary	Luxury
Ordinary	Catastrophic
Controllable	Uncontrollable
Natural	Man-made
-------------------------------	-------------------------------
Large population	Small population
Random and "uncaused"	Non-random, caused

(Source: Taken from Litai, et al., (1983))

TABLE II

Carcinogens (and years) for which Final Regulations have been Promulgated by EPA

1970:	Kanechlor		Sulfamic acid cyclohexyl
1972:	DDT		Safrol
1973:	Beryllium (*)		Arsenic Oxide (*)
			Telvar
1974:	Aldrin		
	Dieldrin	1978:	Paraquat
	Chlordane (*)		Asbestos (*)
	Heptachlor (*)		Hexachlor
			Lindane (*)
1975:	Selenium		Acrylonitrile (*)
	Strobane	1979:	DBCP
	Pestox		Pronamide
			Difluron
1977:	Paris Green		Chlorobenzilate (*)
	Vinyl Chloride (*)		
	Benzidine	1980:	Erbon
	PCBs (*)		PBBs
	Benzac		Tris
	Kepone		Perthane
	Chloranil		
	Mirex	1981:	Benzol

* Shown on Figure 2

Source: U. S. EPA, (1984).

Radon in drinking water[6] (#83) and urban benzene (#27) are objectively the next most serious carcinogens for which regulations have been considered and rejected. Five hazards for which federal regulation is being considered fall below the R_r line and, by the criterion of acceptable risk developed here, represent risks for which regulations are unnecessary. The other 66 hazards fall above the line that demarcates acceptable and unacceptable risks.

Chemical carcinogens have also been regulated by EPA for which both risk and population at risk estimates are not available. Such chemicals cannot be shown in this figure and are listed in Table II.

CONCLUSION

The empirical data and the decisions made and under consideration by federal risk managers and shown in Figure 2 are largely consistent with the acceptable risk equation that expresses lifetime risk as a function of exposed population size. This expression uses the geometric mean of the constant rate of risk and the constant total risk.

By adopting this acceptable risk criterion I have sought to resolve the paradoxical situation whereby neither a constant rate nor a constant total risk of cancer can be selected which provides an acceptable guide to regulating carcinogenic chemicals. The formulation of an acceptable risk criterion that is suggested here is not invariate with respect to population size. Some may well fault it for this reason. But when the size of the population that is at risk is considered, a constant value for either criterion invariably can be shown to be unsatisfactory both from objective and subjective perspectives even though both would seem to fulfill the requirement of legal equity.

Variables other than risk and population size are also generally considered by risk managers to be pertinenet to the decisionmaking process. These have not been addressed in this analysis. In particular, the economic costs of regulation obviously affect the regulatory process, either by influencing the decision whether or not to regulate, or `y influencing how stringently to regulated. Thus a comparison of the pre- and post-regulatory risks posed by those carcinogens that have been regulated would provide further insight into risk-managers' regulatory modus operandi. Two articles that touch on these considerations, by Anderson (1983) and by Byrd and Lave (1986), have appeared recently.

REFERENCES

Anderson, Elizabeth L. "Quantitative Approaches in Use to Assess Cancer Risk", Risk Analysis, 3, #4, 277-295, 1983.
Byrd, Daniel and Lester Lave, "Significant Risk is Not the Antonym of De -Minimis Risk", De Minimis Risk, Whipple, G.H., Ed., In Press, 1986, Plenum Press: New York.
Covello, Vincent T., W. Gary Flamm, Joseph V. Rodricks and Robert G.

---

[6]Indoor radon has not been included in the figure. The average risk from this hazard is about 3×10^{-3} to the U.S. population.

Tardiff, The Analysis of Actual Versus Perceived Risk, 1983, New York: Plenum Press.

Fischhoff, Baruch, Paul Slovic and Sarah Lichtenstein, "Weighing the Risks", Environment, 21 #4, 17-20, 32-38, 1979.

Litai, D., D.D. Lanning and N.C. Rasmussen, "The Public Perception of Risk", The Analysis of Actual Versus Perceived Risk, p. 213, Covello, Vincent T., W. Gary Flamm, Joseph V. Rodricks and Robert G. Tardiff, Eds., 1983, New York: Plenum Press.

Milvy, Paul, "A General Guideline for the Management of Risk from Carcinogens", Risk Analysis, 6,#1, 1986.

National Research Council, Toxicity Testing: Strategies to Determine Needs and Priorities, 1984, Washington, D.C.: National Academy Press.

Slovic, Paul, Baruch Fischhoff and Sarah Lichtenstein, "Rating the Risks", Environment, 21, #3, 14-20, 36-39, 1979.

Slovic, Paul, Baruch Fischhoff and Sarah Lichtenstein, "Facts and Fears: Understanding Perceived Risk", Societal Risk Assessment: How Safe is Safe Enough?, Schwing, R.C. and W.A. Albers, Jr., (Eds.), 1980, New York: Plenum Press.

United States Environmental Protection Agency Status Report Chemical Activities, V. II, Fourth Edition, (EPA 560/TIIS-84-001b) February, 1984

RISK MANAGEMENT IN THE U.S. AND JAPAN: A COMPARATIVE PERSPECTIVE

Kazuhiko Kawamura

Management of Technology Program
Vanderbilt University

Paul F. Lynes

Environmental and Water Resources Engineering
Vanderbilt University

Michael Minor

Department of Political Science
Vanderbilt University

Vincent T. Covello

Program Manager for
Risk Assessment
National Science Foundation
Washington, DC 20550

Saburo Ikeda

Institute of Socio-Economic Planning
The University of Tsukuba
Japan

ABSTRACT

Risk management practices are the result of scientific risk analysis, subjective risk evaluation, governmental policy, economic concerns, interest group pressure, and cultural influences. One way of analyzing the relative influence of scientific, cultural and political factors is to examine how decisions for similar risks are made in different countries. Cross-national comparisons may suggest new or alternative approaches to improving the interaction between risk assessment and risk management.

In this paper we examine the risk management process in the United States and Japan through four cases studies (lead, detergents, pesticides, and seat belts). This requires identification of the involved actors, and an understanding of how they are involved; the role of risk analysis in risk management; and the underlying structure. Finally, we ask how similar or dissimilar the U.S. and Japanese processes are in these terms.

This analysis is based on the results of a two-year comparative study of technological risk management in the U.S. and Japan. The work was sponsored by the National Science Foundation, the Japan Society for the Promotion of Science, and the Environmental Protection Agency.

KEY WORDS: Risk management, Risk assessment, U.S. and Japan.

1. INTRODUCTION

Technological hazards are universal, but the means of dealing with them are not universally the same. Different countries will, based on cultural, economic and political differences, manage the same risks differently. A small number of studies have employed a cross-national perspective to compare risk management approaches in several areas (Brickman, Jasanoff, and Ilgen, 1985; Lave and Menkes, 1985).

The object of these cross-national studies is to, first, learn by sharing experiences. The more long-term objective is to profit from this sharing, in areas related to methodologies, data collection, analysis, or the utilization of the results, that might enhance the effectiveness of future technological risk management practices.

This study, which was sponsored by the National Science Foundation and the Japan Society for the Promotion of Science, examined risk management practices in the United States and Japan. The study was begun in October, 1983, included a bilateral workshop with leading U.S. and Japanese participants in October, 1984, and will soon conclude with the publication of a Workshop Proceedings and a Final Report.

2. HISTORICAL PERSPECTIVE (Covello, et al., 1985)

In the U.S. and Japan major changes have taken place in the nature of the risks that each society faces, as well as in the social and political context for risk analysis and risk management efforts. For example, there has been a significant shift in the nature of the risks to which U.S. and Japanese citizens are subject. In 1900, the leading causes of death in both countries were infectious diseases--pneumonia, influenza, and tuberculosis. By mid-century, infectious diseases had been displaced by chronic degenerative diseases of adulthood--especially heart disease and cancer (National Academy of Science, 1979; Foreign Press Center, 1982).

Although there has been no substantial change in the rank of accidents as another leading cause of death, there has been a shift in the types of accidents. The rate of fatal accidents in mines, for example, has fallen substantially as has the average annual rate of fatal accidents in factories in the U.S. and Japan. Natural hazards still cause substantial property damage in both countries, but such events account for only a small number of annual fatalities.

While these types of accidents have been declining in significance, other types have increased. In 1900, for example, the number of automobile accidents in the United States was insignificant; however, in 1980 automobile accidents accounted for over 50,000 deaths (Claybrook, 1983). Although the number of automobile accidents in Japan is much smaller (around 9,000 in 1982), the fatality rate per vehicle mile in 1980 is 37% higher than that in the U.S. (Kasperson and Sakashita, 1984).

Next, in the U.S. and Japan there has been an increase in the role of the central government in managing risks. There have been dramatic increases in: (1) the number of major environmental laws, and (2) the number of national agencies charged with managing health, safety, and environmental risks. In the U.S. attempts have recently been made to reverse the trend toward growth in federal regulatory involvement; however, several factors have contributed to its continuation, including the increasing health, safety, and environmental consciousness of the nation; a decline in the level of public confidence in business; the emergence of the public interest movement; and the growth of a complex, interdependent, highly technological society. Additional factors leading toward continued national regulatory involvement include:

- An accelerating rate of technological change, resulting in enormous increases in the physical and temporal scale and complexity of risks [for example, approximately 70,000 chemicals are in current use, with perhaps 1,000 new chemicals being introduced each year];

- An increase il the speed of scientific and technological developments, leading to shorter and shorter time lags between scientific experimentation, development, and entrepreneurial production;

- The increasing role of government as a producer of risks through its sponsorship of scientific and technological research and development;

- The rising cost of technological risk control and damages.

In Japan, many of the factors have been pronounced. The rate of technological change in Japan equalled if not exceeded that of the United States. In Japan the devastation of World War II required Japan to rebuild her technological and industrial base (Ikeda, 1984). Japan has been transformed into a technological and economic superpower, bringing in its wake the concomitant problems of advanced industrial society.

The turning point in Japan's governmental involvement in risk assessment and management can probably be traced to the 1970 "pollution Diet," a special session during which 14 pollution bills were passed (Reed, 1981). Japan's Basic Law was revised, for the first time assigning greater priority to environmental protection than to economic growth. On July 1 of the next year, the Japanese government created the Environment Agency, which assumed the leading role in monitoring and regulating environmental issues (Kelly et al., 1976). The changed emphasis on environmental quality, even at the expense of economic growth, was maintained even through the oil crisis, and was in fact only relaxed in 1978 in order to create a situation of "peaceful coexistence" between economic growth and environmental protection requirements (Reed, 1981).

Finally, in the U.S. and Japan there has been an increase in the participation of special interest groups in the societal risk management process. Risk analysis and risk management activities have become increasingly politicized, with virtually every major health, safety, and environmental decision subject to intense lobbying by interest groups representing industry, workers, environmentalists, scientific organizations, and other groups (Edwards and von Winterfeldt, 1984). Not only has there been an increase in the number of such groups and their members, but also substantial growth in their scientific sophistication and modes of operation.

In contrast to the American experience, interest groups on environmental issues in Japan have tended to be localized or issue-

specific. There are in Japan no broadly based environmental or public
health organizations similar to the Sierra Club or Environmental Defense
Fund in the U.S.

In Japan, "kogai" (public nuisance) became a fundamental political
issue during the 1960's and 70's, leading to the rise of "Anti-Kogai"
citizen's movements (jumin undo) consisting of individuals directly or
indirectly impacted, or likely to be impacted, by development projects
(Ikeda, 1984). These jumin undo urged the government to take prompt
remedial measures to mediate the growing conflicts between economic
interests and damage to the environment. Using tactics ranging from
"humble requests" to sitdowns, demonstrations, and challenges through the
court system, they have helped block industry expansion (Kelley et al.,
1976) and in some cases (such as Minamata Disease) helped secure victim
compensation.

3. SUMMARY OF RISK MANAGEMENT APPROACHES IN FOUR CASE STUDIES

Case Study Selection

We approached the task of comparing risk management in both countries
through comparison of several carefully selected cases of technological
risk management. Among the issues which affected case study selection
were:

1) Similarity of the issue in both countries.

2) The representativeness of current risk management practices.

3) Sufficient issue duration.

4) Extensiveness.

5) Availability of data.

Based upon these criteria, four case study topics were selected:

1) risks from detergents;

2) seat belts;

3) risks from lead; and

4) pesticides.

Detergents

The detergents case shows close similarities between the U.S. and
Japan. In both cases it is local, rather than national, governments that
have generated the most stringent enforcement.

In both Japan and the U.S. problems were similar: how to manage
eutrophication risks in bodies of water, risks which might be increased by
the use of phosphates in synthetic detergents? In large part the answers
were the same, with the Japanese response predicated on the U.S.
experience. In the U.S., the detergent industry originally attempted to
substitute NTA; questions about its safety led to a second strategy of
reducing phosphorus use. The phosphorus content of detergents dropped
from 9-12% in 1970 to about 6% in those areas of the U.S. which had not
instituted a phosphorus ban.

636

There is considerable variance in the amount of wastewater which is treated in the two countries. In the U.S., most wastewater is treated in some form. As implementation of wastewater technology in the U.S. continues to increase, more U.S. wastewater will be treated for phosphate removal.

In Japan, a significantly lower percentage of wastewater, about 30%, is treated. In the wake of the Eutrophication Prevention Ordinance, the design of the sewerage plant located closest to Lake Biwa, the largest lake and a principal water supply source in Japan, was altered to include nutrient removal. This plant began service in April, 1982, several years after the problem had become serious.

There are varying perceptions of the role of government in the U.S. and Japan. Sueishi and Nishimura describe the "chushuku" system, which suggests that the Japanese government takes a paternal role, and there is a reluctance on the part of government officials to deal frankly with issues which appear to be outside of governmental control. In the detergent area, the role of governmental control is manifested in information availability. In the U.S., research findings are often disseminated and generally fully disclosed. In Japan, on the other hand, there appears to be an absence of information-sharing outside of the government.

Seat Belts

In both the U.S. and Japan, traffic fatalities increased in the 1960's. By 1970, 16,765 fatalities occurred in Japan. This trend reversed in the 1970's, and in 1979 there were only about half as many traffic fatalities as in 1970. However, fatalities began to increase again in the early 1980's.

The number of annual traffic fatalities in the U.S. passed 50,000 in the middle of the 1960's and stayed around 52,000 or 53,000 until 1972 when traffic fatalities reached an all-time high of 54,589. However, traffic fatalities decreased by almost 9,000 due partially to the federally mandated 55-mph speed limit. Traffic fatalities gradually increased afterward and in 1979, traffic crashes were responsible for the death of 51,093 Americans and the disabling injuries of an additional two million.

It should be noted, however, that the annual fatality rate in Japan declined from 8.0 per 100 million vehicle miles in 1975 in 4.8 in 1980. By comparison, in the U.S. the annual fatality rate showed little change from 3.35 per 100 million vehicle miles in 1975 to 3.34 in 1980.

Seat belt usage is low in both the U.S. and Japan: average usage is under 20 percent. Japan requires the driver to fasten the seat belt and to "strive" to have passengers fasten theirs when driving on national expressways. The U.S. now requires child safety seats in all 50 states and has passed mandatory seat belt usage laws in a few states.

Lead

In Japan, the Ushigome-Yangicho incident in Tokyo (May, 1970), acknowledged the risk of exposure to lead. Although health officials found no significant evidence of elevated blood lead levels in the residents tested, the issue become significant to the unions and local political groups. Responses by the Ministry of International Trade and Industry (MITI) called for a lowering of the lead content in gasoline from 8.96 gm/l to 3.28 gm/l in June, 1970. An expert committee was assembled in August, 1970, and the committee outlined a schedule for reduction of lead content in gasoline which resulted in the level of lead in gasoline being 0.15 gm/l by April, 1975. A total ban of lead was considered, but leaded gasoline remained available as premium gasoline for older cars which required lead for mechanical reasons. Government subsidies assisted refineries to increase the production of unleaded gasoline.

In 1975, the Environmental Protection Agency was sued to list lead as a pollutant under the Clean Air Act. This action was challenged, but lead was listed as a pollutant in 1976, and air quality criteria and the proposed standard were developed. The air quality criteria document determined that over 88% of the ambient air lead resulted from the combustion of leaded gasoline. A phasedown in lead was outlined, but the oil crisis of 1978 delayed the reduction of the lead content in gasoline.

The target population at risk from the health effects of lead in the blood were children under six years of age. Occupational exposure also resulted in ambient air quality limits in the workplace. Misfueling, additional information concerning health effects, and greater consumption than anticipated have resulted in additional reduction of lead in gasoline, from 1.10 gm/gal (0.29 gm/l) to 0.1 gm/gal (0.026 gm/l).

In both cases, the impact of leaded gasoline on the catalytic converters in automobiles played a major role in reducing lead in gasoline. Catalytic converters were installed to reduce non-lead pollutants, but the lead fouled the catalyst making the converters ineffective. In Japan, air quality was a major concern as well as the economic significance of the export market to the U.S. Technological developments provided engines that did not require catalytic converters to achieve the air quality emission standards.

Pesticides

Specially synthesized organic compounds became commercially available for pesticide applications (insecticides, herbicides, fungicides, anti-microbials, and other special applications) beginning in the 1940's. These compounds--organic chemicals such as DDT, parathion, BHC--proved to be highly potent for pest control and relatively rapidly displaced many older, less effective inorganic pesticide formulations. In agriculture, they opened new avenues for managing production, by stabilizing crops against pest destruction, improving yields, and underwriting a shift toward less labor-intensive production. Other important uses have included food and grain storage.

The use of synthetic organic pesticides increased rapidly in both Japan and the United States from the late 1940's onward. In Japan, the use of pesticides has increased dramatically even as agricultural land has slightly declined. The area of agricultural land in Japan averaged 6.2 million hectares in the 1960's but was marginally lower, at 5.8 million hectares in the 1970's. Pesticide use meanwhile climbed from 130 million pounds of on-line pesticide ingredients in 1960, to 180 million pounds by 1970, and more than 350 million pounds by 1980.

While the magnitude of pesticide use in the U.S. is sizeable and growing, the intensity of use has been markedly less than in Japan. U.S. agricultural land averaged 438.9 million hectares in the 1960's and 433.2 million hectares in the 1970's. In 1960 over 304 million pounds of pesticides were being applied annually. Pesticide use increased to 515 million pounds on average during the 1970's and by 1980, was about 605 million pounds. During the 1970's, then, Japanese farmers were using some 31 pounds of pesticides per hectare; by comparison, the American farmer was using an average 1.19 pounds per hectare.

There are numerous parallels in the situation encountered and the regulatory procedures evolved as Japan and the U.S. have sought to cope with chemical pesticides. The content of technical studies undertaken in each country's management process is largely the same. Each country utilizes basically a two-step management process. Prior to commercial sale and use, pesticide compounds are subjected to registration review and assessment (including necessary technical studies). Second, post-registration review and assessment continue as warranted; registration status and conditions may be revised or ultimately rescinded as new evidence on effectiveness and the impacts of use becomes available.

Foremost among the differences is the formal status accorded to risk/benefit evaluations in pesticide assessment. In the U.S., the Special Review procedure formalizes quantitative risk/benefit studies in the management process. There is, however, no parallel for this procedure in Japan. Quantitative risk/benefit studies are not formalized in the Japanese pesticide management process. Such analyses, when conducted, tend to be rather judgmental in character.

4. CONCLUDING REMARKS

Realizing that there are exceptions to any generalizations, and that four case studies and a workshop do not provide a broad foundation, it may nonetheless be useful to compare risk management in the U.S. and Japan along several dimensions. We found it useful to compare the approach to, and the structure of, risk management and draw obvious and non-obvious implications.

Approach to Risk Management. We can compare the Japanese approach, which tends toward negotiation and administrative guidance, with the U.S. approach of management by regulation. Much has been made of the Japanese ability to operate by consensus rather than law. In some cases, this tendency is regarded enviously, as in the tendency to regard management-labor relations and business-government relations in Japan as operating more smoothly than "adversarial" relations in the U.S.

We found that informal coordination was practiced more widely in Japan than in the United States, so there is some basis for accepting these generalizations for both the U.S. and Japan. The Japanese do practice a more coordinative approach to risk management, while we need remind no one of the adversarial and sometimes acrimonious relations between regulators and regulated in the U.S.

Risk Management Structure. Japan has an informal approach to risk management that utilizes an ad hoc committee evaluation. The committee is comprised of experts in the given area, and the committee's results are not publicly disclosed. The risk management structure, in Japan, tends to be centralized.

By contrast, in the U.S., risk management is more formal, open, and information is widely disseminated. Although much of the structure is centralized in the federal government, many of the federal laws encourage decentralization of authority to state agencies. Furthermore, local or state jurisdictions enact regulations that may be more strict than federal regulations.

Risk analysis and management are institutionalized processes in the United States. For example, in the case of pesticides, the RPAR process not only provides for risk analysis, but also for risk/benefit analysis.

There is no institutional analogue in Japan. The same goes for users of restricted pesticides: certification is required in the U.S., but not in Japan.

Centralization/decentralization is also important in the development of risk issues. In Japan, local interest groups, supported by the mass media, tend to bring risk issues into the government's awareness as demonstrated by the blood lead poisoning incident of newspaper workers, in the lead case study, and the water quality of Lake Biwa in the detergents case study. In the U.S., issues tend to gain national recognition through organized national interest groups, such as the Environmental Resources Defense Fund which initiated the law suits resulting in lead regulation under the Clean Air Act.

Obvious Implications. Given that Japan relies on negotiation and coordination to manage technological risks, Japan appears to have a system which is efficient in the economic sense. Issues would not tend to become a matter of public debate, but instead be a matter of negotiation between parties which are relatively "expert," that is, risk producers and risk regulators.

In contrast, the U.S. appears adversarial and therefore inefficient. Relations between risk producers and risk regulators tend to become confrontational. Many issues become a matter of public debate, and after interest groups have become involved, there may be some risk that scientific input loses influence in the public debate.

Non-Obvious Implications. At the same time, we need to ask whether there are non-obvious implications in a consensual versus an adversarial approach. It appears there may be. We found that Japanese participants in the workshop continued to mention the lack of public confidence that the Japanese government was doing a good job of protecting them from risks. Because the debate was most often "behind closed doors," nothing appeared to be happening. Therefore, public perception was that risks were being either mis-managed or simply not managed at all.

By contrast, an open, more adversarial approach in the U.S. at least created the public perception that risks were being dealt with. Of course there is always the strong possibility that risks would be perceived as being mismanaged, but less possibility of a public perception that nothing at all was being done.

This study comparing technological risk management in the U.S. and Japan is part of a small, but growing literature on cross-national risk management comparison. As mentioned earlier, Lester Lave and Joshua Menkes have explored risk management in the U.S. and West Germany. In addition, Ron Brickman, Sheila Jasanoff, and Thomas Ilgen have completed a study which compares policies for regulating toxic chemicals in the U.S., Britain, France and West Germany.

These studies are useful but just scratch the surface. There is a need for both research breadth (more countries entered into a comparative framework) and depth (more cases, and a more finely-structured framework with which to analyze cases).

Attempts are being made to develop a second U.S.-Japan workshop that would examine the technical aspects of risk assessment in both countries. With this study of risk management as a background, examination of techniques regarding risk assessment would provide the basis for further scientific and technical exchange between the two countries.

REFERENCES

Brickman, R., S. Jasanoff, and T. Ilgen, Controlling Chemicals: The
    Politics of Regulation in Europe and the United States, Ithaca:
    Cornell University Press, 1985.
Claybrook, J., "Motor Vehicle Occupant Restraint Policy," pp. 21-47 in V.
    Covello, W. G. Flamm, J. Rodricks, and R. Tardiff, (ed.), The Analysis
    of Actual Versus Perceived Risks, New York: Plenum, 1983.
Covello, V. T., J. Mumpower, K. Kawamura, P. F. Lynes, and M. Minor, "Risk
    Analysis and Risk Management in the U.S. and Japan: A Historical
    Perspective," in the Proceedings of the First U.S.-Japan Workshop on
    Risk Management, October 28-31, 1984, Tsukuba Science City, Japan.
Edwards, W. and D. von Winterfeldt, "Public Disputes About Risky
    Technologies; Stakeholders and Arenas," in V. Covello, J. Menkes, and
    J. Mumpower, (eds.), Risk Evaluation and Management, New York: Plenum
    Press, 1984.
Foreign Press Center, Facts and Figures of Japan, 1982 Edition, Tokyo,
    Japan, 1982.
Ikeda, S., "Risk Management Practices in Japan," Proceedings of the First
    U.S.-Japan Risk Management Workshop, October 28-31, 1984, Tsukuba
    Science City, Japan.
Kasperson, R. and N. Sakashita, "Seat Belt Usage in the United States and
    Japan," Proceedings of the First U.S.-Japan Risk Management Workshop,
    October 28-31, 1984, Tsukuba Science City, Japan.
Kelley, D. R., K. R. Stunkel, and R. R. Wescott, The Economic Superpowers
    and the Environment, San Francisco: W. H. Freeman, 1976.
Lave, L. B. and J. Menkes, "Managing Risk: A Joint U.S.-German
    Perspective," Risk Analysis, Vol. 5, No. 1, March, 1985, pp. 17-24.
National Academy of Sciences, Sciences and Technology: A Five Year
    Outlook, San Francisco: W. H. Freeman, 1979.
Reed, S. R. "Environmental Politics: Some Reflections Based on the
    Japanese Case," Comparative Politics, Vol. 13, No. 3, April, 1981, pp.
    253-270.
Sueishi, T. and S. Nishimura, "The State of the Art in Risk Assessment in
    Japan," in the Proceedings of the First U.S.-Japan Workshop on Risk
    Management, October 28-31, 1984, Tsukuba Science City, Japan.

RISK EVALUATION OF HAZARDOUS WASTE DISPOSAL

SITES USING FUZZY SET ANALYSIS

Randy D. Horsak   Sam A. Damico

NUS Corporation   S.A. Damico & Associates, Inc.
Houston, Texas   Houston, Texas

Evaluation and ranking of controlled hazardous waste sites can be made using a relatively new technique referred to as Fuzzy Set Analysis. The methodology presented is applicable to multiple alternative decision making, when criteria are of unequal importance, and is based on the concept of establishing a subjective value for each alternative according to each criterion, and then raising the subjective value to a power commensurate with the relative importance of the criterion. This exponential weight is calculated on the basis of a preferential analysis of criteria comparisons. Apart from ranking the alternatives, Fuzzy Set Analysis provides a quantitative representation of the community opinion of the order of importance of the criteria, regardless of the sites being considered. Based on the importance factors averaged from a cross section of the community, public concern could also be ranked.

KEY WORDS: Risk, Hazardous Waste, Fuzzy Set, Ranking, Subjective Variable, Alternative Decision Making

INTRODUCTION

Under the Hazardous and Solid Waste Amendments of 1984 (Section 3019 of RCRA), owners of hazardous waste disposal sites using landfill operations or surface impoundments are required to amend RCRA Part B permit applications to include information on the potential for the public to be exposed to hazardous wastes as a result of their operations.

According to the EPA's guidance manual, the owner should draw conclusions regarding the potential for and possible magnitude of human exposure from both normal operations and accidents at or near the unit(s) of concern, for each unit and for each pathway. The owner should also discuss the potential for direct human exposure and the potential for human exposure from the contamination of food chain crops. In particular, the owner should describe the site-specific location, design, and operating factors that reduce the potential for releases as well as factors that increase the potential for exposure.

To comply with EPA guidelines, an analysis should be performed for each of the following potential exposure pathways:

- groundwater
- surface water
- soil
- air
- subsurface gas releases
- transporation-related releases
- worker-management practices

As was the case for the implementation of CERCLA (i.e., Superfund), the EPA may be required to identify the facilities warranting the highest priority for remedial action. When setting priorities, criteria may be established based on relative risk through the Hazard Ranking System (HRS) or a similar model. The ramifications of submitting exposure information could range from "no action" by the EPA to complete shutdown of the facility.

Matrix Evaluation Analysis

Numerical matrix approaches, such as the HRS, have been used to evaluate and rank hazardous waste sites in order to prioritize remediation efforts. Due to the non-quantifiable nature of the criteria, these matrices are built using subjective values whose unitless natures require that the values be weighted according to the importance or significance of the criterion. Consequently, the values are adjusted to account for the inequality of the criteria. Several techniques are used to weight criteria values, and each attempts to reach a decision with a minimum degree of bias. The use of a priori assignment of weighting factors has been widely used in recent years. This approach involves assigning the criteria weights by the study team based upon experience and knowledge of the criteria.

Another popular approach is the "Delphi Technique" of gathering a diverse assembly of individuals who, as a group, assign weights to the criteria. Following the criteria weighting, the values for each alternative are adjusted accordingly, and the sites are then compared. "Sensitivity tests" are performed by changing the criteria weights or criteria values, or both, to determine if the final site ranking is changed by these slight adjustments. The purpose of the sensitivity test is to introduce the element of tolerance limits to the analysis.

Regardless of the inherent shortcomings, it is apparent that subjectively-based, weighted matrix analysis represents the state of the art for disposal site evaluation in today's regulatory environment. Thus, it remains industry's responsibility to seek new approaches to improve the methodology to provide better and more reliable decisions.

Fuzzy Set Analysis

At best, the decision to distinguish one site from several alternatives can be a tortuous and time consuming effort. Advances in decision theory and the availability of computers to store and manipulate large amounts of information can simplify this effort.

One methodology (Yager, 1977) recently developed for multiple alternative decision making, when criteria are of unequal importance, is based on the concept of establishing a subjective value for each alternative according to each criterion, and then raising the subjective value to a power commensurate with the relative importance of the criterion. This exponential weight is calculated on the basis of a preferential analysis of criteria comparisons.

644

A detailed review of Fuzzy Set Analysis can be found in Zadeh (1973) and Kaufman (1975). Briefly, Fuzzy Set Analysis refers to a consideration of multiple alternatives according to multiple criteria. When the number of alternatives and criteria is small, the human mind is capable of "keeping things in order"; however, when the alternatives or criteria are numerous, the "fuzziness" of the matrix is pronounced so that significant information is either suppressed or ignored. To remedy this, the relative importance of the criteria is determined in a separate matrix analysis and is applied as a vector weighting to the alternatives. Yager's procedure to determine the relative importance of the criteria is to calculate the eigenvector of the maximum eigenvalue of a matrix of paired comparisons; this is done according to the importance of one criterion over another, when only those two criteria are considered.

TABLE 1

SITE EVALUATION CRITERIA

- Groundwater

- Surface Water

- Air

- Soil

- Subsurface Gas Release

- Transportation Release

- Worker Practice

Case Study

To illustrate how Fuzzy Set Analysis may be used, consider the following hypothetical example. Hazwaste Disposal Company (HDC) owns and operates five commercial landfills. As a result of the RCRA requirement for exposure information, HDC submitted reports to the EPA for their consideration. However, HDC has also elected to further explore the nature of the risk at each of their five landfills. Because of limited time and money, HDC hopes to determine the nature of the risk at each site, prioritize the risks among sites, and then undertake a program of corrective action, if necessary.

Table 1 lists the site evaluation criteria, and Table 2 summarizes the parameters analyzed within each criterion. The numerical ratings shown in Table 3 are the result of extensive analysis performed by technical experts in their respective fields. In many instances, computer models were used to predict pollutant concentration levels at various receptor points in order to realistically compare sites.

TABLE 2

SUMMARY OF PARAMETERS FOR EACH EXPOSURE PATHWAY

AIR

Observed Releases
Waste Characteristics
Waste Volume
Demographic Distribution
Target Receptors
Land Use
Meteorology - Wind Speed and Dispersion
Waste Volume

GROUNDWATER

Observed Releases
Depth to Aquifer
Precipitation
Permeability
Physical State
Containment
Waste Characteristics
Water Well Use
Subsurface Soil
 Characteristics
Target Receptors

SURFACE WATER

Observed Releases
Terrain
Precipitation
Flooding
Distance to Surface Water
Physical State
Containment
Waste Characteristics
Waste Volume
Target Receptors
Surface Water Use
Ecosystems

SOIL

Observed Releases
Terrain
Permeability
Physical State
Containment
Waste Characteristics
Waste Volume
Area Land Use
Target Receptors

SUBSURFACE GAS

Observed Releases
Waste Characteristics
Waste Volume
Demographic Distribution
Target Receptors
Meteorology

TRANSPORTATION

Observed Accidents
Waste Characteristics
Waste Volume
Routes
Demographic Distribution
Target Receptors
Land Use
Transfers
Containment
Management Training Practices

WORKER

Observed Accidents
Waste Characteristics
Waste Volume
Accessibility
Containment
Target Receptors
Management Training Practices

646

TABLE 3

SUMMARY OF SITE RATINGS

Exposure Pathway	Willow Road Site	Broadfield Site	Osage Site	Weston Site	Fairfield Site
Air	.7	.8	.8	.6	.7
Groundwater	.6	.7	.5	.4	.6
Surface Water	.7	.7	.6	.5	.6
Soil	.9	.8	.9	.9	.9
Subsurface Gas	.7	.4	.6	.9	.8
Transportation	.6	.8	.8	.9	.6
Worker	.9	.9	.9	.9	.9
	5.1	5.1	5.1	5.1	5.1

To determine an average opinion of the relative importance value for each of the 7 criteria, 19 individuals were selected as a representative cross section of a typical community. Each individual was asked to relate his or her preferences in paired comparisons of the criteria. The eigenvector of the maximum eigenvalues for the matrix of paired comparisons was calculated, and the mean value for each criterion was used as an exponential weighting factor for the data listed in Table 3. By weighting the ratings for each site according to the the importance factors of the selection criteria, no single criterion may be considered more important than another when considering the merits of an individual site. Therefore, any criterion from a site may be compared to the same (or any other criterion for another site) on a numerical basis.

As an illustration, if we consider that the worst chain is the chain with the weakest link, then the same logic can apply to the site ranking. In other words, we will review only the lowest weighted values for each site, and rank them accordingly. The results of the combined analysis are presented in Table 4.

For the five sites, the corresponding decision values indicate that the "worst" site is Weston, followed by Fairfield, Willow Road, Osage, and Broadfield.

Apart from concluding the rank of each site, Fuzzy Set Analysis provides a quantitative representation of the community opinion of the order of importance of the criteria, regardless of the sites being considered. Based on the importance factors averaged from a cross section of the community, public concern would be ranked according to the order presented in Table 5.

TABLE 4

SUMMARY OF DECISION VALUES

Exposure Pathway	Willow Road Site	Broadfield Site	Osage Site	Weston Site	Fairfield Site
Air	.3599	.5277	.5277	.2314	.3599
Groundwater	.4537	.5759	.3422	.2423	.4537
Surface Water	.8532	.8532	.7967	.7346	.7967
Soil	.9031	.8059	.9031	.9031	.9031
Subsurface Gas	.8998	.7624	.8596	.9693	.9361
Transportation	.7142	.8632	.8632	.9329	.7142
Worker	.9771	.9771	.9771	.9771	.9771

TABLE 5

ORDER OF IMPORTANCE OF CRITERIA

CRITERION	IMPORTANCE FACTOR
AIR	2.865
GROUNDWATER	1.547
SOILS	0.967
TRANSPORTATION	0.659
SURFACE WATER	0.445
SUBSURFACE GAS	0.296
WORKER PRACTICE	0.220

SUMMARY

Fuzzy Set Analysis can be used not only to rank the various waste disposal sites in terms of risk, but also to focus on the key parameters that affect decision making. HDC can use this technique to focus on potential risks and also to prepare a strategy for site remediation.

REFERENCES

Kaufman, A. (1975). "Theory of Fuzzy Subsets," Vol. 1. Academic Press: New York.
Yager, R. R. (1977). "Multiple Objective Decision-making Using Fuzzy Sets." Int. J. Man-Machine Studies. 9:375-382.
Zadeh, L.A. (1973). "Outline of a New Approach to the Analysis of Complex Systems and Decision Processes." IEEE Transactions on Systems, Man and Cybernetics, SMC-1,28-44.

ON THE EVOLUTION OF RISK ASSESSMENT AND RISK

MANAGEMENT AND THE FUTURE NEEDS

Fred Hoerger

Regulatory and Policy Consultant
Health and Environmental Sciences
The Dow Chemical Company
Midland, Michigan 48674

Only a quarter century ago, health and ecological concerns were dealt with almost exclusively by experts -- scientists and technologists who relied upon their experience, intuition, judgment, empirical rules of thumb, and a sense of safe vs. unsafe.

Since then, advances in medicine, toxicology, related biological sciences, ecology and analytical chemistry have resulted in recognition of risk assessment as a multidisciplinary endeavor.

Concurrently, public expectations for health and environmental quality, as well as direct and indirect public participation, have increased. Thus, today risk management is multivalue oriented.

The case study of the arsenic smelter at Tacoma, Washington, not only illustrates the multidiscipline/multivalue nature of risk assessment and risk management, but also underscores the importance of communicating and understanding risks. Today's roles of hazard assessor, exposure assessor, risk analyst and risk manager, may in the future be augmented by the role of communicator. The need for improving the bases for risk assessment, risk management, and communication of risk information is well recognized by today's leaders in these professions. However, existing efforts in research, pilot programs, and think thanks are limited and fragmentary. It is proposed that significant progress can come in each of the three fields by a collective identification of action oriented programs.

The papers presented in this session on the arsenic smelter in Tacoma provide a vivid, and rather comprehensive, portrayal of the state-of-the-art of the risk assessment and risk management processes as applied in contemporary society. My purpose as wrap-up speaker will be threefold: to briefly review how our U.S. society came to its present status of risk assessment and risk management; to characterize some important aspects of present analysis and policy making; and to suggest a few factors which will shape future policies and practices.

The Past is Prologue

Over the centuries, as societies have progressed from survival to affluent lifestyles, their concerns for risk have become more and more complex, sophisticated and varied. Food adulteration, water and food sanitation, particulates in air and drug efficacy were the major concerns from the mid-nineteenth to mid-twentieth century. (1) Many products of today -- pesticides, plastics, brake fluids, solvents, antibiotics, surfactants, glues, synthetic fibers and aerosol personal care aids, for example -- simply did not exist in 1945. (2) At that time only the experts and science fiction buffs envisioned nuclear power, interstate highway systems, television, electronics, the space age technologies and the medical practices of today.

The technological advances since 1945, however, have spurred great expectations in terms, not only of material goods and services, but also in the interests of health, ecological balances and environmental esthetics.

The controversies, debates and decisions over nuclear energy, automotive safety, worker health practices, the "chemical of the month," air, water and land pollution, all involved identification of new hazards (real or potential) and a ratcheting down of public norms of safety expectations.

Concurrent with these recent technological advances and the heightened sophistication of risk concerns, we have significantly increased our reliance on government for dealing with these health and environmental matters -- and our whole style of decisionmaking has shifted -- until about 1965 the relatively few regulatory officials were regarded as experts. The agencies were staffed largely with scientists, analysts, and technological engineers who relied up judgment to determine the safe or the unsafe; quasi-scientific rules of thumb such as empirical safety factors, augmented simple data bases and analogy to related phenomena and intuition. As issues became more complex, logic and decision-analysis decisionmakers and/or means of rationalization. A considerable body of literature emerged in the seventies dealing with federal analysis for decisionmaking.

The increasing role of government has drastically increased the complexity of our decision process. The numerous laws have decreased the flexibility of the decisionmaker. The Delaney Amendment to the Food, Drug and Cosmetic Act prescribes a way of managing the risks of carcinogens intentionally added to the food supply; the Clean Air Act prescribes a standard of protection for hazardous air pollutants, the Occupational Safety and Health Act prescribes standards to be based on feasibility. The congressional and political pressures have assumed a significant portion of the risk management function. Perhaps even more noteworthy has been the evolution of the public participation function in regulatory proceedings. (1) Self motivated, nonstakeholder individuals and groups have evolved, public hearings are prescribed by law, and stakeholders become advocates and adversaries.

The final aspect of our historical perspective which I would like to mention is the role of technology itself in increasing our ability to detect long-term or low-level hazard potentials.

Analytical chemistry permits the detection of substances at the part per billion, part per trillion, and even the part per quadrillion level. However, toxicology and the related biological sciences are relatively new, still largely empirical sciences without an underlying base of integrating theory. Epidemiology and exposure monitoring involve laborious studies. Consequently, our study of adverse health effects has focused on identification of possible risks and this capacity far exceeds our ability to elucidate and interpret the significance of the possibilities.

The case study of the arsenic smelter further illustrates the unfolding saga of society attempting to deal with risks. The smelter first became operational in 1890 to fulfill a raw material need and reflected the go-west and industrial revolution mentality of simply producing a product and having jobs. It is interesting that the first study of the health effects of arsenic was reported in the English literature about the same time that the Tacoma smelter was built. (3) Occupational health, particulate control, and finally chronic health evolved as concerns largely since 1945, coincident with advances in our science and understanding of health and environmental effects. The roles of EPA, OSHA, and state government certainly became significant since 1970. And more recently, public participation has been direct at the local level, and indirect through influence on formation of national policy on air regulations.

In summary, evolution of U.S. administrative procedures and congressional mandates during the past two decades has directed the regulatory agencies toward probabilistic statements of risk. However, much of the concurrent public and media discussion has been in terms of risk or no-risk with limited focus on the significance of low probabilities.

The Present Status of Risk Assessment and Risk Management

I wish to review several selected aspects of risk assessment and risk management in order to properly characterize our complex decision process. My points of emphasis are those which I believe set the stage for improvements in our processes.

1. Risk assessment is distinguishable from risk management. Today we utilize risk assessment and risk management as a framework for thinking about decisions. The National Academy of Sciences (NAS) highlighted this distinction in 1983. (4) I believe the distinction is an important one. Risk assessment involves the generation, collection and evaluation of scientific and factual information in order to characterize risk as objectively as possible. Risk management, in contrast, involves decisions in a broader context -- social, economic and risk values. The two but interactive. Figure 1 illustrates the interrelationship of risk assessment, laws and social values as inputs to a risk management

The Inputs for a Risk Management Decision

Figure 1

decision. I will speak more about these distinct functions later.

2. Risk assessment is a multidisciplinary process. The NAS subdivided risk assessment into hazard identification, hazard assessment, exposure assessment and risk characterization and estimation. (4) Hazard identification can be equated to testing and screening for hazards and research to elucidate the hazard -- building the data base. Hazard assessment is the evaluation of the data base and includes characterization of cause-effect and dose-response relationships. These steps, along with exposure assessment and risk estimation, include many disciplines such as epidemiology, clinical medicine, toxicology and related biological sciences, statistics or biostatistics, industrial hygiene, engineering, analytical chemistry, and sometimes such specialties as meteorology, hydrogeology and physics.

3. Risk assessment requires interdisciplinary peer involvement and review. Today there is frequently a wide divergence between the widely accepted premise that risk assessment is multidisciplinary and the actual practice or reality of risk assessment. Frequently, an individual or a small staff prepares a risk estimate which is then reviewed by others -- from a supervisory standpoint, from a peer standpoint, and/or from an institutional policy standpoint.

In my view, there are two shortcomings to the present practice of risk estimation. The preparer, whether a single person or a small group, represents a limited range of specialized know-how and experience relative to the complexity of the phenomena being assessed. This sets a particular style and weighting of assumptions in the draft assessment document. To a greater or lesser degree, the subsequent reviews are cast into a narrow format of checking the validity of the data used, the process used, and even the arithmetic of the third decimal place. The significance of the assumptions, the choice of mathematical models, and the consideration of other plausible mechanisms frequently gets rather limited attention in peer review. Even in one of today's best models, review of EPA staff draft carcinogen assessment documents by the Science Advisory Board, the limited resources and the time deadlines of the regulatory process often contribute to limited incorporation of peer review ideas into the final risk assessment. Considering the fact that summaries of draft risk assessments receive widespread circulation in the professional community, are highlighted by the various media, and "streaked" to decisionmakers, the draft assessment with little multidisciplinary input carries much more clout that even the best final assessment.

The point is, better ways to incorporate multidisciplinary thinking into the synthesis of the assessment and to provide for interactive peer review must be found. Only then can the credibility of risk estimates be improved.

4. Risk management decisions involve multivalues. Our regulatory decisions involve a complex set of values, some codified into laws, and some articulated by precedent and administrative policy and practice, and some emerging from the perceptions of the day. Again referring to the figure, the flexibility of the decisionmaker is limited. In my view, the wise administrator will try to clarify, early in the regulatory process, the restraints and the degree of latitude for a decision. The EPA decision to communicate risk information to the people of Tacoma suffered from initial uncertainty as to whether EPA intended to rely on public opinion for the decision or to adhere to the restraints imposed by the Clean Air Act. In contrast, in the saccharin controversy of a few years ago, the FDA made an early decision that the FD&C Act required the Agency to initiate proceedings to ban the substance. Their limited flexibility

to consider a small risk in other ways threw the controversy into the political arena for Congress to become the risk manager. The "zero-risk" statute was amended because the public valued benefits.

The trend in enactment of environmental laws in the seventies and Executive Orders in the eighties illustrates the philosophical dynamics of value emphasis. The National Environmental Protection Act (NEPA) required federal consideration of environmental values. The air and water laws of 1972, and even the 1981 Superfund, were command and control laws to achieve environmental quality values with little consideration of other values. More recently, the Toxic Substances Control Act (TSCA) of 1976 and the Executive Orders of President Carter and President Reagan required a consideration of broader social and economic values (wherever statutes were not restraining).

This year William Lowrance completed a comprehensive book entitled, Modern Science and Human Values. (5) He goes a step further and summarizes the emerging discussions on ethics, morality, equity and professional stewardship -- all values which often subtly underlie the controversial risk debates. He also touches upon the need for newer approaches to dispute resolution such as negotiation, mediation, arbitration and extra-legal dispute tribunals.

5. Communication of risk information is recognized as important but is largely intuitive and value laden. The Tacoma case study illustrates the significant effort involved in communication for a single public hearing and the variety of interpretations placed on both facts and analyses displayed before and at the hearings. The National Science Foundation, EPA, a few companies, universities and journalist groups have initiated, or are supporting programs to highlight the importance of more objective, more complete and less sensational reporting of risk information. By and large, these valuable efforts focus on assessing the problems and encourage greater individual responsibility and discipline on the part of communities, scientists, risk analysts, decisionmakers, reporters, editorial writers and educators. These efforts appear embryonic however.

Research into perceptions of risk, acceptance of risk, intuitive integration of information, relevancy of information, perceptions of information gaps or information over-load, and curriculum content has been very limited and in some cases nonexistent. It is noteworthy that numerous papers at this annual meeting focus on communication. It appears that extensive research, much of it pioneering, and perhaps elementary, is necessary if significant improvements are to be made in the effectiveness of communication and educational efforts.

The Future -- Muddled and Add-on Complexity or a Collective Agenda for Clarity and Progress

Looking to the future is risky business. It is said that in the mid-19th century an artist with a futurist bent was quite highly regarded. One of his works portrayed New York City in the mid-20th century. His masterpiece showed Manhattan filled with busy streets, block after block of offices and apartments, and giant bridges across the rivers to accommodate the needs of a bustling population. However, his portrayal of the buildings was most unusual by the realities of Manhattan today. There were no skyscrapers! All of his buildings were of a uniform five stories in height. The futurist had not foreseen the simple innovation of the elevator!

Today's risk assessors compensate for the 19th century artist's failure to anticipate a specific event by use of probabilistic estimates or by upper bound and lower bound estimates of risk. I'll hedge my views on the future by presenting three scenarios of the future but let you place your estimates on each scenario.

The first scenario involves a snail's pace evolution from the status quo by simply trying to refine and add on to our present approaches. The discipline of risk analysis will inch forward; more screening for hazards, empirical fitting of mathematical models to empirical data, improved peer review, and slow transfer of findings from molecular biology to risk assessment problems will be involved. Risk management will vacillate in its reliance upon the political process in contrast to the expertise and wisdom of science, engineering, and economics. But the trend will be toward innovative approaches such as unilateral corporate decisions to minimize risk, negotiation and resolution among stakeholders or at the community level, and administrative tribunals to lighten the loads on the courts.

The trend to an informed public will continue, but in a haphazard manner. Information availability, media sensationalism, communication and promotion by advocates, and the work of educators may well increase, but it will be capped by two factors -- the availability of resources and the public's ability to rely on common sense in terms of the relative weight to be given values and in their ability to decipher the relevant from the irrelevant.

In this muddled scenario of the future, perhaps the greatest progress will come from the enhanced ability to manage information provided by the computer systems. The ability to file information, to retrieve it, to analyze vertically, horizontally, and for specific criteria and properties are only now coming of age for the data bases used by risk analysts. These tools will provide new hypotheses and focus much more discussion on inconsistencies in estimates, logic paths and the messages of the communicator.

My second scenario includes the probability of discontinuities. First the topics of the risk agenda could change dramatically. Have the risk assessors of today analyzed the probability of oil from the Middle East being shut off for a six month period or a two year period? It seems that this year has seen a very noticeable increase in the number of air transportation fatalities and the damage from storms and earthquakes. Are these apparent increases random deviations, or flaws in our past statistical counting and estimating? Or, consider the plausibility of terrorists tinkering with our storage depots, communication and electrical switching points, or our water reservoirs.

On the optimistic side, it is plausible that significant breakthroughs will come in the biological sciences -- cancer researchers continue to be optimistic on finding cures or real prevention strategies; genetic engineers and investors have gleams in their eyes for new pharmaceuticals, safe pesticides and microorganisms that solve waste clean-up problems. The Health and Human Services Department has recently formulated a national policy which stresses problem solving in environmental health research; interpretation of problems might catch up with our rate of problem identification.

If any of the above events occurs, we will see a shift in our agenda of risks -- for the gloomy possibilities, many of today's low level risk debates will fade into oblivion. For the more optimistic breakthroughs, the scrutiny of new kinds of risk posed by the new technologies and societal activities would follow.

Incidentally, it would be interesting for analysts to compare the probabilities of occurrence of some of the above events with the probabilities for a few of today's concerns and to examine the relative proportion of national resources currently devoted to the different risk potentials.

My third scenario involves what I call a collective action agenda for improvement in risk assessment and risk management. It is based on the premise that we can collectively do much better than the fragmentary snail's pace scenario, and that a collective action plan will help society deal with the discontinuities of the future.

It seems to me that the needs for improving risk assessment, risk management and risk communication are well known and generally accepted. In the field of environmental health, three blue-ribbon reports of the past year articulate needs for research to improve the basis of risk assessment. The reports from a Task Force III group, from a panel of experts convened by the Council of Environmental Quality and the HHS Administration all articulate very similar needs. (6,7,8) These reports, however, stop short of defining an action plan or in defining programs that fit into results oriented institutional programs.

Similarly there is general dissatisfaction on our present approaches to risk management. Stewart, a Harvard law professor, recently pointed out the shortcomings of command and control regulations. (9) Congress is frustrated by the slow progress on waste site clean-up and in the time to write regulations. Clean Sites, Inc., a private sector enterprise was formed by industry and environmental groups to augment the government role in cleaning up waste sites. Mediation of environmental problems has occurred at the community level in recent years. Pilot programs to negotiate proposed rules are underway at OSHA and EPA. The Dubos Center will hold a workshop later this year to explore ways that the private sector can augment the government role in control of hazardous substances. All of these are embryonic attempts to make risk management more cost effective and timely. William Ruckelshaus has, on several recent occasions, emphasized the need to do analytical work and to synthesize new concepts for dealing with risk.

Finally, the emerging recognition that risk communication and education need investigation has already been stated.

As a generalization, the current approaches to all these need areas are largely fragmentary, single individual or single institution projects, often justified principally on the basis of other "more expedient" short-term goals.

My challenge is, instead of more conferences on the needs of risk assessment, management, or communication, we should organize workshops that focus on such questions as: Assuming a large yearly budget, what specific research programs should be initiated to improve the basis of risk assessment? The basis of risk management? The improvement of understanding of risk phenomena? Productive ideas for progress will come only if we change some of our meetings -- the topics must focus on the specifics of action programs, the participants must be those who generate new information and those which represent institutions who can deploy funds.

I believe we can make real progress in the quality of risk decisions and the utilization of our limited national resources if we develop action oriented programs -- research, pilot effort and policy concepts -- that

explore and test the already largely defined needs. Collective agendas
that incorporate and augment the current institutional efforts will
catalyze interests and support. The alternative to real progress is the
muddled snail's pace scenario and limited national capability to
anticipate and plan for the discontinuities of the future.

REFERENCES

Covello, Vincent T. and Jeryl Mumpower. "Risk Analysis and Risk
    Management: An Historical Perspective." Risk Analysis. June, 1985.
Gehring, Perry, J. "On Chemicals and Risks." Chemtech. September, 1985.
Hutchinson, J. Brit. Med. J. 2:1280. 1887.
National Academy of Sciences. Risk Assessment in the Federal
    Government: Managing the Process. National Academy Press. 1983.
Lowrance, William W. Modern Science and Human Values. Oxford University
    Press. 1985.
Upton, Arthur C., Goldstein, Bernard D., et al. "Human Health and the
    Environment: Some Research Needs." Report of the Third Task Force
    for Research Planning in Environmental Health Science. 1985.
Council on Environmental Quality. "Report on Long-term Environmental
    Researah and Development." March, 1985.
Executive Committee, Department of Health and Human Services (DHHS)
    Committee to Coordinate Environmental and Related Programs (CCERP).
    "Risk Assessment and Risk Management of Toxic Substances." A Report to
    the Secretary DHHS. April, 1985.
Steward, Richard B. "Economic, Environment, and the Limits of Legal
    Control." Harvard Environmental Law Review. Vol. 9:1. 1985.

BHOPAL DISASTER AND RISK ANALYSIS: THE SIGNIFICANCE
OF THE BHOPAL DISASTER TO RISK ANALYSIS AT ANY OTHER
CHEMICAL PLANT (SAFETY EXPENDITURE WITH CAPITAL RATIONING)

Ernest V. Anderson

Probabilities, Utilities and Risks
Sun City West, Arizona 85375

ABSTRACT

Current frequency of chemical plant incidents involving the public my
average one every ten years for a fifty man department (one every million
man hours.) Prior to Bhopal these resulted in from 1 to 400 complaints
per incident with visits to a first aid station the most common reaction.
What guides should now be applied to such exposures?

Self regualtion of loss exposures has limitations due to ignorance,
poverty and self deception. Effective safety measures require both
minimum and maximum cost levels on money. Synergism between small
exposures may require that each of us consider the implications of others
following our safety guides and lowers the allowable level of imposed
risk.

KEY WORDS: Bhopal, Negligible-risk, Safe-enough, Stopping-rules,
           Externalities, Synergism, Acceptable-risk-imposition.

OBJECTIVES OF THIS PAPER

The objectives of this paper are to increase public understanding of
some principles that have been useful in the field of loss prevention with
insured risks and with self-insured risks, and to suggest that self-
regulation of the chemical industry while necessary is in three (3)
particular cases not sufficient to prevent material and human loss.

PUBLIC UNDERSTANDING

PUBLIC UNDERSTANDING is pertinent to any discussion of risk
analysis. Indeed, the words "public" and "understanding" each have
implications for decision-making.

UNDERSTANDING is risk analysis is achieved when any concerned citizen
would act with the same sense of urgency or caution as the person who
gives a warning or conveys relevant information. Of course, there can be
disagreements about safety decisions--and I will say more about that--but
if there is UNDERSTANDING, both parties will appreciate why, how, or what
they are evaluating differently.

The other part of PUBLIC UNDERSTANDING--the PUBLIC-- is too often used in condescending manner. The public is the same person you see in the mirror or across the breakfast table. It includes legislators, State or Federal regulators, medical and academic opinion makers, consumers, producers, employees, retirees, and children. We all live on Spaceship Earth.

NEGLIGIBLE RISK

Perhaps the easiest point to make is that zero concentration, zero exposure, and zero risk do not exist. ZERO may be a shorthand term for 10-6, or even one part per million, but the only meaning to attach to a comment that there is "zero risk" is that the risk is negligible, too inconsequential to bother with, and simply not worth the cost of measuring.

Note that a negligible risk may still present a very small chance of a very large loss. Crossing the street or standing on the sidewalk both have such a risk from a car out of control. If the chance that the driver of the oncoming car has lost control is one in a thousand million, and my injury is valued at one million dollars, the resultant expected loss is one tenth of a cent. My worry about this problem with 1000 cars per hour passing my corner may save a dollar's worth of expected loss but will certainly drive me to an insane asylum or cost me more than that in wasted time. Erich Fromm's observations on neurotic worry are pertinent. (See highlighted box.)

RISK AND NEUROSIS

In the popular press, safety messages on risk-adverse and risk-purpose usually are slanted to praise the cautious individual. To even the balance, the following quotes by the eminent psychoanalyst Erich Fromm from an article in the New York Times of 11 December 1975 are instructive:

"If someone will not touch a doorknob because he might catch a dangerous bacillus, we call this person neurotic or his behaviour irrational.

"Normal thinking is based on the belief in a greater or lessor degree of probability. Paranoid-like thinking is based on the assumption of a logical possibility and wants to have absolute certainty that something could not happen even in the most remote circumstances.

"In individual life we know the irrationality of people who strive for absolute security--people such as hypochondriacs who spend most of their energy protecting their health, or overcautious people who avoid any risk because it could interfere with their craving for absolute security. "This craving is irrational (1) because there is no absolute security in life, (2) because once it is established as the dominant goal there is no limit to the means sought for to reach this goal, (3) because in the search for this goal the person cripples himself and loses all pleasure in living. In fact the chase after absolute security is a boomerang: it creates more insecurity than it avoids.

"A goal of absolute security is equally damaging when it dominates government policy. Economically it impoverishes us, politically it restricts freedom, psychologically it creates fear and apathy."

658

"Negligible risk should be tolerated, and severe risk should be reduced until the <u>avoidable residual risk costs</u> (loss-cost <u>plus</u>] risk-cost <u>plus</u> present value of ongoing control-costs imposed on others) are negligible." Note <u>unavoidable</u> costs or risks are compared with the benefits of an activity in determining if the activity should be undertaken at all but have no bearing on control costs if the word unavoidable is correct.

It may be the case that the marginal reduction in the risk imposed has been reduced to the marginal cost of the last safety action and the totals are still above an accepted negligible level. Any continued expenditure by the firm is in effect valuing risk at a higher level than the public and requiring them to pay this higher rate if they wish the product. (Everyone must buy a station wagon to avoid the compact car risk.) It seems more beneficial to publicize the risk questions involved and make both products available so the public may choose.

The key question is not: Should the cost of correction limit the actions taken? Rather, the key question is: What values or trade offs are used to factor in such intangibles as: the importance of livelihood to an employee, of a life to each of us, or of the freedom of the jungle <u>versus</u> the security of the zoo!

Some will deny that a life can be valued; but every safety decision implies a hidden value, and it is better that it be in the open than hidden in a computer. In this century, the changes in society's valuation of a life can be illustrated by the Workers Compensation awards for a death. These awards have risen 10% per year from $1000 to a current maximum of about $1,000,000. This is about 50 times greater than the 20 fold increase in annual wages and 100 times the increase in cost of living. As Aaron Wildavsky says: "Richer is Safer."[1] or as I would say it: "Poverty Compels Risk Taking."

EFFECTIVE SAFETY EXPENDITURES

The willingness of any community to spend thousands of dollars to rescue a child who has fallen into a well is an another example of societal values. The limit in this case is the number of workers who can be effective in the rescue, not the dollar cost. In many industrial situations and government programs you will find that safety expenditure is limited by the lack of opportunities for effective expenditure as much, or as often, as by lack of financial resources or ignorance. The key work in this safety decision theory is "effective." A remedy is effective when the reduction in expected loss-cost is more than the expenditure.

Even if this is not the case, the remedy may still be supported by some in order to shift wealth or to reduce their burden by changing the price of this or that commodity or service. A remedy also may be a marketing or political ploy to appear to be taking "decisive" action, one, that might not be justifiable on the basis of risk alone.

---

[1]Aaron Wildavsky, "Richer is Safer...," the Public Interest 60, 23-30 1980.

You will note that greed or lack of empathy is not included as a major cause of inadequate safety. The reasoning is that self-interest in these litigious times makes it more profitable to prevent than to pay for injury to others. The point you must not forget is that the trial lawyers association and the courts, not Congress or the regulating agencies are setting safety standards in today's society.

When a risk is appreciable but no effective remedy is known there is a need for further study. The hardest problems may require us to go back to the beginning. There may be equally efficacious but less hazardous alternative products or processes available. The question of when to replace existing facilities or product lines must be considered at least annually; and also upon any significant change in information. The latter, of course, includes loss history: both your own and that of your competitors. One of the few advantages of the growth of conglomerates is that it is easier for them to make a decision in favor of change.[2]

HOW SAFE IS SAFE ENOUGH?

Two paragraphs on risk in the field of product liability from the National Business Council for Consumer Affairs are also applicable to environmental risk and to employee risk:

> "Risks of bodily harm are not unreasonable when consumers understand that risks exist, can appraise their probability and severity, know how to cope with them, and voluntarily accept them to get benefits that could not be obtained in less risky ways. When there is a risk of this character, consumers have reasonable opportunity to protect themselves; and public authorities should hesitate to substitute their value judgments about the desirability of the risk for those of the consumers who choose to incur it.

> But preventable risk is not reasonable (a) when consumers do not know that it exist; or (b) when though aware of it, consumers are unable to estimate its frequency and severity; or (c) when consumers do not know how to cope with it, and hence are likely to incur harm unnecessarily; or (d) when risk is unnecessary in that it could be reduced or eliminated at a cost in money or in the performance of the product that consumers would willingly incur if they knew the facts and were given the choice."[3]

And as Ralph Nader says: "The burden of proof rests on the party that

---

[2]See George Terborgh, Dynamic Equipment Policy, McGraw Hill 1949 and Daniel Goldman, "Following the Leader," Science 85 (October): 18, 20.

[3]National Business Council for Consumer Affairs, Action Guide Lines, (date?) p. 218.

initiates the risk, that profits from the risk, and that has the greatest resources to do something about the risk."[4]

If the enternalities are going to be internalized by the courts, self-regulation will tend to become automatic. Another factor promoting self control is that internal plant loss may be much greater than loss outside the fence. The 1979 Three Mile Island nuclear loss, for example, affected the public only via mental uncertainty and travel costs. Yet the cost to shareholders of nuclear utilities has run into the tens of billions. For nuclear as for many other risks, the cost to the initiator is many times that to the public. I would argue that this market incentive for self-regulation is more efficient, effective, and reliable than governmental regulation.

Unfortunately it does not follow that one can do without the latter. There are at least three broad catagories of circumstances where self regulation is wanting. One, the more easily corrected of the three is ignorance. If I the chief executive do not know of the failings or shortcomings in safety practices at the plant they may continue until disaster strikes. Or if I do not appreciate the risk and lack knowledge of the long range effects of chemical (X) or of its synergistic combinations with the life style of the neighborhood; I may condone the storage of large quantities etc.

The second class of circumstances where self regulation may fail are characterized by Poverty. I have bought less than adequate equipment, my wage scale keeps only the least capable workers or supervisors and profits are so questionable that continued operation for any length of time is doubtful. A false claim of inability to pay is always possible but refusal to pay is more often based on exaggerated cost estimates or remedies and minimization of benefit estimates than on claims of poverty. Note that the claim awards and punative damage awards make such tactics a very poor strategy.

The final case is - Self Deception. All parties involved, managers, supervisors and workers may know better but there is a tacit agreement not to rock the boat or raise embarrassing questions. (See the discussion pages 18 & 20 in the October issue of Science 85 by Daniel Goldman).

The answers to ignorance, proverty and self deception are not found at this conference but one can hope that a culture or climate which fosters open discussion of risks and requires a periodic assessment by the risk creator of the hazards and remedies available can reduce the shortcomings of self regulation to that level where outsiders be they government regulators, environmental groups or the insurers of the plant can cope with the risks that are left.

SAFETY EXPENDITURES WITH CAPITAL RATIONING

The general rule is that any improvement where the expenditure is less than the present value of the benefit by reduction in future losses ought to be made. However, where there are multiple candidates which pass

---

[4]Ralph Nader, "Professional Responsibility Revisited," from the Proceedings of the Conference on Science, Technology, and the Public Interest held by the Brookings Institution in Washington, D.C., on 8 October 1973.

this screen or where there are insufficient funds to undertake the desired action further guides are needed. One such guide is a list of procedures to be followed in this less than perfect world for employment, environmental and product hazards.

When ever a known risk, or one which should be known, is imposed by A on B the first act must be disclosure of all the facts known by A. The second should be education of B so that an informed consent can be given, to any agreed upon continuation. When, as in the recent airline union negotiations, there is understanding by the second party that continued employment for enjoyment of some benefit) requires acceptance of a wage cut (or of some other hazard), he or she will elect that option with the minimum risk or maximum benefit. However; the understanding must result in a conviction strong enough to support the required action.

The major disagreements arise from the unwillingness of one side to permit the other to make any contribution in the decision process. In almost all cases both parties at a round table could agree on what is needed and what must be postponed to a more affluent year but neither is willing to abide by the others' unilateral decision. Thus even though the EPA may write the rules for Air Pollutant control, they will have difficulty in accepting a solution which is cost effective for plant A and its stakeholders in the community.

Similar problems arose with the "Pinto" gas tank. In the calculation of the cost of change, who is the customer who approves the trade off. The product safety design guide does not require each car to have the crash resistance of the M1 Tank but it is expected to meet or surpass the standards of a similar product now in use. Since this would never permit any reduction in safety an alternative test is that a buyer fully informed would rather bear the risk than spend the money to have the hazard reduced to a lower level.

But we are still left with the problem of the marginal producer or employer. Should a safety requirement drive him out of business or do the sunk costs and benefits of the ongoing operation offset some possible temporary externalities. Remember we are talking about continuation with full disclosure so there is willing acceptance by the stakeholders - the employees, the neighbors, the customers and the investors. Those who were unwilling have been (or could have been) compensated with the consent of the creditors and of the remaining stakeholders. It is an axiom of a free society that one can elect a course of action which does not interfere with the rights of others and when the continuation aids the lowest income group among the stakeholders not just the pockets of the owners it is presumptious of the crusader to say safety first. The argument that this or that hazard should not be permitted here or overseas is most often made by those yong idealists who would not accept their own parents' advice on risks involving only their own amusement but still have the arrogance to constrain others on the essential of a livelihood or food and shelter.

The Indian acceptance of the hazard at Bhopal was partly ignorance of the magnitude of the possible accident but also the result of their much larger risk of starvation à la Ethopia. Just as DDT is banned in the US and necessary elsewhere, the herbicides and pesticides can perform their needed work to feed the starving if we only learn to manage the inevitable risks of "Living."

To say that a plant should be isolated from a large city to reduce the exposure ignores the transportation problem for workers without cars while the partial remedy of buses operated by the plant does not prevent the movement of squatters to the fence line as occurred in the El Paso lead pollution problem.

STOPPING RULES

The rule that a risk imposed on others must be negligible is not sufficient for reasons related to the Tragedy of the Commons. If you as one of the 5000 drivers in your town were to compute the cost of the added accident risk to a single one of your 10,000 neighbors for the first or should I say the last time you failed to stop at a traffic light or exceded the posted speed to beat the light change, the amount is undoubtedly negligible. Let us suppose it is one ten thousandth of a penny to each of your neighbors or one cent added third party liability to you. This may also be an approximation of the direct injury risk to yourself. (You are definitely at the scene of your unsafe driving practices.)

But his number is multiplied by the 100,000 intersections you pass in a year and by 5000 to compute an annual cost in just your town, IF YOU GRANT EACH OTHER DRIVER THE RIGHT TO DO AS YOU DO. Adding up the costs in each of 20,000 other neighborhoods makes the countrywide total ten billion dollars for even a one cent estimate on a single unsafe practice.

Moreover; the above calculating omits the synergistic effects found in multiple exposures, that is the compounding of risk that will result as more than one driver fails to stop at intersections (or more than one factory fails to limit stack emissions). It is thus an understatement of the costs of a negligible risk change. While such multiplication was most prominent with asbestos and smoking, it is the practice in almost all private risk calculus to consider current life styles as constant and project the effects of the proposed action with no other changes. The problems of synergism are incorrectly left to EPA and Congress. The moral obligation to act only as you would permit all others to act has particular significance when repetition of an act (N) times does much more than (N) times the societal injury (or yield more than N times the advantage to others).[5]

Since the (N) in the case of the U.S. population is of the order of 100,000,000 working adults or car drivers or families, the argument is that one should consider the repetition of your proposed action this number of times and weigh the consequences from the multiple interactions of that many repetitions.

As discussed above in the case of the speeding auto driver, whenever the interaction of two acts leads to greater loss (2 drivers fail to slow up at the same intersection) the total social cost will increase exponentially and all of us have a moral obligation to avoid this overloading of the commons and increasing of the risk load on the common man.

In the attached list of often overlooked costs involved in low probability-high consequence events a fair estimate of the cost from each

---

[5] See pages 272-275 "Foundations of Inductive Logic" by Roy Harrod Harcourt, Brace and Company 1956-7. This book has also the best discussion of probability I have ever read.

item may be 2PL. (Where P is the probability of exceeding loss size L.) However; if there are interactions of this type, between the costs of my taking this action and everyone else following suit the cost of externalities will exceed the sum of all others.

All of the above should be combined with the following new postulate. (An axiom that can only be justified by the utility of the resultants):

THE ANNUAL EXPECTED PUBLIC COSTS FOR A FACTORY CREATED EXPOSURE SHALL NOT BE GREATER THAN 100 DOLLARS PER EMPLOYEE

If my exposure is reaching 1000 neighbors and I have 50 employees- the imposed risk is $5. per capita per year or 10 cents a week- definitely negligible and more than offset by the reduction in the property tax or other benefits of this operation.

The plant with 20 depts of 50 employees each may split its safety budget to secure the greatest returns by extra care on the hazardous operation. It must be remembered that the overall risk includes product liability as well and that this is a constraint on the maximum risk allowed from the entire operation. Where ever possible the plant will thru its safety, environment and quality depts reduce the outside impact. i.e., when ever an action will cut the expected loss by more than the cost of the action.

The figure of $100 per employee per year as the maximum acceptable expected accident cost for any effect outside the plant fence may also be applicable inside. Certainly many firms have a lower cost today both inside and out. Unfortunately not all and the best measure of the management we can think of is the ratio of their costs on such measures to that of their competitors. Many firms have improved but others over the years fail badly due to self deception, to proverty levels of spending on safety and due to ignorance of the interactions between their acts and those of the rest of society.

SOME MAJOR COSTS OMITTED IN JUDGEING LOW PROBABILITY RISKS

1. Expected Loss when (P) is the annual probability of exceeding loss size (L), is in the range 4PL to 8PL per year or 40 to 80PL per lifetime.
2. Disutility of large loss up to 95% of current wealth (W) has an equivalent utility value of approximately 3PL per year or 30 per lifetime.
3. Regret cost equals the value of perfect information, of always making the right decision. Might also be called reputation cost.
4. Sunk costs of other unusable investments if the event occurs.
5. Liquidity cost of reserves equal to the maximum possible loss.
6. Criminal liability for wrong or injury done to society.
7. Cost of frequency reduction measures.
8. Cost of severity reduction measures both by you and by others.
9. Cost of risk management: analysis, implementation, audit and insurance carriers overhead.
10. cost of information acquisition and of experimentation.
11. Externalities including those which will be transferred back by the courts.
12. Reversibility costs if we decide we don't want this risk.
13. Duration costs; how long do we bear this risk?
14. Costs of uncertainties in the values of the parameters and in our future risk portfolio.
15. UNKNOWN UNKNOWNS.

ENHANCING RISK MANAGEMENT BY FOCUSING ON THE LOCAL LEVEL:

AN INTEGRATED APPROACH*

June Fessenden-Raden,** Carole A. Bisogni***
and Keith S. Porter****

Cornell University
Ithaca, New York

ABSTRACT

An integrated approach to risk management that focuses on the local
level will lead to a more satisfactory and timely resolution of localized
risk situations such as chemical contamination of groundwater that serves
as a source of drinking water. More importantly this approach will result
in additional positive long-range effects -- increased local capabilities
to deal with future chemical risk problems and improved prevention of some
types of chemical contamination of groundwater. Conceptualizing the
management of risks as having inputs (the risk situation, laws and
policies, technical context, and community context), process, and outcomes
illustrates that neither outside intervenors nor the local community
should approach a risk situation without regard for all of the inputs or
without understanding the dynamics of the process of managing risks at the
local level.

KEY WORDS: Risk management, community response, groundwater chemical
               contamination, drinking water quality

---

* This paper is part of a series of five related papers entitled
"Enhancing Risk Management by Focusing on the Local Level." Research for
this paper was supported by the Ford Foundation and the National Science
Foundation -- Ethics and Values in Science and Technology (RII-8409912).
All views expressed in this paper are those of the authors and do not
necessarily reflect the views of the Ford Foundation or the National
Science Foundation.

** Associate Professor of Biochemistry and Biology & Society, Program
on Science, Technology, and Society, Division of Biological Sciences,
Institute of Comparative and Environmental Toxicology.

*** Associate Professor of Nutritional Sciences, Division of
Nutritional Sciences, Institute of Comparative and Environmental
Toxicology.

**** Associate Director, Water Resources Institute, Center for
Environmental Research.

INTRODUCTION

On the occasion of receiving the Society for Risk Analysis distinguished contribution award last year, Chauncey Starr (1985) suggested that the operations established for the management of risk were as important as the quantitative description derived from the risk. In our research on chemically contaminated groundwater, we have seen that risk management approaches designed far away from the risk locale have too often resulted in unsatisfactory outcomes from the perspectives of both the community and the risk managers. Our results suggest that the management of risk might be enhanced in terms of both the short-term and long-range effectiveness by taking an integrated, multidisciplinary approach and by focusing on the local level. We consider a successful outcome to be one that not only resolves the particular risk situation, but also provides for increased community competence to prevent and, as needed, to respond to any future chemical contamination problems. An example of prevention would be the establishment of groundwater protection programs, (e.g., establishing aquifer protection zones). We suggest that risk management planners and implementers need to utilize more multidisciplinary, integrated approaches and increase their sensitivity to the local community at risk.

When considering risk management operations that could be enhanced by focusing on the local level, groundwater chemical contamination problems serve as a highly illustrative paradigm. Groundwater contamination can result from a multiplicity of causes and human activities. To successfully deal with these problems, an involvement of many disciplines is necessary. Also, the adoption and implementation of any solution often requires the collective efforts of individuals, communities, industries and government agencies.

In this series of papers different members of our research group will illustrate the importance of considering several aspects of risk management: (1) integration of dimensions of risk management operations, (2) the community context of the risk, and (3) the risk management process itself. The papers reflect our belief that an integrated approach that focuses on the local level could enhance protection of the public health and the environment.

As the introductory paper in the series we first will present brief background information on the chemical contamination of groundwater and associated public health risks. We then will describe a conceptual framework for risk management at the local level, that we have found helpful in our efforts to understand risk management at the local level.

GROUNDWATER, CHEMICAL CONTAMINATION, PUBLIC HEALTH

The water supply for over half of the U.S. population comes from groundwater. In many rural areas, over 95% of residents are dependent on groundwater as an economically irreplaceable source of drinking water. Unfortunately, the purity of groundwater can no longer be assumed. Chemicals contaminate groundwater across the U.S. New risk situations are reported to the public almost daily. More than twenty pesticide residues and hundreds of synthetic organic chemicals have been found in public and private drinking water supplies from groundwater. The length of time and full extent of such contamination is unknown.

Chemical contamination of groundwater is often a localized problem, and contaminants may come from multiple sources -- underground storage

Table 1

Attitudes Toward Additional Pollution Controls

	Support additional controls (no mention of closure)			Support additional control (if closure might result)		
	Yes	No	Don't Know	Yes	No	Don't Know
Hearing	58%	34%	8%	51%	42%	7%
Phone	40%	29%	30%	32%	47%	21%

Table 2

Correlation With Risk Tolerance

Item	Pearson r*
Harmful effects vs benefits of smelter	.863
Do you think the smelter is a health hazard	.818
"Real risks" (in S's judgement) are higher or lower than EPA estimates	.807
Personal immunity to cancer caused by ASARCO emissions	.525
Voluntarines of exposure to ASARCO emissions	.470
Should standards be based on affordability	.454
Personal immunity to general environmentally caused cancer	.387
Agencies should not wait for certainty before acting to reduce risks	.386
Costs versus benefits of pollution controls in general	.374

*All correlations presented are significant at less than the .001 level.

Table 3

Results of Factual Knowledge Questions
for Hearing Respondents

	Risk Estimate Question		Regulation Question	
	Correct	Incorrect(1)	Correct	Incorrect
Less Risk Tolerant	62%	38%	47%	53%
More Risk Tolerant	41%	59%	26%	74%
Overall Percentage	52%	48%	37%	63%

1.   Percentages cited as incorrect include those who gave incorrect answers
as well as those who did not answer or selected the Don't Know response option.

2.   Chi square analyses reveal the differences between MT and LT groups to
be significant at less than the .001 level for both questions.

Table 4

Risk Decision Aspects Used in Item Generation

Risk

    Mortality
        Self
        Others
            General Public
            Workers
            Future generations

    Morbidity
        Self
        Others
            General Public
            Workers
            Future generations

    Knowledge of hazard
        Self
        Science and government
    Dread of hazard
        Self
        Others

Benefits

    Economic
        Self
        Others
    Non-economic
        Self
        Others

Costs

    Property damage
    Income loss

Environmental effects

    Plants and animals
    Non-living environment

tanks, hazardous wastes, sanitary landfills, fertilizers and pesticides, mining wastes, household cleaning agents, leaking public sewage systems and private septic systems, chemical spills, even highway deicing salt. Just one aspect of the potential problem, leaking underground storage tanks, is illustrated by some figures in upstate New York. Of the more than 120,000 underground fuel storage tanks, 20% or 24,000 currently are believed to be leaking. Nationwide there may be as many as 200,000 leaking underground storage tanks.

Because of its complexity, once groundwater is contaminated, it is both technologically difficult and very expensive to decontaminate. Chemical contaminants in groundwater move anywhere from inches to feet per year. They move in plumes with only limited dilution from the point of application to discharge. The amount and concentration of the contaminant in the groundwater, as well as the time it takes for the contaminant to get to the saturated water zone or aquifer, depends on the intrinsic properties of the chemical, the subsurface soil, and the amount and distribution of precipitation in the aquifer recharge area. For example, in Minnesota, arsenic used as a pesticide in the 1930's is only now showing up in the groundwater (Steenhuis, 1985). On the other hand, aldicarb pesticide residue was found in Long Island groundwater within four years of the pesticide's first use (Pacenka and Porter, 1981).

The health effects from drinking, cooking with, and bathing in chemically contaminated water generally are unknown. At the concentrations commonly found in groundwater many chemicals may pose little or no health threat. Others such as toluene, trichloroethylene and tetrachloroethane may cause immediate or acute health effects such as skin rashes, dizziness, headaches, even heart arrhythmias. In addition, chemicals may pose risks of chronic health problems such as cancer, or neurological, immunological and reproductive dysfunctions. Any health risk is dependent not only on the properties of the chemicals and the conditions of the exposure, but also on the exposure to other chemicals, individual susceptibility and lifestyle. The risk to the health of any single individual is just not known. Toxicologists can, at best, with much uncertainty, estimate the risk to some statistically healthy population.

AN INTEGRATED APPROACH TO RISK MANAGEMENT

Over the past five years our interdisciplinary project at Cornell has been considering the problems of management of risks at the local level associated with chemically contaminated groundwater used as a source of drinking water. We have as our overall goal the expansion of risk management capabilities of communities and individuals with respect to groundwater and chemical contamination. Our multidisciplinary research team is utilizing its diverse expertise to study non-metropolitan communities, primarily in New York State (Lemley, et al., 1985; Hughes, et al., 1982; Fitchen, et al., forthcoming). In these communities we are looking into such factors as: the environmental fate of the chemical, the hydrogeological features of the area, evaluation of potential health risks, the community's level of knowledge about the contaminated water situation, and the decisions and responses of individuals and institutional factors.

The conceptual framework we have used to study the management of risks from chemically contaminated groundwater was adapted from the nutrition communication model of Gillespie and Yarbrough (1984). Shown in Figure 1, this conceptual framework has been useful in identifying various

Table 5

Risk Decision Variables Included in Analysis

Endogenous variables

Risk

ASARCO   Mortality/morbidity: Self

Mortality/morbidity: Other

Earthquake   Mortality/morbidity: All

Benefits

ASARCO   Benefits: All

Earthquake   Benefits: Economic

Benefits: Non-economic

Information seeking

(Same for both hazards)

Risk mitigation/reduction

(Same for both hazards)

Exogenous variables

Scientific background

Attitude toward science/technology

Attitude toward government

Concern in hazard information

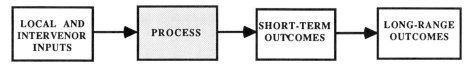

Figure 1

Risk Management

aspects of risk management that are critical to optimal resolution of a situation and in need of more attention from both researchers and the public policy makers.

According to our conceptual framework, the management of risks at the local level has three major components: inputs, process, and outcomes. The inputs include (1) the characteristics of the actual risk situation such as the nature of the chemical and the number of people or wells affected; (2) the laws and policies invoked by that risk situation, and (3) the technical context such as the technological options and limitations for treating the contaminants. To resolve groundwater contamination problems, expertise from a variety of disciplines is needed. However, few technical experts have the full complement of knowledge, skills, and experience in all of the technical areas needed to address groundwater contamination problems. Thus, a variety of technical experts are often involved. Our studies have shown that integration is needed among the technical experts including engineers, toxicologists and hydrogeologists.

Our studies indicate that a second type of integration also is needed in risk management -- integration between the technical and human dimensions of the problem. This series of papers will focus on the need to recognize the human dimension of risk management and actively incorporate this dimension into risk management. Risk managers must be sensitive to the local community context of the risk situation such as economics, demographics, community attitudes, beliefs and values and socio-political institutions.[1] We have seen that intervenors have often ignored this input entirely.

Janet Fitchen, a cultural anthropologist, in the next paper will present research that supports our contention that local response to the risk and the risk management process is shaped by the local context. Fitchen's paper examines the dynamics of the interactions between risk management and the community. She identifies ten local context factors that appear most important in shaping community response. Since local response will affect both short-term and long-range effectiveness of risk management, it is argued that risk management planners and implementers need to pay more attention to the local community context (Fitchen, 1986).

Inputs are brought to the risk management process by outside

---

[1]For the purpose of our research we have defined community as the local population and its local institutions involved or affected by the risk and its management.

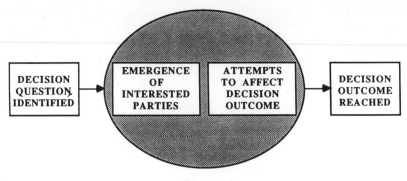

Figure 2

The Process

intervenors and local people. Outside intervenors are defined as
technical experts or representatives of institutions that are involved
with the community because of their technical expertise or statutory
authority. These intervenors include, but are not limited to, engineers,
regulators, lawyers, educators, toxicologists, and public health
specialists. They provide technical input into the risk management
process in terms of their specialized knowledge, skills and experiences.
Intervenors also bring beliefs, attitudes and values about groundwater,
its protection, chemical risks, regulations, other technical experts and
the community at risk. Intervenor inputs affect how intervenors (1) relate
to the community and other intervenors, (2) are perceived by the community
and other intervenors, and (3) participate in the risk management process.
Often we have found intervenors enter a risk management operation with
preset options and predetermined strategies that may or may not be
applicable to the specific community at risk. The dominant risk
management approach seems to be the one-sided intervention of technical
experts (e.g., government personnel or consultants) with technological
solutions to be implemented in the local community under the direction of
the outside intervenor.

The many individuals who live and work in the locality bring another
set of critical inputs to the risk management process, regardless of
whether or not these inputs are acknowledged by intervenors. Local
participants bring a variety of credentialed and non-credentialed
expertise to the risk management process such as knowledge about past use
of an area, successful local management experience, and local folk
wisdom. Unfortunately, intervenors too often ignore such local experience
as irrelevant to the management of the risk. Also, local participants
bring beliefs, attitudes, and values related to themselves, their
community and their risks. How they participate in the risk management
process, whether they accept or reject intervenor technical information
and advice, and how they will react to the outcome(s) are all affected
by these beliefs, attitudes, and values.

Many intervenors seem to believe the locals "can't really understand
the situation." Bonney Hughes, a graduate student in environmental
toxicology, discusses citizens' knowledge, beliefs, and actions related to
chemical contamination of groundwater (Hughes and Bisogni, 1986). One
approach to enhanced risk management at the local level is through

increasing the knowledge of local citizens related to groundwater and chemical contamination. However, for educational programs to be effective or meaningful to citizens, educators must consider citizens' existing beliefs, attitudes, and practices.

Our research shows that regardless of the beliefs of intervenors, local citizens do provide critical inputs and do contribute to the effectiveness of risk management. Management of risks from chemically contaminated groundwater is not conducted exclusively by federal or state governments, but involves inputs from all governmental levels and the private sector. While the risk management processes at the local level vary across the more than a dozen communities that we have studied, we suggest that some features are common. The risk management process is dynamic. It is interactive involving many decisions spread out over time. The process also is iterative. The results in a number of intermediate or short-term outcomes can feedback to influence both concurrent and future decision-making as well as the inputs of the intervenors and the local participants.

Jenifer Heath, a graduate student in environmental toxicology, has focused specifically on the interactive nature of the risk management process. Some details of the process identified as important in influencing short-term and long-range risk management effectiveness are presented in the third paper in this series (Heath and Fessenden-Raden, 1986).

The final paper in this series is by Hank Hughes, a water resource specialist. He will provide evidence that intervenors can work with communities in productive ways in which each learn (Hughes, 1986). In each project, members of the community have worked with the Water Resources staff from Cornell in identifying valid options, in evaluating the technical merits of the options and in selecting the preferred options for community implementation.

CONCLUSION

We conceptualize management of risks from chemically contaminated groundwater as involving inputs, process and outcomes. Neither the outside intervenors nor the local community should approach a risk situation without regard for all the inputs or without understanding for the dynamics of the risk management process.

We take the position that the local community is not merely a passive setting within which outside technical experts briefly perform their specialties in the management of a given risk. The community is an interactive setting in which both the risk and the management of the risk are embedded. We contend that to enhance risk management, an integrated, multidisciplinary approach focusing on the local level where the risk is being experienced, is needed. Improved communication and use of scientific and technical information related to chemical contamination of groundwater, public health, and risk assessment is also essential. Technical responses from engineering to health must be better integrated with each other. The technical response as a whole needs to be integrated with the local inputs. For an optimal outcome of any risk management operation, there should be learning by both the intervenors and the local community. The local community should acquire some competence to (1) more readily deal with any future chemical risk problems, and (2) act to prevent such problems as much as is possible. The community should better know where to go for information and help when it is needed. Ideally

Table 6

ASARCO: LISREL Maximum Likelihood Parameter Estimates
(all t-values greater than 2.0)

Dependent Variable	Predictors	R^2	R^2 (Without Hazard Information)	Total Effects of Concern
MMO1	SCI (-0.21), STA (0.20), GOVA (0.33), CON (0.26)	0.25	0.25	0.26
MMS1	MMS1 (0.43), STA (0.22	0.28	0.28	0.11
BEN1		0.00	0.00	0.00
MIT1	CON1 (0.43)	0.19	0.00	0.43
INFO1	MIT1 (0.17), CON1 (0.40)	0.25	-	0.48
MMO2	MMO1 (0.46), STA (0.21), CON (0.35)	0.45	0.36	0.46
MMS2	MMS1 (0.16), MMO2 (0.37), INFO2 (0.20)	0.28	0.27	0.29
BEN2	BEN1 (0.63)	0.39	0.39	0.00
MIT2	MIT1 (0.40), CON2 (0.42)	0.36	0.27	0.60
INFO2	MMS1 (0.26), CON2 (0.45)	0.27	-	0.48
MMO3	MMO1 (0.25), MMO2 (0.59), INFO3 (0.24)	0.64	0.58	0.47
MMS3	MMS2 (0.53), MMO3 (0.24), CON3 (0.14)	0.46	0.49	0.40
BEN3	BEN1 (0.24), BEN2 (0.46), CON3 (0.25)	0.40	0.40	0.00
MIT3	MIT1 (0.33), MIT2 (0.20), MMO3 (0.24), CON3 (0.25)	0.40	0.36	0.63
INFO3	INFO2 (0.38), CON2 (-.28), CON3 (0.63)	0.48	-	0.53

Table 7

Earthquake: LISREL Maximum Likelihood Parameter Estimates
(All t-values greater than 2.0)

Dependent Variable	Predictors	R^2	R^2 (Without Hazard Information)	Total Effects of Concern
MMA1		0.00	0.00	0.00
EBEN1	MMA1 (0.33), GOVA (-0.27)	0.18	0.18	0.00
NBEN1	EBEN1 (0.40)	0.16	0.16	0.00
MIT1	EBEN1 (0.27)	0.08	0.08	0.00
INFO1	CON1 (0.35)	0.12	-	0.35
MMA2	MMA1 (0.59), INFO2 (0.17), CON2 (0.21)	0.50	0.44	0.28
EBEN2	EBEN1 (0.43)	0.18	0.18	0.00
NBEN2	NBEN1 (0.40), MMA2 (0.14), EBEN2 (0.28), INFO2 (0.16)	0.36	0.35	0.11
MIT2	MIT1 (0.45), NBEN2 (0.27)	0.30	0.29	0.03
INFO2	CON2 (0.42)	0.17	-	0.43
MMA3	MMA2 (0.78), CON3 (0.10)	0.62	0.64	0.32
EBEN3	EBEN1 (0.20), EBEN2 (0.28), MMA3 (.12), NBEN3 (0.48)	0.60	0.61	0.10
NBEN3	NBEN2 (0.58), MMA3 (0.20)	0.42	0.46	0.13
MIT3	MIT2 (0.58), NBEN3 (0.20)	0.44	0.44	0.04
INFO3	INFO2 (0.32), CON3 (0.49)	0.40	-	0.52

the long-range impact of a successful risk management operation also would provide for improved intervenor response elsewhere, and perhaps even improved public policy.

REFERENCES

Fitchen, Janet M., 1986, "The Importance of Community Context in Effective Risks Management" this volume.

Fitchen, Janet M., Jenifer S. Heath and June Fessenden-Raden, forthcoming, "Risk Perception in Community Context: A Case Study," to be published in a volume entitled The Social Construct of Risk, edited by Branden Johnson and Vincent Covello.

Gillespie, A. H. and Paul Yarborough, 1984, "A Model for Communicating Nutrition," J. Nutrition Education, 16(4):168.

Heath, Jenifer S. and June Fessenden-Raden, 1986, "The Relationship Between Risk Management Intervenors and the Community," this volume.

Hughes, Bonney F. and Carole A. Bisogni, 1986, "Citizens' Knowledge, Attitudes, and Actions Regarding Chemical Contamination of Drinking Water," this volume.

Hughes, Henry B.F., 1986, "Incorporating Technical Information and Community Goals into Risk Management Decisions Related to Groundwater," this volume.

Hughes, Henry B.F., Keith S. Porter, et al., 1982, "Reclamation of a Groundwater Supply: Clifton Springs, NY," Center for Environmental Research, Cornell University, Ithaca, NY.

Lemley, A.T., J. Fessenden-Raden, C.A. Bisogni, and J.M. Holway, 1985, "Nitrate Contamination: Public Awareness," J. Amer. Water Works, 77:34-39.

Pacenka, Steven and Keith S. Porter, 1981, "Preliminary Regional Assessment of the Environmental Fate of the Potato Pesticide Aldicarb, Eastern Long Island, New York," Center for Environmental Research, Cornell University, Ithaca, NY.

Steenhuis, Tammo, 1985, "Pollutant Transport Process in Soil and Groundwater" (submitted for publication).

Starr, Chauncey, 1985, "Risk Management, Assessment, and Acceptability," Risk Analysis, 5:97-102.

THE IMPORTANCE OF COMMUNITY CONTEXT

IN EFFECTIVE RISK MANAGEMENT*

Janet M. Fitchen**

Cornell University, Ithaca, NY

ABSTRACT

In studying communities dealing with groundwater contamination, we find that perceptions of the health risk are affected by collective perception of the risk management. Both perception of the risk and perception of the risk management, we find, are shaped by factors in the local context. This paper identifies ten context factors that affect community response and may explain why different communities respond differently. It is suggested that long-range benefits for protection of health and environment could be achieved if these local context factors were taken into account in planning and carrying out risk management.

KEY WORDS: risk perception, risk management, community response, groundwater chemical contamination

INTRODUCTION

The social science component of our inter-disciplinary research project is a process-oriented study of the way communities and outside intervention agencies interact in responding to risks posed by chemical contamination of groundwater.[1] This paper focuses on overall community response, rather then on individual perceptions, and seeks to explain why different communities respond differently.

Our previous case study of a community with contaminated groundwater revealed that perception of the health risk is a complex, dynamic, and interactive phenomenon (Fitchen, et al., forthcoming). Faced with an actual existing risk, people's perceptions changed through time partly reflecting an emerging collective perception of the risk. We found a close interactive connection between perception of the risk management and perception of the risk (as discussed by Starr, 1985 and reported by Schwartz et al., 1985). We found that perception and response are also influenced by the local context in which both the risk and the risk management are embedded.

The present comparative analysis of several communities with contaminated groundwater explores further the role of local context. We are attempting to isolate the specific factors inherent in local contexts that affect perception of and response to risk and risk management. We suggest that if risk managers knew more about these relevant context factors, they could be more effective in achieving both short-term and long-range goals of risk management.

METHODOLOGY

Since differences in the way communities respond to risk and risk management could be attributed to differences in either the risk or the risk management, we have attempted to control for both of these variables. We have selected for research a half dozen non-metropolitan communities that have discovered similar industrial solvents (primarily trichloroethylene) in water supply wells.[2] At the levels of concentration found in these cases, the health effects are characterized by uncertainty, low probability, and long latency. By selecting sites within New York State and further concentrating primarily on those that have been designated federal "Superfund" sites, we can also control for state and federal regulatory standards, for the agencies that become involved (primarily New York State Department of Environmental Conservation, and Department of Health, and the United States Environmental Protection Agency), and for characteristic institutional procedures. We are then able to concentrate on factors inherent in the communities that may be underlying their different responses.

For contrast, however, we have briefly examined two situations of groundwater contamination involving other kinds of toxic chemicals (in one case pesticide residues, in another petroleum products), which pose different health risks and may involve different government agencies. In addition, we are also studying two cases where pollution has not yet occurred within the community's underground water source, but where local awareness of toxic contamination nearby, combined with gentle nudges by regional planning staff and others, have led the community to consider taking protective measures.

In each community we have studied the contamination situation in some depth, including the technical facts, the chronology of events, and the decisions, actions and reactions of local officials and community residents, as well as federal and state officials and outside technical experts. In-depth interviews with local decision makers have been supplemented by informal discussions with local residents, attendance at public hearings and meetings, monitoring of local newspapers, careful researching of public documents and reports, and collection of background information on the community. While some case studies have involved only brief, retrospective research, others have involved many on-site visits spanning more than a year of elasped time, and are still continuing.

LOCAL CONTEXT FACTORS AFFECTING RISK RESPONSE

Preliminary analysis of our field studies has enabled us to identify ten local context factors that appear to be important in shaping local risk perceptions and responses, and may explain the different responses observed among communities. We group these context factors into two separate categories. Community context factors are the relevant characteristics of the community itself, excluding factors specifically related to the contamination. Risk context factors are the relevant aspects of the situation surrounding the contamination, excluding the contamination itself. (The order in which we have listed the factors does not necessarily reflect their actual importance.)

Community Context Factors

1. Vulnerability of local economic base

Economic vulnerability is clearly an important factor shaping perceptions and responses, as both the contamination and its remediation may have a negative impact on a local economy. Among our sample, communities with an unstable, weak, or declining economy, or those undergoing transition (for example out of manufacturing) may be willing to consider accepting a higher level of health risk. They are less eager to have federal or state agencies become involved in risk management, preferring to take care of the problem locally (though perhaps seeking federal/state funds to enable them to do so). In general, we find the communities whose economic base is external to them, as in out-commuting suburbs demand higher standards of protection than communities whose economic base is internal.

2. Demographic stability and households with children

Various studies indicate that expectations of continued local residence and the presence of young children in the household are associated with attitudes towards risk (Fowlkes and Miller, 1982; Edelstein, 1983; and Lemley, et al., 1985). It is reasonable that these factors show up in aggregate response also. While both these characteristics, and also homeownership rates, appear to influence risk response more than such demographic factors as age or education level, our observations do not enable us to specify how or why.

3. Trust in and identification with local government

A general, longstanding trust in local government bodies and officials seems to be one of the most important context factors minimizing public expression of risk anxiety.[3] A "we" feeling of identification with local government fosters perception that local officials are acting effectively to protect public health -- whether or not there is evidence to substantiate the belief. On the other hand, in those communities where there is a general lack of trust in local government, the stage seems to be set for heightened anxiety about the risk and for criticism of the actions of both local and state/federal agencies conducting the risk management. (In communities with a history of a split between residents who implicitly trust local government and those who have little confidence in it, we find two markedly different levels of anxiety about the risk, and two conflicting evaluations of how well the risk managers are doing their job.)

4. Strength of local self-image

Among our cases, those communities that had a fairly strong collective identity at the time contamination was discovered tend to exhibit less public anxiety over the risk. On the other hand, an amorphous residential area that suddenly acquired boundaries and a stigmatized identity as the "the bad water area" exhibited anxiety and seemed to expect inadequacies in the risk management.[4]

The particular attributes of a community's self-definition also influence risk response. One of our communities describes itself as "small" and "rural" (even though technically a "city"), and as "upholding the old-fashioned American pioneer value of self-reliance." Here we find little public concern over the health risk, and a preference for local-level risk management. In contrast, suburban or bedroom communities, where people describe themselves only in terms of invidious comparisons with the city from which they have recently moved, may show greater concern over a similar risk. Residents fear that the evils they sought to escape are following them into the suburbs. But since they do not expect local governments to be capable of protecting them, they call for higher level government action -- though may soon become dissatisfied with the performance of state/federal agencies.

5. Direct or indirect experience with similar environmental/health risks

Perception of a new risk situation is influenced by the level of satisfaction with the handling and outcome of similar problems in the past. Additionally, collective perceptions of an emerging local situation are affected by perceptions of contamination situations that have occurred elsewhere. We found that complaints about the way federal and state agencies conducted risk management in one community traveled quickly along the inter-community grapevine to engender negative attitudes elsewhere. (However, we also found that two communities may form quite divergent interpretations of a single situation elsewhere. For example our communities did not all agree on the implication of Love Canal, even though they watched the same TV news stories. We suggest that their differing interpretations were shaped by differences in local context factors.)

Risk Context Factors

1. Perceived health effects and lifestyle disruptions

A community's response to the risk and risk management is definitely influenced by whether people experience health problems that they attribute to the toxic contamination, and whether these perceptions receive public support. In several of our sample cases where the health effect has a long latency period, the collective perception is that the contaminant has not yet caused adverse health problems and is unlikely to do so in the future. The local media have not found, or have not given credibility to, any individuals' claims of health problems linked to the contaminant. These "unworried" communities contrast sharply with another situation where the contaminants are different and people have experienced health problems that they link to the chemicals in the water. Stories and photographs in local press have given credibility and publicity to these health problems, adding to a collective perception that harm has occurred. There is a high level of citizen arousal, anxiety about future health problems, and criticism of the risk management as incompetent, slow, and inadequate. However, in still another of our cases, citizen anxiety and criticism ran high even though no one claimed health effects. In this case, other factors besides the perception of health effects must be shaping perceptions.

Perceived lifestyle disruptions or dislocations related to the contamination also heighten community arousal about the risk and stir criticism of its management. Water shortages and precautionary measures such as boiling and hauling water, having filters installed in the home, or having large unwieldy jugs of water delivered may all be perceived as inconveniences or disruptions of daily life, even as invasions of the privacy of the home, and tend to create negative attitudes towards the risk and its management (c.f. Edelstein, 1983).

2. Other risks facing the community

The water contamination is likely to be only one of several concerns in the load of risks and problems a community is carrying at the time. (Rayner, 1985, refers to a community's "risk portfolio.") In some cases, perceived economic risks (e.g. future loss of local jobs due to structural changes in the national economy) preoccupy the community; in other cases anxiety centers on perceived deterioration in quality of life (e.g. unwanted and rapid growth due to encroaching sprawl of a nearby city). Communities troubled by other perceived risks may underperceive the health risk or underestimate its possible deleterious effects. In other cases, though, the health risk becomes the focus of general discontent and the symbol of everything that is wrong, leading to general anxiety that public health will be inadequately protected.

3. Social and symbolic role of the "presumed polluters"

Collective attitudes towards both the risk and the risk management are influenced by the relationship the community perceives between itself and the presumed source(s) of chemical pollution. While the most obvious aspect of this relationship may be economic dependence, the social and symbolic significance of the presumed polluter is also very important. A local factory may be woven into the social fabric of the community. Its founders may be local folk heroes, its management personnel may serve as pillars of the community's civic and religious groups. It supports a little league team, and may even have donated the playing field. The plant may have been the employer of several generations of townspeople, and may still be the employer of one's friends, neighbors and relatives. Residents set their watches by the factory's whistles, and regulate their activities by its shifts. The community's self-image may be verbalized in terms of the company's product, which may even be symbolized graphically in the official seal of the city. In communities such as this, a polluting industry may be perceived as internal or "part of the community" in the cognitive sense, even if the physical location is outside the community. In these cases, public expression of concern over risks posed by chemicals from these facilities is muted, and will not be fanned by local press or politicians. On the other hand, where the presumed polluter is perceived as external to the community, as belonging cognitively to the realm of "outside" and "them," (whether or not it is physically located outside of the community) citizens have taken a more active and sometimes adversarial stance against the polluters.[5]

4. Familiarity with the chemicals posing the risk

Several studies have shown that familiarity with a risk may minimize the individual's fear of that risk (Slovic, et al., 1979, 1980, 1984; Fowlkes and Miller, 1982, p. 56). On the level of community, familiarity with the chemicals posing the risk may affect risk response. Local familiarity with the particular chemical comes from direct experience in handling or using the chemical in the workplace (be it factory or farm), and also from indirect or vicarious experience through relatives and neighbors who work with it. There may be a general community assumption that the hazardous materials are "part of life here." The discovery that such a familiar chemical has entered the water supply is not apt to have much shock impact. Collective anxiety may be quite low -- unless people perceive immediate health effects or major lifestyle disruptions. In contrast, where people had no prior familiarity with the chemicals, the initial reaction to the report that unpronounceable, unfamiliar chemicals are in the water supply may stir more public concern.

5. Confidence in sources of information about the risk

        People like to trust their own senses and the informal information
sources of friends, relatives and neighbors (Fitchen, 1985). In cases
where the chemical contaminant in the water produces an odor, taste, or
"off" color, people's own senses may identify contamination long before
water samples are taken for analysis. If the lab tests do not confirm
what the community "knows," the public perception is that the experts and
officials are falsely denying that a problem exists.

        But where the contaminants are undetectable by smell, taste, or
sight, people must seek risk information from other sources. In these
cases, they want clear, unequivocal information, and they want it
delivered quickly. Experts who disagree among themselves or change their
minds lose credibility. When "the people who are supposed to know about
these things" give the impression that they don't really know, the
community's anxiety about the risk is apt to increase, while at the same
time its confidence in the risk management decreases. Delays in providing
information, (e.g. slow return of water-test results), and equivocal
answers to the public's questions about whether they should drink the
water, (e.g. answers hedged with "on the other hand" and indications of
uncertainty), further undermine community confidence in the risk
management. If it also appears that information is purposefully beine
withheld or altered, then the informal channels of information become more
active and more persuasive, and the community's level of anxiety and
distrust increases markedly (see Berry and Stoeckle, 1985). In these
cases, as Schwartz et al. (1985, p. 72) indicates, the elevated community
concern that is sometimes labeled "hysteria" is actually a rational
response.

DISCUSSION AND IMPLICATIONS

        Our ongoing observations have highlighted ten specific factors of the
local context that appear to shape community response in situations of
groundwater contamination. These same context factors might also be
operating where other types of health/environmental risk are involved. We
suggest that at least part of the explanation for intercommunity
differences in response to such risks lies in the ten factors we have
identified. We do not find, however, that any single one of these context
factors explains local response in all of the communities. Nor do we find
all of the context factors operating uniformly in all of our cases. In
fact, our analysis leads us to suggest that in reality there is not a
single context factor operating uniformly in all situations, but rather a
cluster of context factors that underlies and explains particular
responses in particular communities.

        We would like to call special attention here to the clustering of
context factors pertaining to attitudes towards institutions. We find
that community perception of both the risk itself and the risk management
is shaped in large part by trust and confidence in and identification with
such diverse institutions as local government, the "presumed polluter,"
the sources of information about the risk, and the risk management
agencies. While more research is needed on this cluster of factors, our
findings encourage us to make the practical suggestion that risk managers
at all levels should foster trust and open relationships so as to avoid
the development of an us-versus-them adversarial situation. A polarized,
confrontational risk management process is often counterproductive in that
it takes time and attention away from the urgent task at hand, makes

cooperation difficult, and may negatively predispose other communities elsewhere. Furthermore, if a community is "turned off" by a risk management process that fails to take local concerns into account, the community is not apt to undergo the learning, attitude change, and institution-building that could help it protect its own environmental resources in the future.

However, by advocating the minimization of confrontation during risk management, we do not mean to imply that local anxiety over a risk is necessarily bad or to be avoided. Communities should be aroused; and heightened concern may lead them to take initiative in demanding effective action or in developing their own institutional capabilities and protective strategies.[6]

The practical implication of our work is that both governmental agency planners and technical experts involved in risk management need greater understanding of the specific local-level contexts in which risk management is implemented. However, it would be neither feasible nor efficient for risk management administrators and outside technical intervenors to sponsor in-depth studies of each and every community in which environmental risks are to be addressed. We would suggest that the relevant and useful information about a community could be gathered rather efficiently if attention were concentrated on just those aspects of the local context that are most likely to affect local responses to risk and to risk management.

The context factors we have identified here provide a minimal list of what the planners and implementers of risk management ought to know about a community so that they can design and carry out risk management in a way that not only resolves the toxic problem at hand, but also achieves long-range goals of enhancing local ability to prevent and deal with future environmental/health risks.

NOTES

* This paper is part of a series of five related papers entitled "Enhancing Risk Management by Focusing on the Local Level." Research for this paper was funded by the National Science Foundation -- Ethics and Values in Sciences and Technology (RII-8409912). All views expressed in this paper are those of the author and do not necessarily reflect the view of the National Science Foundation.

** Assistant Professor of Anthropology, Ithaca College, and Adjunct Assistant Professor in Science, Technology & Society, Cornell University.

1. This research project at Cornell University is entitled "Environmental Chemicals and Individual/Community Risk Management." See the first paper in this series for general overview of our integrated approach to risk management (Fessenden-Raden, et al., 1986). Some of the social science research reported on here is also analyzed in a forthcoming study by Fitchen, Heath, and Fessenden-Raden, entitled "Risk Perception in Community Context: A Case Study." The author wishes to acknowledge the collaborative effort of Jenifer S. Heath in conducting the field research on which this paper is based. We wish to thank the many people in our study communities who have so generously shared their time, observations, and experiences. Because some of them are still involved in technical investigations and local negotiations, we have elected to protect the anonymity of the communities under study.

2. For the purpose of this research, "community" is defined operationally as a locality (a social, political, or geographical entity, or a mixture thereof) dealing with a chemical contamination problem in the water supply, or briefly, the risk-affected population and its decision-making institutions. Within this definition, we have selected non-metropolitan communities (small cities, villages, sections of townships, with populations ranging from 1,500 to 35,000). The justification for this selection is that groundwater contamination most frequently affects non-metropolitan communities because they are the places most dependent on groundwater for drinking water.

3. Trust in local institutions is also considered important in the work of Rayner (1984, 1985) and Douglas and Wildavsky (1982), who see it as related to the hierarchial nature of communities.

4. Edelstein (1982) found this effect in a study of local reactions to contamination of private wells in New Jersey.

5. Berry, et al. (1984) cites a case in Massachusetts where the polluter was external to the community (physically as well as ideationally), and the level of anger and anxiety were high. Edelstein (1982) presents another interesting case where the polluting dump was perceived as external, although its physical location was clearly within the community.
6. We agree with Schwartz, et al. (1985, p. 73) that "...community concern should be equal to the risks to which people are exposed; no more, no less." Too little anxiety is not necessarily any better than too much. A level of concern that is appropriate to the risk fosters a rational response to the existing risk, and encourages the community to take preventive measures for the future.

REFERENCES

Berry, David, et al., 1984, "Costs and Benefits of Removing Volatile Organic Compounds from Drinking Water," Cambridge, MA: Abt Associates.

Berry, David and J. Andrew Stoeckle, 1985, "Decentralization of Risk Management: The Case of Drinking Water," Cambridge, MA: Abt Associates.

Douglas, Mary and Aaron Wildavsky, 1982, Risk and Culture, Berkeley: University of California Press.

Edelstein, Michael R., 1982, "The Social and Psychological Impacts of Groundwater Contamination in the Legler Section of Jackson, New Jersey," (unpublished ms.).

Fessenden-Raden, June, Carole A. Bisogni, and Keith S. Porter, 1986, "Enhancing Risk Management by Focusing on the Local Level," this volume.

Fitchen, Janet M., 1985, "Cultural Factors Affecting Perception and Management of Environmental Risks: American Communities Facing Chemical Contamination of Their Groundwater," paper presented at Society for Applied Anthropology, Washington, D.C.

Fitchen, Janet M., Jenifer S. Heath, and June Fessenden-Raden, forthcoming, "Risk Perception in Community Context: A Case Study," to be published in a volume entitled The Social Construction of Risk, edited by Branden Johnson and Vincent Covello.

Fowlkes, Martha R. and Patricia Y. Miller, 1982, Love Canal: The Social Construction of Disaster, Washington, D.C.: Federal Emergency Management Agency.

Lemley, A.T., J. Fessenden-Raden, C.A. Bisogni, and J.M. Holway, 1985, "Nitrate Contamination: Public Awareness," J. Amer. Water Works, 77:34-39.

Rayner, Steve, 1984, "A Cultural Analysis of Occupational Risk Perception," Royal Anthropological Institute Newsletter, 60:10-12.

Rayner, Steve, 1985, "Predicting Social Acceptance of Future Technologies: Advanced Concepts for Nuclear Reactors," lecture presented at Cornell University, 2/7/85.

Schwartz, Steven P., Paul E. White, and Robert G. Hughes, 1985, "Environmental Threats, Communities, and Hysteria," Journal of Public Health Policy, 6:58-77.

Slovic, Paul, Baruch Fischoff, and Sara Lichtenstein, 1979, Rating the Risks," Environment, 21:14-39.

Slovic, Paul, Baruch Fischoff, and Sara Lichtenstein, 1980, "Facts and Fears: Understanding Perceived Risk." in R. C. Schwing and W.A. Albers, eds. Social Risk Assessment: How Safe is Safe Enough? New York: Plenum Press, 181-214.

Slovic, Paul, Baruch Fischoff, and Sara Lichtenstein, 1984, "Behavioral Decision Theory Perspectives on risk and Safety," Acta Psychologica, 56:183-203.

Starr, Chauncey, 1985, "Risk Management, Assessment, and Acceptability," Risk Analysis, 5:97-102.

THE RELATIONSHIP BETWEEN RISK MANAGEMENT INTERVENORS

AND THE COMMUNITY*

Jenifer S. Heath** and June Fessenden-Raden***

Cornell University
Ithaca New York

ABSTRACT

The management of toxicologic risk at the community level is a very complex process. It is generally construed as a centrally-directed activity void of interaction. Our observations in communities facing health risks as a result of chemical contamination of groundwater indicate that there is considerable interaction between centralized risk managers and community members. This paper introduces a systematic framework which can be used to describe the risk management process. We have found that the risk management process is iterative, interactive and layered in time, and that the pools of participants overlap. There also is feedback on two levels. We have disaggregated the process into individual decision units, each of which is then broken down into a series of four stages: identification of the decision question, emergence of interested parties, attempts to influence the decision outcome, and reaching the decision outcome. This framework for analyzing the risk management process helps to identify important events that otherwise may go unnoticed.

KEY WORDS: Groundwater, risk management, risk analysis, decision making, toxic chemicals, chemical contaminants, community

INTRODUCTION

Successful risk management should not only satisfactorily deal with the specific risk that precipitated the response, but also provide a learning experience through which the community (and perhaps the outside

---

* This paper was presented as part of a series of five related papers entitled "Enhancing Risk Management by Focusing on the Local Level." Funding for this research was provided by the Jesse Smith Noyes Foundation and the National Science Foundation Ethics and Values in Science and Technology Program (RII-8409912). All view expressed in this paper are those of the authors and do not necessarily reflect the views of the Jesse Smith Noyes Foundation or the National Science Foundation.

** Graduate Student, Environmental Toxicology

*** Associate Professor of Biochemistry and Biology and Society, Program on Science, Technology and Society, Division of Biological Sciences, Institute of Comparative and Environmental Toxicology.

intervenor) develops response patterns or skills that will be helpful in preventing the occurrence of another similar risk in the future or result in an appropriate, productive response should a similar risk be unavoidable. Our observations indicate that, at least in the case of chemically contaminated groundwater used as drinking water, risk management is often less than entirely successful.

While people might disagree about what constitutes a "satisfactory" resolution of the risk situation, some outcomes can easily be classified as unsatisfactory. In one of our study communities, a reliable and inexpensive source of drinking water that was estimated to pose a cancer risk of one additional case per million persons exposed over a lifetime was closed and replaced with an unreliable, more expensive source that was estimated to pose a cancer risk one or two orders of magnitude higher. All parties agreed that this outcome was unsatisfactory.

Unsatisfactory risk management outcomes occur in part because both local participants and intervenors tend to view risk management as a centralized decision making operation. Centralized risk managers tend to view their activities as something that is applied to the community within which the risk occurs; they are the practitioners of risk management and the community is the recipient.[1] Local participants, likewise, often perceive risk management as something that is done to them and their community.

Our experience indicates that in reality the risk management process is an interactive process, one to which both intervenors and local participants provide inputs. We divide the participants in risk management into two groups: local participants and intervenors. Local participants are those actors who are recognized by members of their communities as "one of us." This does not mean that all community members agree about the resolution of the issues facing them, but rather than there is usually some consensus as to whether or not any given individual is an insider or an outsider. Examples of local participants are mayors, department of public works employees, town council members, and active local residents. Intervenors are the "outsiders." Examples include representatives of the federal Environmental Protection Agency or U.S. Geological Survey, and state health or environmental agencies. We suggest that if all participants, both local and non-local, recognized the interactive nature of the risk management process, the resulting perspective would be more conductive to successful risk management.

METHODS

This paper is one outcome of a larger research project designed to study the perception and management of toxicologic risk at the community level. Data were gathered in six non-metropolitan communities in upstate

---

[1]For examples of the perspectives on risk management commonly presented in the literature, see Calabrese (1978), Crandall and Lave (1981), Fischoff, et al. (1979), Keeney (1983), Okrent (1980), and Starr and Whipple (1980). See Berry and Stoeckle (1985) for a discussion of decentralization in the case of drinking water regulation.

New York.[2] All six communities had become involved in a risk management
process as a result of contamination by trichloroethylene and/or
tetrachloroethylene of groundwater serving as the source for public (and
sometimes private) drinking water supplies.

These local risk management situations were followed through time.
For each community, a chronology of past events was reconstructed and
ongoing events were observed. Local, state and federal level participants
in the risk management process were interviewed to obtain their
perspectives. Local newspaper accounts of the events surrounding the risk
management process were analyzed, and we attended public meetings relevant
to the risk situation. Technical (engineering) reports and other
documentation (such as written records of communication between
participants or notes taken by participants at meetings) were also
reviewed when available.

All examples given in this paper are taken from our observations of
communities engaged in the management of public health risks posed by
chemically contaminated groundwater.[3]

The management of toxicologic risks at the community level varies
from community to community and from one situation to another, but
regularities can be identified. The conceptual framework presented in
Figure 1 has proved useful as a means of describing the interactive nature
of risk management.

THE INPUTS

We emphasize the importance of considering the impact of broader
social and political forces and technical capabilities on the process of
managing risks at the community level. The risk management process is
very much embedded within the context of the community as a whole
(Fitchen, et al., forthcoming). It also occurs within a legal and
regulatory framework that varies according to substantive issue area and
governmental level. Laws, policies and actors at the local, state and
federal levels affect the management of risks posed by contaminated
drinking water. Groundwater quality is managed through different laws and

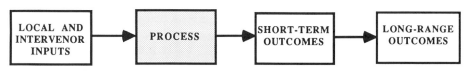

Figure 1

Risk Management

[2]The authors wish to express their gratitude to Janet M. Fitchen, who
participated in the investigation of the communities and has provided
intellectual support throughout the process of preparing this paper.

[3]We appreciate the participation of the many individuals who
cooperated with our research efforts. We protect the anonimity of our
study communities out of respect for ongoing risk management efforts.

policies which were invoked in some of our study communities. Also, the risk management processes in some of these communities were affected by state and federal "superfund" activities. Thus, risk management in these communities is effected by actors from all three levels of government.[4] Because all six study communities face similar risk situations and are in the same state, variation of the inputs into the risk management process was minimized.

THE PROCESS

The risk management process is initiated by the recognition that a risk exists. In the communities in this study, this recognition occurred in one of two ways. Either someone with a specific suspicion about the existence of contaminants in the groundwater decided to sample the drinking water supply, or a sample was taken from a randomly identified supply (as when the U.S. Environmental Protection Agency (U.S. EPA) did a survey of water quality).

Numerous decisions are made in the process of managing a health risk in a community. We have found that looking at each individual decision separately allows us to develop an accurate description of the activities comprising the management of the risk. Thus, we break down the risk management process into individual decision units and focus on each separately. All of these units taken together make up the risk management process.

The risk management process has five important characteristics. (1) It is an iterative process. That is, each successive decision unit brings the process as a whole somewhat closer to the final outcome. (2) The risk management process is also interactive. The interactive nature of the process is so important that our framework focuses not on information gathering and processing, but rather on the interaction itself.[5] (3) The participant population overlaps. There is one pool of participants for the process as a whole, and different subsets of this pool participate in each decision unit. (4) The risk management process is also layered in time. By this we mean that at any given time, many decisions are being made. The passage of time is important because the larger social context within which the whole process is embedded changes with time (Fitchen, et al., forthcoming). (5) Finally, there is feedback in the risk management process on two levels. Within a given decision unit, some activities will affect others. Also, each unit may affect local and intervenor inputs into other concurrent and future decision units.

For each decision unit, we have identified four stages: the identification of the decision question, the emergence of interested parties, attempts to influence the decision outcome, and reaching the decision outcome (see Figure 2). It is helpful to separate these stages conceptually, but in reality they are not necessarily distinct. In particular, the emergence of interested parties and attempts to affect the decision outcome commonly are very closely linked.

---

[4]See Fessenden-Raden, et al. (1986) for elaboration of our definition of inputs into the risk management process.

[5]The decision literature often treats information gathering and processing. See, for example, Anderson (1983), Archer (198), Hill, et al. (1978), and Mintzberg, et al. (1976).

690

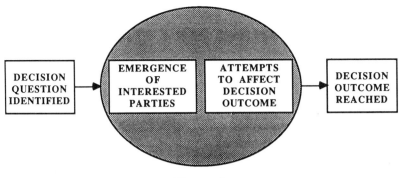

Figure 2

The Process

Identification of Decision Question

The first stage in each unit of the risk management process is the identification of the decision question. That is, one or more participants recognizes that there is some specific question to be addressed. Examples of decision questions include: "Should we issue a boil water notice?" "Should we close well number seven?" or "Which treatment option will we choose?"

Emergence of Interested Parties

Once the decision question has been identified, parties who are interested in the outcome of the decision emerge. Different interested parties have different preferences as to what the decision outcome should be, and so take different sides.

The power relationships involved in decision making at the community level have been studied by Gamson (Gamson, 1968). Some of his concepts help to clarify the interactions both within and across decision units.

Gamson (1968) suggests that for any single decision question, there is some individual or group that has the ability to make a binding decision. He calls that group the "authorities" for that given decision question. All other participants for the decision unit Gamson calls "partisans." (Authority as used here in no way implies expertise.) There may be a different group of authorities for each different decision question. For instance, representatives of the U.S. EPA or the New York State Department of Environmental Conservation are the authorities for decision questions involving the use of Superfund monies.

It is not always clear which group is the authority for a given decision unit. When lines of authority are unclear, the participant who first identified the decision question is often assumed to be the binding decision maker. In New York, this sort of role confusion is common in decision units involving the closing of public supply wells. Since there is no state (or federal) law governing the presence of most organic chemicals in the drinking water, the final decision about closing a public supply well is technically in the domain of local participants. But many local participants are not aware of their authority in this decision unit. The state Department of Health is often the source of the suggestion to close a well (the decision question), and so is often assumed to be the authority.

The other participants who are interested in the decision outcome Gamson (1968) calls "partisans." Because different people may prefer different outcomes for any given decision question, there may be many different partisan groups. But, there is only one group of authorities for each decision question. For instance, if the mayor were the authority for the decision question of whether to close contaminated wells, partisan grmups might be the local department of public works and county health department preferring that the wells remain open, and the state health department preferring that the wells be closed.

Individuals' preferred decision outcomes are not static but may change over time. While some participants tend to share preferences across different decision units, it is not uncommon for participants who align together in one decision unit to oppose each other in another.

Individuals' preferences for decision outcomes seem to be affected by four factors: (1) relevant information and knowledge possessed by the participant, (2) the participant's concerns about broader issues, (3) the participant's affiliations with other participants, and (4) distrust of other participants. This is a preliminary categorization; the four are not entirely distinct from one another, and certainly not independent.

Information and knowledge about the risk situation and about the potential ramifications of a given set of decision outcomes affects individuals' preferences of outcomes (Hughes and Bisogni, 1986). Different individuals have different amounts of knowledge and interpret that knowledge didferently, and so informed, intelligent participants may, on the basis of knowledge alone, prefer different decision outcomes.

Also, different participants often focus on different broader concerns. We have found that risk managers generally expect that participants will focus mn the health risk. But our research indicates that many other concerns may take precedence over the health risk in people's minds. For instance, some participants have a broader concern about the economic risk to the community, others about the issue of adequate water supply, still others about bureaucratic stumbling blocks, and so on.[6] While it is not uncommon for different participants to have different broader concerns, we have found that participants often fail to recognize this absence of consensus. This lack of awareness is often a stumbling block in the risk management process because decision outcomes that seem ideal to participants with one set of over-riding concerns seem inappropriate to participants with different broader concerns. Discord results.

Individuals' affiliations with other participants may also affect their preferences, as when some organization expresses a preference and its members then feel compelled to concur.

Finally, distrust of other participants affects people's preferences. Participants tend to take sides against others whom they distrust. The effect of distrust on the risk management process is particularly noticeable when the activities in other concurrent and previous decision units have caused local participants to distrust

---

[6]Fitchen (1986) described ten factors in the community context that affect broader concerns.

intervenors. In such situations, local participants may almost automatically join together in opposition to the intervenor's preferred outcome, to the detriment of all involved.

Attempts to Affect the Decision Outcome

The third stage in each decision unit is attempts to affect the decision outcome. This is the stage at which the various partisan groups try to get the authorities to reach the decision outcome they favor. Gamson (1968) uses the term "influence" for partisans' attempts to sway authorities. In the study community where the local department of public works and the county health department formed one partisan group active in the decision unit for the question, "Should we close the well?" and the state health department was another, both attempted to influence the authority (the mayor). Representatives of the state health department, preferring that the well be closed, threatened that if the mayor did not close the well, they would tell the local media that the mayor was ignoring a public health risk. The clear implication was that the mayor might not be re-elected if his constituents felt he was not protecting them. The local department of public works and county health department wanted the well to remain open, and attempted to influence the mayor by explaining their reasons to him.

Gamson (1968) suggests that influence attempts can be broken down into three categories or three "means of influence." These are constraint, inducement, and persuasion. The state health department's attempt to affect the mayor's decision about closing the well by threatening him is an example of a constraint. The local department of public works' and county health department's attempt to educate the mayor was a form of persuasion.

In response to partisans' influence attempts, authorities attempt to maintain "social control" (Gamson, 1968). That is, authorities try to maintain their freedom to reach their own preferred outcome despite partisans' influence attempts. In the case of the mayor deciding whether to close the well, it is not clear that any attempts were made to control the partisans. In another community, the U.S. EPA has attempted to control local partisans' ability to affect numerous Superfund-related decisions by reaching decision outcomes without telling other potential participants that such a decision was being considered.

Gamson (1968) identifies three "means of social control": insulation, sanction, and persuasion. When the Environmental Protection Agency makes decisions in isolation, it is using insulation.

It is helpful to borrow these six concepts (three means of influence and three means of social control) for application to the risk management process. The choice of means of influence and control illuminates certain aspects of the relationship between different participants. First, the choice reflects participants' perceptions of current and past relationships. For instance, the use of persuasion usually indicates feelings of mutual respect (Gamson, 1968). Sensitive participants can recognize relationships that need improvement if they pay attention to choice of means. Choice of means of influence and control in one decision unit also affects the relationships between the same participants in other concurrent and future decision units.

Decision Outcome Reached

The fourth stage in the decision unit is that a final decision outcome is reached by the authorities. Decision outcomes and the activities that precede them may have several effects. It may become evident during the resolution of one decision question that another decision question must be addressed. Also, the decision outcome may result in some intermediate risk management outcome, such as the closing of a well or the initiation of a new study. The decision outcome itself is distinct from its implementation.

OUTCOMES

We identify two categories of risk management outcomes. The first, short-term risk management outcomes, are the direct result of the process described above. Activities like issuing a boil water notice, performing a hydrogeologic study, or providing carbon filtration are examples of short-term risk management outcomes. The sum of the effects of all of the short-term outcomes in a given community is the long-range outcome. This outcome, which includes resolution of the risk situation and any relevant learning that may occur within the community, can seldom (if ever) be assessed in a time-frame that is meaningful to the intervenors.[7]

CONCLUSION

We have found that the risk management process is very complex -- much more so than most people realize. Disaggregating the process in a systematic way, as we do using the four stage decision unit, helps to unravel some of its complexities.

As we continue to gather and analyze data, we will expand this perspective on the risk management process. We hope, for instance, to identify associations between means of influence and control used in one decision unit and choice of preferred outcome by the same participants in other concurrent and future decision units. The analysis we have completed thus far will guide our continued efforts.

REFERENCES

Anderson, P.A., 1983, "Decision Making by Objection and the Cuban Missile Crisis," Administrative Science Quarterly, 28:201-222.
Archer, E.R., 1980, "How to Make a Business Decision: An Analysis of Theory and Practice," Management Review, 69(2):54-61.
Berry, David and J. Andrew Stoeckle, 1985, "Decentralization of Risk Management: The Case of Drinking Water," Abt Associates Inc.
Calabrese, Edward J., 1978, Methodological Approaches to Deriving Environmental and Occupational Health Standards, Wiley-Interscience, NY.
Crandall, Robert W. and Lester B. Lave, eds, 1981, The Scientific Basis of Health and Safety Regulations, The Brookings Institute, Washington, DC.
Fessenden-Raden, June, Carole A. Bisogli, and Keith S. Porter, 1986, "Enhancing Risk Management by Focusing on the Local Level: An Integrated Approach," this volume.

---

[7]See Fessenden-Raden, et al. (1986) for more details about our perspective on the outcomes of risk management.

Fischoff, Baruch, Paul Slovic and Sarah Lichtenstein, 1979, "Weighing the Risks," Environment, 21(4):17-20, 32-38.

Fitchen, Janet M., 1986, "The Importance of Community Context in Effective Risk Management," this volume.

Fitchen, Janet M., Jenifer S. Heath, and June Fessenden-Raden, forthcoming, "Risk Perception in Community Context: A Case Study," to be published in a volume entitled The Social Construction of Risk, edited by Branden Johnson and Vincent Covello.

Gamson, William A., 1968, Power and Discontent, The Dorsey Press, Homewood, Ill.

Hill, P.H., H.A. Bedau, R.A. Chechile, W.J. Crochetiere, B.L. Dellerman, D. Ounjiam, S.G. Pauker, and J.Z. Rubin, 1978, Making Decisions, Addison-Wesley Publishing Company, Reading, Massachusetts.

Hughes, Bonney A. and Carole A. Bisogni, 1986, "Citizens' Knowledge, Beliefs and Actions Regarding Chemical Contamination of Drinking Water," this volume.

Keeney, Ralph L., 1983, "Issues in Evaluating Standards," Interfaces, 13(2):12-22.

Mintzberg, H., D. Raisinghani, and A. Theoret, 1976, "The Structure of 'Unstructured' Decision Processes," Administrative Science Quarterly, 21:246-275.

Okrent, David, 1980, "Alternative Risk Management Policies for State and Local Governments," report to the National Science Foundation PB83-128983.

Starr, Chauncey and Chris Whipple, 1980, "Risks of Risk Decisions," Science, 208:1114-1119.

CITIZENS' KNOWLEDGE, BELIEFS AND ACTIONS

REGARDING CHEMICAL CONTAMINATION OF DRINKING WATER*

Bonney F. Hughes** and Carole A. Bisogni***

Cornell University, Ithaca, New York

ABSTRACT

To obtain background information for the development of educational materials, we studied a sample of water supply customers in a non-metropolitan area in New York State. We examined knowledge, beliefs and actions related to chemical contamination of groundwater used as a source of drinking water. Respondents knew many of the key concepts related to water and health to which new information about the chemical contamination of groundwater could be linked. Respondents were less familiar with the terms, groundwater and parts per million. Few misconceptions were observed. Respondents who knew more about water and health tended to have more positive beliefs about seeking information about drinking water quality, be more interested in information, and report reading or learning about drinking water quality more frequently.

KEY WORDS: Risk management, groundwater contamination, drinking water quality, education, environmental toxicology, public perceptions

INTRODUCTION

Individual citizens can influence the management of risks from chemical contamination of groundwater used as a source of drinking water through their actions. One of the ways to enhance the management of such risks is to educate citizens about groundwater and its protection. Before embarking upon educational programs, however, the characteristics of potential audiences must be understood. What an audience already knows about a topic as well as their beliefs and actions will influence how they respond to educational messages and whom they will believe (Gillespie and Yarbrough, 1984).

We studied citizens' knowledge related to chemical contamination of groundwater used as a source of drinking water as background for the development of educational materials. We used Novak's theory of education as a framework for studying citizens' knowledge (Novak, 1977; Novak and Gowin, 1984). According to this theory, new knowledge is acquired meaningfully only when it is related to concepts that the learner already has. Thus, one focus of our study was to identify the concepts that citizens had about water and the health effects of contaminants to which new information might be related.

697

We also studied how frequently citizens had read or heard information about drinking water quality and their beliefs about seeking information on this topic. To investigate the relationships of individual's beliefs to action we were guided by the theory of reasoned action (Ajzen and Fishbein, 1980). According to this theory an important determinant of a person's actions are his/her beliefs about outcomes of the action. A person is more likely to engage in an activity if s/he has a positive attitude about it. The positive attitude will tend to occur if the person thinks that a desirable outcome is likely to result from the action. In our study we explored how citizens' knowledge about water and health effects of contaminants was related to their beliefs about reading or hearing about drinking water quality and to the frequency with which they took these actions. We hypothesized that citizens with greater knowledge about water and the health effects of contaminants would believe that reading or hearing information about drinking water quality would have beneficial outcomes for them and report more involvement in seeking information.

Method

The citizens in our study were the customers of a water supply system in Elmira, New York. A well supplying the water system had been closed in 1980 because of contamination by trichloroethylene, an industrial solvent. In 1984 several private wells were found to be contaminated with the chemical. We sent a mail questionnaire to a systematic random sample of 1100 (6.5%) of the water customers in February 1985. We used Dillman's (1978) method for mail surveys and received 610 (55%) responses.

In developing the measures for knowledge, beliefs and actions we first conducted in-depth interview with a different sample of the water system customers. Among the 26 people interviewed, we discovered some knowledge of simple toxicological concepts, but confusion about groundwater. These people reported seeking information about drinking water to various degrees. Based on the responses to the interviews we designed a mail questionnaire to probe the same topics: knowledge about water, knowledge about the health effects of contaminants and seeking information.

Knowledge about water and and knowledge about health effects of contaminants were measured using a series of true and false statements with the response choices: true, false and don't know. The knowledge instrument measured the extent to which respondents' belief about water and health were in agreement with the latest professional tenets.

To study whether or not respondents' knowledge of water and knowledge of the health effects of contaminants were related to their beliefs about seeking information and frequency of seeking information, we developed scales to measure these variables. Scales were created by summing over the related knowledge items. For each item a correct response was scored as +1, a don't know response as 0, and an incorrect response as -1.

To assess respondents' beliefs about seeking information we asked how likely it was that each of six outcomes would happen as a result of seeking information and how desirable each outcome was. A score of +1 was assigned when an outcome was rated as "likely," -1 for a rating of "unlikely" and 0 for a rating of "neither." Likewise each desirability rating was assigned +1 if the respondent said "desirable," -1 for undesirable and 0 if the respondent said "neither."

The products of the likelihood and desirability ratings were calculated for each outcome. A positive product indicated that the respondent thought that the action was beneficial with respect to that outcome; a negative product indicated that the action was not beneficial with respect to the outcome; a product near or equal to zero indicated that the respondent felt neutral with respect to the outcome. For example, a potential outcome of "reading or hearing about drinking water quality" was "teaches me new ways to protect water quality." If the product of these two ratings was -1, the respondent considered this outcome either desirable and likely or undesirable and unlikely. Both types of responses suggested that the result of the action would be beneficial, assuming that the respondent wants to avoid something undesirable as well as bring about desirable things.

The products of the desirability and likelihood ratings for all listed outcomes for reading or hearing about information listed were added together. If the sum was positive, the respondent believed that the action would be beneficial with respect to the listed outcomes; if negative, not beneficial; and if zero, neutral. To the extent that the listed outcomes were representative of those the respondent considered relevant when deciding whether or not to read or hear information, the sum of the products mentioned above indicated whether or not the respondent believed the outcomes of this action to be beneficial on the whole.

We also asked respondents to rate how interested they were in information about drinking water quality using one of four response choices, "not at all," "a little," "fairly interested," and "very interested."

To measure the extent to which respondents sought information about drinking water quality, we asked how frequently in the last year respondents had read about drinking water quality in newspapers or magazines, heard about drinking water on radio or television or talked about it. Based on respondents' answers to these questions, each respondent was assigned a score for seeking information about drinking water quality.

We examined the relationships among respondents' scores for knowledge of water, knowledge of health effects of contaminants, beliefs about reading or hearing about information about drinking water quality, self-rated interest in information and self-reported frequency of seeking information about drinking water quality. Depending on the characteristics of the data we examined the relationships using either chi square analysis or Spearman's rank correlation.

RESULTS AND DISCUSSION

Knowledge. Only about one-third of the respondents were aware that industrial chemicals had led to the closing of a water supply system well. This level of awareness seemed low especially because newspaper articles had been written about the 1980 closing. However, articles had not appeared until two years after the closing. Another possible explanation for the low awareness was that the system had several other wells in addition to a surface water supply so that the closing of one well was not a major problem. About 70% of the respondents were aware that some private wells had been contaminated by industrial chemicals. Reports of contamination of several private wells in this community had generated considerable publicity the summer before the survey was conducted. In the year before the survey ten articles had been published in local papers about private wells compared to six articles about public wells.

When asked about water under the ground, 70% or more respondents knew that such water moved; could be contaminated; and was replenished by rain, snow, lakes, and streams and water that people use. Less than 25% knew the correct definition of "groundwater," which is all water below the water table.

About 70% of the respondents knew what the term "concentration" meant and knew that the term "parts per million" was a measure of concentration. Only 45% correctly identified the definition of parts per million, however. Some respondents indicated misconceptions for these terms.

In terms of concepts related to effects of contaminants on health, most respondents indicated few misconceptions. About 90% of the respondents knew that chemical contaminants or pollutants could get into people's bodies and could correctly identify routes of exposure. Seventy percent or more knew that exposures to chemical contaminants could affect one's behavior, nervous system, chances of getting cancer, or chances of having a child with birth defects. Only 12% associated exposure to chemical contaminants with the chances of getting diabetes, and association for which the authors know of no research evidence. Seventy-five percent of respondents correctly identified the definition of the term, "a one in a hundred thousand chance of happening in a lifetime."

The results of the knowledge questions indicate that in general the respondents had many of the key concepts related to water and health to which new information about groundwater or associated health risks could be related. The lack of misconceptions for some of the key concepts may make the task of educating easier than if many misconceptions were present. Novak claimed that changing misconceptions is very difficult (Novak and Gowin, 1984).

The area for which respondents indicated the least amount of knowledge was related to technical terms including "groundwater" and "parts per million." These findings indicate that intervenors should be sure to define these terms when communicating with citizens.

Beliefs about Seeking Information. Ninety-one percent of respondents believed that reading or hearing about the quality of drinking water was likely to keep them informed about an important issue; 94% viewed this outcome as desirable. Eighty percent believed that the activity was likely to teach them new ways to protect water quality, and 90% rated this outcome as desirable. Only 31% believed that reading or hearing about drinking water was likely to result in something that they enjoyed, but 93% rated doing something I enjoy as desirable. Only 22% thought that the activity was likely to result in doing their work better, but 92% rated this outcome as desirable. Sixty-six percent believed it was unlikely that reading or hearing about drinking water would take time away from other things, but 54% rated this outcome as desirable. Seventy-one percent thought it was unlikely that reading or hearing about drinking water quality does not help them or their family and 65% rated doing something that does not help me or my family as undesirable.

Thus, in terms of both likelihood and desirability many respondents viewed reading or hearing information about drinking water quality as beneficial with respect to outcomes related to keeping informed about an important issue, helping themselves or their family, and learning new ways to protect water quality. Outcomes related to enjoyment or work performance were viewed as less beneficial.

Respondents rated their interest in information about drinking water quality in the following way. Thirty-four percent indicated "very interested," 42% "fairly interested," 18% "a little" and 6% "not at all." Reading or hearing about drinking water quality. Seventy-four percent of respondents reported that they had read about drinking water quality in newspapers or magazines. Of these, 55% reported reading about drinking water quality more than four times in the last year. Sixty-nine percent of respondents had heard about drinking water quality on the radio or television with 53% of these reporting that they had heard such information more than four times in the last year. Of the 62% who had discussed the quality of drinking water with someone, 56% had discussed it four or more times in the last year.

Relationships Among Knowledge and Beliefs. Respondents with high scores for knowledge of water tended to have high scores for self-reported interest in information about drinking water quality (chi square significant, p = 0.0001). However, respondents' scores for knowledge of health effects of contaminants were not related to scores for self-reported interest in information about drinking water quality.

A relationship between knowledge about health effects of contaminants and beliefs about the outcome of reading or hearing about drinking water quality was observed, however. Respondents with lower scores for knowledge of health effects were less likely to believe that the outcomes of reading or hearing about drinking water quality were beneficial (chi square significant, p = .006). No relationship between knowledge of water and beliefs was observed.

Respondents' scores for beliefs about the outcomes of reading or hearing about drinking water quality were significantly related to their self-rated interest in information about drinking water. Respondents with more positive views about the outcomes of reading or hearing information about drinking water tended to report more interest than other respondents (chi square significant, p = .0001).

Relationships of Knowledge, Beliefs and Actions. Scores on the knowledge scales were related to respondents' self-reported frequency of information-seeking. For both knowledge of water and knowledge of health effects, higher scores were associated with higher frequencies of reading or hearing information about drinking water quality (chi square significant, p = .0001).

Self-rated interest in information about drinking water quality was also positively associated with the frequency with which respondents reported reading or hearing about drinking water quality (Spearman's rho = 0.41, p = .0001).

Respondents who had more positive beliefs about the outcomes listed for reading or hearing about drinking water quality tended to report reading or hearing about drinking water quality more often (chi square significant, p = .0005).

These results provide some support for the hypotheses that individuals who are more knowledgeable about a topic will be more interested in seeking information on drinking water and report more involvement in this behavior. These associations, however, are not necessarily causal. A high level of knowledge could result from interest in a topic and information seeking behavior. The findings suggest, however, that if people acquire some information about water quality, this information may interest them in further information. Furthermore, if they become interested in the information they may believe that seeking information will be beneficial and actually seek information more often than before. More research is needed, however, to support these conclusions.

The study suggests that citizens may be receptive to educational messages about drinking water quality because many citizens have the key concepts related to water and health effects and that once they gain some knowledge they will seek more. The challenge to educators is to present the information in a way that will motivate citizens to learn. Citizens may perceive benefits of information as relating to keeping them informed of important community issues, helping their family and resource protection. Other benefits that we did not explore may also be perceived.

This study has provided initial insight into some characteristics of audiences that must be considered when developing educational messages about drinking water quality. Further work must be conducted to develop effective strategies for communicating with citizens about this important issue.

NOTES

* This paper was presented as one of five papers in an integrated series entitled, "Enhancing Risk Management by Focusing on the Local Level." Funding for this project was provided by the Ford Foundation and the Jessie Smith Noyes Foundation. The opinions expressed in the paper represent those of the authors and not necessarily those of the Foundations.

** Graduate Student, Environmental Toxicology

*** Associate Professor, Division of Nutritional Sciences and Institute for Comparative and Environmental Toxicology

REFERENCES

Ajzen, I. and M. Fishbein. 1980 Understanding Attitudes and Predicting Social Behavior. Englewood Cliffs, N.J.: Prentice-Hall, Inc.
Dillman, D.A. 1978. Mail and Telephone Surveys: The Total Design Method. New York: Wiley.
Gillespie, A.H. and P. Yarbrough. 1984. A conceptual model for communicating nutrition. J. Nutrition Education 16(4):168.
Novak, J.D. 1977. A Theory of Education. Ithaca, N.Y.: Cornell University Press.
Novak, J.D. and D.B. Gowin. 1984. Learning How To Learn. New York: Cambridge University Press.

INCORPORATING TECHNICAL INFORMATION AND COMMUNITY GOALS

INTO RISK MANAGEMENT DECISION RELATED TO GROUNDWATER*

Henry B. F. Hughes**

Cornell University, Ithaca, NY

ABSTRACT

Effective local groundwater management requires technical information which often must be provided by experts from outside the community who become intervenors. We have found that successfully weaving technical information into the decision making process of a community requires a sensitivity to the perspective of the community. Understanding the community context can allow an intervenor to develop technical information that is relevant to the immediate needs of the community. An effective partnership between the intervenor and key individuals in the community facilitates the development of realistic options, and usually leads to a positive outcome.

KEY WORDS: groundwater contamination, groundwater management, risk management, local government

INTRODUCTION

Groundwater management is a responsibility which local governments in New York State are beginning to address as a result of the increasing frequency of groundwater contamination incidents. Effective management requires technical information which often must be provided by experts from outside the community. The Water Resources Program at Cornell has been assisting communities through New York State in dealing with water quality issues. Our goal has been to help communities address the issues currently facing them in a manner that will leave them better prepared to face and deal with future water quality problems. We have also sought to develop and improve methods of assisting communities. The issue which we have dealt with most is groundwater protection which is the subject of this paper.

We have found that successfully weaving technical information into the decision making process of a community requires a sensitivity to the perspectives of the community, since every community we have worked with has approached the problems from a slightly different perspective. Groundwater quality is not always of primary importance to a community and, therefore groundwater management competes with other community goals.

This paper identifies three key components of intervention by outside experts in local groundwater management decisions which we have found from experience to be critical to achieving a positive outcome. The first component consists of gaining an understanding of the community's perspective and establishing a constructive relationship with community leaders. The second is to develop technical information which addresses the most important issues of the current situation. The third component is presenting the technical information in the form of options which give the community as much flexibility as possible to choose how groundwater will be managed locally.

The Local Perspective

The goals which a community has set which are not related to groundwater may either compete with or compliment the goals related to groundwater. The goal which most often conflicts with groundwater protection is economic development. In some communities, development is a goal of local officials because more jobs are needed. In several Long Island towns, where rapid development is already occurring, local officials are trying to reduce or control the development pressure for a number of reasons including groundwater protection and open space or farmland preservation.

Where development is already perceived by community leaders as undesirable, groundwater protection is embraced as one of several complimentary goals. However, the communities that seek development along with groundwater protection are much more skeptical of strict land use controls, such as limiting housing densities. If community leaders want both development and good quality groundwater then the information presented to them should help them understand the risks that particular types of development pose to groundwater quality.

Farmland preservation is a goal which may or may not compliment groundwater protection. The nonintensive type of agriculture practiced in many rural areas of New York State is often consistent with maintaining high quality groundwater in underlying aquifers. In these areas farmland preservation and groundwater protection are natural allies. More chemically intensive agriculture can cause serious groundwater contamination meaning that the need for high quality groundwater must compete with agriculture or at least with certain agricultural practices. This is most evident in potato growing areas of Long Island where nitrogen fertilizers and several pesticides have contaminated large quantities of groundwater.

In each community with which we have worked, the past experiences of the community with groundwater and the other goals have influenced the perception of the risk of groundwater contamination from various local activities. In order for us to intervene in a constructive way it was necessary to take the time to understand the specific community and to realize that while we were the experts on groundwater, the leaders of the community were the experts on the community. Helping the community leaders make use of the information we could provide required us to establish a relationship with the leaders so that we could understand their goals and gain their trust. We could then work together to develop a groundwater protection strategy.

Developing Useful Technical Information

The key to developing useful technical information for a community is understanding what questions need to be answered before community leaders can proceed with a groundwater management program. Groundwater and its contaminants are elusive entities from a technical standpoint. This makes it very difficult to answer questions about contaminant health effects or groundwater movement in precise terms. This, in turn, can cause experts to either shy away from hard to answer questions or to invest a lot of money in trying to precisely define one aspect while ignoring others. Both of these pitfalls can render a technical report useless if they cause key questions to be left unanswered. Answers to the technical questions which can not be calculated precisely can be developed and presented in a way that openly shows the uncertainty.

A question that many communities start with when they address groundwater management is: "Where does the water in our well or wells come from?" The community needs to know where precipitation water infiltrates the land surface and flows toward their well. This area of land, referred to as a recharge area, is very difficult to locate precisely and the price for locating it increases rapidly with precision. However, if groundwater is to be protected the community must answer this question with a precision which it feels comfortable defending.

On Long Island, deep flow recharge areas were identified during a regional study as the most important recharge areas for drinking water. Undeveloped tracts of land in these deep flow recharge areas became natural candidates for areas to protect. In more rural areas there often are not detailed hydrologic studies available, and it was necessary for us to develop estimates of the location of the important recharge areas for public wells in these communities.

One community started with a more basic question which was something like: "Can groundwater contamination happen to our wells?" Many of the members of the town planning board were not familiar with the numerous incidents of groundwater contamination which were highly publicized in other parts of the state. Hence, they were not aware of the risks that their currently high quality groundwater faced. This made it important for us to develop information which could help them envision the types of contamination which they were vulnerable to. This was done by developing hypothetical case studies which showed, in detail, what could happen to their water as a result of a particular development in the recharge area for their wells. The case studies covered contamination from residential development, intensified agricultural activity and underground gasoline storage. Such hypothetical case studies were not necessary on Long Island or in other areas where public officials had been reading about groundwater contamination in their newspapers for years.

Once it has been established that risks do exist and that a particular recharge area is to be the focus of management program, it is necessary to relate particular management actions to levels of risk of contamination from various contaminants. The two classes of groundwater contaminants which we have dealt with most are nitrate and synthetic organic chemicals since these are by far the most common contaminants causing public well closings in New York State.

Nitrate is the simpler example to discuss from a risk management stand point. New York State has had an official nitrate standard for drinking water for a long time. The maximum allowable concentration of nitrate in drinking water in New York State is 10 milligrams per liter (mg/l). Also, nitrate loadings from various land uses are due largely to sewage, animal waste and nitrogen fertilizers. These loadings are predictable, and hence it is possible to determine with reasonable accuracy what land uses can be allowed in a recharge area to be compatible with a chosen planning criterion.

In order to ensure that the concentration of any contaminant is below the standard more than half the time, the average concentration of the contaminant must be less than the standard. Since concentrations vary, this means that a planning criterion must be less than the health standard by an amount that guarantees meeting the health standard a high percentage of the time. This is particularly true of groundwater where relatively little mixing takes place. Porter (1982) evaluated the relationship between the mean concentration of nitrate found in a set of groundwater samples in Nassau County and the percentage of the samples which violated the 10 mg/l nitrate standard. He found that if the average nitrate concentration in an area was 6 mg/l then 10% of the samples from that area had nitrate concentrations exceeding 10 mg/l. In order to achieve better than 90% compliance with the 10 mg/l standard in an area characteristic of Nassau County, an average concentration of less then 6 mg/l would be required. A higher percentage of compliance would require a lower average.

Several Long Island towns adopted unofficial planning criteria for nitrate which reflected their respective philosophies and current situations. In the eastern Long Island towns which are still largely undeveloped there was considerable sentiment for a policy of nondegradation toward the high quality groundwater. Accordingly, planners there used a nitrate criterion of 2 mg/l as a basis for zoning ordinances in recharge areas. The 2 mg/l criterion would ensure a very high percentage of compliance with the 10 mg/l standard, and it had a history of use for protecting similar areas in New Jersey (Hughes and Porter, 1983). It did allow for some development.

A more heavily developed western Long Island town, with which we worked, felt that a 6 mg/l criterion was adequate for the areas they were trying to protect. This higher criterion reflects a number of differences between the western and eastern towns. Development pressures are much higher in western Long Island, there is less public pressure for nondegradation of groundwater and there is less emphasis on maintaining open space.

We helped the towns develop zoning ordinances to ensure that new residential developments would be consistent with their nitrate criteria. The ordinances limited the density of housing and the size of fertilized lawns.

The synthetic organic chemicals we were concerned about did not have official standards, but the State Health Department uses guidelines of 50 micrograms per liter (ug/l) for a single organic, or 100 ug/l combined concentrations if more than one synthetic organic is present, for closing water supply wells. For certain proven carcinogens such as benzene or vinyl chloride the guideline is 5 ug/l. While the nitrate standard is assumed to be a stable quantity for planning purposes, the synthetic organics guidelines are expected to change, and could be lowered. Table 1 shows the calculated water quality criteria which accompany various cancer risks from drinking water for two of the organics most often found in New York's groundwater. These criteria are all less than the 50 ug/l guideline.

The New York State Department of Environmental Conservation which is separate from the Department of Health has established ambient groundwater standards for certain of the synthetic organic chemicals, which specify the maximum concentration of the contaminants which can be released to

Table 1

Water Quality Criteria Suggested by EPA (1980 a,b)

Water Quality Criteria to Allow One
Additional Cancer per:

Chemical	10,000,000 people	people	1,000,000 people	100,000
Trichloroethylene	0.27 ug/l		2.7 ug/l	27 ug/l
Tetrachloroethylene	0.08 ug/l		0.8 ug/l	8 ug/l

groundwater. For trichloroethylene, for example, the standard is 10 ug/l. We used this 10 ug/l standard as a starting point for development planning information. The 10 ug/l standard can be translated into a permissible loading rate per unit area for a particular area. For trichloroethylene the maximum permissible loading rate turns out to be 0.07 pound (3/4 of an ounce of liquid) per acre per year for Long Island's climate (Hughes et al., 1985). For all practical purposes this means that a facility using trichloroethylene must not discharge any of it to the groundwater since even a very small discharge will cause the standard to be violated.

There is much less flexibility for a town in preventing synthetic organic chemical contamination. Most contamination from synthetic organic chemicals comes from industrial and commercial areas. The towns were able to reduce the risk of organic chemical contamination by keeping industrial and commercial development out of the important recharge areas as much as possible. In areas where industrial and commercial activities are already overly important recharge areas, the emphasis needs to be on encouraging and requiring waste disposal practices which do not endanger groundwater. Unlike the situation with nitrate, there was not an opportunity to design land use plans which could be expected to produce water with a certain acceptable concentration of the organic compounds. There are still differences in the ways communities approach prevention, but they are more subtle. A community's strategy for preventing synthetic organic contamination may be governed more by what is possible economically and politically in their situation than by how community leaders feel about the risks.

Presenting Information

The manner in which information is shared with a community has much to do with how well it is accepted. We found that presenting the technical information at the end of a project in terms of specific options has several advantages. It allows the intervenor to map out one or more specific actions that the community can take, but it clearly leaves the ultimate decision up to the community leaders. In most towns, we worked closely with one or more planners who worked for the town and lived in town. We developed a set of options in conjunction with these people, to make them realistic for the community.

In each town, the options were presented and discussed in report form and at one or more meetings bringing together the leaders who would have the responsibility of implementing the options. These meetings typically included representatives from the town, the county health and planning departments, the water supply companies and the cooperative extension service. The process of involving everyone from the beginning gave them a stake in the success of the effort. By the end of a project there was usually a consensus developing around one or more options as being appropriate for the community.

CONCLUSION

To be effective, an intervenor must not enter into a local risk management situation assuming that he or she has all the answers ahead of time. Community leaders are often experts on what their community wants and what type of options are feasible politically and economically. Understanding the community context can allow an intervenor to develop technical information that is relevant to the immediate needs of the community. An effective partnership must exist between the intervenor and key individuals in the community. We feel that our projects have been successful when a community adopts steps for groundwater protection and the intervenors learn from the project how to better assist other communities.

NOTES

* This paper is part of a series of five related papers entitled "Enhancing Risk Management by Focusing on the Local Level."

** Water Resource Specialist, Center for Environmental Research.

REFERENCES

Hughes, H.B.F., J. Pike and K.S. Porter. 1985. Assessment of Groundwater
    Contamination by Nitrogen and Synthetic Organics in Two Water
    Districts in Nassau County, New York. Center for Environmental
    Research, Cornell University, Ithaca, N.Y.
Hughes, H.B.F. and K.S. Porter. 1983. Land Use and Groundwater Quality
    in the Pine Barrens of Southampton. Center for Environmental
    Research, Cornell University, Ithaca, N.Y.
Porter, K.S. 1982. Groundwater Information: Allocation and Data
    Needs. Center for Environmental Research, Cornell University, Ithaca,
    N.Y.
United States Environmental Protection Agency. 1980. Ambient Water
    Quality Criteria for Tetrachloroethylene. National Technical
    Information Service, Washington, D.C.
United States Environmental Protection Agency. 1980. Ambient Water
    Quality Criteria for Trichloroethylene. National Technical
    Information Service, Washington, D.C.

POLICY CONSIDERATION IN THE SELECTION OF NATIONAL EMISSION

STANDARDS FOR HAZARDOUS AIR POLLUTANTS FOR THE TACOMA SMELTER

Robert Ajax* and Janet Meyer**

Environmental Protection Agency*,
Pacific Environmental Services, Inc.**

INTRODUCTION

This paper presents background information and the policy basis for the National Emission Standards for Hazardous Air Pollutants (NESHAP) that were proposed to limit inorganic arsenic emissions from the ASARCO smelter at Tacoma, Washington. The standard-setting approach used and the role public participation played in the development of the final standard are also discussed. Factors considered include the estimated community health risks and the uncertainties in these estimates; the need to reduce public exposure to arsenic and to protect health; the potentially available control measures; the economic impacts of plant closure on smelter employees and the local community; and the opinions of the local community as expressed in 3 days of public hearings and in over 650 comment letters.

The Environmental Protection Agency's (EPA's) initial activities relating to development of standards for inorganic arsenic began when "Standards of Performance for New Stationary Sources - Primary Copper, Zinc, and Lead Smelters," were promulgated in 1976. The Natural Resource Defense Council, Inc. (NRDC), subsequently filed a petition to review the standards because inorganic arsenic emissions from nonferrous smelters were not included among the regulated pollutants. In response to the petition, EPA made a commitment to gather data necessary for setting standards on arsenic emissions from copper smelters. In the fall of 1976 EPA initiated work to assess arsenic emissions from existing primary copper smelters and to evaluate appropriate control technology. Information obtained from this work indicated that fugitive arsenic emissions from copper smelters could also be a major source of arsenic air pollution and the greatest contributor to public exposure. This work eventually led to the proposal of standards in 1983 for glass manufacturing plants and primary copper smelters, with the most prominent part of the rulemaking pertaining to the ASARCO smelter at Tacoma, Washington (48 FR 33112). A final standard had been developed and was being reviewed within the Agency when ASARCO announced its plans to close the smelter. Because of the planned closure (which has now occurred), EPA did not issue a final rule. The period between 1976 and 1983-84 included several changes in EPA's administration and significant shifts in the approach to rulemaking. This paper provides a brief history of this rulemaking and discusses the risk management approach used in development of the standard, including the role local participation played in the development of the final standard.

BACKGROUND

The primary copper smelting industry in the U.S. uses pyrometallurgical processes to extract copper from sulfide copper ores. At all primary copper smelters, two primary operations are conducted: (1) smelting the copper ore concentrates by melting the concentrates together with fluxes to produce an iron-copper sulfide mixture (matte) and an iron oxide slag; and (2) converting the matte to blister copper by oxidizing the sulfur and other impurities for removal in the offgases and oxidizing the iron for removal in slag.

In the pyrometallurgical process, arsenic is separated from the copper and its oxidized and volatilized into the process offgases or removed with the slag. The amount of arsenic emitted to the atmosphere during roasting, smelting, and converting is a direct function of the arsenic content of smelter feed materials and smelter configuration as well as the emission capture and control techniques used.

Arsenic is an impurity frequently found in copper ore deposits. At the 15 primary copper smelters operating in the U.S. in 1983, the average arsenic content of feed material charged to roasters or furnaces ranged from 0.0004 to 4.0 weight percent. As shown in Figure 1, the average arsenic content of the feed materials was well below 0.5 weight percent at the majority of smelters and only one smelter processed feed material with more than 1 percent arsenic. This was the Tacoma smelter which, in addition to processing high-arsenic copper ore concentrates, also recovered arsenic trioxide from waste materials. This significant difference between the Tacoma smelter and the remaining smelters and the urban location of the smelter led to the development of a separate standard for the Tacoma smelter.

Because of the high estimated risks for the ASARCO-Tacoma smelter and the community concerns, the Tacoma smelter became a principal focus of EPA's inorganic arsenic NESHAP development activities. As Dave Patrick and others in this session will describe, the potential for elevated community exposure was confirmed in several studies and risk estimates indicated both high individual and population risks. Consequently, following the listing of inorganic arsenic as a hazardous pollutant, development of a standard to limit emissions from the Tacoma smelter became a high priority.

DEVELOPMENT OF STANDARD

Proposal Risk Management Approach

The basis for the risk management approach to standard-setting is EPA's interpretation that it is not the intent of Section 112 to eliminate totally all risks from airborne carcinogens and that Section 112 standards which permit some level of residual risk can be considered to provide an ample margin of safety to protect public health. The standard-setting approach used to select the control requirements in the arsenic NESHAP was essentially the three-step approach first described in 1979 in the proposed air carcinogen policy (44 FR 58642). The first step consisted of determining whether current controls at the ASARCO-Tacoma shelter reflect application of best available technology (BAT). The BAT is the technology which, in the judgment of EPA, is the most advanced level of control which is adequately demonstrated considering environmental, energy, and economic impacts. For those emission points where BAT is in place, EPA determined whether a NESHAP standard is needed to assure that BAT will remain in place and will be properly operated and maintained. A primary consideration is the existence of other Federally enforceable standards. Also, EPA considered whether standards established under separate authorities (e.g., other EPA standards, other Federal, State, or local requirements) are effective in reducing emissions and whether Section 112 standards will be redundant and unnecessary. If BAT is not in place on specific emission points or if there is reason to expect that BAT may not remain in operation, these emission points are identified for development of standards.

The second step involved the selection of BAT for the emission points identified for development of standards. To select BAT for an emission point, regulatory alternatives were defined based on demonstrated control technology. The environmental, economic, and energy impacts of the alternatives were determined. Based on such an assessment, one of the alternatives was selected at BAT.

The third step involved consideration of regulatory alternatives beyond BAT for all of the inorganic arsenic emission points at the ASARCO-Tacoma smelter. This consisted of consideration of the estimated risk which remains after application of BAT along with considering costs, economic impacts, risk reduction, and other impacts that would result if a more stringent alternative were selected. If the residual risk is judged not to be unreasonable considering the other impacts or beyond BAT controls, more stringent controls than BAT are not required. However, if the residual risk is judged to be unreasonable, then an alternative more stringent than BAT would be required.

Development of Proposed Standard

Consistent with the above policy, EPA examined each inorganic arsenic emission source at the Tacoma smelter to determine whether the level of control reflects BAT. In this review, the Agency found that, except for converter fugitive emission controls, BAT was in place. The converter fugitive emission controls identified as BAT were the air-curtain secondary hoods which ASARCO was installing in a phased program. It was EPA's assessment based on observations of the technology in Japan and review of ASARCO's plans that this technology would be about 95 percent effective in capturing fugitive converter emissions. The capital cost of the three hoods was estimated at $3.5 million and the annual operating cost was estimated at $1.5 million. The EPA performed an economic analysis based upon available data and concluded these controls should not have a significant economic impact on the smelter. Energy, solid waste and other nonair environmental impacts were estimated and judged to be reasonable.

The EPA next assessed the residual health risks remaining after application of BAT and the availability of additional controls beyond BAT. As described in Dave Patrick's paper, the residual estimated health risks were relatively high compared to other sources previously considered for NESHAP. However, EPA's examination identified no additional technological controls that would significantly reduce emissions and associated exposures. Remaining alternatives were, therefore, limited to production curtailments and reduction in arsenic content of copper ore concentrates processed by the smelter. It was EPA's judgment that either would cause closure of the smelter. Thus, the decision involved a balancing of a BAT-based standard with relatively high estimated risks on the one hand against closure of the smelter with potentially serious personal and community impacts on the other. In reaching a decision, two factors became particularly important. One was the significant uncertainty in the many assumptions and data that went into the health risk estimates and the recognition by the Agency that these estimates should not be regarded as accurate estimates of the actual cancer risk. (These uncertainties included the significant uncertainties in the emission estimates, the dispersion modeling of the smelter, and the simplifying assumptions made in the risk analysis.) The second was the heretofore absence of any comments or opportunity for comments by the affected public. Based on this, the decision was made that the proposed standard should not go beyond BAT.

Other Considerations

It is important to note that the information that was available at the time of proposal and the policy approach which was followed were developed during the Costle Administration and the Gorsuch Administration. However, it was Mr. Ruckelshaus, who was appointed Administrator in early 1983, who was left with the responsibility for the actual proposal and final decisions. Due to the short court-ordered time schedule and the managerial changes which were being undertaken during the initial months of the Ruckelshaus Administration, there was little time available for the new Administrator to consider the far reaching implications of the policies embodied in the proposed regulation. These changes included the appointment of a new Administrator for EPA Region X where the smelter is located, and the replacement of the Assistant Administrator for Air, Noise, and Radiation by an Acting Assistant Administration. Consequently, at the time the standard was proposed, the Administrator made very clear that in this case, in particular, the final standard was still open to debate, and that full participation by the public in the process leading up to the publication of the final regulation for arsenic was especially important in order to guide the final decisions.

PUBLIC INVOLVEMENT

Public Participation. Consistent with the Administrator's belief that the opinions of the people directly affected by the rulemaking are important, extraordinary steps were taken to ensure that they were informed and afforded an opportunity for meaningful participation. Specifically, supporting information for the proposed standard was made available for public inspection in the area affected by the ASARCO-Tacoma smelter (Tacoma and Vashon Island). In addition, EPA conducted a series of three public workshops in the area during August 1983, to provide and explain information on the proposed standard. These workshops were well attended and included both formal presentations by EPA personnel and question and answer sessions. Because of these efforts to solicit public comment on the standard, some people perceived that the public was being asked to vote on the standard. The EPA subsequently clarified that the decision on the standard was the Administrator's alone, but that the administrator considered the opinions of the affected people to be an important element in the decisionmaking process.

A public hearing was held on November 2, 3, and 4, 1983, in Tacoma, Washington, and a second public hearing was held in Washington, D.C., on November 8, 1983. In addition, EPA met with the major interested groups (ASARCO, Sierra Club, Puget Sound Air Pollution Control Agency [PSAPCA], NRDC, and United Steelworkers of America [USWA]) on December 20, 1983, to discuss the dispersion modeling study for the ASARCO-Tacoma smelter and additional opportunities for emission control that were listed in the December 16, 1983, Federal Register notice (48 FR 55880).

During the public comment period, more than 650 comment letters were received on the proposed standard, the revised ambient modeling of emissions from the ASARCO-Tacoma smelter, and the additional analyses and proposed requirements described in the December 16, 1983, Federal Register notice. Most of the commenters made multiple comments, and many repeated comments made in other letters or by other commenters.

Overview of Comments. The majority of the comments received on the proposed standard were from members of the public and appear to be motivated by personal concerns and interest in the rulemaking. The public comments reflected the range of concerns of people living in the affected communities over the health and economic impacts of the ASARCO-Tacoma smelter's operations. To present the spectrum of comments, the comments have been categorized into five general positions. These five positions can be described as ranging from "not regulation is needed" to "the smelter should be closed." These general positions are briefly described below.

A small number of commenters expressed the opinion that regulation was unnecessary because existing air pollution controls were adequate. Frequently, these commenters argued that the ASARCO-Tacoma smelter's arsenic emissions did not present any threat to the health of local residents.

A slight majority of all the commenters recommended that EPA adopt only the proposed controls for converter air-curtain secondary emissions. As a group, these commenters tended to believe that there was not evidence of a public health risk from the ASARCO-Tacoma smelter's arsenic emissions and that EPA should evaluate the air quality improvement achieved by the use of the converter secondary hoods before imposing any additional control requirements.

Commenters expressing this opinion included ASARCO, current and retired ASARCO employees, and many residents of Tacoma, Ruston, and surrounding communities. Some of these commenters argued that the jobs and economic benefits to the area were of greater importance than any health risk from the arsenic emissions.

The third category of opinion held by commenters is that to reduce risks to a maximum extent feasible, the EPA should require converter controls and all other controls that may be technically feasible. A number of these commenters further commented that the proposed standard does not require any emission controls beyond those already required by PSAPCA, and the proposed standard was only delaying control of converter fugitive emissions. These opinions were expressed by local regulatory agencies and the USWA, and a number of environmental groups, civic organizations, and private individuals. Many of these groups and individuals (including, in particular, Washington Fair Share, Tacoma City Council, Tacoma-Pierce County Chamber of Council, and Tahomans for a Healthy Environment) emphasized that the Tacoma area can have both jobs and health through application of best controls and new smelting technology. These commenters favored continued operation of the ASARCO-Tacoma smelter as long as emissions are well controlled. To achieve this goal, the groups and individuals made specific recommendations for additional controls.

The fourth category of comments reflects that opinion that the proposed standard does not provide an ample margin of safety and that EPA should require emission reductions so there are no remaining risks or only negligible risks. This opinion was expressed by a significant number of the commenters, predominantly residents of Vashon Island but also including residents of Tacoma and Ruston. Commenters stating this opinion also considered reduction of risks and health protection more important than allowing the smelter to continue operation and the retention of jobs. Within the group, some commenters expressed concerns regarding the effects of the ASARCO-Tacoma smelter's emissions on their health and on the environment in general. Frequently cited concerns of this group are the accumulation of arsenic and heavy metals in the soil and water, the warnings by the local health department against growing and consumption of certain garden vegetables, levels of arsenic measured in the urine and hair of children living in the area, and fallout of emissions on automobiles and property.

The final category in the spectrum of public opinions proposed that the ASARCO-Tacoma shelter should be required to process low-arsenic content copper ore concentrates or be required to cease operation. These commenters believed that arsenic emissions (and other emissions) from the ASARCO-Tacoma smelter present significant health risks to the surrounding population. This opinion was expressed by a significant number (but a smaller number than the preceding category) of public commenters. Frequently, these commenters stressed that the Tacoma area would benefit financially and aesthetically from closure of the smelter. These commenters thought that the ASARCO-Tacoma smelter was a significant contributor to the negative image for the area and to loss of new business opportunities to other locales.

RISK MANAGEMENT POLICY AND APPROACH AFTER PROPOSAL

The final standard that was under consideration within EPA at the time ASARCO announced its decision to close the smelter was based upon an assessment of a wide range of factors and on the risk management policy described previously. The draft standard reflected application of the best technology which was available and could be applied without causing plant closure or imposing costs that far exceed any public health benefit. The factors that were considered during the development of the final standard fall into five broad categories: (1) health risks and the uncertainties in the health risk estimates and the need to reduce exposure in order to protect public health; (2) the potential to reduce emissions; (3) the economic impacts of plant closure on the local community and on the smelter employees; (4) the opinions of the local community as expressed in the hearings and comment letters, and (5) other environmental considerations. These are each described in more detail below, except for the health risk estimates and uncertainties which are discussed in Mr. Patrick's paper.

Potential Emission Reductions. A range of potential emission control options were identified which were, or may have been, applicable to the ASARCO-Tacoma smelter. These included: (1) converter fugitive emission controls; (2) equipment and work practice controls for other low-level fugitive emission sources; (3) control of emissions during malfunctions; (4) more efficient main stack control devices; (5) new smelting technology; (6) new arsenic trioxide production technology; and (7) limits on he arsenic content of copper ore concentrates processed. Table 1 lists the availability of the control options. Figure 2 compares 1982 estimated arsenic emission rates from the ASARCO-Tacoma smelter with estimated arsenic emission rates for the different control options.

The conclusions in Table 1 regarding technical feasibility and affordability reflect the position of EPA technical staff at the time the

714

final rule was being prepared. The conclusions regarding affordability pertain to whether the additional control measures are in themselves affordable, assuming that in the absence of further control the smelter would remain profitable. In addition to the previously cited costs of converter controls, equipment and work practice controls and curtailments during malfunctions were estimated to involve capital costs of $750,000 and annualized costs of $1,540,000. While substantial, EPA's analyses indicated these costs would not cause closure. In contrast, EPA's analysis of the effect of limits on the arsenic content of concentrates showed that even if low arsenic copper ore concentrates were available, it would be affordable to replace only a small proportion of the high-arsenic with low-arsenic concentrates. Even this would be costly. For example, based on EPA's analysis, a 15 percent reduction in the amount of high-arsenic concentrates would result in approximately $2.8 million reduction in net income.

Based on this, it is clear that, from the perspective of risk management there were, in fact, only two options: (1) application of all available, feasible controls which would reduce emissions by approximately 20 percent, and (2) closure of the smelter. There were differences in opinion both within EPA and among the commenters as to what technologies were available, the effectiveness of various technologies, and the appropriate monitoring and enforcement approaches. However, none of these, even in the most effective combinations, could come close to reducing emissions and risk to near zero, and in the broader perspective, did not substantially alter the basic choices which were available.

Effects of Closure. Because the alternative of requiring the ASARCO-Tacoma smelter to process primarily low-arsenic concentrates would likely result in closure, EPA updated a study on the impacts of closure of the smelter on the local business, employment, and tax revenues in the Tacoma area. Other potential societal impacts were considered qualitatively through consideration of public comments on the effects of closure and the desirability of closure of the ASARCO-Tacoma smelter. The updated evaluation indicated that closure would: (1) increase the local unemployment rate by an additional 0.7 percentage points; (2) reduce local business revenues by about $21 million annually; and (3) reduce tax revenues to State and local governments by about $2.7 million annually. The study did not assess the other economic effects of the smelter's operation, such as unemployment insurance costs, retraining costs for employees, effects on property values, health care costs, and home and auto maintenance if the smelter closed.

The above information was considered along with the public comments on the societal impacts of closure of the ASARCO-Tacoma smelter. The majority of public comments on the societal impacts of closure focused on the anticipated employment and local economic impacts. Some commenters argued that closure would improve economic development opportunities for the area, hence an ultimate positive economic impact on the area. In contrast, most commenters believed that closure would have a negative economic impact on the Tacoma area. A majority of commenters did not favor closure because of the negative economic impacts on the area, the lack of demonstrated health effects, and a belief in the possibility for additional significant emission reductions at the smelter. The other societal impacts of concern were discussed in the smelter workers' Union comments on the proposed standards. These additional impacts included health risks due to unemployment and toxic waste disposal problems that would occur in other communities from the need to dispose of the arsenic that ASARCO had been recovering. The Union also argued that EPA should consider the impact of forced closure of the smelter on public health and reject deliberate creation of unemployment as a regulatory strategy. In support of this point, the Union cited the finding of a 1976 Joint Economic Committee of the U.S. Congress that unemployment has been associated with increased deaths and illness. Assuming the results of this study can be applied to counties, and using the risk estimates developed in this study, the USWA estimated that a 1 percent increase in unemployment, sustained over a 6-year period, would represent an increase in the mortality rate in Pierce County of 91 deaths.

Public Opinions. Both specific comments on smelter controls and general public opinions on the proposed standard played an important role in the final assessment of the appropriate level of control for the ASARCO-Tacoma smelter. The specific comments on smelter controls illustrated the need for extensive involvement with day-to-day operations of the smelter, and affected the specific control measures evaluated after proposal. In particular, owing to comments and recommendations by State and local agencies, members of the community, and EPA Region X, increased emphasis was placed on evaluating means of reducing emissions due to upsets and preventable malfunctions and of ensuring proper operation and maintenance of control equipment. In general, the majority of comments supported the position (1) that standards should be designed to reduce emissions and health risks to a minimum, and (2) that setting standards at overly restrictive levels which would result in closure was not appropriate.

Other Pollutants and Past Emissions. Although this rulemaking specifically addressed inorganic arsenic emissions, and was conducted under Section 112, other considerations were the other pollutants emitted by the smelter, other environmental impacts of the smelter, and other environmental standards affecting the smelter. These concerns were raised in the hearing and workshops by a number of commenters, many of whom expressed frustration over the narrow focus of the rulemaking. The EPA shared this concern and recognized that arsenic control at the smelter should not be considered in isolation. Even in the context of Section 112 alone, consideration of other environmental impacts were important because new control technologies and smelter processes that affect arsenic emissions also affect other pollutants. Beyond this, EPA considered other environmental impacts of the smelter, the impact of this standard on emissions of other pollutants, and the adequacy of actions being taken under other environmental statutes to address other environmental impacts of the smelter. Specific actions considered included actions being taken to reduce occupational exposures to arsenic, and actions being taken by EPA to clean up past emissions from the smelter.

On consideration was that the standard for inorganic arsenic emissions would also reduce particulate matter emissions. Consequently, emissions of other pollutants (e.g., lead or antimony) which are also present in particulate matter would also be reduced by BAT controls. Emissions of gaseous pollutants, such as SO_2, would not be reduced; however, there are other regulations that limit emissions of these pollutants from the ASARCO-Tacoma smelter. In particular, ASARCO was required by the 1981 PSAPCA Board Order to achieve 90 percent control of SO_2 emissions by 1987.

The other environmental impacts of the smelter were being studied by EPA, and efforts are underway to solve the problems identified. The Superfund program (Comprehensive Environmental Response Compensation and Liability Act) is designed for EPA to take actions needed to protect public health from exposure to hazardous substances in all environmental media. The EPA is using its Superfund program, therefore, to investigate other pollutants, such as cadmium and lead, and to remedy the problems resulting from exposures to these pollutants. Investigations funded in part or entirely by the Superfund program are underway or being developed to study the potential health problems resulting from the historical accumulation of arsenic, lead, and cadmium in the vicinity of the ASARCO smelter. Efforts are also underway to reduce discharges of pollutants into Commencement Bay. It was EPA's conclusion that this work will aid in the characterization and resolution of the environmental problems associated with the ASARCO-Tacoma smelter's operations that would not be affected by the stringency of standards limiting air emissions.

The Agency also recognized that even at the control levels required by the NESHAP standard, that some degree of accumulation of arsenic and heavy metals in the soil may occur. However, the present levels of these materials in other environmental media are largely the result of the much higher emissions from the smelter before effective control equipment was installed. Emissions had decreased significantly over the past 20 to 30 years. Although the standard would not have eliminated arsenic and heavy metal deposition, EPA believed that the controls would have reduced emissions significantly and would reduce accumulation in the environment.

SUMMARY AND CONCLUSIONS

The policy basis for the rulemaking action affecting the Tacoma smelter was consistent through the development of the proposed and final standard. In particular, the risk management policy continued to be based on EPA's interpretation that it is not the intent of Section 112 to eliminate totally all risks; and that standards which permit some level of residual risk can be considered to protect the public health. The basic standard-setting approach of identifying controls and weighing the broad range of impacts and benefits of the alternatives also was used throughout the rulemaking.

This rulemaking action did, however, differ from other NESHAP rulemakings in the unusual level of public involvement in review and development of the final standard. Public involvement with the arsenic standard was greater than normal due to EPA efforts, under Mr. Ruckelshaus' leadership, to obtain and consider the opinions of the affected people. This was a significant departure from an earlier decision by EPA to discontinue NESHAP development based on the conclusion that BAT controls were already planned. This public involvement affected the regulatory process in several ways. First, the extensive local involvement in the process resulted in increased understanding by EPA of the variations in daily operations of the smelter which were not necessarily evident during brief on-site inspections. This experience showed EPA the value of local involvement and the need for EPA local partnership in the NESHAP process. Second, once the benefits, risks, and uncertainty associated with alternatives were described to the public the majority of those commenting on the standard tended to make decisions similar to those made by EPA.

FRAMEWORK FOR ACID DEPOSITION DECISION MAKING

William E. Balson*, D. Warner North* and
Richard Richels**

Decision Focus Incorporated*
Los Altos, California
Electric Power Research Institute**

ABSTRACT

Acid precipitation and dry deposition of acid materials have emerged
as an important environmental issue. This paper presents a framework for
the analysis of decisions on acid deposition. The decision framework is
intended as a means of summarizing scientific information and
uncertainties on the relation between emissions from electric utilities
and other sources, acid deposition, and impacts on ecological systems.
The methodology for implementing the framework is that of decision
analysis, which proves a quantitative means of analyzing decisions under
uncertainty. The decisions of interest include reductions in sulfur oxide
and other emissions thought to be precursors of acid deposition,
mitigation of acid deposition impacts through means such as liming of
waterways and soils, and choice of strategies for research.

The paper review two versions of a decision tree model that
implements the decision framework. The basic decision tree addressed
decisions on emissions control and mitigation in the immediate future and
a decade hence, and it includes uncertainties in the long-range transport
and ecological impacts. The research emphasis decision tree addresses the
effect of research funding on obtaining new information as the basis for
future decisions.

KEY WORDS: Decision Analysis, Methodology, Acid Rain, Acid Deposition,
            Decision Tree, Research, Air Pollution

INTRODUCTION

The terms "acid rain" and "acid precipitation" are used to describe
the complex chemical changes that result from the presence of oxides of
sulfur, oxides of nitrogen, and other compounds in the air that may lead
to increased acidity in precipitation, in ground and surface waters, and
in soil. A more comprehensive and accurate term is "acid deposition,"
since the transfer of acid material from the atmosphere to the biosphere
may occur not only in the aqueous phase, (e.g., rain snow, fog) but also
as dry deposition, in which gaseous or particulate material is absorbed by
the ground, vegatation, or surface water.

As the debate on acid deposition has intensified, the need for an
integrating framework for balancing the potential environmental effects

719

with the costs of emissions control has grown. Industry and government are faced with the immediate decision of whether to (1) impose additional controls on power plants and other potential sources, (2) take steps to mitigate the possible effects of acid deposition, or (3) wait until additional understanding can be achieved on the relationship between emissions and ecological effects. The choice involves the careful balancing of very different types of risks. Acting now to reduce emissions carries the risk that large expenditures will be made with little or no beneficial effect, while waiting carries the risk that significant ecological damage will be incurred that could have been prevented by prompt action.

If the results of the extensive research programs underway in the United States, Canada, and Europe were available today, the choice might be less difficult. But unfortunately, resolution of crucial uncertainties may not occur for five to ten years or longer. Until that time, it will not be possible to predict accurately how changes in emissions will affect the extent of ecological damage from acid deposition. In the absence of perfect foresight, what is needed is a means of reasoning about the best decision based on the information available today.

The object of the research reported in this paper has been to develop a framework to summarize current information and uncertainties on acid deposition. The framework is intended to aid decisionmakers in assessing strategies for control of anthropogenic emissions and for mitigating the effects of acid deposition. The framework is also intended to aid in the evaluation of research programs for organizations such as the Electric Power Research Institute or the United States Government, which are spending substantial funds to develop better information as a basis for future decisions.

OVERVIEW OF THE DECISION FRAMEWORK

To understand the effects of alternative control strategies, it is necessary to understand the relation that various levels of emissions reduction may have on the impacts of acid deposition. The potential changes in impact must then be balanced with the cost of achieving emission reductions. The comparison of various control strategies is made difficult by several factors:

- There is a large degree of uncertainty about the relationship between emissions and impacts.

- It is difficult to compare the value of changes in impacts with the costs of emission reductions.

- People involved in assessing control and mitigation strategies have different degrees of uncertainty and different opinions about the evaulation of costs and impacts.

- The uncertainty in the relationship between emissions and impacts will only resolve over time.

The decision framework is designed to allow explicit treatment of each of these factors, separating the evaluation of costs and impacts from consideration of the resolution of uncertainty over time. In doing this, the framework provides a vehicle for discussion and investigation of sensitive assumptions, which can lead to the building of a concensus.

Three stages can be distinguished in the relationship between control alternatives and impacts, as shown in figure 1. First, there is the

720

effect that control strategies will have on emissions. Then, changes in emissions must be related to changes in acid deposition. Finally, changes in acid deposition must be related to changes in the various impacts that can be identified, such as decreased forest productivity and the loss of sport fisheries. There is scientific uncertainty about each of these stages. Relatively little is known about how specific changes in acid deposition will affect changes in impacts. The range of estimates given by respected scientist varies by several orders of magnitude. There is somewhat less uncertainty regarding how changes in emissions will affect changes in deposition; however, the range of uncertainty is still quite large, primarily due to the complex nature of the chemical transformations that occur in the atmosphere. There is comparatively little uncertainty about how reduction strategies would affect changes in emissions. Accordingly, in implementing the framework the importance of uncertainty in the other two stages has been stressed.

At present, the scientific evidence regarding the effects of emissions is contradictory and subject to different interpretations by various experts. The decision framework allows an investigation of the implications of the differing assessments and evaluates the importance of the disagreements in terms of their effects on the choice of a control or mitigation strategy. Many experts who disagree about the interpretation of the current state of knowledge, agree that in five to ten years many of those disagreements will be settled. Thus, in the decision framework, the choice is characterized as one in which we may act now, at a large cost, and accept the possibility that emission reduction will have little beneficial impact. Alternatively, we can wait five to ten years to act on better information that may become available, and accept the possibility that damage may occur during that period. In each case, there is a possibility that the decision will turn out to have been incorrect. From our current state of knowledge, we cannot be sure.

The strategies that are available and the resolution of uncertainty at different points in time are represented as a decision tree in figure 2. A decision tree is simply an effective way of describing a set of scenarios. Each particular set of decisions and outcomes representing how uncertainty could resolve comprises a scenario. Each scenario answers a "what if?" question corresponding to what if a particular strategy was chosen followed by a particular change in deposition and finally by a particular change in impacts. The decision tree of figure 2 provides a generic representation of the time sequence of choices among decision alternatives and the resolution of uncertainty in the areas enumerated in

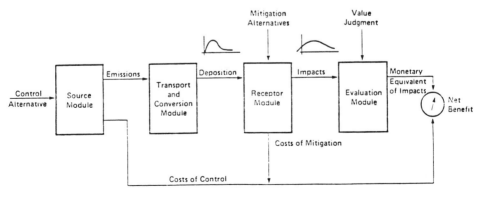

Figure 1

Overview of Decision Framework

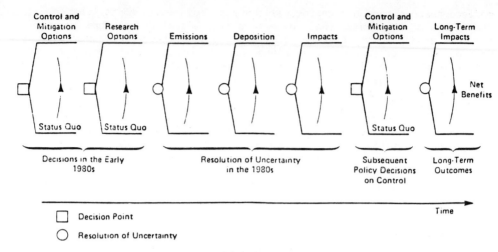

Figure 2

Decision Tree for Acid Deposition Policy

the framework of figure 1. The first two stages, shown at the far left of
the figure, are the decisions within the next few years on control and
mitigation options and on a national research program on acid
deposition. The next two stages represent resolution of uncertainty on
the relation of deposition to emissions and the relation of impacts to
deposition as the research program is carried out and new scientific
knowledge is obtained. Next comes a decision point in the early 1990's,
when national policy on control and mitigation would be reassessed and an
alternative chosen on the basis of the new information that has recently
been made available. Further resolution of uncertainty on deposition, and
impacts of acid deposition then follows. Additional uncertainties can
easily be introduced.

The decision tree of figure 2 provides a rich sequence of scenarios
describing the decisions and outcomes characterizing national policy on
acid rain. It includes two stages of decisionmaking, one with present
information and one with the information that might become available five
to ten years hence following an extensive research program. The decision
tree explicitly includes the option of taking action now to control
emissions or mitigate the effects of acid deposition and the option to
wait until better information becomes available in five to ten years. The
effect of today's research funding decisions and the choice of emphasis in
the research program may strongly affect what information becomes
available in the next five to ten years, and this interaction is
explicitly considered in the decision tree framework. The decision
framework provides a useful separation between value judgments on costs
and benefits and scientific judgments about uncertainties in the impacts
of acid deposition. Each scenario in the decision tree may be considered
as having impacts on a number of concerned parties: consumers who may
have pay more for electricity because of decisions to impose controls on
power plants, fishermen and recreational property owners who stand to lose
if sport fishing in a given lake is degraded by acid deposition, forest
products firms and property owners who suffer economic losses if forest
productivity is reduced, and members of the general public who are

concerned about possible ecological changes from acid deposition. The evaluation of impacts on these diverse parties is difficult because people see that some parties bear more of the costs while other parties receive more of the benefits resulting from a particular decision alternative. People in Ohio benefit from cheaper electricity because their power plants burn coal with a higher level of sulfur emissions than would be allowed in many other Eastern states. People in New York may benefit from reduction in Ohio River Valley sulfur emissions if the reduction improves the fishing in Adirondack lakes. The political reality is that government officials must evaluate how tradeoffs will be made between the costs that one group bears and the benefits that another group receives. Issues of equity and property rights make such value judgments extremely difficult. It is useful to separate these value judgments from the uncertainty in the effects that long-range transport of sulfur and other pollutants may cause. The decision framework accomplishes this desired separation between the answer to the question of what will happen under a given choice of control and mitigation strategies and the societal evaluation of what each outcome is worth.

IMPLEMENTATION OF THE DECISION FRAMEWORK

The decision framework has been implemented as a computer model that represents a set of decision trees that are fast, flexible, and easily used. The model is designed to run on both mainframe computers and the IBM-PC. Two decision trees are available. Both are based on the structure shown in figure 2. The basic tree, illustrated in figure 3, assumes that uncertainty on the relation of emissions to deposition and on the extent of ecological impacts will be resolved by the second decision point five to ten years from now. This basic tree can be used to quickly evaluate strategies and calculate the value of achieving full resolution of uncertainty. The research emphasis decision tree, illustrated in figure 4, allows an explicit characterization of the results of research programs. While this tree is more complex, it allows the investigation of

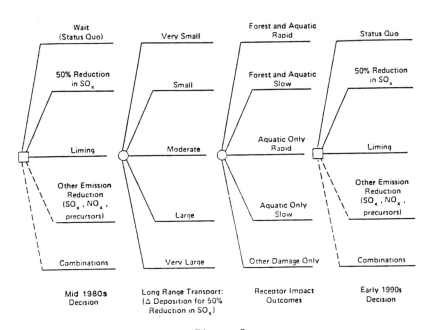

Figure 3

Decision Tree with Full Resolution of Uncertainty by the Early 1990s

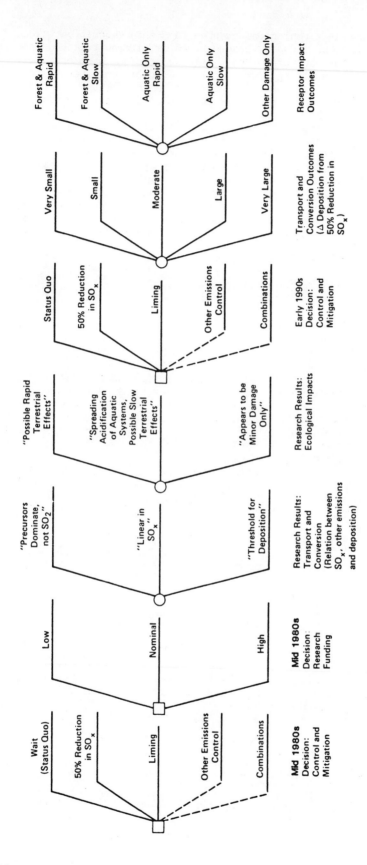

Figure 4

Decision Tree with Resolution of Uncertainty
Dependent on Research Funding Decision

724

research alternatives that result in partial resolution of uncertainty. Both decision trees utilize the same basic assumptions and evaluations, the only difference being the extent of scientific judgment required to understand how uncertainty will resolve over time.

The relations are built up from simple modules that are easily understood graphically. The reduction in emissions resulting from a specific strategy is phased in over time. Various assumptions about the change in deposition that results from a change in emissions can be utilized. The pattern of lake and forest acidification that occurs can be varied. Each of these relationships can be changed within a wide range of possibilities and each is modular so that it can be replaced by an entirely different set of assumptions if desired. For example, the module that calculates the reduction in emissions could be replaced by a specific time pattern of emissions that is input by the user.

The decision framework can aid in generating concensus by testing a wide range of assumptions for their importance to control decisions. The implementation of the framework as a computer model aids this testing process by making changes in assumptions straightforward. The model has been tested on several illustrative cases examining both national and state acid deposition control alternatives.

ACKNOWLEDGEMENTS

This work was sponsored by the Electric Power Research Institute. Portions of this paper have appeared elsewhere. Any opinions expressed are those of the authors alone.

REFERENCES

Balson, W. E., Boyd, D. W. and North, D. W., 1982. "Acid Deposition: Decision Framework--Volume 1: Description of Conceptual Framework and Decision Tree Models--Final Report (RP 2156)," EPRI EA-2540, Palo Alto, CA, Electric Power Research Institute, August.

Balson, W. E. and North, D. W., 1983. "Acid Deposition: Decision Framework--Volume 3: State-level Application--Final Report (RP 2156)," EPRI EA-2540, Palo Alto, CA, Electric Power Research Institute, December.

Balson, W. E., North, D. W. and Colville, G., 1985. "Analysis of Sulfur Dioxide Control Strategies Related to Acid Deposition in Wisconsin-- Volume I," Wisconsin Utilities Acid Deposition Task Force, Milwaukee, WI, May.

A COMPARATIVE ANALYSIS OF AIR POLLUTION STANDARD-SETTING AND

REGULATORY PROCEDURES IN THE UNITED STATES AND WEST GERMANY[1]

Eric H. Bauman* and Ortwin Renn**[2]

Cooperative Power*
Minneapolis, Minnesota 55344
Nuclear Research Centre Juelich**
Federal Republic of Germany

ABSTRACT

    The regulatory processes used to set air pollution standards in the
United States (US) and the Federal Republic of Germany (FRG) are
significantly different. This comparative study (in progress) seeks to
determine if those differences significantly affect the standards finally
promulgated. Ideas for improving the regulatory processes are also being
collected. Interviews are being conducted with the major parties involved
in each of five case studies (i.e. dioxins in municipal waste
incinerators, nitrogen dioxide, cadmium, lead, and smog/ozone). The

---

[1]PROJECT SUPPORT: This research is being supported by general
operating funds of the Nuclear Research Center Juelich, a national
laboratory funded by the West German Federal Ministry of Research and
Technology (90%) and the State of North-Rhine Westphalia (10%). Mr.
Bauman is also supported by the study/travel grant from the German
Marshall Fund of the United States. Additional project support is
acknowledged from the Commission of the European Communities, Sigurd Olson
Environmental Institute at Northland College, and Cooperative Power
Association.

[2]Eric H. Bauman is Supervisor of Environmental Planning,
Environmental Affairs Department, Cooperative Power, 14615 Lone Oak Road,
Eden Prairie (Minneapolis) Minnesota, 55344. Mr. Bauman was a guest
scientist at the Nuclear Research Center Juelich, Program Group Technology
and Society, from February 5 - September 15, 1985.

    Ortwin Renn, is Manager, Man and Technology Department, Program Group
Technology and Society, Nuclear Research Center Juelich, PO Box 1913, D-
5170 Juelich, Federal Republic of Germany.

authors are identifying possibilities of transferring successful elements of each country's process to the other.

KEY WORDS: West Germany, air pollution, standard-setting, regulation, decision-making, public involvement, comparative analysis

This paper outlines the approach being used in a comparative analysis of air pollution standard-setting and regulatory procedures in the United States of America (US) and the Federal Republic of Germany (West Germany, or FRG). In addition, some preliminary conclusions and observations are offered.

STUDY GOALS AND PROCESS

We have three major interests in this comparative analysis. First, we are seeking to determine how the process of setting environmental standards affects the outcome of the regulatory proceedings. Second, we are identifying, through interviews with the major parties involved in each case study, potential improvements that could be made in the standard-setting process. Third, we will determine if elements of one country's process can be transferred to the other country.

The study team initially selected 15 potential case studies in areas of air, water, pesticides, chemical waste handling, and groundwater/soil. These were narrowed to five air pollution case studies. These case studies are: cadmium, lead, NOx, dioxins in municipal waste incinerators, and smog/ozone.

The basic data collection tools are two questionnaires which are being administered to the major parties actively participating in each case study regulatory proceeding. These parties include agency/ministry staff, industrial trade associations, environmental groups, labor, and other relevant organizations.

A detailed questionnaire is being used for each case study interview to obtain information about:

* types of data and information used in the proceeding
* how and when interest groups and agency/ministry staffs were involved
* regulatory options considered, and final rule promulgated
* satisfaction of interest groups with the process.

A second questionnaire was also administered to selected officials and interest group representatives soliciting opinions about the standard-setting process as a whole, and obtaining suggestions for improvement. This study is still "in-progress". We underestimated the number of interviews required in the United States, and interview scheduling was more difficult in the FRG. Interviewing will be continuing through November 1985.

BRIEF OVERVIEW OF THE GERMAN STANDARD-SETTING PROCESS

Anticipating that most of attendees at the conference would be from the US, we will briefly describe the FRG approach to promulgating environmental regulations.

Under FRG law, the Interior Ministry (Bundesinnenministerium, or BMI) in Bonn is responsible for establishing air pollution control regulations, with research support coming from the Federal Environmental Agency (Umweltbundesamt, or UBA) in Berlin. Ambient, point-source, and mobile sources are subject to controls under regulations promulgated by the BMI.

In addition to the BMI and the UBA, there are three other important parties in the standard setting process. These are: the Association of German Engineers (Verband der Deutsche Ingenieur, or VDI), the German Research Society (Deutsche Forschungs Gemeinschaft, or DFG), and the States' Environmental Ministries Conference (Umweltministeriumkonferenz, or UMK). The VDI and the DFG are not governmental institutions.

The VDI is a professional association of engineers, which has standing and ad hoc committees of "experts" that develop recommendations for the BMI about potential standards, or appropriate action regarding chemical pollutants or other environmental management questions.

The DFG, somewhat akin to the US National Academy of Sciences, also has standing and ad hoc committees which investigate environmental management questions and develop recommendations for the Interior Ministry.

The Umweltministeriumkonferenz (UMK) is composed of representatives of state-level environmental ministries. The UMK will often review proposed regulations during or after initial drafting by the BMI. The UMK also has committees (e.g. air, water) where these proposals are discussed, and consensus recommendations are developed. The committees forward recommendations to the full UMK for further discussion and consensus building. Recommendations are then forwarded to the BMI.[3]

It should be noted that the BMI may also form ad hoc committees, or working groups, to investigate specific issues. For example, in 1984, the Interior Ministry formed a dioxins working group comprised of representatives from the states, the research community, federal ministerial staff, and industry. They were charged with the responsibility of assessing the potential public health risks stemming from possible dioxin emissions from municipal waste incinerators.

The BMI is responsible under provisions of the German Air Emissions Act to consult with interested parties during development of regulations, and they must provide opportunities for the interest parties to present comments to the BMI.

After approval by the BMI, regulations are sent to the Bundesrat for concurrence/appproval. Once approved by the Bundesrat, the regulations are given to the President of signature.

Implementation of environmental and pollution control laws, with a few specific exceptions, is totally the responsibility of the states (Laender).

------

[3]The UMK is involved in the review of proposed standards because one house of the German Parliament, the Bundesrat, is comprised of elected officials appointed by their home states to represent that state. We are told that normally the UMK consensus building process sufficiently addresses most of the state concerns before proposed rules reach the Bundersrat for formal approval.

During the BMI's development of draft regulations, there may be substantial contact with relevant outside interest groups who may be potentially affected by the regulations. This contact can include private, "closed door" sessions.

The emphasis of the German system is on negotiation, consultation with directly affected parties, and a balancing of interests.

While economic interests are an important consideration in German rulemaking, a healthy environment is also important. The following principles are embodied in various German environmental laws (Bundesmininsterium des Innern, 1982; von Moltke, 1985):

*Vorsorgeprinzip   ---   encouraging the prevention of problems

*Verursacherprinzip   ---   polluter must pay for cleanup

*Bestantschutzprinzip   ---   nothing should be worse than it has been

*Kooperationsprinzip   ---   all public groups must be involved

There is another concept, Gemeinlast, which is apparently not specifically stated within statutes, but which has guided some political decisions. Within the concept of Gemeinlast, the community or public will pay for cleanup of pollution episodes when a specific source can not be identified.

There are also allowances within German environmental management practices to "ratched down" allowable emissions levels at existing plants through so-called "dynamizing clauses". These levels are to be achieved through the "Stand der Technik"; in US terms, the Best Available Control Technology (BACT).

US PROCESS

It goes almost without saying that the US Environmental Protection Agency is charged with implementing the Clean Air Act (CAA), including the setting of standards for national ambient air quality (NAAQS), new source performance standards (NSPS), hazardous air pollutants (NESHAPS), and mobile source controls.

While many conference attendees are already familiar with the the US process, we will briefly describe the somewhat generalized process for setting NAAQS (Jordan et al, 1983), because the differences in approaches between the US and the FRG are significant.

1. Agency staff and/or contractors prepare a criteria document draft which summarizes the relevant scientific studies.

2. Chapters of the criteria document are reviewed in draft form in open workshops with agency staff, interest groups, etc. and a member of the Clean Air Scientific Advisory Committee (CASAC).

3. Chapters are revised by staff/contractors, where appropriate.

4. The criteria document (C/D) is reviewed by CASAC in an open

meeting, which includes time for presentations by the interested parties.

5. During CASAC's review of the C/D, a "staff paper" is prepared by the Office of Air Quality Planning and Standards which summarizes the scientific studies, identifies the key issues, then makes recommendations for regulatory action.

6. Staff paper, and C/D, is reviewed in an open meeting by CASAC.

7. After C/D and staff paper approval by CASAC, draft rules are developed by staff, and are internally reviewed. This internal review includes the "red border" review by all Assistant Administrators before going to the Administrator.

8. During this time of internal review, the Office of Management and Budget (OMB) reviews the draft rule and a preliminary Regulatory Impact Analysis (RIA) in accordance with Executive Order 12291 to insure that "(b) Regulatory action shall not be taken unless the potential benefits to society for the regulation outweight the potential costs to society" (Office of the President, 1981).

9. After approval by OMB and the "red border" review, the Administrator may publish the proposed regulation in the Federal Register.

10. Public comments are solicited, usually for 45 to 60 days, though extensions may be granted.

11. EPA staff responds to the comments, and makes revisions in the rule as appropriate.

12. The revised rule again receives internal EPA review (including "red border") as well as OMB review.

13. Once approved by OMB, the Administrator publishes the final rule in the Federal Register.

14. Involved parties have 60 days to file a petition with the Administrator asking him to reconsider the final rule.

Notice that the US process is open to any interested party, and the steps in the regulatory process are known. The process leads to a standard with a substantial data base that justifies the standard, and this justification is published. Such justification is a requirement of the US system of government (Shapiro, 1985).

In the setting of NAAQS, the CAA states that EPA must set standards which protect the most sensitive members of the population with a margin of safety. Economics are not to be considered. Economic impacts have been considered, however, in the NAAQS rulemaking processes, through OMB review of proposed rules. OMB's role is controversial.

PRELIMINARY OBSERVATIONS

While this comparative analysis of US and FRG standard-setting is still "in-progress", we can offer some preliminary observations and conclusions.

1. The processes for setting environmental standards appear to be quite different. The US system is open and adversarial, where documentation and justification is critical. The FRG system involves more "closed door" negotiations, and dependence on "expert committees" which are not formal governmental entities. Specific interest groups are involved, but the method of involvement and the invitations for involvement are largely done at the discretion of the BMI. There does appear, however, to be increasing pressure to "open up" the process.

2. Formal risk assessments and formal cost/benefit studies appear to have less of a role in the FRG formal rulemaking process than in the US. However, we were told that industry would like to see risk assessments introduced into the rulemaking process so that its issues can be better aired.

3. Consideration of economic interests seems to be important in West German standard-setting. While economics can be considered in some US air quality standard-setting, economics can not be considered in the establishment of NAAQS.

4. There are different attitudes in the FRG towards the role of government, civil servants, and the role of science. In the FRG, citizens have trusted the civil servants (Beamte) to truly represent their interests and to appropriately balance all interests. Also, the opinions of scientists and experts carries much weight in the FRG, and is well accepted (Coppock, in press).[4]

5. Environmental groups and "Grass Roots organizations" (so-called Burgerinitiativegruppe) have a minimal role, if any, in standard-setting in the FRG. Apparently, this is in part by design. BMI officials simply do not normally consult with these parties early in the rulemaking process because they are not seen as having the capabilities to add significant technical expertise to the discussions, and they are not "stakeholders". These groups, on the other hand, feel that their input, when it is requested later in the process, comes at a time when major decisions have already been made. Therefore, it is not a worthwhile expeditures of their resources to participate.

RECOMMENDATIONS FOR IMPROVEMENT IN STANDARD-SETTING PROCESS

Within the general (i.e. non-case study specific) questionnaire, interviewees are asked to provide ideas for improving the existing regulatory process.

In the FRG, the main comments thus far have been:

* process should be more open to outside groups;
* should involve outside, affected interest groups earlier in the standard-setting process;

---

[4]The authors refer the reader to the following paper which addresses this issue of the role of scientists in the FRG: Rob Coppock, "Interactions Between Scientists and Public Officials: A Comparison of the Use of Science in Regulatory Programs in the United States and West Germany" Policy Sciences, vol. 8, no. 4 (in press).

* should be more use of risk assessment in the formal
  standard-setting process.

In the US, numerous comments have also been received. These include:

* federal funding should be provided to public interest groups so
  that they can adequately and effectively participate in the
  process.
* the open, adversarial process is essentially good and will remain
  with us. The length of the process does "stop stupid things from
  happening," said one interviewee. On the other hand, we probably
  can shorten the process in some ways. For example, many studies
  could be incorporated into the NAAQS Criteria document by reference
  rather then spending much time and resources to include these
  studies in the criteria document for each NAAQS revision. Because
  the time requirements are less, the system can be more responsive
  to changes in scientific information. While numerous interviewees
  would like to see the process shortened, EPA indicates that up to
  80% of its final regulations are challenged (USEPA, no date).
* "Reg neg" or regulatory negotiation seems to be perceived as being
  useful, but in limited applications.
* OMB should be excluded from the rulemaking process, particularly in
  NAAQS rulemaking since ambient standards are supposed to be only
  health-based; others seem to welcome OMB review.
* Standard-setting should consider better whether the marginal
  benefits of a proposed rule are really worth the marginal costs.

We are also receiving comments to questions about: the role of
industry self-regulation; guiding principles that organizations use in
considering positions on proposed rules; and the role of formal risk
assessment.

CLOSING

While this comparative study is still in-progress, we do see that
there are significant differences in the styles of environmental standard-
setting in the FRG and the US; differences in procedures and the
information used. These differences appear to be based in different
political traditions. We can not yet say, however, the extent to which
these differences in the standards resulting from the respective processes
are significant (e.g. stricter), nor can we yet comment on the efficiency,
equity, timeliness, etc. of the standard-setting processes themselves.

There is no question that major changes in laws in each country would
be required to transfer successful elements of one country's process to
the other country, because of significant differences in the basic laws
(including constitutions), and traditions of political decision-making.
For example, FRG does not have a Freedom of Information Act. For the US,
we could not implement "closed door negotiation" sessions.

Perhaps the best way to improve standard-setting and environmental
management, given the differences in political traditions, is though
exchanges of environmental and health risk information and technology
transfer.

REFERENCES

NOTE--Much of the information presented in this paper is based upon
personal interviews conducted by the principal investigators between May,

733

1985 and the present with federal and state agency and ministry officials, industrial trade association representatives, environmental organizational representatives, labor union representatives, and other organizations in the United states and the Federal Republic of Germany. A list of interviewees will be included in the final project reports.

Bundesministerium des Innern, 1982, "Bericht der Bundesrepublik Deutschland zur Unweltpolitik (Report on the environmental policy of the Federal Republic of Germany)," pp. 10-11.

Coppock, Rob, in press, "Interactions Between Scientists and Public Officials: A Comparison of the Use of Science in Regulatory Programs in the United States and West Germany" in Policy Sciences, vol. 8, no. 4.

Jordan, Bruce C., Harvey M. Richmond and Thomas McCurdy, 1983, "The Use of Scientific Information in Setting Ambient Air Standards" in Environmental Health Perspectives, vol. 52, pp. 233-240.

Office of the President, Executive Order 12291 of February 17, 1981, Federal Register, vol 46, no. 33, pp. 13193-13198.

Shapiro, Sidney A., 1985, "Overview of Legal Basis For Rulemaking Requirements of the Federal United States Government", unpublished paper for the Program Group Technology and Society, Nuclear Research Centre Juelich, Federal Republic of Germany.

US Environmental Protection Agency, no date, "The Environmental Protection Agency's Regulatory Negotiation Project," fact sheet.

von Moltke, Konrad, 1985, Interview with Eric H. Bauman, Washington, DC, August 30, 1985.